THE COMPLETE

COOKING FOR TWO

COOKBOOK

Revised & Updated 10th Anniversary Edition

700+ Recipes for Everything
You'll Ever Want to Make

AMERICA'S TEST KITCHEN

Library of Congress Cataloging-in-Publication Data has been applied for.

ISBN 978-1-954210-86-8 (paperback)

America's Test Kitchen
21 Drydock Avenue, Boston, MA 02210

Printed in Canada
10 9 8 7 6 5 4 3 2 1

Distributed by
Penguin Random House Publisher Services
Tel: 800.733.3000

Pictured on front cover Sautéed Chicken Breasts (page 111) with Quick Salsa Verde (page 111)

Pictured on back cover (clockwise from top left) Chicken Pot Pie (page 126), Bistecca alla Fiorentina (page 272), Soupe au Pistou (page 43), Key Lime Pie (page 407), Pesce all'Acqua Pazza (page 183)

Editorial Director, Books Adam Kowit

Executive Food Editor Dan Zuccarello

Deputy Food Editor Stephanie Pixley

Executive Managing Editor Debra Hudak

Project Editor Elizabeth Carduff

Senior Editors Suzannah McFerran and Sara Mayer

Test Cooks Olivia Counter, Danielle DeSiato-Hallman, Laila Ibrahim, José Maldonado, Ashley Moore, Meaghen Walsh, and David Yu

Assistant Test Cook Lainey Seyler

Editorial Assistant Julia Arwine

Design Director Lindsey Timko Chandler

Designers Allison Boales and Jen Kanavos Hoffman

Photography Director Julie Bozzo Cote

Senior Photography Producer Meredith Mulcahy

Senior Staff Photographers Steve Klise and Daniel J. van Ackere

Staff Photographers Kritsada Panichgul and Kevin White

Additional Photography Joseph Keller and Carl Tremblay

Food Styling Joy Howard, Sheila Jarnes, Catrine Kelty, Chantal Lambeth, Gina McCreadie, Kendra McNight, Ashley Moore, Christie Morrison, Marie Piraino, Elle Simone Scott, Kendra Smith, and Sally Staub

Project Manager, Creative Operations Katie Kimmerer

Senior Print Production Specialist Lauren Robbins

Production and Imaging Coordinator Amanda Yong

Production and Imaging Specialists Tricia Neumyer and Dennis Noble

Copy Editor Cheryl Redmond

Proofreader Vicki Rowland

Indexer Elizabeth Parson

Chief Creative Officer Jack Bishop

Executive Editorial Directors Julia Collin Davison and Bridget Lancaster

Contents

Welcome to America's Test Kitchen

This book has been tested, written, and edited by the folks at America's Test Kitchen, where curious cooks become confident cooks. Located in Boston's Seaport District in the historic Innovation and Design Building, it features 15,000 square feet of kitchen space including multiple photography and video studios. It is the home of *Cook's Illustrated* magazine and *Cook's Country* magazine and is the workday destination for more than 60 test cooks, editors, and cookware specialists. Our mission is to empower and inspire confidence, community, and creativity in the kitchen.

We start the process of testing a recipe with a complete lack of preconceptions, which means that we accept no claim, no technique, and no recipe at face value. We simply assemble as many variations as possible, test a half-dozen of the most promising, and taste the results blind. We then construct our own recipe and continue to test it, varying ingredients, techniques, and cooking times until we reach a consensus. As we like to say in the test kitchen, "We make the mistakes so you don't have to." The result, we hope, is the best version of a particular recipe, but we realize that only you can be the final judge of our success (or failure). We use the same rigorous approach when we test equipment and taste ingredients.

All of this would not be possible without a belief that good cooking, much like good music, is based on a foundation of objective technique. Some people like spicy foods and others don't, but there is a right way to sauté, there is a best way to cook a pot roast, and there are measurable scientific principles involved in producing perfectly beaten, stable egg whites.

Our ultimate goal is to investigate the fundamental principles of cooking to give you the techniques, tools, and ingredients you need to become a better cook. It is as simple as that.

To see what goes on behind the scenes at America's Test Kitchen, check out our social media channels for kitchen snapshots, exclusive content, video tips, and much more. You can watch us work (in our actual test kitchen) by tuning in to *America's Test Kitchen* or *Cook's Country* on public television or on our websites. Listen to *Proof*, *Mystery Recipe*, and *The Walk-In* (AmericasTestKitchen.com/podcasts) to hear engaging, complex stories about people and food. Want to hone your cooking skills or finally learn how to bake—with an America's Test Kitchen test cook? Enroll in one of our online cooking classes.

However you choose to visit us, we welcome you into our kitchen, where you can stand by our side as we test our way to the best recipes in America.

facebook.com/AmericasTestKitchen
instagram.com/TestKitchen
youtube.com/AmericasTestKitchen
tiktok.com/@TestKitchen
x.com/TestKitchen
pinterest.com/TestKitchen

AmericasTestKitchen.com
CooksIllustrated.com
CooksCountry.com
OnlineCookingSchool.com

JOIN OUR COMMUNITY OF RECIPE TESTERS

Our recipe testers provide valuable feedback on recipes under development by ensuring that they are foolproof in home kitchens. Help the America's Test Kitchen book team investigate the how and why behind successful recipes from your home kitchen.

The Basics of Cooking for Two

Introduction

The test kitchen has spent more than 25 years developing bulletproof recipes for just about everything imaginable: all-time comfort classics; hundreds of soups and stews; modern and classic salads and sides; vegetarian and vegan dishes; and innumerable pies, tarts, cakes, and other desserts. Like most recipes, ours typically serve four, six, and sometimes more. That said, we've realized that households change over time or through circumstance. Our readers started to echo this sentiment—whether they were single parents, empty nesters, or newlyweds, they wanted recipes for the dishes we'd been developing for years, but they wanted them scaled to serve just two. So in 2014, we published the first edition of *The Complete Cooking for Two Cookbook*. In the ensuing years, the test kitchen has heard from the fans of the first book that they'd love even more recipes scaled for two, recipes that reflected some of the new directions the test kitchen has gone. So this 10th Anniversary Edition of *The Complete Cooking for Two Cookbook* includes more than 200 exciting new recipes, the latest techniques, and new photos throughout.

This book is designed to be an all-purpose cookbook for today's smaller households. We included a wide range of recipes—everything you might want to eat during the course of the year. But once we got cooking, we discovered that our mission wasn't going to be so easy. Often there are amounts that don't divide evenly (one egg, for example) or there is simply no way to buy just the amount you need, think 4 ounces of kale or a half cup of ricotta. Sometimes, an entire dish needs to be re-engineered from the ground up. Just how do you make a lasagna for two? You certainly can't use the standard 13 by 9-inch baking dish. In short, we discovered there are different rules and approaches when cooking for two. And because we have vetted every recipe in our test kitchen, they are just as reliable as our standard recipes—no need to scale recipes yourself and hope they work.

Because households of two can be as time-pressed as larger households, we also looked for new approaches to complicated recipes. We've included streamlined recipes like Modern Beef Pot Pie with Mushrooms and Sherry made in a skillet with a rich sauce and a nearly no-work topping of baguette slices encrusted with Gruyère cheese. A chapter on slow-cooker and air-fryer recipes (new to this edition) will give you lots of convenient lanes to dinner with favorites like Slow-Cooker Meatballs and Marinara, Air-Fryer Lemon-Pepper Chicken Wings, and Air-Fryer Orange-Mustard Glazed Salmon. A big grilling chapter brings the cooking outdoors with many appealing options like Bistecca alla Fiorentina and Grilled Shrimp and Vegetable Kebabs. In short, we wanted this Anniversary Edition to feel fresh and new, and with 17 chapters and more than 700 recipes, there is something here for everyone. So here you will find recipes like Bò Lúc Lắc; Panang Curry with Eggplant, Broccolini, and Tofu; Dan Dan Mian; and Turmeric Scallops with Mango and Noodle Salad. All manner of modern salads and grain dishes like Freekeh Salad with Sweet Potatoes and Walnuts and Charred Chicken Salad will have you upping your salad game. And what about Italian classics? Rest assured, your favorites and more are included, from Classic Pork Ragu (made with 12 ounces of country-style pork ribs) to an ingenious Skillet Eggplant Parmesan and a Weeknight Bolognese, to Pesce all'Acqua Pazza, a dazzlingly easy way to poach fish with a broth you won't be able to resist. And we didn't leave out dessert. Across three baking and dessert chapters we cover quick breads, fruit desserts, cookies, and cakes with recipes such as Garam Masala–Spiced Mango Crisp and Lemon–Poppy Seed Mug Cake.

This book doesn't just include recipes—we also share what we've learned about cooking for two. For example, waste doesn't happen with just leftovers, it starts with shopping for the ingredients themselves. Proper storage of ingredients is also paramount since a smaller household may take longer to make it through a block of feta in brine, a wedge of good cheese, a loaf of bread, a head of cauliflower, or a 14-ounce container of tofu. In the following pages, we share our shopping strategies, no-waste recommendations, and how best to outfit your kitchen. With these strategies, suddenly you will view with new eyes ingredients you may have tossed, like your vegetable scraps; save them and freeze them and then when you have a robust collection, use them to make our savory and delicious vegetable scrap broth. A newly expanded section called Putting Leftover Ingredients to Work is designed to help you run an efficient kitchen with small recipes using ingredients you inevitably have leftover, like 8 ounces of eggplant, extra ricotta, or half a fennel bulb. In addition, we direct you to other recipes in the book using more than 20 ingredients so that you can plan ahead and make the most of what you buy. Above all, we aimed to make cooking for two failproof.

How to Reduce Food Waste

If there is one thing indisputable about the culinary world, it's that collectively, it can be a powerful force for change and for the good of humanity. Think José Andrés, renowned Spanish-American chef and creator of World Central Kitchen, whose mission is to change the world through the power of food. Then there's Sophia Roe, a young James Beard–award winning chef and food activist who gained her culinary chops working at Eleven Madison Park, and whose widely popular blog and videos about the impact of food on the planet have captivated a huge audience. Witness Tamar Adler's latest book, *The Everlasting Meal Cookbook: Leftovers A to Z*, a bible on how to incorporate this important philosophy into your cooking whether cooking for just two or for a crowd. And *Cucina Povera: The Italian Way of Transforming Humble Ingredients into Unforgettable Meals* by Giulia Scarpaleggia, because well, haven't the Italians always known how to cook and eat this way?

One place everyone can have an impact is in their own kitchen by minimizing waste, which affects your time, your wallet, and our landfills. Since it is definitely harder to shop and cook this way when you are cooking for just two, in the pages that follow you will find easy-to-implement ways to get started right away.

USE EVERY PART

Don't be tempted to snap off those beet or radish greens or the lovely web-like fronds that come with fresh-from-the-market carrots. Save them and sauté the hearty ones; and use the carrot fronds to make a terrific pesto—just add a little parsley, garlic, olive oil, cheese, and nuts of any kind and puree it all in a food processor. See our recipe for Basil Pesto (page 235) and swap out the basil for other greens.

STASH SCRAPS IN YOUR FREEZER FOR STOCK

We like to keep a prep bowl for scraps on our cutting board as we prep meals for ease of clean up, and also it helps to remind you to empty most of those scraps into a bag in your freezer.

Vegetable Scrap Broth

Makes 8 cups   `VEGETARIAN`
Total time 1 hour 20 minutes, plus 1 hour cooling

This is an opportunity to transform what might otherwise end up as food waste into a broth that can add layers of flavor to anything from risottos and pilafs to soups and sauces to hearty stews and braises.

Freeze scraps in zipper-lock bags; avoid saving any scraps that are deeply discolored, overly softened, or beginning to mold. We don't recommend saving potato scraps or scraps from vegetables that have sulfuric or bitter notes, such as broccoli, cauliflower, and cabbage. Consider adding additional flavor with aromatics, such as bay leaf, peppercorns, and citrus zest, or savory elements such as Parmesan rind, kombu, soy sauce, miso, and tomato paste.

1½ pounds trimmings from nearly any vegetable
3 quarts water
1 tablespoon table salt

Combine all ingredients in large pot and bring to boil. Partially cover; reduce heat to medium-low; and simmer gently, about 1 hour. Strain broth through fine-mesh strainer into large bowl or container; discard spent scraps. Let broth cool completely. (Cooled broth can be refrigerated for up to 4 days or frozen for up to 2 months.)

IDEAS FOR SCRAPS TO USE FOR BROTH

- Carrot peels and tops
- Celery leaves or trimmings
- Corn cobs
- Fennel stalks and fronds
- Tiny unpeeled garlic cloves or garlic skins
- Herb stems and sprigs
- Mushroom stems
- Onion, leek, and shallot skins and greens
- Radish tops
- Tomato cores and trimmings
- Winter squash peels and seeds
- Root vegetable peels

Quick Pickled Vegetables

Makes about 2 cups   VEGETARIAN
Total time 55 minutes

This recipe works well with a single variety or a combination of vegetables such as onions, shallots, carrots, fennel, cabbage, and radishes. Trim and peel as needed. Halve and core fennel and cabbage before slicing. Shave carrots into ribbons for added contrast. Feel free to add up to 1 teaspoon of your favorite whole spices to the brine.

    1 cup white or red wine vinegar
    ⅓ cup sugar
    ⅛ teaspoon table salt
    2 cups thinly sliced hearty vegetables

Microwave vinegar, sugar, and salt in medium bowl until steaming, 2 to 3 minutes; whisk to dissolve sugar and salt. Add vegetables to hot brine and press to submerge completely. Let sit for 45 minutes. Drain. (Drained pickled vegetables can be refrigerated for up to 1 week.)

STOP THROWING AWAY BREAD

Bread is at the top of the list of the most wasted food product globally. There are easy strategies to avoid contributing to this problem. Start freezing a portion of the bread you buy so that it doesn't go stale and end up in the trash. Find more ways to use it in a variety of recipes like croutons, fattoush, panzanella, fancy grilled cheese sandwiches, and more (see page 15).

SCRUB, DON'T PEEL

Just imagine all the carrots and potatoes and other vegetables you've peeled over the years. And while sometimes it is necessary, oftentimes it's not. Think organic carrots at the peak of freshness. There is no reason to peel, simply scrubbing them is sufficient, especially if you are putting them into a stew or braise or if you are shredding them. The same is true for small Yukon Gold or baby red potatoes. Roast them skin-on or cut them up and put them in a stew or braise. You can also simply steam them skin-on and top them with melted butter and fresh herbs. After all, the bulk of the nutrients are in the skin.

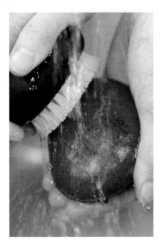

PICKLE IT

If you are left with half a head of cauliflower, extra green beans, a bunch of beets, or more asparagus than you can eat, consider making a batch of quick pickles.

GROW YOUR OWN HERBS

In the for-two kitchen, it can be hard to use up a big bunch of parsley, dill, basil, mint, cilantro, or chives regardless of how careful you are about washing and storing them. One solution, if you have a garden, is to simply grow the herbs you use most often. And in the winter months (and if you live in an apartment), keep a few small pots of herbs in a sunny window.

MAKE YOUR OWN CONDIMENTS, SPICE RUBS, AND SALAD DRESSINGS

You can eliminate a lot of packaging waste if you make an effort to make small batches of things like barbecue sauce, ketchup, mustard, harissa, spice rubs, and salad dressings. Other than salad dressings, these items can be stored for a long time. Throughout the book you will find spice rubs and other condiments and a recipe for Foolproof Vinaigrette, with many appealing variations (page 72). Also see ideas for bottom-of-the-jar sauces and condiments on page 7.

BUY PACKAGING FREE WHEN POSSIBLE

You can buy all manner of vegetables and greens loose with no plastic wrap or packaging whatsoever; these include carrots, celery heads, mushrooms, kale, Swiss chard, heads of romaine and more. Consider buying coffee beans in bulk (and don't use the pods) and buy loose tea rather than tea bags.

NEVER THROW AWAY A CONDIMENT JAR AGAIN
Often the dregs of a condiment container can be mixed with other items in your pantry to make a new and interesting sauce, vinaigrette, or glaze to drizzle on food. So don't throw it away!

MAKE JAM
Fruit goes bad easily, so it's handy to have a simple formula to make it into jam.

Strawberry Refrigerator Jam

Makes about 1 cup   VEGETARIAN
Total time 25 minutes, plus 30 minutes cooling

¾ pound strawberries, hulled and cut into
    ½-inch pieces (3 cups)
½ cup sugar
1½ tablespoons lemon juice

1. Place metal spoon in freezer to chill. Combine strawberries, sugar, and lemon juice in medium saucepan. Bring to boil over medium-high heat, then reduce heat to medium. Mash fruit with potato masher until fruit is mostly broken down. Simmer vigorously until fruit mixture thickens to jamlike consistency, 15 to 20 minutes.

2. To test for set point, remove saucepan from heat. Dip chilled spoon into jam and allow jam to run off spoon; jam should slowly fall off spoon in single thickened clump. If jam is runny, return to medium heat and simmer 2 to 4 minutes before retesting. Transfer finished jam to jar with tight-fitting lid, let cool to room temperature, then cover and refrigerate. (Jam can be refrigerated for up to 3 weeks.)

VARIATIONS
Blueberry Refrigerator Jam
Makes about 1 cup
Substitute ½ pound blueberries for strawberries and leave fruit whole. Reduce sugar to 6 tablespoons and lemon juice to 1 tablespoon. In step 1, simmer mixture for 8 to 12 minutes.

Raspberry Refrigerator Jam
Makes about 1 cup
Substitute ½ pound raspberries for strawberries and leave fruit whole. Reduce sugar to 6 tablespoons and lemon juice to 1 tablespoon.

NOTES FROM THE TEST KITCHEN

COMPOST IT
You may think that your food scraps don't make a difference in pollution, but that's not the case. Americans add billions of pounds of food to landfills each year, producing greenhouses gases like methane that negatively impact the environment. You can stop feeding the problem by reducing the amount of food scraps thrown into landfills. In addition to helping the planet, composting makes perfect (free) plant food and cuts down on food smells in your trash.

We like to use a countertop compost bin, which allows you to neatly store food scraps until you can transfer them to a larger setup: either a community drop-off or your backyard. Our winning countertop bin, the **OXO Good Grips Easy-Clean Compost Bin (1.75 Gal)** is light—weighing around 4 pounds when filled. Its wide opening makes dumping and emptying heaps of scraps a breeze. Even without a filter, it contained odors for a full week. It's spacious, capable of holding up to five days' worth of peels, coffee grounds, and egg shells from a two-person household that likes to cook.

Bottom-of-the-Jar Sauces and Condiments

AN ALMOST-EMPTY JAR OF

honey	+	soy sauce	=	soy honey
	+	melted butter	=	honey butter
	+	hoisin	=	honey-hoisin glaze
	+	Thai chili paste	=	honey-chili paste
jam (microwave jam to melt first)	+	whole-grain/Dijon mustard, vinegar, and oil	=	fruit vinaigrette
	+	fresh fruit	=	glazed fruit topping
	+	melted butter	=	fruity butter spread
	+	water, minced garlic, minced ginger, and soy sauce	=	fruity soy-ginger glaze
	+	chopped fresh herbs and water	=	sweet and herby glaze
mayonnaise	+	Thai curry paste	=	thai curry mayonnaise
	+	lime/lemon juice and zest	=	citrus mayonnaise
	+	horseradish and Worcestershire	=	steakhouse mayonnaise
	+	chipotle chile in adobo	=	chipotle mayonnaise
	+	curry powder or Ras el Hanout (page 58)	=	spiced mayonnaise
sun-dried tomatoes	+	vinegar, mustard, and minced shallot	=	sun-dried tomato vinaigrette
	+	mayonnaise	=	sun-dried tomato mayonnaise
miso	+	mirin, oil, and minced ginger	=	miso dressing
	+	mayo, maple syrup, toasted sesame oil, and vinegar	=	miso-maple vinaigrette
	+	melted or softened butter	=	miso butter
hoisin	+	unseasoned rice vinegar, minced ginger, and chopped scallions	=	hoisin vinaigrette
peanut butter	+	oats and water (1:1 ratio); let sit overnight	=	overnight peanut butter oats
	+	unseasoned rice vinegar, hot water, and curry paste	=	peanut sauce
	+	chocolate syrup and hot milk	=	peanutty hot chocolate
red curry paste	+	coconut milk and lime juice	=	red curry sauce
mustard	+	vinegar, honey, oil, and herbs	=	classic vinaigrette
	+	soy sauce and vinegar	=	tahini-soy dressing
gochujang	+	soy sauce, rice vinegar, minced ginger, minced garlic, and toasted sesame oil	=	gochujang sauce

Befriend Your Freezer

The freezer is key to eliminating food waste, especially when cooking for two. Here are some common ingredients that are hard to buy in small quantities with info on how best to freeze them.

ANCHOVIES AND BACON Coil up individually (to prevent sticking and to minimize surface area for freezer burn), freeze on plate, and transfer to zipper-lock bag.

BANANAS Peel bananas and freeze in zipper-lock freezer bag.

BEANS Drain, pat beans dry with paper towels, and transfer to zipper-lock bag. Lay bag flat to freeze to save space.

BREAD Slice bread, wrap tightly in aluminum foil, and seal in zipper-lock bag before freezing.

BUTTER Stored in the refrigerator, butter can pick up off-flavors. Instead, freeze butter in its wrapper.

BUTTERMILK Place some small paper cups on tray and fill each with ½ cup buttermilk; place tray in freezer.

CANNED TOMATO PASTE Open both ends of can, push out paste, and freeze in zipper-lock bag. To use, cut off only as much paste as needed from frozen log.

CHEESE Yes, you can freeze cheese. We tested extra-sharp cheddar, Brie, fresh goat cheese, and Pecorino Romano. Wrap the cheese tightly in plastic wrap and seal in a zipper-lock bag for up to 2 months. Let it defrost overnight in the fridge (a 2½-hour rest on the counter also works).

CHIPOTLE CHILES IN ADOBO Freeze spoonfuls of chiles and sauce on parchment paper–lined baking sheet. Transfer frozen chiles to zipper-lock bag.

CITRUS ZEST Grate zest from entire fruit, mound into ½- or 1-teaspoon piles on plate, and freeze. Transfer frozen zest to zipper-lock bag.

COCONUT MILK Transfer to airtight container and freeze. If milk separates after defrosting, blend with immersion blender for about 30 seconds to re-emulsify.

COOKED RICE Spread cooked long-grain white or brown rice in single layer on rimmed baking sheet until completely cooled, then transfer to zipper-lock bag and lay flat to freeze.

EGG WHITES Pour leftover egg whites (never yolks) into each well of ice cube tray and freeze.

FRESH HERBS Place chopped herbs in wells of ice cube tray, cover with water, and freeze. Frozen herb cubes can be added directly to sauces, soups, and more.

GARLIC Place minced garlic in small bowl, cover with enough neutral-tasting oil to coat, then spoon heaping teaspoons onto baking sheet to freeze. Transfer frozen garlic to zipper-lock bag.

GINGER Cut fresh ginger into 1-inch pieces and freeze in zipper-lock bag. To use, chop or grate ginger directly from freezer.

NUTS Due to their high fat content, nuts go rancid quickly unless frozen. Freeze nuts in zipper-lock freezer bag.

RICOTTA Ricotta is a fresh cheese that contains a lot of water, so when we considered freezing it, our suspicion was that freezing would cause the extra water to leach out when thawed, giving the cheese a gritty texture. To find out for sure, we froze a few previously opened containers of ricotta for two months, then defrosted them. When sampled plain, the never-frozen cheese was preferred for its smooth, clean taste. The frozen ricotta was looser in texture and slightly watery. Few tasters could detect any differences when the ricotta was baked in the manicotti or lasagna, but the frozen ricotta tossed with pasta was objectionable. In this recipe, the ricotta does not get cooked, and its texture was noticeably granular. So if you have trouble using up ricotta before it spoils, go ahead and freeze the extra—just make sure to use it in a recipe where it will be cooked.

TOFU Tofu is about 88 percent water; as it freezes, the ice crystals expand, pushing apart the protein network. When thawed, the water drains away, leaving the tofu with a spongy consistency that is highly absorbent. We experimented with freezing tofu in the test kitchen and quite liked the results. When stir-fried, the slabs did absorb sauce readily and had a resil-ient, slightly chewy texture that was far more meat-like than fresh tofu. And because the thawed tofu contained less water, it formed a nice crust when deep-fried. To freeze, slice extra-firm tofu into ½- to ¾-inch-thick slabs, spread them in a single layer on a baking sheet or plate, and place them in the freezer overnight. (At this point, the tofu can be placed in zipper-lock bags and stored in the freezer for up to a month.) To use, thaw to room temperature and press each slab gently over a colander to expel any remaining water before cooking.

WINE Measure 1 tablespoon wine into each well of ice cube tray and freeze. Use paring knife or small spatula to remove frozen wine cubes and add as desired to dishes.

How to Shop Smarter

Grocery stores are designed to entice shoppers to buy more, with buy-one-get-one sales, lower prices for bigger quantities, and everything packaged in "family-size" portions. It can seem impossible to shop for two without a lot of waste, but we've found that there are a few simple ways to buy just what you need.

GET CREATIVE IN THE PRODUCE SECTION

Produce is often the most difficult thing to buy for two. Stores sell carrots by the bunch, lettuce by the head, and grapes and cherries in bags of 2 pounds or more. You may have better luck in the organic section, where produce is often sold loose by the pound. Frozen fruits and vegetables are also very useful when cooking for two. Individually quick-frozen produce is often as good or better than what you can get fresh—frozen peas and blueberries are two good examples.

SHOP AT A FARMERS' MARKET

Farmers' markets are a terrific place to buy fantastic fresh produce and much more in just the amounts you want. And it is a great way to ensure that you are eating what is seasonal. Many vendors allow you to pick the amount of loose lettuce greens you want instead of a whole head, for instance, and many sell half loaves of high-quality homemade breads, small containers of freshly dug potatoes, and much more. The offerings are usually organic, freshly harvested, and of the highest quality. These markets offer the opportunity to not only reduce food waste when cooking for two, but the chance to use every part of vegetables like radishes, carrots,

and beets because the quality of the greens attached to them is superb, and they can be used in pestos, stocks, and more. In the fall and winter months, hearty produce and dozens of varieties of apples abound so you can plan around using them and buy only what a recipe requires.

TAKE A NUMBER AT THE MEAT COUNTER

If you can buy your meat at a local butcher shop or if your supermarket has a meat counter, go for it. With everything packaged and priced to order, you can purchase just what you need, whether it's ½ pound of ground beef or two chicken breasts.

SHOP THE BULK BINS FOR DRY GOODS

Buying prepackaged foods such as flour, nuts, rice, and grains is almost always more expensive than buying just what you need from a bulk bin. If your supermarket doesn't have a bulk section, seek out stores that do. It also will help you cut down on packaging that needs to be recycled.

PAY MORE PER POUND

It can seem silly to buy a small package of meat when you could get twice as much for less per pound. However, the alternative is spending more money, buying more than you need, and likely throwing it away when it spoils. Instead, look for six eggs instead of a dozen, a 4-ounce container of sour cream, or a package of just two pork chops. You'll pay more per pound or ounce, but spend less overall—and what you buy won't end up in the garbage.

BE THOUGHTFUL IF BUYING IN BULK

If you do want to shop in bulk to take advantage of lower prices, choose items that will keep well long term. Frozen vegetables and fruits, dried pasta, beans, and rice are all good to buy in bulk. Meat is often significantly cheaper in bulk, so although there will be a slight loss in quality, it can be worth buying in bulk and freezing. Most cuts can be kept frozen for several months; simply buy a large package and separate it into individual portions before freezing. For more information on freezing meat, see pages 114 and 143.

OPT FOR CANNED OR FROZEN

Canning and freezing are both great ways to preserve foods at their peak, and foods preserved in this way will last almost indefinitely, so you can stock up without worrying about looming expiration dates.

Some vegetables, such as peas, corn, spinach, and pearl onions, take particularly well to freezing and may be even higher quality than fresh depending on the time of year. Frozen broccoli, carrots, cauliflower, and green beans work well in dishes like soups and stews, where you're not looking for the crisp texture of fresh vegetables. But beware frozen asparagus, mushrooms, bell peppers, and snow peas: These high-moisture vegetables usually turn mushy once thawed.

SHOP THE SALAD BAR

Your supermarket's salad bar is for more than just salads—it's perfect if you need just half a cup of snap peas or cherry tomatoes, shredded carrots, chopped bell peppers, or a handful of spinach.

INGENIOUS INGREDIENTS

When you cook for two, you know the frustration of recipes calling for just half a cup of chicken broth or a tablespoon of red wine. Here are a few handy ingredients that make it easy to use smaller amounts and avoid waste.

BOUILLON AND BROTH CONCENTRATES Dehydrated and concentrated forms of chicken, vegetable, and beef broth, these shelf-stable products are cost-effective (because you're not paying for the water) and last for up to two years once opened. Simply mix with water to make just as much broth as you need. We particularly like **Better than Bouillon Chicken Base**, which makes 38 cups of broth. See page 50 for more information about these options.

BOXED WINE Once opened, bottles of wine are rarely usable for more than a week. But boxed wine has an air-tight inner bag that prevents exposure to oxygen even after the box is opened, so the wine lasts up to one month.

SHALLOTS Onions add great aromatic flavor to recipes, but a single onion is often too much for a recipe for two.

DRIED HERBS Fresh herbs have a very short shelf life, so in the for-two kitchen a big bunch can often go to waste. Luckily, as long as the herbs are cooked, you can substitute long-lasting dried herbs; this works especially well with sage, rosemary, and thyme. Just use one-third the amount called for. You can also dry your own fresh herbs to keep them from going bad; see page 24 for our recipe for Easy Dried Herbs.

SMALL POUCHES OF OLIVES, MARINARA SAUCE, AND MORE These are everywhere now, so if you want to avoid buying a large container of olives or a 26-ounce jar of marinara sauce, these are a great option. You can also find small pouches of chimichurri sauce, romesco sauce, pesto, and other sauces perfect for saucing chicken or fish for two.

RECYCLABLE BOXES OF CRUSHED AND DICED TOMATOES These lightweight and convenient boxes come in smaller quantities (13 ounces), and it's easy to wash them out and flatten them for recycling.

SMALL JARS AND TUBES OF POWER-PACKED INGREDIENTS Look for small jars of tapenade, sun dried tomato pesto, olive pesto, and tubes of anchovy paste and even harissa. These are great for emergency dinners for two (see our recipe for Spaghetti with Turkey-Pesto Meatballs on page 234) or for a hit of flavor instantly to many dishes.

FROZEN SHRIMP Don't hesitate to buy frozen shrimp; most "fresh" shrimp already has been frozen and defrosted, so it's best to buy it frozen. Most shrimp, including all bagged options, are individually quick-frozen (IQF). You can defrost just what you need in minutes under cold running water.

How to Store Smarter

Despite your best intentions at the supermarket and in the kitchen, there are some ingredients that you might end up tossing out because they've gone bad before you've had time to use them up. In the test kitchen, we've developed useful strategies to help preserve the freshness of these harder-to-finish ingredients.

ASPARAGUS Trim ends and set spears upright in 1 to 2 inches of water. Cover loosely with zipper-lock bag and refrigerate.

AVOCADO Store cut avocados submerged cut side down in lemon water in refrigerator for up to 2 days. (Avocado may have slightly softer texture and tart flavor.)

BERRIES Because they are prone to mold, wash berries before storing. Swish them in a solution of 3 parts water and 1 part vinegar, rinse, then dry thoroughly in a colander or paper towel–lined salad spinner. Store in a loosely covered, paper towel–lined container.

BREAD Crusty bread, like a rustic Italian loaf, will last a few days simply stored cut side down on the counter. Do not store it in plastic (the moisture encourages mold) or in the refrigerator, where bread stales faster than at room temperature. For longer storage, wrap the bread tightly in aluminum foil, place it in a zipper-lock bag, and store in the freezer for up to one month. To serve, bake the frozen foil-wrapped loaf directly on the rack of a 450-degree oven until warm and crisp, 10 to 30 minutes.

CHEESE We find that cheeses are best wrapped in parchment paper and then in aluminum foil and refrigerated. The paper allows the cheese to breathe, and the foil keeps out off-flavors from the refrigerator and prevents the cheese from drying out.

CARROTS Trim leafy tops, place carrots in open zipper-lock bag, and refrigerate.

CELERY Wrap whole heads loosely in aluminum foil to minimize moisture loss.

CUCUMBERS, ZUCCHINI, AND SUMMER SQUASH Wrap tightly in plastic wrap to minimize moisture loss.

CHILES Fresh chiles like jalapeños and serranos quickly lose their flavor and crispness when left loose in the crisper drawer, but they will keep for several weeks halved then stored in a brine of 1 tablespoon salt per cup of water; rinse before using.

CHOCOLATE Because cocoa butter easily picks up off-flavors from other foods, chocolate should never be stored in the refrigerator or freezer. To extend its shelf life, wrap it tightly in plastic wrap and store it in a cool, dry place. When exposed to rapid changes in temperature or humidity, it can develop a discolored surface. This condition, known as bloom, is only cosmetic—bloomed chocolate is safe to eat and cook with.

EGGS Properly stored eggs will last up to three months, but both the yolks and the whites become looser and their flavor will begin to fade over time. Store eggs in the back of the refrigerator (the coldest area) and keep them in the carton, which holds in moisture and protects the eggs from odors.

FLOUR All-purpose flour is one ingredient that is useful to purchase in larger amounts. To keep our flour fresh, we store it in a wide-mouth container, which also makes it easy to dip in a measuring cup and level off the excess back into the container. All-purpose flour can be stored in the pantry for up to a year, but whole-grain flours like whole-wheat and rye are more perishable and should be stored in the freezer.

FRESH HERBS Because they're highly perishable and sold in large bunches, herbs are one of the hardest things to avoid throwing out. To get the most life out of herbs, gently rinse and dry them (a salad spinner works well), wrap them in a damp paper towel, and place in a partially open zipper-lock bag in the crisper drawer. Basil, however, should be handled differently. Don't rinse it before you need to use it; the added moisture will decrease its shelf life. Simply wrap it in clean paper towels, place it in a partially open zipper-lock bag, and refrigerate.

GARLIC Store heads of garlic in a cool, dark place with plenty of air circulation to prevent spoiling and sprouting. Store cut garlic in oil in the refrigerator for no more than four days.

GINGER When wrapped in plastic or foil, ginger will grow mold where the condensation is trapped, so it's best to simply toss it into the refrigerator unwrapped.

GREENS Delicate greens spoil quickly if not stored properly. Wash greens and dry thoroughly in a salad spinner, then store directly in the spinner between layers of paper towels, or lightly roll in paper towels and store in a zipper-lock bag left slightly open. If pre-washed, store in the original plastic container or bag.

LEAVENERS Keep baking powder and baking soda in the pantry and replace them every six months. Keep yeast in the refrigerator or freezer to slow its deterioration. And because yeast is a living organism, observe the expiration date.

MEAT Raw or cooked meat should be refrigerated well wrapped and will keep for two to three days. To freeze meat in small batches for long-term storage, place two pieces of meat (such as chicken breasts, small steaks, or portions of ground meat) at different locations inside a large zipper-lock freezer bag. Flatten out the bag, forcing the air out, so that the meat portions do not touch. Then fold the bag over in the center and freeze it.

MUSHROOMS Thanks to their high moisture content, raw mushrooms are very perishable. To maximize air circulation without drying out mushrooms, store them wrapped in plastic in their original packaging or in a partially open zipper-lock bag.

OILS To prevent rancidity, store cooking oils in a cool, dark pantry. Unopened olive oil lasts for one year; once opened, it will last for about three months. Toasted sesame oil and nut oils, like peanut oil, should be stored in the refrigerator.

ONIONS AND OTHER ALLIUMS Onions and shallots should be stored in a cool place away from light. Don't store onions in the refrigerator; their odor can permeate other foods. Delicate scallions, chives, and leeks do belong in the refrigerator; store them in a glass of water covered loosely with a zipper-lock bag. To store part of a chopped or sliced onion, refrigerate in a zipper-lock bag and rinse before using to remove residual odor.

POTATOES If not stored correctly, potatoes will germinate and grow. To avoid this, keep them in a cool, dark place. Store them in a paper (not plastic) bag and keep them away from onions, which give off gases that will hasten sprouting.

SPICES Keep spices in a cool, dark pantry to prolong their freshness. To keep track of your spices' freshness, it's helpful to label each jar with the date opened; whole spices are good for about two years and ground spices for one year.

SWEETENERS Store brown sugar in an airtight container; a terra-cotta Brown Sugar Bear will help keep it soft. Keep molasses and honey in the pantry (they will crystallize in the refrigerator). Maple syrup should be refrigerated, as it is susceptible to mold. Syrup also can be kept in the freezer (it will not freeze solid because of its high sugar concentration).

TOMATOES Contrary to popular belief, both cut and whole tomatoes actually can be stored in the refrigerator once fully ripe (for 2 days and 5 days respectively). To keep them from picking up off-flavors, put them in an airtight container, which works better than plastic wrap at keeping out odors.

Putting Leftover Ingredients to Work

When cooking in smaller quantities, it's unavoidable that you'll end up with some leftover ingredients. Whether it's half a butternut squash or part of a can of beans or tomatoes, these odds and ends tend to languish in the refrigerator until they have to be thrown away. Our solution? Quick, simple recipes that make it easy to put these ingredients to work. In addition, we've provided a list of recipes across the book that use these ingredients so you can plan ahead to make another distinct recipe and feel good about not wasting ingredients.

■ **FAST** (Start to finish in 30 minutes or less)
■ **VEGETARIAN**

ASPARAGUS

A bunch of asparagus is typically a pound, which is too much for the for-two audience. Here are some ideas of what to do with the remaining spears.

Pan-Roasted Asparagus
Serves 2 **FAST** **VEGETARIAN**

Heat 1 teaspoon vegetable oil in 12-inch skillet over medium heat until shimmering. Add 6 ounces trimmed thick asparagus to skillet with tips pointed in one direction and add 6 ounces trimmed thick asparagus with tips pointed in opposite direction. Using tongs, distribute spears in even layer. Sprinkle with 1 teaspoon water, ¼ teaspoon table salt, and pinch pepper, cover, and cook until asparagus is bright green and still crisp, 3 to 4 minutes. Uncover; increase heat to medium-high; and cook until asparagus is tender and well browned on all sides, 4 to 6 minutes, rearranging spears as needed. Off heat, sprinkle with 1 teaspoon lemon juice and season with salt and pepper to taste. Serve.

Creamy Asparagus Soup
Serves 2 **VEGETARIAN**

Cut tips off ½ pound thin asparagus spears and reserve. Cut spears into ½-inch pieces. Melt ½ teaspoon butter in large saucepan over medium-high heat. Add asparagus tips and cook until just tender, about 2 minutes; transfer to bowl and set aside. Add 1½ teaspoons butter, asparagus spears, ¼ pound thinly sliced leeks, pinch table salt, and pinch pepper to now-empty pan and cook over medium-low heat until vegetables are softened, about 10 minutes. Add ¾ cup vegetable or chicken broth to pan and bring to boil over medium-high heat. Reduce heat to medium-low and simmer until vegetables are tender, about 5 minutes. Stir in 2 tablespoons frozen peas and 2 teaspoons grated Parmesan. Process soup in blender until smooth; transfer to clean pan. Stir in 1 tablespoon heavy cream, ⅛ teaspoon lemon juice, and asparagus tips and cook over medium-low heat until warmed through, about 2 minutes. Season with salt and pepper to taste. Serve.

Stir-Fried Asparagus with Shiitake Mushrooms
Serves 2 **VEGETARIAN**

Combine 1 tablespoon water, ½ tablespoon soy sauce, ½ tablespoon sherry, 1 teaspoon packed brown sugar, 1 teaspoon grated fresh ginger, and ½ teaspoon toasted sesame oil in bowl. Heat ½ tablespoon vegetable oil in 12-inch nonstick skillet over high heat until smoking. Add 12 ounces thin asparagus, sliced into 2-inch lengths on bias and 4 ounces thinly sliced shiitake mushrooms and cook until asparagus is spotty brown, 3 to 4 minutes. Add soy sauce mixture and cook until asparagus is crisp-tender, 1 to 2 minutes. Transfer to serving platter, sprinkle with 1 thinly sliced scallion, and serve.

RECIPES USING UP ASPARAGUS

- Tortellini Salad with Asparagus and Fresh Basil Vinaigrette (page 86)
- Braised Chicken Thighs with Potatoes, Carrots, Asparagus, and Dill (page 132)
- Steamed Sole and Vegetable Bundles with Tarragon (page 172)
- Stir-Fried Shrimp with Lemon-Ginger Sauce (page 191)
- Risotto Primavera (page 213)
- Soft-Cooked Eggs with Steamed Asparagus (page 363)

Stir-Fried Asparagus with Shiitake Mushrooms

Grilled Cheese Sandwiches with Caramelized Onion and Apple

Individual Chocolate Bread Puddings

Serves 2 `VEGETARIAN`

Heat oven to 325 degrees. Whisk 1 large egg and 3 tablespoons sugar together in large bowl. Whisk in 1 cup half-and-half and ½ teaspoon vanilla. Stir in 2 ounces chopped bittersweet chocolate and 2½ cups ½-inch cubes baguette. Cover and soak for 20 minutes, stirring often. Portion mixture into 2 large greased, ovensafe coffee cups (or ramekins) and bake until puddings are set, 25 to 30 minutes. Let cool slightly before serving.

RECIPES USING UP BREAD

- Creamless Creamy Tomato Soup (page 46)
- Catalan Beef Stew (page 55)
- Turkey Burgers (page 95)
- Grilled Cheese Sandwiches with Caramelized Onion and Apple (page 99)
- Grilled Cheese Sandwiches with Tomato and Pesto (page 99)
- Portobello Panini (page 99)
- Tofu Katsu Sandwiches (page 100)
- Pork Schnitzel (page 155)
- Mushroom, Brussels Sprout, and White Bean Gratin (page 219)
- Grilled Vegetable and Bread Salad (page 285)
- Slow-Cooker Meatballs and Marinara (page 298)
- Skillet Strata with Cheddar (page 368)
- Skillet Strata with Sausage and Gruyère (page 368)
- Bourbon Bread Pudding (page 446)

BREAD

A family of two would have to eat sandwiches for days to use up an entire loaf of bread or a whole baguette. Bread can be frozen for up to one month, or you can try our recipes for using up bread before it goes bad.

Garlic Croutons

Makes 2 cups `FAST` `VEGETARIAN`

Heat oven to 350 degrees. Toss 4 slices hearty white sandwich bread, cut into 1-inch pieces, with 2 tablespoons melted unsalted butter and 1 minced garlic clove. Season with salt and pepper. Spread onto rimmed baking sheet and bake until golden brown and crisp, 15 to 20 minutes, stirring occasionally.

Summer Berry Gratin

Serves 2 `VEGETARIAN`

Heat oven to 450 degrees. Pulse 2 slices hearty white sandwich bread, 2 tablespoons brown sugar, 2 tablespoons softened unsalted butter, and pinch ground cinnamon in food processor to coarse crumbs, about 10 pulses. Gently toss 1½ cups blackberries, blueberries, raspberries, and/or quartered strawberries with 1 teaspoon granulated sugar, ¼ teaspoon vanilla extract, and pinch salt, then spread into 7¼ by 5¼-inch baking dish. Sprinkle crumb mixture evenly over fruit and bake until crumbs are deep golden brown and fruit is hot, 15 to 20 minutes, rotating dish halfway through baking. Let cool slightly before serving.

BUTTERMILK

Buttermilk is generally sold only by the quart, so when recipes call for a small amount, you're stuck with lots of leftovers. You can refrigerate it for up to three weeks (with some flavor loss) or freeze it for up to two months, but we prefer to put it to work.

Very Berry Smoothie

Serves 2 `FAST` `VEGETARIAN`

Process 1½ cups buttermilk, 1½ cups frozen berries, 1 peeled and chopped banana, 1 tablespoon sugar, and pinch table salt on low speed in blender until berries are chopped, about 10 seconds. Increase speed to high and continue to process until smooth, 20 to 40 seconds. Season with more sugar and adjust consistency with water as needed. Serve.

Ranch Dressing

Makes 1 cup `FAST` `VEGETARIAN`

Whisk ⅔ cup sour cream, ¼ cup buttermilk, 2 tablespoons minced fresh cilantro (or dill, tarragon, or parsley), 1 tablespoon minced shallot, 2 teaspoons white wine vinegar, ½ teaspoon garlic powder, ¼ teaspoon table salt, and ¼ teaspoon pepper together until smooth. Season with sugar to taste.

Muffin Tin Doughnuts

Makes 4 doughnuts `VEGETARIAN`

Heat oven to 400 degrees. Whisk 1¼ cups cake flour, ⅓ cup sugar, 1¼ teaspoons baking powder, ¼ teaspoon table salt, and pinch nutmeg together in large bowl. In separate bowl, whisk ⅓ cup buttermilk, 3 tablespoons melted unsalted butter, and 1 large egg together. Stir buttermilk mixture into flour mixture until combined. Scoop batter into 4 greased wells of muffin tin and bake until lightly browned and toothpick inserted in center comes out clean, 15 to 18 minutes. Mix ½ cup sugar and ½ teaspoon ground cinnamon together in small bowl. Brush warm donuts with 2 tablespoons melted unsalted butter, then roll in cinnamon sugar to coat. Serve.

Muffin Tin Doughnuts

> ### RECIPES USING UP BUTTERMILK
> - Buttermilk Mashed Potatoes (page 333)
> - Buttermilk Pancakes (page 370)
> - Simple Drop Biscuits (page 378)
> - Fresh Herb Simple Drop Biscuits (page 378)
> - Black Pepper and Bacon Simple Drop Biscuits (page 378)
> - Rosemary and Parmesan Simple Drop Biscuits (page 378)
> - Cinnamon Streusel Coffee Cake (page 382)
> - Skillet Cherry Cobbler (page 395)
> - Glazed Lemon Bundt Cakes (page 426)
> - Fluffy Yellow Layer Cake (page 431)
> - Vanilla Cupcakes (page 435)

BUTTERNUT SQUASH

Once chopped, a single butternut squash can yield up to 8 or 9 cups—far too much for just two people. And since it can't be eaten raw like some vegetables, using it up isn't as easy as tossing it into a salad. Luckily, our recipes for left-over butternut squash are so good, you might not want to wait to have leftovers.

Roasted Butternut Squash Salad

Serves 2 `VEGETARIAN`

Heat oven to 425 degrees. Toss 1 pound butternut squash, peeled, seeded, and cut into 1-inch pieces (2½ cups), with 1 tablespoon extra-virgin olive oil and ¼ teaspoon table salt; spread onto rimmed baking sheet. Roast until squash is spotty brown and tender, 30 to 35 minutes, stirring occasionally. Toss roasted squash with 4 ounces arugula, ¼ cup dried cranberries, 1 tablespoon extra-virgin olive oil, and 2 table-spoons cider vinegar. Season with salt and pepper to taste, and serve.

Butternut Squash Breakfast Hash

Serves 2

Microwave 1 pound butternut squash, peeled, seeded, and cut into ½-inch pieces (2½ cups), and 1 cup water in covered bowl until tender, 5 to 8 minutes; drain. Cook 2 slices chopped bacon in 12-inch nonstick skillet over medium-high heat until crispy, about 5 minutes; transfer to paper towel-lined plate. Add 1 chopped onion and 1 teaspoon paprika to fat left in skillet and cook over medium heat until softened, about 5 minutes. Add squash and cook, stirring often, until lightly browned, about 10 minutes. Sprinkle with bacon, season with salt and pepper to taste, and serve.

Quick Kimchi

RECIPES USING UP BUTTERNUT SQUASH

- Butternut Squash Soup with Blue Cheese and Pepitas (page 44)
- Fattoush with Butternut Squash and Apple (page 81)
- Braised Tofu with Butternut Squash and Eggplant (page 223)
- Slow-Cooker Creamy Butternut Squash and Apple Soup (page 294)
- Butternut Squash Puree (page 337)
- Butternut Squash Puree with Orange (page 338)
- Butternut Squash Puree with Honey and Chipotle Chile (page 338)

CABBAGE

Inexpensive, healthy, and delicious, cabbage is a great addition to any recipe. But what do you do with leftovers? How about making creamy coleslaw, roasting it, or pickling it for kimchi?

Creamy New York Deli Coleslaw

Serves 2   VEGETARIAN

Toss 4½ cups shredded green cabbage (½ small head) and 1 peeled and grated carrot with ½ teaspoon table salt in colander and let drain for 1 hour; rinse and pat dry with paper towels. In large bowl, whisk ¼ cup mayonnaise, 2 tablespoons minced shallot, 1 tablespoon distilled white vinegar, ½ teaspoon Dijon mustard, and ½ teaspoon sugar together. Stir in cabbage and season with salt and pepper to taste. Cover and refrigerate until chilled, at least 30 minutes, before serving.

Roasted Cabbage Wedges

Serves 2   VEGETARIAN

Place rimmed baking sheet on upper-middle rack and heat oven to 450 degrees. Combine ½ teaspoon sugar, ½ teaspoon pepper, and ¼ teaspoon table salt in small bowl. Cut ½ small head green or napa cabbage through core into quarters. Brush with 2 tablespoons vegetable oil and sprinkle with sugar mixture. Place cabbage wedges on hot baking sheet, flat side down, and roast until tender and browned at edges, 15 to 20 minutes, flipping wedges halfway through roasting. Drizzle with 1 teaspoon balsamic vinegar and serve.

Quick Kimchi

Makes 2 cups

Toss 4 cups coarsely chopped napa cabbage (½ small head) with ¼ cup water and microwave until slightly softened, about 3 minutes. Drain cabbage and let cool slightly, about 5 minutes. Toss drained cabbage with 2 thinly sliced scallions, 1 tablespoon unseasoned rice vinegar, 1 tablespoon gochujang, 1 minced garlic clove, 1½ teaspoons sugar, and 1 teaspoon fish sauce. Season with salt to taste. Kimchi can be refrigerated for up to 6 months.

RECIPES USING UP CABBAGE

- Farmhouse Vegetable and Barley Soup (green cabbage) (page 43)
- Sweet and Tangy Coleslaw (green cabbage) (page 89)
- Sweet and Tangy Coleslaw with Bell Pepper and Jalapeño (green cabbage) (page 90)
- Sweet and Tangy Coleslaw with Apple and Tarragon (green cabbage) (page 90)
- Charred Cabbage Salad with Torn Tofu and Plantain Chips (red cabbage) (page 91)
- Tofu Katsu Sandwiches (green cabbage) (page 100)
- Crispy Sesame Pork Chops with Wilted Napa Cabbage Salad (napa cabbage) (page 154)
- Curry Roasted Cabbage Wedges with Tomatoes and Chickpeas (green cabbage) (page 221)
- Ramen with Pork and Cabbage (green cabbage) (page 255)
- Grilled Fish Tacos (green cabbage) (page 280)
- Skillet-Roasted Cabbage with Mustard and Thyme (green, napa, or savoy cabbage) (page 322)

Crispy Spiced Chickpeas

Refried Beans
Makes 1 cup FAST VEGETARIAN

Process ¾ cup rinsed canned pinto beans (or red kidney beans or black beans) and ¼ cup vegetable or chicken broth in food processor until smooth, about 30 seconds. Heat 2 tablespoons extra-virgin olive oil in 10-inch nonstick skillet over medium heat until shimmering. Add ¼ cup finely chopped onion and cook until softened, 2 to 4 minutes. Stir in 1 minced garlic clove and ⅛ teaspoon ground cumin and cook until fragrant, about 30 seconds. Stir in processed beans and cook until thickened, 3 to 5 minutes. Season with salt and pepper to taste, and serve.

Garlicky Sautéed White Beans with Tomatoes
Serves 2 FAST VEGETARIAN

Cook 2 thinly sliced garlic cloves with 2 tablespoons extra-virgin olive oil in 8-inch skillet over medium-low heat until fragrant and lightly golden, about 3 minutes. Stir in ¾ cup rinsed canned cannellini beans (or small white beans), 1 chopped tomato, and ¼ teaspoon table salt. Increase heat to medium-high and cook, stirring often, until tomatoes are softened and beans are heated through, about 3 minutes. Off heat, stir in 1 tablespoon chopped fresh basil (or parsley, cilantro, chives, dill, or scallions). Season with salt and pepper to taste, and serve.

RECIPES USING UP CANNED BEANS

- Soupe au Pistou (cannellini or navy) (page 43)
- Pasta e Fagioli (cannellini) (page 48)
- Chickpea and Vegetable Soup with Warm Spices (page 51)
- Classic Beef Chili (kidney or pinto) (page 64)
- Beef Chili with Bacon (kidney or pinto) (page 64)
- Beef Chili with Chipotle, Black Beans, and Corn (page 64)
- Beef Chili with Chickpeas and Warm Spices (page 64)
- Five-Alarm Chili (pinto) (page 66)
- Turkey Chili (kidney or pinto) (page 67)
- Skillet Brown Rice and Beans with Corn and Tomatoes (black beans) (page 213)
- Spanish-Style Skillet Brown Rice and Chickpeas (page 214)
- Chickpea Cakes with Cucumber-Yogurt Sauce (page 218)
- Black Bean Salad with Corn and Avocado (black beans) (page 353)

CANNED BEANS
Canned beans are particularly convenient when cooking for two because they're quick-cooking and don't require lengthy soaking times. And there's no need to toss the leftovers when you use just part of a can; here are our favorite recipes for using the rest.

Crispy Spiced Chickpeas
Makes ¾ cup FAST VEGETARIAN

Combine ¼ teaspoon smoked paprika, ⅛ teaspoon sugar, ⅛ teaspoon table salt, and pinch pepper in medium bowl. Heat ¼ cup vegetable oil in 8-inch skillet over medium-high heat until just smoking. Carefully add ¾ cup rinsed and dried canned chickpeas to hot oil and cook until crisp throughout and dark brown, 10 to 15 minutes. Using slotted spoon, transfer hot chickpeas to bowl with spices and toss to coat. Let cool slightly before serving.

Kidney Bean Salad
Serves 2 VEGETARIAN

Toss ¾ cup rinsed canned kidney beans (or cannellini beans), 1 peeled and thinly sliced small carrot, 1 thinly sliced celery rib, 1 thinly sliced small shallot, 1 tablespoon white wine vinegar, 1 tablespoon extra-virgin olive oil, 1 tablespoon chopped fresh parsley, and ¼ teaspoon table salt in bowl and let marinate for 30 minutes. Season with salt and pepper to taste, and serve.

CANNED TOMATOES

Because canned tomatoes are of consistent quality year-round, we reach for them often in recipes. But not every recipe uses an entire can. Here's how to avoid letting them go to waste.

Quick Tomato Salsa

Makes ½ cup   `FAST`   `VEGETARIAN`

Pulse ½ cup drained canned diced tomatoes, 1 tablespoon minced shallot, 1 tablespoon minced fresh cilantro, and pinch cayenne pepper in food processor until roughly chopped, about 8 pulses. Transfer to fine-mesh strainer and let drain for 1 minute. Transfer to serving bowl and stir in 1 teaspoon lime juice. Season with salt and pepper to taste.

Spicy Chipotle Barbecue Sauce

Makes about ¾ cup   `VEGETARIAN`

Melt 1 tablespoon unsalted butter in medium saucepan over medium heat. Add 1 minced shallot and ½ teaspoon chili powder and cook until shallot is softened, about 2 minutes. Stir in ½ cup drained canned diced tomatoes and cook until softened and dry, about 1 minute. Add ¼ cup ketchup, ¼ cup vegetable or chicken broth, 2 tablespoons brown sugar, 2 teaspoons white vinegar, and ½ teaspoon minced canned chipotle chile in adobo sauce. Bring to simmer and cook until thickened, about 20 minutes. Process sauce in blender until smooth, about 30 seconds, adjusting consistency with extra broth as needed. Season with salt, pepper, vinegar, and chipotle to taste.

Spicy Chipotle Barbecue Sauce

Easy Tomato Chutney

Makes ¾ cup   `VEGETARIAN`

Combine ¾ cup canned diced tomatoes with their juice, ¾ cup water, 1 minced shallot, 2 tablespoons sugar, 2 tablespoons cider vinegar, 1 tablespoon golden raisins, ⅛ teaspoon table salt, and pinch cayenne together in medium saucepan. Bring to simmer over medium-low heat and cook, stirring occasionally, until thickened and reduced to about ¾ cup, 45 to 50 minutes. Using potato masher, mash any large pieces of tomato. Let cool to room temperature.

Chavela

Serves 2   `FAST`

Mexico's answer to the bloody Mary, chavela is a refreshing cocktail that swaps the usual vodka for lighter beer for a drink perfect for barbecues and brunch.

Process ¾ cup canned diced tomatoes with their juice, 1½ tablespoons lime juice, 1 tablespoon hot sauce, 1 teaspoon Worcestershire sauce, and ⅛ teaspoon table salt in blender until smooth, about 30 seconds; pour evenly into 2 pint glasses or large beer mugs. Divide 12 ounces Mexican lager between 2 glasses. Garnish with celery sticks and serve.

RECIPES USING UP CANNED TOMATOES

- Easy Skillet Cheese Pizza (canned diced tomatoes) (page 103)
- Easy Skillet Pizza with Fontina, Arugula, and Prosciutto (page 103)
- Easy Skillet Pizza with Goat Cheese, Olives, and Spicy Garlic Oil (page 103)
- Easy Skillet Pizza with Ricotta, Bacon, and Scallions (page 103)
- Ultimate Thin-Crust Pizza (canned whole peeled tomatoes) (page 104)
- Chicken and Chorizo Paella (canned diced tomatoes) (page 129)
- Braised Cod Peperonata (canned diced tomatoes) (page 174)
- Quick Marinara Sauce (canned diced tomatoes) (page 199)
- Spaghetti al Tonno (canned diced tomatoes) (page 239)

CAULIFLOWER

Most recipes in this book call for half a head of cauliflower or a few cups of florets, leaving at least half of the head behind. Buying pre-cut florets gives you a mix of giant pieces and dribs and drabs. It is better to buy a whole head and cut it up yourself for more even florets.

Cauliflower Rice

Serves 2 VEGETARIAN

Pulse ½ head cauliflower, cut into 1-inch florets in food processor until finely ground into ¼- to ⅛-inch pieces, 6 to 8 pulses, scraping down sides of bowl as needed. Heat 1 teaspoon vegetable oil in small saucepan over medium-low heat until shimmering. Add 2 tablespoons minced shallot and cook until softened, about 3 minutes. Stir in processed cauliflower, ¼ cup vegetable or chicken broth, and ¼ teaspoon table salt. Cover and cook, stirring occasionally, until cauliflower is tender, 10 to 13 minutes. Uncover and continue to cook, stirring occasionally, until cauliflower rice is almost completely dry, about 3 minutes. Off heat, season with salt and pepper to taste and stir in 1 tablespoon minced fresh parsley, chives, or basil. Serve.

Whipped Cauliflower

Serves 2 VEGETARIAN

Bring 1 cup water to boil in large saucepan over high heat, then add ½ head cauliflower, cut into 1-inch pieces. Cover; reduce heat to medium; and cook until very tender, 16 to 20 minutes, stirring once halfway through cooking. Drain cauliflower and transfer to food processor. Add 1½ tablespoons unsalted butter and ¼ teaspoon table salt and process until completely smooth, about 4 minutes, scraping down sides of bowl as needed. Adjust consistency with hot water as needed. Season with salt and pepper to taste. Serve.

Skillet-Roasted Cauliflower with Capers and Pine Nuts

Serves 2 VEGETARIAN

Combine ½ head cauliflower, cut into 1½ inch florets, 1 tablespoon extra-virgin olive oil, ¼ teaspoon table salt, and ¼ teaspoon pepper in 12-inch nonstick skillet. Cover and cook over medium-high heat until cauliflower starts to brown and edges just start to become translucent, about 5 minutes. Uncover and continue to cook, stirring every 2 minutes, until florets turn golden brown in many spots, about 12 minutes. Push cauliflower to edges of skillet. Add 1 tablespoon oil, 1 tablespoon rinsed and minced capers, and ½ teaspoon grated lemon zest to center and cook, stirring with rubber spatula, until fragrant, about 30 seconds. Stir cauliflower into caper mixture and continue to cook, stirring occasionally, until cauliflower is tender but still firm, about 3 minutes. Off heat, season with salt and pepper to taste and sprinkle with 2 tablespoons toasted pine nuts and 1 tablespoon minced fresh chives, parsley, or basil. Serve with lemon wedges.

RECIPES USING UP CAULIFLOWER

- Creamy Curried Cauliflower Soup (page 44)
- Roasted Grape and Cauliflower Salad with Chermoula (page 90)
- Pasta with Roasted Cauliflower, Garlic, and Walnuts (page 233)
- Roasted Cauliflower (page 324)
- Roasted Cauliflower with Lemon and Capers (page 324)
- Roasted Cauliflower with Chorizo and Smoked Paprika (page 325)
- Cauliflower Gratin (page 325)

CELERY

Celery is usually sold in bunches, yet most recipes call for just a few stalks. These easy recipes will make sure the rest doesn't get forgotten in the crisper drawer.

Cream of Celery Soup

Serves 2

Melt 1 tablespoon unsalted butter in large saucepan over medium-low heat. Add 4 chopped celery ribs; 1 small russet potato, peeled and chopped fine; 1 small chopped onion; ½ tablespoon sugar; ½ teaspoon dried sage; and pinch table salt. Cover and cook until celery and onion are softened, about 15 minutes. Stir in 1½ cups chicken broth and simmer, uncovered, until potato is tender, 10 to 15 minutes. Process soup in blender until smooth, about 2 minutes, then return to clean saucepan. Stir in 3 tablespoons heavy cream (or half-and-half) and return to brief simmer. Season with salt and pepper to taste, and serve.

Celery Salad with Red Onion and Orange

Serves 2 VEGETARIAN

Cut away peel and pith from 1 orange, cut orange into 8 wedges, then slice wedges crosswise into ½-inch-thick pieces. Toss 4 celery ribs, sliced thin on bias, orange pieces, 3 tablespoons finely chopped red onion, 2 tablespoons extra-virgin olive oil, 1 tablespoon cider vinegar, and 1 teaspoon honey together in bowl. Season with salt and pepper to taste and let salad sit for 15 minutes before serving.

CITRUS ZEST

Oftentimes recipes call for a small amount of citrus zest but there is no need to waste the rest, as you can dehydrate it and steep in tea or add to pan sauces, custards, or cooking water for grains to impart subtle citrus flavor.

Dehydrated Citrus Zest

`VEGETARIAN`

Use a vegetable peeler to remove strips of citrus zest, avoiding the bitter pith. Place strips on paper towel–lined plate. Microwave on high power for 2 to 3 minutes, let cool, then store in airtight container for up to 6 months.

COCONUT MILK

Coconut milk is worth putting to use when you're left with extra. Here are a few creamy recipes making the most of part of a can, plus savory recipes throughout the book.

Coconut Rice Pudding

Serves 2   `VEGETARIAN`

Bring 1 cup water to boil in small saucepan. Stir in ½ cup long-grain or medium-grain rice and ⅛ teaspoon table salt. Cover and simmer over low heat, stirring often, until water is almost fully absorbed, 10 to 15 minutes. Stir in 1 cup unsweetened coconut milk, 1½ cups milk, ⅓ cup sugar, ½ teaspoon vanilla extract, and ¼ teaspoon ground cinnamon. Simmer, stirring often, until spoon is able to stand up in pudding, 35 to 40 minutes. Serve warm or chilled.

No-Churn Coconut Ice Milk

Serves 2   `VEGETARIAN`

This cardamom-spiced frozen dessert is similar to ice cream. The vodka is crucial to its texture; do not omit it.

Whisk ¾ cup coconut milk, ¾ cup heavy cream (or half-and-half), ⅓ cup corn syrup, 1 tablespoon vodka, ¼ teaspoon lime zest, ¼ teaspoon ground cardamom, and ⅛ teaspoon table salt in large bowl. Cover with plastic wrap and freeze until mixture begins to freeze around edges, 1½ to 2 hours. Stir mixture until smooth and frothy. Transfer to 2-cup container with tight-fitting lid and freeze until firm, 4 to 5 hours, before serving.

Piña Coladas

Serves 2   `FAST` `VEGETARIAN`

Process ¾ cup unsweetened coconut milk, ¼ cup dark rum, 2 cups pineapple chunks, 1 cup ice, 3 tablespoons sugar, and 2 teaspoons lime juice in blender on low until coarsely pureed, about 10 seconds. Increase speed to high and process until smooth, 20 to 40 seconds. Season with more sugar and lime juice to taste, and serve.

Pina Colada

RECIPES USING UP COCONUT MILK

- Moong Dal Soup with Coconut Milk and Spinach (page 49)
- Thai Red Curry with Chicken (page 62)
- Thai Red Curry with Beef and Eggplant (page 63)
- Halibut and Creamy Coconut Rice Packets (page 181)
- Steamed Mussels in Coconut Milk with Cilantro (page 197)
- Panang Curry with Eggplant, Broccolini, and Tofu (page 222)
- Coconut-Cardamom Rice Pudding (page 447)

**Smashed Sichuan
Cucumbers**

CUCUMBERS

Most recipes in this book call for half a cucumber. Here are some ideas for what to do with the other half.

Smashed Sichuan Cucumbers

Serves 2 `VEGETARIAN`

Trim and cut ½ English cucumber crosswise into 3 equal lengths and place in zipper-lock bag. Seal bag. Using small skillet or rolling pin, firmly but gently smash cucumbers until flattened and split lengthwise into 3 to 4 spears each. Tear spears into rough 1-inch pieces and transfer to colander set in large bowl. Toss cucumbers with ½ teaspoon kosher salt and let sit for at least 15 minutes and up to 30 minutes. Meanwhile, whisk 1 teaspoon Chinese black vinegar and ¼ clove minced garlic together in medium bowl; let sit for at least 5 minutes or up to 15 minutes. Whisk 1 teaspoon soy sauce, ½ teaspoon toasted sesame oil, and ¼ teaspoon sugar into vinegar mixture to dissolve sugar. Add cucumbers, discarding any extracted liquid, and ¼ teaspoon sesame seeds to bowl with dressing and toss to combine. Serve immediately.

Quick Pickle Chips

Makes one ½-pint jar `VEGETARIAN`

Bring ⅛ cup water, ⅓ cup seasoned rice vinegar, ½ garlic clove, ⅛ teaspoon turmeric, pinch black peppercorns, and pinch yellow mustard seeds to boil in medium saucepan over medium-high heat.

Fill one ½-pint jar with hot water to warm. Drain jar, then pack ½ cucumber, sliced ¼ inch thick, and 1 dill sprig into jar. Using funnel and ladle, pour hot brine over cucumber to cover. Let jar cool completely, about 30 minutes. Cover jar with lid and refrigerate for at least 2½ hours before serving.

RECIPES USING UP CUCUMBER

- Gazpacho (page 46)
- Greek Chopped Salad (page 73)
- Panzanella (page 78)
- Fennel, Apple, and Chicken Chopped Salad (page 78)
- Steak and Rice Noodle Salad with Cucumber and Mint (page 82)
- Steamed Bao with Hoisin Chicken and Cucumber (page 98)
- Lamb Pita Sandwiches with Tzatziki (page 101)
- Pomegranate Chicken with Farro and Cucumber Salad (page 131)
- Turmeric Scallops with Mango Noodle Salad (page 194)
- Chickpea Cakes with Cucumber-Yogurt Sauce (page 218)
- Chilled Soba Noodles with Cucumber, Snow Peas, and Radishes (page 251)
- Lemongrass Beef and Rice Noodle Bowl (page 254)
- Bun Cha (page 276)

EGGPLANT

Because it requires cooking, eggplant can be a tricky vegetable to use up. And recipes for two rarely call for a whole eggplant. Here are some tasty ideas for what to do with the other half.

Easy Ratatouille

Serves 2 `VEGETARIAN`

Heat 2 tablespoons extra-virgin olive oil in 12-inch nonstick skillet over medium-high heat until shimmering. Add 8 ounces eggplant, cut into ¾-inch pieces (2 cups), and ⅛ teaspoon table salt and cook until eggplant is browned, 5 to 7 minutes. Stir in 1 tablespoon extra-virgin olive oil and ½ chopped onion and cook until onion is softened, 5 to 7 minutes. Stir in 2 minced garlic cloves and cook until fragrant, about 30 seconds. Stir in 1 large chopped tomato and ¾ cup vegetable or chicken broth and simmer until vegetables are softened and liquid has thickened slightly, 10 to 15 minutes. Season with salt and pepper to taste. Sprinkle with Parmesan cheese and drizzle with more olive oil. Serve.

Easy Eggplant Dip

Makes ⅔ cup   `VEGETARIAN`

Combine 8 ounces eggplant, peeled and cut into ¾-inch pieces (2 cups), 2 tablespoons extra-virgin olive oil, and ¼ teaspoon table salt in 10-inch nonstick skillet. Cover and cook over medium heat, stirring often, until eggplant is lightly browned, very soft, and beginning to break down, about 10 minutes. Pulse cooked eggplant, 2 teaspoons lemon juice, and ⅛ teaspoon ground cumin in food processor until coarsely pureed, about 5 pulses. Transfer mixture to bowl and stir in 2 tablespoons plain Greek yogurt (or sour cream); season with salt and pepper to taste. Cover and refrigerate until chilled, about 30 minutes. Serve with bread or crackers.

RECIPES USING UP EGGPLANT

- Ciambotta (page 59)
- Thai Red Curry with Beef and Eggplant (page 63)
- Garlicky Pork with Eggplant (page 163)
- Baked Snapper with Roasted Ratatouille (page 178)
- Skillet Eggplant Parmesan (page 206)
- Panang Curry with Eggplant, Broccolini, and Tofu (page 222)
- Braised Tofu with Butternut Squash and Eggplant (page 223)

FENNEL

Most recipes in this book call for half a bulb of fennel. Here are some ideas for what to do with the other half so it doesn't go to waste.

Quick Pickled Fennel

Makes one ½-pint jar   `VEGETARIAN`

Pickled fennel makes a nice addition to a cheese board and is also great on a sandwich.

Bring ⅓ cup seasoned rice vinegar, 2 tablespoons water, ½ garlic clove, one ½-inch strip orange zest, ⅛ teaspoon fennel seeds, pinch black peppercorns, and pinch yellow mustard seeds to boil in medium saucepan. Fill one ½-pint jar with hot water to warm. Drain jar, then pack ½ fennel bulb, thinly sliced and trimmed, into jar. Using funnel and ladle, pour hot brine over fennel to cover. Let jar cool completely, cover with lid, and refrigerate for at least 2½ hours before serving. (The fennel can be refrigerated for up to 6 weeks; the fennel will soften significantly after that.)

Fennel Confit

Serves 2   `VEGETARIAN`

Fennel confit makes a savory snack spread on a baguette, toasted bread, or crackers.

Adjust oven rack to middle position and heat oven to 300 degrees. Cut ½ fennel bulb into ½-inch thick pieces and save 2 teaspoons minced fresh fonds, discarding stalks. Arrange half of fennel, cut side down, in single layer in large saucepan. Sprinkle with pinch table salt. Repeat with remaining fennel and additional pinch table salt. Scatter 1 lightly crushed garlic clove, one 1-inch strip lemon zest, pinch caraway seeds, and pinch fennel seeds over top, then add ¾ cup extra virgin olive oil (fennel may not be completely submerged). Cover pan; transfer to oven; and cook until fennel is very tender and is easily pierced with tip of paring knife, about 1 hour. Remove pan from oven. Using slotted spoon, transfer fennel to serving platter, brushing off any garlic, lemon zest, caraway seeds, or fennel seeds that stick to fennel. Drizzle 1 tablespoon cooking oil over fennel, sprinkle with fennel fronds, and sprinkle with sea salt to taste. Serve with lemon wedges.

Quick Pickled Fennel

Fennel Salad with Orange and Olives

Serves 2 `VEGETARIAN`

Whisk 1 tablespoon extra-virgin olive oil, ½ tablespoon lemon juice, pinch table salt, and pinch pepper in large serving bowl until combined; set aside. Cut away peel and pith from 1 blood orange. Quarter orange, then slice crosswise into ¼-inch-thick pieces. Add sliced orange, ½ thinly sliced fennel bulb, 2 tablespoons thinly sliced black olives, and 2 tablespoons chopped fresh mint to bowl with dressing and toss gently to coat. Season with salt and pepper to taste. Serve.

RECIPES USING UP FENNEL

- Hearty Chicken Noodle Soup with Leeks, Fennel, and Orzo (page 36)
- Fish Stew with Chorizo and Fennel (page 59)
- Chef's Salad with Capicola and Provolone (page 83)
- Braised Chicken Thighs with Potatoes, Fennel, and Tarragon (page 132)
- Stuffed Tomatoes with Goat Cheese and Zucchini (page 208)
- Fennel, Olive, and Goat Cheese Tarts (page 211)
- Farro Risotto with Fennel, Radicchio, and Balsamic Vinegar (page 215)

FETA

Feta is often sold in large tubs and can spoil very quickly. While it's great crumbled over a salad or Mediterranean-inspired pasta dish, we came up with a few more creative ideas for putting this tangy cheese to work.

Spicy Whipped Feta

Makes ½ cup `FAST` `VEGETARIAN`

Process ½ cup crumbled feta cheese, 1 tablespoon extra-virgin olive oil, 1 tablespoon water, 1 teaspoon lemon juice, ½ teaspoon paprika (or smoked paprika), and ⅛ teaspoon cayenne pepper together in food processor until smooth, about 20 seconds. Transfer mixture to serving bowl and drizzle with more olive oil. Serve with bread or crackers.

Watermelon and Feta Salad with Mint

Serves 2 `FAST` `VEGETARIAN`

Trim and discard rind from 12 ounces thinly sliced watermelon. Arrange watermelon on plate and sprinkle with ½ cup crumbled feta cheese and 1½ tablespoons chopped fresh mint. Serve.

Creamy Feta Dressing

Makes 1¼ cups `FAST` `VEGETARIAN`

Whisk ¾ cup crumbled feta, ¼ cup whole milk, ⅓ cup mayonnaise, 1 tablespoon lemon juice, ¼ teaspoon pepper, ¼ teaspoon garlic powder, and ¼ teaspoon ground coriander together in bowl. Season with salt and pepper to taste, and serve.

RECIPES USING UP FETA

- Wilted Spinach Salad with Radishes, Feta, and Pistachios (page 74)
- Fattoush with Butternut Squash and Apple (page 81)
- Turkey Burgers with Olives and Feta (page 95)
- Chicken and Orzo with Spinach and Feta (page 129)
- Shrimp Saganaki (page 189)
- Savory Spinach Strudel (page 212)
- Air-Fryer Turkey-Zucchini Meatballs with Orzo, Spiced Tomato Sauce, and Feta (page 305)
- Lentil Salad with Olives, Mint, and Feta (page 354)
- Tofu Scramble with Spinach and Feta (page 364)
- Broccoli and Feta Frittata (page 367)
- Shakshuka (page 367)

FRESH AND DRIED HERBS

Easy Dried Herbs
`FAST` `VEGETARIAN`

Lay sprigs of sage, rosemary, thyme, oregano, mint, or marjoram in single layer between 2 paper towels and microwave until dry and brittle, 1 to 3 minutes. Crumble herbs, discarding any tough stems, and store in airtight container for up to 3 months.

Lemon and Herb Compound Butter

Makes 5 tablespoons `FAST` `VEGETARIAN`

This butter is delicious spread on toast or served over steaks, fish fillets, mashed potatoes, roasted vegetables, or pasta. Using fork, beat 2 teaspoons minced fresh thyme (or rosemary, sage, oregano, mint, or marjoram), 4 tablespoons softened unsalted butter, 1 teaspoon lemon juice, ½ teaspoon lemon zest, and ½ teaspoon table salt in small bowl until combined. Place butter mixture in center of sheet of plastic wrap and roll into thick cylinder, twisting ends of plastic shut. Refrigerate until firm, about 30 minutes. Butter can be kept refrigerated for several days or frozen for up to 1 month.

GROUND TURKEY AND GROUND PORK

Recipes for two typically call for less than 1 pound ground turkey and ground pork. Here are a few quick meals to use up the rest of the package.

Simplest Ground Turkey Tacos

Serves 2 `FAST`

Heat 1 teaspoon vegetable oil in medium saucepan or 10-inch skillet over medium heat until shimmering. Add 3 minced garlic cloves, 2 teaspoons tomato paste, 2 teaspoons chili powder, ¼ teaspoon table salt, and 1 tablespoon minced shallot and cook until fragrant, about 1 minute. Stir in 8 ounces ground turkey and cook, breaking up meat with wooden spoon, until no longer pink, 2 to 4 minutes. Divide filling evenly among 4 taco shells and top with shredded Monterey Jack cheese, pickled jalapeños, and chopped shallot. Serve.

Mango-Turkey Sloppy Joes

Serves 2 `FAST`

Toss ½ cup coleslaw mix and 1½ teaspoons cider vinegar together in small bowl. Season with salt and pepper to taste; set aside. Heat 1 tablespoon vegetable oil in 10- or 12-inch nonstick skillet over medium heat until shimmering. Add ½ finely chopped bell pepper and 1 finely chopped shallot and cook until softened and lightly browned, 4 to 6 minutes. Stir in 1 minced garlic clove and ½ teaspoon chili powder and cook until fragrant, about 30 seconds. Add 4 ounces ground turkey and cook, breaking up meat with wooden spoon, until no longer pink, about 2 minutes. Stir in 1 (8-ounce) can tomato sauce, 1 cup chopped mango, 2 teaspoons packed brown sugar, 1 teaspoon Worcestershire sauce, and 1 teaspoon cider vinegar. Bring to simmer and cook until sauce is slightly thickened, 3 to 5 minutes. Season with salt and pepper to taste. Divide turkey mixture between 2 burger bun bottoms, then top with coleslaw mixture and bun tops. Serve.

Mango-Turkey Sloppy Joes

RECIPES USING UP GROUND TURKEY AND GROUND PORK

- Spaghetti and Turkey-Pesto Meatballs (page 234)
- Air-Fryer Turkey-Zucchini Meatballs with Orzo, Spiced Tomato Sauce and Feta (page 305)
- Dan Dan Mian (pork) (page 252)
- Bun Cha (pork) (page 276)

RADISHES

Radishes typically come in bunches or bags, while recipes for two use only a few. Here are some ideas to use up those extra radishes.

Baguette with Radishes, Butter, and Herbs

Serves 2 `FAST` `VEGETARIAN`

Combine 2 tablespoons European-style softened butter, 1 teaspoon chives, pinch table salt, and pinch pepper in bowl. Whisk 2 teaspoons minced chives, ⅛ teaspoon lemon juice, and ⅛ teaspoon extra-virgin olive oil in medium bowl. Add 1 tablespoon chopped fresh parsley and toss to coat. Season with salt and pepper to taste. Cut 1 (4-inch) piece of baguette lengthwise. Spread butter mixture over cut sides of baguette. Shingle 4 ounces thinly sliced radishes evenly over butter and top with parsley salad. Sprinkle with sea salt to taste. Cut baguette crosswise into 2 or 3 pieces. Serve.

Braised Radishes

Serves 2 `VEGETARIAN`

Melt ½ tablespoon butter in 10-inch skillet over medium-high heat. Add 1 tablespoon minced shallot and ⅛ teaspoon table salt, and cook until softened, 2 to 3 minutes. Add ½ pound trimmed and halved radishes and 3 tablespoons vegetable or chicken broth; cover; and cook until radishes are tender, about 10 minutes, stirring halfway through cooking. Uncover and continue to cook until liquid thickens slightly, about 1 minute. Stir in 1 teaspoon minced fresh chives and season with salt and pepper to taste. Serve.

Quick Pickled Radishes

Makes 1 cup `VEGETARIAN`

These pickled radishes are great on tacos or sandwiches. Whisk ¼ cup lime juice, 1 teaspoon sugar, and ½ teaspoon kosher salt in medium bowl until sugar and salt have dissolved. Stir in 6 large, thinly sliced radishes and 1 thinly sliced shallot and let sit for 15 minutes for flavors to blend (or refrigerate for up to 1 hour). Drain vegetables and serve.

> **RECIPES USING UP RADISHES**
> - Wilted Spinach Salad with Radishes, Feta, and Pistachios (page 74)
> - Seared Scallop Salad with Snap Peas and Radishes (page 85)
> - Salmon and Black Rice Salad with Snap Peas and Radishes (page 187)
> - Chilled Soba Noodles with Cucumber, Snow Peas, and Radishes (page 251)
> - Slow-Cooker Pulled Pork Tacos with Radish-Apple Slaw (page 300)
> - Sautéed Radishes with Crispy Bacon (page 335)

RICOTTA CHEESE

These easy recipes will ensure your leftover ricotta doesn't go to waste.

Herbed Ricotta Spread

Makes ½ cup `VEGETARIAN`

Line fine-mesh strainer with triple layer of coffee filters and place over bowl. Spoon ½ cup ricotta cheese (whole-milk or part-skim) into strainer, cover, and let drain for 1 hour. Transfer to serving bowl and stir in 1 tablespoon minced fresh basil (or parsley, tarragon, cilantro, or dill), 1 tablespoon extra-virgin olive oil, 1 minced garlic clove, ½ teaspoon lemon juice, and ¼ teaspoon grated lemon zest. Season with salt and pepper to taste. Serve with crackers or toasted bread.

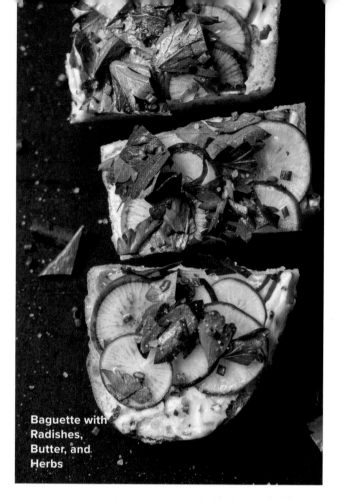

Baguette with Radishes, Butter, and Herbs

Lemon-Herb Ricotta Fritters

Makes 6 fritters `VEGETARIAN`

Combine 1 cup ricotta cheese (whole-milk or part-skim), ⅓ cup panko bread crumbs (or plain dried bread crumbs), ¼ cup grated Parmesan cheese, 2 tablespoons chopped fresh basil (or parsley, cilantro, tarragon, or chives), 1 egg yolk, ½ teaspoon table salt, ¼ teaspoon pepper, and ⅛ teaspoon grated lemon zest in bowl. Using wet hands, shape mixture into six ½-inch-thick patties. Heat ¼ cup olive oil in 12-inch nonstick skillet over medium-high heat until shimmering. Fry patties until golden and crisp on both sides, 4 to 5 minutes, gently flipping halfway through cooking. Serve with green salad or freshly sliced tomato.

Sweet Ricotta Cheese Dip

Makes about ¾ cup `VEGETARIAN`

Process ¾ cup ricotta cheese (whole-milk or part-skim), 3 tablespoons confectioners' sugar, ½ teaspoon vanilla extract, and ¼ teaspoon grated lemon zest together in food processor until smooth, about 1 minute, scraping down sides of bowl as needed. Serve with cinnamon-sugar pita chips, biscotti, or toast, or spoon into bowl with fresh berries.

STOCKS

Many recipes for stock make an enormous amount and require a long ingredient list. These two thrifty recipes eliminate waste and can be made in quantities that make sense for the for-two kitchen.

Rotisserie Chicken Stock

Makes 8 cups

The next time you buy a rotisserie chicken, don't toss the skin and bones after you use the chicken itself. It's easy to make a flavorful stock using them.

Bring 8 cups water, reserved chicken skin and bones from 1 (2½ pound) rotisserie chicken, and 10 parsley stems to simmer in Dutch oven over medium-high heat. Cover, reduce heat to medium-low, and simmer gently for 30 minutes. Using tongs, discard any large pieces of chicken bones. Strain broth through fine-mesh strainer into large bowl, pressing on solids to extract as much broth as possible.

Quick Shrimp Shell Stock

Makes about 1½ cups

It's good to get in the habit of saving and freezing your shrimp shells because they can be used to make an easy and delicious stock you can use in risotto, miso soup, or fish or seafood stews. Not that 1½ pounds shrimp makes 1½ cups shells. Adjust the quantity of water to accommodate fewer or more shrimp shells. The water should cover the majority of the shells in the skillet.

Heat 1 tablespoon vegetable oil in 12 inch skillet over medium-high heat until shimmering. Add 1½ cups shrimp shells and cook until spotty brown, 5 to 7 minutes. Stir in 1 tablespoon tomato paste and cook for 30 seconds. Add 2 cups water and bring to boil. Cover, reduce heat to low, and simmer for 5 minutes. Strain stock, pressing on solids to extract as much liquid as possible; discard shells. (Cooled stock can be refrigerated for up to 1 week or frozen for up to 2 months.)

TOFU

Recipes for two typically call for 7 ounces of tofu. Here are some easy ideas for the other half of the container.

Miso Soup with Tofu

Serves 2   VEGETARIAN

Bring 2 cups vegetable or chicken broth and 1 cup water to simmer in medium saucepan. Off heat, whisk in 2 tablespoons white miso, then stir in 7 ounces drained silken, soft, or firm tofu, cut into 1-inch pieces. Sprinkle with 2 thinly sliced scallions and 1 crumbled toasted sheet nori and season with salt and pepper to taste. Serve. (Soup can be refrigerated for up to 3 days.)

Sriracha-Lime Tofu Bowl

Serves 2

Drain 7 ounces firm or extra firm tofu and cut into ¾-inch pieces. Sprinkle with ⅛ teaspoon table salt and pinch pepper. Heat 1 teaspoon vegetable oil in 10-inch nonstick skillet over medium-high heat until shimmering. Add tofu and cook until lightly browned, 6 to 8 minutes; transfer to bowl. Whisk 1 tablespoon lime juice, 2½ teaspoons honey, 2½ teaspoons fish sauce, 1 teaspoon grated fresh ginger, and 1 teaspoon sriracha together in second bowl. While whisking constantly, slowly drizzle in 1 tablespoon vegetable oil until combined. Toss 6 cups shredded cabbage with half of vinaigrette to coat, then season with salt and pepper to taste. Top with tofu; 1 shredded carrot; ½ thinly sliced bell pepper; ¼ cup fresh cilantro leaves; and ¼ cup chopped fresh Thai basil, basil, or mint; and drizzle with remaining vinaigrette. Serve with lime wedges and drizzle with extra sriracha.

Handy Equipment for Two

Scaling down recipes often requires inventive use of standard kitchen essentials, like using a loaf pan to make a perfectly sized lasagna for two. And some for-two recipes require different-size cooking equipment, from smaller skillets and saucepans to specialty-size pie plates and more. Fortunately, these items are inexpensive and widely available in stores and online. Here is a list of the equipment we reach for when scaling recipes down to size.

SMALL SKILLETS A 12-inch skillet is usually our favorite kitchen workhorse. But once we started scaling down recipes, we found that many recipes required a scaled-down skillet as well—try to make just enough pan sauce for two steaks in a large skillet and it will overreduce and burn. So we recommend buying 10-inch and 8-inch skillets in addition to standard 12-inch skillets. We use both traditional and nonstick 10-inch skillets for sautes and stir-fries throughout the book, and an 8-inch skillet is essential for baking a small strata or soufflé. Our favorite nonstick skillets are all made by **OXO**. Our favorite stainless skillets are made by **All-Clad**.

SMALL, MEDIUM, AND LARGE SAUCEPANS When cooking for two, we frequently reach for a saucepan instead of a larger pot. For braises, we use large (4-quart) saucepans in lieu of a large Dutch oven (most hold as much as 7 or 8 quarts). We use medium (2- to 3-quart) saucepans for soups and stews and small (1- to 2-quart) saucepans for melting just a little butter or chocolate or for making sauces. Our favorite 4- and 2-quart stainless saucepans are made by **All-Clad**.

SMALL RIMMED BAKING SHEETS These smaller rimmed baking sheets (known as quarter sheet pans) can handle all sorts of tasks like roasting vegetables, chicken parts, and more. They are easier to maneuver and easier to clean. They are also great for refrigerating prepped items like burgers and meatballs and resting cooked meats We recommend the **Nordic Ware Naturals Quarter Sheet Pan**.

A LIGHTWEIGHT CUTTING BOARD When you are cooking for just two, you have less prep work and less need for a large cutting board. Weighing just over 3 pounds, our favorite lightweight cutting board is the **OXO Good Grips Carving and Cutting Board**.

MINI WHISKS Sometimes we want a smaller tool for beating a few eggs or emulsifying just enough salad dressing for one or two people. That's where mini whisks come in. At about 5 to 7 inches in total length—they're ideal for these smaller jobs. Our favorite diminuitive whisk is the **Tovolo Stainless Steel 6" Mini Whisk**.

UTILITY KNIFE We have become enamored of these knives that are a cross between a chef's knife and a paring knife. It has more power than a paring knife but gives you more control than a chef's knife. Of course, there are tasks where there are no substitutes for a chef's knife because of its size or leverage, but when cooking for two, the chances are that you can reach for a utility knife for most prep tasks, and as a bonus it is lighter weight and supereasy to use. The winner of our testing is **Tojior 150 mm Petty R-2 Powder Steel Knife**. We also like this somewhat less expensive ultitity knife: **MAC PKF Pro Utility 6-inch Knife**.

KITCHEN SHEARS We rely on kitchen shears for all manner of kitchen tasks from trimming chicken thighs and cutting the tips off green beans to cutting up whole tomatoes right in the can and snipping bunches of chives or scallions into short lengths. We guarantee that they will be especially helpful in prepping recipes for two. **Shun Multi-Purpose Shears** are our favorite.

A SKINNY SPATULA When you are making smaller batches of food, a smaller spatula will be helpful in maneuvering around the corners of a smaller saucepan or bowl. We recommend the **GIR Skinny Spatula**.

GLASS BOWLS IN AN ARRAY OF SIZES There is no need to use or wash a large bowl when cooking for two if you don't have to. That's why it is handy to have a set of bowls that comes in a wide array of sizes. The **Arc International Luminarc 10-Piece Stackable Bowl Set** is perfect for any kitchen, but especially useful in the for-two kitchen.

MINI AND SMALL COLANDERS Mini, collapsible colanders come in handy for rinsing small amounts of food like berries or canned beans. We like the **Progressive Prepworks Collapsible Mini Colander**. For draining 6 ounces of pasta, which most of our for-two recipes call for we like the **Tramontina 1.25 QT. Stainless Steel Colander**.

SMALL BAKING DISHES Small baking dishes come in handy for scaled-down gratins and baked desserts. We use a 4-cup 8½ by 5½-inch baking dish for our Cauliflower Gratin (page 325) and our Potato Gratin (page 330); for a petite Tiramisu (page 440), we reach for a smaller 3-cup rectangular baking dish measuring approximately 7¼ by 5¼ inches, although dishes of comparable size work, too. Look for gratin dishes with straight sides no higher than 2 inches; taller sides inhibit browning.

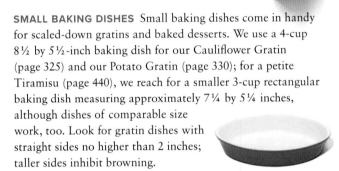

MULTIPLE LOAF PANS We use both traditional loaf pans and mini loaf pans (which measure approximately 5½ by 3 inches) in the for-two kitchen. We've found that standard loaf pans are the perfect size for baking small casseroles, brownies, and bar cookies. Mini loaf pans are ideal for scaled-down baked goods such as quick breads.

LOTS OF RAMEKINS Ramekins, in various sizes, are handy for making scaled-down desserts. We use 5- to 12-ounce ramekins for making individual servings of desserts such as Individual Blueberry Crumbles (page 398), Warm Chocolate Fudge Cakes (page 438), and Crème Brûlée (page 444). We also use 12-ounce ramekins to make elegant individual Chicken Pot Pies (page 126).

SMALL CAKE PANS With 6-inch round cake pans, you can make a perfectly sized coffee cake (like our Cinnamon Streusel Coffee Cake on page 382)and more just for two.

SMALL PIE PLATES We rely on 6-inch pie plates to make perfectly portioned pies for two. A small pie plate also makes it easy to scale down our Classic Cheese Quiche (page 370).

SMALL TART PANS When you want to make individual tarts (sweet or savory), two 4-inch tart pans with removeable bottoms hold just the right amount of crust and filling.

SPRINGFORM PANS Small 4½-inch springform pans are essential for making New York Cheesecakes (page 442) that don't feed a crowd. We also rely on this pan for delicate cakes like our Almond Cakes (page 428) and our Rustic Peach Cakes (page 429).

SMALL BUNDT PANS Bundt pans make beautiful cakes, but a standard pan holds 12 cups and makes a cake large enough for a party. We've found that mini 1-cup Bundt pans are ideal for making two elegant single-serving cakes, like Bold and Spicy Gingerbread Cakes (page 427) or Summer Berry Snack Cakes (page 423).

A SMALL SLOW COOKER For our slow-cooker suppers for two, we found a 4-quart oval slow cooker easier to maneuver and clean and less space-hogging than the standard 6- to 7-quart slow cookers (but the recipes in this book will work equally well with either size). We highly recommend the **Cuisinart 4-Quart Cook Central 3-n-1 Multicooker**.

A SMALL FOOD PROCESSOR While you may need a full-size food processor for making pizza dough or large batches of pesto, there is so much that our winning 4-cup food processor, the **Cuisinart Elite 4-Cup Grinder/Chopper**, can do such as making bread crumbs, chopping nuts, and much more.

AN IMMERSION BLENDER A standard blender is large, the glass jar makes it heavy, and it is hard to clean. Not to mention that if you are pureeing a small batch of soup, you have to get the soup into and out of the blender in batches. The solution to all this work is an immersion blender. You can use it right in your pot or slow-cooker insert. Our winner, the **Braun MultiQuick 5 Hand Blender** is lightweight and compact.

Emergency Substitutions

When you're shopping for just two, it's often impractical to stock half-and-half as well as heavy cream or both light and dark brown sugar, and no one wants to run out to the market for just one ingredient. But often a simple substitution can save you the hassle. Here is a list of common ingredients frequently called for in recipes and their recommended substitutes.

TO REPLACE	AMOUNT	SUBSTITUTE				
Whole Milk	½ cup	5 tablespoons skim milk + 3 tablespoons half-and-half				
		⅓ cup 1 percent low-fat milk + ⅙ cup half-and-half				
		⅜ cup 2 percent low-fat milk + 2 tablespoons half-and-half				
		7 tablespoons skim milk + 1 tablespoon heavy cream				
Half-and-Half	½ cup	⅜ cup whole milk + 2 tablespoons heavy cream				
		⅓ cup skim or low-fat milk + ⅙ cup heavy cream				
Heavy Cream	½ cup	½ cup evaporated milk				
		Not suitable for whipping or baking, but fine for soups and sauces.				
Eggs		LARGE	JUMBO	EXTRA-LARGE	MEDIUM	For half of an egg, whisk the yolk and white together and use half of the liquid.
		1	1	1	1	
		2	1½	2	2	
		3	2½	2½	3½	
		4	3	3½	4½	
		5	4	4	6	
		6	5	5	7	
Buttermilk	½ cup	⅜ cup plain whole-milk or low-fat yogurt + 2 tablespoons whole milk				
		½ cup whole milk + 1½ teaspoons lemon juice or distilled white vinegar				
		Not suitable for raw applications, such as a buttermilk dressing.				
Sour Cream	½ cup	½ cup plain whole-milk yogurt				
		Nonfat and low-fat yogurts are too lean to replace sour cream.				
Plain Yogurt	½ cup	½ cup sour cream				
Cake Flour	1 cup	⅞ cup all-purpose flour + 2 tablespoons cornstarch				
Baking Powder	1 teaspoon	¼ teaspoon baking soda + ½ teaspoon cream of tartar (use right away)				
Light Brown Sugar	½ cup	½ cup granulated sugar + 1½ teaspoons molasses				Pulse the molasses in a food processor along with the sugar or simply add it along with the other wet ingredients.
Dark Brown Sugar	½ cup	½ cup granulated sugar + 1 tablespoon molasses				
Confectioners' Sugar	½ cup	½ cup granulated sugar + ½ teaspoon cornstarch, ground in a blender (not a food processor)				
		Works well for dusting over cakes, less so in frostings and glazes.				
Fresh Herbs	1 tablespoon	1 teaspoon dried herbs				
Unsweetened Chocolate	1 ounce	3 tablespoons cocoa powder + 1 tablespoon vegetable oil				
		1½ ounces bittersweet or semisweet chocolate (remove 1 tablespoon sugar from the recipe)				
Bittersweet or Semisweet Chocolate	1 ounce	⅔ ounce unsweetened chocolate + 2 teaspoons sugar				
		Works well with fudgy brownies. Do not use in a custard or cake.				

Prep School

There are ingredients everyone ends up prepping constantly—think onions, shallots, bell peppers, and more. And some of the prep work can be tedious, like coring tomatoes and apples. Here are a few ideas to make prep work a little easier for you.

APPLES

1. Simply cut planks all around circumference of apple.

2. Slice into thin attractive wedges. This is especially useful when cutting apples to incorporate into salad.

ASPARAGUS

1. Remove 1 spear of asparagus from bunch and bend it at thicker end until it snaps.

2. With broken asparagus spear as guide, trim tough ends from remaining asparagus bunch using chef's knife.

BELL PEPPERS

1. Chop off each end.

2. Slice edges from top to bottom so that you have four pieces. Remove any pith or seeds. Cut pieces into desired size called for in recipe. Chop end pieces.

BROCCOLI

Hold broccoli head level with cutting board. Using kitchen shears, maneuver them so that you can simply cut off florets where stems meet larger stalk.

BRUSSELS SPROUTS

1. Use sharp chef's knife to remove dried end where sprout was attached to stalk.

2. Slice each sprout in half through root end and then in half again to quarter it.

CABBAGE SHREDDING

1. Cut cabbage into quarters, then cut away hard piece of core attached to each quarter.

2. Flatten small stacks of leaves on cutting board and use chef's knife to cut each stack crosswise into ¼-inch-wide shreds.

CELERY

1. Instead of laboriously separating celery stalks and then chopping, simply slice off end of a bunch and proceed to chop celery until you have required amount.

2. Chop or mince until pieces are size required for your recipe.

KALE AND SWISS CHARD

Use kitchen shears to remove leaves following line of stems. Flatten leaves and cut into strips or pieces according to recipe. Chop stems if being used in recipe.

LEEKS

1. Trim root end and cut off upper portion of tough dark green layers. Cut in half horizontally.

2. Cut each half crosswise into pieces, place in colander, and rinse thoroughly; alternatively, use salad spinner. Chop again if necessary.

ONION

1. Halve onion through root end, then peel onion and trim top. Make several horizontal cuts from 1 end of onion to other but don't cut through root end.

2. Make several vertical cuts. Be sure to cut up to but not through root end.

3. Rotate onion so that root end is in back; slice onion thinly across previous cuts. As you slice, onion will fall apart into chopped pieces.

PARSLEY AND CILANTRO

1. Wash bunch of herbs but do not cut stems.

2. Hold bunch in one hand and with knife in other hand simply shave off leaves. Refrigerate what you do not need to use immediately.

3. Mince leaves and any tender stems still attached.

SHALLOT

1. Halve shallot through root end, then make closely spaced horizontal cuts through peeled shallot, leaving root end intact.

2. Make several vertical cuts through shallot.

3. Finally, thinly slice shallot crosswise, creating fine mince.

ROMAINE LETTUCE

1. Cut off stem end of romaine heart. Slice through romaine heart lengthwise. Cut each section in half.

2. Chop each of four sections into ½-inch pieces. Wash in salad spinner.

TOMATOES

1. Simply cut planks at a slight diagonal all around circumference of tomato as close to core as you can until all you have left is the core.

2. Cut planks into desired size called for in recipe.

CHAPTER 1

Soups & Chowders

▪ **FAST** (Start to finish in 30 minutes or less)
▪ **VEGETARIAN**

Opposite: Soupe au Pistou

Hearty Chicken Noodle Soup

Beef and Barley Soup

Hearty Chicken Noodle Soup

Serves 2

Total time 1 hour 25 minutes

WHY THIS RECIPE WORKS We wanted to streamline chicken noodle soup and make it quick enough to prepare for two any night of the week—without losing any of its soul-satisfying flavor. While homemade stock was out, we found that we could get great results from store-bought chicken broth with just a couple of extra steps. Adding sautéed aromatics lent our broth a welcome depth and complexity, while creating a simple roux contributed a nutty flavor and also thickened the broth slightly, giving our soup a long-simmered consistency. A bone-in chicken breast gave our broth more flavor than a boneless one did, and quick-cooking egg noodles turned our soup into a hearty one-dish meal. Be careful not to overcook the chicken in step 3 or it will taste dry.

1 (12-ounce) bone-in split chicken breast, trimmed
⅛ teaspoon table salt
   Pinch pepper
2 teaspoons vegetable oil
1 small onion, chopped fine
1 celery rib, minced
1 carrot, peeled and cut into ½-inch pieces
1 teaspoon minced fresh thyme or ¼ teaspoon dried
1 tablespoon all-purpose flour
3 cups chicken broth
1 bay leaf
½ cup wide egg noodles
1 tablespoon minced fresh parsley

1. Pat chicken dry with paper towels and sprinkle with salt and pepper. Heat oil in medium saucepan over medium-high heat until just smoking. Brown chicken, skin side down, until golden, about 6 minutes; transfer to plate. Pour off all but 1 tablespoon fat from saucepan.

2. Add onion, celery, and carrot to fat left in saucepan and cook over medium heat until softened, about 5 minutes. Stir in thyme and cook until fragrant, about 30 seconds. Stir in flour and cook for 1 minute. Slowly whisk in broth, scraping up any browned bits and smoothing out any lumps.

3. Add browned chicken along with any accumulated juices and bay leaf. Bring to simmer and cook until chicken registers 160 degrees, 20 to 22 minutes, flipping chicken halfway through cooking. Transfer chicken to cutting board, let cool slightly, then shred into bite-size pieces using 2 forks, discarding skin and bones.

4. Discard bay leaf. Return soup to simmer, stir in noodles, and cook until vegetables and noodles are tender, about 8 minutes. Off heat, stir in shredded chicken and let sit until heated through, about 2 minutes. Stir in parsley and season with salt and pepper to taste. Serve.

VARIATIONS

Hearty Chicken Noodle Soup with Leeks, Fennel, and Orzo

Substitute ½ leek, white and light green parts only, halved and sliced ¼ inch thick, for onion; ½ fennel bulb, cored and chopped, for celery; and ¼ cup orzo for egg noodles.

Hearty Chicken Noodle Soup with Tomatoes, Zucchini, and Shells

Omit carrot. Substitute ½ cup medium shells for egg noodles and simmer for 5 minutes. Stir in 1 zucchini, cut into ½-inch pieces, and 1 tomato, cored and chopped, and continue to simmer until pasta and zucchini are tender, about 5 minutes. Stir in shredded chicken and proceed with recipe.

SHREDDING CHICKEN

Hold 1 fork in each hand, with tines facing down. Insert tines into meat and gently pull forks away from each other, breaking meat into bite-size pieces or large chunks.

Beef and Barley Soup

Serves 2

Total time 1 hour 20 minutes

WHY THIS RECIPE WORKS Beef and barley soup is not one that improves as it sits—the barley swells and turns gummy, making for a stodgy soup. To avoid leftovers, we needed a pot of soup for two, and we wanted it to be quick. Using store-bought broth saved us time, while blade steak— readily available in smaller portions—offered beefy flavor and tender, juicy meat without hours of simmering. We gave the meat a head start and added the barley later which ensured that the grains remained pleasantly chewy and didn't overcook. Finally, for maximum flavor, we gave the vegetables time to caramelize, doubled the amount of thyme and garlic, and added some tomato paste and soy sauce for rich, beefy flavor.

1 (8-ounce) beef blade steak, trimmed and cut into ½-inch pieces
  Pinch table salt
  Pinch pepper
1 tablespoon vegetable oil
6 ounces cremini mushrooms, trimmed and sliced thin
2 carrots, peeled and cut into ½-inch pieces
1 small onion, chopped fine
2 tablespoons tomato paste
3 garlic cloves, minced
2 teaspoons minced fresh thyme or ½ teaspoon dried
2 cups beef broth
2 cups chicken broth
4 teaspoons soy sauce
½ cup quick-cooking barley
2 tablespoons chopped fresh parsley

1. Pat beef dry with paper towels and sprinkle with salt and pepper. Heat oil in medium saucepan over medium-high heat until just smoking. Brown beef on all sides, 5 to 7 minutes; transfer to bowl.

2. Add mushrooms, carrots, and onion to fat left in saucepan and cook over medium heat until any mushroom juice has evaporated and vegetables begin to brown, 6 to 8 minutes. Stir in tomato paste, garlic, and thyme and cook until fragrant, about 30 seconds.

3. Stir in beef broth, chicken broth, and soy sauce, scraping up any browned bits. Stir in browned beef along with any accumulated juices, bring to simmer, and cook for 15 minutes.

4. Stir in barley and simmer until barley and beef are tender, 10 to 15 minutes. Stir in parsley and season with salt and pepper to taste. Serve.

TRIMMING BLADE STEAK

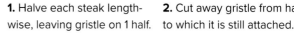

1. Halve each steak lengthwise, leaving gristle on 1 half.

2. Cut away gristle from half to which it is still attached.

**Potato-Leek Soup with
Crispy Ham and Jammy Eggs**

Escarole, Sausage, and Orzo Soup

Serves 2

Total time 1 hour

WHY THIS RECIPE WORKS For a quick yet satisfying weeknight meal, we combined tender bites of sausage, delicate pasta, and hearty greens for a warming Italian-inspired soup. We browned the sausage to create a flavorful fond on the bottom of the pot then added onion and garlic. Red pepper flakes infused our soup with a subtle heat. Cooking orzo pasta right in the broth streamlined our dish, and the starch from the pasta gave the broth body and substance. Chopped escarole contributed a pleasant, mildly bitter flavor. Chicken sausage is available in a wide variety of flavors; feel free to choose one that you think will pair well with the other flavors in this dish.

1 tablespoon extra-virgin olive oil, divided
6 ounces cooked chicken sausage, sliced ½ inch thick
1 small onion, chopped fine
1 garlic clove, minced
⅛ teaspoon red pepper flakes
3 cups chicken broth
2 ounces escarole, trimmed and chopped coarse (2 cups)
¼ cup orzo
¼ cup grated Parmesan cheese
1 tablespoon minced fresh parsley

1. Heat 2 teaspoons oil in medium saucepan over medium-high heat until shimmering. Add sausage and cook until browned, about 5 minutes; transfer to bowl.

2. Heat remaining 1 teaspoon oil in now-empty saucepan over medium heat until shimmering. Add onion and cook until softened and lightly browned, 5 to 7 minutes. Stir in garlic and pepper flakes and cook until fragrant, about 30 seconds.

3. Stir in broth, scraping up any browned bits. Stir in browned sausage, escarole, and orzo. Bring to simmer and cook until orzo is tender, 10 to 12 minutes. Off heat, stir in Parmesan and parsley and season with salt and pepper to taste. Serve.

Potato-Leek Soup with Crispy Ham and Jammy Eggs

Serves 2

Total time 45 minutes

WHY THIS RECIPE WORKS This recipe gives potato-leek soup a modern spin. To add smoky, savory flavor we crisped deli ham in a pan for a garnish. Then we sautéed the leeks in the fat left behind, which added even more depth of flavor. After adding the broth and water, we cooked the potatoes and then mashed them a bit in the pot, which thickened the soup. The crowning touch is a topping of the crispy ham and jammy eggs, which melt into the already creamy soup.

- 2 teaspoons extra-virgin olive oil
- 3 ounces thinly sliced deli ham, chopped
- 1 pound leeks, white and light green parts only, halved lengthwise, sliced thin, and washed thoroughly
- 1 teaspoon minced fresh thyme or ¼ teaspoon dried
- 1½ cups chicken broth
- 1¼ cups water
- 1 pound russet potatoes, peeled and cut into 1-inch pieces
- 2 Easy-Peel Jammy Eggs (page 360), halved lengthwise
- 1 tablespoon minced fresh parsley, tarragon, dill, or chives

1. Heat oil in large saucepan over medium heat until shimmering. Add ham and cook, stirring often, until lightly browned and beginning to crisp, 3 to 5 minutes; using slotted spoon, transfer ham to paper towel–lined plate.

2. Add leeks to oil left in saucepan and cook until softened and lightly browned, 6 to 8 minutes. Stir in thyme and cook until fragrant, about 30 seconds. Stir in broth, water, and potatoes and bring to simmer. Cover and cook until vegetables are tender, 15 to 18 minutes.

PREPARING LEEKS

1. Trim off root and leaves, and cut leek in half lengthwise.

2. Slice leek crosswise as directed. Wash cut leeks to remove dirt and sand.

3. Using potato masher, mash soup in saucepan until potatoes are mostly broken down and soup is thickened. Season with salt and pepper to taste. Top each portion with half of crispy ham, 1 jammy egg, and 1½ teaspoons parsley. Serve.

New England Clam Chowder

Serves 2

Total time 1¼ hours

WHY THIS RECIPE WORKS Many people are intimidated by the thought of preparing clam chowder at home—clams can be expensive and a challenge to cook, and the dairy in chowder has a tendency to curdle. We wanted to make clam chowder accessible to the for-two kitchen, and we started with the clams. Cherrystones offered good value and flavor, and we found that if we steamed them they did not toughen up so long as we removed them from the pot as soon as they opened. A combination of homemade clam broth and chicken broth provided a base that was balanced and not overly salty. Creamy Yukon Gold potatoes held their shape as the chowder simmered so there were hearty bites of potato throughout. Bacon provided a smoky note that completed our scaled down chowder. Serve with oyster crackers.

- 1 cup water
- 2 pounds medium hard-shell clams, such as cherrystones, scrubbed
- 2 slices bacon, chopped fine
- 1 small onion, chopped fine
- 1 celery rib, minced
- ¼ teaspoon minced fresh thyme or pinch dried
- 2½ tablespoons all-purpose flour
- 1½ cups chicken broth
- 1 Yukon Gold potato (8 ounces), peeled and cut into ½-inch pieces
- ⅓ cup heavy cream
- 1 tablespoon minced fresh parsley

1. Bring water to boil in medium saucepan. Add clams, cover, and cook for 5 minutes. Stir clams thoroughly, cover, and continue to cook until they just begin to open, 2 to 5 minutes. As clams open, transfer them to bowl and let cool slightly. Discard any unopened clams.

2. Measure out and reserve 1 cup of clam steaming liquid, avoiding any gritty sediment that has settled on bottom of saucepan. Using paring knife, remove clam meat from shells and chop coarse.

3. In clean saucepan, cook bacon over medium heat until crispy, 5 to 7 minutes. Add onion and celery and cook until softened, about 5 minutes. Stir in thyme and cook until fragrant, about 30 seconds. Stir in flour and cook for 1 minute.

4. Slowly whisk in broth and reserved clam steaming liquid, scraping up any browned bits and smoothing out any lumps. Stir in potatoes, bring to simmer, and cook until potatoes are tender, 20 to 25 minutes. Off heat, stir in chopped clams and cream and let sit until heated through, about 2 minutes. Stir in parsley and season with salt and pepper to taste. Serve.

VARIATION
Pantry Clam Chowder
Omit water and fresh clams and skip steps 1 and 2. Substitute 1 (8-ounce) bottle clam juice for clam steaming liquid and 2 (6.5-ounce) cans minced clams, drained, for chopped clams.

REMOVING CLAM MEAT FROM THE SHELL

1. Steam clams until they just open, as seen on left, rather than completely open, as shown on right.

2. Carefully use oyster knife or paring knife to open clam shell completely.

3. Once open, discard top shell and use knife to cut clam from bottom shell.

Hot-and-Sour Soup with Rice Vermicelli and Shrimp
Serves 2
Total time 40 minutes
WHY THIS RECIPE WORKS Full of energetic flavors inspired by the hot-and-sour Thai soup known as tom yum, this recipe combines a fragrant broth with tender rice vermicelli and succulent shrimp. The broth for tom yum achieves its complexity from steeping a mix of aromatics including lemongrass, makrut lime leaves, and galangal. In this version, we employed jarred Thai curry paste, a wonder ingredient packed with all of those aromatics plus chiles, which provides much of the heat, which we bolstered with a fresh jalapeño. We started by whisking the curry paste and just a hint of sugar into broth, then we staggered the cooking of four key ingredients— mushrooms, fresh chiles, shrimp, and tomato—to be sure they were each cooked perfectly. To finish, we rounded out the flavors with a splash each of briny fish sauce and zesty lime juice, plus a generous hit of fresh herbs. To make this dish spicier, reserve and add the chile seeds as desired.

2 ounces rice vermicelli
3 cups chicken or vegetable broth
2 tablespoons Thai green or red curry paste
1 teaspoon sugar
4 ounces cremini or white mushrooms, trimmed and sliced thin
1 jalapeño chile, stemmed, seeded, and sliced into thin rings
8 ounces extra-large shrimp (21 to 25 per pound), peeled, deveined, and tails removed
1 tomato, cored, seeded, and chopped
1 tablespoon fish sauce
1 tablespoon lime juice
2 tablespoons chopped cilantro, fresh Thai basil, basil, or mint

1. Bring 2 quarts water to boil in medium saucepan. Off heat, add vermicelli and let sit, stirring occasionally, until fully tender, about 5 minutes. Drain, rinse with cold water, drain again, and set aside.

2. Bring broth to simmer in now-empty saucepan over medium-low heat then whisk in curry paste and sugar until dissolved. Add mushrooms and jalapeño and simmer for 1 minute. Stir in shrimp and cook until opaque throughout, about 1 minute. Off heat, stir in tomato, fish sauce, and lime juice and season with salt and pepper to taste. Transfer soup to serving bowl, add noodles, then sprinkle with cilantro. Serve.

Hot-and-Sour Soup
with Rice Vermicelli
and Shrimp

SOUP MAKING

While the world of soup is diverse, there are some underlying principles that apply to most recipes.

SAUTÉ AROMATICS The first step in making many soups is sautéing aromatic vegetables such as onion and garlic. Sautéing not only softens their texture so that there is no unwelcome crunch in the soup, it also tames any harsh flavors and develops more complex flavors in the process.

START WITH GOOD BROTH If you're not inclined to pack your freezer with homemade stock, packaged broth is a convenient option for soup making. But differences among packaged broths are quite significant—some are pretty flavorful, while others taste like salty dishwater. Shop carefully. See page 50 for more information about buying broth.

CUT VEGETABLES TO THE RIGHT SIZE Most soups call for chunks of vegetables. Haphazardly cut vegetables will cook unevenly—some pieces will be underdone and crunchy while others will be soft and mushy. Cutting the vegetables to the size specified in the recipe ensures that the pieces will all be perfectly cooked.

STAGGER THE ADDITION OF VEGETABLES
When a soup contains a variety of vegetables, their addition to the pot must often be staggered to account for their varying cooking times. Hardy vegetables like potatoes and winter squash can withstand much more cooking than delicate asparagus or spinach.

SIMMER, DON'T BOIL A simmer is a restrained version of a boil; fewer bubbles break the surface, and they do so with less vigor. Simmering heats food through more gently and more evenly than boiling; boiling can cause vegetables such as potatoes to break apart or fray at the edges, and it can toughen meat, too.

SEASON JUST BEFORE SERVING It's best to add salt, pepper, and other seasonings after cooking, just before serving. This is because the saltiness of the stock and ingredients such as canned tomatoes and beans can vary greatly.

Miso-Ginger Udon Noodle Soup
Serves 2 VEGETARIAN
Total time 35 minutes

WHY THIS RECIPE WORKS Miso soup is commonly eaten as one part of a larger meal; our version, with assists from noodles, spicy fresh ginger, and a few quick-to-prep vegetables, is ample enough to be a hearty dinner all on its own. We started by boiling thick udon noodles until chewy-tender and then set them aside while we made the soup. Because overheating miso can mute this fermented product's nuanced flavor, we prepared the broth with care. First, we bloomed fragrant ginger in nutty sesame oil. We then added water, carrots, and edamame to the pot and cooked just until the vegetables were tender. Soy sauce seasoned the broth and amped up its umami backbone. Only when the vegetables were cooked did we spoon out a bit of the broth, gently whisk the miso into it off the heat, and then return the broth-miso mixture to the pot with the rest of the soup. (Whisking the miso with a smaller amount of broth before adding it to the pot helps prevent clumps from being left behind.) After we added the udon and portioned the soup into individual bowls, we topped each with scallions, sesame seeds, and a drizzle of toasted sesame oil.

- 6 ounces dried udon noodles
- 4 teaspoons grated fresh ginger
- 2 teaspoons toasted sesame oil, plus extra for drizzling
- 1 carrot, peeled, halved lengthwise, and sliced ¼ inch thick
- ½ cup frozen edamame
- 1 teaspoon soy sauce, plus extra for seasoning
- 2 tablespoons white or red miso
- 2 scallions, sliced thin
- 1 teaspoon sesame seeds, toasted

1. Bring 2 quarts water to boil in large pot. Add noodles and cook, stirring often, until tender. Drain noodles, rinse well, and drain again; set aside.

2. Meanwhile, heat ginger and oil in large saucepan over medium-low heat, stirring often, until ginger is fragrant and beginning to brown, about 2 minutes. Stir in 3¾ cups water, scraping up any browned bits, then stir in carrot, edamame, and soy sauce. Increase heat to medium, bring to simmer, and cook until vegetables are tender, 3 to 5 minutes.

3. Transfer ½ cup hot broth to small bowl or measuring cup and whisk in miso. Stir miso mixture and noodles into soup and return to brief simmer. Off heat, season with extra soy sauce to taste. Top individual portions with scallions, drizzle with extra oil, and sprinkle with sesame seeds before serving.

Soupe au Pistou

Serves 2   VEGETARIAN

Total time 50 minutes

WHY THIS RECIPE WORKS This classic Provençal vegetable soup is light and flavorful, featuring seasonal vegetables, white beans, and a dollop of garlicky pistou, the French equivalent of pesto. Since the delicate flavor of a homemade vegetable stock would be obscured by the flavors of the vegetables and the pistou, we were able to save time by using store-bought broth. Leek, green beans, and zucchini made for a balanced summer lineup. Just one tomato added color and brightness, and canned white beans contributed some substance to our soup and required zero prep. We didn't want to drag out the food processor for such a small amount of pistou, so instead we simply combined the oil, garlic, basil, and Parmesan in a bowl for easy prep (and cleanup).

- 4 teaspoons extra-virgin olive oil, divided
- 1 carrot, peeled and cut into ¼-inch pieces
- ½ leek, white and light green parts only, sliced ½ inch thick and washed thoroughly
- ¼ teaspoon table salt
- 3 garlic cloves, minced, divided
- 1½ cups vegetable broth
- 1½ cups water
- 3 ounces green beans, trimmed and cut into ½-inch lengths
- 1 small zucchini, quartered lengthwise and sliced ¼ inch thick
- ¾ cup canned cannellini or navy beans, rinsed
- 1 plum tomato, cored and chopped
- 2 tablespoons chopped fresh basil
- 2 tablespoons grated Parmesan cheese

1. Heat 1 tablespoon oil in medium saucepan over medium heat until shimmering. Add carrot, leek, and salt and cook until softened, about 5 minutes. Stir in two-thirds of garlic and cook until fragrant, about 30 seconds.

2. Stir in broth and water and bring to simmer. Stir in green beans and simmer until bright green but still crunchy, about 5 minutes. Stir in zucchini, beans, and tomato and continue to simmer until vegetables are tender, about 3 minutes.

3. Combine remaining 1 teaspoon oil, remaining garlic, basil, and Parmesan in bowl and season with pepper to taste. Season soup with salt and pepper to taste. Top individual portions with basil mixture before serving.

Farmhouse Vegetable and Barley Soup

Serves 2   VEGETARIAN

Total time 1 hour 25 minutes

WHY THIS RECIPE WORKS Most recipes for hearty winter vegetable soups are neither quick nor easy. For a satisfying soup for two that wouldn't take the better part of a day to make, we started with canned vegetable broth. To boost its flavor, we added soy sauce and just one dried porcini mushroom. These ingredients gave the soup plenty of savory, meaty flavor. To make the soup seriously satisfying, we added barley to the hearty combination of carrot, parsnip, potato, leek, and cabbage. A pat of butter, some thyme, and lemon juice added richness and brightened the flavors. We prefer an acidic, unoaked white wine such as Sauvignon Blanc for this recipe. Garnish the soup with crumbled cheddar cheese or herbed croutons, if desired.

- 2 parsley stems plus 1 tablespoon minced fresh parsley
- 2 sprigs fresh thyme plus ½ teaspoon chopped
- 1 dried porcini mushroom, rinsed
- 1 bay leaf
- 2 tablespoons unsalted butter, divided
- 1 leek, white and light green parts only, halved lengthwise, sliced ½ inch thick, and washed thoroughly
- 1 small carrot, peeled and cut into ½-inch pieces
- 1 small parsnip, peeled and cut into ½-inch pieces
- 2 tablespoons dry white wine
- ¾ teaspoon soy sauce
- ½ teaspoon table salt
- 2 cups water
- 1½ cups vegetable broth
- 3 tablespoons pearl barley
- 1 small garlic clove, peeled and smashed
- 1 small Yukon Gold potato (6 ounces), peeled and cut into ½-inch pieces
- ½ cup chopped green cabbage
- ¼ cup frozen peas
- 1 teaspoon lemon juice

1. Bundle parsley stems, thyme sprigs, mushroom, and bay leaf in cheesecloth and tie with kitchen twine to secure. Melt 1 tablespoon butter in medium saucepan over medium heat. Add leek, carrot, parsnip, wine, soy sauce, and salt. Cook, stirring occasionally, until liquid has evaporated and leek is softened, about 5 minutes.

2. Add herb and mushroom bundle, water, broth, barley, and garlic and bring to simmer. Reduce heat to medium-low, partially cover, and simmer for 15 minutes.

3. Stir in potato and cabbage and simmer, stirring occasionally, until barley, potato, and cabbage are tender, about 15 minutes.

4. Off heat, discard bundle. Stir in peas and let sit until heated through, about 2 minutes. Stir in minced parsley and chopped thyme, remaining 1 tablespoon butter, and lemon juice. Season with salt and pepper to taste. Serve.

Butternut Squash Soup with Blue Cheese and Pepitas

Serves 2 VEGETARIAN

Total time 55 minutes

WHY THIS RECIPE WORKS For a delicious butternut squash soup that was creamy, aromatic, and hearty, we started by browning squash pieces to slightly caramelize their edges and deepen the flavor; because we needed only a relatively small amount, we found that we could do this on the stovetop (much faster than roasting in the oven). A single shallot emphasized the sweet notes of the squash, and cream provided some richness. Sage, a classic pairing with squash, brought piney, herbal notes, and rich, pungent blue cheese added a salty sharpness that contrasted with the sweet squash. A sprinkling of roasted pepitas added a toasty, crunchy finishing touch. We prefer crumbling a block of blue cheese ourselves, but store-bought blue cheese crumbles will work fine here. You can use an immersion blender to process the soup directly in the pot instead of using a blender. Serve with crusty bread, if desired.

- 1 tablespoon extra-virgin olive oil
- ½ large butternut squash (1¼ pounds), peeled, seeded, and cut into 1-inch pieces (3 cups)
- 1 shallot, chopped
- 1 garlic clove, minced
- 1 teaspoon minced fresh sage
- 2 cups vegetable or chicken broth, plus extra as needed
- ⅛ teaspoon table salt
- ⅛ teaspoon pepper
- 2 tablespoons heavy cream
- ¼ cup crumbled blue cheese
- 2 tablespoons roasted, salted pepitas

1. Heat oil in medium saucepan over medium heat until shimmering. Add squash and shallot and cook until vegetables are softened and lightly browned, about 10 minutes. Stir in garlic and sage and cook until fragrant, about 30 seconds.

Butternut Squash Soup with Blue Cheese and Pepitas

2. Stir in broth, salt, and pepper and bring to simmer, scraping up any browned bits. Reduce heat to medium-low; cover; and cook until squash is tender, about 15 minutes.

3. Process soup in blender until smooth, about 2 minutes. Return soup to saucepan over medium-low heat and stir in cream. Adjust consistency with extra broth as needed. Off heat, season with salt and pepper to taste. Serve, sprinkled with blue cheese and pepitas.

Creamy Curried Cauliflower Soup

Serves 2 VEGETARIAN

Total time 40 minutes

WHY THIS RECIPE WORKS Fragrant curry powder and nutty cauliflower come together in this easy-to-make, creamy, and highly aromatic soup. After building a flavorful base with shallot, ginger, and curry powder, we added cauliflower and broth and briefly simmered it on the stovetop before blending it all together until smooth. Cauliflower blends beautifully—its low insoluble fiber content gives it a leg up to breaking down compared with other vegetables, contributing to the silky, not

PUREEING SOUP

The texture of a pureed soup should be as smooth and creamy as possible. With this in mind, we tried pureeing several soups with a food processor, a hand-held immersion blender, and a countertop blender. It pays to use the right appliance when blending soup. And because pureeing hot soup can be dangerous, follow our safety tips.

IMMERSION BLENDER The immersion blender has appeal because it can be brought to the pot, eliminating the need to ladle hot ingredients from one vessel to another. It is especially good for pureeing smaller batches of soup.

BLENDER A standard blender turns out the smoothest pureed soups but is harder to use for small amounts. The blade on the blender does an excellent job with soups because it pulls ingredients down from the top of the container. No stray bits go untouched by the blade. And as long as plenty of headroom is left at the top of the blender, there is no leakage.

PROCESS WITH CAUTION: FOOD PROCESSOR The food processor does a decent job of pureeing, but some small bits of vegetables can get trapped under the blade and remain unchopped. Even more troubling is the tendency of a food processor to leak hot liquid. Fill the workbowl more than halfway and you are likely to see liquid running down the side of the food processor base.

WAIT BEFORE BLENDING, AND BLEND IN BATCHES When blending hot soup, follow a couple of precautions. Wait 5 minutes for moderate cooling, and never fill the blender jar more than halfway; otherwise, the soup can explode out the top.

KEEP LID SECURE Don't expect the lid on a blender to stay in place. Hold the lid securely with a folded dish towel to keep it in place and to protect your hand from hot steam.

---

chunky, texture. A splash of cream added just the right amount of richness. After cooking, we stirred in cilantro for a fresh finish; a squeeze of lime juice provided a contrasting burst of brightness. You can use an immersion blender to process the soup directly in the pot instead of using a blender.

- 1 tablespoon extra-virgin olive oil
- 1 shallot, chopped
- 1½ teaspoons curry powder
- 1 teaspoon grated fresh ginger or ½ teaspoon ground ginger
- ½ head cauliflower (1 pound), cored and cut into 1-inch florets
- 2 cups vegetable or chicken broth, plus extra as needed
- ⅛ teaspoon table salt
- ¼ cup heavy cream or half-and-half
- 1 tablespoon minced fresh cilantro, parsley, or chives
  Lime wedges

1. Heat oil in medium saucepan over medium-low heat until shimmering. Add shallot and cook until softened and lightly browned, 3 to 5 minutes. Stir in curry powder and ginger and cook until fragrant, about 30 seconds.

2. Stir in cauliflower, broth, and salt, scraping up any browned bits. Bring to simmer and cook until cauliflower is tender, about 15 minutes.

3. Process soup in blender until smooth, about 2 minutes. Return soup to now-empty saucepan, stir in cream, and adjust consistency with extra hot broth as needed. Off heat, stir in cilantro and season with salt and pepper to taste. Serve with lime wedges.

CUTTING CAULIFLOWER

1. Pull off any leaves, then cut out core of cauliflower using paring knife.

2. Separate florets from inner stem using tip of paring knife. Cut larger florets into smaller pieces by slicing them through stem.

Creamless Creamy Tomato Soup

Serves 2 `FAST` `VEGETARIAN`

Total time 30 minutes

WHY THIS RECIPE WORKS While the cream in most tomato soups tempers the acidity of the tomatoes, it also dulls their flavor. We discovered we could achieve a creamy texture without cream by adding bread to our tomato soup. When simmered with the tomatoes and then blended, the bread broke down and disappeared into the soup, adding body and taming the tartness of the tomatoes while still allowing the tomato flavor to shine through. A little brown sugar heightened the sweet tomato flavor, as did a splash of brandy. As for the tomatoes, canned offered consistently better flavor all year round than the fresh offerings at the supermarket. You can use an immersion blender to process the soup directly in the pot instead of using a blender.

- 2 tablespoons extra-virgin olive oil, divided, plus extra for drizzling
- 1 small onion, chopped
- 2 garlic cloves, minced
- 1 (28-ounce) can whole peeled tomatoes
- 2 slices hearty white sandwich bread, crusts removed, torn into 1-inch pieces
- 2 teaspoons packed brown sugar, plus extra for seasoning
- ½ cup vegetable or chicken broth, plus extra as needed
- 1 tablespoon brandy (optional)
- 2 tablespoons minced fresh chives

1. Heat 1 tablespoon oil in medium saucepan over medium heat until shimmering. Add onion and cook until softened, about 5 minutes. Stir in garlic and cook until fragrant, about 30 seconds. Stir in tomatoes and their juice and mash with potato masher until no pieces are larger than 2 inches.

2. Stir in bread and sugar, bring to simmer, and cook until bread is saturated and starts to break down, about 5 minutes. Process soup in blender with remaining 1 tablespoon oil until smooth, about 2 minutes. Return soup to clean saucepan.

3. Stir in broth and brandy, if using, and bring to brief simmer. Adjust soup consistency with extra broth as needed. Season with salt, pepper, and extra sugar to taste. Sprinkle individual portions with chives and drizzle with extra oil before serving.

Gazpacho

Serves 2 `VEGETARIAN`

Total time 25 minutes, plus 4 hours chilling

WHY THIS RECIPE WORKS While a bowl of chilled gazpacho is incredibly appealing on a hot summer day, chopping piles of vegetables is not, making this popular Spanish soup an ideal recipe to scale down. For a chunky soup, we hand-chopped the vegetables. A minced shallot provided a sweet aroma, and marinating the vegetables briefly in sherry vinegar ensured our soup was seasoned throughout. A cup of tomato juice along with a few ice cubes gave our soup just the right consistency and guaranteed that it was thoroughly chilled.

- 1 large tomato, cored, seeded, and cut into ¼-inch pieces
- ½ red bell pepper, cut into ¼-inch pieces
- ½ cucumber, halved lengthwise, seeded, and cut into ¼-inch pieces
- 1 shallot, minced
- 2 tablespoons sherry vinegar
- 1 small garlic clove, minced
- ¼ teaspoon table salt
- ¼ teaspoon pepper
- 1 cup low-sodium tomato juice
- ¼ teaspoon hot sauce (optional)
- 3 ice cubes
- 2 teaspoons extra-virgin olive oil
- 2 tablespoons minced fresh parsley or cilantro

1. Combine tomato, bell pepper, cucumber, shallot, vinegar, garlic, salt, and pepper in medium bowl and let sit for 5 minutes. Stir in tomato juice; hot sauce, if using; and ice cubes. Cover and refrigerate until well chilled and flavors meld, at least 4 hours or up to 24 hours.

2. To serve, discard any unmelted ice cubes. Stir soup to recombine and season with salt and pepper to taste. Ladle soup into individual chilled serving bowls, drizzle with oil, and sprinkle with parsley.

VARIATION

Gazpacho with Shrimp

Add 8 ounces cooked and peeled small shrimp (51 to 60 per pound), chilled, to soup before seasoning with salt and pepper in step 2.

SEEDING RAW TOMATOES

A. For Round Tomatoes: Halve tomato crosswise. Gently squeeze each half and shake out seeds and gelatinous material. Use your finger to scoop out any remaining seeds.

B. For Plum Tomatoes: Halve tomato through core end. Scoop out seeds and gelatinous material with your finger.

Corn Chowder with Chorizo and Poblanos

Serves 2

Total time 45 minutes

WHY THIS RECIPE WORKS We love the salty, spicy, tangy, rich flavors of elote, the popular Mexican street corn—so much so that we turned it into a soup that feels like a treat. Because this soup is all about the toppings, we doubled down on them—first, we sautéed poblano chiles for vegetal depth, and then we cooked Mexican chorizo until it turned deliciously crispy and rendered some flavorful fat, which we used to toast our corn. After we added aromatics and broth to the corn, we pureed most of it until creamy, leaving some corn kernels whole for a pleasant chunky texture. If you don't have a blender, an immersion blender will also work; just puree the soup right in the saucepan, pulsing until soup is thickened slightly, about 5 pulses.

- 1 tablespoon vegetable oil, divided
- 2 poblano chiles, stemmed, seeded, and sliced thin
- 4 garlic cloves, minced, divided
- 1¼ teaspoons chili powder, divided
- 2 ounces Mexican-style chorizo, casings removed
- 4 ears corn, kernels cut from cobs, or 3½ cups frozen
- ⅛ teaspoon table salt
- 1½ cups vegetable or chicken broth
- ¼ cup chopped fresh cilantro or parsley
  Lime wedges

Corn Chowder with Chorizo and Poblanos

1. Heat 1 teaspoon oil in medium saucepan over medium heat until shimmering. Add poblanos and cook until just tender, 3 to 5 minutes. Stir in one-fourth of garlic and ¼ teaspoon chili powder and cook until fragrant, about 30 seconds. Transfer to bowl, cover with aluminum foil, and set aside. In now-empty saucepan, heat remaining 2 teaspoons oil over medium heat until shimmering. Add chorizo and cook until browned. Using slotted spoon, transfer chorizo to bowl with poblanos, covering with foil to keep warm.

2. Pour off all but 1 teaspoon fat from pan. (If necessary, add oil to equal 1 teaspoon.) Add corn and cook over medium heat, stirring occasionally, until lightly browned, about 5 minutes. Stir in remaining garlic, ¾ teaspoon of remaining chili powder, and salt and cook until fragrant, 30 seconds. Stir in broth, scraping up any browned bits. Bring to simmer and cook until corn is tender, 2 minutes.

3. Process 2 cups soup in blender until smooth. Stir pureed soup into remaining soup in saucepan, adjusting consistency with hot water as needed, and season with salt and pepper to taste. Off heat, top with poblano-chorizo mixture, cilantro, and remaining ¼ teaspoon chili powder. Serve with lime wedges.

Pasta e Fagioli

Serves 2

Total time 50 minutes

WHY THIS RECIPE WORKS Pasta e fagioli is a hearty Italian soup composed of pasta and beans with a thick tomato base—we sought to create a perfect weeknight version made from pantry staples. Bacon, onion, and celery gave us a flavorful base. Allowing canned, diced tomatoes to cook down with the aromatics before adding chicken broth and water helped reduce the tomato juice and concentrate its flavor. We also added the beans before the broth to infuse them with the flavor of the bacon and vegetables. Ditalini was the perfect pasta to round out our hearty soup for two. Serve with grated Parmesan cheese and drizzle with extra-virgin olive oil.

- 2   slices bacon, chopped fine
- 1   small onion, chopped fine
- 1   celery rib, minced
    Pinch plus ¼ teaspoon table salt, divided
- 1   garlic clove, minced
- 1   teaspoon minced fresh oregano or ¼ teaspoon dried
    Pinch red pepper flakes
- 1   (14.5-ounce) can diced tomatoes
- ¾   cup canned cannellini beans, rinsed
- 1   cup chicken broth
- 1   cup water
- ⅔   cup small pasta, such as ditalini, tubettini, or mini elbows

1. Cook bacon in medium saucepan over medium heat until crispy, 5 to 7 minutes. Add onion, celery, and pinch salt and cook until softened and lightly browned, 5 to 7 minutes. Stir in garlic, oregano, and pepper flakes and cook until fragrant, about 30 seconds.

2. Stir in tomatoes and their juice, scraping up any browned bits. Stir in beans; bring to simmer; and cook until mixture has thickened slightly, about 5 minutes. Stir in broth, water, and remaining ¼ teaspoon salt and bring to boil. Stir in pasta and cook until al dente, 8 to 12 minutes. Season with salt and pepper to taste, and serve.

5-Ingredient Black Bean Soup

Serves 2   `FAST` `VEGETARIAN`

Total time 20 minutes

WHY THIS RECIPE WORKS Lucky for us (and our taste buds), a single can of beans is so much more than just the beans. The bean liquid did the heavy lifting, providing body, silky texture, and deep flavor—we didn't even need a lot of herbs or aromatics to make these soups sing. For this black bean soup, a base of smoky, fruity chipotle chiles in adobo sauce gave the soup character and depth of flavor in a flash, while lime zest and broth added fresh aroma and subtle complexity. We coarsely mashed the beans after cooking, which helped to thicken the soup, and Greek yogurt brought extra creaminess and tanginess.

- 1   (15-ounce) can black beans, undrained
- 1   cup vegetable or chicken broth, plus extra as needed
- 2–3 teaspoons minced canned chipotle chiles in adobo sauce
- 2   tablespoons plain Greek yogurt
- ½   teaspoon grated lime zest, plus lime wedges for serving

Bring beans and their liquid, broth, and chipotle to simmer in medium saucepan and cook over medium-low heat, stirring occasionally, until beans begin to break down, 5 to 7 minutes. Using potato masher, coarsely mash beans in saucepan. Adjust consistency with extra hot broth as needed. Off heat, stir in yogurt and lime zest, and season with salt and pepper to taste. Serve with lime wedges.

Tuscan White Bean Soup

Serves 2

Total time 40 minutes

WHY THIS RECIPE WORKS With just a handful of ingredients, Tuscan white bean soup embodies the straightforward simplicity that Italian cooking is known for. But while the ingredient list is simple, it typically relies on a lengthy simmering time to build robust flavor. To cut back on cooking time without sacrificing flavor, we started with a potent base of bacon, carrot, onion, and dried rosemary. Allowing canned white beans to simmer for just 5 minutes with the broth gave them a significant flavor boost, and a last-minute addition of spinach brought some extra heartiness to our dish. We prefer the texture of cannellini beans in this soup; however, small white beans can be substituted. Serve with grated Parmesan cheese and drizzle with extra-virgin olive oil.

2 slices bacon, chopped fine
1 small onion, chopped fine
1 carrot, peeled and chopped fine
 Pinch plus ½ teaspoon table salt, divided
1 garlic clove, minced
¼ teaspoon dried rosemary, crumbled
1¾ cups chicken broth
¼ cup water
1 (15-ounce) can cannellini beans, rinsed
5 ounces frozen spinach, thawed and squeezed dry

1. Cook bacon in medium saucepan over medium heat until crispy, 5 to 7 minutes. Add onion, carrot, and pinch salt and cook until softened and lightly browned, 5 to 7 minutes. Stir in garlic and rosemary and cook until fragrant, about 30 seconds.

2. Stir in broth, water, beans, spinach, and remaining ½ teaspoon salt. Bring to simmer and cook until soup has thickened slightly, about 5 minutes. Season with salt and pepper to taste, and serve.

Moong Dal Soup with Coconut Milk and Spinach

Serves 2 `VEGETARIAN`

Total time 45 minutes

WHY THIS RECIPE WORKS This aromatic, creamy soup made from moong dal (buttery, split mung beans) comes together in a snap. In addition to broth and water, we added coconut milk, which played well with the warm spices and bold, fresh ingredients. A punchy salsa-like topping added color, crunch, and heat. If you can't find split mung beans, you can substitute split red lentils; do not use yellow lentils or split pigeon peas (toor dal). To make this dish spicier, reserve and add the chile seeds as desired.

1 tomato, cored and chopped
2 tablespoons chopped fresh cilantro
1 tablespoon lime juice, plus lime wedges for serving
1 jalapeño chile, stemmed, seeded, and minced, divided
2 tablespoons canola oil
1 small onion, chopped fine
1 tablespoon grated fresh ginger
2 garlic cloves, minced
1 teaspoon ground cumin
½ teaspoon turmeric
2½ cups vegetable or chicken broth
1 cup water

Moong Dal Soup with Coconut Milk and Spinach

SQUEEZING SPINACH DRY

To rid thawed spinach of excess water before adding it to recipes, simply wrap it in cheesecloth and squeeze it firmly.

¾ cup split mung beans, picked over and rinsed
⅓ cup canned coconut milk
2 ounces frozen chopped spinach, thawed and squeezed dry

1. Combine tomato, cilantro, lime juice, and half of jalapeño in small bowl. Season with salt and pepper to taste; set aside.

2. Heat oil in large saucepan over medium heat until shimmering. Add onion and cook until softened and lightly browned, 5 to 7 minutes. Stir in ginger, garlic, cumin, turmeric, and remaining jalapeño and cook until fragrant, about 1 minute.

BUYING BROTH
Here are a few good stand-ins for homemade broth that will deliver richly flavored yet speedy soups and stews.

CHICKEN BROTH In search of the best-tasting chicken broth, we discovered a few things that made a big difference in quality. First, look for a sodium content between 400 and 700 milligrams per serving. Too-salty broth can easily ruin a dish, but not enough salt can leave a dish tasting bland. Also, look for a mass-produced broth. Several broths had rancid off-flavors caused by fat oxidation; the worst offenders were made by smaller companies. Last, look for a short ingredient list that includes vegetables like carrots, celery, and onions. Our pick? **Swanson Chicken Stock**, which tastes rich and meaty thanks to its high percentage of meat-based protein.

BEEF BROTH We've found beef broths generally short on beefy flavor, but our winning beef broth, **Rachael Ray Stock-in-a-Box All-Natural Beef Flavored Stock**, has a short ingredient list that starts with concentrated beef stock, so this stock has more fresh, real meat than its competitors without a slew of processed additives.

BOUILLION AND BROTH CONCENTRATES
Dehydrated forms of chicken, beef, and vegetable broth, these shelf-stable products are cost-effective and last for up to two years once opened. Simply mix with water to make just as much broth as you need. We particularly like **Better than Bouillon** brand **Chicken Base and Roasted Beef Base**, which make 38 cups of broth. The beef base has a goodly amount of salt and multiple flavor enhancers; it is economical, stores easily, and dissolves quickly in hot water. Our winning vegetable broth was **Orrington Farms Vegan Chicken Flavored Broth Base and Seasoning**.

3. Stir in broth, water, and beans and bring to simmer. Reduce heat to low and cook, partially covered, until beans are beginning to break down, 10 to 12 minutes.

4. Whisk soup vigorously until beans are completely broken down and soup is thickened, about 30 seconds. Stir in coconut milk and spinach; return to simmer; and cook until spinach is heated through, about 2 minutes. Season with salt and pepper to taste. Top each portion with half of tomato mixture. Serve.

Lentil Soup

Serves 2
Total time 1½ hours

WHY THIS RECIPE WORKS We wanted our scaled-down lentil soup to have just the right consistency (one that was neither too brothy nor overly thick) and a deep, well-rounded flavor. Selecting the right lentils was key, and the earthy flavor and firm texture of lentilles du Puy won out over other varieties, which tended to disintegrate when simmered. We cooked the lentils in a covered pan with the aromatics (along with some tomatoes and salt for an additional flavor boost) prior to adding the liquid, which helped them remain intact. Pureeing a few cups of the soup created a substantial, creamy base. Bacon infused our soup with smoky flavor and offered a welcome textural contrast, while parsley and a splash of balsamic vinegar provided a bright finish. Although we prefer lentilles du Puy (also called French green lentils) for this recipe, it will work with any type of lentil except red or yellow. Note that cooking times may vary depending on the type of lentils you use. You can use an immersion blender to process the soup directly in the pot instead of using a blender.

2 slices bacon, chopped fine
1 small onion, chopped fine
1 carrot, peeled and cut into ¼-inch pieces
1 tomato, cored, seeded, and chopped fine
1 garlic clove, minced
¼ teaspoon minced fresh thyme or pinch dried
½ cup dried lentils, picked over and rinsed
½ teaspoon table salt
2 cups chicken broth
1 cup water
1 bay leaf
1 tablespoon minced fresh parsley
1 teaspoon balsamic vinegar

Lentil Soup

Chickpea and Vegetable Soup with Warm Spices

Serves 2   `VEGETARIAN`

Total time 55 minutes

WHY THIS RECIPE WORKS This simple and hearty soup takes its inspiration from Harira, a classic Moroccan soup usually made with dried legumes and lamb. For our for-two soup repertoire, we kept the earthy, warm spices that are the hallmark of this soup and made an easy vegetarian version using canned chickpeas. Store-bought vegetable broth, along with some onion, provided a streamlined, yet flavorful, base. Tomato paste lent a long-simmered depth to our soup, and cooking it briefly with garlic, paprika, garam masala, and cumin allowed all the flavors to bloom. Some chopped tomato and zucchini contributed freshness and textural interest, and a sprinkling of fresh cilantro provided the perfect finishing touch for this simple, flavorful, one-pot meal.

- 1 tablespoon unsalted butter
- 1 small onion, chopped fine
- ¼ teaspoon table salt
- 2 teaspoons tomato paste
- 2 garlic cloves, minced
- ½ teaspoon paprika
- ½ teaspoon garam masala
- ¼ teaspoon ground cumin
- 2 cups vegetable broth
- 1 cup canned chickpeas, rinsed
- 1 tomato, cored, seeded, and chopped fine
- 1 small zucchini, cut into ½-inch pieces
- 1 tablespoon minced fresh cilantro

1. Melt butter in medium saucepan over medium heat. Add onion and salt and cook until softened, about 5 minutes. Stir in tomato paste, garlic, paprika, garam masala, and cumin, and cook until fragrant, about 30 seconds.

2. Stir in broth and chickpeas, bring to simmer, and cook for 10 minutes. Stir in tomato and zucchini and continue to simmer until zucchini is tender, about 10 minutes. Stir in cilantro and season with salt and pepper to taste. Serve.

1. Cook bacon in medium saucepan over medium heat until crispy, 5 to 7 minutes. Add onion and carrot and cook until softened, about 5 minutes. Stir in tomato, garlic, and thyme and cook until fragrant, about 30 seconds. Stir in lentils and salt. Reduce heat to medium-low; cover; and cook until lentils have darkened, 5 to 8 minutes.

2. Stir in broth, water, and bay leaf, scraping up any browned bits. Bring to simmer; partially cover; and cook until lentils are tender but still hold their shape, 35 to 45 minutes.

3. Process 1½ cups of soup in blender until smooth, about 2 minutes. Return processed soup to saucepan and stir to combine. Season with salt and pepper to taste. Sprinkle individual portions with parsley and drizzle with vinegar before serving.

VARIATION

Curried Lentil Soup

Omit bacon. Heat 1 tablespoon vegetable oil in medium saucepan over medium heat until shimmering. Add onion and carrot and proceed with recipe. Add ¾ teaspoon curry powder and ½ teaspoon garam masala with tomato, garlic, and thyme. Substitute 1 tablespoon minced fresh cilantro for parsley.

Stews, Curries & Chilis

Stews

Chilis

Curries

◼ **VEGETARIAN**

Opposite: Fish Stew with Chorizo and Fennel

Weeknight Beef Stew

Weeknight Beef Stew

Serves 2

Total time 1 hour

WHY THIS RECIPE WORKS Beef stews typically require a lengthy simmering time and a large cut of meat and feed a crowd. For our scaled-down stew, instead of chuck-eye roast, we chose quick-cooking steak tips. To mimic the flavor of a slow-cooked stew, we seared the beef to develop more fond and added tomato paste, a small amount of anchovy, and soy sauce for savory depth. Steak tips, also known as flap meat, are sold as whole steak, cubes, and strips; look for either whole steak tips or strips that are easy to cut into small pieces.

12	ounces sirloin steak tips, trimmed and cut into ½-inch pieces
¼	teaspoon table salt
⅛	teaspoon pepper
4	teaspoons vegetable oil, divided
1	small onion, chopped fine
1	carrot, peeled and sliced ¼ inch thick
2	garlic cloves, minced
1	teaspoon tomato paste
½	anchovy fillet, rinsed and minced
½	teaspoon minced fresh thyme or ⅛ teaspoon dried
1	tablespoon all-purpose flour
3	tablespoons dry red wine
1½	cups beef broth
1	small Yukon Gold potato (6 ounces), peeled and cut into ½-inch pieces
¼	cup frozen peas
1	teaspoon soy sauce

1. Pat beef dry with paper towels and sprinkle with salt and pepper. Heat 2 teaspoons oil in medium saucepan over medium-high heat until just smoking. Brown half of beef on all sides, 5 to 7 minutes; transfer to bowl. Repeat with remaining 2 teaspoons oil and remaining beef; transfer to bowl.

2. Add onion and carrot to fat left in saucepan and cook over medium heat until softened, about 5 minutes. Stir in garlic, tomato paste, anchovy, and thyme and cook until fragrant, about 30 seconds. Stir in flour and cook for 1 minute.

3. Slowly whisk in wine, scraping up any browned bits and smoothing out any lumps. Stir in broth and potato and bring to simmer. Reduce heat to medium-low, cover, and simmer until vegetables are tender, 15 to 20 minutes.

4. Stir in browned beef along with any accumulated juices, peas, and soy sauce and simmer until stew is heated through, about 2 minutes. Season with salt and pepper to taste, and serve.

Classic Beef Stew

Serves 2

Total time 3½ hours

WHY THIS RECIPE WORKS We wanted a recipe for an ultimate beef stew that would keep the cooking process simple without compromising the stew's deep, complex flavor. To start, we swapped out the usual chuck roast for boneless beef short ribs—which have outstanding beefy flavor and become supremely tender after a slow simmer—and browned them to develop a flavorful fond with which we could build the rest of our stew. A little flour added to the sautéed aromatics helped thicken our stew, while some umami-rich tomato paste and beef broth enhanced the meatiness of the ribs. Traditional carrots, potato, and peas worked well here, and cutting the carrots and potatoes into substantial pieces ensured they didn't overcook. You will need a medium ovensafe saucepan for this recipe.

1 pound boneless beef short ribs, trimmed and cut into 1½-inch pieces
¼ teaspoon table salt
⅛ teaspoon pepper
1 tablespoon vegetable oil
1 small onion, chopped fine
2 garlic cloves, minced
1 teaspoon tomato paste
½ teaspoon minced fresh thyme or ⅛ teaspoon dried
1 tablespoon all-purpose flour
¼ cup dry red wine
1½ cups beef broth
1 bay leaf
1 Yukon Gold potato (8 ounces), cut into ¾-inch pieces
2 carrots, peeled and sliced ¾ inch thick
¼ cup frozen peas
1 tablespoon minced fresh parsley

1. Adjust oven rack to middle position and heat oven to 300 degrees. Pat beef dry with paper towels and sprinkle with salt and pepper. Heat oil in medium ovensafe saucepan over medium-high heat until just smoking. Brown beef on all sides, about 8 minutes; transfer to bowl.

2. Add onion to fat left in saucepan and cook over medium heat until softened, about 5 minutes. Stir in garlic, tomato paste, and thyme and cook until fragrant, about 30 seconds. Stir in flour and cook for 1 minute.

3. Slowly whisk in wine, scraping up any browned bits and smoothing out any lumps. Stir in broth, bay leaf, and browned beef along with any accumulated juices and bring to simmer. Cover, transfer saucepan to oven, and cook for 1 hour.

4. Stir in potato and carrots and continue to cook in oven, covered, until beef and vegetables are tender, 1½ to 2 hours.

5. Discard bay leaf. Using large spoon, skim excess fat from surface of stew. Stir in peas and let sit until heated through, about 2 minutes. Stir in parsley and season with salt and pepper to taste. Serve.

VARIATION
Provençal Beef Stew

Omit potato and peas. Increase garlic to 3 cloves, tomato paste to 2 teaspoons, and carrots to 4. Stir in 2 (2-inch) strips orange zest, ¼ ounce dried porcini mushrooms, rinsed and minced, and 1 rinsed anchovy fillet with garlic, tomato paste, and thyme. Stir in 1 (14.5-ounce) can diced tomatoes, drained, and ¼ cup coarsely chopped pitted kalamata olives with broth, bay leaf, and browned beef.

TRIMMING SHORT RIBS

Short ribs can be very fatty, so it's important to trim them well to avoid a greasy stew. Using sharp knife, trim away large piece of fat on top and, if necessary, any fat on bottom of each rib.

Catalan Beef Stew

Serves 2

Total time 3½ hours

WHY THIS RECIPE WORKS For a complexly flavored Catalan beef stew, we started with a sofrito, a slow-cooked mixture of onion, spices, and herbs. Salt and sugar helped the onion to caramelize; then we added a grated plum tomato and cooked it until the mixture was thick and jamlike. Boneless beef short ribs were easy to buy in small amounts and became ultratender after a slow simmer. A broth of water and white wine allowed the rich flavors of the meat and the sofrito to shine. A traditional picada, a mixture of toasted bread, almonds, garlic, and parsley, brightened the stew's flavor and thickened the broth. You will need a medium ovensafe saucepan for this recipe. Serve with potatoes or rice.

STEW

- 1 tablespoon extra-virgin olive oil
- 1 onion, chopped fine
- ¼ teaspoon sugar
- ¾ teaspoon table salt, divided
- 1 plum tomato, halved lengthwise, pulp grated on large holes of box grater, and skin discarded
- ½ teaspoon smoked paprika
- 1 bay leaf
- ¾ cup water
- ½ cup dry white wine
- 8 ounces white mushrooms, trimmed and quartered
- 1 sprig fresh thyme
  Pinch ground cinnamon
- 1½ pounds boneless beef short ribs, trimmed and cut into 1½-inch pieces
- ¼ teaspoon pepper

PICADA

- 2 tablespoons whole blanched almonds
- 2 teaspoons extra-virgin olive oil
- ½ slice hearty white sandwich bread, crust removed, torn into 1-inch pieces
- 1 garlic clove, peeled
- 1½ tablespoons minced fresh parsley
- ¼ teaspoon sherry vinegar

1. FOR THE STEW Adjust oven rack to middle position and heat oven to 300 degrees. Heat oil in medium ovensafe saucepan over medium-low heat until shimmering. Add onion, sugar, and ¼ teaspoon salt and cook, stirring often, until onion is deeply caramelized, 25 to 30 minutes. Stir in tomato, paprika, and bay leaf and cook, stirring often, until mixture is darkened and thick, 5 to 10 minutes.

2. Stir in water, wine, mushrooms, thyme sprig, and cinnamon, scraping up any browned bits. Sprinkle beef with remaining ½ teaspoon salt and pepper, add to stew mixture, and bring to simmer. Transfer saucepan to oven and cook, uncovered, for 1 hour.

3. Stir stew to redistribute meat and continue to cook in oven, uncovered, until beef is tender, 1½ to 2 hours.

4. FOR THE PICADA Meanwhile, combine almonds and oil in bowl and microwave until nuts are light golden, 45 to 60 seconds. Stir in bread and continue to microwave until bread is golden, 60 to 90 seconds; transfer to food processor.

Add garlic and process until mixture is finely ground, about 20 seconds, scraping down sides of bowl as needed. Transfer mixture to bowl and stir in parsley.

5. Discard bay leaf and thyme sprig from stew. Stir in picada and vinegar and season with salt and pepper to taste. Serve.

Brazilian Pork and Black Bean Stew

Serves 2

Total time 1 hour 20 minutes

WHY THIS RECIPE WORKS This hearty Brazilian stew features creamy black beans and smoky, tender pork. We wanted to scale down the yield while preserving its bold, potent flavors. Just one can of black beans provided a good base and saved us the long soaking time dried beans require. Smoky linguiça sausage and meaty country-style ribs (which, unlike other ribs, can be purchased individually) gave us the most pork flavor with the least amount of prep. For rich flavor without hours of simmering, we browned the ribs and added plenty of aromatics and vegetables—garlic, onion, bell pepper, jalapeño, and a tomato. A little flour and mashing some of the beans helped thicken our stew to the proper consistency. Finally, we topped our dish with a salsa for a fresh, bright contrast to the rich stew. To make this dish spicier, add the chile seeds. Serve with rice.

- 1 small green bell pepper, stemmed, seeded, and chopped fine, divided
- 1 small tomato, cored, seeded, and chopped fine, divided
- 1 small onion, chopped fine, divided
- 1 jalapeño chile, stemmed, seeded, and minced, divided
- 2 tablespoons vegetable oil, divided
- 1 tablespoon white wine vinegar
- 1 tablespoon minced fresh cilantro
- ⅛ teaspoon plus ¼ teaspoon table salt, divided
  Pinch plus ⅛ teaspoon pepper, divided
- 12 ounces boneless country-style pork ribs, trimmed and cut into 1½-inch pieces
- 2 garlic cloves, minced
- 2 tablespoons all-purpose flour
- 2 cups chicken broth
- 1 (15-ounce) can black beans, rinsed
- 4 ounces linguiça sausage, cut into ½-inch pieces

1. Combine 2 tablespoons bell pepper, 2 tablespoons tomato, 2 tablespoons onion, 1 tablespoon jalapeño, 1 teaspoon oil, vinegar, cilantro, ⅛ teaspoon salt, and pinch pepper in bowl; set salsa aside.

2. Pat pork dry with paper towels and sprinkle with remaining ¼ teaspoon salt and remaining ⅛ teaspoon pepper. Heat 1 tablespoon oil in medium saucepan over medium-high heat until just smoking. Brown pork lightly on all sides, about 6 minutes; transfer to bowl.

3. Heat remaining 2 teaspoons oil in now-empty saucepan over medium heat until shimmering. Add remaining bell pepper, remaining onion, and remaining jalapeño and cook until softened, about 5 minutes. Stir in garlic and remaining tomato and cook until fragrant, about 30 seconds. Stir in flour and cook for 1 minute.

4. Slowly whisk in broth, scraping up any browned bits and smoothing out any lumps. Stir in browned pork along with any accumulated juices, beans, and linguiça and bring to simmer. Reduce heat to medium-low; cover; and simmer until pork is tender, about 30 minutes.

5. Using back of wooden spoon, mash some of beans against side of pan to thicken stew. Season with salt and pepper to taste. Serve with salsa.

Brazilian Pork and Black Bean Stew

Chicken Tagine

Serves 2

Total time 40 minutes

WHY THIS RECIPE WORKS Tagines of North Africa are warmly spiced, assertively flavored stews that typically involve long lists of ingredients (meats, vegetables, fruits, and numerous spices) and are cooked for hours in conical earthenware vessels, also called tagines. They're exceedingly delicious, but can be a lot of work. We judiciously selected ingredients to make sure we were staying true to the flavors while cutting down on work. We relied on ras el hanout, a Moroccan spice blend that captures the heady flavor of many spices in one, to deliver big flavor in a single ingredient. Quick-cooking chicken thighs were our protein of choice. Chickpeas and dried apricots, traditional additions that also happen to be pantry friendly, contributed to the tagine's sweet-savory balance, and just one sweet potato was plenty to amp up the sweetness of the braise. Coarsely mashing the tagine at the end of cooking helped achieve a creamy texture reminiscent of long-cooked stews but in a fraction of the time. Serve over couscous, rice, or other grains. Top with pomegranate seeds if desired. You can use store-bought ras el hanout or make your own (see page 58).

Chicken Tagine

1 tablespoon vegetable oil
1 shallot, chopped fine
2 garlic cloves, minced
1½ teaspoons ras el hanout
1 (15-ounce) can chickpeas, rinsed
1½ cups chicken or vegetable broth
8 ounces boneless, skinless chicken thighs, trimmed and cut into 1-inch pieces
1 small sweet potato (8 ounces), peeled and cut into 1-inch pieces
¼ cup dried apricots, quartered
2 tablespoons chopped fresh cilantro

1. Heat oil in medium saucepan over medium-low heat until shimmering. Add shallot, garlic, and ras el hanout and cook, stirring often, until shallot and garlic are softened and spices are fragrant, about 3 minutes.

2. Stir in chickpeas, broth, chicken, sweet potato, and apricots, scraping up any browned bits. Bring to simmer and cook until chicken and sweet potato are tender, about 15 minutes. Using potato masher or back of large spoon, coarsely mash stew to desired consistency. Off heat, stir in cilantro and season with salt and pepper to taste. Serve.

Ras el Hanout

Makes ½ cup VEGETARIAN

If you can't find Aleppo pepper, you can substitute ½ teaspoon paprika plus ½ teaspoon red pepper flakes.

16 cardamom pods
4 teaspoons coriander seeds
4 teaspoons cumin seeds
2 teaspoons anise seeds
2 teaspoons ground dried Aleppo pepper
½ teaspoon allspice berries
¼ teaspoon black peppercorns
4 teaspoons ground ginger
2 teaspoons ground nutmeg
2 teaspoons ground cinnamon

Process cardamom pods, coriander seeds, cumin seeds, anise seeds, Aleppo pepper, allspice, and peppercorns in spice grinder until finely ground, about 30 seconds. Stir in ginger, nutmeg, and cinnamon. (Ras el hanout can be stored in airtight container for up to 1 month.)

Shrimp and Sausage Gumbo

Serves 2
Total time 1 hour

WHY THIS RECIPE WORKS Gumbo might hail from the Big Easy, but there's nothing "easy" about the typical hours-long process of making the roux, a low-and-slow-cooked mixture of flour and fat that gives gumbo its deep brown color, toasty flavor, and body. To streamline, we cranked up the heat a bit while cooking the roux—we still achieved dark, flavorful, gravy-like results in a mere 15 minutes. The holy trinity (onion, celery, and bell pepper) provided the base, Cajun seasoning gave us complex, authentic flavor with just one ingredient, and a bottle of clam juice brought piquant saltiness without the need to make shrimp stock. Garlicky andouille sausage and quick-cooking shrimp were simple to prepare and rounded out this bayou stew. Serve on its own or with rice.

¼ cup all-purpose flour
3 tablespoons vegetable oil
8 ounces andouille sausage, halved lengthwise and sliced ½ inch thick
1 small onion, chopped fine
1 red bell pepper, stemmed, seeded, and cut into ½-inch pieces
1 celery rib, minced
2 garlic cloves, minced
1 teaspoon Cajun seasoning
½ teaspoon minced fresh thyme or ⅛ teaspoon dried
1 (8-ounce) bottle clam juice
½ cup water
8 ounces extra-large shrimp (21 to 25 per pound), peeled, deveined, and tails removed
2 scallions, sliced thin

1. Whisk flour and oil together in medium saucepan until smooth. Cook over medium heat, whisking occasionally, until mixture is deep brown and fragrant, about 15 minutes.

2. Add andouille, onion, bell pepper, and celery and cook until vegetables are softened and lightly browned, about 10 minutes. Stir in garlic, Cajun seasoning, and thyme and cook until fragrant, about 30 seconds.

3. Slowly whisk in clam juice and water, scraping up any browned bits and smoothing out any lumps. Bring to simmer and cook until vegetables are tender and mixture has thickened, about 10 minutes. Stir in shrimp and continue to simmer until opaque throughout, 2–3 minutes. Stir in scallions and season with salt and pepper to taste. Serve.

Fish Stew with Chorizo and Fennel

Serves 2

Total time 50 minutes

WHY THIS RECIPE WORKS To build an intensely flavorful base for our fish stew in a short amount of time, we sautéed a generous amount of onion and fennel in fruity extra-virgin olive oil. A few ounces of smoky chorizo sausage contributed hearty flavor and spicy complexity. White wine, diced tomatoes, and a bottle of clam juice gave the broth brightness, a welcome acidity, and just the right amount of brininess. The fish (we liked substantial pieces of cod) needed just a few minutes of simmering in our highly flavorful broth to cook through. Make a quick garnish by stirring together toasted pine nuts, minced fresh mint, and orange zest. Serve with crusty bread or rice.

- 1 tablespoon extra-virgin olive oil, plus extra for serving
- 4 ounces chorizo sausage, cut into ½-inch pieces
- 1 small onion, chopped fine
- ½ fennel bulb, stalks discarded, bulb cored and sliced thin
- 2 garlic cloves, minced
- ⅓ cup dry white wine
- 1 (14.5-ounce) can diced tomatoes
- 1 (8-ounce) bottle clam juice
- 12 ounces skinless cod fillets, 1 to 1½ inches thick, cut into 2-inch pieces
- ¼ teaspoon table salt
- ⅛ teaspoon pepper
- 1 tablespoon minced fresh parsley

1. Heat oil in medium saucepan over medium heat until shimmering. Add chorizo, onion, and fennel and cook until vegetables are softened, about 8 minutes. Stir in garlic and cook until fragrant, about 30 seconds. Stir in wine, scraping up any browned bits. Stir in tomatoes with their juice and clam juice, bring to simmer, and cook until flavors meld, about 10 minutes.

2. Sprinkle cod with salt and pepper. Nestle cod into stew mixture, spoon some of sauce over fish, and bring to simmer. Reduce heat to medium-low, cover, and simmer until fish flakes apart when gently prodded with paring knife and registers 140 degrees, about 5 minutes. Gently stir in parsley and season with salt and pepper to taste. Drizzle individual portions with extra oil before serving.

Ciambotta

Ciambotta

Serves 2   VEGETARIAN

Total time 1 hour 25 minutes

WHY THIS RECIPE WORKS Italy's answer to ratatouille, ciambotta is a dish that turns a bounty of summer vegetables into a fresh, satisfying stew. But given that the mix of vegetables typically includes zucchini, tomatoes, and eggplant, it's no surprise that the result is often a watery, flavorless dish. We browned the eggplant to rid it of excess moisture, which also contributed rich flavor. Similarly, we found that sautéing canned tomatoes drove off excess moisture and developed good caramelization; the addition of a little tomato paste further concentrated the tomato flavor. Just one potato (we liked buttery Yukon Gold) added plenty of starch and heft to this dish; we gave it a jump start in the microwave, which ensured that it was tender at the same time as the other vegetables. Finished with a sprinkling of fresh basil, grated Pecorino Romano, and a drizzle of oil, this is a stew we can enjoy any time of year.

3 tablespoons extra-virgin olive oil, divided,
  plus extra for serving
½ eggplant (8 ounces), cut into 1-inch pieces
1 Yukon Gold potato (8 ounces), peeled and cut into
  ½-inch pieces
1 (14.5-ounce) can whole peeled tomatoes,
  drained with juice reserved
3 garlic cloves, minced
1 teaspoon tomato paste
¼ teaspoon minced fresh oregano or pinch dried
¼ teaspoon table salt
¼ teaspoon pepper
3 cups vegetable broth
1 small zucchini, halved lengthwise, seeded,
  and cut into 1-inch pieces
2 tablespoons chopped fresh basil
¼ cup grated Pecorino Romano cheese

1. Heat 2 tablespoons oil in medium saucepan over medium-high heat until shimmering. Brown eggplant lightly on all sides, 5 to 7 minutes; transfer to bowl. Meanwhile, microwave potato and 1 teaspoon oil in covered bowl until softened, about 5 minutes.

2. Heat remaining 2 teaspoons oil in now-empty saucepan over medium heat until shimmering. Add tomatoes, garlic, tomato paste, oregano, salt, and pepper and cook until mixture is dry and beginning to brown, 11 to 13 minutes.

3. Stir in broth and reserved tomato juice, scraping up any browned bits. Stir in browned eggplant, softened potato, and zucchini and bring to simmer. Reduce heat to medium-low; partially cover; and simmer until vegetables are tender and stew has thickened, 25 to 35 minutes. Gently stir in basil and season with salt and pepper to taste. Sprinkle individual portions with Pecorino and drizzle with extra oil before serving.

SEEDING ZUCCHINI

Cut zucchini in half lengthwise, then run small spoon inside each zucchini half to scoop out seeds.

Quinoa and Vegetable Stew
Serves 2 `VEGETARIAN`
Total time 1 hour

WHY THIS RECIPE WORKS Looking to add a hearty vegetarian meal to our for-two repertoire, we decided to develop a recipe for a quinoa and vegetable stew. A staple in Peru, quinoa stew typically includes a good mix of vegetables, with potatoes and corn at the forefront. We found that red potatoes most closely resembled the flavor and texture of native Peruvian potatoes. Paprika was similar in color and flavor to traditional annatto powder, and cumin and coriander rounded out the spice profile for rich, balanced flavor. We added the spices with the aromatics, which prevented them from burning and allowed time for their flavors to develop. To thicken the stew, we simmered the quinoa for a few extra minutes to release additional starch. This stew tends to thicken as it sits; add additional warm vegetable broth as needed before serving to loosen. We like the convenience of prewashed quinoa; rinsing removes the quinoa's bitter protective coating (called saponin). If you buy unwashed quinoa, rinse it and then spread it out on a clean dish towel to dry for 15 minutes. Serve with lime wedges, diced avocado, and crumbled queso fresco.

1 tablespoon vegetable oil
1 small onion, chopped
½ red bell pepper, cut into ½-inch pieces
2 garlic cloves, minced
1 teaspoon paprika
¾ teaspoon ground coriander
½ teaspoon ground cumin
½ cup water
2 cups vegetable broth
1 red potato (6 ounces), unpeeled, cut into
  ½-inch pieces
⅓ cup quinoa, rinsed
⅓ cup fresh or frozen corn
3 tablespoons minced fresh cilantro

1. Heat oil in medium saucepan over medium heat until shimmering. Add onion, bell pepper, garlic, paprika, coriander, and cumin. Cook, stirring often, until vegetables are softened and spices are fragrant, about 5 minutes. Stir in water, scraping up any browned bits. Stir in broth and potato, bring to simmer, and cook for 10 minutes.

2. Stir in quinoa and simmer for 8 minutes. Stir in corn and continue to simmer until vegetables and quinoa are just tender, 6 to 8 minutes. Season with salt and pepper to taste. Sprinkle individual portions with cilantro before serving.

PREPARING FRESH CORN

To remove kernels from ear of corn, stand cob upright inside bowl, then slice down along sides of cob using sharp knife.

NOTES FROM THE TEST KITCHEN

GUIDELINES FOR USING DRIED HERBS

Dried herbs are more convenient than fresh because they don't spoil and need no more prep than a twist of a lid. But they can add a dusty quality to dishes, especially when added at the end. Here are the tricks we've found for using them successfully.

WHEN DRIED HERBS SHINE AND HOW TO SUBSTITUTE Only some dried herbs give good results, mainly in recipes with longer cooking times (20 minutes or more) and a good amount of moisture. Chili is one dish that is better made with dried oregano than with fresh. Dried rosemary, sage, marjoram, and thyme also fare reasonably well in certain applications; the flavor compounds in these herbs are relatively stable at high temperature, so they maintain their flavor through the drying process. To replace fresh herbs with dried, use one-third the amount, and add them early in the cooking process so they have time to soften.

WHEN FRESH IS BEST Those herbs that we consider delicate (basil, chives, and parsley) lose most of their flavor when dried; we prefer fresh forms of these herbs. Two herbs, tarragon and dill, fall into a middle category: They do add flavor in their dried form, but it is more muted than that provided by other dried herbs.

SMART STORAGE Like spices, dried herbs should be stored in a cool, dark, dry place, not near the stove where heat, light, and moisture will shorten their shelf life. However, even when properly stored, dried herbs lose their potency six to 12 months after opening, so it's important to replace them frequently. You can test dried herbs for freshness by rubbing them between your fingers—if they don't release a bright fragrance, buy a new jar.

Quinoa and Vegetable Stew

Thai Red Curry with Chicken

Thai Red Curry with Chicken

Serves 2

Total time 35 minutes

WHY THIS RECIPE WORKS Thai curries are complexly flavored, boasting a balance of aromatic, funky, tangy, and sweet flavors. Curry paste is an ingredient we go back to again and again, and for good reason—we always have it on hand, it's fast, and it packs an aromatic punch. We whisked it into broth to develop a superflavorful base in a snap. Chicken and a potato gave our curry heft; crunchy bell pepper and snap peas brought texture; sugar, fish sauce, and lime juice provided the balance of flavors we were after; and coconut milk added creamy, slightly sweet richness. Serve on its own or over rice.

1½ cups chicken or vegetable broth
2 tablespoons Thai red or green curry paste
2 teaspoons sugar
8 ounces boneless, skinless chicken thighs, trimmed and cut into 1-inch pieces
1 Yukon Gold potato (8 ounces), peeled and cut into 1-inch pieces
1 small red, orange, or yellow bell pepper, stemmed, seeded, and chopped
4 ounces sugar snap peas, strings removed, cut on bias into ½-inch pieces
½ cup canned coconut milk
2 tablespoons chopped fresh Thai basil, basil, cilantro, or mint
1 tablespoon fish sauce
1 tablespoon lime juice

1. Bring broth to simmer in medium saucepan over medium-low heat, then whisk in curry paste and sugar until dissolved. Add chicken and potato; bring to simmer; and cook until tender, 8 to 10 minutes. Stir in bell pepper and snap peas and cook until just tender, 3 to 5 minutes.

2. Off heat, stir in coconut milk, basil, fish sauce, and lime juice and season with salt and pepper to taste. Serve.

Vindaloo-Style Pork

Vindaloo-Style Pork

Serves 2

Total time 1¼ hours

WHY THIS RECIPE WORKS This recipe is inspired by classic pork vindaloo, an Indian stew of Portuguese origin that combines elements of hot, sweet, and tangy into one boldly flavored dish. We found that just one ingredient, garam masala—a warm blend of spices typically including cumin, cardamom, cloves, and cinnamon, among others—gave our vindaloo its distinct flavor. Tomatoes, mustard seeds, and chicken broth, along with some aromatic onion and garlic, provided a good base. For the pork, we chose country-style ribs, which have more flavor than pork tenderloin and are easier to get in small portions than the more traditional pork butt. Red wine vinegar contributed the classic tanginess, and some chopped fresh cilantro provided a burst of color and a distinct herbal note. Serve with rice.

12 ounces boneless country-style pork ribs, trimmed and cut into 1½-inch pieces
¾ teaspoon table salt, divided
⅛ teaspoon pepper
2 tablespoons vegetable oil, divided
1 small onion, chopped fine
2 garlic cloves, minced
2 teaspoons mustard seeds
1 teaspoon garam masala
1 teaspoon hot paprika
2 tablespoons all-purpose flour
2 cups chicken broth
1 (14.5-ounce) can diced tomatoes, drained
2 tablespoons minced fresh cilantro
1 tablespoon red wine vinegar

1. Pat pork dry with paper towels and sprinkle with ¼ teaspoon salt and pepper. Heat 1 tablespoon oil in medium saucepan over medium-high heat until just smoking. Brown pork lightly on all sides, about 6 minutes; transfer to bowl.

2. Heat remaining 1 tablespoon oil in now-empty saucepan over medium heat until shimmering. Add onion, garlic, mustard seeds, garam masala, paprika, and remaining ½ teaspoon salt. Cook, stirring often, until onion is softened and spices are fragrant, about 5 minutes. Stir in flour and cook for 1 minute.

3. Slowly whisk in broth, scraping up any browned bits and smoothing out any lumps. Stir in browned pork along with any accumulated juices and tomatoes and bring to simmer. Reduce heat to medium-low; cover; and simmer until pork is tender, about 30 minutes. Stir in cilantro and vinegar and season with salt and pepper to taste. Serve.

Thai Red Curry with Beef and Eggplant

Serves 2

Total time 50 minutes

WHY THIS RECIPE WORKS To create a quick Thai beef curry for two we chose sirloin steak tips for their deep, beefy flavor and substantial texture. Jarred red curry paste eliminated much of the prep work, and coconut milk contributed a creamy richness. A combination of fish sauce, brown sugar, and lime juice provided the proper salty, sweet, and sour elements. Hearty eggplant complemented the beef. Steak tips, also known as flap meat, are sold as whole steak, cubes, and strips; look for either whole steak tips or strips that are easy to cut into small pieces for this recipe. To make the beef easier to slice, freeze it for 15 minutes. Depending on the freshness and spice level of your curry paste, you may need to add more or less to taste. If you can't find Thai basil leaves, regular basil will work fine. Serve with rice.

5 teaspoons vegetable oil, divided
½ eggplant (8 ounces), cut into ½-inch pieces
2 teaspoons Thai red curry paste, plus extra for seasoning
¾ cup canned coconut milk
1 tablespoon fish sauce
2 teaspoons packed brown sugar
¾ cup chicken broth
½ teaspoon cornstarch
8 ounces sirloin steak tips, trimmed, cut into strips (if necessary), and sliced thin against grain
¼ cup fresh Thai basil leaves
2 teaspoons lime juice

1. Heat 1 tablespoon oil in 12-inch nonstick skillet over medium-high heat until shimmering. Brown eggplant lightly on all sides, 5 to 7 minutes; transfer to bowl.

2. Heat remaining 2 teaspoons oil in now-empty skillet over medium-high heat until shimmering. Add curry paste and cook until fragrant, about 30 seconds. Whisk in coconut milk, fish sauce, and sugar. Whisk broth and cornstarch together in bowl, then whisk mixture into skillet. Bring to simmer and cook until sauce is slightly thickened, 5 to 8 minutes. Season with extra curry paste to taste.

3. Stir in beef and simmer until strips separate and turn firm, about 5 minutes. Stir in browned eggplant and continue to simmer until beef and eggplant are tender and sauce has thickened, about 8 minutes. Off heat, stir in basil and lime juice and season with salt and pepper to taste. Serve.

Classic Beef Chili

Serves 2

Total time 1½ hours

WHY THIS RECIPE WORKS Recipes for chili are typically geared toward a crowd, so we knew that creating a scaled-down version for two would require a careful balancing act. Starting with the spices, we determined that 1½ tablespoons of chili powder was just right; although this seemed like a modest amount, even for two servings, we found that if we used any more it simply overwhelmed the other layers of flavor in our chili. Cumin, coriander, red pepper flakes, oregano, and cayenne rounded out our spices, and we added them early—along with the aromatics—to develop their flavors fully. Twelve ounces of beef and ¾ cup of canned beans provided just the right meat-to-bean ratio. The juice from a can of diced tomatoes and a little tomato sauce were all the liquid we needed, creating a chili that was thick, rich, and utterly satisfying. Serve with your favorite chili garnishes.

- 1 tablespoon vegetable oil
- 1 small onion, chopped fine
- ½ red, green, or yellow bell pepper, cut into ½-inch pieces
- 1½ tablespoons chili powder
- 3 garlic cloves, minced
- 1 teaspoon ground cumin
- ¾ teaspoon ground coriander
- ¼ teaspoon red pepper flakes
- ¼ teaspoon dried oregano
- ¼ teaspoon table salt
- ⅛ teaspoon cayenne pepper
- 12 ounces 85 percent lean ground beef
- 1 (14.5-ounce) can diced tomatoes
- 1 (8-ounce) can tomato sauce
- ¾ cup canned kidney or pinto beans, rinsed

1. Heat oil in medium saucepan over medium heat until shimmering. Add onion, bell pepper, chili powder, garlic, cumin, coriander, pepper flakes, oregano, salt, and cayenne. Cook, stirring often, until vegetables begin to soften and spices are fragrant, 3 to 5 minutes.

2. Add ground beef and cook, breaking up meat with wooden spoon, until no longer pink and just beginning to brown, 3 to 5 minutes. Stir in tomatoes and their juice, tomato sauce, and beans and bring to simmer. Cover; reduce heat to medium-low; and simmer, stirring occasionally, for 45 minutes.

3. Uncover and continue to simmer, stirring occasionally, until beef is tender and chili is slightly thickened, about 15 minutes. (If chili begins to stick to bottom of pot, stir in ¼ cup water.) Season with salt and pepper to taste, and serve.

Classic Beef Chili

VARIATIONS

Beef Chili with Bacon

Cook 4 slices bacon, cut into ¼-inch pieces, in medium saucepan over medium heat until crispy, 5 to 7 minutes. Omit oil and add vegetables and spices to saucepan with bacon and bacon fat; proceed with recipe.

Beef Chili with Chipotle, Black Beans, and Corn

Omit red pepper flakes and cayenne pepper. Add 1 teaspoon minced canned chipotle chile in adobo sauce with vegetables and spices. Substitute ¾ cup rinsed canned black beans for kidney beans. After chili is thickened, stir in ½ cup frozen corn and let sit 2 minutes until heated through. Stir in 1 to 2 teaspoons more minced chipotle to taste before serving.

Beef Chili with Chickpeas and Warm Spices

Omit chili powder and red pepper flakes. Add 1 teaspoon paprika, 1 teaspoon ground ginger, and ⅛ teaspoon ground cinnamon with vegetables and spices. Substitute ¾ cup rinsed canned chickpeas for kidney beans and add ¼ cup raisins, if desired, with tomatoes and chickpeas. Stir in ¼ teaspoon grated lemon zest plus 1 teaspoon juice before serving.

Texas Chili

Serves 2

Total time 3 hours 20 minutes

WHY THIS RECIPE WORKS We wanted a chili that would be hearty, with satisfying chunks of meat, and spicy, but not overwhelmingly hot. We'd typically choose a chuck-eye roast for this type of chili, but since we didn't need that much meat for our scaled-down version, we found that boneless beef short ribs worked just as well, offering plenty of meaty flavor in every bite. Some kidney beans provided additional heft. A full 2 tablespoons of chili powder and some minced chipotle chile contributed plenty of smoky heat. One can of diced tomatoes pureed with a corn tortilla (a readily available substitute for authentic masa harina) helped thicken the chili to just the right consistency. You will need a medium ovensafe saucepan with a tight-fitting lid for this recipe. Serve with your favorite chili garnishes.

- 1 (14.5-ounce) can diced tomatoes
- 1 (6-inch) corn tortilla, chopped coarse
- 1½ pounds boneless beef short ribs, trimmed and cut into 1½-inch pieces
- ½ teaspoon table salt
- ¼ teaspoon pepper
- 1 tablespoon vegetable oil
- 1 small onion, chopped fine
- 2 tablespoons chili powder
- 2 teaspoons ground cumin
- 2 garlic cloves, minced
- 2 teaspoons minced canned chipotle chile in adobo sauce
- 1 (15-ounce) can kidney beans, rinsed

1. Adjust oven rack to middle position and heat oven to 300 degrees. Process tomatoes with their juice and tortilla pieces in food processor until smooth, about 30 seconds.

2. Pat beef dry with paper towels and sprinkle with salt and pepper. Heat oil in medium ovensafe saucepan over medium-high heat until just smoking. Brown beef on all sides, about 8 minutes; transfer to bowl.

3. Add onion, chili powder, cumin, garlic, and chipotle to fat left in saucepan. Cook over medium heat, stirring often, until onion is softened and spices are fragrant, about 5 minutes. Stir in tomato mixture, scraping up any browned bits. Stir in beans and browned beef with any accumulated juices and bring to simmer. Cover, transfer saucepan to oven, and cook until beef is tender, 2½ to 3 hours.

4. Using large spoon, skim excess fat from surface of chili. Season with salt and pepper to taste. Serve.

NOTES FROM THE TEST KITCHEN

ALL ABOUT SPICES

Here are a few tips to help you get the most from your spice rack.

BUYING SPICES Because grinding releases the compounds that give a spice its flavor and aroma, it's best to buy spices whole and grind them just before using; the longer a spice sits, the more its flavor will fade. If you do buy spices preground, try to buy them in small quantities, preferably from places (like spice shops) more likely to have high turnover.

STORING SPICES PROPERLY Don't store spices and herbs on the counter close to the stove because heat, as well as light and moisture, shortens their shelf life. Keep them in a cool, dark, dry place in well-sealed containers.

CHECKING FOR FRESHNESS Grind or finely grate a small amount of whole spices and take a whiff. If the spice releases a lively aroma, it's still good to go. If the aroma and color have faded, it's time to restock. Label each spice with the date opened; whole spices are generally good for two years and ground spices for one year.

BLOOMING SPICES BUILDS FLAVOR We often bloom spices to remove any raw flavor or dustiness and intensify their flavors. To bloom spices, cook them briefly on the stovetop or in the microwave in a little oil or butter. As they dissolve, their flavorful essential oils are released from a solid state into solution form, where they mix and interact, producing a more complex flavor. Just be careful to avoid burning them.

GETTING A GOOD GRIND Freshly ground spices have superior aroma and vibrancy, and because whole spices have a longer shelf life than preground, grinding your own will help you get more out of the spices you buy. We recommend buying a designated blade-type coffee grinder for grinding spices. Our favorite, the **Krups Coffee and Spice Grinder**, produced an exceptionally fine grind of all spices. We found that it easily ground amounts anywhere from 1 teaspoon to ¼ cup.

Five-Alarm Chili

½ ounce dried ancho chiles, stemmed, seeded, and torn into 1-inch pieces

1⅓ cups water, divided

4 plum tomatoes, cored and halved lengthwise

3 tablespoons crushed corn tortilla chips

1 tablespoon minced canned chipotle chile in adobo sauce

4 teaspoons vegetable oil, divided

12 ounces 85 percent lean ground beef

¼ teaspoon table salt

⅛ teaspoon pepper

1 onion, chopped fine

½ jalapeño chile, stemmed, seeds reserved, and minced

2 garlic cloves, minced

1½ teaspoons ground cumin

1½ teaspoons chili powder

½ teaspoon sugar

⅛ teaspoon cayenne pepper

⅓ cup beer

¾ cup canned pinto beans, rinsed

1. Combine anchos and ⅓ cup water in bowl and microwave until softened, about 2 minutes. Drain and discard liquid. Process anchos, remaining 1 cup water, tomatoes, tortilla chips, and chipotle in blender until smooth, about 1 minute; set aside.

2. Heat 2 teaspoons oil in medium saucepan over medium-high heat until just smoking. Add ground beef, salt, and pepper and cook, breaking up meat with wooden spoon, until all liquid has evaporated and beef begins to sizzle, 5 to 7 minutes. Drain in colander; set aside.

3. Heat remaining 2 teaspoons oil in now-empty saucepan over medium-high heat until shimmering. Add onion, jalapeño, and reserved seeds, if using, and cook until onion is softened and lightly browned, 5 to 7 minutes. Stir in garlic, cumin, chili powder, sugar, and cayenne and cook until fragrant, about 30 seconds. Stir in beer and bring to simmer. Stir in ancho-tomato mixture, cooked beef, and beans and bring to simmer. Cover; reduce heat to medium-low; and simmer, stirring occasionally, until thickened, about 30 minutes. Season with salt to taste, and serve.

Five-Alarm Chili

Serves 2

Total time 1 hour 20 minutes

WHY THIS RECIPE WORKS For a seriously hot five-alarm chili, we combined fresh jalapeños, canned chipotle chiles, dried ancho chiles, cayenne, and chili powder for complex, multilayered flavor. Ground beef and creamy pinto beans bulked up the chili, and fresh tomatoes added brightness. To round out the chili and give it some body, we turned to a few unusual additions: A splash of light-bodied beer gave our chili malty depth and a little bitterness, and crushed corn tortilla chips thickened it and added a subtle background of corn flavor. Dried ancho chiles can be found in the international aisle of most supermarkets. Light-bodied American lagers, such as Budweiser, work best in this recipe. To make this dish spicier, add the chile seeds. Serve with your favorite chili garnishes.

ALL ABOUT CHILE PEPPERS

Chiles get their heat from a group of chemical compounds called capsaicinoids, the best known being capsaicin. Capsaicin in a chile is concentrated mostly in the inner whitish pith (called ribs), with progressively smaller amounts in the seeds and flesh. If you like a lot of heat, you can use the entire chile when cooking. If you prefer a milder dish, remove the ribs and seeds. Here are the chiles we reach for most in the test kitchen.

JALAPEÑO Perhaps the best-known chile, jalapeños are moderately hot and have a bright, grassy flavor similar to a green bell pepper. They can be dark green or scarlet red.

CHIPOTLE Smoky, sweet, and moderately spicy, chipotle chiles are jalapeños that have been smoked over aromatic wood and dried. They are sold as is or canned in adobo, a tangy tomato-and-herb sauce. We recommend using canned chipotles; they can be added straight to a dish and they last indefinitely when frozen.

POBLANO These chiles are very dark green in color—sometimes nearly black. When ripe, they turn a reddish-brown. We love poblanos for their fruity, subtly spicy flavor. Thanks to their large size, they are also ideal for stuffing. Poblanos can be found in Latin markets and many supermarkets. Their peak season is summer and early fall. When dried, they are known as ancho chiles and have a rich, earthy flavor.

ANAHEIM With their acidic, lemony flavor, mild spiciness, and crisp texture, these popular chiles can be eaten raw, roasted, or fried; they are also frequently stuffed or used in salsa. Anaheim chiles are medium green in color and have a long, tapered shape. When dried, they are called New Mexico or Colorado chiles.

SERRANO Similar in appearance to jalapeños but with a slightly more slender shape and brazen heat, these chiles have a fresh, clean, fruity flavor. They are good both raw in salsa and cooked in chilis and curries.

HABANERO These small, lantern-shaped chiles pack intense heat. They have a floral, fruity flavor that makes them—when used sparingly—a great addition to marinades, salsas, and cooked dishes. They range from light green to orange to red in color.

THAI These tiny, multicolored chiles look ornamental, but they mean business. They have a flavor similar to that of black peppercorns and a bold, lingering heat. They are best when used sparingly in cooked dishes. The bird chile is the dried form.

SEEDING CHILES

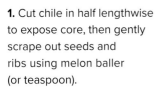

1. Cut chile in half lengthwise to expose core, then gently scrape out seeds and ribs using melon baller (or teaspoon).

2. Use sharp edge of melon baller to cut off stem.

Turkey Chili

Serves 2

Total time 1½ hours

WHY THIS RECIPE WORKS For a turkey chili that would rival its beef counterpart, we found that the type of turkey we used and the point at which we added it to the chili were key. Ground turkey that was 93 percent lean remained moist and had enough fat to flavor our chili. Adding half of the meat to the cooked vegetables in the beginning allowed time for its flavor to infuse the chili, while adding the other half after the chili had simmered for 30 minutes ensured that some of the meat remained in larger pieces. Be sure to use ground turkey, not ground turkey breast (also labeled 99 percent fat free), in this recipe. Serve with your favorite chili garnishes.

- 1 tablespoon vegetable oil
- 1 small onion, chopped fine
- ½ red, green, or yellow bell pepper, cut into ½-inch pieces
- 1½ tablespoons chili powder
- 3 garlic cloves, minced
- 1 teaspoon ground cumin
- ¾ teaspoon ground coriander
- ¼ teaspoon red pepper flakes
- ¼ teaspoon dried oregano
- ¼ teaspoon table salt
- ⅛ teaspoon cayenne pepper
- 12 ounces ground turkey, divided
- 1 (14.5-ounce) can diced tomatoes
- 1 (8-ounce) can tomato sauce
- ¾ cup canned kidney or pinto beans, rinsed

1. Heat oil in medium saucepan over medium heat until shimmering. Add onion, bell pepper, chili powder, garlic, cumin, coriander, pepper flakes, oregano, salt, and cayenne. Cook, stirring often, until vegetables begin to soften and spices are fragrant, 3 to 5 minutes.

2. Add 6 ounces ground turkey and cook, breaking up meat with wooden spoon, until no longer pink and just beginning to brown, 3 to 5 minutes. Stir in tomatoes and their juice, tomato sauce, and beans and bring to simmer. Cover; reduce heat to medium-low; and simmer, stirring occasionally, for 30 minutes.

3. Pat remaining 6 ounces ground turkey together into ball, then pinch off teaspoon-size pieces and stir into chili. Simmer, uncovered, stirring occasionally, until turkey is tender and chili is slightly thickened, about 30 minutes. (If chili begins to stick to bottom of pot, stir in ¼ cup water.) Season with salt and pepper to taste, and serve.

VARIATION
Tequila and Lime Turkey Chili

Add 1 tablespoon tequila with tomatoes and beans in step 2. Stir in 1 tablespoon more tequila and 1 teaspoon grated lime zest plus 2 teaspoons juice before serving.

CRUMBLING GROUND TURKEY

To give ground turkey an appealing crumbled texture, pack half of turkey together into ball, then pinch off teaspoon-size pieces of meat and stir them into simmering chili as directed in recipe.

White Chicken Chili

Serves 2

Total time 1 hour

WHY THIS RECIPE WORKS To achieve the right consistency for our white chicken chili, we utilized two thickeners: flour and pureed hominy. We cooked the flour briefly with the aromatics and spices—poblano chiles, onion, garlic, cumin, and coriander—which not only thickened the chili but also built depth of flavor. For a luxuriously thick texture, we pureed a portion of the hominy. Store-bought tomatillo salsa—a zesty combination of green tomatoes, chiles, and cilantro that is also known as salsa verde—boosted the flavor of our chili at the end. Both white hominy and yellow hominy will work in this chili; however, we prefer the deeper flavor of white hominy here. Be careful not to overcook the chicken in step 3 or it will taste dry. To make this dish spicier, add the chile seeds. Serve with your favorite chili garnishes.

- 1 (15-ounce) can white or yellow hominy, rinsed, divided
- 2 cups chicken broth, divided
- 1 tablespoon vegetable oil
- 2 poblano chiles, stemmed, seeded, and chopped
- 1 small onion, chopped fine
- 2 garlic cloves, minced
- 1 teaspoon ground cumin
- 1 teaspoon ground coriander
- 1 tablespoon all-purpose flour
- 12 ounces boneless, skinless chicken breasts, trimmed
- ¼ teaspoon table salt
- ⅛ teaspoon pepper
- ½ cup jarred tomatillo salsa
- 2 tablespoons minced fresh cilantro

White Chicken Chili

1. Process 1 cup hominy and ½ cup broth in blender until smooth, about 10 seconds.

2. Heat oil in medium saucepan over medium heat until shimmering. Add poblanos, onion, garlic, cumin, and coriander. Cook, stirring often, until vegetables are softened and spices are fragrant, about 5 minutes. Stir in flour and cook for 1 minute.

3. Slowly whisk in remaining 1½ cups broth, scraping up any browned bits and smoothing out any lumps. Stir in pureed hominy mixture and remaining ½ cup hominy. Season chicken with salt and pepper, add to chili mixture, and bring to simmer. Cover; reduce heat to medium-low; and simmer until chicken registers 160 degrees, 10 to 15 minutes, flipping chicken halfway through cooking. Transfer chicken to cutting board, let cool slightly, then shred into bite-size pieces using 2 forks.

4. Return chili to simmer; stir in shredded chicken and tomatillo salsa; and cook until heated through, about 2 minutes. Stir in cilantro and season with salt and pepper to taste. Serve.

Tempeh Chili

Serves 2   VEGETARIAN

Total time 1 hour 20 minutes

WHY THIS RECIPE WORKS To create a true chili—not a bean and vegetable stew—we found it best to keep our ingredient list relatively simple: just one bell pepper and one type of bean were all we needed. Onion, garlic, chili powder, and cumin provided a solid base of flavor, while some minced chipotle chile contributed a subtle warmth and smokiness. Crushed tomatoes gave our chili a hearty, thick consistency. Finally, crumbled tempeh filled out our vegetarian chili, giving it a substantial texture. To make this dish spicier, add the larger amount of chipotle. Serve with your favorite chili garnishes.

- 1 tablespoon vegetable oil
- 1 small red, green, or yellow bell pepper, stemmed, seeded, and cut into ½-inch pieces
- 1 small onion, chopped fine
- 1 tablespoon chili powder
- 2 garlic cloves, minced
- 1–2 teaspoons minced canned chipotle chile in adobo sauce
- 1 teaspoon ground cumin
- ½ teaspoon table salt
- 1 cup water
- 1 (28-ounce) can crushed tomatoes
- 1 (15-ounce) can kidney, black, or pinto beans, rinsed
- 1 (8-ounce) package tempeh, crumbled
- 2 tablespoons minced fresh cilantro

1. Heat oil in medium saucepan over medium heat until shimmering. Add bell pepper, onion, chili powder, garlic, chipotle, cumin, and salt. Cook, stirring often, until vegetables are softened and spices are fragrant, about 5 minutes.

2. Stir in water, scraping up any browned bits. Stir in tomatoes, beans, and tempeh and bring to simmer. Cover; reduce heat to medium-low; and simmer, stirring occasionally, for 30 minutes.

3. Uncover and continue to simmer, stirring occasionally, until vegetables and tempeh are tender and chili is slightly thickened, about 15 minutes. (If chili begins to stick to bottom of pot, stir in ¼ cup water.) Stir in cilantro and season with salt to taste. Serve.

CHAPTER 3

Side
Salads &
Dinner
Salads

■ **FAST** (Start to finish in 30 minutes or less)
■ **VEGETARIAN**

Opposite: Poached Shrimp Salad with Avocado and Grapefruit

Foolproof Vinaigrette

Foolproof Vinaigrette

Makes about ¼ cup, enough to dress 8 to 10 cups lightly packed greens `FAST` `VEGETARIAN`

Total time 10 minutes

WHY THIS RECIPE WORKS Vinaigrettes often seem a little slipshod—harsh and bristling in one bite, dull and oily in the next—plus, they tend to separate soon after being prepared. To get the best flavor, we found that top-notch ingredients were crucial. And for a well-balanced vinaigrette that wouldn't separate, we whisked fruity extra-virgin olive oil and vinegar together with a little mayonnaise, which acts as an emulsifier. Some minced shallot and Dijon mustard rounded out the flavors in our classic vinaigrette. This vinaigrette works with nearly any type of green. Red wine, white wine, or Champagne vinegar will work in this recipe. For a hint of garlic flavor, rub the inside of the salad bowl with a cut clove of garlic before adding the lettuce and dressing. Placing the oil in a small measuring cup will make it easy to pour in a steady stream.

1 tablespoon red wine, white wine, or champagne vinegar
1½ teaspoons very finely minced shallot
½ teaspoon regular or light mayonnaise
½ teaspoon Dijon mustard
⅛ teaspoon table salt
3 tablespoons extra-virgin olive oil

1. Whisk vinegar, shallot, mayonnaise, mustard, and salt together in small bowl until mixture is milky in appearance and no lumps of mayonnaise remain.

2. Whisking constantly, drizzle oil into vinegar mixture in slow, steady stream. If pools of oil gather on surface as you whisk, stop adding oil and whisk mixture well to combine, then resume whisking in oil in slow stream. Vinaigrette should be glossy and lightly thickened, with no pools of oil on its surface. Season with pepper to taste. (Vinaigrette can be refrigerated for up to 2 weeks.)

VARIATIONS

Foolproof Lemon Vinaigrette

This vinaigrette is best for dressing mild greens.

Substitute lemon juice for vinegar. Omit shallot. Add ¼ teaspoon grated lemon zest and pinch sugar along with salt.

Foolproof Balsamic-Mustard Vinaigrette

This vinaigrette is best for dressing assertive greens.

Substitute balsamic vinegar for wine vinegar, increase mustard to 2 teaspoons, and add ½ teaspoon chopped fresh thyme along with salt.

Foolproof Walnut Vinaigrette

Substitute 1½ tablespoons roasted walnut oil and 1½ tablespoons regular olive oil for the extra-virgin olive oil.

Foolproof Herb Vinaigrette

Add 1 tablespoon minced fresh parsley or chives and ½ teaspoon minced fresh thyme, tarragon, marjoram, or oregano to vinaigrette just before using.

Greek Chopped Salad

Serves 2 VEGETARIAN

Total time 25 minutes, plus 15 minutes salting

WHY THIS RECIPE WORKS Most Greek salads consist of iceberg lettuce, chunks of green pepper, and a few pale wedges of tomato, all sparsely dotted with olives and cubes of feta. We wanted a salad with crisp ingredients and bold flavors all blended together with a bright-tasting dressing infused with fresh herbs. We made a simple dressing with olive oil, red wine vinegar, and a little garlic, then tossed it over cucumbers, tomatoes, chickpeas, olives, shallot, and fresh parsley. Salting the cucumber and tomato and letting them drain kept their excess moisture from watering down the salad. We marinated the vegetables in the vinaigrette, which allowed the flavors to meld before we added in crisp romaine lettuce, briny olives, and salty feta cheese. If cherry tomatoes are unavailable, substitute grape tomatoes; cut the grape tomatoes in half crosswise rather than quartering them. Don't skimp on the draining time in step 1 or the salad will taste watery.

½ cucumber, peeled, halved lengthwise, seeded, and cut into ½-inch pieces
4 ounces cherry tomatoes, quartered
¼ teaspoon table salt
1 tablespoon extra-virgin olive oil
1 tablespoon red wine vinegar
1 small garlic clove, minced
¾ cup canned chickpeas, rinsed
¼ cup minced fresh parsley
1 shallot, minced
2 tablespoons chopped pitted kalamata olives
½ romaine lettuce heart (3 ounces), torn into bite-size pieces
1 ounce feta cheese, crumbled (¼ cup)

1. Toss cucumber, tomatoes, and salt together and let drain in colander for 15 minutes.

2. Whisk oil, vinegar, and garlic together in large bowl. Add drained cucumber and tomatoes, chickpeas, parsley, shallot, and olives and toss to combine. Let sit until flavors meld, about 5 minutes. Add lettuce and feta and toss gently to combine. Season with salt and pepper to taste, and serve.

Cucumber Salad with Olives, Oregano, and Almonds

Serves 2 FAST VEGETARIAN

Total time 30 minutes

WHY THIS RECIPE WORKS Cucumbers can make a cool, crisp salad—but not if they're soggy from their own moisture and swimming in a watery dressing. For a cucumber salad with good crunch, we drained the sliced cucumbers on paper towels while we prepared the dressing. Then, to prevent the dressing from getting watered down, we made a concentrated version with 2½ tablespoons of vinegar and just 1 teaspoon of olive oil. To keep the vinegar from tasting harsh, we simmered it for a few minutes. When tossed with the cucumbers, this potent mixture retained its bright flavor. Briny kalamata olives, a thinly sliced shallot, and some toasted almonds added more flavor and crunch and nicely complemented the cool cucumber. The texture of this salad depends upon thinly sliced cucumbers and shallots. Be sure to slice the vegetables ⅛ to 3/16 inch thick. This salad is best served within 1 hour of being dressed.

2 small cucumbers, peeled, halved lengthwise, seeded, and sliced thin
2½ tablespoons white wine vinegar
1 teaspoon extra-virgin olive oil
1 teaspoon sugar
½ teaspoon table salt
Pinch pepper
¾ teaspoon lemon juice
2 tablespoons chopped pitted kalamata olives
1 small shallot, sliced thin
½ teaspoon minced fresh oregano
1½ tablespoons coarsely chopped toasted sliced almonds

1. Line baking sheet with paper towels and evenly spread cucumber slices on sheet. Refrigerate while preparing dressing.

2. Bring vinegar to simmer in small saucepan and cook until reduced to 1 tablespoon, 3 to 5 minutes. Transfer to large bowl and let cool to room temperature, about 5 minutes. Whisk in oil, sugar, lemon juice, salt, and pepper until well combined.

3. Add chilled cucumbers, olives, shallot, and oregano to dressing and toss to combine. Let sit for 5 minutes, then toss to redistribute dressing. Season with salt and pepper to taste and sprinkle with almonds. Serve.

VARIATIONS

Cucumber Salad with Chile, Mint, and Peanuts

Omit pepper, olives, and shallot. Substitute 1 teaspoon vegetable oil for olive oil and increase amount of sugar to 1¼ teaspoons. Substitute ¾ teaspoon lime juice for lemon juice and add 1½ teaspoons fish sauce and 1 seeded and minced Thai chile to dressing in step 2. Substitute 2 tablespoons minced fresh mint for oregano and 2 tablespoons coarsely chopped toasted peanuts for almonds.

Cucumber Salad with Jalapeño, Cilantro, and Pepitas

Omit pepper, olives, and shallot. Substitute ¾ teaspoon lime juice for lemon juice and add 1 teaspoon grated lime zest and ½ seeded and minced jalapeño chile to dressing in step 2. Substitute ½ cup minced fresh cilantro for oregano and 1½ tablespoons toasted pepitas for almonds.

Cucumber Salad with Ginger, Sesame, and Scallions

Omit pepper, olives, and shallot. Substitute 1 teaspoon toasted sesame oil for olive oil and increase amount of sugar to 1¼ teaspoons. Substitute ¾ teaspoon lime juice for lemon juice and add 1 teaspoon grated fresh ginger to dressing in step 2. Substitute 2 thinly sliced scallions for oregano and 1½ tablespoons toasted sesame seeds for almonds.

Wilted Spinach Salad with Radishes, Feta, and Pistachios

Serves 2 `FAST` `VEGETARIAN`

Total time 15 minutes, plus 15 minutes freezing

WHY THIS RECIPE WORKS For a failproof recipe for a wilted spinach salad that would provide a nice alternative to basic greens, we experimented with various types of spinach and found that flat-leaf and baby spinach became soft and mushy, but hardier curly-leaf spinach stood up to the heat. To make the dressing, we began by heating 2 tablespoons of fruity extra-virgin olive oil in a Dutch oven along with some minced shallot. Peppery sliced radishes, crumbled feta, and toasted pistachios rounded out our updated spinach salad. Be sure to cook the spinach just until it begins to wilt.

2 tablespoons crumbled feta cheese
2 tablespoons extra-virgin olive oil
1 (2-inch) strip lemon zest plus 2 teaspoons juice
1 small shallot, minced
1 teaspoon sugar
5 ounces curly-leaf spinach, stemmed and torn into bite-size pieces
3 radishes, trimmed and sliced thin
2 tablespoons chopped toasted shelled pistachios

1. Place feta on plate and freeze until slightly firm, about 15 minutes.

2. Heat oil, lemon zest, shallot, and sugar in Dutch oven over medium-low heat until shallot is softened, 2 to 4 minutes. Discard lemon zest and stir in lemon juice. Add spinach; cover; and cook until spinach is just beginning to wilt, about 30 seconds.

3. Transfer spinach and hot dressing to large bowl. Add chilled feta, radishes, and pistachios, and toss gently to combine. Season with salt and pepper to taste, and serve.

VARIATION

Wilted Spinach Salad with Cherries, Goat Cheese, and Almonds

Substitute 2 tablespoons crumbled goat cheese for feta cheese, 1 (2-inch) strip grapefruit zest for lemon zest, 2 teaspoons grapefruit juice for lemon juice, 2 tablespoons dried cherries for radishes, and 2 tablespoons chopped toasted sliced almonds for pistachios.

Roasted Beet Salad with Goat Cheese and Pistachios

Serves 2 `VEGETARIAN`

Total time 1 hour 10 minutes, plus 20 minutes cooling

WHY THIS RECIPE WORKS To make beets the star of a simple yet elegant salad, we had to find the easiest way to prepare them. Boiling and steaming diluted their flavor, but when wrapped in foil and roasted, the beets were juicy and tender, with a concentrated sweetness. Peeling was easier when the beets were still warm—the skins slid off effortlessly. We also tossed the sliced beets with the dressing while still warm, allowing them to absorb maximum flavor. Crumbled goat cheese, peppery arugula, and toasted pistachios rounded out the dish. Look for bunches of beets that have uniformly sized beets so that they will roast in the same amount of time.

4. Add arugula to beets and toss gently to coat. Season with salt and pepper to taste. Sprinkle with goat cheese and pistachios and serve.

VARIATION
Roasted Beet Salad with Blood Orange and Almonds

Reduce amount of sherry vinegar to 4 teaspoons. Substitute ½ cup shaved ricotta salata for goat cheese and 2 tablespoons toasted sliced almonds for pistachios. Cut away peel and pith from 1 blood orange. Quarter orange, then slice crosswise into ½-inch-thick pieces; add blood orange pieces with arugula.

REMOVING BEET SKINS

To easily skin beets without straining your hands, cradle roasted beet in your hands in several layers of paper towels or clean dish towel, then gently rub off skin.

Roasted Beet Salad with Goat Cheese and Pistachios

1 pound beets, trimmed

2 tablespoons extra-virgin olive oil

5 teaspoons sherry vinegar

¼ teaspoon table salt

¼ teaspoon pepper

1 cup baby arugula

1 ounce goat cheese, crumbled (¼ cup)

2 tablespoons chopped toasted shelled pistachios

1. Adjust oven rack to middle position and heat oven to 400 degrees. Wrap beets individually in aluminum foil and place on rimmed baking sheet. Roast beets until skewer inserted into center meets little resistance, 45 minutes to 1 hour.

2. Remove beets from oven and carefully remove foil (watch for steam). When beets are cool enough to handle, rub off skins with paper towels or clean dish towel and cut into ½-inch-thick wedges; if large, cut wedges in half crosswise.

3. Meanwhile, whisk oil, vinegar, salt, and pepper together in large bowl. Add sliced beets, toss to coat, and let cool to room temperature, about 20 minutes.

Garlicky Broccoli and Chickpea Salad

Serves 2 VEGETARIAN

Total time 45 minutes

WHY THIS RECIPE WORKS Roasted broccoli is one of the kings of the vegetable kingdom: crisp-tender, sweet, and lightly charred at the edges. Combine the roasted florets with a can of creamy chickpeas and you've got an unbelievably easy and hearty salad. Instead of heating up the oven, we pan-roasted the broccoli in a skillet. After softening a red onion, we transfered it to a bowl with the chickpeas and a creamy, lemony-garlicky dressing and then used the same skillet to cook the broccoli. We intentionally slightly overcrowded the pan with broccoli at first; this caused trapped steam to quickly soften the top layer of broccoli, all while the florets on the bottom charred and turned crispy through direct contact with the hot pan. Stirring the broccoli at 5-minute intervals redistributed the broccoli so every bit achieved the perfect balance of tenderness and crispy char in no time. If you use a 10-inch skillet, the skillet will look very full when you first add the broccoli, but the broccoli will shrink as it cooks.

Garlicky Broccoli and Chickpea Salad

3 tablespoons extra-virgin olive oil, divided

2 teaspoons lemon juice

2 garlic cloves, minced

2 teaspoons mayonnaise

¼ teaspoon red pepper flakes

1 (15-ounce) can chickpeas, rinsed

1 small red onion, halved and sliced ½ inch thick

½ teaspoon table salt, divided

¼ teaspoon pepper, divided

12 ounces broccoli florets, cut into 2-inch pieces

1. Whisk 1 tablespoon oil, lemon juice, garlic, mayonnaise, and pepper flakes together in large bowl. Add chickpeas and toss to combine; set aside.

2. Heat 1 tablespoon oil in 10- or 12-inch nonstick skillet over medium heat until shimmering. Add onion, ¼ teaspoon salt, and ⅛ teaspoon pepper and cook until softened and lightly browned, 4 to 6 minutes. Transfer onion to bowl with chickpea mixture.

3. Heat remaining 1 tablespoon oil in now-empty skillet over medium-low heat until shimmering. Add broccoli, remaining ¼ teaspoon salt, and remaining ⅛ teaspoon pepper. Cook until broccoli is well browned and crispy in spots, about 20 minutes, stirring every 5 minutes. Transfer broccoli to bowl with chickpea mixture and toss to combine. Serve warm or at room temperature.

Cherry Tomato Salad with Basil and Fresh Mozzarella

Serves 2   **VEGETARIAN**

Total time 30 minutes, plus 30 minutes salting

WHY THIS RECIPE WORKS Cherry tomatoes can make a great salad, but the liquid they exude can make a soggy mess. To get rid of some of their juice without throwing away flavor, we salted and drained the tomatoes then used a salad spinner to separate the tomato jelly from the flesh. We reduced the liquid to a flavorful concentrate (adding shallot, olive oil, and vinegar) and reunited it with the tomatoes. Some fresh mozzarella and chopped basil rounded out this great all-season salad. If cherry tomatoes are unavailable, substitute grape tomatoes; cut the grape tomatoes in half crosswise rather than quartering them. Don't skimp on the tomato sitting time in step 1, or the salad will taste watery.

Cherry Tomato Salad with Basil and Fresh Mozzarella

6 ounces cherry tomatoes, quartered
½ teaspoon sugar
¼ teaspoon table salt
1 small shallot, minced
1 teaspoon balsamic vinegar
2 teaspoons extra-virgin olive oil
2 ounces fresh mozzarella, cut into ½-inch pieces and patted dry with paper towels (½ cup)
¼ cup chopped fresh basil

1. Toss tomatoes, sugar, and salt together in large bowl; let sit for 30 minutes.

2. Transfer tomatoes to salad spinner and spin until most of seeds and excess liquid have been removed, 45 to 60 seconds, stirring frequently to redistribute tomatoes. Return tomatoes to now-empty bowl and set aside. Strain tomato liquid through fine-mesh strainer, pressing on solids to extract as much liquid as possible. Reserve 2 tablespoons liquid; discard extra liquid and tomato solids.

3. Bring reserved tomato liquid, shallot, and vinegar to simmer in small saucepan and cook until reduced to 1 tablespoon, 2 to 3 minutes. Transfer mixture to small bowl; let cool to room temperature, about 5 minutes. Whisk in oil until combined.

4. Add dressing, mozzarella, and basil to tomatoes and toss to combine. Season with salt and pepper to taste, and serve.

VARIATION

Cherry Tomato Salad with Tarragon and Blue Cheese

Toasted chopped pecans or walnuts are a nice addition here.

Substitute 1 teaspoon cider vinegar for balsamic vinegar, ¼ cup crumbled blue cheese for mozzarella, and 2 teaspoons chopped fresh tarragon for basil. Whisk 2 teaspoons honey and 1 teaspoon Dijon mustard into tomato liquid with oil in step 3.

NOTES FROM THE TEST KITCHEN

BUYING AND STORING FRESH TOMATOES

Buying tomatoes at the height of summer won't guarantee juicy, flavorful fruit, but keeping these guidelines in mind will help.

CHOOSE LOCALLY GROWN TOMATOES If at all possible, this is the best way to ensure a flavorful tomato. The shorter the distance a tomato has to travel, the riper it can be when it's picked. And commercial tomatoes are engineered to be sturdier, with thicker walls and less of the flavorful jelly and seeds.

LOOKS AREN'T EVERYTHING When selecting tomatoes, oddly shaped tomatoes are fine, and even cracked skin is OK. Avoid tomatoes that are overly soft or leaking juice. Choose tomatoes that smell fruity and feel heavy. And consider trying heirloom tomatoes; grown from naturally pollinated plants and seeds, they are some of the best local tomatoes you can find.

BUY SUPERMARKET TOMATOES ON THE VINE If supermarket tomatoes are your only option, look for tomatoes sold on the vine. Although this does not mean that they were fully ripened on the vine, they are better than regular supermarket tomatoes, which are picked when still green and blasted with ethylene gas to develop texture and color.

STORING TOMATOES Once you've brought your tomatoes home, proper storage is important to preserve their fresh flavor and texture for as long as possible. Here are the rules we follow in the test kitchen:

Never refrigerate tomatoes; the cold damages enzymes that produce flavor compounds, and it ruins their texture, turning the flesh mealy. Even when cut, tomatoes should be kept at room temperature (wrap them tightly in plastic wrap).

If the vine is still attached, leave it on and store the tomatoes stem end up. Tomatoes off the vine should be stored stem side down at room temperature. We have found that this prevents moisture from escaping and bacteria from entering, and thus prolongs shelf life.

To quickly ripen hard, unripened tomatoes, store them in a paper bag with a banana or apple, both of which emit ethylene gas, which hastens ripening.

Panzanella

Serves 2   `VEGETARIAN`

Total time 45 minutes

WHY THIS RECIPE WORKS Italian cooks have long been masters of making great dishes out of humble ingredients, and panzanella—a (typically lettuce-free) salad with fresh vegetables and stale bread infused with a vinaigrette—is a prime example. We bypassed using stale bread and opted for a baguette, which is naturally chewy and has enough structure to hold up to a bit of moisture. Since we were cooking for only two people, using the oven to "stale" the bread seemed excessive. Instead, toasting the cubed bread in a 12-inch nonstick skillet was easier and faster. We wanted to mostly avoid leaving parts of vegetables behind, so we decided on one red bell pepper, one small yellow summer squash, cherry tomatoes, and half an English cucumber. Some panzanellas feature all raw vegetables, but we wanted to concentrate the flavor of the squash and red pepper by cooking them; the same skillet we used to toast the baguette pieces worked great for that. A potent Dijon vinaigrette, fortified with briny capers plus minced garlic and shallot, infused the vegetables and bread with a sharp tanginess that only got better as the vegetable mixture sat. A little chopped basil added freshness, while shaved Parmesan added richness. You can substitute grape tomatoes for the cherry tomatoes, if desired.

VINAIGRETTE

- 3 tablespoons extra-virgin olive oil
- 1 shallot, minced
- 2 tablespoons white wine vinegar
- 1 tablespoon capers, rinsed
- 2 garlic cloves, minced
- ¼ teaspoon table salt
- ¼ teaspoon pepper

SALAD

- 3 tablespoons extra-virgin olive oil, divided
- 1 small red bell pepper, stemmed, seeded, and cut into 1-inch pieces
- 1 small yellow summer squash, quartered lengthwise and cut crosswise into 1-inch pieces
- ½ teaspoon table salt, divided
- ¼ teaspoon pepper
- ½ English cucumber, quartered lengthwise and cut crosswise into ½-inch pieces
- 4 ounces cherry tomatoes, halved
- 1 (6-inch) baguette, cut into 1-inch pieces
- ¼ cup chopped fresh basil
- 1 ounce Parmesan cheese, shaved with vegetable peeler

1. FOR THE VINAIGRETTE Whisk all ingredients together in large bowl; set aside.

2. FOR THE SALAD Heat 1 tablespoon oil in 12-inch nonstick skillet over medium-high heat until shimmering. Add bell pepper, squash, ¼ teaspoon salt, and pepper and cook, stirring occasionally, until vegetables are softened and browned, 7 to 9 minutes. Transfer bell pepper mixture to bowl with vinaigrette; add cucumber and tomatoes and toss to combine. Wipe skillet clean with paper towels.

3. Heat remaining 2 tablespoons oil in now-empty skillet over medium heat until shimmering. Add bread and remaining ¼ teaspoon salt and cook, stirring frequently, until golden brown and crisp on all sides, 3 to 5 minutes. Remove from heat and let bread cool in skillet for 10 minutes. Transfer bread and basil to bowl with vegetables; toss to combine. Serve, sprinkling individual portions with Parmesan.

Fennel, Apple, and Chicken Chopped Salad

Serves 2

Total time 20 minutes, plus 15 minutes salting

WHY THIS RECIPE WORKS Great chopped salads are lively mixes of lettuce, vegetables, fruit, nuts, and cheeses, offering a variety of tastes, textures, and visual appeal. Unfortunately, they're more often random collections of leftovers from the crisper drawer doused with a watery, bland dressing. To make a cohesive version that was light and flavorful, we chose a mix of cucumber, fennel, apple, romaine, and chicken. First, we salted the cucumber to remove its excess moisture. To keep the lean chicken breast tender, we browned it on just one side and then poached it. A minced shallot cut the sweetness of the apples nicely, and some creamy goat cheese added richness. For the dressing, an assertive, vinegar-heavy ratio delivered a welcome acidic kick. Fuji and Gala apples are widely available year-round, but Jonagold, Pink Lady, Jonathan, or Macoun can be substituted. Avoid Granny Smith apples here; they are too tart. Don't skimp on the cucumber draining time, or the salad will taste watery.

- ½ cucumber, peeled, halved lengthwise, seeded, and sliced ½ inch thick
- ¼ teaspoon plus ⅛ teaspoon table salt, divided
- 1 (8-ounce) boneless, skinless chicken breast, trimmed Pinch pepper
- 1 tablespoon extra-virgin olive oil, divided
- 1 ounce goat cheese, crumbled (¼ cup)
- 2 tablespoons cider vinegar

- 2 tablespoons minced fresh tarragon
- 1 Fuji or Gala apple, cored, quartered, and sliced crosswise ¼ inch thick
- 1 small fennel bulb, stalks discarded, bulb halved, cored, and sliced ¼ inch thick
- 1 large shallot, minced
- ½ romaine lettuce heart (3 ounces), torn into bite-size pieces

1. Toss cucumber and ¼ teaspoon salt together and let drain in colander for 15 minutes.

2. Meanwhile, pat chicken dry with paper towels and sprinkle with remaining ⅛ teaspoon salt and pepper. Heat 1 teaspoon oil in 8-inch nonstick skillet over medium-high heat until just smoking. Lay chicken in skillet and cook until well browned on first side, 5 to 7 minutes.

3. Flip chicken, add ½ cup water, and reduce heat to medium-low. Cover and continue to cook until chicken registers 160 degrees, 5 to 7 minutes. Transfer chicken to cutting board, let cool slightly, then cut into 1-inch pieces.

4. Whisk goat cheese, vinegar, tarragon, and remaining 2 teaspoons oil together in large bowl until smooth. Add drained cucumber, cut chicken, apple, fennel, and shallot and toss to combine. Let sit until flavors meld, about 5 minutes. Add lettuce and toss gently to coat. Season with salt and pepper to taste, and serve.

Fennel, Apple, and Chicken Chopped Salad

Charred Chicken Caesar Salad

Serves 2

Total time 1 hour

WHY THIS RECIPE WORKS The concept of the chicken Caesar salad is so ingrained in popular consciousness that you might not stop to consider it much—it just is. It's comforting because it's more about the rich dressing, chicken, croutons, and Parmesan than it is about the lettuce. But start talking about wonderfully warm oven-charred romaine hearts, and suddenly the greens have your attention. Whisking together a creamy dressing and brushing some on the romaine halves before putting them in the oven produced a beautifully charred and deeply satisfying salad base. All you have to do to the chicken is pound it thin and bake. And for crunchy croutons far better than anything premade, we tossed cubes of fresh baguette with olive oil and garlic paste before crisping them in the oven. A final drizzle of dressing is all you need (aside from some extra Parmesan, of course).

Charred Chicken Caesar Salad

Fattoush with Butternut Squash and Apple

1 (6-inch) piece baguette, cut into ¾-inch pieces

3 tablespoons extra-virgin olive oil, divided

2 small garlic cloves, minced to paste, divided

1 pound boneless, skinless chicken breasts, trimmed

½ teaspoon pepper, divided

¼ teaspoon table salt

3 tablespoons mayonnaise

3 tablespoons grated Parmesan cheese, plus extra for serving

1½ teaspoons lemon juice

1½ teaspoons white wine vinegar

1½ teaspoons Worcestershire sauce

1½ teaspoons Dijon mustard

1 anchovy fillet, rinsed and minced (optional)

2 romaine lettuce hearts (6 ounces each), halved lengthwise through cores

1. Adjust oven rack to middle position and heat oven to 400 degrees. Toss baguette pieces, 1 tablespoon oil, and half of garlic together in bowl. Arrange baguette pieces in single layer on rimmed baking sheet and bake until light golden brown and crisp, 6 to 8 minutes. Transfer croutons to bowl and season with salt and pepper to taste; set aside.

2. Pound thicker end of chicken breasts between 2 sheets of plastic wrap to uniform thickness. Pat chicken dry with paper towels and sprinkle with ¼ teaspoon pepper and salt. Arrange chicken on now-empty sheet and bake until chicken registers 160 degrees, 18 to 23 minutes, flipping halfway through baking. Transfer chicken to cutting board, tent with aluminum foil, and let rest while preparing dressing and lettuce.

3. Wipe sheet clean with paper towels. Adjust oven rack to upper position and heat broiler. Whisk mayonnaise, Parmesan, lemon juice, vinegar, Worcestershire, mustard, anchovy (if using), remaining 2 tablespoons oil, remaining garlic, and remaining ¼ teaspoon pepper in bowl until smooth.

4. Brush cut sides of each romaine half with 1 tablespoon dressing. Place romaine cut side up on again-empty sheet and broil until lightly charred, 5 to 7 minutes.

5. Slice chicken thin crosswise. Arrange romaine halves on individual plates and drizzle with remaining dressing. Top with chicken and croutons and sprinkle with extra Parmesan. Serve.

Fattoush with Butternut Squash and Apple

Serves 2   VEGETARIAN

Total time 40 minutes

WHY THIS RECIPE WORKS Pitas are a mainstay of Mediterranean cuisine, but they can stale quickly, so dishes designed to use them up abound. Pita bread salad, or fattoush, is a common example—and its appeal goes far beyond leftovers. We developed this pita salad that included distinctly fall flavors with fantastic contrasts in texture.

5 teaspoons extra-virgin olive oil, divided

4 teaspoons lemon juice

1 teaspoon ground sumac, plus extra for serving

8 ounces butternut squash, peeled, seeded, and cut into ½-inch pieces (about 1½ cups)

⅛ teaspoon table salt

⅛ teaspoon pepper

3 cups baked pita chips (page 82), broken into ½-inch pieces

6 ounces chopped romaine lettuce (4 cups)

1 apple, cored and cut into ½-inch pieces

⅔ cup frozen shelled edamame, thawed and patted dry

2 tablespoons chopped fresh parsley

2 scallions, sliced thin

1 ounce feta cheese, crumbled (¼ cup)

1. Adjust oven rack to lowest position and heat oven to 450 degrees. Whisk 4 teaspoons oil, lemon juice, and sumac together in large bowl; set aside.

2. Toss squash with remaining 1 teaspoon oil, salt, and pepper. Spread in even layer on rimmed baking sheet and roast until well browned and tender, 10 to 12 minutes, stirring halfway through roasting. Set aside to cool slightly, about 5 minutes.

3. Add squash, pita chips, lettuce, apple, edamame, parsley, and scallions to bowl with dressing and toss gently to coat. Season with salt and pepper to taste. To serve, top each portion with 2 tablespoons feta and sprinkle with extra sumac.

Baked Pita Chips

Makes about 4 cups **VEGETARIAN**
Total time 35 minutes

Homemade pita chips are a far cry from storebought ones and they are so easy to make. We like to use them in our recipe for fattoush, but they are great to have around for snacking. Both white and whole-wheat pita breads will work in this recipe.

  2 (6½-inch) pita breads
    Olive or canola oil spray
    Pinch table salt
    Pinch pepper

1. Adjust oven rack to middle position and heat oven to 350 degrees. Using kitchen shears, cut around perimeter of each pita and separate into 2 thin rounds.

2. Working with 1 round at a time, spray rough side evenly with oil spray and sprinkle with salt and pepper. Stack rounds on top of one another, rough sides up. Using chef's knife, cut pita stack into 6 wedges. Spread wedges, rough sides up and in single layer on rimmed baking sheet.

3. Bake until wedges are golden and crisp, 10 to 15 minutes, stirring occasionally and rotating sheet halfway through baking. Transfer sheet to wire rack and let chips cool slightly, about 10 minutes. Serve warm or at room temperature.

Steak, Mushroom, and Blue Cheese Salad

Serves 2
Total time 35 minutes

WHY THIS RECIPE WORKS For a flavorful dinner salad: juicy steak, mushrooms, and blue cheese. We cooked the steak until just medium rare, then we used the flavorful fond left in the skillet to cook the mushrooms. Sautéing them with a tablespoon of vinaigrette gave them a bright, tangy flavor that balanced their earthiness. To complement the salad's main components, we made a simple vinaigrette and tossed it with tender baby spinach and briny capers, then topped the greens with the mushrooms, steak, and blue cheese. We prefer the steak cooked to medium-rare, but if you prefer it more or less done, see our guidelines on page 161.

  1 (8-ounce) boneless strip steak, ¾ inch thick, trimmed
 ⅛ teaspoon table salt
    Pinch pepper
 ¼ cup extra-virgin olive oil, divided
  2 tablespoons red wine vinegar
  1 small shallot, minced
1½ teaspoons Dijon mustard
  8 ounces white or cremini mushrooms, trimmed and quartered
  4 ounces (4 cups) baby spinach
  1 tablespoon capers, rinsed and minced
  1 ounce blue cheese, crumbled (¼ cup)

1. Pat steak dry with paper towels and sprinkle with salt and pepper. Heat 1 tablespoon oil in 10-inch skillet over medium-high heat until just smoking. Lay steak in skillet and cook until well browned on first side, 3 to 5 minutes. Flip steak; reduce heat to medium; and continue to cook until meat registers 120 to 125 degrees (for medium-rare), 1 to 4 minutes. Transfer steak to cutting board, tent loosely with aluminum foil, and let rest while finishing salad. Pour off fat from skillet but do not wipe clean.

2. Whisk remaining 3 tablespoons oil, vinegar, shallot, and mustard together in large bowl. Add mushrooms and 1 tablespoon vinaigrette to now-empty skillet and cook over medium heat until mushrooms are golden, 6 to 8 minutes; let cool slightly.

3. Add spinach and capers to remaining vinaigrette and toss gently to coat. Season with salt and pepper to taste. Divide spinach among individual plates or transfer to serving platter and top with mushrooms. Slice steak thin and arrange over salad. Sprinkle with blue cheese and serve.

Steak and Rice Noodle Salad with Cucumber and Mint

Serves 2
Total time 1 hour

WHY THIS RECIPE WORKS This fresh and appealing recipe pairs thinly sliced seared flank steak with dried rice vermicelli and a pungent marinade of vegetable oil, lime juice, fish sauce, and brown sugar. To keep things simple, we marinated the meat after searing it. We let the steak rest, sliced it, then tossed it with the tangy dressing. Meanwhile, we chopped onion, cucumber, and herbs and tossed them with cooked rice noodles and more of the dressing. A garnish of chopped peanuts provided the finishing touch. Do not substitute other types of noodles for the rice vermicelli here. We prefer the steak cooked to medium-rare, but if you prefer it more or less done, see our guidelines on page 161.

2 ounces dried rice vermicelli
1 (8-ounce) flank steak, trimmed
⅛ teaspoon table salt
   Pinch pepper
3 tablespoons vegetable oil, divided
3 tablespoons lime juice (2 limes)
3 tablespoons fish sauce
1 tablespoon packed brown sugar
1 small red onion, halved and sliced thin
½ cucumber, peeled, halved lengthwise, seeded, and sliced thin
4 teaspoons minced fresh mint
½ head Bibb lettuce (4 ounces), leaves separated
2 tablespoons chopped dry-roasted peanuts

1. Bring 2 quarts water to boil in medium saucepan. Off heat, add noodles and let sit, stirring occasionally, until tender, about 10 minutes. Drain noodles, rinse with cold water, and drain again, leaving noodles slightly wet.

2. Meanwhile, pat steak dry with paper towels and sprinkle with salt and pepper. Heat 1 tablespoon oil in 10-inch skillet over medium-high heat until just smoking. Lay steak in skillet and cook until well browned on first side, 3 to 5 minutes. Flip steak; reduce heat to medium; and continue to cook until meat registers 120 to 125 degrees (for medium-rare), 3 to 5 minutes. Transfer steak to cutting board, tent loosely with aluminum foil, and let rest for 5 minutes.

3. Whisk remaining 2 tablespoons oil, lime juice, fish sauce, and sugar together in bowl until sugar dissolves. Slice steak in half lengthwise, then slice thin against grain. Toss sliced steak with 2 tablespoons dressing in separate bowl and let sit for 5 minutes. In third bowl, toss cooked noodles, onion, cucumber, and mint with 3 tablespoons dressing and let sit for 5 minutes.

4. Divide lettuce leaves among individual plates or arrange on serving platter. Drain noodle mixture and arrange over lettuce. Drain steak and arrange over salad. Sprinkle with peanuts and drizzle with remaining dressing. Serve.

Steak and Rice Noodle Salad with Cucumber and Mint

Chef's Salad with Capicola and Provolone

Serves 2   FAST
Total time 15 minutes

WHY THIS RECIPE WORKS We put a new spin on this old classic by swapping out the usual deli ham for flavorful capicola (a nicely seasoned Italian cold cut) and adding sweet cherry peppers and anise-flavored fennel to the mix. We used the liquid from the peppers in our red wine vinaigrette, which helped balance the richness of the meat and cheese and ensured a hint of heat in every bite. Garlic and oregano rounded out the dressing. Although hard-cooked eggs are traditional in chef's salads, we found our version was so fresh and flavorful that we didn't miss the eggs when we left them out. When buying the capicola and provolone for this salad, ask the deli to slice each into ¼-inch-thick slabs so that you can easily cut them into ¼-inch strips. If cherry tomatoes are unavailable, substitute grape tomatoes; cut the grape tomatoes in half crosswise rather than quartering them.

**Chef's Salad with
Capicola and Provolone**

3 tablespoons extra-virgin olive oil

2 tablespoons jarred sliced sweet cherry peppers,
plus 1 teaspoon brine

2 tablespoons red wine vinegar

1 garlic clove, minced

¼ teaspoon minced fresh oregano or pinch dried

1 romaine lettuce heart (6 ounces), torn into
bite-size pieces

½ fennel bulb, stalks discarded, cored, and sliced thin

6 ounces cherry tomatoes, quartered

2 (¼-inch-thick) slices capicola (4 ounces),
cut into ¼-inch-thick strips

2 (¼-inch-thick) slices provolone cheese (4 ounces),
cut into ¼-inch-thick strips

1. Whisk oil, pepper brine, vinegar, garlic, and oregano
together in large bowl. Add lettuce, fennel, and tomatoes and
toss gently to combine. Season with salt and pepper to taste.

2. Divide salad among individual plates or transfer to
serving platter. Top with cherry peppers, capicola, and provolone. Serve.

Poached Shrimp Salad with Avocado and Grapefruit

Serves 2

Total time 45 minutes

WHY THIS RECIPE WORKS Poached shrimp salad makes
a great, naturally light meal, but too-lean versions often leave
us wanting more. We wanted to develop a satisfying yet
healthy salad featuring tender shrimp and a complementary
mix of fresh fruit and vegetables. To poach the shrimp, we
made a flavorful poaching liquid, called a court-bouillon, with
cold water, lemon juice, sugar, salt, peppercorns, and a bay
leaf, then brought the mixture to a gentle simmer over medium
heat. Just 10 minutes on the stove plus a 2-minute rest off
the heat gave us perfectly cooked, tender shrimp infused with the
subtle flavor of the broth. A combination of tart ruby-red
grapefruit, buttery avocado, and a bold dressing with ginger,
honey, and Dijon mustard gave our shrimp salad a balance
of sweet, tart, and tangy flavors. If your grapefruit tastes especially tart, add ¼ teaspoon more honey to the dressing. If
you are short on grapefruit juice, substitute water.

SHRIMP

12 ounces extra-large shrimp (21 to 25 per pound),
peeled, deveined, and tails removed

¼ cup lemon juice, spent halves reserved (2 lemons)

1 tablespoon sugar

1 teaspoon whole black peppercorns

1 teaspoon table salt

1 bay leaf

SALAD AND VINAIGRETTE

½ red grapefruit

1 small shallot, minced

1 tablespoon lime juice

2 teaspoons extra-virgin olive oil

¾ teaspoon grated fresh ginger

¾ teaspoon honey

½ teaspoon Dijon mustard

¼ teaspoon table salt

⅛ teaspoon pepper

½ avocado, cut into ½-inch pieces

1 ounce snow peas, strings removed, sliced thin
on bias

1 tablespoon minced fresh mint

1 head Bibb lettuce (8 ounces), leaves separated

1. FOR THE SHRIMP Combine shrimp, 2 cups cold water, lemon juice, reserved lemon halves, sugar, peppercorns, salt, and bay leaf in medium saucepan. Place saucepan over medium heat and cook shrimp, stirring several times, until opaque throughout, 8 to 10 minutes (water should be just bubbling around edge of pan and register 165 degrees). Off heat, cover saucepan and let shrimp sit in broth for 2 minutes.

2. Meanwhile, fill large bowl halfway with ice and water. Drain shrimp, discarding lemon half and spices. Immediately transfer shrimp to bowl of ice water to stop cooking and let sit until fully chilled, about 5 minutes. Remove shrimp from ice water and pat dry with paper towels.

3. FOR THE SALAD AND VINAIGRETTE Cut away peel and pith from grapefruit. Working over bowl, use paring knife to slice between membranes to release segments. Reserve 2 tablespoons juice; discard any extra.

4. Whisk reserved grapefruit juice, shallot, lime juice, oil, ginger, honey, mustard, salt, and pepper together in large bowl. Add chilled shrimp, grapefruit segments, avocado, snow peas, and mint and toss gently to combine. Season with salt and pepper to taste. Divide lettuce leaves among individual plates or arrange on serving platter. Spoon shrimp mixture over lettuce and drizzle with any dressing left in bowl. Serve.

VARIATION

Poached Shrimp Salad with Avocado, Orange, and Arugula

Substitute 1 whole orange for grapefruit and grapefruit juice and 3 ounces baby arugula for Bibb lettuce. Reduce amount of honey to ¼ teaspoon.

SEGMENTING CITRUS FRUIT

1. Slice off top and bottom of grapefruit or orange, then cut away peel and pith.

2. Slice between membrane and 1 segment to center of fruit. Turn blade and slice along membrane on segment's other side to free segment. Repeat with remaining segments.

PITTING AND DICING AN AVOCADO

1. Slice avocado in half around pit, then lodge edge of knife blade into pit and twist to remove.

2. Don't pull pit off with your hand. Instead, use large wooden spoon to pry pit safely off knife.

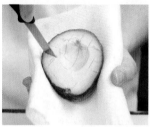

3. Using dish towel to hold avocado steady, make ½-inch crosshatch incisions in flesh of each avocado half, cutting down to but not through skin.

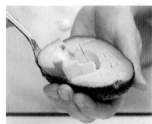

4. Separate diced flesh from skin with soupspoon inserted between skin and flesh, gently scooping out avocado pieces.

Seared Scallop Salad with Snap Peas and Radishes

Serves 2 **FAST**

Total time 30 minutes

WHY THIS RECIPE WORKS For an elegant dinner salad, we wanted to combine tender seared sea scallops with fresh spring vegetables. We sandwiched the scallops between paper towels and allowed them drain before cooking, which rid them of excess moisture that would prevent them from developing a burnished crust in the skillet. Once they were ready to cook, we seared them in a hot skillet for only a few minutes until their centers were just opaque and their exteriors were well browned and flavorful. For the salad, we tossed delicate mesclun greens, fresh sugar snap peas, and thinly sliced, peppery radishes with

**Seared Scallop Salad
with Snap Peas and Radishes**

a simple vinaigrette and arranged the scallops on top. We recommend buying "dry" scallops, which don't have chemical additives and taste better than "wet." Dry scallops will look ivory or pinkish; wet scallops are bright white.

- 12 ounces large sea scallops, tendons removed
- 1 tablespoon red wine vinegar
- ½ teaspoon Dijon mustard
- 3 tablespoons extra-virgin olive oil, divided
- 6 ounces sugar snap peas, strings removed, halved crosswise
- 4 ounces (4 cups) mesclun
- 4 radishes, trimmed and sliced thin
- 1 shallot, sliced thin
- ¼ teaspoon table salt
- ⅛ teaspoon pepper

1. Place scallops on large plate lined with clean dish towel. Place second clean dish towel on top of scallops and press gently on towel to blot liquid. Let scallops sit at room temperature for 10 minutes while towels absorb moisture.

2. Meanwhile, combine vinegar and mustard in large bowl. Whisking constantly, drizzle 2 tablespoons oil into vinegar mixture in slow, steady stream. Add snap peas, mesclun, radishes, and shallot and toss gently to coat. Season with salt and pepper to taste. Divide salad among individual plates or transfer to serving platter.

3. Sprinkle scallops with salt and pepper. Heat remaining 1 tablespoon oil in 12-inch nonstick skillet over high heat until just smoking. Add scallops in single layer, flat side down, and cook, without moving, until well browned, 1½ to 2 minutes. Flip scallops and continue to cook until sides of scallops are firm and centers are opaque, 30 to 90 seconds (remove smaller scallops as they finish cooking). Arrange scallops over salad. Serve.

Tortellini Salad with Asparagus and Fresh Basil Vinaigrette

Serves 2 `VEGETARIAN`

Total time 55 minutes

WHY THIS RECIPE WORKS For a supereasy but attractive pasta salad that would be welcome at any picnic, we paired convenient store-bought cheese tortellini with crisp asparagus and a dressing inspired by the flavors of classic pesto. First, we blanched the asparagus in the same water we later used to cook the cheese tortellini, which gave the pasta some of the asparagus's delicate flavor. We tossed the cooked tortellini in a bold dressing of extra-virgin olive oil, lemon juice, shallot, and garlic. Just before serving, we tossed in some bright, juicy cherry tomatoes; fresh basil; grated Parmesan; toasted pine nuts; and the blanched asparagus. Be sure to set up the ice bath before cooking the asparagus, as plunging it in the cold water immediately after blanching preserves its bright green color and ensures that it doesn't overcook.

½ pound thin asparagus, trimmed and cut into 1-inch lengths
½ teaspoon table salt, plus salt for cooking asparagus and pasta
½ pound dried cheese tortellini
¼ cup extra-virgin olive oil
1½ tablespoons lemon juice, plus extra for seasoning
1½ tablespoons minced shallot
1 garlic clove, minced
¼ teaspoon pepper
6 ounces cherry or grape tomatoes, halved
½ ounce Parmesan or Pecorino Romano cheese, grated (¼ cup)
⅓ cup chopped fresh basil, mint, or parsley
2 tablespoons pine nuts or walnuts, toasted

1. Bring 4 quarts water to boil in large pot. Fill large bowl halfway with ice and water. Add asparagus and 1 tablespoon salt to boiling water and cook until crisp-tender, about 2 minutes. Using slotted spoon, transfer asparagus to ice bath (do not discard cooking water) and let cool, about 2 minutes; drain and pat dry.

2. Return pot of water to boil. Add tortellini and cook, stirring often, until tender. Drain tortellini; rinse with cold water; and drain again, leaving tortellini slightly wet.

3. Whisk oil, lemon juice, shallot, garlic, pepper, and salt together in large bowl. Add tortellini and toss to combine.

4. Add tomatoes, Parmesan, basil, pine nuts, and asparagus and toss gently to combine. Season with salt, pepper, and extra lemon juice to taste. Serve. (Cooled tortellini, cooked asparagus, and dressing can be refrigerated separately for up to 2 days. Toss before serving.)

TOASTING PINE NUTS

Toast pine nuts in dry skillet over medium heat, shaking pan occasionally to prevent scorching, until slightly darkened in color, 3 to 5 minutes.

Freekeh Salad with Sweet Potatoes and Walnuts
Serves 2   VEGETARIAN
Total time 55 minutes

WHY THIS RECIPE WORKS High-fiber freekeh is a wheat-based grain that deserves a spot in your pantry for its grassy, slightly smoky flavor that's absent from other whole-wheat products. We topped our base of freekeh with roasted sweet potatoes and seasoned them with fenugreek, a sweet seed with a unique, maple-like flavor. To bring everything together, we stirred in a rich yet bright tahini-lemon dressing. You can substitute barley for the freekeh; decrease cooking time to 20 to 40 minutes.

¾ cup freekeh
½ teaspoon table salt, divided, plus salt for cooking freekeh
6 ounces sweet potato, peeled and cut into 1-inch pieces (about 1 cup)
1 tablespoon extra-virgin olive oil, divided
¼ teaspoon pepper, divided
¼ teaspoon ground fenugreek or curry powder
2 tablespoons tahini
1 tablespoon lemon juice
1 tablespoon water
½ cup fresh cilantro leaves
2 tablespoons walnuts, toasted and chopped

1. Bring 2 quarts water to boil in large saucepan. Add freekeh and ½ teaspoon salt, return to boil, and cook until grains are tender with slight chew, 30 to 45 minutes. Drain freekeh, spread onto platter or rimmed baking sheet, and let cool completely, 10 to 15 minutes.

2. Meanwhile, microwave potato in covered bowl until tender, 5 to 8 minutes, stirring halfway through microwaving; drain well. Heat 1 teaspoon oil in 8- or 10-inch nonstick skillet over medium heat until shimmering. Add potato, ¼ teaspoon salt, and ⅛ teaspoon pepper and cook, stirring occasionally, until golden brown, 4 to 6 minutes. Off heat, stir in fenugreek.

3. Whisk tahini, lemon juice, water, remaining ¼ teaspoon salt, remaining 2 teaspoons oil, and remaining ⅛ teaspoon pepper together in large bowl. Add freekeh, potato, cilantro, and walnuts and toss to combine. Season with salt and pepper to taste. Serve warm or at room temperature.

Classic Tuna Salad

Serves 2 `FAST`

Total time 20 minutes

WHY THIS RECIPE WORKS You may not think you need a recipe for tuna salad, but a few simple steps can make the difference between one that is just okay and one that is very good. First we mixed some minced shallot with a little olive oil and microwaved it to soften its bite and enhance the flavor of the oil. To eliminate excess moisture, we drained the tuna and pressed it with paper towels.

- 2 tablespoons minced shallot
- 1 tablespoon extra-virgin olive oil
- 2 (5-ounce) cans solid white tuna in water
- ¼ cup mayonnaise
- 1 small celery rib, minced
- 1 teaspoon lemon juice
- Pinch sugar

1. Combine shallot and oil in small bowl and microwave until shallot begins to soften, about 2 minutes; set aside to cool for 5 minutes. Drain tuna in fine-mesh strainer then press dry with paper towels. Transfer tuna to medium bowl and mash with fork until finely flaked.

Tuna Salad with Apples, Walnuts, and Tarragon

2. Add mayonnaise, celery, lemon juice, sugar, and shallot mixture to tuna and mix until well combined. Season with salt and pepper to taste. Serve.

VARIATIONS

Curried Tuna Salad

Add ½ teaspoon curry powder to bowl with shallot and oil before microwaving. Add ½ cup green grapes, halved, to salad in step 2.

Tuna Salad with Apples, Walnuts, and Tarragon

Add ½ apple, cored and cut into ½-inch pieces; ¼ cup walnuts, toasted and chopped coarse; and 1½ teaspoons minced fresh tarragon to salad in step 2.

Tuna Salad with Cornichons and Whole-Grain Mustard

Add ¼ cup finely chopped cornichons, 1½ teaspoons minced fresh chives, and 1½ teaspoons whole-grain mustard to salad in step 2.

Classic Chicken Salad

Serves 2

Total time 35 minutes, plus 30 minutes chilling

WHY THIS RECIPE WORKS There are many varieties of chicken salad, but there's no beating the classic version: tender cubes of moist chicken lightly bound with mayonnaise and freshened up with celery and aromatic flavors. For juicy and tender chicken, we added the chicken to a pot of water, heated the water to 170 degrees, then let the chicken finish cooking through gently off heat. Salting the water helped to season the chicken throughout. Then, while the chicken cooled, we simply mixed up a classic dressing with mayonnaise, lemon juice, mustard, celery, shallot, and fresh parsley or tarragon for a quintessential chicken salad. To ensure that the chicken cooks through, start with cold water in step 1 and don't use breasts that weigh more than 8 ounces or are thicker than 1 inch. Serve over mixed salad greens or in a sandwich.

- Table salt for poaching chicken
- 2 (6- to 8-ounce) boneless, skinless chicken breasts, trimmed
- ¼ cup mayonnaise
- 1 teaspoon lemon juice
- ½ teaspoon Dijon mustard
- 1 celery rib, minced
- 1 small shallot, minced
- 1 tablespoon minced fresh parsley or tarragon

1. Dissolve 1 tablespoon salt in 3 cups cold water in medium saucepan. Submerge chicken in water. Heat saucepan over medium heat until water registers 170 degrees. Off heat, cover saucepan and let sit until chicken registers 165 degrees, 15 to 17 minutes.

2. Transfer chicken to paper towel–lined plate and refrigerate until cool, about 30 minutes. Pat chilled chicken dry with paper towels and cut into ½-inch pieces.

3. Whisk mayonnaise, lemon juice, and mustard together in medium bowl. Add cut chicken, celery, shallot, and parsley and toss to combine. Season with salt and pepper to taste.

Classic Potato Salad

Serves 2   VEGETARIAN

Total time 55 minutes, plus 1 hour chilling

WHY THIS RECIPE WORKS   For our potato salad, we wanted lightly dressed, flavorful, tender potatoes punctuated by crunchy bits of onion and celery. We found that seasoning the potatoes while still hot maximized flavor, so we tossed hot russets with white vinegar, then added a judicious amount of mayonnaise. One small rib of celery and a minced shallot added just the right amount of crunch and onion flavor. Prep-free pickle relish added a subtle sweetness. Celery seeds reinforced the flavor of the fresh celery and provided an underlying complexity. Be careful not to overcook the potatoes or they will become mealy and break apart. If you find the potato salad a little dry for your liking, add more mayonnaise.

> 1 pound russet potatoes, peeled and cut into
>   ¾-inch pieces
>   Table salt for cooking potatoes
> 1 tablespoon distilled white vinegar
> ¼ cup mayonnaise
> 1 small celery rib, minced
> 1½ tablespoons sweet pickle relish
> 1 small shallot, minced
> 1 tablespoon minced fresh parsley
> ½ teaspoon dry mustard
> ½ teaspoon celery seeds
> 1 large Hard-Cooked Egg (page 360), cut into ¼-inch
>   pieces (optional)

1. Place potatoes and 1 tablespoon salt in medium saucepan and add water to cover by 1 inch. Bring to boil over medium-high heat, then reduce heat to medium and simmer, stirring once or twice, until potatoes are tender, about 8 minutes.

2. Drain potatoes and transfer to medium bowl. Add vinegar and, using rubber spatula, toss gently to coat. Let sit until potatoes are just warm, about 20 minutes.

3. Meanwhile, whisk mayonnaise, celery, pickle relish, shallot, parsley, mustard, and celery seeds together in small bowl. Gently fold dressing and egg, if using, into potatoes. Season with salt and pepper to taste. Cover and refrigerate until chilled, at least 1 hour or up to 1 day. Serve.

VARIATION

Garlicky Potato Salad with Tomatoes and Basil

Omit parsley and egg. Add 1 minced small garlic clove to dressing in step 3. Gently fold 2 tablespoons coarsely chopped basil and 3 ounces quartered cherry tomatoes into potatoes with dressing.

Sweet and Tangy Coleslaw

Serves 2   VEGETARIAN

Total time 15 minutes, plus 25 minutes chilling

WHY THIS RECIPE WORKS   For a bright, tangy coleslaw, we ditched the mayonnaise in favor of a light dressing of oil and cider vinegar. To keep the moisture of the cabbage from diluting the dressing, we lightly salted the cabbage and microwaved it, which pulled out its excess water, then quickly dried it in a salad spinner. Chilling the dressing helped to compensate for the warm cabbage. We replaced the usual domineering onion with grated carrot and chopped parsley and added celery seeds for a little zip to make a refreshing slaw that would go with almost anything. A brief chill in the fridge allowed its flavors to meld.

> 2 tablespoons cider vinegar, plus extra for seasoning
> 1 tablespoon vegetable oil
>   Pinch celery seeds
>   Pinch pepper
> ½ small head green cabbage, halved, cored,
>   and shredded (4 cups)
> 2 tablespoons sugar, plus extra for seasoning
> ½ teaspoon table salt
> 1 small carrot, peeled and shredded
> 1 tablespoon minced fresh parsley

1. Combine vinegar, oil, celery seeds, and pepper in medium bowl. Place bowl in freezer until vinegar mixture is well chilled, at least 10 or up to 20 minutes.

2. While vinegar mixture chills, toss cabbage with sugar and salt in separate bowl. Cover and microwave until cabbage is partially wilted and reduced in volume by one-third, 45 to 90 seconds, stirring cabbage halfway through microwaving.

3. Transfer cabbage to salad spinner and spin until excess water is removed, 10 to 20 seconds. Add cabbage, carrot, and parsley to chilled vinegar and toss to combine. Season with extra vinegar, extra sugar, and salt to taste. Cover and refrigerate until chilled, at least 15 minutes or up to 1 day. Toss to redistribute dressing and serve.

VARIATIONS

Sweet and Tangy Coleslaw with Bell Pepper and Jalapeño

To make this dish spicier, reserve and add the chile seeds as desired.

Substitute 2 teaspoons lime juice for celery seeds, ½ thinly sliced small red bell pepper and ½ seeded and minced jalapeño chile for carrot, and 1 thinly sliced small scallion for parsley.

Sweet and Tangy Coleslaw with Apple and Tarragon

Reduce amount of cider vinegar to 1 tablespoon. Substitute ¼ teaspoon Dijon mustard for celery seeds, ½ Granny Smith apple, cored and cut into 2-inch-long matchsticks, for carrot, and 1 teaspoon minced fresh tarragon for parsley.

SHREDDING CABBAGE

1. Cut cabbage into quarters, then cut away hard piece of core attached to each quarter.

2. Flatten small stacks of leaves on cutting board and use chef's knife to cut each stack crosswise into ¼-inch-wide shreds.

Roasted Grape and Cauliflower Salad with Chermoula

Serves 2 VEGETARIAN
Total time 45 minutes

WHY THIS RECIPE WORKS Cauliflower's delicate and versatile flavor makes it an ideal canvas on which to paint other flavors and textures. Here those "paints" come from grapes, cilantro, and shallot, which combine to turn simple roasted cauliflower into a memorable and refined salad. Cauliflower's nutty and sweet flavor shines brightest when roasted, but we didn't stop with roasting just the cauliflower. We tossed sweet red grapes and a sliced scallion onto the same sheet as the cauliflower to roast simultaneously, which brought out the caramelized sweetness of all three. At first glance, a whole head of cauliflower might sound like a lot to serve two, but it cooked down in the oven's intense heat to yield two servings that were substantial but not at all overwhelming. While the vegetables and grapes roasted, we whisked together a quick chermoula, a North African sauce made with hefty amounts of cilantro, lemon, and garlic, to use as a dressing. Fresh cilantro leaves and crunchy walnuts are the finishing touch.

1¼ pounds cauliflower florets, cut into 1-inch pieces
  1 cup seedless red grapes
  1 shallot, sliced thin
  ¼ cup extra-virgin olive oil, divided
  ¾ teaspoon table salt, divided
  ¼ cup chopped fresh cilantro, plus whole leaves for serving
  1 tablespoon lemon juice
  1 garlic clove, minced
  ¼ teaspoon ground cumin
  ¼ teaspoon paprika
  ¼ teaspoon cayenne pepper
  1 tablespoon toasted and chopped walnuts or pecans

1. Adjust oven rack to middle position and heat oven to 450 degrees. Toss cauliflower, grapes, and shallot with 1 tablespoon oil and ½ teaspoon salt and arrange in even layer on rimmed baking sheet. Roast until cauliflower is spotty brown and tender, 20 to 25 minutes, stirring mixture halfway through roasting. Transfer baking sheet to wire rack and let cauliflower mixture cool slightly, about 5 minutes.

2. Whisk chopped cilantro, lemon juice, garlic, cumin, paprika, cayenne, remaining 3 tablespoons oil, and remaining ¼ teaspoon salt together in large bowl. Add cauliflower mixture and toss to coat. Season with salt and pepper to taste. Transfer salad to serving bowls and sprinkle with cilantro leaves and walnuts. Serve warm or at room temperature.

Charred Cabbage Salad with Torn Tofu and Plantain Chips

Serves 2   VEGETARIAN

Total time 55 minutes

WHY THIS RECIPE WORKS This show-stopping salad is a feast for multiple senses, offering up richly colorful bites of red cabbage, emerald-green fresh basil, and golden plantain chips in addition to a wallop of flavor. The flavor inspiration for this salad came from Southeast Asia. We coated the cabbage in a mix of Thai red curry paste and turmeric before roasting it to bring out its natural sweetness, and we marinated torn tofu pieces in a piquant mix of soy sauce, lime juice, ginger, and sugar to infuse each piece with sweet-and-sour flavor. Tearing the tofu produced all sorts of nooks and crannies that allowed the tofu to hold on to the marinade much more efficiently than tofu with straight-cut sides. A scallion added pleasant crispness; plantain chips contributed sweet-salty crunch. And to make a warm and impactful dressing to drizzle over everything, we bloomed more curry paste, turmeric, and ginger in the microwave before whisking in another dose of tart lime juice.

Charred Cabbage Salad with Torn Tofu and Plantain Chips

- 7 ounces firm or extra-firm tofu, torn into bite-size pieces
- 2 tablespoons lime juice, divided
- 1 tablespoon soy sauce
- 2 teaspoons grated fresh ginger, divided
- 1 teaspoon sugar
- 2 tablespoons vegetable oil, divided
- 2 teaspoons Thai red curry paste, divided
- 1½ teaspoons ground turmeric, divided
- ⅛ teaspoon table salt
- ½ head red or green cabbage (1 pound), cut into 4 wedges through core
- 2 tablespoons shredded fresh basil
- 1 scallion, sliced thin
- 2 tablespoons plantain chips, crushed

1. Adjust oven rack to lowest position and heat oven to 500 degrees. Line rimmed baking sheet with aluminum foil. Gently press tofu dry with paper towels. Whisk 1 tablespoon lime juice, soy sauce, 1 teaspoon ginger, and sugar together in medium bowl. Add tofu and toss gently to coat; let sit for 20 minutes. (Tofu can be refrigerated for up to 24 hours.)

2. Whisk 1 tablespoon oil, ½ teaspoon curry paste, 1 teaspoon turmeric, and salt together in small bowl. Arrange cabbage wedges in even layer on prepared sheet, then brush cabbage all over with oil mixture. Cover tightly with foil and roast for 10 minutes. Remove foil and drizzle cabbage with 1½ teaspoons oil. Roast, uncovered, until cabbage is tender and bottoms of wedges are well browned, 10 to 15 minutes. Transfer baking sheet to wire rack and let cabbage cool slightly, about 5 minutes.

3. Whisk remaining 1 teaspoon ginger, 1½ teaspoons oil, 1½ teaspoons curry paste, and ½ teaspoon turmeric together in second bowl. Microwave until fragrant, about 10 seconds. Whisk in remaining 1 tablespoon lime juice.

4. Transfer cabbage to cutting board, chop coarse, then transfer to serving plates. Top with basil, scallion, and tofu. Drizzle with dressing and sprinkle with plantain chips. Serve warm or at room temperature.

CHAPTER 4

Burgers, Sandwiches, Pizza & More

Burgers

Tacos and Sandwiches

Pizzas, Calzones, and Stromboli

■ **FAST** (Start to finish in 30 minutes or less)
■ **VEGETARIAN**

Opposite: Tofu Katsu Sandwiches

Juicy Pub-Style Burgers

Serves 2

Total time 40 minutes, plus 25 minutes freezing

WHY THIS RECIPE WORKS Few things are as satisfying as a thick, juicy, pub-style burger. But avoiding the usual gray band of overcooked meat is a challenge. We wanted a patty that was well-seared, juicy, and evenly rosy from center to edge. Grinding our own meat in the food processor was a must for this ultimate burger, and sirloin steak tips were the right cut for the job. Cutting the meat into small, ½-inch chunks before grinding and lightly packing the meat to form patties gave the burgers just enough structure to hold their shape in the skillet. A little melted butter improved their flavor and juiciness, but our biggest discovery came when we transferred the burgers from the stovetop to the oven to finish cooking—the stovetop provided intense heat for searing, while the oven's gentle ambient heat allowed for even cooking, thus eliminating the overcooked gray zone. Steak tips, also known as flap meat, are sold as whole steak, cubes, and strips; look for either whole steak tips or strips that are easy to cut into small pieces for this recipe. When stirring the butter and pepper into the ground meat and shaping the patties, take care not to overwork the meat, or the burgers will become dense. We prefer these burgers cooked to medium-rare, but if you prefer them more or less done, see our guidelines on page 161. Serve with your favorite burger toppings.

Juicy Pub-Style Burgers

- 1 pound sirloin steak tips, trimmed and cut into ½-inch pieces
- 2 tablespoons unsalted butter, melted and cooled
- 1 teaspoon pepper, divided
- ½ teaspoon table salt
- 1 teaspoon vegetable oil
- ¼ cup mayonnaise
- 2 teaspoons soy sauce
- 2 teaspoons minced fresh chives
- 1 teaspoon packed brown sugar
- ¾ teaspoon Worcestershire sauce
- 1 small garlic clove, minced
- 2 large hamburger buns, toasted if desired

1. Place beef on rimmed baking sheet in single layer. Freeze beef until very firm and starting to harden around edges but still pliable, about 25 minutes.

2. Pulse half of beef in food processor until finely ground into ¹⁄₁₆-inch pieces, about 35 pulses, scraping down sides of bowl as needed to ensure that beef is evenly ground. Return ground beef to empty side of sheet. Repeat with remaining half of beef; return to sheet. Spread ground beef on sheet and inspect carefully, removing any long strands of gristle and large chunks of hard meat or fat.

3. Adjust oven rack to middle position and heat oven to 300 degrees. Drizzle melted butter over ground beef and add ½ teaspoon pepper. Toss gently with fork to combine, being careful not to overwork meat. Divide meat mixture into 2 lightly packed balls, and gently flatten each ball into ¾-inch-thick patty.

4. Sprinkle patties with salt and ¼ teaspoon pepper. Heat oil in 10-inch skillet over high heat until just smoking. Using spatula, place burgers in skillet and cook without moving for 2 minutes. Flip burgers and continue to cook for 2 minutes. Transfer patties to clean, dry rimmed baking sheet and bake until burgers register 120 to 125 degrees (for medium-rare), 3 to 6 minutes. Transfer burgers to plate and let rest for 5 minutes.

5. Whisk mayonnaise, soy sauce, chives, sugar, Worcestershire, garlic, and remaining ¼ teaspoon pepper together in bowl. Serve burgers on buns with sauce.

Juicy Pub-Style Burgers with Peppered Bacon and Aged Cheddar

While beef is in freezer, sprinkle ½ teaspoon coarsely ground pepper over 3 slices bacon. Cook bacon in 10-inch skillet over medium heat until crispy, about 10 minutes. Using slotted spoon, transfer bacon to paper towel–lined plate; cut bacon in half crosswise. Pour off all but 1 teaspoon fat from skillet; substitute bacon fat for vegetable oil. Top each burger with ¼ cup shredded aged cheddar cheese before transferring to oven. Top burgers with sauce and bacon just before serving.

Juicy Pub-Style Burgers with Crispy Shallots and Blue Cheese

While beef is in freezer, heat ⅓ cup vegetable oil and 2 thinly sliced shallots in small saucepan over medium-high heat. Cook, stirring frequently, until shallots are golden, 6 to 8 minutes. Using slotted spoon, transfer shallots to paper towel–lined plate and season with salt to taste. Proceed with recipe, topping each burger with ¼ cup crumbled blue cheese before transferring to oven. Top burgers with sauce and crispy shallots just before serving.

Turkey Burgers

Serves 2   FAST

Total time 30 minutes

WHY THIS RECIPE WORKS In theory, turkey burgers are an easy, healthy weeknight meal, but in practice they often turn out bland, dry, and boring. To keep our turkey burgers moist and tender, we mixed a panade—a paste of bread and milk—into the ground turkey. Pantry-friendly Worcestershire sauce and Dijon mustard gave the burgers a complex meaty flavor. To cook the burgers to a safe temperature without burning them or drying out the meat, we first seared the burgers to ensure they got nicely browned, then we partially covered the pan and turned the heat to low during the last few minutes of cooking to cook them through gently. Be sure to use ground turkey, not ground turkey breast (also labeled 99 percent fat free), in this recipe. Serve with your favorite burger toppings.

½ slice hearty white sandwich bread, crusts removed, torn into quarters
1 tablespoon whole milk
12 ounces ground turkey
1 teaspoon Worcestershire sauce
1 teaspoon Dijon mustard
¼ teaspoon table salt
⅛ teaspoon pepper
1 tablespoon vegetable oil
2 large hamburger buns, toasted if desired

1. Mash bread and milk into paste with fork in large bowl. Using your hands, mix in ground turkey, Worcestershire, mustard, salt, and pepper until thoroughly combined. Divide meat mixture into 2 lightly packed balls and gently flatten each ball into 1-inch-thick patty.

2. Heat oil in 10-inch nonstick skillet over medium heat until shimmering. Gently place burgers in skillet and cook until lightly browned and crusted on both sides, 3 to 4 minutes per side.

3. Reduce heat to low; partially cover; and cook until burgers register 160 degrees, 8 to 10 minutes, flipping burgers halfway through cooking. Serve burgers on buns.

Turkey Burgers with Olives and Feta

Omit Worcestershire and mustard. Mix 3 tablespoons chopped pitted kalamata olives, ¼ cup crumbled feta cheese, 1 small minced shallot, and 1 minced garlic clove into turkey mixture in step 1.

Make-Ahead Lentil and Mushroom Burgers

Makes 6 patties   VEGETARIAN

Total time 40 minutes

WHY THIS RECIPE WORKS Ever wish that serving up made-from-scratch plant-based burgers was as easy as reaching into the freezer and browning up a couple of frozen patties? These supersavory lentil and mushroom burgers make six patties and can be frozen for up to a month, so you can cook up a couple now and save the rest to enjoy later. We made these patties with earthy brown lentils, bulgur (which absorbs excess moisture), and meaty mushrooms, plus a combo of egg and panko for crumble-proof binding power. Half a cup of buttery cashews added richness and a pleasant chew when ground and mixed into the patties. Don't confuse bulgur with cracked wheat, which has a much longer cooking time and will not work in this recipe. Look for medium-grind bulgur (labeled "#2"), which is roughly the size of mustard seeds. Avoid coarsely ground bulgur; it will not cook through in time. This recipe makes six patties. Two patties are cooked immediately; the remaining four are frozen for later.

8 ounces cremini or white mushrooms, trimmed and quartered
½ cup raw cashews
1 celery rib, cut into 1-inch pieces
1 shallot, quartered
½ cup medium-grind bulgur
¼ cup water
3 tablespoons plus 2 teaspoons extra-virgin olive oil, divided
½ teaspoon table salt
1 (15-ounce) can brown lentils, rinsed
½ cup panko bread crumbs
1 large egg
2 slices (1½ ounces) cheddar or mozzarella cheese (optional)
2 burger buns, toasted if desired
2 leaves Bibb or Boston lettuce
1 small tomato, sliced thin

1. TO MAKE PATTIES Pulse mushrooms, cashews, celery, and shallot in food processor until finely chopped, about 10 pulses, scraping down sides of bowl as needed. Transfer vegetable mixture to large bowl and stir in bulgur, water, 3 tablespoons oil, and salt. Microwave, stirring occasionally, until bulgur is softened and most of liquid has been absorbed, about 6 minutes; let cool slightly.

2. Vigorously stir lentils, panko, and egg into vegetable-bulgur mixture until well combined and mixture forms cohesive mass. Using your moistened hands, divide mixture into 6 equal portions (about ½ cup each), then tightly pack each portion into 3½-inch-wide patty. To freeze up to 6 patties, evenly space patties on parchment paper–lined rimmed baking sheet and freeze until firm, about 1 hour. Stack patties between pieces of parchment, wrap in plastic wrap, and place in zipper-lock freezer bag. (Patties can be frozen for up to 1 month. Do not thaw patties before cooking.)

3. TO COOK PATTIES Heat remaining 2 teaspoons oil in 10- or 12-inch nonstick skillet over medium heat until shimmering. Gently lay 2 patties in skillet and cook until well browned and crispy on first side, 3 to 5 minutes. Using 2 spatulas, gently flip patties; top with cheddar, if using; and cook until well browned and crispy on second side, 3 to 5 minutes. Serve burgers on buns, topped with lettuce and tomato.

Salmon Tacos with Cabbage Slaw and Lime Crema

Serves 2   FAST
Total time 30 minutes

WHY THIS RECIPE WORKS The fish in fish tacos can come in a range of styles but for this recipe we took a simple and healthy approach: simply searing a fillet of salmon. Salmon has so much richness that all we needed to do was rub it with chipotle chile powder and a little salt before we seared it. And because salmon is a good reheater, you can make the slaw and salmon ahead and take them to taco in no time. If using wild salmon, decrease cook time slightly and cook fillet to 120 degrees (for medium-rare).

⅓ cup plain Greek yogurt
½ teaspoon grated lime zest plus 2 tablespoons juice, divided, plus lime wedges for serving
½ teaspoon table salt, divided
1 cup (2 ounces) coleslaw mix
½ small red onion, sliced thin
2 tablespoons fresh cilantro leaves
1 (6-ounce) skin-on salmon fillet, 1 to 1½ inches thick
¼ teaspoon chipotle chile powder
½ teaspoon vegetable oil
6 (6-inch) corn tortillas, warmed

1. Whisk yogurt, ¼ teaspoon lime zest, 1 tablespoon juice, and ⅛ teaspoon salt together in small bowl; set crema aside. Whisk remaining ¼ teaspoon lime zest, remaining 1 tablespoon juice, and ⅛ teaspoon salt together in large bowl. Add coleslaw mix, onion, and cilantro and toss to combine; set slaw aside.

2. Pat salmon dry with paper towels and sprinkle with chile powder and remaining ¼ teaspoon salt. Heat oil in 8- or 10-inch nonstick skillet over medium-high heat until shimmering. Cook salmon, skin side up, until well browned, 3 to 5 minutes. Flip and continue to cook until salmon is still translucent when checked with tip of paring knife and registers 125 degrees (for medium-rare), 3 to 5 minutes.

3. Transfer salmon to plate and let cool slightly, about 2 minutes. Using 2 forks, flake salmon into rough 1-inch pieces; discarding skin. Divide salmon among tortillas, then top with cabbage slaw and drizzle with crema. Serve with lime wedges.

Steak Tacos with Nectarine Salsa

Serves 2

Total time 35 minutes

WHY THIS RECIPE WORKS For hearty and easy-to-make steak tacos, we turned to quick-cooking flank steak, which we rubbed with cumin, paprika, and salt before cooking. And for an appealing and fresh touch we made a nectarine salsa. The nectarines added pleasant sweetness and a lively tang when combined with more assertive ingredients like bell pepper, cilantro, shallot, jalapeño and lime juice. To make this dish spicier, reserve and add the chile seeds. We prefer the steak cooked to medium-rare, but if you prefer it more or less done, see our guidelines on page 161.

- 1 nectarine or peach, halved, pitted, and cut into ¼-inch pieces
- ½ red, orange, or yellow bell pepper, chopped fine
- 2 tablespoons chopped fresh cilantro
- 1 small shallot, minced
- ½ jalapeño pepper, seeded and minced
- 1 tablespoon lime juice, plus lime wedges for serving
- ½ teaspoon table salt, divided
- ⅛ teaspoon pepper
- ½ teaspoon ground cumin
- ½ teaspoon ground paprika
- 6 ounces flank steak, trimmed
- 1 teaspoon vegetable oil
- 6 (6-inch) corn tortillas, warmed (page 124)

1. Combine nectarine, bell pepper, cilantro, shallot, jalapeño, lime juice, ¼ teaspoon salt, and pepper in bowl and toss to combine; set salsa aside.

2. Combine cumin, paprika, and remaining ¼ teaspoon salt in small bowl. Pat steak dry with paper towels and rub with spice mixture.

3. Heat oil in 10- or 12-inch skillet over medium-high heat until just smoking. Add steak and cook until well browned and meat registers 120 to 125 degrees (for medium-rare), 3 to 6 minutes per side. Transfer steak to cutting board, tent loosely with aluminum foil, and let rest for 5 minutes.

4. Slice steak thin against grain. Toss salsa to recombine and season with salt and pepper to taste. Divide steak among tortillas, then top with salsa. Serve with lime wedges.

Steak Tacos with Nectarine Salsa

Steamed Bao with Hoisin
Chicken and Cucumber

Grilled Cheese Sandwich with
Caramelized Onion and Apple

Steamed Bao with Hoisin Chicken and Cucumber

Serves 2

Total time 40 minutes

WHY THIS RECIPE WORKS A beloved street food in many parts of Asia, pleasantly sweet, pillowy stuffed bao buns (here with glazed chicken instead of the traditional pork) are surprisingly easy to make at home. For the appealing chicken filling, we first created a simple hoisin-based sauce in which to cook boneless skinless chicken. Once cooked, we shredded it, returned it to the skillet with the sauce, and let it heat through, adding sesame seeds and scallion greens at the end. We cooked the frozen bao buns in a parchment-lined steamer basket, then filled them with the chicken mixture and topped with thinly sliced cucumber and cilantro. These buns are both beautiful and irresistibly delicious. You can find frozen, presteamed lotus leaf bao, distinguished by their flat and folded shape, at Asian grocery stores and online.

1 teaspoon vegetable oil
2 scallions, white and green parts separated and sliced thin
¼ cup hoisin sauce
2 tablespoons water
1 (6-to 8-ounce) boneless, skinless chicken breast, trimmed
2 teaspoons toasted sesame seeds
6 (1-ounce) frozen lotus leaf bao
¼ English cucumber, quartered lengthwise and sliced thin
½ cup fresh cilantro leaves and stems, trimmed
Lime wedges
Sriracha

1. Heat oil in small saucepan over medium heat until shimmering. Add scallion whites and cook until softened, about 1 minute. Stir in hoisin and water and bring to simmer. Nestle chicken into sauce. Reduce heat to medium-low; cover; and cook until chicken registers 160 degrees, 10 to 12 minutes, flipping chicken halfway through cooking.

2. Remove saucepan from heat. Transfer chicken to cutting board, let cool slightly, then shred into bite-size pieces using 2 forks. Return chicken to saucepan and cook over low heat until sauce is thickened and chicken is heated through, 2 to 4 minutes. Stir in sesame seeds and scallion greens.

3. Cut piece of parchment slightly smaller than diameter of bamboo or collapsible steamer basket; place parchment in basket. Poke 20 small holes in parchment and lightly spray with vegetable oil spray. Place bao on parchment, making sure they are not touching. Set basket over simmering water and cook, covered, until puffed and heated through, 4 to 6 minutes. Remove basket from water and let bao cool for 5 minutes. (Or, wrap frozen bao in damp dish towel. Place on plate and microwave for about 1 minute, flipping halfway through microwaving.) Divide chicken among bao, then top with cucumber and cilantro. Serve with lime wedges and sriracha.

Grilled Cheese Sandwiches with Caramelized Onion and Apple

Serves 2 VEGETARIAN

Total time 45 minutes

WHY THIS RECIPE WORKS These sandwiches are at once sophisticated and easy to make, with sweet quick-caramelized onion, woodsy thyme, tangy mustard, and crisp apple all bound up with cheddar cheese. Weighing the sandwiches down with a heavy Dutch oven helped the cheese melt more thoroughly for mess-free flipping; to save on dishes, we made the sandwiches in the same skillet we used to caramelize the onion. Any variety of sweet apple can be used here. We like to use rustic artisanal bread for this recipe; look for a wide loaf that will yield big slices. Wrap the bottom of your Dutch oven in aluminum foil for easy cleanup. You will need a 12-inch nonstick skillet with a tight-fitting lid for this recipe.

CARAMELIZED ONION

- 2 teaspoons extra-virgin olive oil
- 1 onion, halved and sliced thin
- 6 tablespoons water, divided
- ¼ teaspoon table salt
- ⅛ teaspoon pepper
- 1 teaspoon Dijon mustard
- ¼ teaspoon minced fresh thyme or pinch dried

SANDWICHES

- 4 (½-inch-thick) slices rustic bread
- 2 teaspoons extra-virgin olive oil, divided
- 1 small apple, cored and sliced thin
- 4 slices cheddar cheese

1. FOR THE CARAMELIZED ONION Heat oil in 12-inch nonstick skillet over medium heat until shimmering. Add onion, ¼ cup water, salt, and pepper; cover; and cook until onion has softened and water has evaporated, 5 to 7 minutes. Uncover; reduce heat to medium-low; and continue to cook, stirring occasionally, until onion is golden brown, 13 to 15 minutes.

2. Stir in remaining 2 tablespoons water, scraping up any browned bits, and cook until liquid evaporates, about 1 minute. Off heat, stir in mustard and thyme; transfer to small bowl and let cool slightly. (Caramelized onion can be refrigerated for up to 3 days.)

3. FOR THE SANDWICHES Place bread slices on cutting board and brush each slice with ½ teaspoon oil. Flip 2 slices oil-side down and arrange onion, apple, and cheddar in even layers on top. Arrange remaining 2 slices of bread on top oil-side up.

4. Wipe skillet clean with paper towels. Place sandwiches in now-empty skillet and weigh down with large pot or Dutch oven. Cook (keeping pot on sandwiches, but not pressing down) over medium-low heat until first side is golden brown, 5 to 7 minutes. Using 2 spatulas, carefully flip sandwiches, then replace pot and cook until second side is golden brown, 5 to 7 minutes. Serve.

VARIATION

Grilled Cheese Sandwiches with Tomato and Pesto

Omit caramelized onion. Substitute 4 thin tomato slices for apple and mozzarella for cheddar. Spread 1 tablespoon pesto on non-oiled sides of bread slices before layering tomatoes and mozzarella.

Portobello Panini

Serves 2 VEGETARIAN

Total time 40 minutes

WHY THIS RECIPE WORKS Add fontina cheese, roasted red peppers, and garlic-rosemary mayonnaise to meaty portobellos and you are guaranteed an irresistible sandwich. To ensure that the mushrooms would be tender, we precooked them in a grill pan before assembling and toasting the sandwiches. Using shredded fontina helped speed the melting process and guaranteed an even layer of gooey cheese. A nonstick grill pan and a Dutch oven mimicked the signature marks of a panini press. Wrapping the bottom of your Dutch oven will make for easy cleanup. Do not substitute sandwich bread for the crusty Italian loaf. We like to use rustic, artisanal bread for this recipe; do not use a baguette, but rather look for a wide loaf that will yield big slices. We like the attractive grill marks that a grill pan gives the panini, but you can substitute a 12-inch nonstick skillet.

3 large portobello mushroom caps, halved

2 tablespoons extra-virgin olive oil, divided

¼ teaspoon table salt

⅛ teaspoon pepper

2 tablespoons mayonnaise

2 garlic cloves, minced

1 teaspoon minced fresh rosemary

4 (½-inch-thick) slices crusty bread

4 ounces fontina cheese, shredded (1 cup)

¼ cup jarred roasted red peppers, rinsed, patted dry, and sliced ½ inch thick

1. Preheat 12-inch nonstick grill pan over medium heat for 2 minutes. (Droplets of water should just sizzle when flicked onto pan.) Toss mushrooms, 1 tablespoon oil, salt, and pepper together. Place mushrooms, gill side up, in pan and weight with Dutch oven. Cook until mushrooms are well browned on both sides, about 5 minutes per side. Transfer mushrooms to plate and wipe pan clean.

2. Combine mayonnaise, garlic, and rosemary in bowl. Spread mayonnaise mixture evenly over 1 side of each slice of bread. Assemble 2 sandwiches by layering ingredients as follows between prepared bread (with mayonnaise mixture inside sandwich): half of fontina, cooked mushrooms, red peppers, and remaining fontina. Press gently on sandwiches to set.

3. Reheat now-empty pan over medium heat for 1 minute. Brush outside of sandwiches lightly with remaining 1 table-spoon oil, place sandwiches in pan and weigh down with large pot or Dutch oven. Cook sandwiches until bread is golden brown and crisp on both sides and cheese is melted, about 4 minutes per side. Serve.

A PANINI PRESS ALTERNATIVE

Place sandwiches in hot 12-inch nonstick grill pan or skillet and weight with Dutch oven. Cook until bread is golden and crisp on both sides, flipping sandwiches halfway through cooking.

Tofu Katsu Sandwiches

Serves 2

Total time 35 minutes

WHY THIS RECIPE WORKS Japanese katsu involves frying a thin, panko-breaded cutlet and serving it with a sweet and savory tonkatsu sauce. The sandwiches of the same name add shredded cabbage and layer it all between slices of fluffy milk bread. In this vegetarian take, we recreated the mouthwatering sandwich using tofu "cutlets." To help the panko adhere, we dredged tofu slices in a mixture of flour and egg. For the tonkatsu sauce we combined ketchup, Worcestershire, soy sauce, garlic powder, and a little sugar. The cabbage needed nothing more than a toss with rice vinegar, toasty sesame oil, and a pinch of sugar before it was ready to be piled atop the bread (soft white sandwich bread in lieu of milk bread) and drizzled with sauce. You will need a 10-inch nonstick skillet for this recipe; the tofu won't crisp as evenly in a larger skillet.

2 tablespoons ketchup

2 teaspoons Worcestershire sauce

1 teaspoon soy sauce

½ teaspoon garlic powder

½ teaspoon sugar, divided

1 large egg

1 tablespoon all-purpose flour

⅔ cup panko bread crumbs

7 ounces firm or extra-firm tofu

¼ teaspoon table salt

½ cup vegetable oil, for frying

1¼ teaspoons unseasoned rice vinegar

¾ teaspoon toasted sesame oil

1½ cups shredded red or green cabbage

4 slices soft white sandwich bread

1. Whisk ketchup, Worcestershire, soy sauce, garlic powder, and ¼ teaspoon sugar together in small bowl; set aside.

2. Whisk egg and flour together in shallow dish. Place panko in large zipper-lock bag and lightly crush with rolling pin; transfer crumbs to second shallow dish. Slice tofu length-wise into four ½-inch-thick slabs, pat dry with paper towels, and sprinkle with salt. Working with 1 slab at a time, dip tofu in egg mixture, allowing excess to drip off, then coat all sides with panko, pressing gently to adhere; transfer to large plate.

3. Place wire rack in rimmed baking sheet and line rack with triple layer of paper towels. Heat vegetable oil in 10-inch nonstick skillet over medium-high heat until shimmering. Add tofu and cook until deep golden brown, 2 to 3 minutes per side. Transfer tofu to prepared rack and let drain.

4. Combine vinegar, sesame oil, and remaining ¼ teaspoon sugar in small bowl. Add cabbage, toss to coat, and season with salt and pepper to taste. Arrange cabbage and tofu on 2 slices of bread. Drizzle with reserved sauce and top with remaining bread slices. Serve.

Lamb Pita Sandwiches with Tzatziki

Serves 2 FAST

Total time 30 minutes

WHY THIS RECIPE WORKS We wanted a shawarma-style sandwich with straight-off-the-rotisserie flavor, but without constructing an actual at-home vertical rotisserie (or ordering takeout). Our solution? Creating cinnamon- and garlic-spiked lamb patties that we seared in a hot nonstick skillet. This cooking method developed a flavorful crust on both sides, mimicking the deeply savory exterior achieved from a restaurant-style roaster. A quick tzatziki sauce of Greek yogurt, cooling cucumber, lemon juice, garlic, and fresh herbs completed this stunner.

¼ cup plain Greek yogurt

½ cucumber, ¼ cucumber grated and ¼ cucumber sliced thin, divided

½ teaspoon minced fresh mint or dill

1 garlic clove, minced, divided

⅛ teaspoon plus ½ teaspoon table salt, divided

12 ounces ground lamb

½ teaspoon ground cinnamon

⅛ teaspoon pepper

1 teaspoon vegetable oil

2 (8-inch) pita breads

½ romaine lettuce heart (3 ounces), sliced thin

4 thin slices tomato

1. Combine yogurt, grated cucumber, mint, half of garlic, and ⅛ teaspoon salt in bowl; cover and refrigerate tzatziki until ready to serve. Break up ground lamb into small pieces in bowl, then add cinnamon, pepper, remaining garlic, and remaining ½ teaspoon salt. Lightly knead with hands until combined. Pinch off and shape mixture into six ½-inch-thick patties.

2. Heat oil in 12-inch nonstick skillet over medium-high heat until just smoking. Add patties and cook until well browned on first side, about 4 minutes. Flip patties, reduce heat to medium, and cook until well browned on second side and tender through-out, about 4 minutes. Transfer to paper towel–lined plate.

Lamb Pita Sandwiches with Tzatziki

3. Cut top 2 inches from pitas; discard or reserve for other use. Place pitas on plate, cover, and microwave until warm, about 30 seconds. Spread half of tzatziki inside each pita, then fill each with half of lettuce, sliced cucumber, tomato, and lamb patties. Serve.

Basic Pizza Dough

Makes 8 ounces dough VEGETARIAN

Total time 1¼ hours

WHY THIS RECIPE WORKS We wanted a recipe for a great-tasting pizza dough that would make just enough for a small pizza or a large calzone. The first key was getting the right ratio of flour to water. High-protein bread flour ensured our dough baked up chewy with a crisp crust. A little olive oil added richness and made the dough easier to roll out. All-purpose flour can be substituted for the bread flour, but the resulting crust will be a little less chewy. If desired, you can slow down the dough's rising time by letting it rise in the refrigerator for 8 to 16 hours in step 2; let the refrigerated dough soften at room temperature for 30 minutes before using.

Easy Skillet
Cheese Pizza

1 cup (5½ ounces) bread flour, plus extra
    as needed
¾ teaspoon instant or rapid-rise yeast
½ teaspoon table salt
1½ teaspoons extra-virgin olive oil
7 tablespoons warm water (110 degrees)

1. Process flour, yeast, and salt in food processor until combined, about 2 seconds. With processor running, slowly add oil, then water, and process until dough forms sticky ball that clears sides of bowl, 1½ to 2 minutes. (If, after 1 minute, dough is sticky and clings to blade, add extra flour, 1 tablespoon at a time, as needed until it clears sides of bowl.)

2. Transfer dough to lightly floured counter and shape into tight ball. Place dough in large, lightly oiled bowl and cover tightly with greased plastic wrap. Let rise at room temperature until doubled in size, 1 to 1½ hours.

VARIATION
Whole-Wheat Pizza Dough
Substitute ½ cup whole-wheat flour for ½ cup of bread flour.

Easy Skillet Cheese Pizza
Serves 2 | VEGETARIAN
Total time 45 minutes

WHY THIS RECIPE WORKS We wanted to come up with an easier, quicker way to make pizza at home. Our idea was to build the pizza in a skillet, give the crust a jump start with heat from the stovetop, then transfer it to the oven to cook through—no pizza stone required. We oiled the skillet to keep the dough from sticking and to encourage browning, then we added the dough and turned up the heat. A simple no-cook sauce of diced tomatoes, olive oil, and garlic and a combination of mozzarella and a little Parmesan were all the toppings this easy pizza needed. You can substitute 8 ounces of store-bought pizza dough for the dough in this recipe. Let the dough sit out at room temperature while preparing the remaining ingredients and heating the oven.

3 tablespoons extra-virgin olive oil, divided
½ cup canned diced tomatoes, drained with juice reserved
1 small garlic clove, minced
⅛ teaspoon table salt
1 recipe Basic Pizza Dough (page 101),
    room temperature
4 ounces whole-milk mozzarella cheese, shredded (1 cup)
2 tablespoons grated Parmesan cheese

1. Adjust oven rack to upper-middle position and heat oven to 500 degrees. Grease 12-inch ovensafe skillet with 2 tablespoons oil.

2. Pulse tomatoes, garlic, salt, and remaining 1 tablespoon oil together in food processor until coarsely ground, about 12 pulses. Transfer mixture to liquid measuring cup and add reserved tomato juice until sauce measures ½ cup.

3. Place dough on lightly floured counter. Press and roll dough into 11-inch round. Transfer dough to prepared skillet; reshape as needed. Spread sauce over dough, leaving ½-inch border at edge. Sprinkle mozzarella and Parmesan evenly over sauce.

4. Set skillet over high heat and cook until outside edge of dough is set, pizza is lightly puffed, and bottom crust is spotty brown when gently lifted with spatula, about 3 minutes.

5. Transfer pizza to oven and bake until crust is brown and cheese is golden in spots, 7 to 10 minutes. Using potholders (skillet handle will be hot), remove skillet from oven and slide pizza onto cutting board. Let pizza cool for 5 minutes before slicing and serving.

VARIATIONS
Easy Skillet Pizza with Fontina, Arugula, and Prosciutto
Toss 1 cup baby arugula with 2 teaspoons extra-virgin olive oil and salt and pepper to taste in bowl. Omit Parmesan and substitute 1 cup shredded fontina for mozzarella. Immediately after baking, sprinkle 2 ounces thinly sliced prosciutto, cut into ½-inch strips, and dressed arugula over top of pizza.

Easy Skillet Pizza with Goat Cheese, Olives, and Spicy Garlic Oil
Mix 1 tablespoon olive oil, 1 minced small garlic clove, and ⅛ teaspoon red pepper flakes together in bowl. Brush garlic-oil mixture over top of pizza dough before adding sauce in step 3. Omit Parmesan and reduce amount of mozzarella to ¼ cup. Sprinkle ½ cup crumbled goat cheese and ¼ cup pitted and halved kalamata olives on top of mozzarella before baking.

Easy Skillet Pizza with Ricotta, Bacon, and Scallions
Cook 2 slices bacon, cut into ¼-inch pieces, in 8-inch skillet over medium heat until crispy, 5 to 7 minutes. Using slotted spoon, transfer bacon to paper towel–lined plate. Mix ½ cup whole-milk ricotta, 1 thinly sliced scallion, ⅛ teaspoon salt, and pinch pepper together in bowl. Omit Parmesan and reduce amount of mozzarella to ¼ cup. Dollop ricotta mixture, 1 tablespoon at a time, on top of mozzarella, then sprinkle with bacon. Sprinkle pizza with 1 more sliced scallion before serving.

PIZZA 101

Making your own pizza should be fun, not stressful. Here are some of our favorite tips for easy, parlor-worthy pizza.

EASY CHEESE SHREDDING Use a clean plastic bag (a large zipper-lock bag works best) to hold the grater and the cheese. By placing the bag around both, you can grate without getting your hands dirty, and you don't have to worry about rogue pieces flying off into your kitchen. The best part? Leftover shredded cheese is ready for storage, no transfer needed.

KEEP TOPPINGS ON HAND Homemade pizza is like a blank canvas for the creative use of myriad toppings. The problem is that you don't always have that many topping options on hand. Try this simple solution: Whenever cooking something such as roasted red peppers, caramelized onions, or sausage, reserve some in a plastic container, label it, and freeze it. The next time you're making pizza, simply defrost and top away.

NO PEEL? NO STONE? NO PROBLEM A baking stone is a terrific investment if you enjoy making bread and pizza, and a peel makes the process easier. But you can also make do with rimless or inverted baking sheets for both the stone and the peel. To improvise a baking stone, preheat a rimless or inverted baking sheet for 30 minutes. As for an improvised peel, simply cover a rimless or overturned baking sheet with parchment paper, shape and top the pizza on the parchment, and slide it directly onto the hot, preheated stone (or baking sheet).

CLEAN CUTTING GUARANTEED If you use a knife to cut pizza, you risk pulling cheese in every direction. A pizza wheel negates this risk. In search of one large and sharp enough to glide through thick and thin crusts without dislodging toppings, we tested five types: three with stainless-steel blades, one with polycarbonate plastic, and one dual wheel. For overall comfort, extreme sharpness, and heft, one pizza wheel was named the test kitchen's favorite. The **OXO Good Grips 4-Inch Pizza Wheel** won points for its thumb guard; the large, soft handle that absorbed extra pressure; and its well-designed wheel, which was easy to clean and safe for nonstick surfaces.

Ultimate Thin-Crust Pizza

Serves 2   VEGETARIAN

Total time 1 hour 40 minutes, plus 24 hours chilling

WHY THIS RECIPE WORKS With home ovens that reach only 500 degrees and dough that's impossible to stretch thin, even the savviest cooks can struggle to produce New York–style parlor-quality pizza. High-protein bread flour gave us a chewy tanned pizza crust, and the right ratio of flour, water, and yeast gave us dough that stretched and retained moisture as it baked. We kneaded the dough quickly in a food processor, then let it proof overnight in the refrigerator to develop its flavors. After we shaped and topped the pizza, it went onto a blazing hot baking stone to cook. Placing the stone near the top of the oven allowed the top of the pizza to brown as well as the bottom. If you don't have a peel or a stone, see Pizza 101 for alternatives. It is important to use ice water to prevent overheating the dough while in the food processor.

DOUGH

1½ cups (8¼ ounces) bread flour
1 teaspoon sugar
¼ teaspoon instant or rapid-rise yeast
⅔ cup ice water
1½ teaspoons vegetable oil
¾ teaspoon table salt

SAUCE

½ cup canned whole peeled tomatoes, drained
1 teaspoon extra-virgin olive oil
1 small garlic clove, minced
¼ teaspoon red wine vinegar
¼ teaspoon dried oregano
⅛ teaspoon table salt
⅛ teaspoon pepper

¼ cup grated Parmesan cheese
4 ounces whole-milk mozzarella cheese, shredded (1 cup)

1. FOR THE DOUGH Process flour, sugar, and yeast in food processor until combined, about 2 seconds. With processor running, slowly add water and process until dough is just combined and no dry flour remains, about 10 seconds. Let dough sit for 10 minutes.

2. Add oil and salt to dough and process until dough forms satiny, sticky ball that clears sides of bowl, about 30 seconds. Transfer dough to lightly oiled counter and knead briefly until smooth, about 1 minute. Shape dough into tight ball, place in large, lightly oiled bowl, and cover tightly with greased plastic wrap. Refrigerate for at least 24 hours or up to 3 days.

3. FOR THE SAUCE Process all ingredients together in food processor until smooth, about 15 seconds, scraping down sides of bowl as needed. Transfer to bowl and refrigerate until ready to use.

4. One hour before baking, position oven rack 4½ inches from top of oven, set baking stone on rack, and heat oven to 500 degrees. Meanwhile, place dough on lightly oiled baking sheet, cover loosely with lightly greased plastic, and let sit at room temperature for 1 hour.

5. Coat dough generously with flour and place on well-floured counter. Using your fingertips, gently flatten into 8-inch disk, leaving 1 inch of outer edge slightly thicker than center. Using your hands, gently stretch disk into 12-inch round, working along edge and giving disk quarter-turns as you stretch.

6. Transfer dough to well-floured peel and stretch into 13-inch round. Spread tomato sauce over dough, leaving ¼-inch border around edge. Sprinkle Parmesan evenly over sauce, followed by mozzarella.

7. Carefully slide pizza onto stone and bake until crust is well browned and cheese is bubbly and beginning to brown, 10 to 12 minutes, rotating pizza halfway through baking. Transfer pizza to wire rack and let cool for 5 minutes. Slice and serve.

SHAPING THIN-CRUST PIZZA

Flatten dough into 8-inch disk on floured counter, leaving edge slightly thicker. Stretch into 12-inch round, giving dough quarter turns. Transfer dough to floured peel and stretch into 13-inch round.

Spinach Calzone

Spinach Calzone

Serves 2 | **VEGETARIAN**

Total time 50 minutes

WHY THIS RECIPE WORKS With soggy fillings and bready crusts, bad calzones are a dime a dozen. We wanted to balance a crisp crust with plenty of chew and a hearty proportion of rich, creamy, flavorful filling. A combination of ricotta and mozzarella plus a little flavorful Parmesan cheese made for an indulgently cheesy filling. Frozen spinach was an easy addition; carefully squeezing it dry kept it from watering down the filling. We bumped up the flavor with garlic, oregano, and red pepper flakes and added an egg yolk to help bind everything together. Cutting vents in the dough let off some steam, and cooling the calzone on a wire rack prevented a soggy bottom. You can substitute 8 ounces of store-bought pizza dough for the dough in this recipe. Let the dough sit out at room temperature while preparing the remaining ingredients and heating the oven; otherwise, it will be difficult to stretch. Serve with your favorite tomato sauce.

5 ounces frozen spinach, thawed and squeezed dry

4 ounces (½ cup) whole-milk ricotta cheese

2 ounces mozzarella cheese, shredded (½ cup)

¼ cup Parmesan cheese, grated

1 tablespoon extra-virgin olive oil

1 large egg yolk, plus 1 large egg, lightly beaten with 2 tablespoons water, divided

1 garlic clove, minced

¼ teaspoon table salt

Pinch pepper

Pinch dried oregano

Pinch red pepper flakes (optional)

1 recipe Basic Pizza Dough (page 101), room temperature

1. Adjust oven rack to lower-middle position and heat oven to 500 degrees. Cut one 9-inch-square piece of parchment paper. Combine spinach, ricotta, mozzarella, Parmesan, oil, egg yolk, garlic, salt, pepper, oregano, and pepper flakes, if using, in bowl.

2. Place dough on lightly floured counter. Press and roll dough into 9-inch round. Transfer dough to parchment square and reshape as needed.

3. Spread spinach filling evenly over bottom half of dough round, leaving 1-inch border at edge. Brush edge with some of egg wash. Fold top half of dough over bottom half, leaving ½-inch border of bottom layer uncovered. Press edges of dough together and crimp to seal.

4. With sharp knife, cut 5 steam vents, about 1½ inches long, in top layer of dough. Brush with remaining egg wash. Slide calzone (still on parchment) onto baking sheet, trimming parchment as needed to fit. Bake until golden brown, about 15 minutes, rotating sheet halfway through baking. Transfer calzone to wire rack and let cool for 5 minutes before slicing and serving.

VARIATIONS

Sausage and Broccoli Rabe Calzone

Omit spinach. Microwave 2 ounces Italian sausage, casings removed and broken into ½-inch pieces, with 4 ounces broccoli rabe, trimmed and cut into 1-inch pieces, and 1 tablespoon water in covered bowl until sausage is no longer pink and broccoli rabe is crisp-tender, about 4 minutes. Drain mixture well, let cool slightly, and add to ricotta mixture.

Meat Lover's Calzone

Omit spinach and salt. Arrange 2 ounces thinly sliced salami, 2 ounces thinly sliced capicola, and 1 ounce thinly sliced pepperoni, all cut into quarters, between double layer of coffee filters on plate. Microwave until fat begins to render, about 30 seconds. Add microwaved meats and 1 tablespoon chopped fresh basil to ricotta mixture.

ASSEMBLING CALZONE

1. Place filling in center of bottom half of dough round. Spread or press filling in even layer over bottom half of dough round, leaving 1-inch border at edge.

2. Brush bottom edge with egg wash. Fold top half of dough over filling, leaving ½-inch border of bottom dough uncovered. Lightly press edges of dough together to seal.

3. Starting at 1 end of seam, place your index finger diagonally across edge and gently pull bottom layer of dough over tip of your finger; press into dough to seal.

4. Cut 5 steam vents, about 1½ inches long, across top of calzone. Cut through only top layer of dough.

Salami, Capicola, and Provolone Stromboli

Serves 2

Total time 1 hour 10 minutes

WHY THIS RECIPE WORKS With a crisp, golden-brown exterior and a layered meat and cheese filling, stromboli makes a great casual dinner. We wanted a streamlined recipe that had a flavorful filling, a crispy crust, and a properly cooked interior. A combination of salami, capicola, and provolone cheese plus jarred roasted red peppers made an easy, no-prep filling with bold flavor. Patting the peppers dry kept their liquid from turning the stromboli soggy. You can substitute 8 ounces of store-bought pizza dough for the dough in this recipe. Let the dough sit out at room temperature while preparing the remaining ingredients and heating the oven; otherwise, it will be difficult to stretch. Serve with your favorite tomato sauce.

  1 recipe Basic Pizza Dough (page 101),
      room temperature
  2 ounces thinly sliced deli salami
  2 ounces thinly sliced deli capicola
  2 ounces thinly sliced deli provolone cheese
  ¼ cup jarred roasted red peppers, rinsed, patted dry,
      and sliced thin
  ¼ cup grated Parmesan cheese
  1 large egg, lightly beaten with 2 tablespoons water
  1 teaspoon sesame seeds
      Kosher salt (optional)

1. Adjust oven rack to middle position and heat oven to 400 degrees. Spray rimmed baking sheet with vegetable oil spray.

2. Place dough on lightly floured counter. Press and roll dough into 10 by 7½-inch rectangle, about ¼ inch thick, with long side facing you.

3. Lay salami, capicola, and provolone over dough, leaving ¾-inch border at edge. Top with red peppers and Parmesan. Brush edge with some of egg wash. Starting from long side, roll dough tightly into long cylinder, then pinch seam and ends to seal. Transfer stromboli to prepared baking sheet, seam side down.

4. Brush top of stromboli with remaining egg wash and sprinkle with sesame seeds and salt, if using. Cover loosely with greased aluminum foil and bake for 15 minutes. Remove foil and continue to bake until crust is golden, about 20 minutes, rotating sheet halfway through baking. Transfer stromboli to wire rack and let cool for 5 minutes before slicing and serving.

ASSEMBLING STROMBOLI

1. Place dough on lightly floured counter. Press and roll dough into 10 by 7½-inch rectangle, about ¼ inch thick, with long side facing you.

2. Arrange meat and provolone over dough, leaving ¾-inch border at edge. Top with red peppers and Parmesan, then brush edge with egg wash.

3. Starting from long side, roll dough tightly into long cylinder.

4. Pinch seam and ends of dough to seal them securely.

VARIATION

Ham and Cheddar Stromboli

Swiss cheese also works well here.

Omit Parmesan. Substitute 4 ounces thinly sliced deli ham for salami and capicola and 2 ounces thinly sliced deli cheddar for provolone. After laying ham on dough in step 3, spread with 1 tablespoon yellow mustard, then top with cheddar. Substitute 1 small dill pickle, cut into matchsticks and patted dry, for red peppers.

CHAPTER 5

Chicken

▪ **FAST** (Start to finish in 30 minutes or less)

Opposite: Pomegranate Chicken with Farro and Cucumber Salad

Chicken Saltimbocca

Serves 2

Total time 45 minutes

WHY THIS RECIPE WORKS Chicken saltimbocca—a spin on veal saltimbocca—sounds promising, but most versions take this dish too far from its roots. We wanted to give each of its three main elements—chicken, prosciutto, and sage—their due. Starting with already thin chicken cutlets made this recipe quick cooking, and we floured the chicken to brown evenly and prevent gummy, uncooked spots. We used thinly sliced prosciutto, which prevented its flavor from overwhelming the dish. A single fried sage leaf is the usual garnish, but we wanted more sage flavor, so we also sprinkled some minced fresh sage over the floured chicken before adding the prosciutto. Most supermarkets carry chicken cutlets, but if you can't find them (or they look ragged), simply buy two boneless, skinless chicken breasts and slice your own. Make sure to buy prosciutto that is thinly sliced, but not shaved. The prosciutto slices should be large enough to fully cover one side of each cutlet; if the slices are too large, simply cut them down to size. If you prefer not to make the garnish, leave out the four fresh sage leaves and skip step 2.

¼ cup plus ½ teaspoon all-purpose flour, divided
4 (4-ounce) chicken cutlets, ¼ inch thick, trimmed
¼ teaspoon pepper
2 teaspoons minced fresh sage, plus 4 large fresh leaves
4 thin slices prosciutto (1½ ounces)
2 tablespoons extra-virgin olive oil, plus extra as needed
1 small shallot, minced
⅓ cup chicken broth
¼ cup dry vermouth or dry white wine
1 tablespoon unsalted butter, chilled
2 teaspoons minced fresh parsley
1 teaspoon lemon juice

1. Spread ¼ cup flour in shallow dish. Pat chicken dry with paper towels and sprinkle with pepper. Working with 1 cutlet at a time, dredge cutlets in flour. Sprinkle 1 side of each cutlet with minced sage, then top with 1 slice prosciutto and press firmly to help it adhere.

2. Heat oil in 12-inch skillet over medium-high heat until shimmering. Add sage leaves and cook until leaves begin to change color and are fragrant, 15 to 20 seconds. Using slotted spoon, transfer fried sage leaves to paper towel–lined plate.

3. Lay cutlets, prosciutto side down, in oil left in skillet and cook over medium-high heat until golden brown on first side, about 2 minutes. Flip cutlets and continue to cook until lightly browned on second side, about 1 minute; transfer to plate and tent loosely with aluminum foil.

4. Pour off all but 1 teaspoon oil from skillet (or add more oil, if necessary). Add shallot and cook over medium heat until softened, about 2 minutes. Stir in remaining ½ teaspoon flour and cook for 1 minute. Whisk in broth and vermouth, scraping up any browned bits and smoothing out any lumps. Bring to simmer and cook until sauce is slightly thickened and reduced to ⅓ cup, 3 to 5 minutes.

5. Return cutlets to skillet, prosciutto side up, along with any accumulated juices, and simmer until heated through, about 30 seconds; transfer cutlets to serving platter. Off heat, whisk butter, parsley, and lemon juice into sauce and season with salt and pepper to taste. Pour sauce over cutlets, garnish with fried sage leaves, and serve.

MAKING CHICKEN CUTLETS

You can buy packaged chicken cutlets at the supermarket. But if they look ragged or are uneven in thickness, you can easily make your own using two 8-ounce boneless, skinless chicken breasts.

1. If small strip of meat (tenderloin) is loosely attached to underside of breast, simply pull it off and reserve for another use.

2. Lay chicken smooth side up on cutting board. With your hand on top of chicken, carefully slice it in half horizontally to yield 2 pieces between ⅜ and ½ inch thick.

3. Lay each cutlet between 2 sheets of plastic wrap and pound with meat pounder or small skillet until roughly ¼ inch thick.

Sautéed Chicken Breasts with White Wine and Herb Pan Sauce

Serves 2

Total time 50 minutes

WHY THIS RECIPE WORKS Nothing dresses up a simple sautéed chicken breast like a good pan sauce. We wanted an elegant, easy chicken dinner with a white wine and herb sauce. We pounded the breasts, which ensured even cooking, and dredged them in flour for a golden-brown crust and plenty of flavorful fond to use as a base for the sauce. We sautéed a minced shallot and then deglazed the skillet with wine and chicken broth. A little flour thickened the sauce, then we finished it with a pat of butter and some fresh parsley. Since we were only cooking enough for two, we were able to cook everything in one batch in a 10-inch skillet, making this already simple dish even faster and easier.

- ¼ cup plus ½ teaspoon all-purpose flour, divided
- 2 (6- to 8-ounce) boneless, skinless chicken breasts, trimmed and pounded to even thickness
- ¼ teaspoon table salt
- ⅛ teaspoon pepper
- 2 tablespoons vegetable oil, divided
- 1 small shallot, minced
- ½ cup chicken broth
- ¼ cup dry white wine or dry vermouth
- 1 tablespoon unsalted butter, chilled
- 2 teaspoons minced fresh parsley or tarragon

1. Spread ¼ cup flour in shallow dish. Pat chicken dry with paper towels and sprinkle with salt and pepper. Working with 1 breast at a time, dredge breasts in flour.

2. Heat 1 tablespoon oil in 10-inch skillet over medium-high heat until just smoking. Lay chicken in skillet and cook until well browned on first side, 6 to 8 minutes. Flip chicken; reduce heat to medium; and continue to cook until chicken registers 160 degrees, 6 to 8 minutes; transfer to serving platter and tent loosely with aluminum foil.

3. Heat remaining 1 tablespoon oil in now-empty skillet over medium heat until shimmering. Add shallot and cook until softened, about 2 minutes. Stir in remaining ½ teaspoon flour and cook for 1 minute. Whisk in broth and wine, scraping up any browned bits and smoothing out any lumps. Bring to simmer and cook until sauce is slightly thickened, about 5 minutes. Stir in any accumulated chicken juices and simmer for 30 seconds. Off heat, whisk in butter and parsley and season with salt and pepper to taste. Pour sauce over chicken and serve.

Sautéed Chicken Breasts with White Wine and Herb Pan Sauce

Quick Salsa Verde

Makes 1 cup   FAST

Total time 10 minutes

This zippy sauce is incredible and brings a welcome brightness to chicken or fish.

- 1 cup minced fresh parsley
- ½ cup extra-virgin olive oil
- 2 tablespoons capers, rinsed and minced
- 4 teaspoons lemon juice
- 2 anchovy fillets, rinsed and minced
- 1 garlic clove, minced
- ¼ teaspoon table salt

Whisk all ingredients together in bowl. (Salsa verde can be refrigerated for up to 2 days. Bring to room temperature and whisk to recombine before serving.)

Chicken Marsala

Serves 2

Total time 55 minutes

WHY THIS RECIPE WORKS Chicken Marsala is an Italian restaurant standby, and we wanted a home version that rivaled the one at our favorite restaurant—with juicy chicken, meaty mushrooms, and a well-balanced Marsala sauce. We began by testing cooking methods. We found that the classic method of sautéing the meat, removing it from the pan, and then building a sauce from the browned bits left in the pan proved best. We also liked the flavor of a chopped onion added in with the mushrooms. For the sauce, we liked sweet Marsala (rather than dry) for its depth of flavor and smooth finish. We finished our sauce with butter for silky richness and added a dash of fresh parsley.

¼ cup plus ½ teaspoon all-purpose flour, divided

2 (6- to 8-ounce) boneless, skinless chicken breasts, trimmed and pounded to even thickness

¼ teaspoon table salt

⅛ teaspoon pepper

1 tablespoon vegetable oil

3 tablespoons unsalted butter, chilled, divided

4 ounces white mushrooms, trimmed and sliced thin

1 small onion, chopped coarse

1 garlic clove, minced

½ cup sweet Marsala

¼ cup chicken broth

1 tablespoon minced fresh parsley

1. Spread ¼ cup flour in shallow dish. Pat chicken dry with paper towels and sprinkle with salt and pepper. Working with 1 breast at a time, dredge breasts in flour.

2. Heat oil in 10-inch skillet over medium-high heat until just smoking. Lay chicken in skillet and cook until well browned on first side, 6 to 8 minutes. Flip chicken; reduce heat to medium; and continue to cook until chicken registers 160 degrees, 6 to 8 minutes; transfer to plate and tent loosely with aluminum foil.

3. Melt 1 tablespoon butter in now-empty skillet over medium heat. Add mushrooms and onion and cook until mushrooms have released their liquid and vegetables are softened and lightly browned, 5 to 7 minutes. Stir in garlic and cook until fragrant, about 30 seconds; transfer mixture to bowl.

4. Add remaining ½ teaspoon flour to again-empty skillet and cook over medium heat for 1 minute. Whisk in Marsala and broth, scraping up any browned bits and smoothing out any lumps. Bring to simmer and cook until sauce is slightly thickened, about 5 minutes. Return chicken along with any accumulated juices to skillet and simmer until heated through, about

Chicken Marsala

1 minute; transfer chicken to serving platter. Off heat, whisk mushroom mixture, remaining 2 tablespoons butter, and parsley into sauce and season with salt and pepper to taste. Pour sauce over chicken and serve.

Chicken Piccata

Serves 2

Total time 50 minutes

WHY THIS RECIPE WORKS Chicken piccata is a simple dish that should be easy to get right. But many recipes miss the mark with extraneous ingredients or paltry amounts of lemon juice and capers. We wanted properly cooked chicken and a streamlined sauce that would keep the star ingredients at the forefront. To ensure the chicken cooked evenly, we pounded the breasts and then sautéed them in one batch in a 10-inch skillet. For bold lemon flavor that wasn't harsh or overly acidic, we simmered strips of lemon zest in the sauce and added lemon juice at the end of cooking to keep its flavor bright. A generous 1 tablespoon of capers perfectly balanced the rich sauce.

¼ cup plus ½ teaspoon all-purpose flour, divided

2 (6- to 8-ounce) boneless, skinless chicken breasts, trimmed and pounded to even thickness

¼ teaspoon table salt

⅛ teaspoon pepper

2 tablespoons vegetable oil, divided

1 small shallot, minced

1 garlic clove, minced

½ cup chicken broth

¼ cup dry white wine

2 (2-inch) strips lemon zest plus 1 tablespoon juice

1 tablespoon capers, rinsed

1 tablespoon unsalted butter, chilled

1 tablespoon minced fresh parsley

1. Spread ¼ cup flour in shallow dish. Pat chicken dry with paper towels and sprinkle with salt and pepper. Working with 1 breast at a time, dredge breasts in flour.

2. Heat 1 tablespoon oil in 10-inch skillet over medium-high heat until just smoking. Lay chicken in skillet and cook until well browned on first side, 6 to 8 minutes. Flip chicken; reduce heat to medium; and continue to cook until chicken registers 160 degrees, 6 to 8 minutes; transfer to serving platter and tent loosely with aluminum foil.

3. Heat remaining 1 tablespoon oil in now-empty skillet over medium heat until shimmering. Add shallot and cook until softened, about 2 minutes. Stir in garlic and cook until fragrant, about 30 seconds. Stir in remaining ½ teaspoon flour and cook for 1 minute. Whisk in broth, wine, lemon zest, and capers, scraping up any browned bits and smoothing out any lumps. Bring to simmer and cook until sauce is slightly thickened, about 5 minutes. Stir in any accumulated chicken juices and simmer for 30 seconds. Off heat, discard zest and whisk in butter, parsley, and lemon juice. Season with salt and pepper to taste. Pour sauce over chicken and serve.

MAKING ZEST STRIPS

Use vegetable peeler to remove long, wide strips of citrus zest from fruit. Try not to remove any white pith beneath zest, as it is bitter.

CHICKEN SAFETY AND HANDLING

It's important to follow some basic safety procedures when storing, handling, and cooking chicken.

REFRIGERATING Keep chicken refrigerated until just before cooking. Bacteria thrive at temperatures between 40 and 140 degrees. This means leftovers should also be promptly refrigerated.

FREEZING AND THAWING Chicken can be frozen in its original packaging or after repackaging. If you are freezing it for longer than two months, rewrap (or wrap over packaging) with foil or plastic wrap, or place inside a zipper-lock freezer bag. You can keep chicken frozen for several months, but after two months the texture and flavor will suffer. Don't thaw frozen chicken on the counter; this puts it at risk of growing bacteria. Thaw it in its packaging in the refrigerator overnight (in a container to catch its juices), or in the sink under cold running water. Count on one day of defrosting in the refrigerator for every 4 pounds of bird.

HANDLING RAW CHICKEN When handling raw chicken, make sure to wash hands, knives, cutting boards, and counters (and anything else that has come into contact with the raw bird, its juices, or your hands) with hot, soapy water. Be careful not to let the chicken, its juices, or your unwashed hands touch foods that will be eaten raw. When seasoning raw chicken, touching the saltshaker or pepper mill can lead to cross-contamination. To avoid this, set aside the necessary salt and pepper before handling the chicken.

RINSING The U.S. Department of Agriculture advises against washing chicken. Rinsing chicken will not remove or kill much bacteria, and the splashing of water around the sink can spread the bacteria found in raw chicken.

COOKING AND LEFTOVERS Chicken should be cooked to an internal temperature of 160 degrees to ensure any bacteria have been killed (however, we prefer the flavor and texture of thigh meat cooked to 175 degrees). Leftover cooked chicken should be refrigerated and consumed within three days.

Crispy Chicken Breasts

Serves 2   FAST

Total time 30 minutes

WHY THIS RECIPE WORKS For a foolproof recipe for this classic comfort food, we started with a standard flour, egg wash, and bread-crumb coating. We found that ultracrisp panko bread crumbs gave us the crunchiest coating. Pounding the chicken to an even thickness ensured that the chicken browned evenly. Cooking for two meant we could cook everything in one batch in a 10-inch skillet; thanks to the smaller vessel, just 6 tablespoons of oil was enough to get a crispy fried coating.

¼ cup all-purpose flour
1 large egg
1 cup panko bread crumbs
2 (6- to 8-ounce) boneless, skinless chicken breasts, trimmed and pounded to even thickness
¼ teaspoon table salt
⅛ teaspoon pepper
6 tablespoons vegetable oil
  Lemon wedges

1. Spread flour in shallow dish. Beat egg in second shallow dish. Spread bread crumbs in third shallow dish. Pat chicken dry with paper towels and sprinkle with salt and pepper. Working with 1 breast at a time, dredge breasts in flour, dip in egg, then coat with bread crumbs, pressing gently to adhere.

2. Line large plate with triple layer of paper towels. Heat oil in 10-inch nonstick skillet over medium-high heat until shimmering. Lay chicken in skillet and cook until golden brown on both sides and chicken registers 160 degrees, 4 to 6 minutes per side. Drain chicken briefly on paper towel–lined plate. Serve with lemon wedges.

Chicken Parmesan

Serves 2

Total time 1 hour

WHY THIS RECIPE WORKS Chicken Parmesan is a perennial favorite, but its multiple components can make it a time-consuming affair. We wanted to streamline this dish to make it feasible for two. We made a quick but flavorful tomato sauce by whirring canned tomatoes in a food processor. Garlic sautéed in olive oil provided a rich backbone, and basil, sugar, and salt rounded it out. For the chicken, we coated breasts in flour, dipped them in an egg wash, then rolled them in a crumb coating of ultracrisp panko bread crumbs and freshly grated Parmesan cheese. Pan-frying the chicken produced an evenly browned crust that stayed crisp even when topped with a mix of mozzarella and fontina and broiled until the cheese turned gooey. Spooning the sauce over the cheese, not the chicken, also ensured a crisp crust. We saved the remaining sauce for tossing with a side of hot spaghetti.

SAUCE

- 1 (28-ounce) can whole peeled tomatoes, drained
- 2 tablespoons extra-virgin olive oil
- 2 garlic cloves, minced
- 2 tablespoons chopped fresh basil
- ¼ teaspoon sugar, plus extra as needed

CHICKEN AND SPAGHETTI

- ¼ cup all-purpose flour
- 1 large egg
- ¾ cup panko bread crumbs
- ¼ cup grated Parmesan cheese
- 2 (6- to 8-ounce) boneless, skinless chicken breasts, trimmed and pounded to even thickness
- ¼ teaspoon table salt, plus salt for cooking pasta
- ¼ teaspoon pepper
- 6 tablespoons vegetable oil
- 1 ounce whole-milk mozzarella cheese, shredded (¼ cup)
- 1 ounce fontina cheese, shredded (¼ cup)
- 1 tablespoon chopped fresh basil
- 4 ounces spaghetti

1. FOR THE SAUCE Pulse tomatoes in food processor until coarsely ground, 6 to 8 pulses. Cook oil and garlic in medium saucepan over medium heat, stirring often, until garlic is fragrant but not browned, about 2 minutes. Stir in pulsed tomatoes; bring to simmer; and cook until sauce is slightly thickened, 10 to 15 minutes. Off heat, stir in basil and sugar and season with salt and extra sugar to taste; cover to keep warm.

2. FOR THE CHICKEN AND SPAGHETTI Adjust oven rack 4 inches from broiler element and heat broiler. Spread flour in shallow dish. Beat egg in second shallow dish. Combine bread crumbs and Parmesan in third shallow dish. Pat chicken dry with paper towels and sprinkle with salt and pepper. Working with 1 breast at a time, dredge breasts in flour, dip in egg, then coat with bread-crumb mixture, pressing gently to adhere.

3. Line large plate with triple layer of paper towels. Heat oil in 10-inch nonstick skillet over medium-high heat until shimmering. Lay chicken in skillet and cook until golden brown on both sides and chicken registers 160 degrees, 4 to 6 minutes per side. Drain chicken briefly on paper towel–lined plate, then transfer to rimmed baking sheet.

4. Combine mozzarella and fontina in bowl. Sprinkle cheese mixture evenly over chicken, covering as much surface area as possible. Broil until cheese is melted and beginning to brown, 2 to 4 minutes. Transfer chicken to serving platter, top each breast with 2 tablespoons tomato sauce, and sprinkle with basil.

5. Meanwhile, bring 4 quarts water to boil in large pot. Add pasta and 1 tablespoon salt and cook, stirring often, until al dente. Reserve ½ cup cooking water, then drain pasta and return it to pot. Add remaining sauce to pasta and toss to combine. Season with salt and pepper to taste and add reserved cooking water as needed to adjust consistency. Serve chicken with pasta.

Chicken Tikka Masala

Serves 2

Total time 50 minutes, plus 30 minutes chilling

WHY THIS RECIPE WORKS It is said that chicken tikka masala was created in a London curry house in the 1970s. It has remained a very popular dish. To create a failproof method, we first coated chicken breasts in a salt-spice mixture and refrigerated them briefly; then we dipped the chicken in yogurt mixed with garlic, ginger, and oil and broiled it. Leaving the breasts whole helped to keep them moist under the heat of the broiler. The ingredients in the sauce depend on the whim of the cook, although tomatoes and cream are always present. We added onions, ginger, garlic, chile, and convenient garam masala. This dish tastes best when made with whole-milk yogurt, but low-fat yogurt can be substituted; do not use non-fat yogurt. Serve with rice. To make this dish spicier, reserve and add the chile seeds as desired.

CHICKEN

- ½ teaspoon table salt
- ½ teaspoon garam masala
- ⅛ teaspoon cayenne pepper
- 2 (6- to 8-ounce) boneless, skinless chicken breasts, trimmed and pounded to even thickness
- ½ cup plain whole-milk yogurt
- 1 tablespoon vegetable oil
- 2 garlic cloves, minced
- 2 teaspoons grated fresh ginger

SAUCE

- 1 (14.5-ounce) can whole peeled tomatoes
- 2 tablespoons vegetable oil
- 1 small onion, chopped fine
- 1 small serrano chile, stemmed, seeded, and minced
- 1½ teaspoons tomato paste
- 1½ teaspoons garam masala
- 1 garlic clove, minced
- 1 teaspoon grated fresh ginger
- 1 teaspoon sugar
- ¼ teaspoon table salt
- ⅓ cup plain whole-milk yogurt
- 2 tablespoons chopped fresh cilantro

1. FOR THE CHICKEN Combine salt, garam masala, and cayenne in bowl. Pat chicken dry with paper towels and sprinkle thoroughly with spice mixture. Place chicken on plate, cover, and refrigerate for 30 minutes to 1 hour. Whisk yogurt, oil, garlic, and ginger together in medium bowl, cover, and refrigerate until needed.

2. FOR THE SAUCE Process tomatoes and their juice in food processor until smooth, about 15 seconds. Heat oil in large saucepan over medium heat until shimmering. Add onion and cook until softened and lightly browned, 5 to 7 minutes. Stir in serrano, tomato paste, garam masala, garlic, and ginger and cook until fragrant, about 30 seconds. Stir in processed tomatoes, sugar, and salt and bring to simmer. Reduce heat to low; cover; and simmer, stirring occasionally, until flavors meld, about 15 minutes. Off heat, stir in yogurt; cover to keep warm.

3. Meanwhile, adjust oven rack 6 inches from broiler element and heat broiler. Set wire rack in aluminum foil–lined rimmed baking sheet. Using tongs, dip chicken into yogurt mixture (chicken should be coated with thick layer of yogurt) and arrange on prepared wire rack. Discard excess yogurt mixture. Broil chicken until lightly charred in spots and chicken registers 160 degrees, 10 to 18 minutes, flipping chicken halfway through cooking.

4. Transfer chicken to cutting board, let rest for 5 minutes, then cut into 1-inch pieces. Stir chicken pieces into warm sauce (do not simmer chicken in sauce). Stir in cilantro, season with salt to taste, and serve.

Braised Chicken with Green Olives and Figs

Serves 2
Total time 50 minutes

WHY THIS RECIPE WORKS Inspired by North African tagines (aromatic braises of meat, vegetables, and fruits), we wanted to devise a weeknight chicken braise seasoned with lemon, figs, and olives. We settled on flavorful but quick-cooking boneless thighs. Poaching the chicken in a savory broth infused it with flavor and ensured the chicken was tender. When it came to choosing spices, we liked the convenience of garam masala, an Indian spice mix that can include cardamom, coriander, cumin, black peppercorns, and cinnamon; we gave it a further flavor boost with paprika. Coarsely chopped dried figs added a hint of sweetness. Look for large, pitted green olives at the olive bar in the supermarket. Pimento-stuffed olives can be substituted for the large green olives in a pinch. Serve with rice or couscous. You will need a 10-inch skillet with a tight-fitting lid for this recipe. Serve with rice or couscous.

- 1 tablespoon extra-virgin olive oil
- 1 small onion, halved and sliced thin
- 1 (3-inch) strip lemon zest plus 1½ teaspoons juice
- 2 garlic cloves, minced
- 1 teaspoon garam masala
- ½ teaspoon paprika
- ½ cup chicken broth
- ¼ cup pitted large green olives, chopped coarse
- ¼ cup dried figs, stemmed and chopped coarse
- 4 (3-ounce) boneless, skinless chicken thighs, trimmed
- ¼ teaspoon table salt
- ⅛ teaspoon pepper
- 1 tablespoon minced fresh cilantro

1. Heat oil in 10-inch skillet over medium heat until shimmering. Add onion and cook until softened, about 5 minutes. Stir in lemon zest, garlic, garam masala, and paprika and cook until fragrant, about 30 seconds. Stir in broth, olives, and figs, scraping up any browned bits.

2. Sprinkle chicken with salt and pepper, lay in skillet, and bring to simmer. Reduce heat to medium-low; cover; and simmer until chicken is very tender, about 15 minutes; transfer chicken to serving platter and tent loosely with aluminum foil.

3. Discard lemon zest. Continue to simmer sauce until slightly thickened, about 3 minutes. Stir in any accumulated chicken juices and simmer for 30 seconds. Stir in cilantro and lemon juice and season with salt and pepper to taste. Pour sauce over chicken and serve.

Three-Cup Chicken

Serves 2

Total time 45 minutes

WHY THIS RECIPE WORKS Originating in Dadu (modern Beijing), Three-Cup Chicken, or San Bei Ji, was named for its sparse ingredient list: a sauce made with 1 cup each of soy sauce, toasted sesame oil, and rice wine. Eventually adopted by neighboring Taiwan, it has evolved into a national dish. We aimed to scale this dish to serve two. First, we streamlined prep by calling for boneless, skinless chicken thighs. For deep flavor, we marinated the chicken in the requisite soy sauce and rice wine along with a bit of brown sugar. Thinly sliced scallions, ginger, garlic cloves, and red pepper flakes contributed a balance of flavors and textures. We eliminated the step of browning which allowed the chicken and sauce to cook in about 30 minutes. A bit of cornstarch mixed with water thickened the sauce to a perfect consistency. Thai basil added welcome freshness, and toasted sesame oil stirred in at the end provided a final flavor punch. We prefer the flavor of Thai basil in this recipe, but Italian basil can be substituted. Serve with white rice.

Braised Chicken with Green Olives and Figs

3	tablespoons soy sauce
3	tablespoons Shaoxing wine
1½	teaspoons packed brown sugar
12	ounces boneless, skinless chicken thighs, trimmed and cut into 2-inch pieces
1½	tablespoons vegetable oil
1	(1-inch) piece ginger, peeled, halved lengthwise, and sliced into thin half-rounds
6	garlic cloves, peeled and halved lengthwise
¼–½	teaspoon red pepper flakes
3	scallions, white and green parts separated and sliced thin on bias
1½	teaspoons water
½	teaspoon cornstarch
½	cup Thai basil leaves, large leaves halved lengthwise
1½	teaspoons toasted sesame oil

1. Whisk soy sauce, Shaoxing wine, and sugar together in medium bowl. Add chicken and toss to coat; set aside.

2. Heat vegetable oil, ginger, garlic, and pepper flakes in 14-inch flat-bottomed wok or 10-inch nonstick skillet over medium-low heat. Cook, stirring frequently, until garlic is golden brown and beginning to soften, 8 to 10 minutes.

Three-Cup Chicken

3. Add chicken and marinade to wok, increase heat to medium-high, and bring to simmer. Reduce heat to medium-low and simmer for 10 minutes, stirring occasionally. Stir in scallion whites and continue to cook until chicken registers about 200 degrees, 8 to 10 minutes.

4. Whisk water and cornstarch together in small bowl, then stir into sauce; simmer until sauce is slightly thickened, about 1 minute. Remove wok from heat. Stir in basil, sesame oil, and scallion greens. Transfer to platter and serve.

Chicken Teriyaki

Serves 2

Total time 50 minutes

WHY THIS RECIPE WORKS Our chicken teriyaki started with bone-in chicken thighs, not because we wanted the bones (we promptly removed them), but because we wanted the skin, which protects the meat from the heat of the skillet and adds succulence. Cutting the thighs into bite-size pieces created plenty of surface area for browning and, eventually, for the glaze. A pretreatment with sake boosted savory flavor. Adding cornstarch to the sake had a triple benefit: It formed an extra layer of protection around the chicken, which left it supple; it provided a surface that "grabbed" the glaze; and some of it sloughed off into the glaze, thickening it a bit more. Serve with rice, scallions, and peppery greens such as watercress.

Chicken Teriyaki

1 pound bone-in chicken thighs
5 teaspoons sake, divided
1½ teaspoons cornstarch
1½ tablespoons soy sauce
1½ teaspoons sugar
1½ teaspoons grated fresh ginger
1 teaspoon vegetable oil

1. Place 1 chicken thigh skin side down on cutting board. Using sharp paring knife, trim excess skin and fat, leaving enough skin to cover meat. Cut slit along length of thigh bone to expose bone. Using tip of knife, cut/scrape meat from bone. Slip knife under bone to separate bone from meat. Discard bone and trim any remaining cartilage from thigh. Keeping thigh skin side down, cut into 1½-inch pieces, leaving as much skin attached as possible. Transfer to medium bowl and repeat with remaining thighs. Add 2 teaspoons sake and cornstarch and stir gently until chicken is evenly coated.

2. Combine soy sauce, sugar, and remaining 1 tablespoon sake in small bowl. Microwave until sugar is dissolved, about 20 seconds. Place fine-mesh strainer over bowl containing soy sauce mixture. Add ginger to strainer and press to extract juice. Discard solids, but do not wash strainer.

3. Line plate with paper towels. Heat oil in 10-inch nonstick skillet over medium heat until shimmering. Place chicken skin side down in skillet (skillet may be very full). Increase heat to medium-high; place splatter screen, if using, on skillet; and cook, without moving chicken, until all pieces have ¼- to ½-inch perimeter of white, 6 to 8 minutes. Slide skillet off heat and flip chicken. Return skillet to burner and reduce heat to medium. Continue to cook until chicken is just cooked through, 1 to 2 minutes.

4. Remove skillet from heat. Using slotted spoon, transfer chicken to prepared plate. Pour off fat, scrape any browned bits out of skillet, and wipe skillet clean with paper towels. Return chicken to skillet. Add soy sauce mixture and cook over medium heat, stirring frequently, until chicken is thinly coated and sauce has consistency of maple syrup, 1 to 2 minutes. Using slotted spoon, transfer chicken to serving bowl. Pour glaze in skillet through now-empty strainer set over small serving bowl. Drizzle 1 tablespoon glaze over chicken and serve, passing remaining glaze (there will be only a small amount, but it's very potent) separately.

DEBONING CHICKEN THIGHS

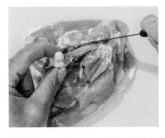
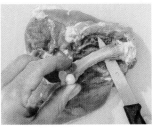

1. Using a sharp paring knife, cut a slit along length of thigh bone to expose bone.

2. Using tip of knife, cut/scrape meat from bone. Slip knife under bone to separate bone from meat.

Chicken Mole

Serves 2

Total time 1½ hours

WHY THIS RECIPE WORKS Mole refers to a variety of Mexican sauces, but the most famous is mole poblano, a rich blend of chiles, nuts, dried fruits, spices, and chocolate. Taking inspiration from mole poblano, we obtained depth of flavor from a combination of chili powder, chipotle chiles, warm spices, raisins, sesame seeds, peanut butter, and a little chocolate. Downsizing this recipe to a 10-inch skillet prevented the sauce from burning. For a smooth, velvety texture, we processed the sauce in a blender, then poured it over chicken breasts and baked them until they were tender. If the spice and chocolate mixture begins to scorch, add a small splash of water or broth to the skillet. Instead of using a blender, you can use an immersion blender to puree the sauce right in the saucepan.

- 1 tablespoon vegetable oil
- 1 small onion, chopped fine
- ½ ounce bittersweet, semisweet, or Mexican chocolate, chopped coarse
- 1 tablespoon chili powder
- 1 teaspoon minced canned chipotle chile in adobo sauce
- ¼ teaspoon ground cinnamon
  Pinch ground cloves
- 1 garlic clove, minced
- 1¼ cups chicken broth
- 1 tomato, cored, seeded, and chopped
- 2 tablespoons raisins
- 1 tablespoon peanut butter

- 1 tablespoon sesame seeds, toasted, plus extra for serving
- 2 (10- to 12-ounce) bone-in split chicken breasts, skin removed, trimmed
- ½ teaspoon table salt
- ¼ teaspoon pepper

1. Adjust oven rack to middle position and heat oven to 400 degrees. Heat oil in 10-inch skillet over medium heat until shimmering. Add onion and cook until softened, about 5 minutes.

2. Reduce heat to medium-low; stir in chocolate, chili powder, chipotle, cinnamon, and cloves; and cook, stirring frequently, until spices are fragrant and chocolate is melted and bubbly, about 1 minute. Stir in garlic and cook until fragrant, about 30 seconds. Stir in broth, tomato, raisins, peanut butter, and sesame seeds. Bring to simmer and cook, stirring occasionally, until sauce is slightly thickened and reduced to about 1¾ cups, 10 to 15 minutes. Transfer sauce to blender and process until smooth, about 30 seconds. Season with salt, pepper, and sugar to taste.

3. Pat chicken dry with paper towels and sprinkle with salt and pepper. Place chicken, skinned side down, in 8-inch square baking dish and pour pureed sauce over top, turning chicken to coat evenly. Bake chicken for 20 minutes. Flip chicken skinned side up and continue to bake until chicken registers 160 degrees, 15 to 25 minutes. Let chicken rest in sauce for 5 minutes. Sprinkle with extra sesame seeds and serve.

Murgh Makhani

Serves 2

Total time 1 hour

WHY THIS RECIPE WORKS Murgh makhani, or Indian butter chicken, tastes rich, creamy, vibrant, and complex. We started our version for two by softening onion, garlic, ginger, and chile in butter followed by garam masala, coriander, cumin, and black pepper. Cream gave the sauce lush, velvety body, and we whisked in another tablespoon of butter for extra richness. To imitate the charring produced by a tandoor, we broiled chicken thighs coated in yogurt (its milk proteins and lactose brown quickly and deeply) before cutting them and stirring them into the sauce. To make this dish spicier, reserve and add the chile seeds as desired. Serve with basmati rice and/or warm naan.

Murgh Makhani

and pepper and cook, stirring frequently, until very fragrant, about 3 minutes. Add water and tomato paste and whisk until no lumps of tomato paste remain. Add sugar and ½ teaspoon salt and bring to boil. Off heat, stir in cream. Using immersion blender or blender, process until smooth, 30 to 60 seconds. Return sauce to simmer over medium heat and whisk in remaining 1 tablespoon butter. Remove saucepan from heat and cover to keep warm. (Sauce can be refrigerated for up to 4 days; gently reheat sauce before adding hot chicken.)

2. Adjust oven rack 6 inches from broiler element and heat broiler. Combine chicken, yogurt, and remaining ½ teaspoon salt in bowl and toss well to coat. Using tongs, transfer chicken to wire rack set in aluminum foil–lined rimmed baking sheet. Broil until chicken is evenly charred on both sides and registers 175 degrees, 16 to 20 minutes, flipping chicken halfway through broiling.

3. Let chicken rest for 5 minutes. While chicken rests, warm sauce over medium-low heat. Cut chicken into ¾-inch pieces and stir into sauce. Stir in 1 tablespoon cilantro and season with salt to taste. Transfer to serving dish, sprinkle with remaining 1½ teaspoons cilantro, and serve.

Roasted Chicken Breasts with Lemon and Thyme

Serves 2

Total time 1 hour

WHY THIS RECIPE WORKS: While chicken is a weeknight staple, recipes for roasted chicken breasts often produce dry meat and flabby skin. We started with flavorful bone-in, skin-on chicken to insulate the meat and keep it juicy. We infused the chicken with flavor by spreading butter, flavored with simple stir-ins, under the skin before cooking. Then we brushed the chicken breast with melted butter and roasted it in a 400-degree oven to encourage crisp skin.

- 2 tablespoons unsalted butter, softened, plus 1 tablespoon melted
- 1 teaspoon table salt, divided
- ½ teaspoon grated lemon zest
- ½ teaspoon minced fresh thyme or ⅛ teaspoon dried
- ¼ teaspoon pepper, divided
- 2 (10- to 12-ounce) bone-in split chicken breasts, trimmed

- 2 tablespoons unsalted butter, cut into 2 pieces and chilled, divided
- ½ onion, chopped fine
- 3 garlic cloves, minced
- 2 teaspoons grated fresh ginger
- 2 teaspoons minced serrano chile
- 1½ teaspoons garam masala
- ½ teaspoon ground coriander
- ¼ teaspoon ground cumin
- ¼ teaspoon pepper
- ¾ cup water
- ¼ cup tomato paste
- 1½ teaspoons sugar
- 1 teaspoon table salt, divided
- ½ cup heavy cream
- 1 pound boneless, skinless chicken thighs, trimmed
- ¼ cup plain Greek yogurt
- 1½ tablespoons chopped fresh cilantro, divided

1. Melt 1 tablespoon butter in medium saucepan over medium heat. Add onion, garlic, ginger, and serrano and cook, stirring frequently, until mixture is softened and onion begins to brown, 6 to 8 minutes. Add garam masala, coriander, cumin,

1. Adjust oven rack to lower-middle position and heat oven to 400 degrees. Combine softened butter, ½ teaspoon salt, lemon zest, thyme, and ⅛ teaspoon pepper in bowl.

2. Pat chicken dry with paper towels. Use your fingers to gently loosen center portion of skin covering breasts. Place half of butter mixture under skin on each breast and gently press on skin to spread mixture evenly over meat. Arrange chicken skin side up on rimmed baking sheet. Brush chicken skin with melted butter and sprinkle with remaining ½ teaspoon salt and remaining ⅛ teaspoon pepper.

3. Roast chicken until it registers 160 degrees, 35 to 40 minutes, rotating sheet halfway through roasting. Let rest for 5 minutes before serving.

VARIATIONS
Roasted Chicken Breasts with Lime and Chipotle

Substitute lime zest for lemon zest and minced canned chipotle chile for thyme.

Roasted Chicken Breasts with Ginger and Five-Spice

Substitute grated fresh ginger for lemon zest and five-spice powder for thyme.

Pan-Roasted Chicken Breasts with Garlic and Sherry Sauce

Serves 2

Total time 50 minutes

WHY THIS RECIPE WORKS Pan roasting is a restaurant technique in which food is browned in a skillet and then slid, skillet and all, into a hot oven to finish cooking. After we browned the chicken on both sides, we placed the skillet in a 450-degree oven. Finally, we used the caramelized drippings left in the pan to make a quick and flavorful sauce of garlic, sherry, and chicken broth. You will need an ovensafe 10-inch skillet for this recipe.

- 2 (10- to 12-ounce) bone-in split chicken breasts, trimmed
- ½ teaspoon table salt
- ¼ teaspoon pepper
- 2 teaspoons vegetable oil
- 3 garlic cloves, sliced thin

- ½ teaspoon all-purpose flour
- ½ cup chicken broth
- ¼ cup dry sherry
- 2 sprigs fresh thyme
- 1 tablespoon butter, chilled
- ½ teaspoon lemon juice

1. Adjust oven rack to lowest position and heat oven to 450 degrees. Pat chicken dry with paper towels and sprinkle with salt and pepper.

2. Heat oil in 10-inch ovensafe skillet over medium-high heat until just smoking. Lay chicken skin side down in skillet and cook until well browned on first side, 6 to 8 minutes, reducing heat if pan begins to scorch. Flip chicken and continue to cook until lightly browned, about 3 minutes.

3. Flip chicken skin side down and transfer skillet to oven. Roast until chicken registers 160 degrees, 15 to 18 minutes.

4. Using potholders (skillet handle will be hot), remove skillet from oven. Transfer chicken to serving platter and tent loosely with aluminum foil.

5. Being careful of hot skillet handle, pour off all but 1 tablespoon fat from skillet; add garlic; and cook over medium heat until softened, about 2 minutes. Stir in flour and cook for 1 minute. Whisk in broth, sherry, and thyme sprigs, scraping up any browned bits and smoothing out any lumps. Bring to simmer and cook until slightly thickened, about 5 minutes. Stir in any accumulated chicken juices and simmer for 30 seconds. Off heat, remove thyme sprigs and whisk in butter and lemon juice. Season with salt and pepper to taste. Pour sauce over chicken and serve.

TRIMMING SPLIT CHICKEN BREASTS

To remove rib section of a split chicken breast, use kitchen shears to trim rib section from each breast, following vertical line of fat from tapered end of breast up to socket where wing was attached.

Skillet-Roasted Chicken Breasts with Harissa-Mint Carrots

Serves 2

Total time 1¼ hours

WHY THIS RECIPE WORKS This recipe is a twofer from one skillet. First, we seasoned bone-in, skin-on chicken breasts under the skin with salt. We placed them skin side down in a cold skillet and then turned on the heat to slowly render the fat and brown the skin without overcooking the delicate flesh just beneath it. Once the skin was well browned, we flipped the breasts and placed them in a 325-degree oven for about 30 minutes to cook through. While the cooked chicken breasts rested, we added shallot, harissa, and salt to the skillet and cooked them until the chicken juices reduced and the aromatics began to sizzle in the chicken fat and release flavor. We then added carrots to the pan along with a little water, covered the pan, and let the carrots cook through. With the skillet uncovered, the savory, chicken-y liquid thickened to coat the carrots. Be sure to remove excess fatty skin from the thick ends of the breasts when trimming. You will need an ovensafe 12-inch skillet with a lid for this recipe.

2 (10- to 12-ounce) bone-in split chicken breasts, trimmed
1¼ teaspoons kosher salt, divided
Vegetable oil spray
1 small shallot, sliced thin
1 teaspoon harissa
12 ounces carrots, peeled and sliced on bias ¼ inch thick
¼ cup water
1 teaspoon lemon juice
2 teaspoons chopped fresh mint, divided

1. Adjust oven rack to lower-middle position and heat oven to 325 degrees. Working with 1 breast at a time, use your fingers to carefully separate skin from meat. Peel back skin, leaving skin attached at top and bottom of breast and at ribs. Sprinkle ¾ teaspoon salt evenly over chicken (⅜ teaspoon per breast). Lay skin back in place. Using metal skewer or tip of paring knife, poke 6 to 8 holes in fat deposits in skin of each breast. Spray skin with oil spray.

2. Place chicken, skin side down, in 12-inch ovensafe skillet and set over medium-high heat. Cook, moving chicken as infrequently as possible, until skin is well browned, 7 to 9 minutes, reducing heat if pan begins to scorch.

3. Carefully flip chicken and transfer skillet to oven. Roast until chicken registers 160 degrees, 25 to 30 minutes.

4. Transfer chicken to plate; do not discard liquid in skillet. Add shallot, harissa, and remaining ½ teaspoon salt to skillet and cook over medium-high heat, stirring occasionally and scraping up any browned bits, until moisture has evaporated and mixture begins to sizzle, 1 to 3 minutes. Add carrots and water and bring to simmer. Cover skillet; reduce heat to medium; and cook until carrots are tender, 10 to 12 minutes, stirring halfway through cooking. Uncover and continue to cook, stirring frequently, until sauce begins to coat carrots, 2 to 4 minutes. Add lemon juice, 1 teaspoon mint, and any accumulated chicken juices to skillet and toss to combine. Season with salt to taste. Transfer carrots to serving platter and sprinkle with remaining 1 teaspoon mint. Top with chicken and serve.

Weeknight Roast Chicken

Serves 2

Total time 1½ hours, plus 20 minutes resting

WHY THIS RECIPE WORKS To get a beautifully browned, perfectly roasted chicken for two on the table any night of the week, we skipped brining and turned to a hybrid roasting technique. We began by roasting a small chicken in a ripping-hot skillet. We started the chicken thigh side down to give the longer-cooking dark meat a head start so that both thighs and breasts would cook through in sync. After the skin crisped, we turned the oven off to cook the breast meat through gently, which yielded flawless results every time. And while the chicken rested before carving, we simply moved the skillet to the stovetop to turn the flavorful pan juices into a tasty sauce. You will need a 12-inch ovensafe skillet for this recipe.

CHICKEN
1 tablespoon kosher salt
½ teaspoon pepper
1 (3- to 3½-pound) whole chicken, giblets discarded
1 tablespoon extra-virgin olive oil

PAN SAUCE
1 shallot, minced
1 cup chicken broth
2 teaspoons Dijon mustard
2 tablespoons unsalted butter, chilled
2 teaspoons minced fresh tarragon
2 teaspoons lemon juice

1. **FOR THE CHICKEN** Adjust oven rack to middle position, place 12-inch ovensafe skillet on rack, and heat oven to 450 degrees. Combine salt and pepper in bowl. Pat chicken dry with paper towels. Rub entire surface with oil. Sprinkle evenly all over with salt mixture and rub in mixture with your hands to coat evenly. Tie legs together with kitchen twine and tuck wingtips behind back.

2. Transfer chicken, breast side up, to preheated skillet in oven. Roast chicken until breast registers 120 degrees and thighs register 135 degrees, 25 to 35 minutes. Turn off oven and leave chicken in oven until breast registers 160 degrees and thighs register 175 degrees, 25 to 35 minutes.

3. Using potholders (skillet handle will be hot), remove skillet from oven. Transfer chicken to carving board and let rest, uncovered, for 20 minutes.

4. **FOR THE PAN SAUCE** Being careful of hot skillet handle, remove all but 1 tablespoon fat from skillet using large spoon, leaving any fond and jus in skillet. Place skillet over medium-high heat, add shallot, and cook until softened, about 2 minutes. Stir in broth and mustard, scraping up browned bits. Bring to simmer and cook until reduced to ¾ cup, about 3 minutes. Stir in any accumulated chicken juices and simmer for 30 seconds. Off heat, whisk in butter, tarragon, and lemon juice. Season with pepper to taste; cover to keep warm. Carve chicken and serve with pan sauce.

Chicken Fajitas

Serves 2
Total time 35 minutes

WHY THIS RECIPE WORKS Grilled chicken fajitas are a backyard favorite. We wanted to create full-of-flavor fajitas that we could enjoy year-round. First, we cooked the chicken quickly in a skillet to give it a well-browned exterior while keeping the interior juicy. Then we tossed the chicken with a tangy marinade of lime juice, cilantro, and Worcestershire sauce, which mimicked the savory smokiness of the grill. While the chicken rested, we took advantage of the flavorful fond left in the skillet to sauté the peppers and onions. To make these fajitas spicy, add a sliced jalapeño along with the bell pepper. Serve with your favorite fajita toppings.

- 2 (6- to 8-ounce) boneless, skinless chicken breasts, trimmed and pounded to even thickness
- ¾ teaspoon table salt, divided
- ⅛ teaspoon pepper
- 2 tablespoons vegetable oil, divided
- 1 red, green, or yellow bell pepper, stemmed, seeded, and cut into ½-inch-wide strips
- 1 small red onion, halved and sliced thin
- 2 tablespoons water
- 1 teaspoon chili powder
- 2 tablespoons lime juice
- 1 tablespoon chopped fresh cilantro
- 1 teaspoon Worcestershire sauce
- ½ teaspoon brown sugar
- 6 (6-inch) flour tortillas, warmed

CARVING A WHOLE CHICKEN

1. Cut chicken where leg meets breast.

2. Pull leg quarter away from carcass. Separate joint by gently pressing leg out to side and pushing up on joint. Cut through joint to remove leg quarter.

3. Cut through joint that connects drumstick to thigh. Repeat steps 1 through 3 on chicken's other side.

4. Cut down along side of breastbone, pulling breast meat away from breastbone as you cut. Remove wing from breast by cutting through wing joint. Slice breast crosswise into slices. Repeat with other side.

1. Pat chicken dry with paper towels and sprinkle with ¼ teaspoon salt and pepper. Heat 1 tablespoon oil in 10-inch nonstick skillet over medium-high heat until just smoking. Lay chicken in skillet and cook until well browned on first side, 6 to 8 minutes. Flip chicken; reduce heat to medium; and continue to cook until chicken registers 160 degrees, 6 to 8 minutes. Transfer chicken to cutting board, tent loosely with aluminum foil, and let rest while preparing vegetables.

2. Add bell pepper, onion, water, chili powder, and ¼ teaspoon salt to now-empty skillet and cook over medium heat until vegetables are softened, 5 to 7 minutes; transfer to serving platter.

3. Meanwhile, whisk lime juice, cilantro, Worcestershire, brown sugar, remaining ¼ teaspoon salt, and remaining 1 tablespoon oil together in large bowl. Cut chicken into ¼-inch-thick slices and toss with lime juice mixture. Arrange chicken on platter with vegetables and serve with warm tortillas.

WARMING TORTILLAS

Warming tortillas to soften them is crucial. If your tortillas are dry, pat each with a little water before warming them. Wrap warm tortillas in foil or a clean dish towel to keep them warm and soft.

Warm tortillas, one at a time, directly on cooking grate over medium gas flame until slightly charred around edges, about 30 seconds per side. Or warm, one at a time, in dry skillet over medium-high heat until softened and speckled brown, 20 to 30 seconds per side.

Gai Pad Krapow

Serves 2 `FAST`

Total time 30 minutes

WHY THIS RECIPE WORKS Gai pad krapow is a Thai street food that stars stir-fried bite-size pieces of chicken and the bright flavor of basil. Stir-frying at a low temperature (versus the high-heat method often used) allowed us to add aromatics and basil in the beginning so they infused the dish with flavor. Grinding the chicken in a food processor gave us

coarse-textured meat that retained moisture during cooking. Oyster sauce and vinegar added rich but bright flavor. Stirring in more basil at the end added a fresh finish and bold basil flavor. For a mild version of the dish, remove the seeds and ribs from the chiles. If fresh Thai chiles are unavailable, substitute two serranos or one medium jalapeño. If you can't find Thai basil leaves, Italian basil will work fine. Serve with rice.

1 cup Thai basil leaves, divided
2 green or red Thai chiles, stemmed
1 garlic clove, peeled
2½ teaspoons fish sauce, divided, plus extra for serving
1½ teaspoons oyster sauce
1½ teaspoons sugar, plus extra for serving
½ teaspoon distilled white vinegar, plus extra for serving
8 ounces boneless, skinless chicken breast, trimmed and cut into 2-inch pieces
1 shallot, sliced thin
1 tablespoon vegetable oil
Red pepper flakes

1. Pulse ½ cup basil, Thai chiles, and garlic in food processor until finely chopped, 10 to 12 pulses, scraping down sides of bowl as needed. Transfer 1½ teaspoons of basil mixture to small bowl and stir in 1½ teaspoons fish sauce, oyster sauce, sugar, and vinegar. Transfer remaining basil mixture to 14-inch flat-bottomed wok or 10-inch nonstick skillet.

2. Without washing food processor bowl, pulse chicken and remaining 1 teaspoon fish sauce in food processor until meat is coarsely chopped, 6 to 8 pulses; transfer to medium bowl and refrigerate for 15 minutes.

3. Stir shallot and oil into basil mixture in wok. Cook over medium-low heat, stirring constantly, until garlic and shallot are golden brown, 5 to 8 minutes. (Mixture should start to sizzle after about 1½ minutes; if it doesn't, adjust heat accordingly.)

4. Stir in chopped chicken and cook over medium heat, breaking up chicken with wooden spoon, until only traces of pink remain, 2 to 4 minutes. Add reserved basil–fish sauce mixture and cook, stirring constantly, until chicken is no longer pink, about 1 minute. Stir in remaining ½ cup basil leaves and cook, stirring constantly, until basil is wilted, 30 to 60 seconds. Serve immediately, passing extra fish sauce, sugar, vinegar, and pepper flakes separately.

Gai Pad Krapow

Gōngbǎo Jīdīng

Serves 2

Total time 40 minutes

WHY THIS RECIPE WORKS Gōngbǎo Jīdīng, otherwise known as Kung Pao Chicken, is a Sichuan classic said to be named after a Qing Dynasty official who was particularly enamored of the dish (gongbao refers to his title while jiding means diced chicken). We started our spicy, tingly Kung Pao Chicken by putting together the chicken and sauce, the stir-fry aromatics, and then toasting peanuts in a skillet to maximize their crunch before setting them aside to cool. Next, we toasted crushed Sichuan peppercorns and arbol chiles that we'd halved lengthwise to release their heat. We stirred in plenty of garlic and ginger and then added the marinated diced chicken thighs. When it was almost cooked through, we added some celery for crisp freshness and then a quick and concentrated sauce mixture that cooked down to a glaze. To adjust the heat level, use more or fewer chiles, depending on the size (we used 2-inch-long chiles) and your taste. Have your ingredients prepared and your equipment in place before you begin to cook. Use a spice grinder or mortar and pestle to coarsely grind the Sichuan peppercorns. If Chinese black vinegar is unavailable, substitute sherry vinegar. Serve with white rice. Do not eat the chiles. You will need a 14-inch flat-bottomed wok or 10-inch nonstick skillet with a tight-fitting lid for this recipe.

CHICKEN AND SAUCE

- 12 ounces boneless, skinless chicken thighs, trimmed and cut into ½-inch pieces
- 2 tablespoons soy sauce, divided
- 1½ teaspoons cornstarch
- 1½ teaspoons Shaoxing wine or dry sherry
- ¼ teaspoon white pepper
- 1½ teaspoons Chinese black vinegar
- 1½ teaspoons packed dark brown sugar
- 1 teaspoon toasted sesame oil

STIR-FRY

- 1½ teaspoons minced garlic
- 1 teaspoon grated fresh ginger
- 3½ teaspoons vegetable oil, divided
- ¼ cup dry-roasted peanuts
- 5–7 dried arbol chiles, halved lengthwise and seeded
- ½ teaspoon Sichuan peppercorns, ground coarse
- 1 celery rib, cut into ½-inch pieces
- 3 scallions, white and light green parts only, cut into ½-inch pieces

1. FOR THE CHICKEN AND SAUCE Combine chicken, 1 tablespoon soy sauce, cornstarch, Shaoxing wine, and white pepper in medium bowl and set aside. Stir vinegar, sugar, oil, and remaining 1 tablespoon soy sauce together in small bowl.

2. FOR THE STIR-FRY Stir garlic, ginger, and 1½ teaspoons oil together in second small bowl. Combine peanuts and ½ teaspoon oil in 14-inch flat-bottomed wok or 10-inch nonstick skillet over medium-low heat. Cook, stirring constantly, until peanuts just begin to darken, 3 to 5 minutes. Transfer peanuts to plate and spread into even layer to cool. Return now-empty skillet to medium-low heat. Add remaining 1½ teaspoons oil, arbols, and peppercorns and cook, stirring constantly, until arbols just begin to darken, 1 to 2 minutes. Add garlic mixture and cook, stirring constantly, until all clumps are broken up and mixture is fragrant, about 30 seconds.

3. Add chicken and spread into even layer. Cover wok; increase heat to medium-high; and cook, without stirring, for 1 minute. Stir chicken and spread into even layer. Cover and cook, without stirring, for 1 minute. Add celery and cook uncovered, tossing slowly but constantly, until chicken is cooked through, 2 to 3 minutes. Add soy sauce mixture and cook, stirring constantly, until sauce is thickened and shiny and coats chicken, about 2 minutes. Stir in scallions and peanuts. Transfer to platter and serve.

Chicken Pot Pie

Serves 2

Total time 1 hour 10 minutes, plus 10 minutes cooling

WHY THIS RECIPE WORKS To simplify chicken pot pie for two, we opted to make two individual pies. Two 12-ounce ramekins were the perfect size vessels. A single boneless, skinless chicken breast was easy to work with and substantial enough for two pies when combined with the rest of the ingredients. Cooking the chicken right in the sauce enriched its flavor and cut down on dishes. A little soy sauce added complex, meaty flavor without a lengthy simmer. Parcooking the crusts on a baking sheet ensured that they didn't collapse into the filling. We prefer the flavor and texture of homemade pie dough here; however, you can substitute 1 (9-inch) store-bought pie dough round. If using store-bought pie dough, bake the crusts for about 8 minutes in steps 1 and 5. You will need two ovensafe 12-ounce ramekins or bowls for this recipe.

1 recipe Classic Single-Crust Pie Dough (page 400)
2 tablespoons unsalted butter
2 carrots, peeled and sliced ¼ inch thick
1 small onion, chopped fine
1 small celery rib, sliced ¼ inch thick
½ teaspoon table salt
2 garlic cloves, minced
1 teaspoon minced fresh thyme
3 tablespoons all-purpose flour
1¾ cups chicken broth
⅓ cup heavy cream
½ teaspoon soy sauce
8 ounces boneless, skinless chicken breast, trimmed
¼ cup frozen peas
2 teaspoons minced fresh parsley
¼ teaspoon lemon juice

1. Adjust oven rack to middle position and heat oven to 450 degrees. Roll out dough on parchment paper to 12-inch round about ¼ inch thick. Using 12-ounce ovensafe ramekin as guide, cut out 2 rounds of dough about ½ inch larger than diameter of ramekin. Fold under and crimp outer ½ inch of dough round, then cut 3 vents in center of each crust. Slide parchment paper with crusts onto rimmed baking sheet. Bake until crusts just begin to brown and no longer look raw, 10 to 12 minutes; set aside.

2. Meanwhile, melt butter in medium saucepan over medium heat. Add carrots, onion, celery, and salt and cook until vegetables are softened and browned, 8 to 10 minutes. Stir in garlic and thyme and cook until fragrant, about 30 seconds. Stir in flour and cook for 1 minute.

3. Slowly whisk in broth, cream, and soy sauce, scraping up any browned bits and smoothing out any lumps. Nestle chicken into sauce and bring to simmer. Cover; reduce heat to medium-low; and cook until chicken registers 160 degrees, 10 to 15 minutes. Transfer chicken to cutting board, let cool slightly, then shred into bite-size pieces using 2 forks.

4. Meanwhile, return pan with sauce to medium heat and simmer until thickened and sauce measures 2 cups, about 5 minutes. Off heat, return shredded chicken along with any accumulated juices to pan. Stir in peas, parsley, and lemon juice and season with salt and pepper to taste.

5. Divide filling between ramekins and place parbaked crusts on top of filling. Place pot pies on baking sheet and bake until crusts are deep golden brown and filling is bubbling, 10 to 15 minutes. Let pot pies cool for 10 minutes before serving.

Chicken Pot Pie

Lemon-Herb Couscous with
Chicken and Dried Cherries

Lemon-Herb Couscous with Chicken and Dried Cherries

Serves 2 FAST

Total time 30 minutes

WHY THIS RECIPE WORKS For an easy, flavor-studded couscous and chicken dinner, we first whisked together a fragrant olive oil–lemon vinaigrette to toss with the cooked couscous. Cooking the couscous was as simple as tossing it with boiling water and a little salt in a covered bowl for 10 minutes. While the couscous finished steaming, we sautéed the chicken pieces in a skillet and then tossed everything together with our bright vinaigrette, sweet dried tart cherries, and fresh herbs. For an accurate measurement of boiling water, bring a kettle of water to a boil and then measure out the desired amount.

- 1 tablespoon extra-virgin olive oil, divided
- 1 tablespoon lemon juice
- 1 small shallot, minced
- 1 garlic clove, minced
- ¾ cup boiling water
- ¾ cup couscous
- ½ teaspoon table salt, divided
- 8 ounces boneless, skinless chicken breast, trimmed and cut into ¾-inch pieces
- ⅛ teaspoon pepper
- 2 tablespoons chopped dried tart cherries
- ¼ cup chopped fresh dill, parsley, mint, and/or tarragon

1. Whisk 2 teaspoons oil, lemon juice, shallot, and garlic together in small bowl; set aside. Combine boiling water, couscous, and ¼ teaspoon salt in large bowl. Cover and let sit for 10 minutes. Fluff couscous with fork; set aside.

2. Pat chicken dry with paper towels and sprinkle with remaining ¼ teaspoon salt and pepper. Heat remaining 1 teaspoon oil in 8- or 10-inch skillet over medium-high heat until shimmering. Add chicken and cook until lightly browned on all sides and cooked through, 3 to 5 minutes.

3. Transfer chicken to bowl with couscous. Add oil-shallot mixture, cherries, and dill and toss gently to combine. Season with salt and pepper to taste. Serve warm or at room temperature.

Chicken and Orzo with Spinach and Feta

Chicken and Orzo with Spinach and Feta

Serves 2

Total time 50 minutes

WHY THIS RECIPE WORKS To make this simple skillet chicken supper memorable, we wanted the side to be the star of the show. We chose orzo, a small pasta that's quick and easy to cook. To add deep, complex flavor, we toasted the orzo until golden brown, then simmered it in just the right amount of chicken broth until perfectly tender. To give the dish Mediterranean flair and vibrant flavor, we added garlic, oregano, and red pepper flakes and stirred in baby spinach, briny feta, and a squeeze of bright lemon juice just before serving. You will need a 10-inch skillet with a tight-fitting lid for this recipe.

- ¾ cup orzo
- 2 (6- to 8-ounce) boneless, skinless chicken breasts, trimmed and pounded to even thickness
- ¼ teaspoon table salt
- ⅛ teaspoon pepper
- 1 tablespoon extra-virgin olive oil, divided
- 2 garlic cloves, minced
- 1 teaspoon minced fresh oregano or ¼ teaspoon dried Pinch red pepper flakes
- 1¼ cups chicken broth, plus extra as needed
- 4 ounces (4 cups) baby spinach
- 2 ounces feta cheese, crumbled (½ cup)
- 1½ teaspoons lemon juice

1. Toast orzo in 10-inch nonstick skillet over medium-high heat until golden brown, 3 to 5 minutes; transfer to bowl.

2. Pat chicken dry with paper towels and sprinkle with salt and pepper. Heat 1 teaspoon oil in now-empty skillet over medium-high heat until just smoking. Brown chicken lightly, 3 to 4 minutes per side; transfer to plate.

3. Add remaining 2 teaspoons oil, garlic, oregano, and pepper flakes to now-empty skillet and cook until fragrant, about 30 seconds. Stir in broth and toasted orzo.

4. Nestle browned chicken into orzo, along with any accumulated juices, and bring to simmer. Reduce heat to medium-low; cover; and simmer until chicken registers 160 degrees, 10 to 12 minutes, flipping chicken halfway through cooking. Transfer chicken to serving platter, brushing any orzo that sticks to chicken back into skillet; tent loosely with aluminum foil.

5. Continue to cook orzo until al dente and creamy, 2 to 5 minutes, stirring in additional broth, 1 tablespoon at a time, as needed to loosen consistency. Stir in spinach, 1 handful at a time, until wilted, about 2 minutes. Stir in feta and lemon juice and season with salt and pepper to taste. Serve chicken with orzo.

Chicken and Chorizo Paella

Serves 2

Total time 55 minutes

WHY THIS RECIPE WORKS Paella is a fragrant Spanish rice dish usually loaded with meat, seafood, and vegetables. While delicious, it's quite a labor of love. We wanted to translate this classic into a streamlined weeknight version with all the flavor of the original. A combination of chorizo sausage and a chicken breast was hearty enough that we could forgo the seafood altogether. A rich sofrito of onion, garlic, and tomato gave our dish a deep flavor, and bright peas and briny olives added color and dimension. Just a pinch of pricey saffron was enough to give our paella flavor. We like to use short-grain Valencia rice for this dish, but you can substitute Arborio rice if you cannot find Valencia. Do not substitute long-grain rice. Look for large, pitted green olives at the olive bar in the supermarket. Pimento-stuffed olives can be substituted for the large green olives in a pinch. To make the chicken easier to slice, freeze it for 15 minutes. You will need a 10-inch nonstick skillet with a tight-fitting lid for this recipe.

- 1½ cups water, divided
- ½ cup Valencia or Arborio rice
- ¼ teaspoon table salt, divided
- 4 teaspoons vegetable oil, divided
- 4 ounces chorizo sausage, halved lengthwise and sliced ¼ inch thick
- 8 ounces boneless, skinless chicken breast, trimmed and sliced ¼ inch thick Pinch pepper
- 1 small onion, chopped fine
- ¾ cup canned diced tomatoes, drained with juice reserved
- 2 garlic cloves, minced
- ⅛ teaspoon saffron threads, crumbled
- ¼ cup pitted large green olives, quartered
- ¼ cup frozen peas

Chicken and Chorizo Paella

4. Stir in browned chorizo and chicken along with any accumulated juices, olives, and peas and increase heat to medium-high. Cook, uncovered, until bottom layer of rice is golden and crisp, about 5 minutes, rotating skillet halfway through cooking to ensure even browning. Season with salt and pepper to taste and serve.

SLICING CHICKEN BREASTS THIN

Slice breast across grain into ¼-inch-thick strips that are 1½ to 2 inches long. Cut center pieces in half so that they are approximately same length as end pieces.

Chicken and Rice

Serves 2

Total time: 1 hour 20 minutes

WHY THIS RECIPE WORKS For the ultimate easy weeknight dinner, we wanted to streamline classic chicken and rice. To get perfectly al dente rice without overcooking the chicken, we microwaved the rice to parcook it, then added it to the pot with the chicken to cook through gently in the even heat of the oven. We chose bone-in, skin-on chicken thighs for rich flavor and seared them to get nicely browned skin. For aromatics, we quickly sautéed onion, garlic, and a little fresh thyme. A sprinkling of parsley finished the dish. You will need a medium ovensafe saucepan for this recipe.

1¼ cups chicken broth, divided
½ cup long-grain white rice
1 teaspoon table salt, divided
4 (5- to 7-ounce) bone-in chicken thighs, trimmed
¼ teaspoon pepper
1 teaspoon vegetable oil
1 small onion, chopped fine
2 garlic cloves, minced
¾ teaspoon minced fresh thyme or ⅛ teaspoon dried
¼ cup dry white wine
2 tablespoons chopped fresh parsley

1. Combine 1 cup water, rice, and ⅛ teaspoon salt in bowl. Cover and microwave until rice is softened and most of liquid is absorbed, 6 to 8 minutes.

2. Meanwhile, heat 2 teaspoons oil in 10-inch nonstick skillet over medium-high heat until just smoking. Add chorizo and cook until lightly browned, about 2 minutes. Using slotted spoon, transfer chorizo to plate. Pat chicken dry with paper towels and sprinkle with remaining ⅛ teaspoon salt and pepper. Add chicken to fat left in skillet; break up any clumps; and cook until lightly browned on all sides, about 4 minutes; transfer to plate with chorizo.

3. Heat remaining 2 teaspoons oil in now-empty skillet over medium heat until shimmering. Add onion and cook until softened, about 5 minutes. Stir in tomatoes and cook until beginning to soften and darken, 3 to 5 minutes. Stir in garlic and saffron and cook until fragrant, about 30 seconds. Stir in remaining ½ cup water and reserved tomato juice, scraping up any browned bits. Stir in parcooked rice, breaking up any large clumps, and bring to simmer. Reduce heat to medium-low; cover; and simmer until rice is tender and liquid is absorbed, 8 to 12 minutes.

1. Adjust oven rack to lower-middle position and heat oven to 350 degrees. Combine ¾ cup broth, rice, and ¼ teaspoon salt in bowl. Cover and microwave until rice is softened and most of liquid is absorbed, 6 to 8 minutes.

2. Meanwhile, pat chicken dry with paper towels and sprinkle with ½ teaspoon salt and pepper. Heat oil in medium ovensafe saucepan over medium-high heat until just smoking. Brown chicken well, about 5 minutes per side; transfer to plate.

3. Pour off all but 1 teaspoon fat from saucepan. Add onion and remaining ¼ teaspoon salt and cook over medium-low heat until softened and lightly browned, 5 to 7 minutes. Stir in garlic and thyme and cook until fragrant, about 30 seconds. Stir in remaining ½ cup broth and wine, scraping up any browned bits. Stir in parcooked rice, breaking up any large clumps, and bring to simmer. Place browned chicken skin side up on rice, cover, and bake until rice is cooked through and chicken registers 175 degrees, about 25 minutes.

4. Using potholders (saucepan handle will be hot), remove saucepan from oven. Transfer chicken to serving platter and tent chicken loosely with aluminum foil. Fluff rice with fork, cover, and let sit for 10 minutes. Stir in parsley and season with salt and pepper to taste. You will need a medium ovensafe saucepan with a tight-fitting lid for this recipe. Serve chicken with rice.

VARIATIONS

Chicken and Rice with Five-Spice and Scallions

Substitute ¼ teaspoon five-spice powder for thyme and 2 thinly sliced scallions for parsley.

Chicken and Rice with Smoked Paprika and Cilantro

Substitute ¼ teaspoon smoked paprika for thyme and 2 tablespoons chopped fresh cilantro for parsley.

Pomegranate Chicken with Farro and Cucumber Salad

Serves 2
Total time 1 hour
WHY THIS RECIPE WORKS In this pan-roasted method, we took advantage of a shortcut for roasting chicken breasts by utilizing the pan's lid to create a stovetop oven. The chicken was enveloped in heat that created satisfying juiciness reminiscent of a whole bird. We served the chicken with a farro and cucumber salad with pomegranate vinaigrette. Do not use quick-cooking or presteamed farro. The cooking time for farro can vary across brands, so check for doneness after 15 minutes. You will need an 8- or 10-inch nonstick skillet with a tight-fitting lid for this recipe.

¾ cup whole farro
½ teaspoon table salt, divided, plus salt for cooking farro
1 (10-to 12-ounce) bone-in split chicken breast, trimmed and pounded to even thickness
⅛ teaspoon pepper
2 tablespoons extra-virgin olive oil
5 teaspoons pomegranate molasses, divided
1 small shallot, minced
1 teaspoon grated orange zest plus 1 tablespoon juice
⅛ teaspoon ground cinnamon
⅓ English cucumber, quartered lengthwise and sliced thin
¼ cup pomegranate seeds
2 tablespoons chopped fresh mint, parsley, cilantro, or basil
1 tablespoon chopped toasted walnuts, pecans, almonds, or pistachios

1. Bring 2 quarts water to boil in large saucepan. Add farro and ½ teaspoon salt, return to boil, and cook until grains are tender with slight chew, 15 to 30 minutes. Drain farro, spread onto plate or rimmed baking sheet, and let cool completely, 10 to 15 minutes.

2. Pat chicken dry with paper towels and sprinkle with ¼ teaspoon salt and pepper. Place chicken, skin side down, in cold 8- or 10-inch nonstick skillet. Cover skillet; place over medium-low heat; and cook chicken, without moving, until skin is deep golden brown, 12 to 18 minutes. Flip chicken and continue to cook, uncovered, until chicken registers 160 degrees, 5 to 10 minutes. Transfer chicken, skin side up, to cutting board and let rest for 5 minutes.

3. Whisk oil, 4 teaspoons pomegranate molasses, shallot, orange zest and juice, 1 teaspoon water, cinnamon, and remaining ¼ teaspoon salt together in large bowl. Add farro, cucumber, pomegranate seeds, mint, and walnuts and toss to combine. Season with salt and pepper to taste. Carve chicken from bones, slice ½ inch thick, and drizzle with remaining 1 teaspoon pomegranate molasses. Serve chicken with salad.

Braised Chicken Thighs with Potatoes, Fennel, and Tarragon

Serves 2

Total time 2 hours

WHY THIS RECIPE WORKS When done right, braised chicken thighs are the ultimate comfort food, with juicy meat surrounded by a rich pan sauce and tender vegetables. But most recipes make enough for a crowd; we wanted a simplified formula for braised chicken that could easily be made in a skillet. For the chicken, we chose bone-in thighs, which would retain more flavor and moisture over the extended cooking time thanks to their fat and connective tissue. We started by browning the thighs to develop a flavorful fond in the pan, then we removed the skin to prevent the final dish from being greasy. For the braising liquid, a combination of chicken broth and wine lent the dish acidity and depth of flavor. To make this dish a hearty meal, we added red potatoes, carrots, and onions, plus some sliced fennel and tarragon for a fresh finish. You will need a 10-inch skillet with a tight-fitting lid for this recipe.

4 (5- to 7-ounce) bone-in chicken thighs, trimmed
¾ teaspoon table salt, divided
¼ teaspoon pepper
2 teaspoons vegetable oil
8 ounces red potatoes, unpeeled, cut into ½-inch pieces
3 carrots, peeled and sliced ½ inch thick
1 small onion, chopped fine
1 garlic clove, minced
½ teaspoon minced fresh thyme or ⅛ teaspoon dried
1¼ cups chicken broth
¼ cup dry white wine
½ fennel bulb, stalks discarded, bulb cored and sliced thin
2 tablespoons minced fresh tarragon
1 teaspoon lemon juice

1. Pat chicken dry with paper towels and sprinkle with ½ teaspoon salt and pepper. Heat oil in 10-inch skillet over medium-high heat until just smoking. Brown chicken well, about 5 minutes per side. Transfer chicken to plate, let cool slightly, then remove skin.

2. Pour off all but 1 tablespoon fat from skillet. Add potatoes, carrots, onion, and remaining ¼ teaspoon salt and cook over medium heat until onion is softened, about 5 minutes. Stir in garlic and thyme and cook until fragrant, about 30 seconds. Stir in broth and wine, scraping up any browned bits.

3. Nestle browned chicken into vegetables, along with any accumulated juices, and bring to a simmer. Reduce heat to medium-low; cover; and simmer until chicken is very tender and almost falling off bone, about 1 hour, flipping chicken halfway through cooking. Transfer chicken to serving dish and tent loosely with aluminum foil.

4. Increase heat to medium, stir in fennel, and continue to simmer, uncovered, until vegetables are tender and sauce is slightly thickened, about 8 minutes. Stir in any accumulated chicken juices and simmer for 30 seconds. Off heat, stir in tarragon and lemon juice and season with salt and pepper to taste. Spoon vegetables and sauce over chicken and serve.

VARIATION

Braised Chicken Thighs with Potatoes, Carrots, Asparagus, and Dill

Substitute 4 ounces asparagus, trimmed and cut on bias into 2-inch lengths, for fennel and 2 tablespoons minced fresh dill for tarragon.

REMOVING CHICKEN SKIN

Chicken skin is often slippery, making it a challenge to remove by hand, even when the chicken has been browned. To remove skin easily, use a paper towel to provide extra grip while pulling.

Chicken Scarpariello

Serves 2

Total time 1¼ hours

WHY THIS RECIPE WORKS If you (and whoever is joining you) like strong flavors, try this dish of chicken and sausage bathed in a garlicky sauce full of onions, bell peppers, and pickled hot cherry peppers. We browned the chicken and sausage and then cooked the bell pepper and onion in the rendered fat until softened and charred in spots. Chopped hot pickled cherry peppers, plus a splash of their spicy brine, delivered the dish's signature shot of bright heat, while flour cooked with the vegetables ensured that the sauce would have enough body to make a cohesive dish. You will need a 10-inch skillet with a tight-fitting lid for this recipe.

2 (10-ounce) chicken leg quarters, trimmed
¼ teaspoon table salt
¼ teaspoon pepper
2 teaspoons extra-virgin olive oil

Chicken Scarpariello

are softened and charred in spots, stirring occasionally, about 7 minutes. Add cherry peppers, garlic, flour, and oregano and cook until fragrant, about 1 minute. Stir in broth, sausage, and cherry pepper brine and bring to simmer, scraping up any browned bits.

4. Nestle chicken, skin side up, into sauce along with any accumulated juices. Reduce heat to medium-low; cover; and simmer until chicken registers 200 degrees, about 20 minutes.

Crispy Chicken with Cabbage Slaw and Tonkatsu Sauce

Serves 2 `FAST`

Total time 30 minutes

WHY THIS RECIPE WORKS This simple pan-fried Japanese chicken dish with a quick, homemade tonkatsu sauce and crunchy cabbage salad will add a real spark to your rotation of chicken meals. We achieved craveable, crispy chicken with just a little oil by using a 10-inch skillet; we needed only 3 tablespoons oil to create an even fry. For the crispy coating, we dredged each cutlet in beaten egg and then coated both sides with panko. You can substitute 1½ cups shredded red or green cabbage for the coleslaw mix. To lightly crush panko, place in a zipper-lock bag and use a rolling pin. Be sure to remove any tenderloin from the breast before halving it; reserve for another use.

6 ounces sweet Italian sausage, casings removed
1 cup thinly sliced red bell pepper
1 cup thinly sliced onion
1 tablespoon chopped hot pickled cherry peppers,
 plus 1 tablespoon brine
2 garlic cloves, minced
1 teaspoon all-purpose flour
½ teaspoon dried oregano
¾ cup chicken broth
1 tablespoon chopped fresh parsley

1. Pat chicken dry with paper towels and sprinkle with salt and pepper. Heat oil in 10-inch nonstick skillet over medium-high heat until just smoking. Add chicken skin side down and cook, without moving it, until well browned, about 5 minutes. Flip chicken and continue to cook until browned on second side, about 4 minutes. Transfer chicken to plate.

2. Add sausage to fat left in skillet and cook until browned, breaking up meat with wooden spoon, about 2 minutes. Using slotted spoon, transfer sausage to paper towel–lined plate.

3. Heat leftover fat in skillet over medium-high heat until shimmering. Add bell pepper and onion and cook until vegetables

2 teaspoons lemon juice
2 teaspoons soy sauce, divided
½ teaspoon toasted sesame oil
1½ cups coleslaw mix
2 scallions, sliced thin
1 tablespoon ketchup
1 tablespoon water
1½ teaspoons Worcestershire sauce
½ teaspoon Dijon mustard
¾ cup panko bread crumbs, lightly crushed
1 large egg
1 (6-to 8-ounce) boneless, skinless chicken breast,
 trimmed, halved horizontally, and pounded
 ¼ inch thick
3 tablespoons vegetable oil
2 cups cooked white rice (page 344), warmed

1. Whisk lemon juice, 1 teaspoon soy sauce, and sesame oil together in medium bowl. Add coleslaw mix and scallions and toss to combine. Season with salt and pepper to taste; set aside for serving.

Crispy Chicken with Cabbage Slaw and Tonkatsu Sauce

Parmesan and Basil–Stuffed Chicken with Roasted Carrots

2. Whisk ketchup, water, Worcestershire, mustard, and remaining 1 teaspoon soy sauce together in small bowl; set aside. Spread panko in shallow dish. Beat egg in second shallow dish. Working with 1 chicken cutlet at a time, dip cutlets in egg, allowing excess to drip off, then coat both sides with panko, pressing gently to adhere.

3. Heat oil in 10-inch skillet over medium-high heat until shimmering. Add cutlets and cook until deep golden brown, 2 to 3 minutes per side. Serve cutlets with rice, coleslaw, and tonkatsu sauce.

Parmesan and Basil–Stuffed Chicken with Roasted Carrots

Serves 2

Total time 1 hour 5 minutes

WHY THIS RECIPE WORKS We wanted an elegant yet easy recipe for stuffed chicken breasts and roasted carrots. We started with a no-fuss cream cheese filling with basil and garlic. Rather than turn to a fussy preparation for stuffing the breasts, we simply spooned the filling under the skin of bone-in chicken breasts; the skin held the filling in place, and the meat emerged from the oven moist and juicy. Brushing the skin with melted butter and baking the breasts in a hot 450-degree oven ensured crisp, golden-brown skin. For a simple side, we tossed carrots with melted butter and a little brown sugar and roasted them alongside the chicken. It is important to buy chicken breasts with the skin still attached and intact; otherwise, the stuffing will leak out. Be sure to spread the carrots in an even layer halfway through baking to ensure that they cook through and brown properly.

- 1 ounce Parmesan cheese, grated (½ cup)
- 1 ounce cream cheese, softened
- 2 tablespoons chopped fresh basil
- 1 tablespoon extra-virgin olive oil
- 1 small garlic clove, minced
  Pinch plus ¼ teaspoon plus ⅛ teaspoon table salt, divided
- 2 pinches plus ⅛ teaspoon pepper, divided
- 2 (10 - to 12-ounce) bone-in split chicken breasts, trimmed
- 1 tablespoon unsalted butter, melted
- 6 small carrots, peeled and sliced ½ inch thick on bias
- 1½ teaspoons packed dark brown sugar

1. Adjust oven rack to middle position and heat oven to 450 degrees. Line rimmed baking sheet with aluminum foil. Mix Parmesan, cream cheese, basil, oil, garlic, pinch salt, and pinch pepper together in bowl.

2. Pat chicken dry with paper towels and sprinkle with ¼ teaspoon salt and ⅛ teaspoon pepper. Use your fingers to gently loosen center portion of skin covering each breast. Using spoon, place half of cheese mixture underneath skin over center of each breast. Gently press on skin to spread out cheese mixture.

3. Arrange chicken skin side up on 1 side of baking sheet. Brush chicken with half of melted butter. Toss carrots with remaining melted butter and sugar and sprinkle with remaining ⅛ teaspoon salt and remaining pinch pepper. Mound carrots in pile on baking sheet, opposite chicken.

4. Bake until chicken registers 160 degrees and carrots are browned and tender, 30 to 35 minutes, rotating sheet and spreading out carrots into even layer halfway through baking. Let chicken and carrots rest on sheet for 5 minutes before serving.

VARIATION

Goat Cheese and Olive–Stuffed Chicken with Roasted Carrots

Omit Parmesan, basil, and olive oil. Add 1½ ounces softened goat cheese, 2 tablespoons finely chopped pitted kalamata olives, and 1 teaspoon minced fresh oregano to cream cheese mixture.

STUFFING BONE-IN CHICKEN BREASTS

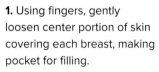

1. Using fingers, gently loosen center portion of skin covering each breast, making pocket for filling.

2. Using spoon, place filling underneath loosened skin, over center of each breast. Gently press on skin to spread out filling.

Chicken Sausage Hash

Serves 2
Total time 40 minutes

WHY THIS RECIPE WORKS While making hash for a crowd might mean endless chopping, all it takes is two small potatoes to get this scaled-down version going. For the classic flavor combination of potatoes and cabbage, we used tiny brussels sprouts to stand in for their larger counterpart. To ensure that everything was evenly cooked, we sautéed the components in stages, added everything back to steam briefly, and then uncovered the pan and cooked until the edges were crispy. Last, we cleared two small wells in the center of the skillet and cracked 2 eggs into each for a poached/fried hybrid that delivered a luxuriously oozy yolk (if desired). You will need a 12-inch nonstick skillet with a tight-fitting lid for this recipe.

- 2 small Yukon Gold potatoes, peeled and cut into ½-inch pieces
- 2 tablespoons vegetable oil, divided
- ¼ teaspoon table salt, divided
- ¼ teaspoon pepper, divided
- 8 ounces chicken sausage, casing removed
- 4 ounces brussels sprouts, trimmed and quartered
- 2 tablespoons water
- 2 large eggs

1. Toss potatoes, 2 teaspoons oil, ⅛ teaspoon salt, and ⅛ teaspoon pepper together in bowl. Cover and microwave until tender, about 5 minutes, stirring once halfway through microwaving; set aside. Heat 2 teaspoons oil in 12-inch nonstick skillet over medium heat until shimmering. Add sausage and cook, breaking up meat with wooden spoon, until sausage is lightly browned, about 5 minutes; add sausage to bowl with potatoes.

2. Heat remaining 2 teaspoons oil in now-empty skillet over medium heat until shimmering. Add brussels sprouts and cook, stirring occasionally, until browned, about 5 minutes. Stir in water and sausage-potato mixture. Reduce heat to medium-low; cover; and cook until brussels sprouts are tender, 3 to 4 minutes, stirring once halfway through. Flip hash, 1 scoop at a time, then lightly repack hash into pan. Repeat flipping and repacking hash every minute until potatoes are well browned, about 4 minutes.

3. Off heat, make 2 shallow wells in hash with back of spoon. Break 1 egg into each well in hash, sprinkle eggs with remaining ⅛ teaspoon salt and remaining ⅛ teaspoon pepper, then cover skillet and place over medium-low heat. Cook to desired doneness: 4 to 5 minutes for runny yolks or 6 to 7 minutes for set yolks. Season with salt and pepper to taste, and serve.

CHAPTER 6

Beef, Pork & Lamb

▦ **FAST** (Start to finish in 30 minutes or less)

Opposite: Pan-Seared Pork Chops with Dirty Rice

Pan-Seared Rib-Eye Steaks with Sweet-Tart Red Wine Sauce

Serves 2 **FAST**

Total time 30 minutes

WHY THIS RECIPE WORKS For easy-to-prepare pan-seared steaks, we selected rib eyes for their beefy flavor. Patting the steaks dry before cooking encouraged browning. Heating the oil over medium-high heat until just smoking ensured that our steaks developed a crisp, caramelized crust, and reducing the heat to medium once we flipped them allowed the steaks to cook through without developing a tough exterior. The fond left behind in the skillet formed the base for a classic red wine sauce featuring balsamic vinegar, Dijon mustard, and a touch of brown sugar for a balanced sweet yet tart flavor. We prefer these steaks cooked to medium-rare, but if you prefer them more or less done, see our guidelines on page 161.

- 2 (8-ounce) boneless rib-eye steaks, ¾ inch thick, trimmed
- ¼ teaspoon table salt
- ⅛ teaspoon pepper
- 1 tablespoon vegetable oil
- 1 shallot, minced
- 1 teaspoon packed brown sugar
- ¼ cup dry red wine
- ¼ cup chicken broth
- 2 teaspoons balsamic vinegar
- ½ teaspoon Dijon mustard
- 1 bay leaf
- 2 tablespoons unsalted butter, chilled
- ½ teaspoon minced fresh thyme

1. Pat steaks dry with paper towels and sprinkle with salt and pepper. Heat oil in 12-inch skillet over medium-high heat until just smoking. Lay steaks in skillet and cook until well browned on first side, 3 to 5 minutes. Flip steaks; reduce heat to medium; and continue to cook until meat registers 120 to 125 degrees (for medium-rare), 1 to 4 minutes; transfer to plate and tent loosely with aluminum foil.

2. Add shallot and sugar to fat left in skillet and cook over medium heat until shallot is just softened and browned and sugar is melted, about 1 minute. Stir in wine, broth, vinegar, mustard, and bay leaf, scraping up any browned bits. Bring to simmer and cook until sauce is slightly thickened, 2 to 4 minutes. Stir in any accumulated meat juices and simmer for 30 seconds. Discard bay leaf. Off heat, whisk in butter and thyme and season with salt and pepper to taste. Serve steaks with sauce.

One-Pan Coffee-Rubbed Steak with Sweet Potatoes and Apples

Serves 2

Total time 55 minutes

WHY THIS RECIPE WORKS A feast for the eyes as well as the soul, this autumnal sheet-pan meal is a winner. First we roasted sweet potato wedges and an abundance of quartered shallots in a hot oven until just softened. Meanwhile, we tossed a thinly sliced apple with oil and salt and prepared the rub for the steak. Then we roasted the steak on the empty side of the sheet pan and added the apple slices on top of the shallots. We made a quick parsley vinaigrette that we tossed with the potatoes, shallots, and apples while the steak rested. Look for shallots that weigh about 1 ounce each. We prefer this steak cooked to medium-rare, but if you prefer it more or less done, see our guidelines on page 161.

- 1 pound sweet potatoes, unpeeled, cut lengthwise into 1-inch wedges
- 4 shallots, peeled and quartered lengthwise
- 2 tablespoons extra-virgin olive oil, divided
- ½ teaspoon table salt, divided
- ½ teaspoon pepper, divided
- 1 large apple, cored, halved, and sliced thin
- 1 teaspoon packed dark brown sugar
- 1 teaspoon finely ground coffee
- 1 teaspoon chili powder
- 1 (6-ounce) boneless strip steak, 1 to 1½ inches thick, trimmed
- 2 tablespoons minced fresh parsley, plus extra for serving
- 1 tablespoon red wine vinegar

1. Adjust oven rack to lower-middle position and heat oven to 450 degrees. Toss potatoes and shallots with 2 teaspoons oil, ⅛ teaspoon salt, and ¼ teaspoon pepper in large bowl. Arrange potatoes skin side down on half of rimmed baking sheet and arrange shallots in single layer next to potatoes. Roast until vegetables are softened and lightly browned, 20 to 25 minutes.

2. Toss apple with 1 teaspoon oil and ⅛ teaspoon salt in now-empty bowl. Combine sugar, coffee, chili powder, remaining ¼ teaspoon salt, and remaining ¼ teaspoon pepper in small bowl. Pat steak dry with paper towels and rub with spice mixture.

3. Place steak on empty portion of baking sheet. Arrange apple slices on top of shallots. Roast until potatoes, shallots, and apples are fully tender and meat registers 120 to 125 degrees

One-Pan Coffee-Rubbed Steak with Sweet Potatoes and Apples

(for medium-rare), 10 to 15 minutes. Transfer steak, bottom side up, to cutting board, tent loosely with aluminum foil, and let rest for 5 minutes.

4. Combine parsley, vinegar, and remaining 1 tablespoon oil in large bowl. Add potatoes, shallots, and apples and toss to combine. Season with salt and pepper to taste. Slice steak thin against grain and sprinkle with extra parsley. Serve steak with sweet potato mixture.

Perfect Filets Mignons with Horseradish Sauce

Serves 2
Total time 40 minutes

WHY THIS RECIPE WORKS We wanted to develop a recipe for restaurant-style filets mignons we could make at home. For a rich, browned crust with a tender interior, we pan-seared oiled filets in a hot skillet until they were well browned on both sides. We then moved the steaks to the oven to finish cooking—this prevented the fond from burning and allowed the steaks to cook through evenly to a perfect medium-rare.

Extremely tender yet mild, filets mignons benefit from a rich sauce, so while the steaks rested we prepared a creamy horseradish sauce to accompany them by combining sour cream, horseradish, a little mayonnaise, garlic, and a squeeze of lemon juice. We prefer these steaks cooked to medium-rare, but if you prefer them more or less done, see our guidelines on page 161.

> 5 teaspoons vegetable oil, divided
> 2 (8-ounce) center-cut filets mignons, 1½ to 2 inches thick
> ¼ teaspoon table salt
> ⅛ teaspoon pepper
> ½ cup sour cream
> 2 tablespoons prepared horseradish
> 1 tablespoon mayonnaise
> 2 teaspoons lemon juice
> 1 small garlic clove, minced

1. Adjust oven rack to lower-middle position, place rimmed baking sheet on oven rack, and heat oven to 450 degrees. When oven reaches 450 degrees, heat 1 tablespoon oil in 10-inch skillet over high heat until just smoking.

2. Meanwhile, rub each side of steaks with ½ teaspoon oil and sprinkle with salt and pepper. Lay steaks in skillet and cook, without moving them, until well browned on both sides, about 3 minutes per side. Transfer steaks to hot sheet in oven and roast until meat registers 120 to 125 degrees (for medium-rare), about 4 minutes. Transfer steaks to plate, tent loosely with aluminum foil, and let rest for 5 minutes.

3. While steaks rest, combine sour cream, horseradish, mayonnaise, lemon juice, and garlic in bowl and season with salt and pepper to taste. Serve steaks with sauce.

Steak Tips with Red Wine Pan Sauce

Serves 2 **FAST**
Total time 30 minutes

WHY THIS RECIPE WORKS Sirloin steak tips have a rich, beefy flavor and satisfying texture, and since they're quick-cooking, they're a good option for an easy weeknight meal. A 10-inch skillet was just the right size for our scaled-down portion of meat, and cooking the tips over medium-high heat gave them a well-seared exterior and allowed them to cook through in just a matter of minutes. While the meat rested we prepared a simple yet flavorful red wine pan sauce, which we used to coat the steak tips just before serving. Steak tips, also

Steak Tips with Red Wine Pan Sauce

known as flap meat, are sold as whole steak, cubes, and strips; look for either whole steak tips or strips that are easy to cut into small pieces for this recipe. Use a good-quality medium-bodied wine, such as a Côtes du Rhône or Pinot Noir. We prefer these steak tips cooked to medium-rare, but if you prefer them more or less done, see our guidelines on page 161. Note that the cooking times may change depending on the size of the steak tips.

- 1 pound sirloin steak tips, trimmed and cut into 2-inch pieces
- ¼ teaspoon table salt
- ⅛ teaspoon pepper
- 1 tablespoon vegetable oil
- 2 tablespoons unsalted butter, divided
- 1 small shallot, minced
- ¼ cup dry red wine
- ½ teaspoon brown sugar
- ½ cup beef broth
- ⅛ teaspoon minced fresh thyme

1. Pat beef dry with paper towels and sprinkle with salt and pepper. Heat oil in 10-inch skillet over medium-high heat until just smoking. Add beef and cook until well browned on all sides and meat registers 120 to 125 degrees (for medium-rare), 5 to 7 minutes; transfer to plate and tent loosely with aluminum foil.

2. Add 1 tablespoon butter to fat left in skillet and melt over medium heat. Add shallot and cook until softened, about 2 minutes. Stir in wine and sugar, scraping up any browned bits. Bring to simmer and cook until nearly evaporated, about 3 minutes. Stir in broth; bring to simmer; and cook until sauce is slightly thickened, about 3 minutes. Stir in any accumulated meat juices and simmer for 30 seconds. Off heat, whisk in remaining 1 tablespoon butter and thyme and season with salt and pepper to taste. Return browned steak tips to skillet and turn to coat with sauce. Serve.

Seared Steak with Crispy Potatoes and Herb Sauce

Serves 2

Total time 50 minutes

WHY THIS RECIPE WORKS The true star of this simple meat-and-potatoes skillet meal is the potent herb sauce that coats everything. Inspired by the bright, garlicky flavors of Argentinean chimichurri, we created a bold parsley sauce by stirring fresh parsley with olive oil, red onion, and red wine

---

NOTES FROM THE TEST KITCHEN

PAN SAUCES 101: THE FOUR-STEP PROCESS

BROWN THE MEAT In a skillet large enough to avoid crowding, heat oil over medium-high heat until just smoking. Add the meat and cook until well browned on both sides and cooked to the desired doneness. Transfer the meat to a platter and tent with foil.

BROWN THE AROMATICS Add minced aromatics, such as garlic, shallot, or oregano, to the skillet and cook until fragrant, about 30 seconds.

ADD THE LIQUID Add the liquid (usually about ½ cup broth, wine, or juice for two servings) and use a wooden utensil to scrape up the bits left from browning the meat. Simmer until the liquid has reduced by about half. Pour in any accumulated juices from the resting meat.

FINISH THE SAUCE Simmer the sauce until thickened. Whisk in 1 to 2 tablespoons of butter. Season with salt and pepper and serve with the meat.

vinegar. Adding one garlic clove promised plenty of kick, and red pepper flakes delivered a bit of pleasant heat. With our sauce ready, we seared beefy, well-marbled strip steak in a hot skillet until well browned. Cooking the steak to medium-rare kept the meat moist and tender. For a perfectly crisp side of potatoes that used the same pan, we cut red potatoes into wedges and jump-started their cooking in the microwave. Using the meaty juices left behind in the skillet, we imparted some flavorful browning onto the wedges, giving them an appealing golden hue and crisp bite. Feel free to use a single herb or a combination of herbs for the sauce. We prefer this steak cooked to medium-rare, but if you prefer it more or less done, see our guidelines on page 161.

6 tablespoons extra-virgin olive oil, divided
¼ cup minced fresh parsley, basil, and/or cilantro
1 small shallot, minced
1 tablespoon red wine vinegar
1 garlic clove, minced
½ teaspoon plus ⅛ teaspoon table salt, divided
⅛ teaspoon red pepper flakes
12 ounces red potatoes, unpeeled, cut into
    1-inch wedges
¼ teaspoon pepper, divided
1 (1-pound) boneless strip or rib-eye steak,
    1½ to 1¾ inches thick, trimmed

1. Combine ¼ cup oil, parsley, shallot, vinegar, garlic, ¼ teaspoon salt, and pepper flakes in bowl; set aside for serving.

2. Toss potatoes with 1 teaspoon oil, ⅛ teaspoon salt, and ⅛ teaspoon pepper in bowl. Cover and microwave, stirring occasionally, until potatoes begin to soften, 5 to 7 minutes; drain well.

3. Heat 2 teaspoons oil in 10-inch nonstick skillet over medium-high heat until just smoking. Pat steak dry with paper towels and sprinkle with remaining ¼ teaspoon salt and remaining ⅛ teaspoon pepper. Place steak in skillet and cook, without moving, until well browned on first side, 3 to 5 minutes. Flip steak; reduce heat to medium; and continue to cook until meat registers 120 to 125 degrees (for medium-rare), 5 to 7 minutes. Transfer steak to cutting board, tent with aluminum foil, and let rest while finishing potatoes.

4. Heat remaining 1 tablespoon oil in now-empty skillet over medium heat until shimmering. Add potatoes and cook, stirring occasionally, until well browned, about 10 minutes. Slice steak ¼ inch thick and serve with potatoes, passing parsley sauce separately.

PREPARING RED POTATOES

Because the skins will be in the final dish, it's important to scrub the potatoes well before cutting them into wedges to ensure that no dirt or grit is left behind.

Sirloin Steak with Boursin Mashed Potatoes

Serves 2

Total time 45 minutes

WHY THIS RECIPE WORKS We wanted a steak-and-potatoes dinner that we could get on the table with a minimum number of ingredients—without sacrificing flavor. A one-pound boneless top sirloin steak was just the right size for two servings, and searing it over high heat then turning down the heat allowed the steak to develop a well-browned exterior without overcooking. For quick mashed potatoes to accompany our steak, we simply simmered potatoes until tender, then stirred in warm milk and Boursin cheese, a garlic-and-herb flavored cheese that gave our potatoes a creamy texture and loads of flavor with just one ingredient. A sprinkling of fresh chives folded into the potatoes was the perfect finishing touch. We prefer this steak cooked to medium-rare, but if you prefer it more or less done, see our guidelines on page 161.

12 ounces russet potatoes, peeled and
    sliced ½ inch thick
1 tablespoon vegetable oil
1 (1-pound) boneless top sirloin steak,
    ¾ to 1 inch thick, trimmed
¼ teaspoon table salt
⅛ teaspoon pepper
¼ cup whole milk, warmed, plus extra as needed
½ (5.2-ounce) package Boursin Garlic and
    Fine Herbs cheese
1 tablespoon minced fresh chives

1. Cover potatoes by 1 inch of water in medium saucepan. Bring to boil over medium-high heat, then reduce to simmer and cook, stirring once or twice, until potatoes are tender, 16 to 18 minutes.

2. Meanwhile, heat oil in 10-inch skillet over medium-high heat until just smoking. Pat steak dry with paper towels and sprinkle with salt and pepper. Lay steak in skillet and cook until well browned on first side, 3 to 5 minutes. Flip steak; reduce heat to medium; and continue to cook until meat registers 120 to 125 degrees (for medium-rare), 5 to 7 minutes. Transfer steak to cutting board, tent loosely with aluminum foil, and let rest for 5 minutes.

3. While steak rests, drain potatoes and return to saucepan. Cook over low heat, stirring constantly, until potatoes are thoroughly dried, about 2 minutes. Off heat, mash potatoes with potato masher until smooth. Gently fold in warm milk and Boursin until incorporated. Adjust consistency with extra warm milk as needed. Stir in chives and season with salt and pepper to taste. Slice steak thin. Serve with potatoes.

Seared Flank Steak with Oat Berries, Zucchini, and Peppers

Serves 2

Total time 1 hour

WHY THIS RECIPE WORKS This one-dish meal features nutty oat berries, seared flank steak, and caramelized vegetables. The oat berries were a nice change of pace from rice, and their hearty texture added flavor and heft to this simple meal. Plus, they don't require hands-on cooking, so you can sear the steak and caramelize vegetables on the stovetop. We jazzed up the cooked oat berries with dill, lemon zest and juice, and olive oil, which ensured they were anything but bland. After searing the steak, we simply caramelized chunks of zucchini and bell pepper until gloriously golden brown. We prefer this steak cooked to 120 to 125 degrees (medium-rare), but if you prefer it more or less done, see our guidelines on page 161.)

¾ cup oat berries (groats), rinsed

½ teaspoon table salt, divided, plus salt for cooking oat berries

2 tablespoons minced fresh dill, tarragon, or parsley

¼ teaspoon lemon zest plus 1 tablespoon juice, plus lemon wedges for serving

1 tablespoon extra-virgin olive oil, divided

6 ounces flank steak, trimmed

¼ teaspoon pepper

1 large zucchini, halved lengthwise and cut into 1-inch pieces

1 red, orange, or yellow bell pepper, stemmed, seeded, and cut into 1-inch pieces

¼ cup dried tart cherries, chopped

Seared Flank Steak with Oat Berries, Zucchini, and Peppers

1. Bring 2 quarts water to boil in large saucepan. Add oat berries and 1½ teaspoons salt and cook until grains are tender with slight chew, 40 to 50 minutes. Drain oat berries. Combine dill, lemon zest and juice, 2 teaspoons oil, and ¼ teaspoon salt in large bowl. Add oat berries and toss to combine; set aside.

2. Pat steak dry with paper towels and sprinkle with pepper and remaining ¼ teaspoon salt. Heat remaining 1 teaspoon oil in 10- or 12-inch nonstick skillet over medium-high heat until just smoking. Add steak and cook until well browned and meat registers 120 to 125 degrees (for medium-rare), 3 to 6 minutes per side; adjust heat as needed to prevent scorching. Transfer steak to cutting board, tent loosely with aluminum foil, and let rest while cooking vegetables.

3. Heat fat left in now-empty skillet over medium-high heat until just smoking. Add zucchini and bell pepper and cook, stirring occasionally, until just tender and deep golden brown, 6 to 10 minutes.

4. Slice steak thin against grain. Stir vegetables, cherries, and any accumulated juices from steak into oat berry mixture. Season with salt and pepper to taste. Serve steak with oat berry mixture and lemon wedges.

Pot-Roasted Steaks with Root Vegetables

Serves 2

Total time 2½ hours

WHY THIS RECIPE WORKS For a hearty, warming winter meal, we wanted to braise steaks and root vegetables for a satisfying dinner. Blade steak proved an ideal cut for pot-roasting, given its meaty flavor and plenty of collagen that broke down into gelatin when slow-cooked for a supremely tender texture. Searing the steaks added flavor and color, and 1½ cups of liquid (a combination of chicken broth and water) provided ample braising liquid. Onion, garlic, celery, and thyme added another layer of flavor, and potatoes turned our dish into a one-pot meal. Finally, we reduced the braising liquid at the end and finished it with a little red wine to create a flavorful sauce. The vegetables in the braising liquid do not get strained out before serving, so cut them into fairly even pieces. For more information on trimming blade steak, see page 37.

- 2 (6- to 8-ounce) beef blade steaks, ¾ to 1 inch thick
- ⅛ teaspoon table salt
- Pinch pepper
- 2 tablespoons vegetable oil, divided
- 4 ounces baby carrots
- 1 small onion, chopped fine
- 1 celery rib, chopped
- 2 garlic cloves, minced
- 1 teaspoon minced fresh thyme or ¼ teaspoon dried
- ½ teaspoon sugar
- 1 cup chicken broth
- ½ cup water
- 8 ounces red potatoes, unpeeled, cut into 1-inch pieces
- 2 tablespoons dry red wine
- 2 teaspoons chopped fresh parsley

1. Adjust oven rack to lower-middle position and heat oven to 350 degrees. Pat steaks dry with paper towels and sprinkle with salt and pepper. Heat 1 tablespoon oil in 12-inch ovensafe nonstick skillet over medium-high heat until just smoking. Lay steaks in skillet and cook until well browned on both sides, 3 to 5 minutes per side; transfer to plate.

2. Add remaining 1 tablespoon oil to fat left in skillet and heat over medium heat until shimmering. Add carrots, onion, and celery and cook until onion is softened, about 5 minutes. Stir in garlic, thyme, and sugar and cook until fragrant, about 30 seconds. Stir in broth and water, scraping up any browned bits, and bring to simmer.

NOTES FROM THE TEST KITCHEN

STORING MEAT SAFELY

Throwing away meat because it went bad before you had a chance to cook it is frustrating, particularly when you've spent a lot of money on a nice steak or cut of lamb. Proper storage is the best way to prolong its shelf life and prevent waste.

REFRIGERATING MEAT Raw meat should be refrigerated well wrapped and never on shelves that are above other food. Check regularly to ensure your refrigerator's temperature is between 35 and 40 degrees. Raw or cooked meat will keep for two to three days in the refrigerator; raw ground meat and raw poultry will keep for two days. Smoked ham or bacon will keep for up to two weeks (see page 8 for information on freezing bacon).

FREEZING MEAT In general, meat tastes best when it hasn't been frozen. The slow process of freezing that occurs in a home freezer (as compared with a commercial freezer) causes large ice crystals to form. The crystals rupture the cell walls of the meat, permitting the release of juices during cooking, resulting in drier meat. If you're going to freeze meat, wrap it well in plastic and then place the meat in a zipper-lock bag and squeeze out excess air. Label the bag with the contents and date and use the meat within a few months.

THAWING MEAT All meat can be thawed safely on a plate or rimmed baking sheet in the refrigerator (and this is the only safe method for large cuts). Never thaw meat on the counter, where bacteria will rapidly multiply. According to the USDA, frozen food that is properly thawed is safe to refreeze. However, a second freeze-thaw cycle aggravates moisture loss, reducing the quality of the meat, so we don't recommend it.

QUICK THAW FOR SMALL CUTS Flat cuts like pork chops or steaks will thaw more quickly when left on a metal surface rather than a wood or plastic one; metal can transfer ambient heat much more quickly. To thaw frozen wrapped steaks, chops, or ground meat (flattened to 1 inch thick before freezing), place in a skillet (heavy steel and cast-iron skillets work best) in a single layer. Flip the meat every half hour until it's thawed.

Modern Beef Pot Pie with
Mushrooms and Sherry

3. Nestle potatoes and browned steaks into skillet along with any accumulated juices and bring to simmer. Cover; transfer skillet to oven; and cook until steaks are fully tender and fork slips easily in and out of meat, about 1¼ hours, flipping steaks halfway through cooking.

4. Using potholders (skillet handle will be hot), remove skillet from oven. Transfer steaks to plate and tent loosely with aluminum foil.

5. Being careful of hot skillet handle, bring cooking liquid left in skillet to simmer over medium-high heat and cook until slightly thickened, 5 to 7 minutes. Stir in wine along with any accumulated juices and continue to simmer for 1 minute. Off heat, stir in parsley and season with salt and pepper to taste. Serve steaks with vegetables and sauce.

Modern Beef Pot Pie with Mushrooms and Sherry

Serves 2

Total time 2 hours

WHY THIS RECIPE WORKS To create a simplified version of beef pot pie with a savory beef filling, we knew that browning boneless short ribs (which we liked for their richness) for deeper flavor was a must, so we seared the meat in a skillet and then used the leftover fat to cook the carrots and onion. A little flour helped thicken the filling to a rich consistency. To satisfy our craving for crust without requiring another pan, we pondered easy yet delicious alternatives. Ultimately, we landed on slices of crusty bread brushed with oil and sprinkled with Gruyère cheese. Toasted under the broiler, the cheesy top browned and crisped while the underside of the bread absorbed some of the pot pie's juices. Minced chives lent a little freshness and color to our easy and delicious beef pot pie. You will need a 10-inch broiler-safe skillet with a tight-fitting lid for this recipe.

1 pound boneless beef short ribs, trimmed and cut into ¾-inch pieces
¼ teaspoon table salt
⅛ teaspoon pepper
2 tablespoons vegetable oil, divided
12 ounces cremini mushrooms, trimmed and quartered
1 small onion, chopped fine
1 tablespoon tomato paste
1 teaspoon minced fresh thyme or ¼ teaspoon dried
1½ tablespoons all-purpose flour
¼ cup dry sherry
1¼ cups beef broth

1 (8-inch) baguette, sliced ½ inch thick, ends discarded
1 ounce Gruyère cheese, shredded (¼ cup)
2 tablespoons minced fresh chives

1. Adjust oven rack to middle position and heat oven to 400 degrees. Pat beef dry with paper towels and sprinkle with salt and pepper. Heat 2 teaspoons oil in 10-inch broiler-safe skillet over medium-high heat until just smoking. Brown beef on all sides, 8 to 10 minutes; transfer to bowl.

2. Add mushrooms, onion, and 1 teaspoon oil to fat left in skillet and cook over medium heat until mushrooms have released their liquid and vegetables are softened and lightly browned, about 8 minutes. Stir in tomato paste and thyme and cook until fragrant, about 30 seconds. Stir in flour and cook for 1 minute.

3. Stir in sherry, scraping up any browned bits, and cook until almost completely evaporated, about 2 minutes. Slowly stir in broth, smoothing out any lumps. Bring to simmer, then stir in beef along with any accumulated juices. Cover; transfer skillet to oven; and cook until beef is tender, about 1 hour, stirring once halfway through cooking.

4. Using pot holder (skillet handle will be hot), remove skillet from oven. Adjust oven rack 8 inches from broiler element and heat broiler. Being careful of hot skillet handle, season filling with salt and pepper to taste.

5. Brush bread with remaining 1 tablespoon oil and shingle around edge of skillet, leaving center open. Sprinkle Gruyère over bread. Broil until cheese is melted and bread is browned, about 2 minutes. Remove skillet from oven and let casserole cool for 5 minutes. Sprinkle with chives and serve.

Prime Rib for Two

Serves 2

Total time 1¼ hours

WHY THIS RECIPE WORKS Even the smallest prime rib roast is too big for two, so we turned to bone-in rib steak. It's from the same juicy, tender rib section of the cow but is the perfect size for two. To get both the crusty, browned exterior and juicy, rosy interior of perfect prime rib, we seared the meat in a skillet, then moved it to a wire rack set in a rimmed baking sheet to cook through in a low oven. Then we used the skillet to make a quick jus with shallot, thyme, beef broth, and red wine. Be sure to brown the edges by using tongs to hold the steak on its side in the hot skillet. We prefer these steaks cooked to medium-rare, but if you prefer them more or less done, see our guidelines on page 161.

1 (1½-pound) bone-in rib-eye steak, 1¾ to 2 inches thick, trimmed
½ teaspoon table salt
¼ teaspoon pepper
1 tablespoon vegetable oil
1 shallot, minced
1 teaspoon ketchup
1 teaspoon minced fresh thyme or ¼ teaspoon dried
½ cup beef broth
¼ cup dry red wine

1. Adjust oven rack to lowest position and heat oven to 200 degrees. Pat steak dry with paper towels and sprinkle with salt and pepper.

2. Heat oil in 12-inch skillet over medium-high heat until just smoking. Brown steak well on all sides, 10 to 12 minutes; transfer to wire rack set in rimmed baking sheet. Roast steak until meat registers 120 to 125 degrees (for medium-rare), 25 to 30 minutes. Transfer steak to cutting board, tent loosely with aluminum foil, and let rest for 5 to 10 minutes.

3. Meanwhile, pour off all but 2 teaspoons fat from skillet. Add shallot and cook over medium heat until softened, about 2 minutes. Stir in ketchup and thyme and cook until fragrant, about 30 seconds. Stir in broth and wine, scraping up any browned bits. Bring to simmer and cook until jus is reduced to ⅓ cup, about 10 minutes. Stir in any accumulated meat juices and simmer for 30 seconds. Cut steak neatly away from bone and slice into ½-inch-thick slices on bias. Serve steak with jus.

Glazed Meatloaf with Root Vegetables

Serves 2

Total time 1¼ hours

WHY THIS RECIPE WORKS There's something nostalgic about a classic meatloaf supper, but a traditional meatloaf recipe makes way too much for two people. Here, we scaled it down, made it an easy-to-prep recipe, and as an added bonus made it a one-dish meal with vegetables roasted alongside the meatloaf. A panade of crushed saltines, egg, and water held the meatloaf together and kept the ground beef moist in the oven. Soy sauce and Parmesan cheese imparted savory depth, while fresh thyme and garlic powder added pep. Finally, a coating of ketchup contributed a sweet and tangy glaze that nicely complemented the meat. Hearty carrots and a turnip were the perfect vegetables to roast alongside the meatloaf

because they only got better the longer they cooked. In the 400-degree oven, they became creamy inside and golden brown and slightly caramelized. To brighten the vegetables' deep roasted flavor, we gave them a sprinkle of chives just before serving. Parsnips can be substitute for the turnips.

10 square saltines
¼ cup grated Parmesan cheese
1 large egg
2 tablespoons water
2 teaspoons soy sauce
¾ teaspoon minced fresh thyme or ⅛ teaspoon dried
½ teaspoon garlic powder
½ teaspoon pepper, divided
12 ounces 85 percent lean ground beef
3 tablespoons ketchup
3 carrots, peeled and cut into 2½-inch lengths, halved or quartered lengthwise to create ½-inch-diameter pieces
6 ounces turnips, peeled and cut into 1-inch pieces
¼ teaspoon table salt
2 teaspoons extra-virgin olive oil
2 teaspoons minced fresh chives

1. Adjust oven rack to lowest position and heat oven to 400 degrees. Line rimmed baking sheet with aluminum foil and spray with vegetable oil spray.

2. Transfer saltines to 1-gallon zipper-lock bag, seal bag, and crush fine with rolling pin. Combine saltine crumbs, Parmesan, egg, water, soy sauce, thyme, garlic powder, and ¼ teaspoon pepper in large bowl. Mix until all crumbs are moistened and mixture forms paste. Add beef and mix with your hands to thoroughly combine.

3. Transfer meatloaf mixture to center of prepared sheet. Using your wet hands, shape into 7 by 3½-inch rectangle; top should be flat and meatloaf should be an even 1½ inches thick. Brush top and sides of meatloaf with ketchup.

4. Toss carrots, turnips, salt, oil, and remaining ¼ teaspoon pepper together in bowl. Place vegetables cut sides down on sheet around meatloaf. Bake until meatloaf registers 160 degrees, 25 to 30 minutes, rotating sheet halfway through baking.

5. Remove sheet from oven. Using 2 spatulas, transfer meatloaf to cutting board. Tent with foil and let rest while vegetables finish baking. Return vegetables to oven and continue to bake until tender and beginning to brown, 5 to 10 minutes. Slice meatloaf, sprinkle vegetables with chives, and serve.

Bò Lúc Lắc

Serves 2

Total time 1 hour

WHY THIS RECIPE WORKS Bò Lúc Lắc or shaking beef is a Vietnamese cross between a beef stir-fry and a watercress salad. We used sirloin steak tips (aka flap meat) for their beefy flavor and pleasant chewy texture. We first marinated the meat in a mixture of soy sauce, fish sauce, and molasses and then reserved the marinade to make the glaze. We coated the meat with oil (to prevent splattering) and then cooked it in two batches to give it ample room in the skillet. True to the dish's name, we shook and stirred the beef to develop good browning and to deglaze the skillet, which prevented the fond from burning. After setting aside the meat, we lightly softened a red onion in butter, added the reserved marinade (along with garlic, water, and cornstarch) to the skillet, and cooked it down to a glossy consistency. We coated the meat with the sauce and then placed it atop the watercress, which had been lightly dressed with a mixture of lime juice and pepper (the rest of which served as a dipping sauce for the meat). Steak tips, also known as flap meat, are sold as whole steak, cubes, and strips; look for either whole steak tips or strips that are easy to cut into small pieces for this recipe. Maggi Seasoning can be used in place of the soy sauce, if desired. Serve with white rice.

Bò Lúc Lắc

2 teaspoons fish sauce
2 teaspoons soy sauce
1 teaspoon molasses
8 ounces sirloin steak tips, trimmed and cut into ¾-inch pieces
2 ounces (2 cups) watercress, torn into bite-size pieces
2 tablespoons lime juice
½ teaspoon pepper
¼ cup water
1 garlic clove, minced
¼ teaspoon cornstarch
2 teaspoons vegetable oil, divided
1½ teaspoons unsalted butter
½ small red onion, sliced thin

1. Whisk fish sauce, soy sauce, and molasses together in medium bowl. Add beef and toss to coat. Let sit at room temperature for 15 minutes. Spread watercress in shallow serving bowl. Combine lime juice and pepper in small bowl and set aside.

2. Using tongs, transfer beef to second medium bowl, letting as much marinade as possible drain back into first bowl. Add water, garlic, and cornstarch to marinade in first bowl and whisk to combine; set aside. Add 1 teaspoon oil to beef and toss to coat.

3. Heat remaining 1 teaspoon oil in 14-inch flat-bottomed wok or 12-inch nonstick skillet over medium-high heat until just smoking. Using tongs, wipe wok clean with paper towels. Add beef to wok, leaving space between pieces. Cook, shaking wok gently and occasionally to capture any fond that collects on bottom of wok, until beef is browned on first side, 3 to 4 minutes. Continue to cook, stirring and shaking wok frequently, until beef is coated and browned and center is just barely pink (to check for doneness, remove larger piece and cut in half), 2 to 4 minutes. Transfer beef to clean bowl.

4. Melt butter in now-empty wok over medium heat. Add onion and cook, stirring occasionally, until just beginning to soften, about 1 minute. Add reserved marinade and bring to boil. Cook, stirring occasionally, until marinade is thickened and glossy, about 2 minutes. Add beef along with any accumulated juices and toss to coat. Scatter beef mixture and sauce over watercress. Drizzle 1 teaspoon lime juice mixture over salad. Divide remaining lime juice mixture among 2 small bowls for dipping and serve with salad.

Stir-Fried Beef and Gai Lan

Stir-Fried Cumin Beef

Stir-Fried Beef and Gai Lan

Serves 2

Total time 45 minutes

WHY THIS RECIPE WORKS Our take on this ever-evolving Chinese American standard features gai lan (Chinese broccoli) and filet mignon: The luxe cut is ideal for quick, high-heat cooking; is readily available in small portions; and just needed a brief chill in the freezer to firm up for easy slicing before being coated in a simple mixture of soy sauce, Shaoxing wine, and cornstarch. While the meat chilled, we sliced the gai lan stalks thin on the bias and cut the tender leaves into wide ribbons. We started the stir-fry by cooking the stalks in oil in a hot wok. As they sizzled, the oil smoldered, infusing the dish with the distinct charred smoky flavor known as wok hei. We then set the stalks aside and stir-fried the leaves with garlic and toasted sesame oil, speeding their cooking with a small but flavorful addition of chicken broth before arranging them on a serving platter. Finally, we stir-fried the marinated beef; returned the stalks to the wok; and stirred in a blend of chicken broth, oyster sauce, soy sauce, Shaoxing wine, toasted sesame oil, and cornstarch. The sauce thickened in less than a minute. If gai lan is unavailable, you can use broccolini, substituting the florets for the gai lan leaves. Do not use standard broccoli. Serve with white rice.

1 (4-ounce) center-cut filet mignon, trimmed

8 ounces gai lan, stalks trimmed

2½ teaspoons Shaoxing wine or dry sherry, divided

1½ teaspoons soy sauce, divided

1 teaspoon cornstarch, divided

¼ cup plus 2 tablespoons chicken broth, divided

1 tablespoon oyster sauce

¾ teaspoon toasted sesame oil, divided

1 tablespoon vegetable oil, divided

¾ teaspoon grated fresh ginger

⅜ teaspoon minced garlic, divided

1. Cut beef into 2 equal wedges. Transfer to plate and freeze until very firm, 20 minutes. While beef freezes, prepare gai lan. Remove leaves, small stems, and florets from stalks; slice leaves crosswise into 1½-inch strips (any florets and stems can go into pile with leaves); and cut stalks on bias into ¼-inch-thick pieces. Set aside. When beef is firm, stand 1 piece on its side and slice against grain ¼ inch thick. Repeat with remaining pieces. Transfer to bowl. Add ½ teaspoon Shaoxing wine, ½ teaspoon soy sauce, and ½ teaspoon cornstarch and toss until beef is evenly coated. Set aside.

2. In second bowl, whisk together ½ cup broth, oyster sauce, ¼ teaspoon sesame oil, remaining 2 teaspoons Shaoxing wine, remaining 1 teaspoon soy sauce, and remaining ½ teaspoon cornstarch; set aside. In third bowl, combine 2 teaspoons vegetable oil, ginger, and ⅛ teaspoon garlic.

3. Heat ½ teaspoon vegetable oil in 14-inch flat-bottomed wok or 12-inch nonstick skillet over high heat until just smoking. Add stalks and cook, stirring slowly but constantly, until spotty brown and crisp-tender, 2 to 3 minutes. Transfer to bowl.

4. Add remaining ½ teaspoon sesame oil, remaining ½ teaspoon vegetable oil, and remaining ¼ teaspoon garlic to wok and cook, stirring constantly, until garlic is fragrant, about 10 seconds. Add leaves and cook, stirring frequently until vibrant green, about 45 seconds. Add remaining 2 tablespoons broth and cook, stirring constantly, until broth evaporates, 1 to 2 minutes. Spread evenly on serving dish.

5. Add ginger-garlic mixture to wok and cook, stirring constantly, until fragrant, about 20 seconds. Add beef and cook, stirring slowly but constantly, until no longer pink, about 1½ minutes. Return stalks to wok and add oyster sauce mixture. Cook, stirring constantly, until sauce thickens, 20 to 40 seconds. Place mixture on top of leaves. Serve.

PREPPING GAI LAN FOR STIR-FRYING

1. Cut leaves off stalks.

2. Slice leaves crosswise into 1½-inch strips.

3. Cut stalks on bias into ¼-inch-thick pieces.

SLICING FILET THIN

This supertender, premium cut is optimal for quick, high-heat wok cookery.

1. Cut beef into 2 equal wedges and freeze until very firm, 20 minutes.

2. Stand each wedge on its side and slice against grain ¼ inch thick.

Stir-Fried Cumin Beef

Serves 2

Total time 40 minutes

WHY THIS RECIPE WORKS With roots in Hunan cuisine, cumin beef typically features tender pieces of meat stir-fried with onions and/or peppers and aromatics (garlic and ginger), lightly glossed in a soy sauce–based glaze, seasoned with spices (cumin, Sichuan peppercorns, and dried chiles or chili flakes), and finished with cilantro. Before cooking, we briefly treated slices of beefy flank steak with baking soda, which raised the meat's pH so that it stayed moist and tender during cooking. We then stir-fried the meat until its juices reduced to a sticky fond that coated each slice. Quickly stir-frying sliced onion allowed it to soften but retain a hint of its raw bite and crunch. Grinding whole cumin seeds and Sichuan peppercorns released vibrant aromatic compounds that gave the dish plenty of fragrance, while Sichuan chili flakes added moderate heat. You can substitute 1½ teaspoons of ground cumin for the cumin seeds. If you can't find Sichuan chili flakes, Korean red pepper flakes (gochugaru) are a good substitute. Another alternative is ¾ teaspoon of ancho chile powder plus ⅛ teaspoon of cayenne pepper. There is no substitute for Sichuan peppercorns. We like this stir-fry with steamed white rice and stir-fried baby bok choy.

1½ teaspoons water
⅛ teaspoon baking soda
8 ounces flank steak, trimmed, cut with grain into 2- to 2½-inch-wide strips, each strip sliced against grain ¼ inch thick
2 garlic cloves, minced
1½ teaspoons grated fresh ginger
1½ teaspoons cumin seeds, ground
1 teaspoon Sichuan chili flakes
½ teaspoon Sichuan peppercorns, ground
¼ teaspoon table salt, divided
1½ teaspoons Shaoxing wine or dry sherry
1½ teaspoons soy sauce
1 teaspoon molasses
¼ teaspoon cornstarch
2 tablespoons vegetable oil, divided
¼ small onion, sliced thin
1 tablespoon coarsely chopped fresh cilantro

1. Combine water and baking soda in medium bowl. Add beef and toss to coat. Let sit at room temperature for 5 minutes.

2. While beef rests, combine garlic and ginger in small bowl. Combine cumin, chili flakes, peppercorns, and ⅛ teaspoon salt in second small bowl. Add Shaoxing wine, soy sauce, molasses, cornstarch, and remaining ⅛ teaspoon salt to beef mixture. Toss until well combined.

3. Heat 1 tablespoon oil in 14-inch flat-bottomed wok or 12-inch nonstick skillet over medium-high heat until just smoking. Add beef mixture and increase heat to high. Using tongs, toss beef slowly but constantly until exuded juices have evaporated and meat begins to sizzle, 2 to 6 minutes. Transfer to clean bowl.

4. Heat remaining 1 tablespoon oil in now-empty wok over medium heat until shimmering. Add garlic mixture (oil will splatter) and cook, stirring constantly, until fragrant, about 15 seconds. Add onion and cook, tossing slowly but constantly with tongs, until onion begins to soften, 1 to 2 minutes. Return beef to wok and toss to combine. Sprinkle cumin mixture over beef and toss until onion takes on pale orange color. Transfer to serving platter, sprinkle with cilantro, and serve immediately.

1. To make it easier to slice steak thin, freeze it for 15 minutes. Slice partially frozen steak with grain into roughly 2-inch-wide pieces

2. Slice each piece against grain into very thin slices.

Steak Fajitas

Serves 2
Total time 35 minutes

WHY THIS RECIPE WORKS For indoor steak fajitas we could make any time of year, we pan-seared steak over medium-high heat to mimic the caramelized exterior and crisp edges of grilled steak. Flank steak had great beefy flavor; we sliced it against the grain, which kept it tender. Tossing it with a squeeze of lime juice after cooking added the bright tang and flavor of a marinade in a fraction of the time. Bell pepper and onion are traditional for fajitas; just one of each was plenty for our scaled-down recipe. Chili powder, cumin, and hot sauce added the smoky, spicy notes we wanted. To make these fajitas spicy, add a sliced jalapeño with the bell pepper. We prefer this steak cooked to medium-rare, but if you prefer it more or less done, see our guidelines on page 161. Serve with your favorite fajita toppings.

12 ounces flank steak, trimmed
½ teaspoon table salt, divided
⅛ teaspoon pepper
2 tablespoons vegetable oil, divided
1 tablespoon lime juice
1 red, green, or yellow bell pepper, stemmed, seeded, and cut into ½-inch-wide strips
1 small red onion, halved and sliced thin
2 tablespoons water
1 teaspoon chili powder
¼ teaspoon ground cumin
¼ teaspoon hot sauce
6 (6-inch) flour tortillas, warmed

1. Pat steak dry with paper towels and sprinkle with ¼ teaspoon salt and pepper. Heat 1 tablespoon oil in 10-inch skillet over medium-high heat until just smoking. Lay steak in skillet and cook until well browned on first side, 3 to 5 minutes. Flip steak; reduce heat to medium; and continue to cook until meat registers 120 to 125 degrees (for medium-rare), 3 to 5 minutes; transfer to cutting board and drizzle with lime juice. Tent loosely with aluminum foil.

2. Heat remaining 1 tablespoon oil in now-empty skillet over medium heat until shimmering. Add bell pepper, onion, water, chili powder, cumin, hot sauce, and remaining ¼ teaspoon salt. Cook, scraping up any browned bits, until vegetables are softened, 5 to 7 minutes; transfer to serving platter.

3. Slice steak thin against grain, arrange on platter with vegetables, and serve with warm tortillas.

Keema

Serves 2

Total time 50 minutes

WHY THIS RECIPE WORKS Keema is a rich and savory spiced ground meat dish that's been a staple of South Asian cuisine for centuries, even gracing the tables of the Turkic sultans and Mughal emperors of the 15th and 16th centuries. Whether it's made with ground goat, lamb, beef, or poultry, the meat is broken into small bits and coated with a complexly spiced, velvety sauce that's rich and savory. Our version features a garam masala, or warming spice mix, comprising whole cinnamon and black and green cardamom as well as ground coriander, cumin, turmeric, and Kashmiri chile powder. We bloomed the whole spices early to coax out their oil-soluble compounds. Then we carefully browned red onion to deepen its flavor before spiking the mixture with garlic and ginger pastes. Next, we added 90 percent lean ground beef, and when it sizzled and browned, we stirred in the ground spices in the masala. As soon as these were fragrant, in went tomatoes and whole-milk yogurt. The tomatoes broke down as the keema cooked, and the yogurt added subtle richness. Together, they created a clingy sauce that flavored every bite of beef. Have your ingredients in place before you begin to cook. Look for black and green cardamom pods, Kashmiri chile powder, and 4- to 5-inch long green chiles at Indian or Pakistani markets. If you can't find Kashmiri chile powder, toast and grind one large guajillo chile and use 1 teaspoon; if a long green chile is unavailable, substitute a serrano. For a milder keema, omit the fresh chile or use only half of it. A rasp-style grater makes quick work of turning the garlic and ginger into pastes. Serve with roti, naan, or basmati rice.

Keema

1 tablespoon vegetable oil
3 black peppercorns
2 green cardamom pods
1 black cardamom pod
1 small cinnamon stick
½ red onion, sliced thin crosswise
½ teaspoon grated garlic
½ teaspoon grated fresh ginger
8 ounces 90 percent lean ground beef
⅜ teaspoon table salt
1 teaspoon ground coriander
1 teaspoon Kashmiri chile powder
¼ teaspoon ground turmeric
¼ teaspoon ground cumin
1 (6-ounce) vine-ripened tomato, cored and chopped
2 tablespoons plain whole-milk yogurt
1 long green chile, halved lengthwise (optional)
2 tablespoons chopped fresh cilantro, plus extra for garnish

1. Heat oil in medium saucepan over medium heat until shimmering. Add peppercorns, green and black cardamom pods, and cinnamon stick and cook, stirring occasionally, until fragrant, about 30 seconds. Add onion and cook, stirring occasionally, until onion is browned, 4 to 7 minutes.

2. Add garlic and ginger and cook, stirring constantly, until fragrant, about 30 seconds. Add beef and salt. Increase heat to medium-high and cook, stirring to break up meat into very small pieces and scraping up any browned bits. Continue to cook, stirring occasionally, until mixture sizzles and bottom of saucepan appears dry, 6 to 9 minutes.

3. Add coriander, chile powder, turmeric, and cumin and cook, stirring constantly, until spices are well distributed and fragrant, about 1 minute. Add tomato; yogurt; and chile, if using, and cook, stirring frequently, until tomato releases its juice and mixture begins to simmer, about 2 minutes. Adjust heat to maintain gentle simmer. Cover and cook, stirring occasionally, until tomato has broken down and wooden spoon scraped across bottom of saucepan leaves clear trail, 10 to 13 minutes. Stir in cilantro and season with salt and pepper to taste. If desired, remove cinnamon stick and cardamom pods. Transfer to serving bowl, garnish with extra cilantro, and serve.

Sautéed Pork Cutlets with Mustard-Cider Sauce

Serves 2
Total time 35 minutes

WHY THIS RECIPE WORKS Pork cutlets offer everything a time-pressed cook could want in a weeknight meal: thrift, minimal preparation, and dinner on the table in minutes. But store-bought cutlets are often lean and unevenly portioned and end up dry, stringy, and unevenly cooked. To solve these problems, we decided to make our own cutlets from boneless country-style ribs. These ribs contain flavorful shoulder meat and little connective tissue, and they are portioned into small pieces and available in small packages. After cutting the ribs into pieces and pounding them thin, our cutlets required just 4 minutes in a hot skillet for a deep brown crust and tender, juicy interior. A simple pan sauce featuring mustard, apple cider, and fresh herbs was the perfect finishing touch. Look for ribs that are 3 to 5 inches long. If your ribs are more than 5 inches long, cut them in half crosswise before slicing them lengthwise to ensure more evenly sized cutlets.

12 ounces boneless country-style pork ribs, trimmed
⅛ teaspoon table salt
Pinch pepper
½ teaspoon sugar
1 tablespoon extra-virgin olive oil
1 tablespoon unsalted butter, cut into 2 pieces, divided
1 shallot, minced
½ teaspoon all-purpose flour
¼ cup chicken broth
¼ cup apple cider
¼ teaspoon minced fresh sage, parsley, or thyme
2 teaspoons whole-grain mustard

1. Cut each rib lengthwise into 2 or 3 pieces about ⅜ inch wide. Lay each piece between 2 sheets of plastic wrap and pound until roughly ¼ inch thick. Pat cutlets dry with paper towels and sprinkle with salt and pepper. Sprinkle sugar evenly over each cutlet.

2. Heat oil in 12-inch skillet over medium-high heat until just smoking. Add 1 piece butter, let melt, then quickly add cutlets. Brown cutlets on both sides, about 2 minutes per side; transfer to plate and tent loosely with aluminum foil.

3. Add shallot to fat left in skillet and cook over medium heat until softened, about 2 minutes. Stir in flour and cook for 1 minute. Whisk in broth, cider, and sage, scraping up any browned bits. Bring to simmer and cook until sauce is slightly thickened, 2 to 3 minutes.

4. Return browned cutlets along with any accumulated juices to skillet and simmer until heated through, about 30 seconds; transfer cutlets to serving platter. Off heat, whisk mustard and remaining 1 piece butter into sauce and season with salt and pepper to taste. Pour sauce over cutlets and serve.

VARIATION
Sautéed Pork Cutlets with Lemon-Caper Sauce
Substitute ¼ cup dry white wine for apple cider. Substitute 2 tablespoons rinsed capers, 1 teaspoon grated lemon zest, and 1 teaspoon lemon juice for mustard.

CUTTING COUNTRY-STYLE RIBS INTO CUTLETS

1. Slice each rib lengthwise to create 2 or 3 cutlets, each about ⅜ inch wide.

2. Lay each piece between 2 sheets of plastic wrap and pound until roughly ¼ inch thick.

Sautéed Boneless Pork Chops with Sage-Butter Sauce

Serves 2

Total time 35 minutes

WHY THIS RECIPE WORKS For perfectly cooked, juicy pan-seared pork chops, we found that the thickness of the chops was key: A ¾-inch chop was thick enough to stay moist during cooking but thin enough that we could cook it entirely on the stovetop. We also sautéed the chops over two different heat levels. First, we seared them on one side over medium-high heat for a nicely browned exterior, then we flipped them over and turned the heat down to let them finish cooking through without drying out. To dress up our simple chops, we created two effortless yet impressive pan sauces—one a simple sage-butter sauce and the other a robust port wine and cherry sauce—with the browned bits left behind in the pan.

2 (6- to 8-ounce) boneless pork chops, ¾ to 1 inch thick, trimmed
⅛ teaspoon table salt
Pinch pepper
2 teaspoons vegetable oil, divided
1 shallot, minced
2 tablespoons minced fresh sage or 2 teaspoons dried
2 garlic cloves, minced
½ cup chicken broth
¼ cup dry white wine
2 tablespoons unsalted butter, chilled

1. Cut 2 slits, about 2 inches apart, through outer layer of fat and silverskin on each chop. Pat chops dry with paper towels and sprinkle with salt and pepper.

2. Heat 1 teaspoon oil in 10-inch skillet over medium-high heat until just smoking. Lay chops in skillet and cook until well browned on first side, about 3 minutes. Flip chops; reduce heat to medium; and continue to cook until meat registers 140 to 145 degrees, 5 to 10 minutes; transfer to serving platter and tent loosely with aluminum foil.

3. Add remaining 1 teaspoon oil to fat left in skillet and heat over medium heat until shimmering. Add shallot and cook until softened, about 2 minutes. Stir in sage and garlic and cook until fragrant, about 30 seconds. Stir in broth and wine, scraping up any browned bits. Bring to simmer and cook until sauce is slightly thickened, about 5 minutes. Stir in any accumulated meat juices and simmer for 30 seconds. Off heat, whisk in butter and season with salt and pepper to taste. Pour sauce over chops and serve.

VARIATION
Sautéed Boneless Pork Chops with Port Wine and Cherry Sauce
Substitute ½ teaspoon minced fresh rosemary for sage and ¼ cup ruby port for wine. Add ¼ cup dried cherries to skillet with broth in step 3.

PREVENTING CURLED PORK CHOPS

To prevent pork chops from curling while cooking, cut 2 slits, about 2 inches apart, through outer layer of fat and silverskin of each chop (this method works for both bone-in and boneless chops).

Crispy Sesame Pork Chops with Wilted Napa Cabbage Salad

Pan-Seared Thick-Cut, Bone-In Pork Chop

Crispy Sesame Pork Chops with Wilted Napa Cabbage Salad

Serves 2
Total time 50 minutes

WHY THIS RECIPE WORKS For breaded pork chops that stayed crispy, we coated our chops in panko bread crumbs and sesame seeds, which added nutty flavor and even more crunch to the coating. Using a generous ⅓ cup of oil to pan-fry the chops ensured that the coating came out crisp and golden. For a slaw-like salad, we wilted napa cabbage to soften it slightly along with garlic and ginger. Don't let the pork chops drain on the paper towels for longer than 30 seconds, or the heat will steam the crust and make it soggy.

- ¼ cup all-purpose flour
- 1 large egg
- ⅔ cup panko bread crumbs
- ⅓ cup sesame seeds
- 4 (3- to 4-ounce) boneless pork chops, ½ to ¾ inch thick, trimmed
- ⅛ teaspoon table salt
  Pinch pepper
- 1½ tablespoons vegetable oil
- 1½ teaspoons toasted sesame oil
- 1 garlic clove, minced
- ½ teaspoon grated fresh ginger
- ½ small head napa cabbage, cored and shredded (4 cups)
- 1 carrot, peeled and shredded
- 1 tablespoon unseasoned rice vinegar, plus extra for seasoning
- ⅓ cup vegetable oil, for frying

1. Set wire rack in rimmed backing sheet. Spread flour in shallow dish. Beat egg in second shallow dish. Combine panko and sesame seeds in third shallow dish.

2. Pat chops dry with paper towels and sprinkle with salt and pepper. Working with 1 chop at a time, dredge chops in flour, dip in egg, then coat with panko mixture, pressing gently to adhere; transfer to prepared rack.

3. Heat 1½ tablespoons vegetable oil and sesame oil in 12-inch nonstick skillet over medium heat until shimmering. Add garlic and ginger and cook until fragrant, about 30 seconds. Stir in cabbage and carrot and cook until just wilted, about 1 minute. Off heat, add rice vinegar and toss to combine. Transfer to serving bowl and season with salt, pepper, and extra vinegar to taste. Wipe skillet clean.

4. Line large plate with triple layer of paper towels. Heat remaining ⅓ cup vegetable oil in 12-inch nonstick skillet over medium-high heat until shimmering. Carefully lay chops in skillet and cook until golden brown and crisp on both sides and meat registers 140 to 145 degrees, 2 to 5 minutes per side. Drain chops briefly on paper towel–lined plate. Serve with cabbage salad.

Pan-Seared Thick-Cut, Bone-In Pork Chop

Serves 2 `FAST`

Total time 25 Minutes

WHY THIS RECIPE WORKS Achieving deeply browned, juicy bone-in pork chops starts with choosing the right chop: 1½-inch-thick rib chops were thick enough to build up a browned exterior before cooking through. We started the chops in a cold (not preheated) nonstick skillet over high heat and flipped them every 2 minutes so that the meat's temperature increased gradually, allowing a crust to build up on the outside without overcooking the interior. Starting over high heat drove off moisture and prevented the chops from steaming, and lowering the heat to medium encouraged browning without smoking. Bone-in rib chops may be labeled as rib cut, end cut, or center cut. To be sure that you are purchasing the correct chop, look for one that features one large eye of loin muscle. If you have time, salt the chop for at least 1 hour or up to 24 hours before cooking: Sprinkle the chop with 1½ teaspoons of Diamond Crystal Kosher Salt (if using Morton, which is denser, use only 1⅛ teaspoons), refrigerate it, and pat it dry with paper towels before cooking. If the pork is enhanced (injected with a salt solution), do not salt the chop ahead. Make sure to include the bone when serving.

- 1 (14- to 16-ounce) bone-in pork rib chop, 1½ inches thick, trimmed
- ¼ teaspoon pepper

1. Pat chop dry with paper towels and sprinkle both sides with pepper. Place chop in cold 10-inch nonstick or carbon-steel skillet. Place skillet over high heat and cook chop for 2 minutes. Flip chop and cook on second side for 2 minutes. (Neither side of chop will be browned at this point.)

2. Flip chop; reduce heat to medium; and continue to cook, flipping chop every 2 minutes, until exterior is well browned and meat registers 140 to 145 degrees, 10 to 15 minutes. (Chop should be sizzling; if not, increase heat slightly. Reduce heat if skillet starts to smoke.)

3. Transfer chop to carving board and let rest for 5 minutes. Carve meat from bone and slice ½ inch thick. (When carving chop, meat at tapered end near bone may retain slightly pink hue despite being cooked.) Season meat with coarse or flake sea salt to taste. Serve with bone.

VARIATIONS

Pan-Seared Thick-Cut, Bone-In Pork Chop with Maple Agrodolce

Bring ¼ cup balsamic vinegar, 2 tablespoons maple syrup, 2 tablespoons minced shallot, 2 tablespoons chopped golden raisins, pinch red pepper flakes, and pinch table salt to boil in small saucepan over medium heat. Reduce heat to low and simmer until reduced and slightly thickened, 8 to 10 minutes (sauce will continue to thicken as it cools). Cover to keep warm until ready to serve. Serve with pork chop.

Pan-Seared Thick-Cut, Bone-In Pork Chop with Creamy Apple-Mustard Sauce

Stir ¼ cup whole grain mustard, 3 tablespoons unsweetened applesauce, 2 tablespoons Dijon mustard, 4 teaspoons cider vinegar, 1 tablespoon honey, 1 tablespoon minced fresh chives, and ¼ teaspoon table salt in bowl until combined. Serve with pork chop.

TEMPING BONE-IN PORK CHOPS

When taking the temperature of your chop, use tongs to lift the meat from the pan and then insert the thermometer sideways into the center of the chop, avoiding the bone.

Pork Schnitzel

Serves 2

Total time 55 minutes

WHY THIS RECIPE WORKS For tender pork schnitzel with a crisp but not greasy coating, we first considered the cut of pork. One small pork tenderloin was just the right size for two servings, and its tenderness and mild flavor are similar to those of veal (the traditional cutlet for schnitzel). Cutting the tenderloin crosswise at an angle and pounding the pieces gave us two oblong cutlets that fit perfectly in the pot. Cubing and microwaving bread before processing it gave us instant dry bread crumbs for a coating that cooked up extra-crisp. Cooking the cutlets in plenty of oil and shaking the pot the entire time gave our schnitzel the characteristic puffed, crinkled appearance. If the pork is enhanced (injected with a salt solution), do not season with salt in step 2. The 2 cups of oil called for in this recipe may seem like a lot, but it's necessary to achieve an authentic crinkled, puffed texture on the finished cutlets. When properly cooked, the cutlets absorb very little oil. You will need at least a 6-quart Dutch oven for this recipe.

PORK

- 4 slices hearty white sandwich bread, crusts removed, cut into ¾-inch cubes (4 cups)
- ¼ cup all-purpose flour
- 2 large eggs
- 1 tablespoon vegetable oil
- 1 (12-ounce) pork tenderloin, trimmed
- ⅛ teaspoon table salt
-   Pinch pepper
- 2 cups vegetable oil, for frying

GARNISHES

-   Lemon wedges
- 1 tablespoon minced fresh parsley
- 1 tablespoon capers, rinsed
- 1 large Hard-Cooked Egg (page 360), yolk and white separated and passed separately through a fine-mesh strainer

1. Set wire rack in rimmed baking sheet. Place bread cubes in single layer on large plate and microwave until bread is dry and a few pieces start to brown lightly, 4 to 6 minutes, stirring halfway through microwaving. Process dry bread in food processor to very fine crumbs, about 45 seconds (you should have about ⅔ cup crumbs); transfer to shallow dish. Spread flour in second shallow dish. Beat eggs with 1 tablespoon oil in third shallow dish.

2. Cut tenderloin crosswise on angle into 2 pieces. Lay each piece between 2 sheets of plastic wrap and pound until roughly ¼ inch thick. Pat cutlets dry with paper towels and sprinkle with salt and pepper. Working with 1 cutlet at a time, dredge cutlets in flour, dip in egg mixture, then coat with bread crumbs, pressing gently to adhere. Transfer to prepared rack and let coating dry for 5 to 10 minutes.

3. Line large plate with triple layer of paper towels. Add 2 cups oil to large Dutch oven until it measures about ½ inch deep and heat over medium-high heat to 375 degrees.

Pork Schnitzel

Carefully lay one cutlet in hot oil and cook, shaking pot gently and continuously, until cutlet is wrinkled and light golden brown on both sides, 1 to 2 minutes per side. Transfer cutlet to paper towel–lined plate and blot well on both sides to absorb excess oil. Repeat with remaining cutlet. Serve cutlets with garnishes.

TURNING TENDERLOIN INTO CUTLETS

1. Cut tenderloin crosswise on angle into 2 equal pieces.

2. Lay each piece between 2 sheets of plastic wrap and pound with meat pounder until roughly ¼ inch thick.

Sautéed Pork Chops with Pears and Blue Cheese

Serves 2 FAST

Total time 30 minutes

WHY THIS RECIPE WORKS Caramelized pears have a mild sweetness that is nicely balanced by the pungent flavor of blue cheese, and we looked to this pairing to give our sautéed pork chops sophisticated flavor in a snap. Bone-in chops stayed juicy and moist, and a dual-heat approach to cooking them—searing one side over medium-high, then turning the heat down to cook the second side—allowed the chops to develop nice browning without overcooking. A simple pan sauce of chicken broth, butter, and balsamic vinegar complemented our dish without overwhelming the other flavors. Bosc pears, a firm, russet-colored variety, work great here. For the boldest flavor, use an assertive blue cheese such as Gorgonzola or Roquefort. Serve with polenta or a green salad.

- 2 (8- to 10-ounce) bone-in pork rib or center-cut chops, ¾ to 1 inch thick, trimmed
- ½ teaspoon table salt, divided
- ¼ teaspoon pepper, divided
- 2 teaspoons vegetable oil, divided
- 1 pear, halved, cored, and cut into ¾-inch wedges
- ½ teaspoon sugar
- ¾ cup chicken broth
- 2 tablespoons unsalted butter, chilled
- 2 teaspoons balsamic vinegar
- 1 ounce blue cheese, crumbled (¼ cup)

1. Cut 2 slits, about 2 inches apart, through outer layer of fat and silverskin on each chop. Pat chops dry with paper towels and sprinkle with ¼ teaspoon salt and ⅛ teaspoon pepper.

2. Heat 1 teaspoon oil in 10-inch skillet over medium-high heat until just smoking. Lay chops in skillet and cook until well browned on first side, about 3 minutes. Flip chops; reduce heat to medium; and continue to cook until meat registers 140 to 145 degrees, 5 to 10 minutes; transfer to serving platter and tent loosely with aluminum foil.

3. Toss pear with sugar, remaining ¼ teaspoon salt, and remaining ⅛ teaspoon pepper in bowl. Heat remaining 1 teaspoon oil over medium-high heat until shimmering. Lay pear slices cut side down in skillet and cook until golden brown on both sides, 1 to 2 minutes per side. Stir in broth, scraping up any browned bits. Bring to simmer and cook until pears are softened, about 5 minutes. Transfer pears to platter with pork.

4. Stir any accumulated meat juices into sauce and simmer until slightly thickened, 1 to 2 minutes. Off heat, whisk in butter and vinegar and season with salt and pepper to taste. Pour sauce over chops and pear, sprinkle with blue cheese, and serve.

Pan-Seared Pork Chops with Dirty Rice

Serves 2

Total time 1 hour 5 minutes

WHY THIS RECIPE WORKS For a weeknight meal with a Southern spin, we combined quick and flavorful pan-seared pork chops with rich and earthy dirty rice. We went with bone-in rib chops, which are higher in fat than other types and therefore less prone to drying out. Browning the chops on just one side gave us the golden, crisp crust we sought while still ensuring juicy meat (and the side of the pork that was getting nestled into the rice lost its crispness anyway). Then we browned some spicy chorizo; sautéed celery, bell pepper, and onion; added the rice and chicken broth (which contributed more flavor to the rice than water); and simmered until the rice was tender. A sprinkling of scallions provided a fresh finish to our one-skillet meal. If you can't find chorizo sausage, use andouille or linguiça.

- 2 (12- to 14-ounce) bone-in pork rib or center-cut chops, 1½ inches thick, trimmed
- ½ teaspoon table salt
- ¼ teaspoon pepper
- 2 tablespoons vegetable oil
- 4 ounces chorizo, halved lengthwise and cut crosswise into ¼-inch pieces
- 1 small onion, chopped fine
- 1 celery rib, minced
- ½ red bell pepper, stemmed, seeded, and chopped fine
- ½ cup long-grain white rice, rinsed
- 2 garlic cloves, minced
- ½ teaspoon minced fresh thyme or ⅛ teaspoon dried
- ⅛ teaspoon cayenne pepper
- 1¾ cups chicken broth
- 2 scallions, sliced thin

1. Cut 2 slits, about 2 inches apart, through outer layer of fat and silverskin on each chop. Pat chops dry with paper towels and sprinkle with salt and pepper. Heat oil in 10-inch skillet over medium-high heat until just smoking. Lay chops in skillet and cook until well browned on one side, 4 to 6 minutes. Transfer chops to plate browned side up.

2. Pour off all but 1 tablespoon fat from skillet. Add chorizo and cook over medium heat until browned, 2 to 3 minutes. Stir in onion, celery, and bell pepper and cook until vegetables are softened, about 5 minutes. Stir in rice, garlic, thyme, and cayenne and cook until fragrant, about 30 seconds. Stir in broth, scraping up any browned bits.

3. Nestle chops into rice, browned side up, along with any accumulated juices, and bring to simmer. Reduce heat to medium-low; cover; and simmer until meat registers 140 to 145 degrees, 8 to 10 minutes. Transfer chops to serving platter, brushing any rice that sticks to chops back into skillet; tent loosely with aluminum foil.

4. Continue to cook rice, covered, stirring occasionally, until liquid has been absorbed and rice is tender, about 15 minutes. Off heat, gently fold in scallions and season with salt and pepper to taste. Serve chops with rice.

Roasted Pork Chops and Zucchini with Basil Vinaigrette

Serves 2

Total time 40 minutes

WHY THIS RECIPE WORKS Pan-searing may be the most common cooking method for bone-in pork chops, but roasting them on a sheet pan in the oven turns out tender, juicy meat and provides extra space to cook a vegetable side at the same time. We cooked the pork chops for 5 minutes in a hot oven and then added chunks of zucchini, which we had tossed with oil and salt and pepper. Once the zucchini had softened and taken on some color, the pork chops were perfectly cooked as well. Finally, we whisked together a simple basil-balsamic vinaigrette to drizzle over the pork and zucchini, ensuring that our meal would end on an herbal note.

- 2 (12-ounce) bone-in pork rib or center-cut chops, 1 to 1½ inches thick, trimmed
- ½ teaspoon plus ⅛ teaspoon table salt, divided
- ¼ teaspoon plus ⅛ teaspoon pepper, divided
- 1 pound zucchini, quartered lengthwise and cut into 2-inch pieces
- 1 tablespoon chopped fresh basil
- 1 tablespoon balsamic vinegar
- ½ small shallot, minced
  Pinch sugar

1. Adjust oven rack to upper-middle position and heat oven to 450 degrees. Using sharp knife, cut 2 slits, about 2 inches apart, through fat on edge of each pork chop. Pat chops dry with paper towels, rub with 1 teaspoon oil, then sprinkle with ¼ teaspoon salt and ⅛ teaspoon pepper. Arrange pork chops in center of rimmed baking sheet and roast for 5 minutes.

2. Meanwhile, toss squash with 2 teaspoons oil, ¼ teaspoon salt, and ⅛ teaspoon pepper in bowl. Distribute in even layer around pork chops on sheet and continue to roast until pork registers 145 degrees and vegetables are tender, 5 to 10 minutes.

3. Remove sheet from oven and let pork chops rest for 5 minutes. Whisk remaining 3 tablespoons oil, remaining ⅛ teaspoon salt, remaining ⅛ teaspoon pepper, basil, vinegar, shallot, and sugar together in bowl. Drizzle vinaigrette over pork and squash. Serve.

Smothered Pork Chops

Serves 2

Total time 2½ hours

WHY THIS RECIPE WORKS For tender smothered pork chops with plenty of flavor, bone-in blade-cut chops were our cut of choice—their higher fat content protected them from drying out during braising. A potent spice rub of onion powder, paprika, and cayenne gave us boldly seasoned meat. Sautéing the onion in butter until lightly browned before adding the other sauce components deepened its flavor. Because both the chops and the onion released a significant amount of liquid during braising, we thickened a small amount of the sauce with cornstarch for a velvety consistency. Be sure to use blade-cut pork chops, which are cut from the shoulder end of the loin and contain a significant amount of fat and connective tissue. You will need a 10-inch ovensafe skillet with a tight-fitting lid for this recipe.

- ½ teaspoon onion powder
- ¼ teaspoon paprika
- ¼ teaspoon table salt
- ¼ teaspoon pepper
- ⅛ teaspoon cayenne pepper
- 2 (8- to 10-ounce) bone-in blade-cut pork chops, ¾ to 1 inch thick, trimmed
- 1 tablespoon vegetable oil
- 1 tablespoon unsalted butter
- 1 onion, halved and sliced thin
- 1 garlic clove, minced
- ½ teaspoon minced fresh thyme or ⅛ teaspoon dried
- ½ cup plus 1 tablespoon beef broth, divided
- 1 bay leaf
- ¾ teaspoon cornstarch
- ½ teaspoon cider vinegar

1. Adjust oven rack to middle position and heat oven to 300 degrees. Combine onion powder, paprika, salt, pepper, and cayenne in bowl. Cut 2 slits, about 2 inches apart, through outer layer of fat and silverskin on each chop. Pat chops dry with paper towels and rub evenly with spice mixture.

2. Heat oil in 10-inch ovensafe skillet over medium-high heat until just smoking. Brown chops well on both sides, 3 to 5 minutes per side; transfer to plate. Add butter to fat left in skillet and melt over medium heat. Add onion and cook until softened and well browned, 8 to 10 minutes. Stir in garlic and thyme and cook until fragrant, about 30 seconds. Stir in ½ cup broth and bay leaf, scraping up any browned bits, and bring to simmer.

3. Nestle browned chops into skillet along with any accumulated juices, cover, and transfer to oven. Cook until chops are fully tender and fork slips easily in and out of meat, about 1½ hours.

4. Using potholders (skillet handle will be hot), remove skillet from oven. Transfer chops to serving platter and tent loosely with aluminum foil. Strain braising liquid through fine-mesh strainer into liquid measuring cup. Discard bay leaf, then transfer onion to bowl.

5. Let braising liquid settle for 5 minutes, then remove fat from surface using large spoon. Being careful of hot skillet handle, return ⅓ cup defatted pan juices to now-empty skillet and bring to simmer. Whisk remaining 1 tablespoon broth and cornstarch together in small bowl, then whisk into skillet. Continue to simmer until sauce is thickened, about 30 seconds. Stir in onions and vinegar and season with salt and pepper to taste. Pour sauce over chops and serve.

Maple-Glazed Pork Tenderloin

Serves 2

Total time 1 hour

WHY THIS RECIPE WORKS Maple-glazed pork tenderloin is a New England tradition—and a small tenderloin serves two perfectly. Searing the meat gave it a flavorful browned exterior and created a fond on which we could build our glaze. Maple syrup, mustard, cider vinegar, a little bourbon, and a pinch of cayenne provided a balanced glaze with sweet, smoky, tart, and spicy notes. A sugar-and-cornstarch coating helped the glaze adhere so that every bite had plenty of maple flavor. Don't be tempted to substitute imitation maple syrup—it will be too sweet. Be sure to pat off the cornstarch mixture thoroughly in step 2, as any excess will leave gummy spots on the tenderloin. You will need a 10-inch nonstick ovensafe skillet for this recipe.

Maple-Glazed
Pork Tenderloin

⅓ cup plus 1 tablespoon maple syrup, divided
2 tablespoons whole-grain mustard
1 tablespoon bourbon
2 teaspoons cider vinegar
½ teaspoon table salt, divided
¼ teaspoon pepper
   Pinch cayenne pepper
1 tablespoon cornstarch
1 teaspoon sugar
1 (12-ounce) pork tenderloin, trimmed
2 teaspoons vegetable oil

1. Adjust oven rack to middle position and heat oven to 350 degrees. Stir ⅓ cup maple syrup, mustard, bourbon, vinegar, ¼ teaspoon salt, and cayenne together in small bowl.

2. Combine cornstarch, sugar, remaining ¼ teaspoon salt, and pepper in shallow dish. Pat tenderloin dry with paper towels, then roll in cornstarch mixture until evenly coated on all sides; thoroughly pat off excess cornstarch mixture.

3. Heat oil in 10-inch ovensafe nonstick skillet over medium-high heat until just smoking. Brown tenderloin well on all sides, 6 to 8 minutes; transfer to plate.

4. Pour off fat from skillet and return to medium heat. Add syrup mixture to now-empty skillet, bring to simmer, scraping up any browned bits, and cook until reduced to ⅓ cup, 30 seconds to 1 minute. Return browned tenderloin to skillet and turn to coat with glaze. Transfer skillet to oven and roast tenderloin until meat registers 135 to 140 degrees, 8 to 12 minutes.

5. Using potholders (skillet handle will be hot), remove skillet from oven. Transfer tenderloin to cutting board, tent loosely with aluminum foil, and let rest for 10 minutes.

6. Meanwhile, being careful of hot skillet handle, transfer glaze left in skillet to small bowl and stir in remaining 1 tablespoon maple syrup. Brush tenderloin with 1 tablespoon glaze, then slice into ¼-inch-thick slices. Serve pork, passing remaining glaze separately.

VARIATIONS
Maple-Glazed Pork Tenderloin with Orange and Chipotle

Substitute 1 teaspoon Dijon mustard for whole-grain mustard and 2 teaspoons minced chipotle chile for cayenne. Add 1 tablespoon orange marmalade to bowl along with maple syrup, mustard, bourbon, vinegar, and salt.

Maple-Glazed Pork Tenderloin with Smoked Paprika and Ginger

Substitute 1 teaspoon Dijon mustard for whole-grain mustard, 1 tablespoon dry sherry for bourbon, and ¾ teaspoon grated fresh ginger and ½ teaspoon smoked paprika for cayenne.

TRIMMING PORK TENDERLOIN

To remove silverskin from pork tenderloin, slip knife underneath it, angle knife slightly upward, and use gentle back-and-forth motion to cut it away from meat.

Spice-Rubbed Pork Tenderloin with Mango Relish
Serves 2
Total time 55 minutes

WHY THIS RECIPE WORKS Lean pork tenderloin is a great canvas for dressing up with rubs and relishes, and that's a good thing since it is so lean and its flavor alone is so mild. In general, we like to sear pork tenderloin on the stovetop for some good browning and then let the oven do the rest. But its leanness also means it is quick to dry out. Here, a warm spice rub of cocoa powder, chili powder, and salt boosted the flavor of the pork. And for moisture and textural contrast, we added a bright mango relish flavored with cilantro, lime juice, and shallot—plus jalapeño for a little kick. We prefer fresh mango here, but you can substitute 1 cup frozen mango. If your mango is unripe, add sugar as needed in step 4. Note that the cocoa and chili powders will make the exterior of the pork look almost blackened. To make this dish spicier, reserve and add the chile seeds as desired.

 2 teaspoons chili powder
 ½ teaspoon unsweetened cocoa powder
 ¼ teaspoon plus ⅛ teaspoon table salt, divided
 1 (12-ounce) pork tenderloin, trimmed
 2 teaspoons vegetable oil
 ½ mango, peeled and cut into ½-inch pieces (1 cup)
 2 tablespoons chopped fresh cilantro
 1 tablespoon lime juice
 1 small shallot, minced
 1 teaspoon minced jalapeño chile, seeds and ribs removed

1. Adjust oven rack to middle position and heat oven to 425 degrees. Combine chili powder, cocoa, and ¼ teaspoon salt in bowl. Pat tenderloin dry with paper towels and rub evenly with spice mixture.

2. Heat oil in 10-inch ovensafe nonstick skillet over medium-high heat until just smoking. Brown tenderloin well on all sides, 6 to 8 minutes, reducing heat if spices begin to burn. Transfer skillet to oven and roast tenderloin until meat registers 135 to 140 degrees, 12 to 15 minutes.

3. Using potholders (skillet handle will be hot), remove skillet from oven. Transfer tenderloin to cutting board, tent loosely with aluminum foil, and let rest for 10 minutes.

4. Meanwhile, combine mango, cilantro, lime juice, shallot, jalapeño, and remaining ⅛ teaspoon salt in bowl. Slice tenderloin into ¼-inch-thick slices and serve with mango relish.

Herb-Rubbed Pork Tenderloin with Fennel and Artichokes

Serves 2

Total time 1 hour 5 minutes

WHY THIS RECIPE WORKS Inspired by the flavors of Provence, this pork tenderloin features a bright spice rub: some herbes de Provence (plus a little salt and pepper) hit the mark, and its potent flavor allowed us to skip the step of browning the tenderloin before putting it in the oven. To make this a one-dish meal, we added a flavorful combination of fennel, artichoke hearts, olives, and cherry tomatoes. Because the pork cooked quickly, we found that the fennel needed a jump start in the microwave before being added to the baking dish with the other vegetables. To thaw the artichokes quickly, microwave them in a covered bowl for about 3 minutes and pat dry before using.

- 1 (12-ounce) pork tenderloin, trimmed
- 1 teaspoon herbes de Provence
- ¼ teaspoon plus ⅛ teaspoon table salt, divided
- ⅛ teaspoon plus pinch pepper, divided
- 1 fennel bulb, stalks discarded, bulb halved, cored, and sliced ½ inch thick
- 5 ounces frozen artichoke hearts, thawed and patted dry
- ¼ cup pitted niçoise or kalamata olives, halved
- 1 tablespoon extra-virgin olive oil
- 6 ounces cherry tomatoes, halved
- 1 teaspoon grated lemon zest
- 1 tablespoon minced fresh parsley

1. Adjust oven rack to lower-middle position and heat oven to 450 degrees. Pat tenderloin dry with paper towels, rub evenly with herbes de Provence, ¼ teaspoon salt, and ⅛ teaspoon pepper.

2. Combine fennel and 1 tablespoon water in medium bowl; cover; and microwave until fennel is softened, 2 to 3 minutes. Drain fennel well, then toss with artichokes, olives, and oil and sprinkle with remaining ⅛ teaspoon salt and pinch pepper.

3. Arrange vegetables in 8-inch square baking dish. Lay tenderloin on top of vegetables and roast until center of meat registers 135 to 140 degrees, 25 to 30 minutes, flipping tenderloin halfway through roasting. Transfer tenderloin to cutting board and tent loosely with aluminum foil.

4. Stir cherry tomatoes and lemon zest into vegetables and continue to roast until fennel is tender and tomatoes have softened, about 10 minutes. Stir parsley into vegetables and season with salt and pepper to taste. Slice tenderloin into ¼-inch-thick slices and serve with vegetables.

NOTES FROM THE TEST KITCHEN

TAKING THE TEMPERATURE OF MEAT

Whether cooking a burger or roasting a pork tenderloin, you should always take the temperature of the area of the meat that will be the last to finish cooking, which is the thickest part or, in some cases, the center. Bones conduct heat, so if the meat you are cooking contains bone, make sure that the thermometer is not touching it. For roasts, take more than one reading to confirm you're at the right point of doneness.

Since the temperature of meat will continue to rise as it rests, an effect called carryover cooking, meat should be removed from the oven, grill, or pan when it's 5 to 10 degrees below the desired serving temperature. Carryover cooking doesn't apply to poultry and fish (they don't retain heat as well as the dense muscle structure in meat), so they should be cooked to the desired serving temperatures. The following temperatures should be used to determine when to stop the cooking process.

	COOK UNTIL IT REGISTERS
Beef/Lamb	
Rare	115 to 120 degrees
Medium-Rare	120 to 125 degrees
Medium	130 to 135 degrees
Medium-Well	140 to 145 degrees
Well-Done	150 to 155 degrees
Pork	
Pork Chops and Pork Loins	140 to 145 degrees
Pork Tenderloins	135 to 140 degrees

Smoky Indoor Ribs

Garlicky Pork with Eggplant

Smoky Indoor Ribs

Serves 2

Total time 3½ hours, plus 30 minutes resting

WHY THIS RECIPE WORKS Smoked ribs take as much as a day in a smoker to become fall-off-the-bone tender. This low-and-slow method is effective, but it isn't very convenient when cooking for two, so we sought to move our ribs indoors. We braised the ribs in the oven until the meat was tender, then brushed them with a simple barbecue sauce and roasted them until they had a crusty exterior like the "bark" of real barbecue. But the ribs were light on smoky flavor. Adding liquid smoke and espresso powder to both our braising liquid and our barbecue sauce and swapping regular paprika for smoked paprika solved the problem. Now our indoor ribs boasted intense depth and tasted as if they'd been in the smoker all day long. Look for liquid smoke that contains no salt or additional flavorings. Slicing the rack of ribs in half ensures that it fits perfectly in the baking dish.

RIBS

- 1 cup water
- 1 tablespoon instant espresso powder
- 1 tablespoon liquid smoke
- 1½ teaspoons table salt
- 1 (2½- to 3-pound) rack pork spareribs, preferably St. Louis cut, trimmed, membrane removed, and rack cut in half

BARBECUE SAUCE

- 2 teaspoons vegetable oil
- 1 small onion, chopped fine
- ⅛ teaspoon table salt
- 1½ teaspoons smoked paprika
- ¾ cup chicken broth
- ⅓ cup cider vinegar
- ⅓ cup dark corn syrup
- ⅓ cup ketchup
- ¼ cup molasses
- 1 tablespoon brown mustard
- 1½ teaspoons hot sauce
- 1½ teaspoons instant espresso powder
- ¼ teaspoon liquid smoke

1. FOR THE RIBS Adjust oven rack to middle position and heat oven to 300 degrees. Bring water, espresso powder, liquid smoke, and salt to boil in small saucepan. Pour mixture into 13 by 9-inch baking dish. Place rib halves, meat side down, in liquid. Cover dish tightly with aluminum foil and bake for 1½ hours.

2. FOR THE BARBECUE SAUCE Meanwhile, heat oil in medium saucepan over medium heat until shimmering. Add onion and salt and cook until softened, about 5 minutes. Stir in paprika and cook until fragrant, about 30 seconds. Stir in broth, vinegar, corn syrup, ketchup, molasses, mustard, hot sauce, and espresso powder. Bring to simmer and cook, stirring occasionally, until thickened and reduced to 1 cup, 20 to 25 minutes. Stir in liquid smoke and season with salt and pepper to taste. Let cool for 20 minutes. Reserve ¼ cup sauce for serving.

3. Set wire rack in aluminum foil–lined baking sheet. Remove ribs from baking dish and transfer, meat side up, to prepared rack; discard braising liquid. Brush both sides of ribs with sauce. Bake until tender and fork inserted into meat meets no resistance, about 1½ hours, brushing meat with sauce after 30 and 60 minutes of cooking. Tent ribs loosely with foil and let rest for 30 minutes. Slice meat between bones. Serve with reserved sauce.

Garlicky Pork with Eggplant

Serves 2

Total time 40 minutes, plus 10 minutes marinating

WHY THIS RECIPE WORKS Pork tenderloin is ideal for stir-fries—it's easy to slice thin, cooks quickly, and is the perfect amount for two servings—plus its mild flavor benefits from a bold stir-fry sauce. A simple sauce of brown sugar, fish sauce, soy sauce, and lime juice did the trick, and it also doubled as a marinade for the pork. Eggplant and onion provided heft and textural interest to our stir-fry, while a generous dose of garlic and black pepper provided a final punch of flavor. To make the pork easier to slice, freeze it for 15 minutes. Do not peel the eggplant, as the skin helps hold it together during cooking. Stir-fries cook quickly, so have everything prepped before you begin cooking. You will need a 14-inch flat-bottomed wok or 12-inch nonstick skillet with a tight-fitting lid for this recipe. Serve with rice.

¼ cup chicken broth
3 tablespoons vegetable oil, divided
1 tablespoon packed light brown sugar
2 teaspoons fish sauce
2 teaspoons soy sauce
1 teaspoon lime juice

1 (12-ounce) pork tenderloin, trimmed and sliced thin
½ teaspoon cornstarch
6 garlic cloves, minced
½ teaspoon pepper
½ eggplant (8 ounces), cut into ¾-inch pieces
1 small onion, halved and sliced ¼ inch thick
2 tablespoons coarsely chopped fresh cilantro

1. Whisk broth, 1 tablespoon oil, sugar, fish sauce, soy sauce, and lime juice together in small bowl. Measure 1 tablespoon sauce into medium bowl, then stir in pork, cornstarch, and 1 tablespoon oil. Cover and marinate pork in refrigerator for at least 10 minutes or up to 30 minutes. Meanwhile, in separate bowl, combine garlic, pepper, and 1 teaspoon oil.

2. Heat remaining 2 teaspoons oil in 14-inch flat-bottomed wok or 12-inch nonstick skillet over high heat until just smoking. Add eggplant and onion; cover; and cook until vegetables are softened and lightly browned, about 3 minutes. Uncover and continue to cook until vegetables are tender, about 5 minutes; transfer to bowl.

3. Return now-empty wok to high heat. Add pork; break up any clumps; and cook until no longer pink and liquid has evaporated, 4 to 6 minutes. Push pork to sides of wok. Add garlic mixture to center and cook, mashing mixture into wok, until fragrant, about 1 minute. Stir garlic mixture into pork.

4. Stir in cooked vegetables. Whisk sauce to recombine, then add to wok. Cook, stirring constantly, until sauce is thickened, about 1 minute. Transfer to serving platter, sprinkle with cilantro, and serve.

SLICING PORK FOR STIR-FRIES

1. To make pork easier to slice, freeze it for 15 minutes. Slice partially frozen pork crosswise into ¼-inch-thick medallions.

Stir-Fried Pork with Shiitakes

Serves 2

Total time 30 minutes, plus 10 minutes marinating

WHY THIS RECIPE WORKS For an easy pork stir-fry, we paired pork tenderloin with mushrooms, snow peas, and crisp bean sprouts. A bold sauce of sweet hoisin sauce, soy sauce, rice vinegar, and spicy red pepper flakes added complexity. Marinating the pork in some of the sauce and a little cornstarch ensured that it was well seasoned and stayed tender when cooked over high heat. Ginger and garlic rounded out the flavors. To make the pork easier to slice, freeze it for 15 minutes. You will need a 14-inch flat-bottomed wok or 12-inch nonstick skillet with a tight-fitting lid for this recipe. Serve with rice.

½ cup water, divided

3 tablespoons vegetable oil, divided

2 tablespoons hoisin sauce

2 tablespoons soy sauce

1 teaspoon unseasoned rice vinegar

¼ teaspoon red pepper flakes

1 (12-ounce) pork tenderloin, trimmed and sliced thin

½ teaspoon cornstarch

2 garlic cloves, minced

2 teaspoons grated fresh ginger

6 ounces shiitake mushrooms, stemmed and sliced thin

4 ounces snow peas, strings removed

4 ounces (2 cups) bean sprouts

1. Whisk ¼ cup water, 1 tablespoon oil, hoisin, soy sauce, vinegar, and pepper flakes together in small bowl. Measure 1 tablespoon sauce into medium bowl, then stir in pork, cornstarch, and 1 tablespoon oil. Cover and marinate pork in refrigerator for at least 10 minutes or up to 30 minutes. Meanwhile, in separate bowl, combine garlic, ginger, and remaining 1 tablespoon oil.

2. Cook mushrooms, snow peas, and remaining ¼ cup water, covered, in 14-inch flat-bottomed wok or 12-inch nonstick skillet over high heat until water is boiling and vegetables begin to soften, about 3 minutes. Uncover and cook until water has evaporated and vegetables are crisp-tender, about 30 seconds; transfer to bowl.

3. Return now-empty wok to high heat. Add pork; break up any clumps; and cook until no longer pink and liquid has evaporated, 4 to 6 minutes. Push pork to sides of wok. Add garlic mixture to center of wok and cook, mashing mixture into wok, until fragrant, 15 to 30 seconds. Stir garlic mixture into pork.

4. Stir in cooked vegetables and bean sprouts. Whisk sauce to recombine, then add to wok. Cook, stirring constantly, until sauce is thickened, about 1 minute. Serve.

Pork Fajitas

Serves 2 **FAST**

Total time 30 minutes

WHY THIS RECIPE WORKS Fajitas are by design a quick-cooking, all-in-one meal, making them the perfect choice for a busy evening. And while they are more traditionally made with chicken or beef, for something a little different, we decided to develop a recipe for juicy pork fajitas. Slicing pork tenderloin into thin pieces before cooking sped up the cooking process. A duo of bell pepper and red onion added just the right texture, color, and sweetness to our meal. A little chili powder, added to the skillet while the vegetables cooked, gave our dish a flavor boost. Once the vegetables were done, we set them aside and added the pork to the pan to cook for just a few minutes. Lime juice, cilantro, and cumin contributed brightness and complexity. To make the pork easier to slice, freeze it for 15 minutes. Serve with your favorite fajita toppings.

1 tablespoon lime juice

2 tablespoons minced fresh cilantro

2 tablespoons vegetable oil, divided

1 red, green, or yellow bell pepper, stemmed, seeded, and cut into ½-inch-wide strips

1 small red onion, halved and sliced thin

1 teaspoon chili powder

¾ teaspoon table salt, divided

1 (12-ounce) pork tenderloin, trimmed, halved lengthwise and sliced crosswise ¼ inch thick

⅛ teaspoon pepper

¼ teaspoon ground cumin

6 (6-inch) flour tortillas, warmed

1. Whisk lime juice, cilantro, and 2 teaspoons oil together in bowl.

2. Heat 1 tablespoon oil in 12-inch skillet over medium-high heat until shimmering. Add bell pepper, onion, chili powder, and ½ teaspoon salt and cook until vegetables are softened, 5 to 7 minutes; transfer to serving platter and tent loosely with aluminum foil.

3. Pat pork dry with paper towels and sprinkle with remaining ¼ teaspoon salt and pepper. Heat remaining 1 teaspoon oil in now-empty skillet over high heat until just smoking. Add pork; break up any clumps; and cook until no longer pink and liquid has evaporated, 4 to 6 minutes. Stir in cumin and cook until fragrant, about 30 seconds. Off heat, stir in lime juice mixture and season with salt and pepper to taste; transfer to platter with vegetables. Serve pork with warm tortillas.

Pork Tacos with Mango Salsa

Serves 2 `FAST`

Total time 25 minutes

WHY THIS RECIPE WORKS We wanted to capture the flavor of tacos al pastor—a Mexican taco filling of slow-cooked, chile-rubbed pork with chopped onion, cilantro, and lime—in a weeknight recipe. Since the traditional large cut of pork shoulder was out of the question for two, we aimed to infuse quick-cooking ground pork with smoky flavor. Chipotle chiles were exactly what we needed: They provided a slow-smoked flavor and a subtle, lingering heat. A generous dose of cilantro and lime juice gave our dish an authentic flavor profile. A little shredded Monterey Jack cheese melted into the pork created a cohesive filling. Spooned into warm corn tortillas and topped with a bright mango salsa, this was a dish we could easily enjoy any night of the week. We prefer fresh mangos here, but you can substitute 1½ cups frozen mango. If your mango is unripe, add sugar as needed in step 1.

- 1 pound mangos, peeled, pitted, and cut into ¼-inch pieces
- ¼ cup minced fresh cilantro, divided
- 1 shallot, minced, divided
- 4 teaspoons lime juice, divided
- ⅛ teaspoon plus ¼ teaspoon table salt, divided
- ⅛ teaspoon pepper
- 2 teaspoons vegetable oil
- 1 teaspoon minced canned chipotle chile in adobo sauce
- 12 ounces ground pork
- 1 ounce Monterey Jack cheese, shredded (¼ cup)
- 6 (6-inch) corn tortillas, warmed
  Lime wedges

1. Combine mangos, 2 tablespoons cilantro, half of shallot, 2 teaspoons lime juice, ⅛ teaspoon salt, and pepper in bowl; set aside.

2. Heat oil in 10-inch skillet over medium heat until shimmering. Add remaining shallot, chipotle, and remaining ¼ teaspoon salt and cook until shallot is softened, about 2 minutes. Add pork and cook, breaking meat up with wooden spoon, until pork is no longer pink, about 5 minutes.

3. Off heat, stir in remaining 2 tablespoons cilantro, remaining 2 teaspoons lime juice, and Monterey Jack and season with salt and pepper to taste. Serve pork with warm tortillas, mango salsa, and lime wedges.

Pork Tacos with Mango Salsa

Braised Lamb Chops with Tomatoes, Olives, and Rosemary

Roast Rack of Lamb with Whiskey Sauce

Braised Lamb Chops with Tomatoes, Olives, and Rosemary

Serves 2

Total time 55 minutes

WHY THIS RECIPE WORKS When buying lamb, many people turn to the tried and true (and expensive) loin or rib chops. But shoulder chops deliver good flavor and are easy to prepare, making them an ideal choice for a simple weeknight braise. Rich lamb stands up well to bold flavors, so we created a Mediterranean-inspired braise with tomatoes, fragrant rosemary, briny olives, and a sprinkling of fresh parsley. Because they are generally leaner, round bone chops, also called arm chops, are preferable for this braise. If available, however, lean blade chops also braise nicely. Serve with polenta or rice. You will need a 12-inch skillet with a tight-fitting lid for this recipe.

  2 (10-ounce) shoulder lamb chops, ¾ to 1 inch thick, trimmed
  ¼ teaspoon table salt
  ⅛ teaspoon pepper
  1 tablespoon extra-virgin olive oil
  1 small onion, chopped fine
  2 garlic cloves, minced
  2 teaspoons minced fresh rosemary or ½ teaspoon dried
  ¼ cup dry red wine
  1 (14.5-ounce) can diced tomatoes
  ¼ cup pitted kalamata olives, chopped
  2 tablespoons minced fresh parsley

1. Pat chops dry with paper towels and sprinkle with salt and pepper. Heat oil in 12-inch skillet over medium-high heat until just smoking. Brown chops well on both sides, 3 to 5 minutes per side; transfer to plate.

2. Pour off all but 1 tablespoon fat from skillet. Add onion and cook over medium heat until softened, about 5 minutes. Stir in garlic and rosemary and cook until fragrant, about 30 seconds. Stir in wine, scraping up any browned bits, and bring to simmer.

3. Stir in tomatoes and their juice and olives. Nestle browned chops into skillet along with any accumulated juices and bring to simmer. Reduce heat to medium-low; cover; and simmer until chops are fully tender and fork slips easily in and out of meat, 20 to 30 minutes. Transfer chops to serving platter and tent loosely with aluminum foil.

4. Continue to simmer sauce until thickened, 2 to 3 minutes. Stir in parsley and season with salt and pepper to taste. Pour sauce over chops and serve.

Mustard-Rosemary Lamb Chops with Roasted Parsnips

Serves 2

Total time 45 minutes

WHY THIS RECIPE WORKS Lean, tender, mildly flavored lamb loin chops are a great option for a weeknight sheet pan meal. We roasted them atop a bed of parsnips, coating both with a glaze of mustard, honey, garlic, lemon zest and juice, and fresh rosemary. While the parsnips emerged caramelized and the lamb perfectly pink, the exterior of the chops lacked color. We suspected that the moisture in our glaze was preventing the lamb from browning during its quick roast. Instead, we brushed the chops with oil and honey before cooking and dabbed on the mustard mixture after, which gave us the best of both worlds—browned chops accented with a fragrant and flavorful glaze. We prefer the subtler flavor of lamb labeled "domestic" or "American" for this recipe. If your lamb chops are smaller than 6 ounces, you may need to continue cooking the parsnips in step 2 after the chops are done. Warming the honey makes it easier to brush onto the lamb. We prefer the lamb cooked to medium-rare, but if you prefer it more or less done, see our guidelines on page 161.

1 pound parsnips, peeled and cut into 2-inch lengths, thick ends quartered lengthwise

2 tablespoons plus 1 teaspoon extra-virgin olive oil, divided

⅛ teaspoon plus ¼ teaspoon table salt, divided

¼ teaspoon pepper, divided

1 tablespoon honey, warmed, divided

4 (6-ounce) lamb loin chops, 1¼ inches thick, trimmed

1 tablespoon Dijon mustard

1 teaspoon minced fresh rosemary

1 garlic clove, minced

1 teaspoon grated lemon zest plus 1 teaspoon juice

1 teaspoon water

1. Adjust oven rack to middle position and heat oven to 450 degrees. Toss parsnips with 1 tablespoon oil, ⅛ teaspoon salt, and ⅛ teaspoon pepper and spread in single layer on rimmed baking sheet. Roast until beginning to soften, about 10 minutes.

2. Combine 1½ teaspoons honey and 2 teaspoons oil in small bowl. Pat lamb chops dry with paper towels, brush with honey-oil mixture, and sprinkle with remaining ¼ teaspoon salt and remaining ⅛ teaspoon pepper. Arrange lamb chops on top of parsnips and continue to roast until chops register 120 to 125 degrees (for medium-rare) and parsnips are tender, 10 to 15 minutes, rotating sheet halfway through roasting.

3. Microwave mustard, rosemary, garlic, lemon zest and juice, water, remaining 2 teaspoons oil, and remaining 1½ teaspoons honey in large bowl until fragrant, about 15 seconds, stirring once halfway through microwaving. Transfer lamb chops to plate and brush with 1 tablespoon mustard mixture. Tent with aluminum foil and let rest while finishing parsnips.

4. Transfer parsnips to bowl with remaining mustard mixture and toss to coat. Season with salt and pepper to taste. Serve lamb with parsnips.

NOTES FROM THE TEST KITCHEN

DOMESTIC VERSUS IMPORTED LAMB

While most of the beef and pork sold in American markets is raised domestically, you can purchase both imported and domestic lamb. Domestic lamb has a larger size and milder flavor, while lamb imported from Australia or New Zealand has a gamier taste. Imported lamb is pasture-fed on mixed grasses, while lamb raised in the United States begins on a diet of grass but finishes with grain. The switch to grain impacts the composition of the animal's fat—and ultimately leads to sweeter-tasting meat.

Roast Rack of Lamb with Whiskey Sauce

Serves 2

Total time 1 hour

WHY THIS RECIPE WORKS Roast rack of lamb for two? No problem. Searing the rack of lamb in a skillet to get a good caramelized crust was key. We used tongs to sear it well on the sides and bottom before transferring the lamb to the oven. We roasted the rack on a rimmed baking sheet until it reached just the right temperature. A smoky, slightly sweet whiskey sauce was the perfect accompaniment to the rich flavor of the lamb. We prefer the milder taste and bigger size of domestic lamb. If using lamb from New Zealand or Australia, the rack will probably be smaller and cook more quickly. We like the smoky flavor of Scotch whiskey, but Irish or American whiskey can be substituted. Have the butcher french the racks for you; the ribs will need some cleaning up, but it will minimize your prep work. We prefer the lamb cooked to medium-rare, but if you prefer it more or less done, see our guidelines on page 161.

LAMB

- 1 (1¼- to 1½-pound) rack of lamb (8 to 9 ribs), frenched and trimmed
- ½ teaspoon table salt
- ¼ teaspoon pepper
- 1 teaspoon vegetable oil

WHISKEY SAUCE

- 1 shallot, minced
- 1 sprig fresh rosemary
- 1 garlic clove, minced
- ½ teaspoon all-purpose flour
- 5 tablespoons Scotch whiskey, divided
- ¾ cup chicken broth
- 1 tablespoon chopped fresh parsley
- 1 tablespoon unsalted butter
- ½ teaspoon lemon juice

1. FOR THE LAMB Adjust oven rack to lower-middle position, place rimmed baking sheet on rack, and heat oven to 425 degrees.

2. Pat lamb dry with paper towels and sprinkle with salt and pepper. Heat oil in 10-inch skillet over medium-high heat until just smoking. Lay lamb in skillet meat side down and cook, without moving, until well browned, 3 to 5 minutes. Reduce heat to medium and, using tongs, hold rack upright in skillet to brown bottom, 2 to 3 minutes.

3. Transfer lamb meat side up to hot sheet in oven, setting skillet aside for sauce. Roast lamb until meat registers 120 to 125 degrees (for medium-rare), 12 to 15 minutes. Transfer lamb to carving board, tent loosely with aluminum foil, and let rest for 5 to 10 minutes.

4. FOR THE WHISKEY SAUCE Meanwhile, pour off all but 1 teaspoon fat from skillet. Add shallot and rosemary sprig and cook over medium heat until shallot is softened, about 2 minutes. Stir in garlic and cook until fragrant, about 30 seconds. Stir in flour and cook for 1 minute.

5. Off heat, slowly stir in ¼ cup whiskey, scraping up any browned bits, and let sit until bubbling subsides, about 1 minute. Carefully return skillet to medium heat and simmer until whiskey has almost completely evaporated, 2 to 3 minutes. Stir in broth and continue to simmer, stirring occasionally, until sauce is slightly thickened and reduced to ⅓ cup, 3 to 5 minutes. Stir in any accumulated meat juices and simmer for 30 seconds.

6. Off heat, discard rosemary sprig. Whisk in remaining 1 tablespoon whiskey, parsley, butter, and lemon juice and season with salt and pepper to taste. Carve lamb, slicing between each rib into individual chops. Serve lamb with sauce.

PREPARING RACK OF LAMB

1. Using boning knife, scrape rib bones clean of any scraps of meat or fat.

2. Trim off outer layer of fat, thin flap of meat underneath it, and fat underneath that flap.

3. Remove silverskin by sliding boning knife between silverskin and flesh.

Lamb Meatballs with Lemony Rice and Artichokes

Serves 2

Total time 1 hour

WHY THIS RECIPE WORKS This appealing and fresh-tasting one-dish dinner features tender lemony lamb meatballs and lemon-infused rice along with artichoke hearts and bright cherry tomatoes. After browning the meatballs, we added chicken broth, scraping up all the tasty browned bits, which flavored the rice as it cooked; we nestled the browned meatballs in the mixture of rice, lemon zest and juice, and the artichokes, and let it all simmer until the rice was fragrant and tender. We chose convenient frozen artichoke hearts that we cooked directly in the flavored rice. To thaw the artichokes quickly, microwave them in a covered bowl for about 3 minutes and pat dry before using. You will need a large saucepan with a tight-fitting lid for this recipe.

¼ cup panko bread crumbs

2 tablespoons milk

3 tablespoons chopped fresh parsley, divided

4 garlic cloves, minced

1¾ teaspoons grated lemon zest, divided, plus
1 tablespoon lemon juice, plus lemon wedges
for serving

¼ plus ⅛ teaspoon table salt, divided

½ teaspoon pepper

8 ounces ground lamb

2 teaspoons extra-virgin olive oil

1¼ cups chicken broth

¾ cup long-grain white rice

4 ounces frozen artichoke hearts, thawed, patted dry,
and quartered

4 ounces cherry or grape tomatoes, halved
Lemon wedges

1. Combine panko, milk, 2 tablespoons parsley, garlic,
1½ teaspoons lemon zest, ¼ teaspoon salt, and pepper in
large bowl. Add lamb and gently knead with hands until well
combined. Using lightly moistened hands, pinch off and roll
lamb mixture into 8 meatballs.

2. Heat oil in large saucepan over medium-high heat until
shimmering. Brown meatballs on all sides, 4 to 6 minutes;
transfer to paper towel–lined plate. Add broth to now-empty
saucepan, scraping up any browned bits, and bring to boil
over medium-high heat. Stir in rice, artichokes, remaining
¼ teaspoon lemon zest and the juice, and remaining ⅛ teaspoon salt and return to boil.

3. Nestle meatballs into rice mixture. Reduce heat to low;
cover; and simmer until rice is tender and liquid is absorbed,
16 to 18 minutes. Off heat, scatter tomatoes over rice. Lay
clean folded dish towel underneath lid and let rest for 10 minutes. Fluff rice with fork and season with salt and pepper to
taste. Sprinkle with remaining 1 tablespoon parsley and serve
with lemon wedges.

Lamb Meatballs
with Lemony Rice
and Artichokes

Fish &
Shellfish

■ **FAST** (Start to finish in 30 minutes or less)
■ **VEGETARIAN**

Opposite: Shrimp Saganaki

Fish Meunière

3 tablespoons unsalted butter, divided
2 teaspoons lemon juice
1½ teaspoons minced fresh parsley
   Lemon wedges

1. Adjust oven rack to lower-middle position, set 2 ovensafe dinner plates on rack, and heat oven to 200 degrees. Spread flour in shallow dish. Pat sole dry with paper towels and sprinkle with salt and pepper. Let sit until fillets are glistening with moisture, about 5 minutes. Working with 1 fillet at a time, dredge fillets in flour.

2. Heat oil in 12-inch nonstick skillet over high heat until shimmering, then add 1 tablespoon butter and swirl to coat skillet bottom. Lay fillets skinned side up in skillet. Immediately reduce heat to medium-high and cook, without moving fillets, until edges of fillets are opaque and bottom is golden brown, about 3 minutes. Using 2 spatulas, gently flip fillets and cook until fish flakes apart when gently prodded with paring knife, about 2 minutes. Transfer fillets, one to each heated dinner plate, keeping skinned side down; return plates to oven.

3. Melt remaining 2 tablespoons butter in 8-inch skillet over medium-high heat. Continue to cook, swirling skillet constantly, until butter is golden brown and has nutty aroma, about 2 minutes. Off heat, stir in lemon juice and season with salt and pepper to taste. Using potholders (plates will be hot), remove plates from oven. Spoon sauce over fillets and sprinkle with parsley. Serve immediately with lemon wedges.

Fish Meunière

Serves 2

Total time 45 minutes

WHY THIS RECIPE WORKS Fish meunière features perfectly cooked fillets that are crisp and golden brown on the outside, napped with a nutty browned butter sauce. For the fish, we liked sole or flounder; using ⅜-inch-thick fillets prevented them from overcooking. We seasoned the fish and let it sit for 5 minutes until beads of moisture appeared on the surface before dredging it with flour. This gave us a crisp, not heavy, coating. For the sauce, we browned butter in a traditional skillet (which allowed us to monitor the color of the butter) and brightened it with lemon. Try to purchase fillets that are similar in size; avoid those that weigh less than 5 ounces because they will cook too quickly.

¼ cup all-purpose flour
2 (5- to 6-ounce) boneless, skinless sole or flounder fillets, ⅜ inch thick
¼ teaspoon table salt
⅛ teaspoon pepper
2 tablespoons vegetable oil

Steamed Sole and Vegetable Bundles with Tarragon

Serves 2

Total time 50 minutes

WHY THIS RECIPE WORKS For a light and easy supper with an elegant presentation, we steamed delicate bundles of vegetables wrapped in fillets of sole. A combination of asparagus, carrot, and red onion made a tasty and visually appealing filling. To ensure that they were nicely crisp-tender, we steamed the vegetables on their own for 5 minutes before rolling them in the fish fillets. To flavor the mild fish and add some richness, we rubbed it with a compound butter made with tarragon, minced shallot, garlic, and lemon zest and juice. Propping up the bundles on lemon slices reinforced the citrus flavor and prevented them from sticking to the steamer basket. Avoid using frozen fish in this recipe. If your asparagus spears are very thick, halve them lengthwise before using. You will need a steamer basket for this recipe.

8 ounces asparagus, trimmed and cut into
  2-inch lengths
1 carrot, peeled and cut into 2-inch-long matchsticks
½ red onion, sliced thin
1 tablespoon unsalted butter, softened
1 tablespoon chopped fresh tarragon, divided
1 small shallot, minced
1 garlic clove, minced
¼ teaspoon grated lemon zest plus ½ teaspoon juice
¼ teaspoon table salt, divided
2 pinches pepper
4 (3-ounce) boneless, skinless sole or flounder fillets,
  ⅛ to ¼ inch thick
8 (¼-inch-thick) slices lemon, divided

1. Fit Dutch oven with steamer basket. Fill pot with water until it just touches bottom of basket and bring to boil. Add asparagus, carrot, and onion to basket, cover, and steam until just tender, about 5 minutes. Remove steamer basket and vegetables from pot, rinse vegetables with cool water, then pat dry. Cover pot to keep water warm.

2. Meanwhile, mix butter, 2 teaspoons tarragon, shallot, garlic, lemon zest and juice, ⅛ teaspoon salt, and pinch pepper together in bowl.

3. Pat sole dry with paper towels and sprinkle with remaining ⅛ teaspoon salt and remaining pinch pepper. Arrange fillets skinned side up with tail end pointing away from you. Spread one-quarter of tarragon butter over each fillet. Divide vegetables among fillets, laying them across wider end of each piece of fish. Tightly roll fillets around vegetables from thick end to thin end to form tidy bundles.

CUTTING CARROTS INTO MATCHSTICKS

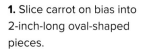

1. Slice carrot on bias into 2-inch-long oval-shaped pieces.

2. Lay ovals flat on cutting board, then slice into 2-inch-long matchsticks, about ¼ inch thick.

4. Return steamer basket to pot with steaming water and line with 4 lemon slices. Lay fish bundles seam side down on top of each lemon slice. Sprinkle bundles with remaining 1 teaspoon tarragon and lay remaining 4 lemon slices on top.

5. Bring water in pot to boil. Cover and steam until fish flakes apart when gently prodded with paring knife, 5 to 7 minutes. Gently transfer bundles to individual plates; discard lemon slices. Serve.

NOTES FROM THE TEST KITCHEN

BUYING AND STORING FISH

WHAT TO LOOK FOR Always buy fish from a trusted source (preferably one with high volume to help ensure freshness). The store, and the fish in it, should smell like the sea, not fishy or sour. And all the fish should be on ice or be properly refrigerated. Fillets and steaks should look bright, shiny, and firm; whole fish should have moist, taut skin; clear eyes; and bright red gills.

WHAT TO ASK FOR It is best to have your fishmonger slice steaks and fillets to order rather than buying precut pieces that may have been sitting around. Don't be afraid to be picky at the seafood counter.

BUYING FROZEN FISH Thin fish fillets like flounder and sole are the best choice if you have to buy your fish frozen because thin fillets freeze quickly, minimizing moisture loss. Firm fillets like halibut, snapper, tilapia, and salmon are acceptable to buy frozen if they will be cooked beyond medium-rare, but at lower degrees of doneness they will have a dry, stringy texture.

DEFROSTING FISH To defrost fish in the refrigerator overnight, remove the fish from its packaging, place it in a single layer on a rimmed plate or dish, and cover with plastic wrap. Do not use a microwave to defrost fish; it will alter the texture of the fish or, worse, partially cook it.

HOW TO STORE IT It's best to buy fish the day it will be cooked. To store, unwrap it, pat it dry, put it in a zipper-lock bag, press out the air, and seal the bag. Then set the fish on a bed of ice in a bowl or other deep container and refrigerate. The fish should keep for one day.

Braised Cod Peperonata

Serves 2

Total time 45 minutes

WHY THIS RECIPE WORKS This Italian-inspired braised cod features a flavorful condiment made from tomatoes, red bell pepper, onion, and garlic. We sautéed the bell pepper and onion until softened and browned, added garlic, thyme, and diced tomatoes, and brought everything to a simmer before nestling the fish into the sauce. The sauce infused the fish fillets with flavor as they braised and protected them from the heat. Chopped basil and a dash of balsamic vinegar added freshness and reinforced our Italian theme. Try to purchase cod fillets that are similar in size so that they cook at the same rate. If the fillets are much thinner than 1 inch, simply fold them over to make them thicker. Halibut and haddock are good substitutes for the cod. You can substitute smoked paprika for the sweet paprika. You will need a 10-inch nonstick skillet with a tight-fitting lid for this recipe.

- 2 teaspoons extra-virgin olive oil
- 1 red bell pepper, stemmed, seeded, and cut into ¼-inch-wide strips
- 1 small onion, halved and sliced thin
- 1 teaspoon paprika
- ½ teaspoon table salt, divided
- 2 garlic cloves, minced
- ½ teaspoon minced fresh thyme or ⅛ teaspoon dried
- ½ cup canned diced tomatoes, drained
- ¼ cup dry white wine
- 2 (6- to 8-ounce) skinless cod fillets, 1 to 1½ inches thick
- ⅛ teaspoon pepper
- 1 tablespoon chopped fresh basil
- 1 teaspoon balsamic or sherry vinegar

1. Heat oil in 10-inch nonstick skillet over medium heat until shimmering. Add bell pepper, onion, paprika, and ¼ teaspoon salt and cook until vegetables are softened and lightly browned, 8 to 10 minutes. Stir in garlic and thyme and cook until fragrant, about 30 seconds. Stir in tomatoes, wine, and ⅛ teaspoon pepper and bring to simmer.

2. Sprinkle cod with remaining ¼ teaspoon salt and pepper. Nestle fillets into skillet, spoon some of sauce over fillets, and bring to simmer. Reduce heat to medium-low; cover; and simmer until fish flakes apart when gently prodded with paring knife and registers 135 degrees, 8 to 10 minutes.

3. Gently transfer fillets to individual plates. Off heat, stir basil and vinegar into sauce and season with salt and pepper to taste. Spoon sauce over fillets and serve.

FOLDING FILLETS

Because fish fillets can often differ in thickness, you may end up with a thin fillet or with fillets of fish with thinner tail ends. If fillets are thin or have thinner tail ends, simply fold them over to make them thicker.

Oven-Steamed Fish with Scallions and Ginger

Serves 2

Total time 1 hour

WHY THIS RECIPE WORKS Classic Chinese and French methods for steaming fish produce moist, flavorful results. We used the best of both approaches to come up with an entirely new method that's easy and equally impressive. We started by swapping the steamer for a tightly covered baking pan and the stovetop for a hot oven. Placing the skinless fillets on a foil sling allowed the fish to flavor the cooking liquid and made it easy to transfer the fish to a serving platter without the fillets falling apart. Removing the fish from the oven before it was fully cooked prevented it from overcooking when finished with sizzling ginger-infused oil. Haddock, red snapper, halibut, and sea bass can be substituted for the cod as long as the fillets are about 1 inch thick. Try to purchase cod fillets that are similar in size so that they cook at the same rate. If the fillets are uneven, fold the thinner ends under when placing the fillets in the pan. This recipe works best in a metal baking pan; if using a glass baking dish, add 5 minutes to the cooking time. To ensure that the fish doesn't overcook, remove it from the oven when it registers 125 to 130 degrees; it will continue to cook as it is plated. Serve with steamed rice and vegetables.

- 4 scallions, trimmed, divided
- 1 (1½-inch) piece ginger, peeled
- 2 small garlic cloves, sliced thin
- 2 (6-ounce) skinless cod fillets, about 1 inch thick
- 1½ tablespoons soy sauce
- 1 tablespoon Shaoxing wine or dry sherry
- ¾ teaspoon toasted sesame oil
- ¾ teaspoon sugar
- ⅛ teaspoon table salt
- ⅛ teaspoon white pepper
- 1 tablespoon vegetable oil
- 3 tablespoons fresh cilantro leaves and thin stems

Oven-Steamed Fish with Scallions and Ginger

on solids to extract liquid; discard solids. Pour strained liquid over cod. Sprinkle reserved scallion over cod. Heat vegetable oil in small skillet over high heat until shimmering. Reduce heat to low, add reserved ginger, and cook, stirring, until ginger begins to brown and crisp, 20 to 30 seconds. Drizzle oil and ginger over cod (oil will crackle). Top with cilantro and serve.

EASY TRANSFER

Steaming the fillets on top of an aluminum foil sling allows us to easily transfer them from the baking pan to the serving platter without breaking them.

1. Grasping both ends, carefully lift sling so that fillets slide to center and are cradled in middle. Place sling gently on serving platter.

2. Place spatula at 1 end of fillets to hold in place. Carefully slide out sling from underneath fish.

1. Adjust oven rack to middle position and heat oven to 450 degrees. Chop 3 scallions coarse and spread evenly in 8-inch square baking pan. Slice remaining scallion thin on bias and set aside. Quarter ginger lengthwise. Chop three-quarters of ginger coarse and spread in pan with chopped scallions. Slice remaining ginger into matchsticks and set aside. Sprinkle garlic over scallions and ginger in pan.

2. Fold 12 by 12-inch piece of aluminum foil lengthwise to create 12 by 6-inch sling and spray lightly with vegetable oil spray. Place sling in pan, with extra foil hanging over ends of pan. Arrange cod on sling.

3. Whisk soy sauce, wine, sesame oil, sugar, salt, and white pepper in small bowl until combined. Pour around cod. Cover pan tightly with foil and bake until fish registers 135 degrees, 12 to 14 minutes.

4. Grasping sling at both ends, carefully transfer sling and cod to deep platter. Place spatula at 1 end of fillets to hold in place and carefully slide out sling from under cod. Strain cooking liquid through fine-mesh strainer set over bowl, pressing

Baked Sole Fillets with Herbs and Bread Crumbs

Serves 2

Total time 1 hour 10 minutes

WHY THIS RECIPE WORKS We wanted a fuss-free, failproof sole recipe suitable for a weeknight, yet elegant enough for a special occasion. We found that rolling the fillets into compact bundles eased the transport from baking dish to plate, and covering the baking dish with foil protected the delicate fish from the drying heat of the oven. To ramp up the sole's mild flavor, we brushed the fillets with Dijon mustard, seasoned them with fresh herbs and lemon zest, and drizzled them with melted butter and garlic. For texture, we topped the fillets with a mixture of herbs and panko bread crumbs browned in butter. Try to purchase sole fillets that are similar in size so that they cook at the same rate. Avoid using frozen fish in this recipe; it will be hard to roll.

Baked Sole with Herbs and Bread Crumbs

3. Pat sole dry with paper towels and sprinkle with salt and pepper. Arrange fillets skinned side up with tail end pointing away from you. Spread ½ teaspoon mustard over each fillet, sprinkle each evenly with half of herb–lemon zest mixture, and drizzle each with 1 teaspoon garlic butter. Tightly roll fillets from thick end to thin end to form cylinders. Set fillets seam side down in 8-inch square baking dish. Drizzle remaining garlic butter over fillets, cover baking dish with aluminum foil, and bake for 25 minutes.

4. Meanwhile, wipe skillet clean. Melt remaining 1 table-spoon butter in now-empty skillet over medium heat. Add panko and cook, stirring often, until panko is deep golden brown, 5 to 8 minutes. Reduce heat to low, add remaining garlic, and cook, stirring constantly, until garlic is fragrant and evenly distributed throughout panko, about 1 minute. Transfer mixture to small bowl and season with salt and pepper to taste. Let cool slightly, then stir in reserved 1 teaspoon herb mixture.

5. Remove baking dish from oven. Baste fillets with melted garlic butter from baking dish and sprinkle with all but 1 tablespoon panko mixture. Continue to bake, uncovered, until fish flakes apart when gently prodded with paring knife, 6 to 10 minutes. Gently transfer fillets to individual plates and sprinkle with remaining 1 tablespoon panko mixture. Serve with lemon wedges.

---

2 tablespoons minced fresh chives
1 teaspoon minced fresh tarragon, basil, or dill
¼ teaspoon grated lemon zest
2 tablespoons unsalted butter, divided
1 garlic clove, minced
2 (5- to 6-ounce) boneless, skinless sole or
   flounder fillets, ⅜ inch thick
¼ teaspoon table salt
⅛ teaspoon pepper
1 teaspoon Dijon mustard
⅓ cup panko bread crumbs
   Lemon wedges

1. Adjust oven rack to middle position and heat oven to 325 degrees. Combine chives and tarragon in small bowl. Measure out 1 teaspoon herb mixture and set aside. Stir lemon zest into remaining herb mixture.

2. Melt 1 tablespoon butter in 8-inch skillet over medium heat. Add half of garlic and cook, stirring often, until fragrant, about 1 minute. Remove skillet from heat.

Nut-Crusted Cod Fillets

Serves 2
Total time 1 hour

WHY THIS RECIPE WORKS Hearty cod fillets take well to roasting and a multitude of toppings. Here, for a playful topping, we chose a nut-based crust. Ground pistachios offered nice texture, appealing color, and a gentle sweetness that empha-sized the subtly sweet cod. We added panko bread crumbs to the pistachios and pretoasted the mixture in the microwave along with herbs and minced shallot. To adhere this rich crust to the fillets, we brushed the fish with a mixture of yogurt, egg yolk, and lemon zest before pressing on the crumbs. Haddock, red snapper, halibut, and sea bass can be substituted for the cod as long as the fillets are about 1 inch thick. Thin tail-end fillets can be folded to achieve proper thickness. Try to pur-chase cod fillets that are similar in size so that they cook at the same rate.

¼ cup shelled pistachios, chopped fine
¼ cup panko bread crumbs
1 shallot, minced
1 tablespoon vegetable oil

½ teaspoon minced fresh thyme or ⅛ teaspoon dried
¼ teaspoon table salt, divided
⅛ teaspoon pepper, divided
1 tablespoon minced fresh parsley
1 tablespoon plain yogurt
1 large egg yolk
¼ teaspoon grated lemon zest, plus lemon wedges
   for serving
2 (6- to 8-ounce) skinless cod fillets, 1 inch thick

1. Adjust oven rack to middle position and heat oven to 300 degrees. Set wire rack in rimmed baking sheet and spray rack with vegetable oil spray.

2. Toss pistachios, panko, shallot, oil, thyme, ⅛ teaspoon salt, and pinch pepper in bowl until evenly combined. Microwave, stirring frequently, until panko is light golden brown, 2 to 4 minutes. Transfer to shallow dish and let cool slightly. Stir in parsley.

3. Whisk yogurt, egg yolk, and lemon zest together in bowl. Pat cod dry with paper towels and sprinkle with remaining ⅛ teaspoon salt and remaining pinch pepper. Brush tops of fillets evenly with yogurt mixture. Working with 1 fillet at a time, press coated side in nut mixture, pressing gently to adhere. Transfer cod, crumb side up, to prepared rack.

4. Cook until cod flakes apart when gently prodded with paring knife and registers 135 degrees, 25 to 30 minutes. Serve with lemon wedges.

Lemon-Herb Cod with Crispy Garlic Potatoes

Serves 2

Total time 1 hour 10 minutes

WHY THIS RECIPE WORKS This is a fabulous one-dish dinner that is both elegant and immensely practical. The thinly-sliced potatoes required a headstart on the delicate fish so we shingled them in two piles on a roasting pan and gave them a 30-minute headstart before topping them with the fish. After we placed the cod on top of the potatoes we topped them with pieces of butter, sprigs of thyme, and slices of lemon and slid it all back into the oven. After just 15 minutes more, we had a perfect dinner of moist, subtly flavored cod and crispy, garlicky potatoes. Try to purchase cod fillets that are similar in size so that they cook at the same rate. If the fillets are much thinner than 1 inch, simply fold them over to make them thicker. Halibut and haddock are good substitutes for the cod.

2 tablespoons extra-virgin olive oil, divided
2 (8-ounce) russet potatoes, sliced ¼ inch thick
   (about 18 slices)
2 garlic cloves, minced
½ teaspoon table salt, divided
¼ teaspoon pepper, divided
2 (6- to 8-ounce) skinless cod fillets,
   1 to 1½ inches thick
1 tablespoon unsalted butter, cut into ¼-inch pieces
2 sprigs fresh thyme
½ lemon, sliced thin

1. Adjust oven rack to lower-middle position and heat oven to 425 degrees. Brush 13 by 9-inch baking dish with 1 tablespoon oil.

2. Toss potatoes with remaining 1 tablespoon oil and garlic and sprinkle with ¼ teaspoon salt and ⅛ teaspoon pepper. Shingle potatoes onto baking sheet in 2 rectangular piles measuring 4 by 6 inches. Roast potatoes until spotty brown and just tender, 30 to 35 minutes, rotating dish halfway through roasting.

3. Pat cod dry with paper towels and sprinkle with remaining ¼ teaspoon salt and remaining ⅛ teaspoon pepper. Carefully place 1 fillet skinned side down on top of each potato pile. Top fillets with butter pieces, thyme sprigs, and lemon slices. Roast cod and potatoes until fish flakes apart when gently prodded with paring knife and registers 135 degrees, about 15 minutes.

4. Slide spatula underneath potatoes and fillets and gently transfer to individual plates. Serve.

ARRANGING COD WITH POTATOES AND LEMON

1. Shingle potato slices into 2 piles of 3 tight rows, each measuring about 4 by 6 inches. Gently push rows together so that potatoes are tidy and cohesive.

2. After parcooking potatoes, carefully place 1 cod fillet skinned side down on top of each set of potatoes. Top fish with butter pieces, thyme sprigs, and lemon slices and return to oven to finish cooking.

Lemon-Poached Halibut with Roasted Fingerling Potatoes

1 (6-ounce) skinless halibut fillet, 1 to 1½ inches thick, halved crosswise
¼ teaspoon dried oregano, divided
1 lemon, sliced thin
1 tablespoon minced fresh parsley

1. Adjust oven rack to lower-middle position and heat oven to 450 degrees. Toss potatoes with 1 tablespoon oil, ½ teaspoon salt, and pepper on rimmed baking sheet. Arrange potatoes, cut sides down, in even layer. Roast until bottoms are lightly browned, 10 to 12 minutes.

2. Lay two 16 by 12-inch rectangles of aluminum foil on counter with short sides parallel to counter edge. Divide tomatoes evenly between foil rectangles, arranging in center of lower half of each sheet of foil. Pat halibut dry with paper towels, sprinkle with oregano and remaining ⅛ teaspoon salt, and place one piece on top of each tomato pile. Top each piece of halibut with 2 lemon slices and drizzle each with 1½ teaspoons oil. Fold top half of foil over halibut, then tightly crimp edges.

3. Remove baking sheet from oven; place packets on top of potatoes; and bake until halibut registers 130 degrees (insert thermometer through packet into thickest part of fillet) and cut sides of potatoes are crisp and skins are spotty brown, 10 to 15 minutes. Carefully open packets, allowing steam to escape away from you, and let cool slightly, about 2 minutes. Season potatoes with salt and pepper to taste and divide between serving plates. Using thin metal spatula, gently slide halibut and tomatoes onto potatoes. Top with any accumulated juices. Sprinkle with parsley. Serve.

Lemon-Poached Halibut with Roasted Fingerling Potatoes

Serves 2

Total time 50 minutes

WHY THIS RECIPE WORKS Make-ahead-friendly foil packets mean you can prep most of this meal the day before. We love the one-pan roasting method because the lean, meaty halibut stays moist and absorbs flavor, while the starchy potatoes, cooked on a sheet pan, get crisp on the outside and creamy on the inside. We gave them a head start in the oven before placing the packets on top. Use potatoes that are approximately 1 inch in diameter. You can substitute mahi-mahi, red snapper, striped bass, or swordfish for the halibut. Try to purchase halibut fillets that are similar in size so that they cook at the same rate.

1½ pounds fingerling potatoes, halved lengthwise
2 tablespoons extra-virgin olive oil, divided
½ teaspoon plus ⅛ teaspoon table salt, divided
⅛ teaspoon pepper
6 ounces cherry or grape tomatoes, halved

Baked Snapper with Roasted Ratatouille

Serves 2

Total time 1 hour 25 minutes

WHY THIS RECIPE WORKS We wanted a simple, sophisticated seafood dish with the bright and sunny flavors of Mediterranean cuisine. Ratatouille, a Provençal dish that combines tomatoes, eggplant, and squash seasoned with garlic and herbs, fit the bill. We thought that the clean, mild flavor and firm texture of red snapper paired well with the roasted vegetables. To keep our dish weeknight-friendly, we wanted to cook all the vegetables together in one dish. Roasting them at 375 degrees proved best; it was hot enough to evaporate the vegetables' exuded liquid, keeping the dish from becoming waterlogged, but not so hot that the vegetables scorched. To give the fish its own distinct flavor, we marinated it in olive oil flavored with basil, lemon, and garlic while the vegetables roasted. Then we simply nestled the fillets into the vegetables for the final 10 minutes of roasting. You can substitute Arctic char, catfish, cod, grouper, or tilefish fillets for the snapper. Be sure to remove the fish from the marinade after 30 minutes.

 1 (14.5-ounce) can diced tomatoes
 1 zucchini or summer squash, cut into ½-inch pieces
 ½ eggplant (8 ounces), cut into ½-inch pieces
 2 shallots, halved and sliced ¼ inch thick
 ¼ cup extra-virgin olive oil, divided
 4 garlic cloves, minced, divided
 ½ teaspoon minced fresh thyme or ⅛ teaspoon dried
   Pinch plus ¼ teaspoon table salt, divided
   Pinch plus ⅛ teaspoon pepper, divided
 1 tablespoon chopped fresh basil, divided
 1 teaspoon grated lemon zest
 2 (6-ounce) skin-on snapper fillets, 1 to 1¼ inches thick
 1½ teaspoons red wine vinegar
   Lemon wedges

1. Adjust oven rack to middle position and heat oven to 375 degrees. Combine tomatoes and their juice, zucchini, eggplant, shallots, 1 tablespoon oil, half of garlic, and thyme in bowl and sprinkle with pinch salt and pinch pepper.

2. Spread vegetable mixture in 8-inch square baking dish. Roast until vegetables are browned and softened, 50 to 60 minutes, stirring halfway through cooking.

3. Meanwhile, whisk remaining 3 tablespoons oil, remaining garlic, 2 teaspoons basil, and lemon zest together in bowl. Pat snapper dry with paper towels and sprinkle with remaining

CUTTING UP EGGPLANT

Cutting up an awkwardly shaped vegetable like eggplant can be tricky. Here's how we do it.

1. To cut eggplant into tidy pieces, first cut eggplant crosswise into ½-inch-thick rounds.

2. Then cut each round into pieces as directed in recipe.

¼ teaspoon salt and remaining ⅛ teaspoon pepper. Add fillets to bowl and turn to coat. Cover and refrigerate for 30 minutes.

4. Remove fillets from marinade and gently nestle into roasted vegetables. Bake until fish flakes apart when gently prodded with paring knife and registers 130 degrees, about 10 minutes. Sprinkle with remaining 1 teaspoon basil and vinegar. Serve with lemon wedges.

Pan-Roasted Thick-Cut Fish Fillets

Serves 2

Total time 35 minutes

WHY THIS RECIPE WORKS We set out to develop a failproof recipe for succulent, well-browned fillets. We quickly learned that we needed thick fillets; thinner pieces overcooked by the time they browned. To ensure the fillets didn't overcook, we seared them in a hot pan, flipped them, then moved the skillet to the oven to finish cooking. Seasoning the fillets with a little sugar accelerated browning, shortening the cooking time to prevent the fish from drying out. The fish emerged from the oven well browned, tender, and moist. Try to purchase cod fillets that are similar in size so that they cook at the same rate; if the fillets are thicker or thinner, be sure to adjust the cooking time as needed. Halibut and haddock are good substitutes for the cod. You will need a 10-inch nonstick, ovensafe skillet for this recipe.

 2 (6- to 8-ounce) skinless cod fillets, 1 to 1½ inches thick
 ¼ teaspoon table salt
 ⅛ teaspoon pepper
 ¼ teaspoon sugar
 2 teaspoons vegetable oil
   Lemon wedges

1. Adjust oven rack to middle position and heat oven to 425 degrees. Pat cod dry with paper towels and sprinkle with salt and pepper. Sprinkle ⅛ teaspoon sugar evenly over skinned side of each fillet.

2. Heat oil in 10-inch ovensafe nonstick skillet over high heat until just smoking. Place fillets in skillet, sugared sides down, and press down lightly to ensure even contact with skillet. Cook until browned on first side, 1 to 1½ minutes. Using 2 spatulas, gently flip fillets and transfer skillet to oven.

3. Roast fillets until fish flakes apart when gently prodded with paring knife and registers 135 degrees, 7 to 10 minutes. Serve immediately with lemon wedges.

VARIATION

Pan-Roasted Thick-Cut Fish Fillets with Green Olive, Almond, and Orange Relish

Pimento-stuffed olives can be substituted for the large green olives in a pinch.

Omit lemon wedges. Pulse ¼ cup pitted large green olives, ¼ cup toasted slivered almonds, 1 minced small garlic clove, and ½ teaspoon grated orange zest in food processor until nuts and olives are finely chopped, 10 to 12 pulses, scraping down sides of bowl as needed. Transfer mixture to medium bowl and stir in 2 tablespoons orange juice, 2 tablespoons extra-virgin olive oil, 2 tablespoons minced fresh mint, and 1 teaspoon white wine vinegar. Season with salt and pepper to taste. Spoon relish over fillets before serving.

Cod and Couscous Packets with Chermoula

NOTES FROM THE TEST KITCHEN

JUDGING THE DONENESS OF FISH

The trick to perfectly cooked fish—fish that is cooked all the way through, but not dried out and flavorless— is knowing when to remove it from the heat so that it is just slightly underdone, and then allowing the residual heat to finish the cooking. The most accurate way to make sure that thicker fish fillets and steaks are properly cooked is to use an instant-read thermometer. However, a thermometer is not practical if you are cooking very thin fish fillets. In these cases, use a paring knife to peek inside; the fish should separate into neat flakes and the flesh should look opaque but appear moist.

Rare	110 degrees (tuna only)
Medium-Rare	125 degrees (tuna or salmon)
	120 degrees (farm-raised salmon)
Medium	135 degrees (flaky white-fleshed fish like cod and haddock)
	130 degrees (firm white-fleshed fish like swordfish or halibut)

Cod and Couscous Packets with Chermoula

Serves 2

Total time 50 minutes

WHY THIS RECIPE WORKS Cooking fish en papillote is a French technique where fish and a side are artfully folded into a parchment paper packet to steam together in the oven, concentrating and marrying their flavors. We found that aluminum foil was easier to work with than parchment. White fish fillets worked best; oilier fishes like salmon or tuna ended up greasy and overwhelmingly pungent. For a simple side, we liked quick-cooking couscous, and we dressed it up with a zesty chermoula sauce—a flavorful Moroccan condiment of cilantro, ginger, garlic, lemon, and spices. Try to purchase cod fillets that are similar in size so that they cook at the same rate. If the fillets are much thinner than 1 inch, simply fold them over to make them thicker. Halibut and haddock are good substitutes for the cod. For an accurate measurement of boiling water, bring a full kettle of water to a boil and then measure out the desired amount.

¼ cup minced fresh cilantro, divided
2 tablespoons extra-virgin olive oil
1 tablespoon grated fresh ginger
2 teaspoons smoked paprika
2 garlic cloves, minced
2 teaspoons grated lemon zest, divided,
  plus 1 tablespoon juice
1 teaspoon ground cumin
⅛ teaspoon red pepper flakes
  Brown sugar
¾ cup couscous
1 cup boiling water
2 (6- to 8-ounce) skinless cod fillets,
  1 to 1½ inches thick
¼ teaspoon table salt
⅛ teaspoon pepper
  Lemon wedges

1. Adjust oven rack to middle position and heat oven to 400 degrees. Combine 3 tablespoons cilantro, oil, ginger, paprika, garlic, 1½ teaspoons lemon zest and juice, cumin, and pepper flakes in small bowl. Season with salt, pepper, and sugar to taste.

2. Place couscous in medium bowl. Pour boiling water over couscous. Immediately cover with plastic wrap and let sit until liquid is absorbed and couscous is tender, about 5 minutes. Fluff couscous with fork, stir in remaining ½ teaspoon lemon zest, and season with salt and pepper to taste.

3. Pat cod dry with paper towels and sprinkle with salt and pepper. Cut two 14 by 12-inch rectangles of aluminum foil and lay them flat on counter. Divide couscous in half evenly, mound in center of each piece of foil, then place fillets on top. Spread 1 tablespoon of sauce over top of each fillet, then tightly crimp foil into packets.

4. Set packets on rimmed baking sheet and bake until fish flakes apart when gently prodded with paring knife and registers 135 degrees, 14 to 18 minutes. Carefully open packets, allowing steam to escape away from you. Sprinkle fillets with remaining 1 tablespoon cilantro and serve with remaining sauce and lemon wedges.

Halibut and Creamy Coconut Rice Packets

Serves 2
Total time 45 minutes

WHY THIS RECIPE WORKS For a Thai-inspired take on fish en papillote, we combined meaty halibut fillets and rice with a quick yet potent sauce made from coconut milk, green curry paste, lime zest, and a little cilantro, which we simply whisked together. The sauce did more than infuse the fish with flavor—it also provided a burst of color and transformed the rice into a rich, creamy accompaniment for our hearty halibut fillets. Try to purchase halibut fillets that are similar in size so that they cook at the same rate. If the fillets are much thinner than ¾ inch, simply fold them over to make them thicker. Cod and haddock are good substitutes for the halibut. You can use leftover rice or store-bought precooked rice here.

½ cup canned coconut milk
¼ cup minced fresh cilantro, divided
4 teaspoons Thai green curry paste
1 teaspoon lime zest
2 (6- to 8-ounce) skinless halibut fillets,
  ¾ inch to 1 inch thick
¼ teaspoon table salt
⅛ teaspoon pepper
2 cups cooked rice
  Lime wedges

1. Adjust oven rack to middle position and heat oven to 400 degrees. Whisk coconut milk, 3 tablespoons cilantro, curry paste, and lime zest together in bowl.

2. Pat halibut dry with paper towels and sprinkle with salt and pepper. Cut two 14 by 12-inch rectangles of aluminum foil and lay them flat on counter. Mound 1 cup cooked rice in center of each piece of foil, then place fillets on top. Spoon coconut mixture over top of fillets, then tightly crimp foil into packets.

3. Set packets on rimmed baking sheet and bake until fish flakes apart when gently prodded with paring knife and registers 130 degrees, 18 to 20 minutes. Carefully open packets, allowing steam to escape away from you. Sprinkle fillets with remaining 1 tablespoon cilantro and serve with lime wedges.

Spiced Swordfish with Avocado-Grapefruit Salsa

Pesce all'Acqua Pazza

Spiced Swordfish with Avocado-Grapefruit Salsa

Serves 2 FAST

Total time 30 minutes

WHY THIS RECIPE WORKS For a quick but satisfying weeknight dinner, we started with meaty swordfish, a fish with an assertive flavor that fares well in robustly flavored dishes. One-inch-thick steaks made it easy to brown the fish nicely without overcooking. For bold flavor, we brushed the steaks with a chili powder and cayenne–spiced oil. To get a nice char and get dinner on the table fast, we took advantage of the intense heat of the broiler, which cooked the steaks in less than 10 minutes. A tangy grapefruit and avocado salsa gave the fish a burst of fresh flavor. Try to purchase swordfish steaks that are about 1 inch thick; if the steaks are thicker or thinner, be sure to adjust the cooking time as needed. Other firm-fleshed fish such as bluefish, red snapper, or grouper can be used in place of the swordfish. If you can find ruby red grapefruit, its color and tangy sweetness work well in this dish.

SALSA

- ½ grapefruit
- ½ avocado, cut into ½-inch pieces
- 1 small shallot, sliced thin
- 1 tablespoon minced fresh mint
- 1½ teaspoons lime juice

SWORDFISH

- 1 tablespoon vegetable oil
- 1 teaspoon chili powder
  Pinch cayenne pepper
- 2 (6- to 8-ounce) skinless swordfish steaks, 1 inch thick
- ¼ teaspoon table salt
- ⅛ teaspoon pepper

1. FOR THE SALSA Cut away peel and pith from grapefruit. Cut into 4 wedges, then slice each wedge crosswise into ½-inch-thick pieces. Combine grapefruit, avocado, shallot, mint, and lime juice in bowl and season with salt and pepper to taste; set aside.

2. FOR THE SWORDFISH Adjust oven rack 6 inches from broiler element and heat broiler. Line rimmed baking sheet with aluminum foil and spray with vegetable oil spray. Combine oil, chili powder, and cayenne in bowl. Pat swordfish dry with paper towels, brush with spiced oil, and sprinkle with salt and pepper. Lay steaks on prepared sheet and broil until fish flakes apart when gently prodded with paring knife and registers 130 degrees, 6 to 9 minutes. Serve with salsa.

Sesame-Crusted Tuna with Wasabi Dressing

Serves 2 FAST

Total time 25 minutes

WHY THIS RECIPE WORKS In our opinion, pan-seared tuna should have a nice crust, a rare to medium-rare center, and simple, complementary flavors. We found that a coating of sesame seeds helped us accomplish all of these things in one fell swoop. Our simple sesame-seed crust minimized the time the fish needed to spend in the skillet and all but eliminated the risk of overcooking. A creamy, spicy dressing of wasabi paste, mayonnaise, and lime juice was the perfect accent. We prefer the flavor and texture of yellowfin tuna here; however, any type of fresh tuna will work. Try to purchase tuna steaks that are about 1 inch thick; if the steaks are thicker or thinner, be sure to adjust the cooking time as needed.

DRESSING

- 2 tablespoons mayonnaise
- 1½ teaspoons lime juice
- 1½ teaspoons wasabi paste

TUNA

- ¼ cup sesame seeds
- 2 (6- to 8-ounce) tuna steaks, 1 inch thick
- 1½ tablespoons vegetable oil, divided
- ¼ teaspoon table salt
- ⅛ teaspoon pepper

1. FOR THE DRESSING Whisk all ingredients together in bowl and season with salt and pepper to taste; set aside.

2. FOR THE TUNA Spread sesame seeds in shallow dish. Pat tuna dry with paper towels, rub with 1½ teaspoons oil, and sprinkle with salt and pepper. Press both sides of each steak in sesame seeds to coat.

3. Heat remaining 1 tablespoon oil in 10-inch nonstick skillet over medium-high heat until just smoking. Lay steaks in skillet and cook until seeds are golden brown, about 2 minutes. Using 2 spatulas, gently flip steaks and continue to cook until seeds are just golden and fish registers 110 degrees (for rare), about 1½ minutes (steaks will be opaque at perimeters and translucent red at center when checked with tip of paring knife), or 125 degrees (for medium-rare), about 3 minutes (steaks will be opaque at perimeters and reddish pink at center). Transfer steaks to cutting board and immediately slice on bias. Serve with wasabi dressing.

VARIATION

Sesame-Crusted Tuna with Ginger-Soy Sauce

Substitute 2 tablespoons soy sauce, 2 tablespoons water, 1 thinly sliced small scallion, 1 tablespoon unseasoned rice vinegar, 1 tablespoon sugar, 1 teaspoon grated fresh ginger, 1 teaspoon toasted sesame oil, and pinch red pepper flakes for mayonnaise, lime juice, and wasabi paste.

Pesce all'Acqua Pazza

Serves 2

Total time 35 minutes

WHY THIS RECIPE WORKS "Acqua pazza," or "crazy water," refers to the southern Italian tradition of cooking the day's catch in seawater. Modern recipes feature longer ingredient lists: Parsley, tomato, white wine, and garlic are common. For the fish, we chose skin-on haddock fillets. The flesh held up nicely during simmering, and the abundant collagen in the skin suffused the broth with rich flavor and body. Halved cherry tomatoes provided sweetness and pops of color. We also liked the addition of white wine, which contributed brightness and light acidity. After just a few minutes, the haddock absorbed the heady flavor of the broth and the broth was enriched by the fish. Try to purchase haddock fillets that are similar in size so that they cook at the same rate. You can substitute skin-on fillets of other firm, white-fleshed fish such as sea bass, branzino, and red snapper for the haddock. You will need a 10-inch skillet with a tight-fitting lid for this recipe. Serve with crusty bread.

- 12 ounces skin-on haddock fillets, ¾ to 1 inch thick
- ½ teaspoon kosher salt, divided
- ⅛ teaspoon pepper
- 1 tablespoon extra-virgin olive oil
- 2 small garlic cloves, sliced thin
- ⅛ teaspoon red pepper flakes
- ½ small onion, chopped fine
- 1 small bay leaf
- 4 ounces cherry or grape tomatoes, halved
- ¾ cup water
- 2 tablespoons dry white wine
- 6 fresh parsley stems, plus 1½ tablespoons chopped fresh parsley, divided

1. Sprinkle haddock all over with ¼ teaspoon salt and pepper and set aside.

2. Heat oil, garlic, and pepper flakes in 10-inch skillet over medium heat, stirring constantly, until garlic begins to sizzle gently, 1½ to 2 minutes. Add onion, bay leaf, and remaining

¼ teaspoon salt and cook, stirring constantly, until onion just starts to soften, 2 to 3 minutes. Add tomatoes and cook, stirring constantly, until tomatoes begin to soften, 2 to 3 minutes. Stir in water, wine, parsley stems, and half of chopped parsley and bring to boil. Nestle haddock skin side down in liquid, moving aside solids as much as possible (it's fine if fillets fold over slightly at ends; liquid will not quite cover fillets). Spoon some liquid and solids over haddock. Reduce heat to low; cover; and simmer gently until fish registers 110 degrees at thickest point, 4 to 7 minutes. Let stand off heat, covered, until fish is opaque and just cooked through (fish should register at least 135 degrees), 3 to 7 minutes.

3. Divide haddock between 2 shallow soup bowls. Discard bay leaf and parsley stems; stir remaining chopped parsley into broth. Season broth with salt and pepper to taste. Spoon portion of broth and solids over each serving of haddock and serve immediately.

Pan-Seared Salmon with Braised Lentils and Swiss Chard

Serves 2

Total time 1¼ hours

WHY THIS RECIPE WORKS We wanted to pair earthy braised lentils and Swiss chard with buttery pan-seared salmon for a hearty, satisfying meal for two. First, we braised the lentils in a skillet (to cut down on dishes) with onion, garlic, thyme, chicken broth, and the chard stems to infuse the lentils with flavor. Once they were tender, we removed them from the skillet and quickly pan-seared the salmon until it had a beautiful browned, caramelized crust and a moist, medium-rare interior. While the salmon rested, we rewarmed the lentils, stirring in the chard leaves until they were just wilted. Try to purchase center-cut salmon fillets of similar size so that they cook at the same rate. If you purchase skin-on fillets, follow the instructions at right to remove the skin. Although we prefer brown lentils for this recipe, it will work with any type of lentil except red or yellow. Note that cooking times may vary depending on the type of lentils you use. If using wild salmon, decrease the cooking time slightly and cook fillets to 120 degrees (for medium-rare). You will need a 10-inch nonstick skillet with a tight-fitting lid for this recipe.

2 tablespoons unsalted butter, divided
6 ounces Swiss chard, stems chopped, leaves cut into 1-inch pieces
¼ cup finely chopped onion

1 garlic clove, minced
¼ teaspoon minced fresh thyme or pinch dried
2 cups chicken broth, divided
½ cup brown lentils, picked over and rinsed
½ teaspoon lemon juice
2 (6- to 8-ounce) skinless salmon fillets, 1½ inches thick
¼ teaspoon table salt
⅛ teaspoon pepper
1 tablespoon vegetable oil
Lemon wedges

1. Melt 1 tablespoon butter in 10-inch nonstick skillet over medium heat. Add chard stems and onion and cook until vegetables are softened, about 5 minutes. Stir in garlic and thyme and cook until fragrant, about 30 seconds. Stir in 1¾ cups broth, lentils, and lemon juice and bring to simmer. Reduce heat to low; cover; and simmer until lentils are tender, about 30 minutes. Season with salt and pepper to taste, transfer to bowl, and cover to keep warm.

2. Wipe skillet clean. Pat salmon dry with paper towels and sprinkle with salt and pepper. Heat oil in now-empty skillet over medium-high heat until just smoking. Lay fillets in skillet and cook until browned on first side, about 5 minutes. Using tongs, gently flip fillets and continue to cook until center of fish is still translucent when checked with tip of paring knife and registers 125 degrees (for medium-rare), 3 to 5 minutes; transfer to plate and tent loosely with aluminum foil.

3. Wipe skillet clean and return to medium-high heat. Add cooked lentil mixture and remaining ¼ cup broth to now-empty skillet and cook until hot, about 1 minute. Stir in chard leaves and remaining 1 tablespoon butter and cook, stirring constantly, until chard is wilted, 2 to 3 minutes. Serve fillets with lentils and lemon wedges.

SKINNING SALMON FILLETS

To remove the skin from raw fillets, use the tip of a boning knife or a chef's knife to cut the skin away from the flesh at the corner of the fillet. Grasp the skin with a paper towel and slice the remaining skin off the flesh.

Chili-Glazed Salmon with Bok Choy

Serves 2 `FAST`

Total time 30 minutes

WHY THIS RECIPE WORKS We wanted a failproof way to get perfectly cooked fish with a crisp, well-browned crust alongside an easy vegetable side. Cooking the fillets in a nonstick skillet kept the browned crust on the fish, not stuck to the pan. We started our glaze with sweet chili sauce; a little savory fish sauce and fresh ginger were all we needed to turn it into a boldly flavored glaze. A pinch of cornstarch helped to thicken the glaze. Baby bok choy paired perfectly with the rich salmon. Try to purchase center-cut salmon fillets of similar size so that they cook at the same rate. If you purchase skin-on fillets, follow the instructions on page 184 to remove the skin. If using wild salmon, decrease cook time slightly and cook fillets to 120 degrees (for medium-rare).

- 2 tablespoons sweet chili sauce
- 1 tablespoon fish sauce
- 1½ teaspoons grated fresh ginger
- ¼ teaspoon cornstarch
- 2 tablespoons vegetable oil, divided
- 2 heads baby bok choy (4 ounces each), halved
- 2 (6- to 8-ounce) skinless salmon fillets, 1½ inches thick
- ¼ teaspoon table salt
- ⅛ teaspoon pepper
  Lime wedges

1. Whisk chili sauce, fish sauce, ginger, and cornstarch together in small bowl. Heat 1 tablespoon oil in 10-inch nonstick skillet over high heat until shimmering. Add bok choy cut side down to skillet and cook until lightly browned on both sides, 1 to 2 minutes per side; transfer to plate.

2. Pat salmon dry with paper towels and sprinkle with salt and pepper. Heat remaining 1 tablespoon oil in now-empty skillet over medium-high heat until just smoking. Lay fillets in skillet and cook until browned on first side, about 5 minutes. Using tongs, gently flip fillets and continue to cook until center of fish is still translucent when checked with tip of paring knife and registers 125 degrees (for medium-rare), 3 to 5 minutes. Holding fillets in place with spatula, carefully pour off any rendered fat in skillet. Off heat, add chili sauce mixture to skillet with salmon and gently flip fillets once or twice to coat. Transfer fillets to serving platter.

3. Add bok choy to skillet with glaze and toss until coated; transfer to platter with fillets. Serve with lime wedges.

Chili-Glazed Salmon with Bok Choy

Roast Salmon with Broccoli Rabe and Pistachio Gremolata

Serves 2 FAST

Total time 30 minutes

WHY THIS RECIPE WORKS Salmon cooks quickly and doesn't flood the pan with rendered juices, so roasting it right alongside an equally quick-cooking vegetable is a great way to streamline a delicious dinner for two. We matched rich salmon with pleasantly bitter broccoli rabe, using skin-on salmon fillets that readily cooked through as the baking sheet heated up. We reinforced the broccoli rabe's bite with some red pepper flakes and minced garlic but kept the seasoning of the salmon simple. After we rubbed the flesh with oil and sprinkled it with salt and pepper, we placed the salmon on half of the baking sheet next to the broccoli rabe. Roasting together in the hot oven, the fillets cooked through to a silky medium-rare right as the broccoli rabe turned tender. A vibrant pistachio gremolata spooned over the salmon added some crunch and fresh flavor. If using wild salmon, decrease the cooking time slightly and cook fillets to 120 degrees (for medium-rare). Try to purchase center-cut salmon fillets of similar size so that they cook at the same rate.

- 2 tablespoons finely chopped toasted pistachios
- 1 tablespoon minced fresh parsley
- 1 garlic clove, minced, divided
- ½ teaspoon grated lemon zest, plus lemon wedges for serving
- 8 ounces broccoli rabe, trimmed and cut into 1½-inch pieces
- 4 teaspoons extra-virgin olive oil, divided, plus extra for drizzling
- ½ teaspoon table salt, divided
- ⅛ teaspoon pepper, divided
  Pinch red pepper flakes
- 2 (6- to 8-ounce) skin-on salmon fillets, 1 to 1½ inches thick

1. Adjust oven rack to lowest position and heat oven to 450 degrees. Combine pistachios, parsley, half of garlic, and lemon zest in small bowl; set gremolata aside for serving.

2. Toss broccoli rabe, 1 tablespoon oil, ¼ teaspoon salt, pinch pepper, pepper flakes, and remaining garlic together on rimmed baking sheet, then arrange in even layer on one half of sheet. Pat salmon dry with paper towels, rub with remaining 1 teaspoon oil, and sprinkle with remaining ¼ teaspoon salt and remaining pinch pepper. Arrange salmon skin side down on empty side of sheet.

3. Roast salmon until centers of fillets are still translucent when checked with tip of paring knife and register 125 degrees (for medium-rare), and broccoli rabe is tender, 10 to 15 minutes. Slide spatula along underside of fillets and transfer to individual serving plates, leaving skin behind. Drizzle broccoli rabe with extra oil and season with salt and pepper to taste. Sprinkle salmon with gremolata and serve with broccoli rabe and lemon wedges.

NOTES FROM THE TEST KITCHEN

BUYING SALMON

FRESH VS. FARMED In season, we prefer the more pronounced flavor of wild-caught salmon to farmed Atlantic salmon (traditionally the main farm-raised variety in the United States). If you're going to spend the extra money for wild salmon, make sure it looks and smells fresh, and realize that high-quality salmon is available only from late spring through the end of summer. We love the taste of wild salmon, but because it doesn't have the cushion of as much lubricating fat, we like it cooked to 120 degrees (for medium-rare) rather than 125 degrees for farmed salmon. Wild salmon is also thinner, so you need to check for doneness earlier than you would for recipes calling for farmed salmon.

CUTS OF SALMON There are many ways to buy salmon. Our preference is to buy thick, center-cut fillets, which can be poached, steamed, pan-seared, roasted, or grilled. Cut from the head end or center, these fillets are the prime cut of the fish. They are thick enough to sear nicely without overcooking and are easy to skin (if desired). Buy the total amount you need in one piece and cut the individual fillets yourself. You will also see thin fillets at the market. Stay away from these. These are cut from the tail end, and they cook so fast that it is impossible to get a nice sear before the fish is overcooked—plus, one end is very, very thin while the other is always much thicker.

SKIN-ON OR BONE-IN For some recipes you will want to buy the salmon skin-on; for recipes that call for skinless salmon, you can easily remove it yourself (see page 184) or ask your fishmonger to do it for you. Bone-in steaks are an excellent choice for pan searing, grilling, or roasting, but they should not be poached. You may also see boneless steaks rolled and tied into a circular shape.

**Pomegranate-Glazed
Salmon with Black-Eyed
Peas and Walnuts**

Pomegranate-Glazed Salmon with Black-Eyed Peas and Walnuts

Serves 2 `FAST`

Total time 25 minutes

WHY THIS RECIPE WORKS For a failproof way of cooking salmon hands-free with a nicely browned exterior and a silky, moist interior, we developed a hybrid roasting method, preheating the oven to 500 degrees but then turning down the heat to 275 just before placing the fish in the oven. The initial blast of high heat firmed the exterior and rendered some excess fat from the skin. The fish gently cooked in the oven and stayed moist as the temperature slowly dropped. Pomegranate molasses, a sweet-and-sour syrup, did double-duty here, acting as both a glaze for the salmon itself as well as a main ingredient in our black-eyed pea salad dressing, tying the two elements together. If using wild salmon, decrease the cooking time slightly and cook fillets to 120 degrees (for medium-rare). Try to purchase center-cut salmon fillets of similar size so that they cook at the same rate. Add a handful of baby spinach or baby arugula to the salad, if desired.

2 (6- to 8-ounce) skin-on salmon fillets, 1 inch thick
½ teaspoon plus 2 tablespoons extra-virgin olive oil, divided
4 teaspoons plus 2 tablespoons pomegranate molasses, divided
½ teaspoon table salt, divided
½ teaspoon pepper, divided
4 teaspoons lemon juice
1½ cups canned black-eyed peas, rinsed and drained well
¼ cup minced fresh parsley, mint, or chives
¼ cup pomegranate seeds
¼ cup toasted chopped walnuts, pecans, or pistachios

1. Adjust oven rack to lowest position and heat oven to 500 degrees. Line rimmed baking sheet with aluminum foil and place sheet on rack. Pat salmon dry with paper towels. Brush with ½ teaspoon oil and 2 teaspoons pomegranate molasses, then sprinkle with ¼ teaspoon salt and ¼ teaspoon pepper.

2. Once oven reaches 500 degrees, reduce oven temperature to 275 degrees. Remove sheet from oven and carefully place salmon, skin side down, on hot sheet. Roast salmon until center is still translucent when checked with tip of paring knife and registers 125 degrees (for medium-rare), 9 to 13 minutes.

3. Meanwhile, whisk lemon juice, 2 tablespoons pomegranate molasses, remaining 2 tablespoons oil, remaining ¼ teaspoon salt, and remaining ¼ teaspoon pepper together in bowl until combined. Add black-eyed peas, parsley, pomegranate seeds, and walnuts and toss to combine. Season salad with salt and pepper to taste.

4. Remove salmon from oven and brush with remaining 2 teaspoons pomegranate molasses. Transfer salmon to plate and serve with black-eyed pea salad.

Salmon and Black Rice Salad with Snap Peas and Radishes

Serves 2

Total time 45 minutes

WHY THIS RECIPE WORKS To make this flavorful flaked salmon and crunchy snap pea salad we used earthy black rice as a base. Then we bolstered these ingredients with a lively dressing of ginger, toasted sesame oil, honey, and rice vinegar. If using wild salmon, decrease the cooking time slightly and cook fillets to 120 degrees (for medium-rare). You can substitute brown rice for the black rice; it may need a few extra minutes of cooking. Try to purchase center-cut salmon fillets of similar size so that they cook at the same rate.

¾ cup black rice

½ teaspoon plus ⅛ teaspoon table salt, plus salt for cooking rice

1 tablespoon unseasoned rice vinegar, divided

1 (6-ounce) skin-on salmon fillet, 1 to 1½ inches thick

2 teaspoons vegetable oil, divided

1 teaspoon toasted sesame oil

1 teaspoon grated fresh ginger

1 teaspoon honey

4 ounces sugar snap peas, strings removed, halved crosswise

1 red bell pepper, stemmed, seeded, and chopped fine

4 radishes, trimmed, halved, and sliced thin

2 tablespoons minced fresh cilantro

1. Bring 2 quarts water to boil in large saucepan over medium-high heat. Add rice and 1½ teaspoons salt and cook until rice is tender, 20 to 25 minutes. Drain rice, spread onto platter or rimmed baking sheet, drizzle with 1 teaspoon vinegar, and let cool completely, 10 to 15 minutes.

2. Meanwhile, pat salmon dry with paper towels and sprinkle with ⅛ teaspoon salt. Heat ½ teaspoon vegetable oil in 8- or 10-inch nonstick skillet over medium-high heat until shimmering. Cook salmon, skin side up, until well browned, 3 to 5 minutes. Flip and continue to cook until salmon is still translucent when checked with tip of paring knife and registers 125 degrees (for medium-rare), 3 to 5 minutes. Transfer salmon to plate and let cool slightly, about 2 minutes. Using 2 forks, flake salmon into rough 2-inch pieces; discard skin.

3. Whisk sesame oil, ginger, honey, remaining ½ teaspoon salt, remaining 2 teaspoons vinegar, and remaining 1½ teaspoons vegetable oil in large bowl. Add cooled rice, salmon, snap peas, bell pepper, radishes, and cilantro and toss to combine. Season with salt and pepper to taste. Serve.

Crispy Salmon Cakes with Sweet and Tangy Tartar Sauce

Serves 2

Total time 35 minutes

WHY THIS RECIPE WORKS We wanted to give classic New England cod cakes a new spin by swapping in rich, meaty salmon. We were after pure salmon flavor with just a few choice ingredients and minimal binder. Fresh salmon easily beat out canned, and we ditched the typical potato binder in favor of mayonnaise and bread crumbs. To chop the salmon, we quickly pulsed 1-inch pieces in the food processor. This gave us both larger chunks for a substantial texture and smaller pieces that helped the cakes hold together. Coating the cakes in ultracrisp panko bread crumbs ensured a good crust. Dijon mustard, shallot, lemon juice, and parsley boosted the flavor of the cakes, and a quick tartar sauce completed our dish. Be sure to use raw salmon here; do not substitute cooked salmon. Do not overprocess the salmon in step 2 or the cakes will have a pasty texture. If you purchase skin-on fillets, follow the instructions on page 184 to remove the skin.

TARTAR SAUCE

⅓ cup mayonnaise

1 tablespoon sweet pickle relish

1½ teaspoons capers, rinsed and minced

1 teaspoon white wine vinegar

¼ teaspoon Worcestershire sauce

SALMON CAKES

1 (10-ounce) skinless salmon fillet, cut into 1-inch pieces

2 tablespoons plus ½ cup panko bread crumbs, divided

1 tablespoon minced fresh parsley

1 tablespoon mayonnaise

1 small shallot, minced

2 teaspoons lemon juice

½ teaspoon Dijon mustard

½ teaspoon table salt

¼ teaspoon pepper

Pinch cayenne pepper

⅓ cup vegetable oil, for frying

1. FOR THE TARTAR SAUCE Whisk all ingredients together in bowl and season with salt and pepper to taste; set aside.

2. FOR THE SALMON CAKES Pulse salmon in food processor until there is an even mix of finely minced and coarsely chopped pieces of salmon, about 2 pulses, scraping down sides of bowl as needed.

3. Combine 2 tablespoons panko, parsley, mayonnaise, shallot, lemon juice, mustard, salt, pepper, and cayenne in bowl. Gently fold in processed salmon until just combined.

4. Spread remaining ½ cup panko in shallow dish. Scrape salmon mixture onto small baking sheet. Divide mixture into 4 equal portions and gently flatten each portion into 1-inch-thick patty. Carefully coat each cake with panko, then return to sheet.

5. Line large plate with triple layer of paper towels. Heat oil in 10-inch skillet over medium-high heat until shimmering. Gently place salmon cakes in skillet and cook, without moving, until golden brown and crisp on both sides, 2 to 3 minutes per side. Drain cakes briefly on paper towel–lined plate. Serve with tartar sauce.

VARIATION

Crispy Salmon Cakes with Smoked Salmon, Capers, and Dill

Reduce amount of fresh salmon to 8 ounces and salt to ⅛ teaspoon. Substitute 1 tablespoon chopped fresh dill for parsley. Fold in 2 ounces finely chopped smoked salmon and 1½ teaspoons rinsed and minced capers with processed salmon in step 3.

Shrimp Saganaki

Serves 2

Total time 45 minutes

WHY THIS RECIPE WORKS Quick-cooking shrimp is one of the easiest things to make for two; for an exciting one-dish shrimp dish to add to our repertoire, we turned to shrimp saganaki, a Greek specialty of tender shrimp baked in a tomato sauce under crumbles of feta. First, we marinated the shrimp with oil; garlic; lemon zest; and sweet, anise-flavored ouzo. For the tomato sauce, we sautéed bell pepper and shallot, then added garlic, pepper flakes, ouzo, white wine, and canned diced tomatoes. Even nestled in the sauce, the shrimp baked unevenly in the oven, so we moved the dish to the stovetop. Simmered gently in the sauce over medium-low heat, the shrimp came out perfectly tender. This dish is fairly spicy; to make it milder, reduce the amount of red pepper flakes. You can substitute 1 tablespoon Pernod or 1 tablespoon vodka plus ⅛ teaspoon anise seeds for the ouzo. You will need a 10-inch skillet with a tight-fitting lid for this recipe. Serve with crusty bread or white rice.

- 12 ounces extra-large shrimp (21 to 25 per pound), peeled and deveined
- 2 tablespoons extra-virgin olive oil, divided
- 1½ tablespoons ouzo, divided
- 3 garlic cloves, minced, divided
- ½ teaspoon grated lemon zest
- ¼ teaspoon table salt
- ⅛ teaspoon pepper

- 2 shallots, minced
- ½ red or green bell pepper, cut into ¼-inch pieces
- ¼ teaspoon red pepper flakes
- 1 (14.5-ounce) can diced tomatoes, drained with ¼ cup juice reserved
- 2 tablespoons dry white wine
- 3 ounces feta cheese, crumbled (¾ cup)
- 1 tablespoon minced fresh dill

1. Toss shrimp with 1½ teaspoons oil, 1½ teaspoons ouzo, one-third of garlic, and lemon zest in bowl. Sprinkle with salt and pepper and set aside.

2. Heat 1 tablespoon oil in 10-inch skillet over medium heat until shimmering. Add shallots, bell pepper, and ⅛ teaspoon salt; cover; and cook, stirring occasionally, until vegetables release their moisture, 3 to 5 minutes. Uncover and continue to cook, stirring occasionally, until moisture evaporates and vegetables have softened, 3 to 5 minutes. Stir in remaining garlic and pepper flakes and cook until fragrant, about 30 seconds. Stir in remaining 1 tablespoon ouzo, tomatoes and reserved juice, and wine. Bring to simmer and cook, stirring occasionally, until flavors meld and sauce is slightly thickened, about 5 minutes. Season with salt and pepper to taste.

3. Stir in shrimp along with any accumulated juices. Reduce heat to medium-low; cover; and simmer, stirring occasionally, until shrimp are opaque throughout, 6 to 9 minutes. Off heat, sprinkle with feta and dill and drizzle with remaining 1½ teaspoons oil. Serve.

DEVEINING SHRIMP

Although the vein running along the back of shrimp has no adverse effect on flavor or texture, removing it improves the appearance.

1. After removing shell, use paring knife to make shallow cut along back of shrimp so that vein is exposed.

2. Use tip of knife to lift vein out of shrimp. Discard vein by wiping blade against paper towel.

SHRIMP 101

BUYING SHRIMP Virtually all of the shrimp sold in supermarkets today have been previously frozen, either in large blocks of ice or by a method called "individually quick-frozen," or IQF for short. Supermarkets simply defrost the shrimp before displaying them on ice at the fish counter. We highly recommend purchasing bags of still-frozen shrimp and defrosting them as needed at home, since there is no telling how long "fresh" shrimp may have been kept on ice at the market. IQF shrimp have a better flavor and texture than shrimp frozen in blocks, and they are convenient for two because it's easy to defrost just the amount you need. We find shell-on shrimp to be firmer and sweeter. Also, shrimp should be the only ingredient listed on the bag; some packagers add preservatives, but we find treated shrimp to have an unpleasant, rubbery texture.

SORTING OUT SHRIMP SIZES Shrimp are sold both by size (small, medium, etc.) and by the number needed to make 1 pound, usually given in a range. Choosing shrimp by the numerical rating is more accurate, because the size label varies from store to store. Here's how the two sizing systems generally compare:

Small	51 to 60 per pound
Medium	41 to 50 per pound
Medium-Large	31 to 40 per pound
Large	26 to 30 per pound
Extra-Large	21 to 25 per pound
Jumbo	16 to 20 per pound

DEFROSTING SHRIMP You can thaw frozen shrimp overnight in the refrigerator in a covered bowl or place them in a colander under cold running water; they will be ready in a few minutes. Thoroughly dry the shrimp before cooking.

PEELING SHRIMP To peel shrimp, break the shell under the swimming legs; the legs will come off as the shell is removed. Leave the tail end intact if desired, or tug the tail end to remove the shell. If buying shrimp labeled "E-Z" peel, pull the shell around and off shrimp, leaving the tail end intact, if desired. See page 189 for information on deveining shrimp.

Pan-Seared Shrimp with Spicy Orange Glaze

Serves 2 FAST

Total time 20 minutes

WHY THIS RECIPE WORKS A good recipe for pan-seared shrimp is hard to find. Most recipes produce shrimp that are either dry and flavorless or pale, tough, and gummy. We wanted shrimp that were well caramelized but still moist and tender. We sometimes brine shrimp to boost flavor and texture, but brining the peeled shrimp inhibited browning. Instead, we seasoned the shrimp with salt, pepper, and sugar, which brought out their natural sweetness and encouraged browning. Since we only needed enough for two, we could easily cook the shrimp in a single batch without overcrowding. A piping-hot skillet browned the shrimp in just 90 seconds, then we coated the shrimp with a sweet and spicy orange glaze (made in minutes with just four ingredients) and simmered it until the glaze was nicely thickened. This dish is fairly spicy; to make it milder, use less chili-garlic sauce. Serve with rice.

GLAZE

- 1 tablespoon minced fresh cilantro
- 1 teaspoon sugar
- ½ teaspoon chili-garlic sauce
- ½ teaspoon grated orange zest plus 2 tablespoons juice

SHRIMP

- 12 ounces extra-large shrimp (21 to 25 per pound), peeled and deveined
- ⅛ teaspoon sugar
- ¼ teaspoon table salt
- ⅛ teaspoon pepper
- 2 teaspoons vegetable oil

1. FOR THE GLAZE Whisk all ingredients together in bowl.

2. FOR THE SHRIMP Pat shrimp dry with paper towels and sprinkle with sugar, salt, and pepper. Heat oil in 10-inch nonstick skillet over medium-high heat until just smoking. Add shrimp in single layer and cook until curled and lightly browned, about 1½ minutes. Whisk glaze mixture to recombine, then add to skillet. Bring to simmer and cook, tossing shrimp to coat, until glaze is slightly thickened, about 30 seconds. Serve.

VARIATION

Pan-Seared Shrimp with Ginger-Hoisin Glaze

Substitute 1 thinly sliced scallion, 1 tablespoon hoisin sauce, 1 tablespoon water, 2 teaspoons grated fresh ginger, 1½ teaspoons unseasoned rice vinegar, ¾ teaspoon soy sauce, and pinch red pepper flakes for cilantro, sugar, chili-garlic sauce and orange zest and juice.

Stir-Fried Shrimp with Lemon-Ginger Sauce

Serves 2 FAST

Total time 30 minutes

WHY THIS RECIPE WORKS For a bright-tasting shrimp stir-fry, we added a hefty dose of lemon juice and fresh ginger to our classic stir-fry sauce. Fresh asparagus and carrot gave our stir-fry heft and paired well with the lemony-ginger shrimp. Cooking the vegetables, shrimp, and aromatics in separate batches was important to ensure that the pan stayed hot and the vegetables and shrimp cooked evenly and quickly. Steaming the vegetables before combining them with the shrimp and sauce yielded perfectly crisp-tender asparagus and carrots without adding extra oil. You will need a 14-inch flat-bottomed wok or 12-inch nonstick skillet with a tight-fitting lid for this recipe.

Stir-Fried Shrimp with Lemon-Ginger Sauce

- ¼ cup chicken broth
- 2 tablespoons lemon juice
- 2 tablespoons Shaoxing wine
- 1 tablespoon soy sauce
- 1 teaspoon sugar
- 1 teaspoon cornstarch
- ⅛ teaspoon pepper
- 12 ounces extra-large shrimp (21 to 25 per pound), peeled, deveined, and tails removed
- 2 teaspoons toasted sesame oil, divided
- 2 scallions, minced
- 2 garlic cloves, minced
- 2 teaspoons grated fresh ginger
- 8 ounces asparagus, trimmed and cut on bias into 2-inch lengths
- 1 carrot, peeled and cut into 2-inch-long matchsticks
- ¼ cup water

1. Whisk broth, lemon juice, Shaoxing wine, soy sauce, sugar, cornstarch, and pepper together in small bowl. Toss shrimp with 1 teaspoon oil in medium bowl. In separate bowl, combine scallions, garlic, ginger, and remaining 1 teaspoon oil.

2. Cook asparagus, carrot, and water, covered, in 14-inch flat-bottomed wok or 12-inch nonstick skillet over high heat until water is boiling and vegetables begin to soften, about 3 minutes. Uncover and continue to cook until water has evaporated and vegetables are crisp-tender, about 2 minutes; transfer to separate bowl.

3. Return now-empty wok to high heat. Add shrimp and cook, tossing slowly but constantly, until nearly opaque, about 1 minute. Push shrimp to sides of wok. Add garlic mixture and cook, mashing into wok, until fragrant, about 30 seconds. Stir garlic mixture into shrimp.

4. Stir in cooked vegetables. Whisk sauce to recombine, then add to wok. Cook, stirring constantly, until shrimp are opaque throughout and sauce is thickened, about 1 minute. Serve.

Shrimp and Grits with
Andouille Cream Sauce

Shrimp and Grits with Andouille Cream Sauce

Serves 2

Total time 40 minutes

WHY THIS RECIPE WORKS For this version of shrimp and grits, we opted for a thick, rich gravy (a departure from the typical thinner shrimp and grits sauce) served over creamy cheddar grits seasoned with a hefty pinch of black pepper. For the shrimp and sauce we sautéed just a couple ounces of chopped andouille sausage until its fat had rendered and the pieces were lightly crisped. Then we poached 12 ounces of extra-large shrimp in plenty of heavy cream. To punch up the flavors, we added a bit of garlic and bracing Tabasco. For further seasoning, we auditioned cayenne, dried thyme, and paprika but ultimately decided to use Louisiana seasoning (often labeled Cajun or Creole seasoning), which did a lot of work for just a single teaspoon. We prefer untreated shrimp, but if your shrimp are treated with salt or additives such as sodium tripolyphosphate (STPP), reduce the Louisiana seasoning to ¾ teaspoon.

GRITS

- 2 cups water, plus extra as needed
- ½ teaspoon table salt
- ⅓ cup old-fashioned grits
- 2 ounces extra-sharp cheddar cheese, shredded (½ cup)
- 2 tablespoons heavy cream
- ¼ teaspoon pepper

SHRIMP AND SAUCE

- 12 ounces extra-large shrimp (21 to 25 per pound), peeled, deveined, and tails removed
- 1 teaspoon Louisiana seasoning
- 1 tablespoon unsalted butter
- 2 ounces andouille sausage, cut into ½-inch pieces (scant ½ cup)
- 2 scallions, white and green parts separated and sliced thin
- 2 garlic cloves, minced
- ½ cup heavy cream
- ½ teaspoon Tabasco sauce, plus extra for serving
  Lemon wedges

1. FOR THE GRITS Bring water and salt to boil in medium saucepan over high heat. Slowly whisk in grits to ensure no lumps form. Reduce heat to medium-low and cook, whisking frequently and scraping sides and bottom of saucepan to make sure grits do not stick, until grits are tender and have consistency of thick pancake batter, 20 to 25 minutes.

2. Off heat, whisk cheddar, cream, and pepper into grits until fully combined. Cover to keep warm.

3. FOR THE SHRIMP AND SAUCE Sprinkle shrimp with Louisiana seasoning and set aside. Melt butter in 10-inch nonstick skillet over medium-high heat. Add andouille and cook until browned, 3 to 5 minutes.

4. Add scallion whites and garlic and cook until fragrant, about 1 minute. Stir in cream and shrimp and bring to simmer. Reduce heat to medium and cook, stirring occasionally, until shrimp are just cooked through and sauce is slightly thickened, 4 to 6 minutes. Off heat, stir in hot sauce and season with salt and pepper to taste.

5. If grits have set, whisk in extra hot water, a little at a time, until creamy; season with salt and pepper to taste. Serve shrimp and sauce over grits, sprinkled with scallion greens, passing lemon wedges and extra hot sauce separately.

Pan-Seared Scallops

Serves 2 `FAST`

Total time 30 minutes

WHY THIS RECIPE WORKS Producing crisp-crusted restaurant-style scallops at home means overcoming a major obstacle: weak stovetops. We wanted pan-seared scallops with perfectly brown crusts and moist, tender centers. Blotting the scallops dry, waiting until the oil was just smoking to add them to the skillet, and switching to a nonstick skillet were all steps in the right direction. But it wasn't until we tried a restaurant technique—butter basting—that our scallops really improved. We seared the scallops on one side then added butter to the skillet to encourage browning. (Butter contains milk proteins and sugars that brown rapidly when heated.) We then used a large spoon to ladle the foaming butter over the scallops. Adding the butter partway through cooking ensured that it had just enough time to work its browning magic on the scallops but not enough time to burn. We recommend buying "dry" scallops, which don't have chemical additives and taste better than "wet."

- 12 ounces large sea scallops, tendons removed
- ¼ teaspoon table salt
- ⅛ teaspoon pepper
- 1 tablespoon vegetable oil
- 1 tablespoon unsalted butter
  Lemon wedges

1. Place scallops on large plate lined with clean dish towel. Place second clean dish towel on top of scallops and press gently on towel to blot liquid. Let scallops sit at room temperature for 10 minutes while towels absorb moisture.

2. Sprinkle scallops with salt and pepper. Heat oil in 12-inch nonstick skillet over high heat until just smoking. Add scallops flat side down in single layer and cook, without moving, until well browned, 1½ to 2 minutes.

3. Add butter to skillet. Using tongs, flip scallops and continue to cook, using large spoon to baste scallops with melted butter (tilt skillet so butter runs to 1 side) until sides of scallops are firm and centers are opaque, 30 to 90 seconds. Serve immediately with lemon wedges.

VARIATIONS
Pan-Seared Scallops with Lemon Browned Butter

Cook 2 tablespoons unsalted butter in small saucepan over medium heat, swirling saucepan constantly, until butter is golden brown and has nutty aroma, 3 to 4 minutes. Add 1 minced small shallot and cook until fragrant, about 30 seconds. Off heat, stir in 2 teaspoons minced fresh parsley, ¼ teaspoon minced fresh thyme, and 1 teaspoon lemon juice. Season with salt and pepper to taste. Serve with scallops

Pan-Seared Scallops with Tomato-Ginger Sauce

Cook 3 tablespoons unsalted butter in small saucepan over medium heat, swirling saucepan constantly, until butter turns golden brown and has nutty aroma, 3 to 4 minutes. Add 1 small plum tomato, cored, seeded, and chopped fine, 1½ teaspoons grated fresh ginger, 1½ teaspoons lemon juice, and pinch red pepper flakes. Cook, stirring constantly, until fragrant, about 1 minute. Season with salt to taste. Serve with scallops.

Turmeric Scallops with Mango Noodle Salad

Serves 2

Total time 35 minutes

WHY THIS RECIPE WORKS This recipe dials up the flavors to bring excitement to a scallop dinner. Here we created a vermicelli noodle salad with a turmeric-lime dressing sweetened with a touch of honey. In addition to the bright dressing, we added sweet mango pieces and crisp slices of cucumber to the noodles for flavor and texture. The buttery, rich seared

Turmeric Scallops with Mango Noodle Salad

scallops proved to be the perfect foil for this unusual noodle salad. Fresh or thawed frozen mango will work here. We recommend buying "dry" scallops, which don't have chemical additives and taste better than "wet."

- 4 ounces rice vermicelli noodles
- 2½ teaspoons vegetable oil, divided
- 8 ounces large sea scallops, tendons removed
- 2 teaspoons grated fresh ginger
- ¾ teaspoon ground turmeric, divided
- ¾ teaspoon ground coriander, divided
- 1 teaspoon grated lime zest plus 1 tablespoon juice, plus lime wedges for serving
- 2 teaspoons honey
- 1 cup ½-inch mango pieces
- ¼ English cucumber, halved lengthwise and sliced ¼ inch thick
- ¼ cup fresh cilantro leaves, plus extra for serving
- 1 shallot, sliced thin
- 2 tablespoons unsalted roasted pepitas
- ¼ teaspoon table salt

1. Bring 2 quarts water to boil in large saucepan. Off heat, add noodles and let sit, stirring occasionally, until tender, about 5 minutes. Drain noodles, rinse well, and drain again. Toss noodles with ½ teaspoon oil; set aside. Meanwhile, place scallops on clean dish towel, then top with second clean dish towel and gently press to dry. Let scallops sit between towels at room temperature for 10 minutes.

2. Microwave 1 teaspoon oil, ginger, ½ teaspoon turmeric, and ½ teaspoon coriander together in large bowl until fragrant, about 10 seconds; let cool slightly. Whisk in lime zest and juice and honey. Add noodles, mango, cucumber, cilantro leaves, shallot, and pepitas; toss to combine. Season with salt and pepper to taste. Divide noodles between serving bowls.

3. Sprinkle scallops with salt, remaining ¼ teaspoon turmeric, and remaining ¼ teaspoon coriander. Heat remaining 1 teaspoon oil in 10- or 12-inch nonstick skillet over medium-high heat until just smoking. Add scallops and cook, without moving, until well browned, 1½ to 2 minutes. Flip scallops and continue to cook until sides of scallops are firm and centers are opaque, 30 to 90 seconds. Transfer to bowls with noodles. Sprinkle with extra cilantro. Serve with lime wedges.

Clams with Pearl Couscous, Kielbasa, and Fennel

Serves 2

Total time 45 minutes

WHY THIS RECIPE WORKS To infuse this simple clam dish with big flavor, we added spicy kielbasa and bright scallions to white wine for a potent broth to steam the clams. A pat of butter contributed ample richness to counter the bright, briny notes of the wine and clams. To make this dish a well-rounded meal, we added juicy cherry tomatoes, fennel, and couscous. Using larger-grained pearl couscous instead of the more traditional, small-grain Moroccan couscous gave our dish great texture and visual appeal. To cook the couscous, we simply simmered it like pasta, drained it, then tossed it into the broth once the clams had steamed open so it could absorb the bright, briny flavors. Small quahogs or cherrystones are good alternatives to the littleneck clams. Be sure to use pearl couscous in this dish; regular (or fine) couscous won't work here.

- 1 cup pearl couscous
- 1 tablespoon unsalted butter
- 1 small onion, chopped coarse
- 1 small fennel bulb (8 ounces), stalks discarded, bulb halved, cored, and chopped coarse

- 4 ounces kielbasa sausage, halved lengthwise and sliced ½ inch thick
- 1 garlic clove, minced
- ¼ cup dry white wine or dry vermouth
- 1½ pounds littleneck clams, scrubbed
- 6 ounces cherry tomatoes, quartered
- ¼ cup coarsely chopped fresh parsley

1. Bring 2 quarts water to boil in medium saucepan. Add couscous and cook, stirring often, until al dente; drain well.

2. Meanwhile, melt butter in large saucepan over medium heat. Add onion, fennel, and kielbasa; cook until vegetables are softened, about 5 minutes. Stir in garlic and cook until fragrant, about 30 seconds. Stir in wine, scraping up any browned bits, and cook until slightly reduced, about 30 seconds. Stir in clams, cover, and cook, stirring occasionally, until clams open, 8 to 10 minutes.

3. Using slotted spoon, transfer opened clams to large bowl; discard any clams that have not opened. Stir drained couscous, tomatoes, and parsley into cooking liquid left in saucepan and season with salt and pepper to taste. Portion couscous into individual bowls, top with clams, and serve.

Steamed Mussels in White Wine with Parsley

Serves 2 FAST

Total time 20 minutes

WHY THIS RECIPE WORKS This French bistro classic, known as moules à la marinière, has just a few simple ingredients—mussels, shallot, parsley, white wine, and butter—but the effect is astonishing. To make our own version, we sautéed a shallot plus a little garlic in butter, added wine and a bay leaf, and nestled in the mussels to gently steam in the broth. Once the mussels opened, we removed them and enriched the broth with butter and heavy cream. A sprinkling of fresh parsley finished this remarkably easy dish. Serve with crusty bread, garlic toasts, or rice.

- 2 tablespoons unsalted butter, divided
- 1 shallot, minced
- 2 garlic cloves, minced
- ⅔ cup dry white wine
- 1 bay leaf
- 2 pounds mussels, scrubbed and debearded
- 2 tablespoons heavy cream
- 3 tablespoons minced fresh parsley

Steamed Mussels in White Wine with Parsley

1. Melt 1 tablespoon butter in Dutch oven over medium heat. Add shallot and cook until softened, about 2 minutes. Stir in garlic and cook until fragrant, about 30 seconds. Stir in wine and bay leaf, bring to simmer, and cook until flavors meld, about 2 minutes.

2. Increase heat to high and add mussels. Cover and cook, stirring occasionally, until mussels open, 3 to 7 minutes.

3. Using slotted spoon, transfer opened mussels to large serving bowl, leaving cooking liquid in pot. Discard bay leaf and any mussels that have not opened.

4. Stir remaining 1 tablespoon butter and cream into cooking liquid, bring to simmer, and cook until butter is melted and liquid is slightly thickened, about 1 minute. Off heat, stir in parsley and season with salt and pepper to taste. Pour sauce over mussels and serve immediately.

VARIATIONS

Steamed Mussels in Coconut Milk with Cilantro

Add 1 sliced jalapeño chile to pot with shallot. Substitute ¾ cup canned coconut milk for wine and 3 tablespoons minced fresh cilantro for parsley. Stir in 1 teaspoon lime juice, 1 teaspoon packed brown sugar, and 1 teaspoon fish sauce with cilantro in step 4.

Steamed Mussels in White Wine with Tomato and Basil

Substitute 3 tablespoons chopped fresh basil for parsley. Add 1 finely chopped tomato with basil in step 4.

NOTES FROM THE TEST KITCHEN

MUSSELS 101

The two main varieties of mussels you'll see at the store are the Atlantic blue mussel and the Pacific green-lipped (also called New Zealand) mussel. These mussels are interchangeable when it comes to cooking. Most mussels sold are farmed or rope-cultured, and are minimally gritty.

To remove the small, weedy beard that often pro-trudes, hold the mussel in your hand, pull the beard firmly out of the shell, using your thumb and the side of a paring knife to grip it firmly. Don't debeard mussels until you are ready to cook them.

You can refrigerate mussels for one day in a colander covered with a damp dish towel. If the mussels won't close when tapped, discard them.

Maryland Crab Cakes

Serves 2

Total time 35 minutes, plus 1 hour chilling

WHY THIS RECIPE WORKS When it comes to crab cakes, Maryland is king. We wanted authentic Maryland-style crab cakes for two. We kept the ingredients simple: Just a little mustard, hot sauce, scallion, and Old Bay seasoning gave us plenty of flavor without overwhelming the crab. We liked the flavor of saltines for our binder, but our crab cakes fell apart in the pan. Adding a little mayonnaise and an egg yolk, patting the crabmeat dry with paper towels, and broiling rather than pan-frying the cakes were easy fixes. To give our cakes a little extra succulence, we added a tablespoon of melted butter to the crab mixture. Greasing the baking sheet with butter helped the bottoms of the cakes crisp to a perfect golden brown. Jumbo lump crabmeat is available at the fish counter of most grocery stores. If you can't find it, you can use pasteurized lump crabmeat.

    7 square or 8 round saltines
    8 ounces lump crabmeat, picked over for shells
    2 scallions, minced
    1 tablespoon unsalted butter, melted,
       plus 1 tablespoon softened
    1 tablespoon mayonnaise
    1 egg yolk
 1½ teaspoons Dijon mustard
    1 teaspoon hot sauce
   ½ teaspoon Old Bay seasoning
       Lemon wedges

1. Process saltines in food processor until finely ground, about 25 seconds; transfer to shallow dish. Dry crabmeat well with paper towels. Using rubber spatula, gently combine crabmeat, 2 tablespoons saltine crumbs, scallions, melted butter, mayonnaise, egg yolk, mustard, hot sauce, and Old Bay in large bowl.

2. Divide mixture into 2 equal portions and shape into tight, mounded cakes. Press 1 side of each cake in remaining crumbs. Place cakes crumb side down on large plate and refrigerate, covered, for at least 1 hour or up to 8 hours.

3. Adjust oven rack 8 inches from broiler element and heat broiler. Grease 8 by 4-inch area in center of rimmed baking sheet with softened butter. Transfer crab cakes to greased portion of prepared sheet, crumb side down. Broil until crab cakes are golden brown, 12 to 15 minutes. Serve with lemon wedges.

Fried Calamari

Serves 2

Total time 40 minutes

WHY THIS RECIPE WORKS Our fried calamari features tender, lightly springy squid encased in a crispy, lacy, golden-brown crust. Slicing the squid bodies into ¾-inch-thick rings prolonged tenderness during frying. Dipping the squid in milk helped just enough of the dredge cling; proteins in the milk also encouraged browning when the milk soaked into the flour. Salting the milk bath, not the dredge or the fried pieces, seasoned the squid evenly. Dredging the squid in all-purpose flour (which contains proteins that brown) ensured that the coating turned deep golden brown before the squid had a chance to toughen. Adding baking powder to the dredge lightened the texture of the coating, and shaking off excess dredge prevented the coating from clumping. Letting the coated pieces rest while the oil heated gave the coating time to hydrate, preventing a dusty film from forming on the exterior. Frying in two batches prevented the oil temperature from dropping too much, so the pieces browned and crisped quickly. If desired, serve the calamari with Quick Marinara Sauce or Spicy Mayonnaise; make the sauce before preparing the squid. Precut squid will not cook up quite as tender as whole bodies that you cut yourself, but they are acceptable.

¼ cup milk
½ teaspoon table salt
¾ cup all-purpose flour
1½ teaspoons baking powder
¼ teaspoon pepper
8 ounces squid, bodies sliced crosswise ¾ inch thick, any extra-long tentacles trimmed to match length of shorter ones
1 quart vegetable oil for frying
Lemon wedges

1. Set wire rack in rimmed baking sheet. Set second rack in second sheet and line with triple layer of paper towels. Heat oven to 200 degrees.

2. Whisk milk and salt together in medium bowl. Combine flour, baking powder, and pepper in second medium bowl. Add squid to milk mixture and toss to coat. Using your hands or slotted spoon, remove half of squid, allowing excess milk mixture to drip back into bowl, and add to bowl with flour mixture. Using your hands, toss squid to coat evenly. Gently shake off excess flour mixture and place coated squid in single layer on unlined rack. Repeat with remaining squid. Let sit for 10 minutes.

3. While squid rests, heat oil in large saucepan over high heat to 350 degrees. Carefully add half of squid and fry for exactly 3 minutes (squid will be golden brown). Using slotted

---

NOTES FROM THE TEST KITCHEN

SQUID 101

GOOD SQUID LOOKS PRISTINE Squid should look moist, shiny, and ivory-colored.

CLEANED SQUID IS SOLD IN TWO PARTS
Fishmongers typically sell both bodies and tentacles. Squid bodies tend to be smooth and tender, while tentacles offer pleasant chew and more surface area.

BUY WHOLE BODIES WHEN POSSIBLE Though we've found the quality of precut rings to be just fine, buying whole bodies allows you to cut them to your own specification.

MOST SQUID HAS BEEN FROZEN Unless you have access to squid direct from the boat, anything you buy has been previously frozen and treated with additives such as sodium citrate and sodium carbonate to inhibit spoilage and enhance texture. But that's fine: We found

the quality of frozen squid—both frozen in the supermarket freezer section and thawed at the fish counter—to be good, and we didn't detect any off-flavors or textures as we have in other types of treated seafood.

IF YOU BUY THAWED Ask the fishmonger how long it's been thawed. For the best quality, thawed squid should be cooked within two days.

IF YOU BUY FROZEN Many supermarkets carry frozen squid packaged in blocks of whole bodies or rings. To use part of a frozen block, wrap the block in a dish towel and press it against the edge of a counter or table to break it.

STORE UNCOOKED SQUID ON ICE Like all seafood, squid deteriorates rapidly. Keep it in the back of the refrigerator, where it's coldest, in a zipper-lock bag resting on a bed of ice.

spoon or spider skimmer, transfer calamari to paper towel–lined rack and transfer to oven to keep warm. Return oil to 350 degrees and repeat with remaining squid. Transfer calamari to platter and serve immediately with lemon wedges.

Quick Marinara Sauce

Makes ¾ cup `FAST` `VEGETARIAN`
Total time 15 minutes

Our fast but full-flavored version of this Italian staple comes together in less than 10 minutes. We briefly sautéed garlic in olive oil in a large skillet (its large surface area promoted speedy evaporation, so the sauce cooked quickly) and then added canned crushed tomatoes and simmered the sauce for about 5 minutes. We then stirred in fresh basil and seasoned the sauce with salt and a touch of sugar (to balance acidity).

  1 tablespoon extra-virgin olive oil
  1 garlic clove, minced
  1 cup canned crushed tomatoes
  2 teaspoons minced fresh basil leaves
    Pinch sugar

Heat oil and garlic in 10-inch skillet over medium heat, stirring frequently, until fragrant but not browned, about 2 minutes. Stir in tomatoes and simmer until slightly thickened, about 5 minutes. Stir in basil and sugar and season with salt to taste.

Spicy Mayonnaise

Makes ½ cup `FAST` `VEGETARIAN`
Total time 5 minutes

Creamy, tangy, spicy, and faintly smoky, this quick stir-together mayonnaise works equally well as a spread or dipping sauce. The combination of smoked paprika and sriracha delivered complex smoke and heat, while lime juice and zest added brightness.

  ½ cup mayonnaise
  1 tablespoon sriracha
  1 teaspoon grated lime zest
    plus 1 tablespoon juice
  ¼ teaspoon smoked paprika

Whisk all ingredients together in bowl.

Fried Calamari

Couscous with Smoked Trout, Apricots, and Pickled Peppers

Couscous with Smoked Trout, Apricots, and Pickled Peppers

Serves 2 `FAST`

Total time 25 minutes

WHY THIS RECIPE WORKS Here, couscous becomes a mild and lovely canvas for featuring bites of rich, savory smoked fish. A tangy dressing soaks into and livens up the grains, which we tossed with tomatoes, parsley, and banana peppers. The brine from the banana peppers doesn't go to waste, as we used it instead of vinegar in the dressing. A surprise addition, dried apricots, added sweetness that offset the dressed grains and smoky fish. For an accurate measurement of boiling water, bring a kettle of water to a boil and then measure out the desired amount.

- ¾ cup boiling water
- ¾ cup couscous
- ½ teaspoon table salt, divided
- 1 tablespoon extra-virgin olive oil, plus extra for drizzling
- ½ cup jarred sliced banana peppers, plus 1 tablespoon brine
- 1 garlic clove, minced
- 1 teaspoon honey
- 4-6 ounces cherry or grape tomatoes, halved
- ¼ cup fresh parsley leaves
- 3 tablespoons chopped dried apricots
- 2 scallions, sliced thin
- 4 ounces hot-smoked trout, mackerel, or salmon, skin and pin bones removed, flaked
  Lemon wedges

1. Combine boiling water, couscous, and ¼ teaspoon salt in medium bowl. Cover and let sit for 10 minutes. Fluff couscous with fork.

2. Whisk oil, banana pepper brine, garlic, honey, and remaining ¼ teaspoon salt together in large bowl. Add couscous, peppers, tomatoes, parsley, apricots, and scallions and toss to combine. Season with salt and pepper to taste. Top each portion with smoked trout. Serve with lemon wedges.

Cataplana

Cataplana

Serves 2

Total time 55 minutes

WHY THIS RECIPE WORKS Cataplana captures the treasures of the Algarve region of Portugal: abundant fresh seafood, smoky cured meat, and paprika, all in rich broth. Book a table at any of the seaside restaurants on the country's southernmost coast, and you will soon see a local spectacle: a server bringing a hammered copper pot to a table. Both the vessel and the stew go by the same name: cataplana. We cooked our version for two in a large saucepan with a tight-fitting lid to mimic the steamy cooking environment of a traditional copper cataplana pot. We added clams and shrimp at the very end of cooking, preserving their delicate textures and rendering them plump, juicy, and tender. We included clam juice in addition to wine not only to boost the seafood flavor of the dish but also to ensure that it had ample, flavorful broth to soak up with crusty bread. We prefer untreated shrimp, but if your shrimp are treated with salt or additives such as sodium tripolyphosphate (STPP), do not add the salt in step 1. Look for small littleneck or Manila clams that are all about 2 inches across so that they cook at the same rate. We call for linguica sausage, but if it's unavailable, you can substitute chouriço or Spanish chorizo. Serve with crusty bread.

- 6 ounces extra-large shrimp (21 to 25 per pound), peeled, deveined, and cut in half crosswise
- ⅛ teaspoon plus ¼ teaspoon table salt, divided
- 1 tablespoon extra-virgin olive oil
- 6 ounces linguica sausage, quartered lengthwise and sliced ¼ inch thick
- 1 garlic clove, minced
- ½ teaspoon smoked paprika
- ¼ teaspoon red pepper flakes
- 1 small onion, halved and sliced thin
- 1 small fennel bulb, stalks discarded, bulb halved, cored, and sliced thin lengthwise
- 1 small red bell pepper, stemmed, seeded, and cut into ¼-inch-wide strips
- 1 (14.5-ounce) can whole peeled tomatoes, drained and chopped coarse
- ½ cup bottled clam juice
- ¼ cup dry white wine
- 1½ pounds littleneck or Manila clams, scrubbed
- ¼ cup chopped fresh parsley
  Lemon wedges

1. Combine shrimp and ⅛ teaspoon salt in bowl; refrigerate until needed. Heat oil in large saucepan over medium-high heat until shimmering. Add linguica and cook, stirring occasionally, until browned and fat is slightly rendered, about 4 minutes. Stir in garlic, paprika, and pepper flakes and cook until fragrant, about 30 seconds.

2. Add onion, fennel, bell pepper, and remaining ¼ teaspoon salt and cook, stirring occasionally, until vegetables are softened, 8 to 10 minutes. Stir in tomatoes, clam juice, and wine. Bring to simmer and cook, stirring occasionally, until thickened slightly, about 5 minutes.

3. Increase heat to high and bring mixture to boil. Stir in clams; cover and cook until clams have opened, 5 to 7 minutes, stirring halfway through cooking. Off heat, stir in shrimp. Cover and let stand off heat until shrimp are opaque and just cooked through, about 5 minutes. Discard any unopened clams. Stir in parsley; season with salt to taste; and serve, passing lemon wedges separately.

NOTES FROM THE TEST KITCHEN

CLEANING AND STORING HARD-SHELL CLAMS
Fresh clams should smell clean, like the ocean, and their shells should be tightly closed. Gently tap the shells of any open clams and wait a few seconds; discard those that don't close, along with any that have cracked shells or smell fishy.

CLEANING Scrub the clams with a stiff brush under cold water to remove exterior mud. If you've ever received gritty clams from your fishmonger, we recommend purging them to remove interior sand.

HOW TO PURGE Dissolve 2 tablespoons kosher salt for every quart of cool water in bowl. Fully submerge clams in saltwater solution. Allow them to sit for 2 hours at cool room temperature, or refrigerate overnight. Carefully lift clams from bowl, leaving grit behind. Rinse again in cool water before using or storing.

STORING Fresh clams must be stored in the refrigerator (except during purging). Do not store them directly over a bowl of ice. Our method: Place the clams in a bowl, cover them with a wet paper towel or newspaper, and place that bowl in a larger bowl full of ice. Check the ice daily; replenish as needed. Clams will stay fresh for up to one week.

CHAPTER 8

Vegetarian

Vegetables, Rice, Grains, and Beans

Tempeh and Tofu

■ FAST (Start to finish in 30 minutes or less)

■ VEGETARIAN

Opposite: Stuffed Tomatoes with Goat Cheese and Zucchini

Roasted Acorn Squash with Bulgur and Chickpeas

Roasted Acorn Squash with Bulgur and Chickpeas

Serves 2 `VEGETARIAN`

Total time 45 minutes

WHY THIS RECIPE WORKS There's a reason for the perennial popularity of stuffed vegetables: They're a great way to get a vegetable-forward dinner on the table in a tidy package. Here, acorn squash quarters overflow with a hearty bulgur filling, while roasted spiced chickpeas, toasted walnuts, dried figs, and cheese contribute to the meal's array of flavors and textures. To save time, we roasted the squash and chickpeas simultaneously on the same rimmed baking sheet after tossing both elements with a fragrant mixture of coriander and cinnamon. While they roasted, we whisked together a quick vinaigrette and simmered the bulgur until tender. Assembly was easy: We tossed the bulgur and chickpeas with the vinaigrette, layered this mixture atop the squash quarters, and then sprinkled it with the crunchy nuts, sweet figs, and creamy feta. When shopping, don't confuse bulgur with cracked wheat, which has a much longer cooking time and will not work in this recipe.

1 (1-pound) acorn squash, quartered lengthwise, seeds removed
1 (15-ounce) can chickpeas, rinsed
¼ cup extra-virgin olive oil, divided, plus extra for drizzling
1 teaspoon ground coriander
½ teaspoon table salt, divided, plus salt for cooking bulgur
  Pinch ground cinnamon
2 tablespoons cider vinegar
½ cup medium-grind bulgur
¼ cup chopped fresh parsley
2 tablespoons chopped toasted walnuts
2 tablespoons chopped dried figs
2 tablespoons crumbled feta cheese

1. Adjust oven rack to middle position and heat oven to 450 degrees. Line rimmed baking sheet with parchment paper. Toss squash, chickpeas, 1 tablespoon oil, coriander, ¼ teaspoon salt, and cinnamon together in large bowl.

2. Arrange squash quarters in single layer on half of prepared sheet and roast until bottoms are lightly browned, 10 to 15 minutes. Add chickpeas to empty side of sheet and roast until squash is tender and well browned and chickpeas are lightly browned, 15 to 20 minutes. Whisk vinegar, remaining 3 tablespoons oil, and remaining ¼ teaspoon salt together in now-empty bowl; set aside.

3. Meanwhile, bring 2 quarts water to boil in large saucepan. Add bulgur and ½ teaspoon salt and return to boil. Reduce heat to medium-low and simmer until tender, 5 to 8 minutes. Drain.

4. Add bulgur, parsley, and chickpeas to bowl with dressing and toss to combine. Transfer two squash quarters to each serving plate, top with bulgur mixture, walnuts, figs, and feta, and drizzle with extra oil. Serve.

Stuffed Eggplant with Lentils, Pomegranate, and Ricotta

Serves 2 VEGETARIAN

Total time 1 hour

WHY THIS RECIPE WORKS For a showstopping main that puts a vegetable squarely (and beautifully) in the spotlight, we stuffed tender roasted eggplant halves with a flavorful lentil and couscous filling full of spices, herbs, and textural contrast. A 1-pound eggplant is the perfect size to serve two people, so we first scored its flesh (to help it release its moisture and cook more quickly) and then roasted it until tender but still sturdy enough not to collapse when filled. While the eggplant roasted, we made a simple but flavorful filling of canned lentils, which require no additional time or prep, and quick-cooking couscous flavored with lemon, baharat, fresh parsley, and sweet-tart pomegranate molasses. Green pistachios added crunch and contrasting color, and dollops of ricotta added creamy richness. For an accurate measurement of boiling water, bring a kettle of water to a boil and then measure out the desired amount. You can use store-bought baharat or make your own.

   3 tablespoons boiling water
   3 tablespoons couscous
   1 (1-pound) eggplant, halved lengthwise
   2 tablespoons extra-virgin olive oil, divided
   ½ teaspoon baharat, divided
   ½ teaspoon table salt, divided
   2 teaspoons pomegranate molasses, plus extra
      for serving
   2 teaspoons lemon juice
   1 (15-ounce) can lentils, rinsed
   ¼ cup fresh parsley leaves
   2 tablespoons chopped toasted pistachios, plus extra
      for serving
   ¼ cup ricotta cheese

Stuffed Eggplant with Lentils, Pomegranate, and Ricotta

Baharat

Makes 3 tablespoons FAST VEGETARIAN

Total time 5 minutes

   1 tablespoon ground nutmeg
   1 tablespoon paprika
   1 teaspoon ground coriander
   1 teaspoon ground cinnamon
   1 teaspoon ground cumin

Combine nutmeg, paprika, coriander, cinnamon, and cumin in small bowl.

1. Adjust oven rack to lower-middle position, place parchment paper–lined rimmed baking sheet on rack, and heat oven to 400 degrees. Combine boiling water and couscous in small bowl. Cover and let sit for 10 minutes. Fluff couscous with fork and season with salt and pepper to taste; set aside.

2. Score flesh of each eggplant half in 1-inch diamond pattern, about 1 inch deep. Brush scored sides of eggplant with 1 tablespoon oil and sprinkle with ¼ teaspoon baharat and ¼ teaspoon salt. Arrange eggplant cut sides down on hot sheet and roast until flesh is tender, 40 to 50 minutes. Transfer eggplant, cut sides down, to paper towel–lined baking sheet and let drain.

3. Meanwhile, whisk pomegranate molasses, lemon juice, remaining 1 tablespoon oil, remaining ¼ teaspoon baharat, and remaining ¼ teaspoon salt together in large bowl. Add lentils, parsley, pistachios, and couscous and toss to combine. Season with salt and pepper to taste.

4. Transfer eggplant cut sides up to serving plates. Using 2 forks, gently push eggplant flesh to sides to make room for filling. Gently mound lentil mixture into eggplant halves and pack lightly with back of spoon. Dollop ricotta mixture evenly over lentils. Sprinkle with extra pistachios and drizzle with extra pomegranate molasses before serving.

Skillet Eggplant Parmesan

Serves 2

Total time 1 hour

WHY THIS RECIPE WORKS Eggplant Parmesan typically involves a large, satisfying casserole meant to serve a crowd. But it is notoriously tedious to make and often seems out of the question for just two. Enter skillet eggplant Parmesan. We reinvented this comfort food classic so we could make it in a fraction of the time. To start, we skipped the step of slowly simmering the tomato sauce and made a simple one in the food processor—no cooking required. To quickly prepare our eggplant slices, we tossed them with flour in a zipper-lock bag and then dipped them in beaten egg and coated them in a savory mixture of homemade bread crumbs mixed with a hefty ¾ cup of grated Parmesan cheese. After frying the eggplant in batches, we assembled our skillet casserole with sauce, circles of fried eggplant, more sauce, and a topping of cheese. Just 15 minutes in a hot oven and our generously sized eggplant Parmesan for two was ready to serve. Be sure to leave the outer edges of the eggplant slices unsauced in step 5 so that they remain crisp once baked.

TOMATO SAUCE

- 1 (14.5-ounce) can whole peeled tomatoes, drained with juice reserved
- 1 tablespoon extra-virgin olive oil
- 1 garlic clove, minced
- ¼ teaspoon table salt

EGGPLANT

- 4 slices high-quality white sandwich bread, torn into quarters
- 1½ ounces Parmesan cheese, grated (¾ cup), divided
- ¼ teaspoon table salt
- ¾ teaspoon pepper, divided
- 2 large eggs
- ½ cup unbleached all-purpose flour
- 1 small globe eggplant (about 12 ounces), sliced into ¼-inch-thick rounds
- ½ cup vegetable oil
- 4 ounces mozzarella cheese, shredded (1 cup)
- ¼ cup chopped fresh basil (optional)

1. FOR THE TOMATO SAUCE Process tomatoes, olive oil, garlic, and salt together in food processor until pureed, about 15 seconds. Transfer mixture to liquid measuring cup and add reserved tomato juice as needed until sauce measures 1½ cups. (Wash and dry bowl of food processor before making bread crumbs.)

2. FOR THE EGGPLANT Adjust oven rack to lower-middle position and heat oven to 425 degrees. Pulse bread in food processor to fine, even crumbs, about 15 pulses (you should have about 4 cups). Transfer crumbs to pie plate and stir in ½ cup Parmesan, ¼ teaspoon salt, and ¼ teaspoon pepper. Beat eggs in second pie plate. Combine flour and remaining ½ teaspoon pepper in large zipper-lock bag.

3. Place eggplant slices in bag of flour, shake bag to coat eggplant, then remove eggplant from bag and shake off excess flour. Using tongs, coat floured eggplant with egg mixture, allowing excess to drip off. Coat all sides of eggplant with bread crumbs, pressing on crumbs to help them adhere. Lay breaded eggplant slices on wire rack set over rimmed baking sheet.

4. Heat oil in 12-inch ovensafe nonstick skillet over medium-high heat until shimmering. Add half of breaded eggplant slices to skillet and cook until well browned on both sides, about 4 minutes, flipping them halfway through cooking. Transfer eggplant to wire rack and repeat with remaining breaded eggplant.

5. Pour off oil left in skillet and wipe out skillet with wad of paper towels. Spread 1 cup of tomato sauce over bottom of skillet. Layer eggplant slices evenly into skillet, overlapping them slightly. Dollop remaining ½ cup sauce on top of eggplant and sprinkle with remaining ¼ cup Parmesan and mozzarella, leaving outer 1 inch of eggplant slices clean.

6. Transfer skillet to oven and bake until bubbling and cheese is browned, 13 to 15 minutes. Let eggplant cool for 5 minutes, then sprinkle with basil (if using) and serve.

Skillet Eggplant
Parmesan

Stuffed Tomatoes with Goat Cheese and Zucchini

Serves 2   `VEGETARIAN`

Total time 45 minutes, plus 30 minutes salting

WHY THIS RECIPE WORKS Warm summer nights call for a simple supper that makes the most of the season's best fresh produce: bright, juicy tomatoes. Filled with zucchini, cheese, and nuts and served alongside a light green salad and a crusty baguette, stuffed tomatoes make a perfect light meal for two. We salted the tomatoes and let them drain to rid them of excess water that would otherwise turn the stuffing to mush. For the filling, we started with easy-to-make couscous. Toasting the couscous before cooking gave it a rich, nutty flavor and ensured fluffy, distinct grains in the finished dish. Chopped zucchini and fennel freshened up the filling, and sautéed shallot and garlic deepened the flavors. A combination of nutty Parmesan and tangy goat cheese contributed a rich creaminess and made the filling more cohesive, and toasted walnuts added crunch and more nutty flavor. Finally, fresh basil added a bright, herbal note that nicely accented our summery supper.

- 4 large tomatoes (8 ounces each)
- ½ teaspoon table salt, divided
- 3 tablespoons extra-virgin olive oil, divided
- ½ fennel bulb, stalks discarded, bulb cored and chopped fine
- 1 shallot, minced
- 1 small zucchini, cut into ¼-inch pieces
- ¼ cup couscous
- 2 garlic cloves, minced
- ⅓ cup vegetable broth
- 1 ounce Parmesan cheese, grated (½ cup), divided
- 1 ounce goat cheese, crumbled (¼ cup)
- ¼ cup walnuts, toasted and chopped coarse
- 2 tablespoons chopped fresh basil

1. Adjust oven rack to upper-middle position and heat oven to 375 degrees. Slice off ⅛ inch of stem end of each tomato and remove core and seeds. Sprinkle inside of each tomato with ⅛ teaspoon salt, place cut side down on paper towel–lined plate, and let drain for 30 minutes.

2. Meanwhile, heat 1 tablespoon oil in medium saucepan over medium heat until shimmering. Add fennel and shallot and cook, stirring occasionally, until softened, 5 to 7 minutes. Stir in zucchini and cook, stirring occasionally, until tender, about 10 minutes. Stir in couscous and garlic and cook until fragrant, about 1 minute.

3. Stir in broth and bring to brief simmer. Off heat, cover and let sit until liquid is absorbed and grains are tender, about 5 minutes. Uncover and fluff grains with fork. Stir in ¼ cup Parmesan, goat cheese, walnuts, and basil. Season with salt and pepper to taste.

4. Line 8-inch square baking dish with aluminum foil and spray with vegetable oil spray. Pat insides of tomatoes dry with paper towels and brush cut edges with 2 teaspoons oil. Mound filling evenly in tomatoes, then arrange cut side up in prepared baking dish. Sprinkle tomatoes with remaining ¼ cup Parmesan and drizzle with remaining 4 teaspoons oil. Bake until cheese is lightly browned and tomatoes are tender, about 20 minutes. Serve.

PREPARING TOMATOES FOR STUFFING

1. Using sharp knife, slice off top ⅛ inch of stem end of tomato.

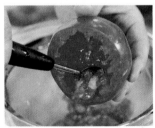

2. Using your fingers or melon scoop, remove and discard tomato core and seeds.

3. Sprinkle inside of cored tomatoes with salt, then place cut side down on paper towel-lined plate to drain for 30 minutes.

Vegetable and Bean Tostadas

Serves 2 `VEGETARIAN`

Total time 40 minutes

WHY THIS RECIPE WORKS Warm tostadas loaded with peppers and onions and creamy beans make a speedy and satisfying supper. For fresh, crisp tortilla shells in just 10 minutes—without the hassle of deep-frying—we baked store-bought tortillas until they were crisp and browned. For the beans, we found that we could get a surprisingly smooth, creamy texture from canned pinto beans by simply mashing the beans with their canning liquid. Pickled jalapeños, along with some of their brine, added a nice amount of heat and tang. To let the fresh flavor of the peppers and onions shine through, we cooked them briefly in a hot skillet and seasoned them with just a squeeze of fresh lime juice. The beans, peppers, and onions made a great-tasting tostada, but we wanted to add some freshness. Topping the tostadas with crunchy coleslaw mix flavored with more of the spicy jalapeño brine did the trick. If you prefer, you can substitute ready-made tostadas. Queso fresco is a fresh, soft Mexican cheese available in many markets; if it's not available, feta works well too.

Vegetable and Bean Tostadas

6 (6-inch) corn tortillas
  Vegetable oil spray
1 tablespoon vegetable oil, divided
1½ green bell peppers, stemmed, seeded, and sliced thin
1 onion, halved and sliced thin
2 garlic cloves, minced
1½ tablespoons lime juice, divided
1 (15-ounce) can pinto beans, undrained
1½ teaspoons minced jarred jalapeños, plus
  2 tablespoons brine, divided
2 cups (5½ ounces) green coleslaw mix
2 ounces queso fresco or feta cheese, crumbled
  (½ cup)
¼ cup sour cream
1 tablespoon minced fresh cilantro

1. Adjust oven rack to middle position and heat oven to 450 degrees. Spray tortillas with oil spray and spread on rimmed baking sheet. Bake until lightly browned and crisp, 8 to 10 minutes.

2. Meanwhile, heat 1½ teaspoons oil in 10-inch skillet over medium heat until shimmering. Add bell peppers and onion and cook until softened and lightly browned, 5 to 7 minutes. Stir in garlic and cook until fragrant, about 30 seconds. Off heat, stir in 1½ teaspoons lime juice and season with salt and pepper to taste. Transfer vegetables to bowl and cover to keep warm.

3. Heat remaining 1½ teaspoons oil in now-empty skillet over medium heat until shimmering. Add beans and their liquid, jalapeños, and 1½ teaspoons jalapeño brine. Cook, mashing beans with potato masher, until mixture is thickened, about 5 minutes. Season with salt and pepper to taste.

4. Toss coleslaw mix with remaining 1½ tablespoons jalapeño brine in bowl and season with salt and pepper to taste.

5. Spread bean mixture evenly over crisp tortillas, then top with queso fresco, cooked vegetables, and slaw. Whisk sour cream and remaining 1 tablespoon lime juice together and drizzle over top. Sprinkle with cilantro and serve.

MAKING TOSTADAS

To turn store-bought tortillas into crispy tostadas, spray tortillas with vegetable oil spray and bake on rimmed baking sheet until lightly browned and crisp, 8 to 10 minutes.

Zucchini, Tomato, and Ricotta Tarts

Fennel, Olive, and Goat Cheese Tarts

Zucchini, Tomato, and Ricotta Tarts

Serves 2 VEGETARIAN

Total time 40 minutes, plus 30 minutes salting and 20 minutes cooling

WHY THIS RECIPE WORKS A great vegetable tart boasts a tender crust, a rich layer of cheese, and plenty of fresh vegetables. We started with our recipe for All-Butter Tart Shells, using the food processor to cut the butter into the flour quickly, then pressing the dough into two individual-size tart pans. Parbaking the crusts ensured that they wouldn't slump, shrink, or get soggy. Next, a layer of chewy mozzarella and creamy ricotta made a rich base layer for our vegetables. For the vegetables, fresh zucchini and tomatoes nicely balanced the cheese and rich, buttery crust and were conveniently quick-cooking. Salting and draining the vegetables before layering them in the tart shells kept the tarts from getting waterlogged. For a final boost of flavor, we drizzled garlic-spiked olive oil over the tarts before baking. Yellow squash can be substituted for the zucchini.

- 9 cherry tomatoes, divided
- ½ teaspoon table salt, divided
- ½ small zucchini (3 ounces), halved lengthwise and sliced ⅛ inch thick
- 2 tablespoons extra-virgin olive oil, divided
- 1 small garlic clove, minced
- 2 ounces (¼ cup) whole-milk or part-skim ricotta cheese
- 2 tablespoons shredded whole-milk mozzarella cheese
- 1 recipe All-Butter Tart Shells (page 411), fully baked and cooled
- 1 tablespoon chopped fresh basil

1. Slice 7 tomatoes into ⅛-inch-thick rounds (you should get about 5 slices from each tomato); quarter remaining 2 tomatoes. Toss tomatoes with ¼ teaspoon salt and spread out onto paper towel–lined plate. Toss zucchini with remaining ¼ teaspoon salt and spread out onto paper towel–lined plate. Let vegetables drain for 30 minutes; gently blot vegetables dry before using.

2. Meanwhile, adjust oven rack to middle position and heat oven to 425 degrees. Combine 1 tablespoon oil and garlic in small bowl. In separate bowl, combine remaining 1 tablespoon oil, ricotta, and mozzarella and season with salt and pepper to taste.

3. Spread ricotta mixture evenly over bottom of cooled prebaked tart shells. Shingle alternating slices of tomato and zucchini around outside edge of tarts. Place quartered tomatoes in center of tarts. Drizzle garlic-oil mixture over vegetables.

4. Bake tarts on rimmed baking sheet until cheese is bubbling and vegetables are slightly wilted, 20 to 25 minutes. Let tarts cool on baking sheet for 20 minutes.

5. To serve, remove outer metal ring of each tart pan, slide thin metal spatula between tart and tart pan bottom, and carefully slide tart onto plate. Sprinkle with basil and serve warm or at room temperature.

Shingle alternating slices of tomato and zucchini around outside edge of tart. Place quartered tomatoes in center of each tart.

Fennel, Olive, and Goat Cheese Tarts

Serves 2 **VEGETARIAN**

Total time 40 minutes

WHY THIS RECIPE WORKS We wanted to make elegant savory tarts inspired by the flavors of the Mediterranean. To keep it easy enough for a weeknight dinner, we pulled store-bought puff pastry from the freezer to form the base. For the filling, fresh, anise-flavored fennel and briny cured olives made a light but flavorful combination. Tangy goat cheese brightened with fresh basil contrasted nicely with the rich, flaky pastry and helped bind the vegetables and pastry together. Parbaking the pastry without the weight of the filling allowed it to puff up nicely. To keep the filling firmly in place, we cut a border around the edges of the baked crusts and lightly pressed down the centers to make neat beds for the cheese and vegetables. Just 5 minutes more in the oven heated the filling through and browned the crusts beautifully. To thaw frozen puff pastry, let it sit either in the refrigerator for 24 hours or on the counter for 30 minutes to 1 hour.

½ (9½ by 9-inch) sheet puff pastry, thawed

4 ounces goat cheese, softened

¼ cup chopped fresh basil, divided

1½ tablespoons extra-virgin olive oil, divided

½ teaspoon grated lemon zest plus 2 teaspoons juice

¼ teaspoon pepper

½ fennel bulb, stalks discarded, bulb cored and sliced thin

1 garlic clove, minced

¼ cup dry white wine

¼ cup pitted oil-cured black olives, chopped

1. Adjust oven rack to middle position and heat oven to 425 degrees. Line baking sheet with parchment paper. Cut pastry sheet in half widthwise to make 2 squares and lay on prepared sheet. Poke pastry squares all over with fork and bake until puffed and golden brown, 12 to 15 minutes, rotating sheet halfway through baking. Using tip of paring knife, cut ½-inch-wide border into top of each pastry shell, then press centers down with your fingertips.

2. While pastry bakes, mix goat cheese, 2 tablespoons basil, 2 teaspoons oil, lemon zest, and pepper together in small bowl. Heat remaining 2½ teaspoons oil in 8-inch skillet over medium heat until shimmering. Add fennel and cook until softened and lightly browned, about 5 minutes. Stir in garlic and cook until fragrant, 30 seconds. Stir in wine, scraping up any browned bits; cover; and cook for 5 minutes. Uncover and continue to cook until liquid has evaporated and fennel is very soft, 3 to 5 minutes. Off heat, stir in lemon juice and olives.

3. Spread goat cheese mixture evenly over centers of pre-baked tart shells, leaving raised edges clean, then spoon fennel mixture evenly over cheese layer. Transfer filled tarts to oven and bake until cheese is heated through and crust is deep golden brown, about 5 minutes. Sprinkle with remaining 2 tablespoons basil and season with salt and pepper to taste. Serve.

Creating a bed for the filling within the tart shell ensures that none of the filling will leak during baking.

1. Lay pastry squares on parchment paper–lined baking sheet and poke them all over with fork. Bake pastry until puffed and golden, 12 to 15 minutes.

2. Using tip of paring knife, cut ½-inch border into top of each pastry shell and press center down with your fingertips to create bed for filling.

Savory Spinach Strudel

Serves 2 `VEGETARIAN`

Total time 55 minutes, plus 10 minutes cooling

WHY THIS RECIPE WORKS Spanakopita is a savory spinach and feta pie with roots in Greek culture. We wanted a streamlined version for two with a zesty spinach filling and a crispy phyllo crust. Spinach, feta, and ricotta flavored with scallions, raisins, pine nuts, oregano, and garlic made a rich, satisfying filling. Using store-bought phyllo was an easy time-saver. And rather than assembling it into a fussy pie, we simply greased and stacked several phyllo sheets, mounded the filling on top, then rolled it up to make an easy spanakopita strudel. Cutting a few steam vents into the top of the strudel kept the top crust crisp. Make sure to thoroughly squeeze the spinach dry, or the filling will leak. Phyllo dough is also available in larger 18 by 14-inch sheets; if using, cut them in half to make 14 by 9-inch sheets. Don't thaw the phyllo in the microwave; let it sit in the refrigerator overnight or on the countertop for 4 to 5 hours.

- 2 ounces feta cheese, crumbled (½ cup)
- 2 ounces (¼ cup) whole-milk ricotta cheese
- 3 scallions, sliced thin
- ¼ cup golden raisins
- 1 tablespoon pine nuts, toasted
- 1 tablespoon minced fresh oregano
- 1 tablespoon lemon juice
- 1 garlic clove, minced
- ¼ teaspoon ground nutmeg
- 5 ounces frozen spinach, thawed, squeezed dry, and chopped coarse
- 5 (14 by 9-inch) phyllo sheets, thawed
  Extra-virgin olive oil

1. Adjust oven rack to middle position and heat oven to 400 degrees. Line rimmed baking sheet with parchment paper. Mix feta, ricotta, scallions, raisins, pine nuts, oregano, lemon juice, garlic, and nutmeg together in medium bowl. Stir in spinach until well combined. Season with salt and pepper to taste.

2. Lay 1 phyllo sheet on clean counter with short side facing you and brush with oil, making sure to cover entire surface. Repeat and layer with remaining 4 phyllo sheets, brushing each with oil.

3. Mound spinach mixture into narrow log along bottom edge of phyllo, leaving 2-inch border at bottom and ½-inch border on sides. Fold bottom edge of dough over filling, then continue to roll dough around filling into tight log, leaving ends open.

4. Gently transfer strudel seam side down to prepared sheet and brush with oil. Cut four 1½-inch vents diagonally across top of strudel.

5. Bake strudel until golden brown, 20 to 25 minutes, rotating sheet halfway through baking. Let cool on sheet for 10 minutes before serving.

MAKING SPINACH STRUDEL

1. On clean counter, layer phyllo sheets on top of one another, brushing each sheet with olive oil.

2. Mound spinach mixture into narrow log along bottom edge of phyllo, leaving 2-inch border at bottom and ½-inch border on sides.

3. Fold bottom edge of dough over filling, then continue to roll dough around filling into tight log, leaving sides open.

4. Transfer strudel seam side down to prepared baking sheet and brush with olive oil. Cut four 1½-inch vents diagonally across top of strudel.

Risotto Primavera

Serves 2 `VEGETARIAN`

Total time 1 hour 5 minutes

WHY THIS RECIPE WORKS Most risotto recipes require constant stirring from start to finish, but with just two to feed, we weren't willing to spend all that time glued to the stove. To streamline the process, we tried cooking the risotto hands-off until it was partially tender, then stirring constantly while it finished cooking. We found that just 6 minutes of stirring at the end was enough to release the necessary starch to give us remarkably creamy risotto. To make the risotto a meal, we added vegetables inspired by pasta primavera: asparagus, mushrooms, onion, and peas. Sautéing the mushrooms and onion in the pan before adding the rice deepened their flavor. Lemon juice and fresh basil brightened the dish, and Parmesan and butter added richness. White, shiitake, or portobello (caps only) mushrooms can be substituted for the cremini in this recipe.

1¾ cups vegetable broth
½ cup water
4 teaspoons extra-virgin olive oil, divided
3 ounces cremini mushrooms, trimmed and sliced thin
½ teaspoon table salt, divided
1 small onion, chopped fine
½ cup Arborio rice
3 ounces asparagus, trimmed and cut into ½-inch pieces
¼ cup frozen peas
¼ cup grated Parmesan cheese, plus extra for serving
2 tablespoons chopped fresh basil
1 tablespoon unsalted butter
2 teaspoons lemon juice

1. Bring broth and water to simmer in small saucepan over medium heat. Remove from heat, cover, and keep warm.

2. Heat 2 teaspoons oil in medium saucepan over medium heat until shimmering. Add mushrooms and ¼ teaspoon salt and cook, covered, until just starting to brown, about 4 minutes; transfer to bowl. Return now-empty saucepan to medium heat, add remaining 2 teaspoons oil, and heat until shimmering. Add onion and remaining ¼ teaspoon salt and cook until just beginning to soften, about 2 minutes. Add rice and cook, stirring constantly, until grains are translucent around edges, about 1 minute.

3. Stir in 1½ cups warm broth, reduce heat to medium-low, cover, and simmer until almost all liquid is absorbed, about 12 minutes. Stir in asparagus, cover, and cook for 2 minutes. Add ½ cup broth and cook, stirring constantly, until broth is absorbed, about 3 minutes. Add remaining ¼ cup broth and peas and cook, stirring constantly, until rice is creamy and al dente, about 3 minutes.

4. Off heat, stir in cooked mushrooms; cover; and let sit until heated through, about 2 minutes. Stir in Parmesan, basil, butter, and lemon juice. Season with salt and pepper to taste. Serve, passing extra Parmesan separately.

Risotto Primavera

Skillet Brown Rice and Beans with Corn and Tomatoes

Serves 2 `VEGETARIAN`

Total time 1 hour 25 minutes

WHY THIS RECIPE WORKS The hearty, sustaining combination of rice and beans is found in many cuisines. We wanted to make a simple weeknight version with black beans and corn and bold flavors. Although white rice is traditional, we preferred the texture, chew, and robust flavor of brown rice. After sautéing an onion, we added fresh corn and the uncooked rice to the skillet and toasted them until fragrant. Then we stirred in vegetable broth and simmered the rice until tender. Canned black beans kept the dish easy; to keep them from getting blown out and mushy, we stirred them in partway through cooking. Garlic, cumin, and cayenne gave the dish a potent aromatic backbone, and a flavorful salsa of grape tomatoes, scallions, cilantro, and lime juice added a fresh counterpoint to the spicy rice and beans. You can substitute ¾ cup frozen corn, thawed and patted dry, for the fresh corn. You will need a 10-inch nonstick skillet with a tight-fitting lid for this recipe.

- 4 teaspoons extra-virgin olive oil, divided
- 1 small onion, chopped fine
- 1 ear corn, kernels cut from cob
- ½ cup long-grain brown rice, rinsed
- 2 garlic cloves, minced
- ½ teaspoon ground cumin
- Pinch cayenne pepper
- 2 cups vegetable broth
- ¾ cup canned black beans, rinsed
- 6 ounces grape tomatoes, quartered
- 2 scallions, sliced thin
- 2 tablespoons minced fresh cilantro
- 2 teaspoons lime juice

1. Heat 2 teaspoons oil in 10-inch nonstick skillet over medium heat until shimmering. Add onion and cook until softened and lightly browned, 5 to 7 minutes. Stir in corn and cook until lightly browned, about 4 minutes. Stir in rice, garlic, cumin, and cayenne and cook until fragrant, about 30 seconds.

2. Stir in broth, scraping up any browned bits, and bring to simmer. Reduce heat to medium-low; cover, and simmer gently; stirring occasionally, for 25 minutes.

3. Stir in beans, cover, and continue to simmer until liquid has been absorbed and rice is tender, 20 to 25 minutes. Season with salt and pepper to taste.

4. Meanwhile, combine remaining 2 teaspoons oil, tomatoes, scallions, cilantro, and lime juice in bowl and season with salt and pepper to taste. Sprinkle tomato mixture over rice and beans before serving.

VARIATION

Spanish-Style Skillet Brown Rice and Chickpeas
Substitute 1 finely chopped red bell pepper for corn and pinch saffron threads, crumbled, for cumin. Substitute ¾ cup rinsed canned chickpeas for black beans. Substitute 2 tablespoons minced fresh parsley for cilantro and 2 teaspoons lemon juice for lime juice.

Farro Risotto with Arugula, Cherry Tomatoes, and Lemon

Farro Risotto with Arugula, Cherry Tomatoes, and Lemon
Serves 2 VEGETARIAN
Total time 1 hour
WHY THIS RECIPE WORKS Farro, a whole-grain relative of wheat, is commonly used in Italy to make farrotto, a dish similar to risotto but with a distinct nutty flavor and satisfying chew. We wanted to come up with our own recipe for farrotto—one that would simplify the tedious risotto-cooking method. We quickly found that this hearty grain didn't require the nonstop stirring or incremental additions of liquid traditionally used to make risotto. We simply added all the liquid to the grain and simmered it uncovered, stirring every few minutes, until the farro was tender. Then we added classic risotto flavorings (Parmesan, butter, and lemon) plus bright cherry tomatoes and peppery arugula for a fresh and hearty meal. For a creamy texture, be sure to stir the farro often in step 2. Serve with a simple green salad.

OUR FAVORITE GRAINS

The following grains are the ones we use most often. We've also included cornmeal and couscous here since they are prepared and served like grains. You can store many grains in the pantry—just make sure they are in an airtight container, and use them within six months. To prevent oxidation, whole grains like farro are best stored in the freezer.

BARLEY This high-fiber grain has a nutty, subtly sweet flavor that makes it an ideal accompaniment to meat, chicken, and fish. Both hulled and pearl barley are stripped of their tough outer covering, but we prefer quicker-cooking pearl barley, which has been polished to remove the bran layer.

FARRO These hulled whole-wheat kernels boast a nutty flavor and chewy bite. Farro is available in three sizes, but the midsize type (farro medio) is most common in the United States. Farro takes best to the pasta cooking method because abundant water cooks the grains evenly.

QUINOA Quinoa is often called a "super-grain" because it's a nutritionally complete protein. When cooked, the grains will unfurl and expand to about three times their size. Quinoa should be rinsed to remove its bitter coating (known as saponin). Toast quinoa in a dry pot before adding water.

WHEAT BERRIES These are whole husked wheat kernels that have an earthy flavor and firm chew. Because they're unprocessed, they remain firm (though softened), smooth, and distinct when cooked, which makes them great for salads. We toast wheat berries in oil before adding them to the water, because it brings out their nutty flavor.

CORNMEAL/POLENTA When shopping for polenta, avoid instant and quick-cooking polenta, which are parcooked and comparatively bland. We find whole-grain cornmeal to be slightly gritty. We prefer degerminated cornmeal, in which the hard hull and germ are removed (check the back label or ingredient list; if it's not labeled as degerminated, you can assume it's whole-grain). As for grind, coarser grains are best for polenta, while finer grinds work well for baking muffins or cornbread.

COUSCOUS Couscous is a starch made from high-protein wheat flour. Traditional Moroccan couscous is made by rubbing coarse-ground durum semolina and water between the hands to form small granules that are then steamed. The boxed couscous found in most supermarkets is a precooked version that needs only a few minutes of steeping in hot liquid. Pearl couscous is larger than traditional couscous (about the size of a caper) and is not precooked. It has a unique, nutty flavor.

---

1 tablespoon extra-virgin olive oil
1 small onion, chopped fine
  Pinch table salt
1 garlic clove, minced
½ teaspoon minced fresh thyme or ⅛ teaspoon dried
¾ cup farro
1½ cups vegetable broth
1 cup water
6 ounces cherry tomatoes, quartered
2 ounces (2 cups) baby arugula
¼ cup grated Parmesan cheese
1 tablespoon unsalted butter
¼ teaspoon grated lemon zest plus 1 teaspoon juice

1. Heat oil in medium saucepan over medium heat until shimmering. Add onion and salt and cook until softened, about 5 minutes. Stir in garlic and thyme and cook until fragrant, about 30 seconds.

2. Stir in farro and cook until lightly toasted, about 2 minutes. Stir in broth and water and bring to simmer. Reduce heat to medium-low and continue to simmer, stirring often, until farro is tender, 20 to 25 minutes.

3. Stir in tomatoes and arugula and cook until vegetables are softened, about 1 minute. Off heat, stir in Parmesan, butter, and lemon zest and juice. Season with salt and pepper to taste, and serve.

VARIATION

Farro Risotto with Fennel, Radicchio, and Balsamic Vinegar

Substitute ½ fennel bulb, cored and chopped fine, for onion. Substitute ½ small head radicchio, cored and sliced thin, for tomatoes and arugula. Substitute 2 teaspoons balsamic vinegar for lemon zest and juice. Drizzle with additional balsamic vinegar to taste before serving.

Savory Dutch Baby with Shaved Mushroom and Celery Salad

Serves 2   `VEGETARIAN`

Total time 45 minutes

WHY THIS RECIPE WORKS For a sophisticated treat, we transformed the traditionally sweet, pancakelike Dutch baby into a savory dish with crisp sides and a tender bottom. For a fluffy rise we used milk and eggs in the batter—their liquid content steamed in the oven, creating lift. A 9-inch metal pie pan gave us the most even rise due to its sloping sides, and to jump-start this rise, we oiled and preheated the pan. You can use whole or low-fat milk instead of skim, but the Dutch baby won't be as crisp. You will need a 9-inch metal pie pan for this recipe; do not substitute a glass pie plate. If your celery came without its leaves, you can substitute fresh parsley leaves. Slice the mushrooms and celery thinly.

DUTCH BABY

- 2 tablespoon extra-virgin olive oil, divided
- ½ cup (2½ ounces) plus 2 tablespoons all-purpose flour
- ¼ teaspoon table salt
- 2 large eggs
- ½ cup skim milk

SHAVED MUSHROOM AND CELERY SALAD

- 4 cremini or white mushrooms, stemmed and sliced thin
- ½ shallot, sliced thin
- 1 tablespoon extra-virgin olive oil, plus extra for drizzling
- 1 teaspoon lemon juice
  Pinch table salt
  Pinch pepper
- 1 celery rib, sliced thin on bias plus ½ cup celery leaves
- ¼ cup shaved Parmesan cheese

1. FOR THE DUTCH BABY Adjust oven rack to lowest position and heat oven to 450 degrees. Brush surface of 9-inch metal pie pan with 1 tablespoon oil. Place pan on rack and heat until oil is shimmering, 3 to 5 minutes.

2. Meanwhile, combine flour and salt in medium bowl. Whisk eggs in separate bowl until frothy, then whisk in milk and remaining 1 tablespoon oil until incorporated. Whisk half of egg mixture into flour mixture until no lumps remain, then slowly whisk in remaining egg mixture until smooth.

3. Working quickly, remove preheated pan from oven and pour batter into pan. Return pan to oven and bake until Dutch baby puffs and turns golden brown (edges will be dark brown), 14 to 19 minutes.

4. FOR THE SHAVED MUSHROOM AND CELERY SALAD In small bowl, combine mushrooms, shallot, oil, lemon juice, salt, and pepper and let sit for 10 minutes. Stir in celery and celery leaves. Top Dutch baby with mushroom-celery mixture and shaved Parmesan. Drizzle with extra oil and serve immediately.

VARIATIONS

Savory Dutch Baby with Smoked Salmon and Avocado

Omit shaved mushroom and celery salad. While Dutch baby bakes, combine ½ shallot, sliced thin; 1 tablespoon extra-virgin olive oil; 1 teaspoon lemon juice; ¼ teaspoon sugar; and pinch table salt in small bowl and let sit for 10 minutes. Top Dutch baby with 4 ounces smoked salmon; 1 avocado, sliced ¼ inch; and shallot mixture. Drizzle with extra oil and sprinkle with 1 teaspoon minced fresh parsley or chives before slicing and serving.

Savory Dutch Baby with Burrata and Prosciutto

If burrata is unavailable, substitute fresh mozzarella.

Omit shaved mushroom and celery salad. While Dutch baby bakes, place 4 ounces room temperature burrata on plate and cut into rough 1½-inch pieces, collecting creamy

Savory Dutch Baby with Burrata and Prosciutto

liquid. Toss ¾ cup baby arugula with ½ teaspoon extra-virgin olive oil and ½ teaspoon balsamic vinegar and season with salt and pepper to taste. Top Dutch baby with arugula mixture, followed by 1 ounce thinly sliced prosciutto, torn into bite sized pieces, and burrata, along with any accumulated liquid. Drizzle with extra oil and vinegar before slicing and serving.

Quinoa Cakes

Serves 2   VEGETARIAN

Total time 1 hour 10 minutes, plus 15 minutes cooling and 30 minutes chilling

WHY THIS RECIPE WORKS Thanks to its high protein content, quinoa makes a satisfying entrée. We set out to develop a recipe for hearty quinoa patties with bright, fresh flavors. To keep our cakes from turning out dry and crumbly, we simmered the quinoa in extra liquid so that it cooked up moist. For the binder, a whole egg plus some cheese worked best—we chose Monterey Jack for its flavor and meltability. Chilling the patties for 30 minutes after forming them ensured that they stayed together in the pan. A combination of scallions, lemon zest and juice, and spinach added freshness. Sun-dried tomatoes and garlic gave the cakes a savory boost, and using the oil from the sun-dried tomatoes to sauté the scallions and garlic wasn't only convenient; it deepened the flavor as well. We like the convenience of prewashed quinoa; rinsing removes the quinoa's bitter protective coating (called saponin). If you buy unwashed quinoa, rinse it and then spread it out on a clean dish towel to dry for 15 minutes. To keep the patties from falling apart, be sure to wait until they are well browned on the first side before attempting to flip them. Serve over mixed greens with a creamy yogurt sauce such as tzatziki.

- 2 tablespoons coarsely chopped oil-packed sun-dried tomatoes, plus 1 tablespoon packing oil
- 2 scallions, chopped fine
- 2 garlic cloves, minced
- 1½ cups water
- ½ cup quinoa, rinsed
- ½ teaspoon table salt
- 1 large egg, lightly beaten
- 1 ounce (1 cup) baby spinach, chopped
- 1 ounce Monterey Jack cheese, shredded (¼ cup)
- ¼ teaspoon grated lemon zest plus 1 teaspoon juice
- 1 tablespoon extra-virgin olive oil

Quinoa Cakes

1. Heat tomato oil in medium saucepan over medium heat until shimmering. Add scallions and cook until softened, about 3 minutes. Stir in garlic and cook until fragrant, about 30 seconds. Stir in water, quinoa, and salt and bring to simmer. Reduce heat to medium-low; cover; and simmer until quinoa is tender but still soupy, 16 to 18 minutes. Off heat, cover and let quinoa mixture sit until liquid is fully absorbed and grains are tender, about 10 minutes. Transfer to large bowl and let cool for 15 minutes.

2. Add tomatoes, egg, spinach, Monterey Jack, and lemon zest and juice to cooled quinoa and mix until uniform. Divide mixture into 2 firmly packed balls, flatten each ball into 1-inch-thick patty, and place on large plate. Refrigerate, uncovered, until patties are chilled and firm, about 30 minutes.

3. Heat olive oil in 10-inch nonstick skillet over medium heat until shimmering. Gently place patties in skillet and cook until well browned on first side, 8 to 10 minutes. Gently flip patties and continue to cook until golden on second side, 8 to 10 minutes. Serve.

Chickpea Cakes with Cucumber-Yogurt Sauce

Serves 2 VEGETARIAN

Total time 30 minutes, plus 15 minutes salting

WHY THIS RECIPE WORKS Buttery, nutty chickpeas make a great foundation for a light yet satisfying veggie burger. To break down the firm chickpeas, we gave them a quick spin in the food processor. Processing them just until we had both some finely chopped beans (to help the patties hold together) and some larger pieces (for a satisfying texture) was key. One egg bound the cakes together nicely and some Greek yogurt added moisture and a subtle tang. Garam masala gave the cakes complex flavor, and a pinch of cayenne added just enough heat. A simple, creamy cucumber-yogurt sauce balanced the rich chickpea cakes. To keep the patties from falling apart, be sure to wait until they are well browned on the first side before flipping. Serve over mixed greens.

- ½ cucumber, peeled, halved lengthwise, seeded, and shredded
- ¼ teaspoon plus ⅛ teaspoon table salt, divided
- ½ cup plus 2 tablespoons 2 percent Greek yogurt, divided
- 3 scallions, sliced thin, divided
- 3 tablespoons minced fresh cilantro, divided
- ¾ cup canned chickpeas, rinsed
- 1 large egg
- 4 teaspoons extra-virgin olive oil, divided
- ¼ teaspoon garam masala
  Pinch cayenne pepper
- ⅓ cup panko bread crumbs
- 1 small shallot, minced
  Lime wedges

1. Toss cucumber and ¼ teaspoon salt together and let drain in colander for 15 minutes. Combine drained cucumber, ½ cup yogurt, 1 tablespoon scallions, and 1 tablespoon cilantro in bowl and season with salt and pepper to taste; set aside.

2. Pulse chickpeas in food processor to coarse puree with large pieces remaining, 5 to 8 pulses, scraping down sides of bowl as needed. In medium bowl, whisk egg, 2 teaspoons oil, garam masala, remaining ⅛ teaspoon salt, and cayenne together. Gently stir in panko, processed chickpeas, remaining 2 tablespoons yogurt, remaining scallions, remaining 2 tablespoons cilantro, and shallot until just combined. Divide bean mixture into 2 lightly packed balls and gently flatten each ball into 1-inch-thick patty.

3. Heat remaining 2 teaspoons oil in 10-inch nonstick skillet over medium heat until shimmering. Gently place patties in skillet and cook until well browned on first side, 4 to 5 minutes. Gently flip patties and continue to cook until well browned on second side, 4 to 5 minutes. Serve with cucumber-yogurt sauce and lime wedges.

Black Bean Burgers

Serves 2 FAST VEGETARIAN

Total time 30 minutes

WHY THIS RECIPE WORKS Our black bean burgers are a far cry from the dense varieties of frozen veggie burgers in the supermarket. We found that mashing most of the beans while leaving a third of them whole made a burger that was neither too soft and crumbly nor too dense and pasty. To bind the burgers, we added an egg and some bread crumbs. Cayenne and cumin added warmth, and chopped red bell pepper and cilantro contributed fresh flavor. Avoid overmixing the bean mixture in step 1 or the burgers will be mealy. To keep the patties from falling apart, be sure to wait until they are well browned on the first side before attempting to flip them. Serve with your favorite burger toppings.

- 1 large egg
- 2 tablespoons extra-virgin olive oil, divided
- ½ teaspoon ground cumin
- ¼ teaspoon table salt
- ⅛ teaspoon cayenne pepper
- 1 (15-ounce) can black beans, rinsed, divided
- 1 cup panko bread crumbs
- ½ red bell pepper, chopped fine
- 2 tablespoons minced fresh cilantro
- 1 small shallot, minced
- 2 hamburger buns, toasted (optional)

1. Whisk egg, 1 tablespoon oil, cumin, salt, and cayenne together in small bowl. In separate bowl, mash 1¼ cups beans with potato masher until mostly smooth. Gently stir in egg mixture, remaining beans, panko, bell pepper, cilantro, and shallot until just combined. Divide bean mixture into 2 lightly packed balls and gently flatten each ball into 1-inch-thick patty.

2. Heat remaining 1 tablespoon oil in 10-inch nonstick skillet over medium heat until shimmering. Gently place patties in skillet and cook until well browned on first side, 4 to 5 minutes. Gently flip patties and continue to cook until well browned on second side, 4 to 5 minutes. Serve on buns, if desired.

VARIATION
Black Bean Burgers with Corn and Chipotle

Substitute 1½ teaspoons minced canned chipotle chile in adobo sauce for cayenne. Stir in ⅓ cup frozen corn, thawed and patted dry, with bell pepper.

Mushroom, Brussels Sprout, and White Bean Gratin

Serves 2   `VEGETARIAN`

Total time 1 hour

WHY THIS RECIPE WORKS Gratins don't need cheese or dairy to qualify as elevated comfort food. This rendition features creamy white beans, meaty cremini mushrooms, tender brussels sprouts, and a crisp, toasty bread layer. For a complex savoriness, we started by sautéing the mushrooms and aromatics until a flavorful browned fond developed on the bottom of the skillet and then deglazed the skillet with wine, scraping up all that concentrated umami flavor and stirring it back into the dish. A small amount of flour—just 1 teaspoon—added sauce-thickening starch. We baked the gratin in a low oven after topping it with bread cubes doused in olive oil seasoned with garlic, thyme, and lemon zest. As the gratin baked, the lower portion of the bread soaked up moisture from the beans below, almost melting into the sauce, while the tops of the cubes dried out and crisped. A last-minute drizzle of the remaining seasoned oil gave the gratin a rich and fragrant finish. You will need a 10- or 12-inch ovensafe skillet for this recipe.

3 tablespoons extra-virgin olive oil

3 garlic cloves, minced

1 teaspoon minced fresh thyme or ¼ teaspoon dried

½ teaspoon grated lemon zest plus 2 teaspoons juice

4 ounces brussels sprouts, trimmed and quartered

4 ounces cremini mushrooms, trimmed and sliced ½ inch thick

1 small onion, sliced thin

½ teaspoon table salt

¼ teaspoon pepper

2 teaspoons tomato paste

1 teaspoon all-purpose flour

¼ cup dry white wine or dry vermouth

1 (15-ounce) can great northern beans, rinsed

1 cup vegetable broth

2–3 slices country-style bread, cut into ½-inch cubes (2 cups)

1 tablespoon chopped fresh parsley

Black Bean Burgers

Mushroom, Brussels Sprout, and White Bean Gratin

1. Adjust oven rack to middle position and heat oven to 350 degrees. Microwave oil, garlic, thyme, and lemon zest in small bowl until fragrant, 10 to 20 seconds.

2. Toss brussels sprouts, mushrooms, and onion with salt, pepper, and 1 tablespoon oil mixture in large bowl. Transfer vegetables to 10- or 12-inch ovensafe skillet and cook over medium-high heat, stirring occasionally, until well browned, 8 to 12 minutes.

3. Stir in tomato paste and flour and cook until fragrant, about 1 minute. Stir in wine, scraping up any browned bits and smoothing out any lumps. Stir in beans and broth and bring to brief simmer; remove from heat.

4. Toss bread with half of remaining oil mixture in now-empty bowl. Arrange bread mixture evenly over top of vegetable-bean mixture. Transfer skillet to oven and bake until bread is golden brown, 18 to 24 minutes.

5. Using potholder, carefully remove skillet from oven (skillet handle will be hot) and let rest for 5 minutes. Stir parsley and lemon juice into remaining oil mixture and drizzle over gratin. Serve.

Roasted Cauliflower Steaks with Chimichurri

Serves 2 VEGETARIAN

Total time 35 minutes

WHY THIS RECIPE WORKS Cauliflower steaks are the ideal vegetarian dinner to whip up in your oven when you want a hearty meal without a long cook time or many-stepped process. Brushing the cauliflower steaks with oil, salt, and pepper and flipping them while cooking meant that they roasted quickly to an enticing, toasty brown. We topped the steaks with vibrant chimichurri while they were still warm, which allowed them to soak up the robust flavors of the sauce. To achieve two perfectly cooked cauliflower steaks without needing to sear them in a skillet, we cooked them on a rimmed baking sheet on the lowest rack at 450 degrees. Look for fresh, firm, bright white heads of cauliflower that feel heavy for their size and are free of blemishes or soft spots; florets are more likely to separate from older heads of cauliflower.

1 head cauliflower (2 pounds)
2 tablespoons extra-virgin olive oil
¼ teaspoon table salt
⅛ teaspoon pepper
1 recipe Chimichurri (page 221)
  Lemon wedges

Roasted Cauliflower Steaks with Chimichurri

1. Adjust oven rack to lowest position and heat oven to 450 degrees. Discard outer leaves of cauliflower and trim stem flush with bottom florets. Halve cauliflower lengthwise through core. Cut one 1½-inch-thick slab lengthwise from each half, trimming any florets not connected to core. You should have 2 steaks; reserve remaining cauliflower for another use.

2. Place steaks on rimmed baking sheet and drizzle both sides with oil. Sprinkle both sides with salt and pepper and rub to distribute. Roast until bottoms of steaks are browned around edges, 17 to 22 minutes. Gently flip and continue to roast until tender and second sides are well browned, 5 to 10 minutes. Brush cauliflower with chimichurri while still warm and serve with lemon wedges.

Curry Roasted Cabbage Wedges with Tomatoes and Chickpeas

Serves 2   VEGETARIAN
Total time 1 hour

WHY THIS RECIPE WORKS Cabbage may lack the dramatic appearance of other cruciferous vegetables, but cut it into wedges and roast it, creating charred, crispy edges with tender, sweet layers underneath, and this humble vegetable absolutely deserves to be at the center of your plate. We first brushed the wedges with oil spiked with curry powder and a little sugar to help with browning. We then covered the cabbage with aluminum foil before putting the baking sheet on the lower rack of a hot oven to steam the wedges and jump-start browning on the undersides. Uncovering the wedges for the last part of cooking crisped and browned their upper sides while maximizing browning underneath. To complete the meal, we simmered chickpeas, tomatoes, and more curry powder on the stovetop while the cabbage roasted. When slicing the cabbage into wedges, be sure to slice through the core, leaving it intact so the wedges don't fall apart.

    3 tablespoons vegetable oil, divided
    1½ teaspoons curry powder, divided
    ½ teaspoon sugar
    ¼ teaspoon table salt
    ⅛ teaspoon pepper
    ½ small head green cabbage (1 pound)
    2 garlic cloves, minced
    1 teaspoon grated fresh ginger
    1 (15-ounce) can chickpeas
    5 ounces grape or cherry tomatoes, halved
    2 tablespoons chopped fresh cilantro

1. Adjust oven rack to lowest position and heat oven to 450 degrees. Combine 2 tablespoons oil, 1 teaspoon curry powder, sugar, salt, and pepper in small bowl. Cut cabbage into four roughly 2-inch-wide wedges, leaving core intact.

2. Arrange cabbage wedges evenly on rimmed baking sheet, then brush all over with oil mixture. Cover tightly with aluminum foil and roast for 10 minutes. Remove foil and continue to roast until cabbage is tender and sides touching sheet are well browned, about 15 minutes longer.

3. Combine remaining 1 tablespoon oil, garlic, ginger, and remaining ½ teaspoon curry powder in large saucepan and cook over medium-high heat until fragrant, about 30 seconds. Stir in chickpeas and their liquid and tomatoes and bring to simmer. Cook, stirring frequently, until tomatoes begin to break down and mixture has thickened slightly, 6 to 8 minutes. Divide cabbage among serving plates and top with chickpea mixture and cilantro. Serve.

Crispy Tempeh with Sambal

Serves 2   FAST   VEGETARIAN
Total time 30 minutes

WHY THIS RECIPE WORKS Tempeh, a traditional Javanese food made from fermented, cooked soybeans, is hugely popular across Indonesia. "Sambal" refers to a class of condiments made primarily of red chile peppers, salt, and vinegar; there are hundreds of versions in Indonesia, but our go-to is sambal oelek, in which the chiles and spices are ground to a thick paste. Fried in oil to deepen its flavor and then combined with tempeh (which has also been fried!), it makes up the foundation of the spicy, savory, utterly satisfying dish known as tempeh sambal goreng. Shallow frying cubes of tempeh delivered irresistibly crispy edges without the hassle of deep-frying. Last-minute additions of kecap manis (an Indonesian soy sauce with a viscous consistency and sweet, molasses-like flavor) and aromatic Thai lemon basil added dimension.

Panang Curry with Eggplant, Broccolini, and Tofu

½ cup vegetable oil for frying
8 ounces tempeh, cut into ½-inch pieces
¾ cup sambal oelek
¼ cup water
1 tablespoon kecap manis
¾ cup fresh Thai lemon basil leaves

1. Heat oil in 14-inch flat-bottomed wok or 12-inch nonstick skillet over medium-high heat to 375 degrees. Carefully add tempeh to hot oil and increase heat to high. Cook, turning tempeh as needed, until golden brown, 3 to 5 minutes, adjusting burner if necessary to maintain oil temperature between 350 and 375 degrees. Transfer tempeh to paper towel–lined plate.

2. Carefully pour off all but 2 tablespoons oil from wok. Add sambal oelek to oil left in wok and cook over medium-high heat, tossing slowly but constantly, until darkened in color and dry paste forms, 7 to 10 minutes. Off heat, stir in water and kecap manis until well combined. Add tempeh and basil and toss until well coated. Serve.

Panang Curry with Eggplant, Broccolini, and Tofu

Serves 2   VEGETARIAN
Total time 50 minutes

WHY THIS RECIPE WORKS Savory-sweet, fragrant, and deeply rich, panang curry is a full-bodied, velvety, coconut milk–spiked curry often made with beef or shrimp. This vegan for-two version puts the vegetables at the forefront, using eggplant, bell pepper, and broccolini to provide a variety of flavors and textures, plus tofu to fortify the dish with plenty of satisfying protein. We started by sautéing the onion and eggplant to soften them and cook off their excess water. We then fried the panang curry paste in oil to enhance its flavor. To complete the sweet, rich, and nutty flavor profile of this panang curry we used a combination of coconut milk and water to create a lush sauce for the vegetables, and then we threw in a handful of roasted peanuts, another traditional panang element. Some Thai basil and a quick squeeze of lime juice finished the dish on a fresh note. You will need a 10- or 12-inch nonstick skillet with a tight-fitting lid for this recipe.

2 tablespoons vegetable oil, divided
1 small onion, chopped fine
¼ teaspoon table salt
8 ounces eggplant, cut into 1-inch pieces
3 tablespoons panang curry paste

1 cup canned coconut milk
¼ cup water, plus extra as needed
5 ounces broccolini, florets cut into 1-inch pieces, stalks cut on bias into ½-inch pieces
1 small red, orange, or yellow bell pepper, stemmed, seeded, and cut into 1-inch pieces
7 ounces firm or extra-firm tofu, cut into 1-inch pieces
8 fresh Thai basil leaves, torn
⅓ cup dry-roasted peanuts, chopped
  Lime wedges

1. Heat 1 tablespoon oil in 10- or 12-inch nonstick skillet over medium-high heat until shimmering. Add onion and salt and cook until softened and lightly browned, 5 to 7 minutes. Stir in eggplant and cook until beginning to soften, 2 to 4 minutes. Transfer to bowl. Heat remaining 1 tablespoon oil in now-empty skillet over medium-high heat until shimmering. Add curry paste and cook, stirring frequently, until paste is fragrant and darkens in color to brick red, 5 to 8 minutes.

2. Stir in coconut milk and water, scraping up any browned bits, then stir in broccolini, bell pepper, tofu, and eggplant mixture and bring to boil. Reduce heat to low; cover; and simmer, stirring occasionally, until vegetables are fully tender, 14 to 16 minutes.

3. Adjust consistency with extra hot water as needed. Off heat, stir in basil and season with salt and pepper to taste. Sprinkle with peanuts and serve with lime wedges.

Braised Tofu with Butternut Squash and Eggplant

Serves 2 VEGETARIAN

Total time 1 hour

WHY THIS RECIPE WORKS Braising is a great method for preparing tofu because the tofu will literally soak up the flavors of the braising liquid as it cooks. Sautéed onion, garlic, ginger, and lemongrass gave the sauce a bold aromatic foundation. Cutting the tofu into cubes maximized its surface area, allowing it to absorb the most flavor. To round out the dish, we wanted hearty, earthy vegetables that would benefit from a quick braise: Sweet, creamy butternut squash and meaty eggplant won over tasters. To deepen their flavors, we browned the vegetables in the pan before adding the tofu and braising liquid. If using prepeeled and seeded squash from the supermarket, you will need 8 ounces for this recipe. The tofu and vegetables are delicate and can break apart easily, so be gentle when stirring. You will need a 10-inch nonstick skillet with a tight-fitting lid for this recipe.

14 ounces extra-firm tofu, cut into ¾-inch pieces
1 tablespoon vegetable oil, divided
1 pound butternut squash, peeled, seeded, and cut into ½-inch pieces (1½ cups)
½ eggplant (8 ounces), cut into ½-inch pieces
1 small onion, chopped fine
4 garlic cloves, minced
1 tablespoon grated fresh ginger
1 lemongrass stalk, trimmed to bottom 6 inches and bruised with back of knife
¾ cup vegetable broth
½ cup canned light coconut milk
2 teaspoons soy sauce
¼ cup minced fresh cilantro
2 teaspoons lime juice

1. Line baking sheet with triple layer of paper towels. Spread tofu over prepared sheet and let drain for 15 minutes.

2. Meanwhile, heat 1 teaspoon oil in 10-inch nonstick skillet over medium-high heat until shimmering. Add squash and cook until spotty brown and tender, 7 to 10 minutes; transfer to bowl. Return now-empty skillet to medium-high heat, add 1 teaspoon oil, and heat until shimmering. Add eggplant and cook until golden brown, 5 to 7 minutes; transfer to bowl with squash.

3. Heat remaining 1 teaspoon oil in again-empty skillet over medium heat until shimmering. Add onion and cook until softened and lightly browned, 5 to 7 minutes. Stir in garlic, ginger, and lemongrass and cook until fragrant, about 30 seconds. Gently stir in tofu, broth, coconut milk, soy sauce, and cooked vegetables and bring to simmer. Reduce heat to medium-low; cover; and cook, stirring occasionally, until vegetables are softened, about 10 minutes. Uncover and continue to simmer until sauce is slightly thickened, about 2 minutes.

4. Off heat, discard lemongrass. Stir in cilantro and lime juice and season with salt and pepper to taste. Serve.

BRUISING LEMONGRASS

To smash lemongrass so that it releases its flavorful oils, set stalk on cutting board and smash it with meat pounder or back of knife. This keeps stalk intact so that it can be easily removed from dish.

CHAPTER 9

Pasta & Noodles

■ **FAST** (Start to finish in 30 minutes or less)
■ **VEGETARIAN**

Opposite: Chilled Soba Noodles with Cucumber, Snow Peas, and Radishes

Spaghetti with Garlic and Olive Oil

Serves 2 `FAST` `VEGETARIAN`

Total time 30 minutes

WHY THIS RECIPE WORKS Made from kitchen staples—pasta, olive oil, garlic, and red pepper flakes—pasta with garlic and oil, or aglio e olio, is the perfect last-minute pantry supper for two. To make the most of its flavors, we started by sautéing the garlic slowly and gently over low heat until it developed a mellow, nutty, rich flavor. For a little kick, we also stirred a small amount of raw garlic minced to a paste into the pasta. Three tablespoons of extra-virgin olive oil (using good olive oil was a must in this simple dish) was just enough to coat the pasta and evenly distribute the garlic without making the dish greasy. Minced parsley, fresh lemon juice, and a dash of red pepper flakes brightened the flavors. A rasp-style grater makes quick work of turning the garlic into a paste.

- 3 tablespoons extra-virgin olive oil, divided
- 5 garlic cloves, minced, plus 1 garlic clove, minced to paste
- ⅛ teaspoon red pepper flakes
- ¼ teaspoon table salt, plus salt for cooking pasta
- 6 ounces spaghetti
- 2 tablespoons minced fresh parsley
- 1 teaspoon lemon juice
- Grated Parmesan cheese

1. Cook 2 tablespoons oil, minced garlic, pepper flakes, and ¼ teaspoon salt in 10-inch nonstick skillet over low heat, stirring often, until garlic foams and is sticky and straw-colored, about 10 minutes. Transfer to bowl and stir in remaining 1 tablespoon oil and garlic paste.

2. Meanwhile, bring 2 quarts water to boil in large pot. Add pasta and 1½ teaspoons salt and cook, stirring often, until al dente. Reserve ½ cup cooking water, then drain pasta and return it to pot. Add 1 tablespoon reserved cooking water to garlic mixture to loosen it. Add garlic mixture, parsley, and lemon juice to pasta and toss to combine. Season with salt and pepper to taste, and adjust consistency with remaining reserved cooking water as needed. Serve with Parmesan.

VARIATIONS

Spaghetti with Garlic, Olive Oil, and Fennel

After transferring cooked garlic mixture to bowl in step 1, cook 1 fennel bulb, cored and sliced thin, ½ cup water, and 2 teaspoons extra-virgin olive oil, covered, in now-empty skillet over medium-high heat until fennel is crisp-tender, about 3 minutes. Uncover and continue to cook until water has evaporated and fennel is lightly browned and fully tender, about 5 minutes. Add cooked fennel to pasta with garlic mixture.

Spaghetti with Garlic, Olive Oil, and Artichokes

To thaw the artichokes quickly, microwave them in a covered bowl for about 3 minutes and pat dry before using.

After transferring cooked garlic mixture to bowl in step 1, heat 2 teaspoons extra-virgin olive oil in now-empty skillet over medium-high heat until shimmering. Add 9 ounces frozen artichoke hearts, thawed and patted dry, and ⅛ teaspoon table salt and cook until artichokes are lightly browned and tender, 4 to 6 minutes. Add cooked artichokes to pasta with garlic mixture.

MINCING GARLIC TO A PASTE

Mince garlic, then sprinkle with pinch salt. Scrape side of chef's knife blade across garlic, mashing it into cutting board to make sticky garlic paste.

Cacio e Pepe

Serves 2 `FAST` `VEGETARIAN`

Total time 30 minutes

WHY THIS RECIPE WORKS The famed Roman pasta dish cacio e pepe ("cheese and pepper" in Italian) is, at its heart, a showcase for Pecorino Romano, a sharp, nutty, pleasantly funky sheep's-milk cheese from the region. For a top-notch version for two, we started by cooking 8 ounces of spaghetti in 1½ quarts of boiling water until it was al dente. Using the right amount of cooking water was important because we reserved some of it to stir back into the pasta later. The correct measurement ensured that the water had just the right starch content to produce a creamy, silky sauce. Once the pasta was finished cooking, we reserved ½ cup of the cooking water, drained the pasta, and returned it to the pot. Grating 2½ ounces of Pecorino Romano cheese on a rasp-style grater ensured that it dissolved readily. Reserved cooking water and 2 tablespoons of butter stirred in with the cheese helped create the sauce. After thoroughly tossing the pasta with tongs, we covered it and allowed it to sit for a minute so that the residual heat could fully melt the cheese and butter and the pasta could drink up all the excess liquid. We added a generous amount of freshly ground black pepper and tossed the pasta again to break up any clumps of cheese that may have formed and to thoroughly coat every noodle with the creamy sauce. The pepper wasn't a gimmick here; its clean, spicy flavor cut through the richness of the butter and cheese, earning its place in the dish's name. An extra sprinkle of grated cheese gave the pasta another layer of salty richness, and a drizzle of bright extra-virgin olive oil added sheen and reinforced the peppery punch. High-quality ingredients are essential in this dish; most important, use imported Pecorino Romano—not the bland domestic cheese labeled "Romano." For the best results, grate the cheese on a rasp-style grater. Do not adjust the amount of water for cooking the pasta; the starchy cooking water is essential for the sauce.

- 8 ounces spaghetti
  Table salt for cooking pasta
- 2½ ounces Pecorino Romano cheese, grated (1¼ cups), divided
- 2 tablespoons unsalted butter
- ¾ teaspoon pepper, plus extra for serving
  Extra-virgin olive oil

1. Bring 1½ quarts water to boil in large saucepan. Add pasta and 1 teaspoon salt and cook, stirring frequently, until al dente. Reserve ½ cup cooking water, then drain pasta and return it to pot.

2. Add 1 cup Pecorino, butter, and reserved cooking water to pasta. Set pot over low heat and, using tongs, toss and stir vigorously to thoroughly combine, about 1 minute. Remove pot from heat, cover, and let pasta sit for 1 minute.

3. Add pepper and toss pasta vigorously once more so sauce thoroughly coats pasta and any cheese clumps are emulsified into sauce, about 30 seconds. (Mixture may look wet at this point, but pasta will absorb excess moisture as it cools slightly.)

4. Transfer pasta to individual bowls. Sprinkle with remaining ¼ cup Pecorino and drizzle with oil. Serve immediately, passing extra pepper separately.

Cacio e Pepe

COOKING PASTA 101

Cooking pasta seems simple, but perfect pasta takes some finesse. Here's how we do it in the test kitchen.

USE PLENTY OF WATER To prevent sticking, you'll need 2 quarts water for 6 ounces dried pasta. Pasta leaches starch as it cooks; without plenty of water to dilute it, the starch will coat the noodles and they will stick together. Use a pot with at least a 4-quart capacity so that the water won't boil over.

SALT THE WATER Adding salt to the pasta cooking water is essential; it seasons and adds flavor to the pasta. Add 1½ teaspoons of salt per 2 quarts of water. Be sure to add the salt with the pasta, not before, so that it will dissolve and not stain the pot.

SKIP THE OIL It's a myth that adding oil to pasta cooking water prevents the pasta from sticking together as it cooks. Adding oil to cooking water just creates a slick on the surface of the water, doing nothing for the pasta. And when you drain the pasta, the oil prevents the pasta sauce from adhering. To prevent pasta from sticking, simply stir the pasta for a minute or two when you add it to the boiling water, then stir occasionally while it's cooking.

CHECK OFTEN FOR DONENESS The timing instructions given on the box are almost always too long and will result in mushy, overcooked pasta. Tasting is the best way to check for doneness. We typically prefer pasta cooked al dente, when it still has a little bite left in the center.

RESERVE SOME WATER Reserve about ½ cup cooking water before draining the pasta—the water is flavorful and can help loosen a thick sauce.

DON'T RINSE Drain the pasta in a colander, but don't rinse the pasta; it washes away starch and makes the pasta taste watery. Do let a little cooking water cling to the cooked pasta to help the sauce adhere.

KEEP IT HOT If you're using a large serving bowl for the pasta, place it under the colander while draining the pasta. The hot water heats up the bowl, which keeps the pasta warm longer.

Pasta with Tomato and Almond Pesto

Serves 2 FAST VEGETARIAN

Total time 30 minutes

WHY THIS RECIPE WORKS For a fresh spin on classic basil pesto, we looked to a Sicilian variation featuring almonds and tomatoes. Cherry tomatoes worked best, offering fruity vibrancy and reliable quality year-round. We found that slivered almonds browned evenly and were preferable to whole almonds (their papery skins proved problematic). Basil played a supporting role here; just ¼ cup offered freshness without dominating the other ingredients. A dash of red wine vinegar contributed brightness, and some Parmesan cheese finished our dish with a nutty richness, for a satisfying meal that came together in no time.

- 6 ounces cherry or grape tomatoes
- ¼ cup fresh basil leaves
- 2 tablespoons slivered almonds, toasted
- 1 small garlic clove, minced
- ½ teaspoon table salt, plus salt for cooking pasta
- ¼ teaspoon red wine vinegar
- ⅛ teaspoon red pepper flakes (optional)
- 3 tablespoons extra-virgin olive oil
- 6 ounces spaghetti or linguine
- ¼ cup grated Parmesan cheese, plus extra for serving

1. Process tomatoes; basil; almonds; garlic; salt; vinegar; and pepper flakes, if using, in food processor until smooth, about 1 minute, scraping down sides of bowl as needed. With processor running, slowly add oil until incorporated, about 30 seconds.

2. Meanwhile, bring 2 quarts water to boil in large pot. Add pasta and 1½ teaspoons salt and cook, stirring often, until al dente. Reserve ½ cup cooking water, then drain pasta and return it to pot. Add pesto and Parmesan and toss to combine. Season with salt to taste, and adjust consistency with reserved cooking water as needed. Serve with extra Parmesan.

VARIATION

Pasta with Tomato, Pine Nut, and Arugula Pesto

Substitute ½ cup baby arugula for basil and 2 tablespoons toasted pine nuts for almonds. Add ¾ teaspoon grated lemon zest plus ½ teaspoon juice with tomatoes in step 1.

Linguine with Quick Tomato Sauce

Serves 2   VEGETARIAN
Total time 35 minutes

WHY THIS RECIPE WORKS While popping open a jar of tomato sauce is easy enough, the truth is, preparing a simple, from-scratch sauce doesn't take that much longer—and the flavor can't be beat. Canned tomatoes provided more consistent results than fresh, and whole tomatoes processed briefly in the food processor gave our sauce just the right consistency: mostly smooth, with just a few small bites of tomato. Draining the tomatoes before processing allowed our sauce to become nicely thickened in just a short amount of time, which was essential for retaining fresh tomato flavor. A little bit of sugar provided a sweetness that balanced the acidity of the tomatoes. Garlic and basil contributed classic background notes, and some fruity extra-virgin olive oil offered just enough richness. For a spicy sauce, add ½ teaspoon red pepper flakes to the oil with the garlic.

- 1 (28-ounce) can whole peeled tomatoes, drained
- 5 teaspoons extra-virgin olive oil
- 2 garlic cloves, minced
- 2 tablespoons chopped fresh basil
- ¼ teaspoon sugar, plus extra as needed
  Table salt for cooking pasta
- 6 ounces linguine

1. Pulse tomatoes in food processor until coarsely chopped and no large pieces remain, 6 to 8 pulses. Cook oil and garlic in medium saucepan over medium heat, stirring often, until fragrant but not browned, about 2 minutes. Stir in pulsed tomatoes, bring to simmer, and cook until slightly thickened, 10 to 15 minutes. Off heat, stir in basil and sugar. Season with salt and additional sugar to taste.

2. Meanwhile, bring 2 quarts water to boil in large pot. Add pasta and 1½ teaspoons salt and cook, stirring often, until al dente. Reserve ½ cup cooking water, then drain pasta and return it to pot. Add sauce and toss to combine. Season with salt and pepper to taste, and adjust consistency with reserved cooking water as needed. Serve.

VARIATION

Linguine with Quick Fire-Roasted Tomato Sauce

Substitute 1 (28-ounce) can drained whole fire-roasted tomatoes for whole tomatoes. Add ¼ teaspoon smoked paprika to oil with garlic.

Hands-Off Spaghetti and Meatballs

Serves 2
Total time 1¼ hours

WHY THIS RECIPE WORKS An entirely hands-off dinner of spaghetti and meatballs sounds like a dream: no long wait for the water to boil, no tedious browning of the meatballs, no time-consuming sauce. For our super-simple version of one-pot spaghetti and meatballs, we pared it down to the basics. An easy combination of ground beef, store-bought pesto, and panko bread crumbs yielded meatballs with plenty of flavor. We wanted the pasta to cook right in the sauce, so we spread spaghetti in a casserole dish and covered it with jarred marinara sauce; thinning the sauce with water ensured that there would be enough moisture to properly cook the strands. We then nestled the meatballs into the sauce and let everything bake, covered, in a very hot oven for 30 minutes. These conditions simulated boiling on the stovetop, which enabled our pasta to cook in the sauce and absorb the flavors surrounding it. Once our pasta was al dente, we uncovered it, gave it a stir, and let the meatballs brown and the sauce thicken for the last few minutes of baking. A sprinkling of nutty Parmesan and fresh basil was the perfect finishing touch.

- 6 ounces spaghetti
- 1½ cups jarred marinara sauce
- 1 cup water, plus extra as needed
- ⅓ cup panko bread crumbs
- 3 tablespoons milk
- 8 ounces 85 percent lean ground beef
- 2 tablespoons basil pesto
- ½ teaspoon table salt
- ⅛ teaspoon pepper
- 1 tablespoon chopped fresh basil

1. Adjust oven rack to middle position and heat oven to 475 degrees. Spray 8-inch square baking dish with vegetable oil spray. Loosely wrap pasta in dish towel, then press bundle against corner of counter to break noodles into 6-inch lengths. Spread pasta in prepared dish. Pour marinara sauce and water over pasta and toss gently with tongs to coat.

2. Using fork, mash panko and milk in large bowl until smooth paste forms. Add beef, pesto, salt, and pepper and knead mixture with your hands until well combined. Pinch off and roll mixture into 1½-inch meatballs (you should have about 8 meatballs). Place meatballs on top of pasta in dish. Cover dish tightly with aluminum foil and bake for 30 minutes.

3. Remove dish from oven and stir pasta thoroughly, scraping sides and bottom of dish. Return uncovered dish to oven and continue to bake until pasta is tender and sauce is thickened, 5 to 8 minutes.

4. Remove dish from oven. Toss to coat pasta and meatballs with sauce, adjusting sauce consistency with extra hot water as needed. Let cool for 10 minutes. Season with salt and pepper to taste. Sprinkle with basil and serve.

Pasta alla Norma

Serves 2

Total time 1 hour

WHY THIS RECIPE WORKS To make it work for two, we streamlined the preparation for pasta alla norma—a dish featuring tender eggplant, rich tomato sauce, and salty, milky shreds of ricotta salata. Salting the eggplant drew out excess moisture, then we microwaved it to cause its air pockets to collapse and compress. This meant that the eggplant soaked up much less oil when sautéed, resulting in perfectly browned eggplant. We pureed canned diced tomatoes for a quick tomato sauce that complemented the eggplant. Do not peel the eggplant, as the skin helps the eggplant hold together during cooking. Other pasta shapes can be substituted for the rigatoni; however, their cup measurements may vary (see page 237). Ricotta salata is traditional, but French feta, Pecorino Romano, and cotija are acceptable substitutes.

- 1 (14.5-ounce) can diced tomatoes
- 1 pound eggplant, cut into ¾-inch pieces
- ¼ teaspoon table salt, plus salt for cooking pasta
- 3 tablespoons extra-virgin olive oil, divided, plus extra for serving
- 2 garlic cloves, minced
- 1 anchovy fillet, rinsed, patted dry, and minced
- ⅛ teaspoon red pepper flakes
- 1 cup water
- 3 tablespoons chopped fresh basil
- 6 ounces (2⅓ cups) rigatoni
- 1½ ounces ricotta salata cheese, shredded (⅓ cup)

1. Process tomatoes and their juice in food processor until smooth, about 10 seconds.

2. Line large plate with double layer of coffee filters and lightly spray with vegetable oil spray. Toss eggplant with salt, then spread out over coffee filters. Microwave eggplant until dry to touch and slightly shriveled, 8 to 10 minutes, tossing halfway through microwaving. Let cool slightly.

3. Transfer eggplant to large bowl, drizzle with 1 teaspoon oil, and toss gently to coat. Heat 1 tablespoon oil in 12-inch nonstick skillet over medium-high heat until shimmering. Add eggplant and cook, stirring occasionally, until well browned and fully tender, about 8 minutes; transfer to clean plate.

4. Let skillet cool slightly, about 1 minute. Add 2 teaspoons oil, garlic, anchovy, and pepper flakes to now-empty skillet and cook over medium heat until fragrant, about 30 seconds. Stir in processed tomatoes and water, bring to simmer, and cook until slightly thickened, about 8 minutes. Stir in eggplant and continue to simmer, stirring occasionally, until eggplant is heated through, 3 to 5 minutes. Stir in basil and remaining 1 tablespoon oil and season with salt and pepper to taste.

5. Meanwhile, bring 2 quarts water to boil in large pot. Add pasta and 1½ teaspoons salt and cook, stirring often, until al dente. Reserve ½ cup cooking water, then drain pasta and return it to pot. Add sauce and toss to combine. Season with salt and pepper to taste, and adjust consistency with reserved cooking water as needed. Serve with ricotta salata and extra oil.

VARIATION

Pasta with Eggplant, Olives, and Capers

Substitute 1 tablespoon minced fresh parsley for basil and add ¼ cup thinly sliced pitted kalamata olives and 1 tablespoon drained and rinsed capers to sauce with parsley and oil in step 4.

Rigatoni with Quick Mushroom Ragu

Serves 2 VEGETARIAN

Total time 40 minutes

WHY THIS RECIPE WORKS This 40-minute ragu is hearty, comforting, and nuanced thanks to umami-rich tomato paste, mushrooms, and a glug of white wine. We blitzed the mushrooms, carrot, and shallot for the base of the ragu in a food processor to get the prep work done in a flash, no fancy knife skills necessary. We cooked the vegetables until softened and a layer of fond (browned bits) formed on the bottom of the pan and then scraped up that flavorful browning and incorporated it back into the sauce to capture all its deep, savory flavor. Tomato paste, garlic, and dry white wine gave the sauce its undeniable ragu essence; a splash of pasta cooking water provided its pasta-coating consistency. Letting the rigatoni sit in the sauce for a few minutes helps it soak up the sauce's flavor and excess liquid.

Rigatoni with Quick Mushroom Ragu

8 ounces cremini or white mushrooms, trimmed and quartered
1 small carrot, peeled and chopped
1 shallot, chopped
1 tablespoon extra-virgin olive oil
½ teaspoon table salt, plus salt for cooking pasta
2 tablespoons tomato paste
2 garlic cloves, minced
¼ teaspoon red pepper flakes
¼ cup dry white wine
6 ounces (2⅓ cups) rigatoni
2 tablespoons grated Parmesan cheese, plus extra for serving

1. Pulse mushrooms, carrot, and shallot in food processor until finely chopped, about 8 pulses, scraping down sides of bowl as needed. Heat oil in large saucepan over medium heat until shimmering. Add mushroom mixture and salt; cover; and cook, stirring occasionally, until vegetables have released their liquid, about 5 minutes. Uncover; increase heat to medium-high; and cook until vegetables begin to brown, 3 to 5 minutes.

2. Stir in tomato paste, garlic, and pepper flakes and cook until fragrant, about 1 minute. Stir in wine, scraping up any browned bits, and cook until nearly evaporated, about 30 seconds. Remove from heat and cover to keep warm.

3. Meanwhile, bring 2 quarts water to boil in large pot. Add pasta and 1½ teaspoons salt and cook, stirring often, until nearly al dente. Reserve 1 cup cooking water, then drain pasta.

4. Add pasta and ½ cup reserved cooking water to saucepan with vegetable mixture and cook over medium heat, stirring occasionally, until pasta is al dente, about 3 minutes. Off heat, let sit for 5 minutes. Stir pasta to recombine and adjust consistency with remaining reserved cooking water as needed. Stir in Parmesan and season with salt and pepper to taste. Serve with extra Parmesan.

NOTES FROM THE TEST KITCHEN

ALL ABOUT CANNED TOMATOES
Canned tomatoes are processed at the height of freshness, so they deliver more flavor than off-season fresh tomatoes.

WHOLE TOMATOES Whole tomatoes are peeled tomatoes packed in either their own juice or puree. Whole tomatoes are soft and break down quickly when cooked. Our favorite brand is **Cento San Marzano.**

DICED TOMATOES Diced tomatoes are peeled, machine-diced, and packed in either their own juice or puree. We favor diced tomatoes packed in juice for their fresh flavor; our favorite is **San Merican.**

CRUSHED TOMATOES Crushed tomatoes are whole tomatoes ground finely and enriched with tomato puree. We like **San Merican.**

TOMATO PUREE Tomato puree is made from cooked tomatoes that have been strained to remove seeds and skins. Our favorite brand is **Muir Glen Organic.**

TOMATO PASTE Tomato paste is tomato puree that has been cooked to remove most moisture. Because it's naturally full of glutamates, tomato paste brings out savory notes. Our preferred brand is **Cento Double Concentrated** (tubed).

Classic Pork Ragu

Pasta with Roasted Cauliflower, Garlic, and Walnuts

Classic Pork Ragu

Serves 2

Total time 2¼ hours

WHY THIS RECIPE WORKS Featuring tender, shredded meat in a rich tomato sauce, classic pork ragu is a rustic alternative to more complicated meat sauces and delivers big, meaty flavor without a lot of work. Determining the right cut of pork was our biggest challenge, since many of the most flavorful cuts of pork are also the largest. Country-style ribs proved ideal; they are available in smaller portions and have plenty of fat and connective tissue to keep the meat moist during the long cooking time. Slowly simmered with a can of whole tomatoes and flavored with shallot, garlic, rosemary, and red wine, these meaty ribs delivered rich, savory flavor. Pork spareribs can be substituted for the country-style ribs. Other pasta shapes can be substituted for the ziti; however, their cup measurements may vary (see page 237).

- 1 (28-ounce) can whole peeled tomatoes, drained with ¼ cup juice reserved
- 12 ounces bone-in country-style pork ribs, trimmed
- ½ teaspoon table salt, divided, plus salt for cooking pasta
- ⅛ teaspoon pepper
- 2 teaspoons extra-virgin olive oil
- 1 large shallot, minced
- 2 garlic cloves, minced
- 1½ teaspoons minced fresh rosemary
- ½ cup dry red wine
- 6 ounces (2 cups) ziti
  Grated Pecorino Romano cheese

1. Pulse tomatoes in food processor until coarsely chopped and no large pieces remain, 6 to 8 pulses.

2. Pat pork dry with paper towels and sprinkle with ¼ teaspoon salt and pepper. Heat oil in 10-inch skillet over medium-high heat until just smoking. Brown pork well on all sides, 8 to 10 minutes; transfer to plate.

3. Add shallot and remaining ¼ teaspoon salt to fat left in skillet and cook over medium heat until softened, 2 to 3 minutes. Stir in garlic and rosemary and cook until fragrant, about 30 seconds. Stir in wine, scraping up any browned bits. Bring to simmer and cook until reduced by half, about 2 minutes.

4. Stir in pulsed tomatoes and reserved juice. Nestle browned ribs into sauce, along with any accumulated juices, and bring to simmer. Reduce heat to low; cover; and simmer gently, turning ribs occasionally, until meat is very tender and falling off bones, about 1½ hours.

5. Transfer ribs to cutting board; let cool slightly; then shred into bite-size pieces using 2 forks, discarding bones. Return shredded meat to sauce; bring to simmer; and cook until heated through and slightly thickened, 2 to 3 minutes. Season with salt and pepper to taste.

6. Meanwhile, bring 2 quarts water to boil in large pot. Add pasta and 1½ teaspoons salt and cook, stirring often, until al dente. Reserve ½ cup cooking water, then drain pasta and return it to pot. Add sauce and toss to combine. Season with salt and pepper to taste, and adjust consistency with reserved cooking water as needed. Serve with Pecorino.

Pasta with Roasted Cauliflower, Garlic, and Walnuts

Serves 2   VEGETARIAN

Total time 1¼ hours

WHY THIS RECIPE WORKS For a warming winter dinner, we wanted to unite a roasted vegetable, pasta, and cheese with a simple sauce. We selected cauliflower as the vegetable, which becomes sweet and nutty when roasted. We cut it into small pieces and sprinkled it with a little sugar, which maximized caramelization, and we cooked it on a preheated baking sheet, which reduced the roasting time. Roasted garlic mashed with extra-virgin olive oil and lemon juice created a creamy puree. Other pasta shapes can be substituted for the campanelle; however, their cup measurements may vary (see page 237).

- 1 head garlic, outer papery skins removed and top quarter of head cut off and discarded
- ½ teaspoon plus 3 tablespoons extra-virgin olive oil, divided
- 1 tablespoon lemon juice, plus extra for seasoning
- ⅛ teaspoon red pepper flakes
- ½ head cauliflower (1 pound), cored and cut into 1-inch florets
- ½ teaspoon table salt, plus salt for cooking pasta
- ⅛ teaspoon pepper
- ⅛ teaspoon sugar
- 6 ounces (2 cups) campanelle
- ¼ cup grated Parmesan cheese, plus extra for serving
- 2 teaspoons minced fresh parsley
- 2 tablespoons chopped toasted walnuts

1. Adjust oven racks to middle and lower-middle positions and heat oven to 500 degrees. Place garlic head cut side up in center of 12-inch square of aluminum foil. Drizzle ½ teaspoon oil over garlic and wrap securely. Place packet on lower rack

1. Rinse garlic head and remove outer papery skin. Cut top quarter off of garlic head so that tops of cloves are exposed.

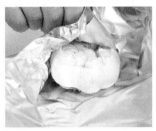

2. Place garlic head cut side up in center of 12-inch square of aluminum foil, drizzle with oil, and wrap securely.

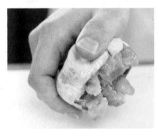

3. After roasted garlic head has cooled, remove from foil. Using your hand or flat edge of chef's knife, squeeze garlic cloves from skins, starting from root end and working up.

and place rimmed baking sheet on upper rack. Roast garlic for 35 minutes. Transfer packet to cutting board, let cool for 10 minutes, then unwrap garlic. Gently squeeze to remove cloves from skin, transfer cloves to small bowl, and mash smooth with fork. Stir in lemon juice and pepper flakes, then slowly whisk in 2 tablespoons oil.

2. While garlic roasts, toss cauliflower, remaining 1 tablespoon oil, salt, pepper, and sugar together in large bowl. Working quickly, carefully arrange cauliflower in single layer on hot sheet. Roast cauliflower until well browned and tender, 10 to 15 minutes, stirring cauliflower halfway through cooking. Transfer cauliflower to cutting board, let cool slightly, then chop into ½-inch pieces.

3. Meanwhile, bring 2 quarts water to boil in large pot. Add pasta and 1½ teaspoons salt and cook, stirring often, until al dente. Reserve ½ cup cooking water, then drain pasta and return it to pot. Add garlic sauce, chopped cauliflower, 2 tablespoons of reserved cooking water, Parmesan, and parsley and toss to combine. Season with salt, pepper, and extra lemon juice to taste, and adjust consistency with remaining reserved cooking water as needed. Sprinkle individual portions with walnuts. Serve with extra Parmesan.

Pasta with Roasted Broccoli, Garlic, and Almonds

Substitute 12 ounces broccoli florets for cauliflower and reduce roasting time to 8 to 10 minutes in step 2. Substitute ¼ cup grated Manchego cheese for Parmesan, 2 tablespoons chopped fresh basil for parsley, and 2 tablespoons toasted slivered almonds for walnuts. Serve with extra grated Manchego.

Pasta with Roasted Mushrooms, Garlic, and Pine Nuts

Substitute 1½ pounds portobello mushroom caps, gills removed, and caps sliced ¾ inch thick, for cauliflower and reduce amount of salt to ⅛ teaspoon in step 2; roast as directed, flipping mushrooms halfway through cooking. Substitute ¼ cup grated Pecorino Romano cheese for Parmesan, 1 teaspoon minced fresh rosemary for parsley, and 2 tablespoons toasted pine nuts for walnuts. Serve with extra Pecorino.

Pasta with Roasted Cherry Tomatoes, Garlic, and Basil

Serves 2   **VEGETARIAN**

Total time 1 hour

WHY THIS RECIPE WORKS Typically we turn to canned tomatoes when we want a sauce we can make year-round, but we thought that a recipe for fresh tomato sauce we could make any time of year was a worthy goal. Cherry tomatoes offer the most reliable flavor and texture out of season, and roasting them is a surefire way to enhance their sweetness and intensify their flavor; just 30 minutes of roasting in a moderate oven yielded tomatoes with sweet, concentrated flavor and an appealing texture. We roasted some garlic and shallot along with the tomatoes, which streamlined our dish, and we liked the tartness and heat provided by a little balsamic vinegar and red pepper flakes. You can substitute grape tomatoes for the cherry tomatoes. Other pasta shapes can be substituted for the penne; however, their cup measurements may vary (see page 237).

  1 small shallot, sliced thin
  2 tablespoons extra-virgin olive oil, divided
  1 pound cherry tomatoes, halved
  3 garlic cloves, sliced thin
1½ teaspoons balsamic vinegar
  ¾ teaspoon sugar
  ¼ teaspoon table salt, plus salt for cooking pasta

  ⅛ teaspoon pepper
  ⅛ teaspoon red pepper flakes
  6 ounces (2 cups) penne
  2 tablespoons chopped fresh basil

1. Adjust oven rack to middle position and heat oven to 350 degrees. Toss shallot with 1 teaspoon oil in small bowl. In medium bowl, toss gently remaining 5 teaspoons oil, tomatoes, garlic, vinegar, sugar, salt, pepper, and pepper flakes together. Spread tomato mixture evenly into 13 by 9-inch baking dish and scatter shallot mixture over top. Roast vegetables, without stirring, until edges of shallot begin to brown and tomato skins are slightly shriveled but tomatoes still retain their shape, about 30 minutes. Remove vegetables from oven and let cool slightly, about 5 minutes.

2. Meanwhile, bring 2 quarts water to boil in large pot. Add pasta and 1½ teaspoons salt and cook, stirring often, until al dente. Reserve ½ cup cooking water, then drain pasta and return it to pot. Transfer vegetable mixture to pot with pasta, add basil, and toss to combine. Season with salt and pepper to taste, and adjust consistency with reserved cooking water as needed. Serve.

Spaghetti and Turkey-Pesto Meatballs

Serves 2

Total time 40 minutes

WHY THIS RECIPE WORKS Turkey meatballs make a great alternative to the traditional beef and pork meatballs—if you can find a way to infuse them with flavor and keep them moist. One convenient product helped us on both fronts. Store-bought basil pesto offered big garlic and herb flavors without any prep, and it contributed richness and kept our meatballs moist. Panko bread crumbs helped to bind the mixture, and grated Parmesan added a rich, savory flavor. After browning the meatballs, we simmered them in a simple tomato sauce (seasoned with just a little garlic and sugar) to finish cooking through. Be sure to use ground turkey, not ground turkey breast (also labeled 99 percent fat free), in this recipe. You can make your own pesto (page 235) or use your favorite store-bought brand from the refrigerated section of the supermarket—they have a fresher flavor than jarred pesto sold in the grocery aisles. You will need a 10-inch skillet with a tight-fitting lid for this recipe.

  8 ounces ground turkey
  ⅓ cup panko bread crumbs
  ¼ cup basil pesto

Spaghetti and Turkey-Pesto Meatballs

simmer gently, turning meatballs occasionally, until meatballs are cooked through, about 5 minutes. Season with salt, pepper, and extra sugar to taste.

3. Meanwhile, bring 2 quarts water to boil in large pot. Add pasta and 1½ teaspoons salt and cook, stirring often, until al dente. Reserve ½ cup cooking water, then drain pasta and return it to pot. Add several large spoonfuls of tomato sauce (without meatballs) and toss to combine. Season with salt and pepper to taste, and adjust consistency with reserved cooking water as needed. Divide pasta between 2 bowls, top each bowl with remaining sauce and meatballs, and sprinkle with basil. Serve with Parmesan.

¼ teaspoon table salt, plus salt for cooking pasta
⅛ teaspoon pepper
1 tablespoon extra-virgin olive oil
1 garlic clove, minced
1 (28-ounce) can crushed tomatoes
¼ teaspoon sugar, plus extra for seasoning
6 ounces spaghetti
1 tablespoon shredded fresh basil
Grated Parmesan cheese

1. Using your hands, gently mix ground turkey, panko, pesto, salt, and pepper together in bowl until uniform. Roll mixture into eight 1-inch meatballs. Heat oil in 10-inch skillet over medium-high heat until just smoking. Brown meatballs well on all sides, about 8 minutes; transfer to paper towel–lined plate.

2. Add garlic to fat left in skillet and cook over medium heat until fragrant, about 30 seconds. Stir in tomatoes and sugar, scraping up any browned bits. Bring to simmer and cook until sauce is slightly thickened, 5 to 8 minutes. Return meatballs to skillet and reduce heat to medium-low. Cover and

Basil Pesto

Makes about ¾ cup `FAST` `VEGETARIAN`
Total Time 15 minutes

Aromatic basil and sweet toasted garlic live in harmony in this fragrant green pesto. Basil tends to darken in homemade pesto; the optional parsley provides bright green color that doesn't fade. Two cups of fresh basil leaves weigh about 2 ounces.

3 garlic cloves, unpeeled
2 cups fresh basil leaves
2 tablespoons fresh parsley leaves (optional)
¼ cup pine nuts, toasted
3 tablespoons grated Parmesan
¼ teaspoon table salt
7 tablespoons extra-virgin olive oil

1. Toast garlic in 8-inch skillet over medium heat, stirring occasionally, until fragrant and skins are just beginning to brown, about 5 minutes. Remove garlic from saucepan and let cool, about 5 minutes. Once cool enough to handle, peel garlic and mince. Place basil and parsley, if using, in heavy-duty quart-size zipper-lock bag; pound with flat side of meat pounder or rolling pin until all leaves are bruised.

2. Process bruised herbs, pine nuts, Parmesan, salt, and garlic in food processor until smooth, scraping down sides of bowl as needed, about 1 minute. With processor running, slowly add oil until incorporated, about 30 seconds. Transfer pesto to bowl and season with salt and pepper to taste. (Pesto can be refrigerated for up to 3 days or frozen for up to 3 months. To prevent browning, press plastic wrap flush to surface, or top with thin layer of olive oil.)

Pasta with Chicken, Broccoli, and Sun-Dried Tomatoes

Serves 2

Total time 45 minutes

WHY THIS RECIPE WORKS Popular versions of this recipe often produce bland chicken and limp broccoli drowning in a fatty cream sauce. We wanted a fresh sauce that would highlight the fresh, crisp broccoli and tender chicken. First, we lightly browned chicken breast strips in butter to build great flavor. To keep the chicken tender and add flavor, we finished cooking it in the sauce, and we blanched the broccoli in the boiling pasta water to keep it crisp. But our real breakthrough came when we replaced the typical cream sauce with a broth-based sauce, which we rounded out with a little butter, Asiago cheese, and some sun-dried tomatoes. Other pasta shapes can be substituted for the ziti; however, their cup measurements may vary (see page 237). Parmesan cheese can be substituted for the Asiago. To make the chicken easier to slice, freeze it for 15 minutes.

- 8 ounces boneless, skinless chicken breast, trimmed and sliced ¼ inch thick
- ¼ teaspoon table salt, divided, plus salt for cooking pasta and vegetables
  Pinch pepper
- 3 tablespoons unsalted butter, divided
- 1 small onion, chopped fine
- 3 garlic cloves, minced
- 1 teaspoon minced fresh thyme or ¼ teaspoon dried
- 1 teaspoon all-purpose flour
- ⅛ teaspoon red pepper flakes
- 1 cup chicken broth
- ½ cup dry white wine
- 12 ounces broccoli, florets cut into 1-inch pieces, stalks peeled and sliced ¼ inch thick
- 6 ounces (2 cups) ziti
- 1 ounce Asiago cheese, grated (½ cup), plus extra for serving
- ½ cup oil-packed sun-dried tomatoes, patted dry and cut into ¼-inch strips
- 1 tablespoon chopped fresh parsley

1. Pat chicken dry with paper towels and sprinkle with ⅛ teaspoon salt and pepper. Melt 1 tablespoon butter in 10-inch nonstick skillet over high heat until beginning to brown. Add chicken; break up any clumps; and cook, without stirring, until beginning to brown, about 1 minute. Stir chicken and continue to cook until nearly cooked through, about 2 minutes; transfer to bowl.

2. Melt 1 tablespoon butter in now-empty skillet over medium heat. Add onion and remaining ⅛ teaspoon salt and cook until softened and lightly browned, 5 to 7 minutes. Stir in garlic, thyme, flour, and pepper flakes and cook until fragrant, about 30 seconds. Whisk in broth and wine, scraping up any browned bits and smoothing out any lumps; bring to simmer; and cook until sauce is slightly thickened and measures about ⅔ cup, about 10 minutes. Remove from heat and cover to keep warm.

3. Meanwhile, bring 2 quarts water to boil in large pot. Add broccoli florets and stalks and 1½ teaspoons salt and cook, stirring often, until florets are crisp-tender, about 2 minutes. Using slotted spoon, transfer broccoli to paper towel–lined plate.

4. Return pot of water to boil. Add pasta and cook, stirring often, until al dente. Reserve ½ cup cooking water, then drain pasta and return it to pot. Stir remaining 1 tablespoon butter, browned chicken along with any accumulated juices, Asiago, and tomatoes into sauce; bring to simmer; and cook until chicken is cooked through, about 1 minute. Add chicken mixture, broccoli, and parsley to pasta and toss to combine. Season with salt and pepper to taste, and adjust consistency with reserved cooking water as needed. Serve with extra Asiago.

Orecchiette with Broccoli Rabe and Italian Sausage

Serves 2

Total time 45 minutes

WHY THIS RECIPE WORKS The Italian region of Puglia is known for its simple, rustic cuisine. We wanted to create a version of one popular dish that features orecchiette paired with bitter broccoli rabe and sweet Italian sausage. Boiling the broccoli rabe allowed the stalks to become tender without overcooking the florets and, as a bonus, we were able to use the richly flavored water to cook the pasta. Browning the sausage provided a good flavor base for the sauce. Chicken broth plus garlic and red pepper flakes contributed a rich backbone, and just one minced anchovy fillet deepened the overall flavor of the dish immensely. A little flour thickened our sauce to a luxurious consistency. Other pasta shapes can be substituted for the orecchiette; however, their cup measurements may vary (see page 237). Don't confuse broccoli rabe with broccoli or broccolini; broccoli rabe is a member of the turnip family and has a peppery bite.

2 tablespoons extra-virgin olive oil

8 ounces sweet Italian sausage, casings removed

3 garlic cloves, minced

1 anchovy fillet, rinsed, patted dry, and minced

1 teaspoon all-purpose flour

¼ teaspoon red pepper flakes

¾ cup chicken broth

½ pound broccoli rabe, trimmed and cut into
1½-inch pieces
Table salt for cooking vegetables and pasta

6 ounces (1¾ cups) orecchiette

¼ cup grated Pecorino Romano cheese,
plus extra for serving

1. Heat oil in 12-inch nonstick skillet over medium-high heat until shimmering. Add sausage and cook, breaking up meat with wooden spoon, until browned and crisp, 5 to 7 minutes. Stir in garlic, anchovy, flour, and pepper flakes and cook until fragrant, about 30 seconds. Stir in broth, scraping up any browned bits and smoothing out any lumps. Bring to simmer and cook, stirring occasionally, until sauce is slightly thickened, about 1 minute. Remove from heat and cover to keep warm.

2. Meanwhile, bring 2 quarts water to boil in large pot. Add broccoli rabe and 1½ teaspoons salt and cook, stirring often, until broccoli rabe turns bright green, about 2 minutes. Using slotted spoon, transfer broccoli rabe to paper towel–lined plate.

3. Return pot of water to boil. Add pasta and cook, stirring often, until al dente. Reserve ½ cup cooking water, then drain pasta and return it to pot. Return sausage mixture to simmer. Add to pasta with broccoli rabe and Pecorino; toss to combine. Season with salt and pepper to taste, and adjust consistency with reserved cooking water as needed. Serve with extra Pecorino.

VARIATION

Orecchiette with Broccoli Rabe and White Beans

Omit sausage and anchovy. Increase amount of garlic to 4 cloves and substitute ¾ cup vegetable broth for chicken broth. Add ¾ cup rinsed canned cannellini beans to skillet with broth. Add 2 tablespoons toasted pine nuts and 1½ teaspoons red wine vinegar to pasta with sauce in step 3.

NOTES FROM THE TEST KITCHEN

PASTA SHAPES AND SIZES

MEASURING PASTA It's easy enough to measure out a pound of pasta, as most packages are sold in this quantity. But a pound of pasta is way too much when cooking for two; most of the recipes in this book call for 6 ounces. Obviously, you can weigh out partial pounds of pasta using a scale or judge by how full the box is, but we think it's easier to measure short pasta shapes using a dry measuring cup and strand pasta by determining the diameter.

Pasta Type	4 Ounces	6 Ounces
Elbow Macaroni and Small Shells	1 cup	1½ cups
Orecchiette	1 cup	1¾ cups
Penne, Ziti, and Campanelle	1¼ cups	2 cups
Rigatoni, Rotini, Fusilli, Medium Shells, Wagon Wheels, and Wide Egg Noodles	1½ cups	2 ⅓ cups
Farfalle	1 ⅔ cups	2½ cups

*These amounts do not apply to whole-wheat pasta.

When 6 ounces of uncooked strand pasta are bunched together into a tight circle, the diameter measures about 1⅛ inches.

MATCHING PASTA SHAPES AND SAUCES

Pairing a pasta shape with the right sauce might be an art form in Italy, but we think there's only one basic rule to follow: Thick, chunky sauces go with short pastas, and thin, smooth, or light sauces with strand pasta. (Of course, there are a few exceptions—but that's where the art comes in.) Although we specify pasta shapes for every recipe in this book, you should feel free to substitute other pasta shapes. Short tubular or molded pasta shapes do an excellent job of trapping and holding on to chunky sauces. Sauces with very large chunks are best with rigatoni or other large tubes. Sauces with small chunks make more sense with fusilli or penne. Long strands are best with smooth sauces or sauces with very small chunks. In general, wider noodles, such as pappardelle and fettuccine, can support slightly chunkier sauces, like a classic ragu.

Spaghetti al Tonno

Spaghetti al Tonno

Serves 2

Total time 40 minutes

WHY THIS RECIPE WORKS For this Italian pantry pasta dish, we used one jar (or can) of olive oil–packed tuna and a small amount of canned whole tomatoes, crushed by hand to produce small, supple pieces. Lots of garlic, some cooked in olive oil and the rest simply warmed through, contributed potent flavor, along with red pepper flakes for heat and anchovies for a briny backbone. To ensure that the tuna stayed moist and silky, we stirred it into slightly underdone spaghetti along with the tomato mixture off the heat and let it warm through. For a spicier dish, use the full ¼ teaspoon of red pepper flakes.

- 1 (5- to 7-ounce) jar/can olive oil–packed tuna, drained
- 1½ teaspoons lemon juice
- ½ teaspoon table salt, divided, plus salt for cooking pasta
- ¼ teaspoon pepper, divided
- 2 tablespoons extra-virgin olive oil, divided, plus extra for drizzling (optional)
- 1 tablespoon capers, rinsed
- 2 teaspoons minced garlic, divided
- 2 small anchovy fillets, rinsed, patted dry, and minced
- ⅛–¼ teaspoon red pepper flakes
- 1 cup canned whole peeled tomatoes, drained with juice reserved, crushed by hand to small pieces
- 6 ounces spaghetti
- 3 tablespoons chopped fresh parsley, divided

1. Bring 2 quarts water to boil in large pot. While water comes to boil, stir tuna, lemon juice, ⅛ teaspoon salt, and ⅛ teaspoon pepper together in small bowl.

2. Heat 1 tablespoon oil, capers, 1½ teaspoons garlic, anchovies, and pepper flakes in small saucepan over medium heat, stirring occasionally, until oil sizzles gently and anchovies break down, 1½ to 2 minutes. Stir in tomatoes and their juice and ¼ teaspoon salt. Increase heat to high and bring to strong simmer. Adjust heat to maintain gentle simmer and cook, stirring occasionally, until slightly thickened, 6 to 7 minutes. Cover and keep warm over low heat.

3. Add spaghetti and 1½ teaspoons salt to boiling water. Cook, stirring often, until barely al dente. Reserve ½ cup cooking water. Drain pasta and return it to pot. Off heat, add tomato mixture, remaining ⅛ teaspoon salt, remaining ⅛ teaspoon pepper, and remaining ½ teaspoon garlic and toss until pasta is well coated. Add tuna mixture and toss gently to distribute. Cover and set aside for 3 minutes so flavors can meld and pasta can finish cooking.

4. Adjust consistency of sauce with reserved cooking water as needed. Add 2 tablespoons parsley and remaining 1 tablespoon oil and toss to combine. Season with salt and pepper to taste. Distribute between 2 pasta bowls. Drizzle each portion with extra oil, if using. Sprinkle with remaining 1 tablespoon parsley and serve.

Spaghetti with Lemon, Basil, and Shrimp

Serves 2

Total time 35 minutes

WHY THIS RECIPE WORKS For an easy shrimp and pasta dish we could get on the table in short order, we opted for a no-cook sauce: A combination of extra-virgin olive oil, lemon juice, and garlic provided the base for a simple vinaigrette we could toss with the warm pasta. Lemon zest added more citrus flavor without adding more acidity; some Parmesan cheese helped thicken the sauce slightly and contributed a nutty flavor; and a pat of butter added richness. We cooked the pasta in the same water we used to cook the shrimp, saving us from dirtying an extra pan. The flavor of this dish depends on high-quality extra-virgin olive oil, fresh-squeezed lemon juice, and fresh basil.

- 3 tablespoons extra-virgin olive oil
- 1 teaspoon grated lemon zest plus 2½ tablespoons juice
- 1 garlic clove, minced to paste
- ¼ teaspoon table salt, plus salt for cooking shrimp and pasta
- 1 ounce Parmesan cheese, grated (½ cup)
- 8 ounces extra-large shrimp (21 to 25 per pound), peeled, deveined, and tails removed
- 6 ounces spaghetti
- 2 tablespoons shredded fresh basil
- 1 tablespoon unsalted butter, softened

1. Whisk oil, lemon zest and juice, garlic, and salt together in bowl, then stir in Parmesan until thick and creamy.

2. Meanwhile, bring 2 quarts water to boil in large pot. Add shrimp and 1½ teaspoons salt and cook until opaque throughout, about 1 minute. Using slotted spoon, transfer shrimp to bowl, season with salt and pepper to taste, and cover to keep warm.

3. Return pot of water to boil. Add pasta and cook, stirring often, until al dente. Reserve ½ cup cooking water, then drain pasta and return it to pot. Add oil-garlic mixture, cooked shrimp, basil, and butter and toss to combine. Season with salt and pepper to taste, and adjust consistency with reserved cooking water as needed. Serve.

Garlicky Spaghetti with Clams
Serves 2 FAST
Total time 30 minutes

WHY THIS RECIPE WORKS For a busy cook wanting a seafood pasta that doesn't require reaching past the pantry to get the flavor of the sea (and good protein), canned clams proved to be a worthy solution. A judicious handful of minced anchovies added to the garlicky spaghetti provided seafood brininess and accentuated the flavor of the clams. You can substitute traditional pasta for the whole-wheat.

6 ounces spaghetti
¼ teaspoon table salt, plus salt for cooking pasta
3 garlic cloves, minced
4 teaspoons extra-virgin olive oil
⅛ teaspoon red pepper flakes
1 (6½-ounce) can chopped clams
2 anchovy fillets, rinsed, patted dry, and minced
1 teaspoon lemon juice
2 tablespoons grated Parmesan cheese
2 tablespoons chopped fresh basil or parsley

1. Bring 2 quarts water to boil in large pot. Add pasta and 1½ teaspoons salt and cook, stirring frequently, until tender. Reserve ½ cup cooking water, then drain pasta and return it to pot.

2. Meanwhile, cook garlic and oil in 8- or 10-inch nonstick skillet over medium-low heat, stirring occasionally, until garlic is lightly browned, 6 to 8 minutes. Off heat, stir in pepper flakes.

3. Add garlic mixture, clams and their juice, anchovies, lemon juice, salt, and reserved cooking water to pasta. Stir until pasta is well coated with sauce and no water remains in bottom of pot, about 1 minute. Season with salt and pepper to taste. Sprinkle each portion with Parmesan and basil before serving.

Cheese Ravioli with Roasted Red Pepper and Pistachio Pesto
Serves 2 VEGETARIAN
Total time 40 minutes

WHY THIS RECIPE WORKS Store-bought ravioli make for a convenient weeknight dinner, but because they trap so much water during cooking, they tend to dilute whatever sauce accompanies them. To solve this problem, we ditched the traditional tomato sauce and paired our ravioli with pesto; its thick texture and concentrated flavor held up well once tossed with the hot ravioli. For an updated version of simple basil pesto, we combined roasted red peppers and sweet pistachios with the classic basil, garlic, and Parmesan cheese. Blanching the garlic mellowed its bite, and the Parmesan helped thicken our pesto to the proper consistency. This recipe calls for fresh ravioli, but you can substitute 12 ounces frozen ravioli.

1 garlic clove, unpeeled
¾ cup jarred roasted red peppers, rinsed and patted dry
½ cup fresh basil leaves
⅓ cup grated Parmesan cheese
¼ cup shelled pistachios, toasted
2 tablespoons extra-virgin olive oil
Table salt for cooking pasta
1 (9-ounce) package fresh cheese ravioli

1. Bring 2 quarts water to boil in large pot. Add garlic to water and cook for 1 minute. Using slotted spoon, transfer garlic to bowl and rinse under cold water to stop cooking. Peel and mince garlic

2. Pulse garlic, red peppers, basil, Parmesan, and pistachios in food processor until smooth, 20 to 30 pulses, scraping down sides of bowl as needed. With processor running, slowly add oil until incorporated, about 30 seconds. Transfer to bowl and season with salt and pepper to taste.

3. Return pot of water to boil. Add pasta and 1½ teaspoons salt and cook, stirring often, until tender. Reserve ½ cup cooking water, then drain pasta and return it to pot. Add ½ cup pesto and toss gently to combine. Season with salt and pepper to taste, and adjust consistency with reserved cooking water as needed. Serve, passing remaining pesto separately.

VARIATIONS
Cheese Ravioli with Sage, Walnut, and Browned Butter Pesto
Melt 3 tablespoons butter in 8-inch skillet over medium-high heat. Continue to cook, swirling skillet constantly, until butter is golden brown and has nutty aroma, 2 to 4 minutes. Off heat,

add ¼ cup chopped fresh sage and let sit until cool, about 10 minutes. Omit oil and substitute butter-sage mixture for roasted red peppers, ½ cup fresh parsley leaves for basil, and ¼ cup toasted walnuts for pistachios in step 2.

Cheese Ravioli with Kale and Sunflower Seed Pesto

Substitute 1 cup chopped stemmed kale for roasted red peppers and ¼ cup toasted sunflower seeds for pistachios. Add ⅛ teaspoon red pepper flakes to food processor in step 2 and increase amount of oil to ¼ cup.

Classic Lasagna

Serves 2

Total time 1½ hours, plus 20 minutes cooling

WHY THIS RECIPE WORKS Lasagna is a crowd-pleaser: What's not to love about a dish layered with tender noodles, meaty sauce, and gooey cheese baked until golden and bubbling? But it's also time-consuming to prepare. We didn't think this hearty and satisfying favorite should be off-limits when cooking for less than a crowd. Our goal was a streamlined version for two. For an easy meaty tomato sauce, we found that meatloaf

Classic Lasagna

mix lent more flavor and richness than ground beef. A little cream with diced tomatoes and canned tomato sauce gave us a velvety sauce reminiscent of a Bolognese. A baking dish made far too much for two, but the noodles fit perfectly in a loaf pan. We simply layered noodles with the sauce and a combination of mozzarella, ricotta, and Parmesan for a perfectly proportioned two-person lasagna. If you can't find meatloaf mix, substitute 4 ounces each of ground pork and 90 percent lean ground beef. Do not substitute fat-free ricotta.

SAUCE

- 1 tablespoon extra-virgin olive oil
- 1 small onion, chopped fine
- ⅛ teaspoon table salt
- 2 garlic cloves, minced
- 8 ounces meatloaf mix
- 2 tablespoons heavy cream
- 1 (14.5-ounce) can diced tomatoes, drained with ¼ cup juice reserved
- 1 (8-ounce) can tomato sauce

FILLING, NOODLES, AND CHEESE

- 4 ounces (½ cup) whole-milk or part-skim ricotta cheese
- 1 ounce Parmesan cheese, grated (½ cup), plus 2 tablespoons, grated, divided
- 3 tablespoons chopped fresh basil
- 1 large egg, lightly beaten
- ⅛ teaspoon table salt
- ⅛ teaspoon pepper
- 4 no-boil lasagna noodles, divided
- 4 ounces whole-milk mozzarella cheese, shredded (1 cup), divided

1. FOR THE SAUCE Adjust oven rack to middle position and heat oven to 400 degrees. Heat oil in large saucepan over medium heat until shimmering. Add onion and salt and cook until softened, about 5 minutes. Stir in garlic and cook until fragrant, about 30 seconds. Stir in meatloaf mix and cook, breaking up meat with wooden spoon, until no longer pink, about 2 minutes.

2. Stir in cream, bring to simmer, and cook until liquid evaporates, about 2 minutes. Stir in tomatoes and reserved juice and tomato sauce. Bring to simmer and cook until flavors are blended, about 2 minutes. Season with salt and pepper to taste.

3. FOR THE FILLING, NOODLES, AND CHEESE Combine ricotta, ½ cup Parmesan, basil, egg, salt, and pepper in bowl.

4. Spread ½ cup sauce over bottom of loaf pan, avoiding large chunks of meat. Lay 1 noodle in pan, spread one-third of ricotta mixture over noodle, sprinkle with ¼ cup mozzarella, and top with ½ cup sauce; repeat layering 2 more times. Lay remaining noodle in pan and top with remaining sauce, remaining ¼ cup mozzarella, and remaining 2 tablespoons Parmesan.

5. Cover pan tightly with aluminum foil that has been sprayed with vegetable oil spray. Bake until sauce bubbles lightly around edges, 25 to 30 minutes. Remove foil and continue to bake until hot throughout and cheese is browned in spots, about 10 minutes. Let cool for 20 minutes before serving.

Baked Macaroni and Cheese

Serves 2 VEGETARIAN

Total time: 1 hour

WHY THIS RECIPE WORKS For this take on macaroni and cheese, we cooked the pasta directly in the oven without even heating up the water. Cooking the pasta at 375 degrees in a mixture of water and evaporated milk gave us tender noodles, and the starchy water provided a creamy base for the cheese sauce. Stirring in shredded cheddar (for flavor) and American cheese (for meltability) at the end of baking gave us a perfectly lush, smooth sauce. We topped our dish with panko bread crumbs, browned in the microwave, for irresistible crunch. The macaroni mixture will seem loose after step 3, but will continue to thicken as it sits.

- 6 ounces (1½ cups) elbow macaroni
- 1 (12-ounce) can evaporated milk
- ½ cup water
- ¼ teaspoon dry mustard
- ¼ teaspoon table salt
- ⅛ teaspoon pepper
- 3 ounces sharp cheddar cheese, shredded (¾ cup)
- 3 ounces American cheese, shredded (¾ cup)
- ¼ cup panko bread crumbs
- 2 teaspoons extra-virgin olive oil
- 2 tablespoons grated Parmesan cheese
- 2 teaspoons minced fresh parsley, basil, or chives (optional)

1. Adjust oven rack to middle position and heat oven to 375 degrees. Spread macaroni into greased 8-inch square baking dish or pan. Whisk evaporated milk, water, dry mustard, salt, and pepper together in bowl. Pour into baking dish and stir gently to combine.

2. Cover dish tightly with aluminum foil and bake, stirring occasionally, until macaroni is nearly tender, 30 to 35 minutes, rotating dish halfway through baking.

3. Remove dish from oven and stir macaroni thoroughly, scraping sides and bottom of dish. Stir in cheddar cheese and American cheese. Cover dish with foil and bake until macaroni is tender and cheese is melted, 10 to 15 minutes (mixture will seem loose).

4. Remove dish from oven. Stir to coat pasta evenly in sauce, and let cool while preparing topping. Toss panko with oil in bowl until evenly coated, then microwave, stirring occasionally, until deep golden brown, 1 to 4 minutes. Transfer dish to wire rack and let cool for 5 minutes, then stir in Parmesan and parsley, if using. Sprinkle casserole with panko and serve.

Baked Ziti with Creamy Leeks, Kale, and Sun-Dried Tomatoes

Serves 2 VEGETARIAN

Total Time: 1 hour

WHY THIS RECIPE WORKS The often-underestimated leek is the backbone of the aromatic sauce in this vegetable-forward baked ziti. We sautéed 1 pound of sliced leeks until they began to caramelize, added some thyme, deglazed the pan with a splash of white wine, and then simmered the mixture in water until the leeks were meltingly soft and ready to be blended into a velvety sauce. Sun-dried tomatoes, garlic and red pepper flakes delivered robust flavor, while baby kale provided another hearty vegetable element.

- ¼ cup panko bread crumbs
- 2 tablespoons extra-virgin olive oil, divided
- ½ teaspoon grated lemon zest, plus lemon wedges for serving
- 1 pound leeks, white and light green parts only, halved lengthwise, sliced thin, and washed thoroughly
- ½ teaspoon table salt, divided, plus salt for cooking pasta
- 1 teaspoon minced fresh thyme or ½ teaspoon dried
- ¼ cup dry white wine
- 3 garlic cloves, minced
- ⅛ teaspoon red pepper flakes
- 3 cups (3 ounces) baby kale
- 2 tablespoons oil-packed sun-dried tomatoes, chopped coarse
- 6 ounces (2 cups) ziti
- 1 tablespoon chopped fresh parsley

1. Adjust oven rack to upper-middle position and heat oven to 450 degrees. Combine panko, 1½ teaspoons oil, and lemon zest in small bowl; set aside.

2. Heat 1 tablespoon oil in large saucepan over medium heat until shimmering. Add leeks and ¼ teaspoon salt and cook until softened and lightly browned, 8 to 10 minutes. Stir in thyme and cook until fragrant, about 30 seconds. Stir in wine, scraping up any browned bits, and cook until nearly evaporated, about 1 minute. Stir in 1 cup water and bring to boil. Reduce heat to low; cover; and simmer until leeks are very tender, 6 to 8 minutes. Process leek mixture in blender until smooth, about 2 minutes; set aside.

3. Cook remaining 1½ teaspoons oil, garlic, and pepper flakes in now-empty saucepan over medium heat until fragrant, about 1 minute. Add kale, sun-dried tomatoes, and remaining ¼ teaspoon salt and cook, stirring occasionally, until kale is wilted and tomatoes are softened, about 2 minutes.

4. Meanwhile, bring 2 quarts water to boil in large pot. Add pasta and 1½ teaspoons salt and cook, stirring often, until al dente. Reserve ¾ cup cooking water, then drain pasta. Add pasta, leek mixture, and ½ cup reserved cooking water to saucepan with kale mixture. Adjust consistency with remaining reserved cooking water as needed (sauce should be thick but still creamy) and season with salt and pepper to taste.

5. Transfer pasta mixture to broiler-safe 8-inch square baking dish, smoothing top with rubber spatula. Cover tightly with aluminum foil and bake until sauce is bubbling, 10 to 12 minutes. Remove dish from oven and heat broiler. Remove aluminum foil and sprinkle panko mixture evenly over pasta. Broil until panko mixture is golden brown, about 2 minutes. Sprinkle with parsley and serve with lemon wedges.

Baked Manicotti

Serves 2 `VEGETARIAN`

Total time 1¼ hours, plus 15 minutes cooling

WHY THIS RECIPE WORKS Well-made versions of this Italian American classic, with tender pasta tubes stuffed with rich ricotta filling and blanketed with tomato sauce, can be eminently satisfying. But when cooking for two, the hassle of putting it all together hardly seems worth it. Stuffing and baking raw pasta tubes proved problematic, but soaking no-boil noodles until just pliable and rolling them up around the filling worked perfectly—and saved us the trouble of boiling the pasta separately. To ensure that our filling was thick and creamy, we mixed ricotta with a generous amount of mozzarella.

Baked Manicotti

Finally, just six ingredients whirred in the food processor gave us a fresh, bright tomato sauce in minutes. Do not substitute fat-free ricotta cheese.

SAUCE

- 1 (14.5-ounce) can diced tomatoes
- 1 tablespoon extra-virgin olive oil
- 2 garlic cloves, minced
- ¼ teaspoon table salt
- ⅛ teaspoon red pepper flakes (optional)
- 1 tablespoon chopped fresh basil

FILLING AND PASTA

- 8 ounces (1 cup) whole-milk or part-skim ricotta cheese
- 3 ounces whole-milk mozzarella cheese, shredded (¾ cup)
- 2 ounces Parmesan cheese, grated (1 cup), divided
- 1 large egg, lightly beaten
- 1 tablespoon chopped fresh basil
- ¼ teaspoon table salt
- ⅛ teaspoon pepper
- 6 no-boil lasagna noodles

1. FOR THE SAUCE Adjust oven rack to middle position and heat oven to 400 degrees. Process tomatoes and their juice, olive oil, garlic, salt, and pepper flakes, if using, in food processor until smooth, about 10 seconds. Transfer mixture to bowl and stir in basil.

2. FOR THE FILLING AND PASTA Combine ricotta, mozzarella, ½ cup Parmesan, egg, basil, salt, and pepper in bowl.

3. Fill large bowl halfway with boiling water. Slip noodles into water, one at a time. Let noodles soak until pliable, about 5 minutes, separating noodles with tip of knife to prevent sticking. Remove noodles from water and place in single layer on clean dish towels.

4. Spread ½ cup sauce over bottom of 9 by 5-inch loaf pan. Transfer noodles to counter with short sides facing you. Spread ¼ cup ricotta mixture evenly over bottom three-quarters of each noodle. Roll noodles up around filling and lay them seam side down in pan. Spoon remaining sauce over top to cover noodles completely. Sprinkle with remaining ½ cup Parmesan.

5. Cover pan tightly with aluminum foil and bake until bubbling, about 25 minutes. Remove foil and continue to bake until cheese is browned in spots, about 10 minutes. Let cool for 15 minutes before serving.

MAKING MANICOTTI

1. Using spoon, spread about ¼ cup of filling evenly over bottom three-quarters of each soaked noodle, leaving top quarter of noodles exposed.

2. Starting at bottom, roll each noodle up around filling, and lay in prepared loaf pan, seam side down.

Ultracreamy Spaghetti with Zucchini

Ultracreamy Spaghetti with Zucchini

Serves 2   VEGETARIAN

Total time 40 minutes

WHY THIS RECIPE WORKS When gardens and farmers' markets are teeming with zucchini, Spaghetti alla Nerano is the way to put pounds of the squash to work. From its verdant hue to its basil-tinged aroma, it is a celebration of summertime. To start, we microwaved thinly sliced rounds of zucchini with salt and water and then sautéed the drained, softened coins until they were lightly browned. Tossing al dente spaghetti with the zucchini, black pepper, basil, starchy pasta water, and butter created an emulsion that served as the base of a sauce, and adding a combination of mild provolone and Parmesan (to replicate the blend of local Italian cheeses traditionally used) made the sauce luxuriously creamy. Be sure to use zucchini that are smaller than 8 ounces because they contain fewer seeds. Use a 1¼-ounce block of mild provolone from the deli counter rather than presliced cheese.

1 pound small zucchini, sliced ⅛ inch thick

½ teaspoon table salt, plus salt for cooking pasta

1 tablespoon extra-virgin olive oil

6 ounces spaghetti

1 tablespoon unsalted butter

1 tablespoon chopped fresh basil

¼ teaspoon pepper

1¼ ounces mild provolone cheese, shredded (⅔ cup)

3 tablespoons grated Parmesan cheese

1. In large bowl, stir together zucchini, 2 tablespoons water, and salt. Cover and microwave until zucchini is softened (some slices will curl at edges) and liquid is released, 8 to 10 minutes, stirring halfway through microwaving. Drain zucchini in colander and let cool slightly, about 5 minutes.

2. Heat oil in 10-inch nonstick skillet over medium-high heat until shimmering. Add zucchini (do not wash colander) and spread into even layer. Cook, stirring every 4 minutes and then reflattening into even layer, until zucchini is very tender and about half of slices are lightly browned, 8 to 10 minutes (it is OK if some pieces fall apart). (Zucchini can be refrigerated for up to 2 days.)

3. Meanwhile, bring 2 quarts water to boil in large pot. Add pasta and 1½ teaspoons salt and cook, stirring often, until al dente. Reserve ¾ cup cooking water, then drain pasta and return it to pot.

4. Add ½ cup reserved cooking water, zucchini, butter, basil, and pepper to pasta. Set pot over low heat and cook, stirring and tossing pasta constantly, until ingredients are evenly distributed and butter is melted, about 1 minute. Off heat, add provolone and Parmesan. Stir vigorously until cheeses are melted and pasta is coated in creamy, lightly thickened sauce, about 1 minute, adjusting consistency with remaining reserved cooking water as needed. Transfer pasta to platter and serve immediately.

Skillet Pasta with Fresh Tomato Sauce

Serves 2   VEGETARIAN

Total time 45 minutes

WHY THIS RECIPE WORKS Most of the year, canned tomatoes offer better tomato flavor than their fresh counterparts do, but when fully ripe, juicy tomatoes are at their peak, we like to go with the real deal. For an effortless but flavorful pasta dinner featuring fresh tomatoes, we simmered the tomatoes briefly so they'd break down and release their juice, then added the pasta right to the pan to cook through. Not only

did the released pasta starch help to thicken the sauce, making it nicely clingy, but the pasta picked up good flavor from cooking in the sauce. A little tomato paste added depth, and a small amount of white wine contributed a brightness that rounded out the flavor of our sauce. Other pasta shapes can be substituted for the campanelle; however, their cup measurements may vary (see page 237). Serve with Parmesan cheese. You will need a 12-inch nonstick skillet with a tight-fitting lid for this recipe.

1 tablespoon extra-virgin olive oil

1 small onion, chopped fine

2 garlic cloves, minced

1½ teaspoons tomato paste

1 pound tomatoes, cored and cut into ½-inch pieces

½ teaspoon table salt

¼ teaspoon pepper

¼ cup dry white wine

2 cups water, plus extra as needed

6 ounces (2 cups) campanelle

2 tablespoons chopped fresh basil

1. Heat oil in 12-inch nonstick skillet over medium heat until shimmering. Add onion and cook until softened, about 5 minutes. Stir in garlic and tomato paste and cook until fragrant, about 1 minute. Stir in tomatoes, salt, and pepper and cook until tomato pieces lose their shape, 5 to 7 minutes. Stir in wine and simmer for 2 minutes.

2. Stir in water and pasta. Cover, increase heat to medium-high, and cook at vigorous simmer, stirring often, until pasta is nearly tender, 10 to 12 minutes.

3. Uncover and continue to simmer, tossing pasta gently, until pasta is tender and sauce is thickened, 3 to 5 minutes; if sauce becomes too thick, add extra water as needed. Off heat, stir in basil and season with salt and pepper to taste. Serve with Parmesan.

Skillet Penne with Chicken, Mushrooms, and Gorgonzola

Serves 2

Total time 50 minutes

WHY THIS RECIPE WORKS Looking for a hearty one-skillet pasta supper to add to our repertoire, we decided to pair tender chicken with earthy mushrooms and rich Gorgonzola cheese. Briefly sautéing a thinly sliced chicken breast was easy and created a flavorful fond on which we could build our sauce. Cooking the pasta right in the sauce was beneficial on two fronts:

The starch from the pasta thickened the sauce, while the pasta absorbed maximum flavor as it simmered. Cooking the mushrooms over medium heat and not crowding them in the skillet ensured that they browned rather than steamed. Other pasta shapes can be substituted for the penne; however, their cup measurements may vary (see page 237). You will need a 10-inch nonstick skillet with a tight-fitting lid for this recipe.

- 8 ounces boneless, skinless chicken breast, trimmed and sliced ¼ inch thick
- ⅛ teaspoon plus ¼ teaspoon table salt, divided Pinch pepper
- 2 tablespoons extra-virgin olive oil, divided
- 4 ounces white mushrooms, trimmed and quartered
- 3 garlic cloves, minced
- 1 teaspoon minced fresh oregano or ¼ teaspoon dried Pinch red pepper flakes
- ½ cup dry white wine
- 6 ounces (2 cups) penne
- 1½ cups chicken broth
- 1 cup water, plus extra as needed
- 1 ounce Gorgonzola cheese, crumbled (¼ cup), plus extra for serving
- 1 tablespoon unsalted butter
- 1 tablespoon minced fresh parsley

1. Pat chicken dry with paper towels and sprinkle with ⅛ teaspoon salt and pepper. Heat 1 tablespoon oil in 10-inch nonstick skillet over medium-high heat until just smoking. Add chicken; break up any clumps; and cook, without stirring, until beginning to brown, about 1 minute. Stir chicken and continue to cook until nearly cooked through, about 2 minutes; transfer to bowl.

2. Add remaining 1 tablespoon oil and mushrooms to now-empty skillet and cook over medium heat, stirring occasionally, until mushrooms have released their moisture and are golden brown, 7 to 10 minutes. Stir in garlic, oregano, and pepper flakes and cook until fragrant, about 30 seconds. Stir in wine; bring to simmer; and cook until nearly evaporated, about 2 minutes.

3. Stir in pasta, broth, water, and remaining ¼ teaspoon salt. Cover; increase heat to medium-high; and cook at vigorous simmer, stirring often, until pasta is tender and sauce is thickened, 12 to 15 minutes; if sauce becomes too thick, add extra water as needed.

4. Reduce heat to low and stir in cooked chicken along with any accumulated juices, Gorgonzola, and butter. Cook, uncovered, tossing pasta gently, until well coated with sauce, 1 to 2 minutes. Season with salt and pepper to taste and sprinkle with parsley. Serve with extra Gorgonzola.

VARIATIONS

Skillet Penne with Chicken, Cherry Tomatoes, and Olives

Substitute 1 small finely chopped onion for mushrooms and cook until softened, about 5 minutes. Add 6 ounces quartered cherry tomatoes and ¼ cup coarsely chopped pitted kalamata olives to pasta along with cooked chicken in step 4. Substitute ½ cup grated Parmesan cheese for Gorgonzola.

Skillet Penne with Chicken, Arugula, Pine Nuts, and Lemon

Substitute 1 small finely chopped onion for mushrooms and cook until softened, about 5 minutes. Add 3 ounces baby arugula to pasta along with cooked chicken in step 4. Substitute ½ cup grated Parmesan cheese for Gorgonzola. Stir 2 tablespoons toasted pine nuts and ¼ teaspoon grated lemon zest plus 1½ teaspoons juice into pasta along with parsley.

Skillet Weeknight Bolognese with Linguine

Serves 2
Total time 55 minutes

WHY THIS RECIPE WORKS Recipes for Bolognese typically feed a crowd and require hours of simmering, so we wanted to reinvent this dish as a weeknight meal for two. We skipped the step of browning the ground meat, which reduced the simmering time needed to make the meat tender; to replace the flavor lost from not browning the meat, we added pancetta, dried porcini, and a little minced anchovy. We chopped our aromatic ingredients in the food processor to save time, and cooked the pasta right in the sauce. If you can't find meatloaf mix, substitute 3 ounces each of ground pork and 90 percent lean ground beef. You will need a 12-inch nonstick skillet with a tight-fitting lid for this recipe.

- 1 small onion, cut into 1-inch pieces
- 1 carrot, peeled and cut into 1-inch pieces
- 1½ ounces pancetta, cut into 1-inch pieces
- ¼ ounce dried porcini mushrooms, rinsed
- ½ anchovy fillet, rinsed and patted dry
- 1 (14.5-ounce) can diced tomatoes
- 1 tablespoon unsalted butter
- 1 garlic clove, minced
- ½ teaspoon sugar
- 6 ounces meatloaf mix
- ¾ cup whole milk

1 tablespoon tomato paste
¼ cup dry white wine
2 cups water, plus extra as needed
6 ounces linguine
Grated Parmesan cheese

1. Pulse onion, carrot, pancetta, porcini, and anchovy in food processor until finely chopped, 10 to 15 pulses; transfer to bowl. Pulse tomatoes and their juice until mostly smooth, about 8 pulses.

2. Melt butter in 12-inch nonstick skillet over medium heat. Add pulsed onion mixture and cook until softened and lightly browned, 5 to 7 minutes. Stir in garlic and sugar and cook until fragrant, about 30 seconds. Stir in meatloaf mix, breaking up meat with wooden spoon, and cook for 1 minute. Stir in milk, scraping up any browned bits. Bring to simmer and cook until milk is almost completely evaporated, 8 to 10 minutes.

3. Stir in tomato paste and cook for 1 minute. Stir in wine; bring to simmer; and cook until almost completely evaporated, 3 to 5 minutes.

4. Stir in pulsed tomatoes, water, and pasta. Cover; increase heat to medium-high; and cook at vigorous simmer, stirring often, until pasta is tender and sauce is thickened, 12 to 16 minutes; if sauce becomes too thick, add extra water as needed. Off heat, season with salt and pepper to taste. Serve with Parmesan.

RINSING DRIED PORCINI

To remove dirt or grit from dried porcini, place porcini in fine-mesh strainer and run under water, using fingers as needed to rub grit out of crevices.

Skillet Mussels Marinara with Spaghetti

Serves 2

Total time 50 minutes

WHY THIS RECIPE WORKS Creating a one-skillet mussels marinara—featuring mussels draped in a mildly spicy, brothy tomato sauce—turned out to be easier than we thought. Not only could we cook the pasta right in the sauce but we added the mussels to the simmering sauce as well, which saved us

Skillet Mussels Marinara with Spaghetti

the step of steaming them in a separate pot. Any type of mussel will work here. When adding the pasta in step 3, stir gently to avoid breaking the noodles; after a minute or two they will soften enough to be stirred more easily. You will need a 12-inch nonstick skillet with a tight-fitting lid for this recipe.

1 (28-ounce) can whole peeled tomatoes
4 teaspoons extra-virgin olive oil, divided, plus extra for serving
1 small onion, chopped fine
3 garlic cloves, minced
½ anchovy fillet, rinsed, patted dry, and minced
¼ teaspoon red pepper flakes
1½ cups water, plus hot water as needed
½ cup bottled clam juice
6 ounces spaghetti
1 pound mussels, scrubbed and debearded
2 tablespoons minced fresh parsley

ALL ABOUT PARMESAN

Parmesan is classified as a grana-type cheese: a hard, grainy cheese made from cow's milk. It has a rich, sharp flavor and a melt-in-your mouth texture. We frequently reach for it to sprinkle on top of pasta dishes or to add a rich, salty flavor to sauces, soups, and stews. Note that not all Parmesan is vegetarian.

BUYING PARMESAN We recommend authentic Italian Parmigiano-Reggiano, which has a complex flavor and smooth, melting texture that none of the others can match. Most of the other Parmesan-type cheeses are too salty and one-dimensional. When shopping, make sure some portion of the words "Parmigiano-Reggiano" is stenciled on the golden rind. To ensure that you're buying a properly aged cheese, examine the condition of the rind. It should be a few shades darker than the straw-colored interior and penetrate about ½ inch deep (younger or improperly aged cheeses will have a paler, thinner rind). And closely scrutinize the center of the cheese. Those small white spots found on many samples are actually good things—they signify the presence of calcium phosphate crystals, which are formed only after the cheese has been aged for the proper amount of time.

STORING PARMESAN After a number of tests to find the optimal storage method for Parmesan, we found that the best way to preserve its flavor and texture is to wrap it in parchment paper, then aluminum foil. However, if you have just a small piece of cheese, tossing it in a zipper-lock bag works almost as well; just be sure to squeeze out as much air as possible before sealing the bag. Note that these methods also work for Pecorino Romano.

PARMESAN VS. PECORINO ROMANO

While Parmesan is a cow's milk cheese, Pecorino Romano is made from sheep's milk. We have found that Parmesan and Pecorino Romano generally can be used interchangeably, especially when the amount called for is moderate. However, when Parmesan is called for in larger quantities, it is best to stick with the Parmesan, as Pecorino Romano can be fairly pungent.

1. Pulse tomatoes and their juice in food processor until coarsely chopped and no large pieces remain, 6 to 8 pulses.

2. Heat 1 tablespoon oil in 12-inch nonstick skillet over medium heat until shimmering. Add onion and cook until softened, about 5 minutes. Stir in garlic, anchovy, and pepper flakes and cook until fragrant, about 30 seconds. Stir in pulsed tomatoes; bring to gentle simmer; and cook, stirring occasionally, until tomatoes no longer taste raw, about 10 minutes.

3. Stir in water, clam juice, and pasta. Cover; increase heat to medium-high; and cook at vigorous simmer, stirring often, for 12 minutes. Stir in mussels; cover; and continue to simmer vigorously until pasta is tender and mussels have opened, about 2 minutes.

4. Reduce heat to low and stir in remaining 1 teaspoon oil and parsley. Cook, uncovered, tossing pasta gently, until pasta is well coated with sauce, 1 to 2 minutes. If sauce is too thick, add hot water, 1 tablespoon at a time, as needed. Discard any mussels that have not opened and season with salt and pepper to taste. Drizzle individual portions with extra oil and serve.

Skillet Tortellini with Crispy Prosciutto and Spring Vegetables

Serves 2

Total time 40 minutes

WHY THIS RECIPE WORKS The convenience of store-bought tortellini is undeniable, but when simply topped with store-bought pasta sauce, it can be bland and uninspired. We wanted properly cooked tortellini, fresh vegetables, and a luxurious, flavor-packed sauce—all cooked in one skillet. Simmering the tortellini in chicken broth rather than water infused it with savory flavor. A little cream added sweet richness to our sauce, and some lemon juice contributed a contrasting brightness. Fennel, spinach, and peas offered color and fresh spring flavor, and a sprinkling of salty, crisp prosciutto provided a welcome meatiness. Fresh tortellini won out over frozen or dried for its superior texture and flavor. Because the tortellini cooks right in the sauce, fresh tortellini should be used; do not substitute dried or frozen tortellini. You will need a 12-inch nonstick skillet with a tight-fitting lid for this recipe.

- 1 ounce thinly sliced prosciutto, cut into ¼-inch pieces
- 1 tablespoon unsalted butter
- 1 small fennel bulb, stalks discarded, bulb halved, cored, and cut into ½-inch pieces
- 2 garlic cloves, minced
- 2 cups chicken broth

1 (9-ounce) package fresh cheese tortellini
3 ounces (3 cups) baby spinach
½ cup frozen peas
¼ cup heavy cream
¼ cup grated Parmesan cheese, plus extra for serving
2 teaspoons lemon juice

1. Cook prosciutto in 12-inch nonstick skillet over medium heat until browned and crisp, 5 to 7 minutes. Using slotted spoon, transfer prosciutto to paper towel–lined plate; set aside.

2. Add butter to fat left in skillet and heat over medium heat until melted. Add fennel and cook until softened and lightly browned, 6 to 9 minutes. Stir in garlic and cook until fragrant, about 30 seconds.

3. Stir in broth and pasta. Cover; increase heat to medium-high; and cook at vigorous simmer, stirring often, until pasta is tender and sauce is thickened, 6 to 9 minutes; if sauce becomes too thick, add water as needed.

4. Reduce heat to low; stir in spinach, peas, and cream; and cook, stirring gently but constantly, until spinach is wilted and pasta is well coated with sauce, 2 to 3 minutes. Off heat, stir in Parmesan and lemon juice and season with salt and pepper to taste. Sprinkle individual portions with reserved crisp prosciutto and serve with extra Parmesan.

Meaty Skillet Lasagna

Serves 2

Total time 50 minutes

WHY THIS RECIPE WORKS We wanted a recipe for meaty lasagna that we could make entirely on the stovetop, and we wanted to scale it down in size. Half a pound of 85 percent lean ground beef offered good flavor and plenty of richness. A large can of whole tomatoes, pulsed briefly in the food processor, gave our sauce a substantial texture—and provided enough liquid to cook the noodles. Stirring in the mozzarella and Parmesan provided a cohesive structure to the dish, but we decided to dollop the ricotta on top so that it remained its own distinct element. Do not substitute no-boil lasagna noodles for the traditional, curly-edged lasagna noodles here. You can substitute part-skim ricotta if desired, but do not use non-fat ricotta. You will need a 10-inch nonstick skillet with a tight-fitting lid for this recipe.

1 (28-ounce) can whole peeled tomatoes
2 teaspoons extra-virgin olive oil
1 small onion, chopped fine

¼ teaspoon table salt
1 garlic clove, minced
Pinch red pepper flakes
8 ounces 85 percent lean ground beef
5 curly-edged lasagna noodles, broken into 2-inch lengths
¼ cup shredded mozzarella cheese, divided
2 tablespoons grated Parmesan cheese, divided
3 ounces (⅓ cup) whole-milk ricotta cheese
2 tablespoons chopped fresh basil

1. Pulse tomatoes and their juice in food processor until coarsely ground and no large pieces remain, 6 to 8 pulses.

2. Heat oil in 10-inch nonstick skillet over medium heat until shimmering. Add onion and salt and cook until softened, about 5 minutes. Stir in garlic and pepper flakes and cook until fragrant, about 30 seconds. Add ground beef and cook, breaking up meat with wooden spoon, until no longer pink, 3 to 5 minutes.

3. Scatter noodles over meat, then pour pulsed tomatoes over pasta. Cover; increase heat to medium-high; and cook at vigorous simmer, stirring often, until pasta is tender, about 20 minutes.

4. Off heat, stir in 2 tablespoons mozzarella and 1 tablespoon Parmesan. Season with salt and pepper to taste. Dollop heaping tablespoons of ricotta over noodles, then sprinkle with remaining 2 tablespoons mozzarella and remaining 1 tablespoon Parmesan. Off heat, cover and let sit until cheese is melted, 2 to 4 minutes. Sprinkle with basil and serve.

VARIATION

Skillet Lasagna with Italian Sausage and Bell Pepper

Substitute 8 ounces hot or sweet Italian sausage, casings removed, for ground beef. Add ½ red bell pepper, chopped coarse, to skillet with onion.

BREAKING LASAGNA NOODLES

To make sure lasagna noodles cook through evenly in skillet, we break them into 2-inch pieces using our hands. Be sure to use traditional curly-edged, not no-boil, lasagna noodles here.

Fideos with Chickpeas and Goat Cheese

Fideos with Chickpeas and Goat Cheese

Serves 2   `VEGETARIAN`

Total time 50 minutes

WHY THIS RECIPE WORKS Fideos, a richly flavored and incredibly popular Spanish dish, calls for breaking noodles into small lengths and toasting them before cooking them with seafood and chorizo in a garlicky tomato stock. We thought the base of bold tomatoes and toasted noodles would work well with chickpeas, so we developed a plant-forward version using the bean and creamy goat cheese. You can substitute traditional spaghetti for the whole-wheat spaghetti.

- 4 ounces 100 percent whole-wheat thin spaghetti
- 4 teaspoons extra-virgin olive oil, divided
- 1 small onion, chopped fine
- 2 tomatoes, cored and chopped
- 2 garlic cloves, minced
- 1 teaspoon smoked paprika
- 1½ cups vegetable or chicken broth
- 1 (15-ounce) can chickpeas, rinsed
- ¼ cup dry white wine
- ½ teaspoon pepper
- ½ cup crumbled goat cheese
- 1 tablespoon chopped fresh parsley
  Lemon wedges

1. Break spaghetti into 1- to 2-inch lengths. Toast pasta in 1 teaspoon oil in 10- or 12-inch broiler-safe skillet over medium-high heat, tossing frequently with tongs, until pasta is well browned and releases nutty aroma (pasta should be color of peanut butter), 6 to 10 minutes; transfer to bowl.

2. Heat 2 teaspoons oil in now-empty skillet over medium heat until shimmering. Add onion and cook until softened and lightly browned, 4 to 6 minutes. Stir in tomatoes and cook until softened, 3 to 5 minutes. Stir in garlic and paprika and cook until fragrant, about 30 seconds. Stir in toasted pasta, broth, chickpeas, wine, and pepper and bring to simmer. Cook, stirring gently and often, until liquid is thickened and pasta is just tender, 8 to 10 minutes.

3. Adjust oven rack 6 inches from broiler element and heat broiler. Off heat, sprinkle goat cheese over fideos and drizzle with remaining 1 teaspoon oil. Transfer skillet to oven and broil until surface of pasta is dry with crisped, browned spots, 3 to 5 minutes. Using pot holder, remove skillet from oven and let sit for 5 minutes. Sprinkle each portion with parsley and serve with lemon wedges.

Japchae

Chilled Soba Noodles with Cucumber, Snow Peas, and Radishes

Serves 2 | VEGETARIAN

Total time 35 minutes

WHY THIS RECIPE WORKS Soba noodles, made from buckwheat flour or a buckwheat-wheat flour blend, have a chewy texture and nutty flavor and are often enjoyed chilled. For a refreshing cold noodle salad, we cooked soba noodles in unsalted boiling water until tender but still resilient and rinsed them under cold running water to remove excess starch and prevent sticking. We then tossed the soba with a miso-based dressing, which clung to and flavored the noodles without overpowering their distinct taste. We also cut a mix of vegetables into varying sizes so they'd incorporate nicely into the noodles while adding crunch and color. Sprinkling strips of toasted nori over the top added more texture and a subtle briny taste. Sheets of nori, a dried seaweed that adds a subtle briny umami flavor and crisp texture to this salad, can be found in packets at Asian markets or in the Asian section of the supermarket. Plain pretoasted seaweed snacks can be substituted for the roasted nori, and yellow, red, or brown miso can be substituted for the white miso, if desired. This dish isn't meant to be overtly spicy, but if you prefer more heat, use the full ¼ teaspoon of red pepper flakes. These chilled noodles pair nicely with salmon, shrimp, tofu, or chicken for lunch or a light dinner.

  4 ounces dried soba noodles
  ½ (8-inch square) sheet nori (optional)
  1½ tablespoons white miso
  1½ tablespoons mirin
  1 tablespoon toasted sesame oil
  1½ teaspoons sesame seeds
  ½ teaspoon grated fresh ginger
  ⅛–¼ teaspoon red pepper flakes
  ¼ English cucumber, quartered lengthwise, seeded, and sliced thin on bias
  2 ounces snow peas, strings removed, cut lengthwise into matchsticks
  2 radishes, trimmed, halved, and sliced into thin half-moons
  2 scallions, sliced thin on bias

1. Bring 2 quarts water to boil in large pot. Stir in noodles and cook, stirring occasionally, until noodles are cooked through but still retain some chew. Drain noodles and rinse under cold water until chilled. Drain well and transfer to large bowl.

2. Grip nori sheet, if using, with tongs and hold about 2 inches above low flame on gas burner. Toast, flipping nori every 3 to 5 seconds, until nori is aromatic and shrinks slightly, about 20 seconds. If you do not have a gas stove, toast nori on rimmed baking sheet in 275-degree oven until it is aromatic and shrinks slightly, 20 to 25 minutes, flipping nori halfway through toasting. Using scissors, cut nori into 1-inch strips.

3. Combine miso, mirin, oil, 1½ teaspoons water, sesame seeds, ginger, and pepper flakes in small bowl and whisk until smooth. Add dressing to noodles and toss to combine. Add cucumber; snow peas; radishes; scallions; and nori, if using, and toss well to evenly distribute. Season with salt to taste, and serve.

Japchae

Serves 2 | VEGETARIAN

Total time 40 minutes

WHY THIS RECIPE WORKS One of Korea's most beloved celebratory dishes often reserved for Korean royalty throughout history, japchae is made using semi-transparent sweet potato starch noodles and a riot of colorful vegetables for a result that is both stunning and delicious. The sauce is made from toasted sesame oil, soy sauce, sugar, sesame seeds, and garlic. After we cooked the noodles, we stir-fried earthy shiitake mushrooms with carrot and onion until just crisp-tender before we stirred in a generous portion of baby spinach, which wilted in mere minutes. You will need a 14-inch flat-bottomed wok or 12-inch nonstick skillet with a tight-fitting lid for this recipe. Sweet potato noodles are sometimes sold as sweet potato starch noodles or sweet potato glass noodles.

  6 ounces (⅛-inch-wide) dried sweet potato noodles, broken into 12-inch lengths
  1 tablespoon toasted sesame oil, divided
  2 tablespoons vegetable oil, divided
  2 scallions, white and green parts separated and sliced thin
  2 garlic cloves, minced, divided
  2 tablespoons soy sauce
  1½ teaspoons sugar
  1½ teaspoons sesame seeds, toasted
  4 ounces shiitake mushrooms, stemmed and sliced thin
  1 carrot, peeled and cut into 2-inch-long matchsticks
  1 small onion, sliced thin
  4 ounces (4 cups) baby spinach

1. Bring 2 quarts water to boil in large pot. Off heat, add noodles and let sit, stirring occasionally, until softened and pliable but not fully tender, about 10 minutes. Drain noodles, rinse well, and drain again. Toss noodles with 1 teaspoon sesame oil; set aside.

2. Meanwhile, combine 1 tablespoon vegetable oil, scallion whites, and half of garlic in small bowl; set aside. Whisk soy sauce, sugar, sesame seeds, remaining 2 teaspoons sesame oil, and remaining garlic in second small bowl until sugar has dissolved; set aside.

3. Heat remaining 1 tablespoon vegetable oil in 14-inch flat-bottomed wok or 12-inch nonstick skillet over medium-high heat until just smoking. Add mushrooms, carrot, and onion; increase heat to high; and cook, stirring often, until vegetables are crisp-tender and lightly browned, 5 to 7 minutes. Stir in spinach and cook until wilted, about 2 minutes.

4. Push vegetables to 1 side of wok. Add scallion white mixture to clearing and cook, mashing mixture into wok, until fragrant, about 30 seconds. Stir scallion white mixture into vegetables. Add noodles and soy sauce mixture and cook, tossing gently, until noodles are well coated and tender, 2 to 4 minutes. Transfer noodles to serving bowls and sprinkle with scallion greens. Serve.

Dan Dan Mian

Serves 2

Total time 1¼ hours

WHY THIS RECIPE WORKS Sichuan's most popular street food, dan dan mian, consists of chewy noodles bathed in a spicy, fragrant chili sauce and topped with crispy, deeply savory bits of pork and plump lengths of baby bok choy. Gently heating Sichuan chili flakes, ground Sichuan peppercorns, and cinnamon in vegetable oil yielded a flavorful chili oil base for the sauce. Whisking in soy sauce, Chinese black vinegar, sweet wheat paste, and Chinese sesame paste added earthy, faintly sweet depth and appropriately thickened the mixture. We smeared the ground pork into a thin layer across the wok with a rubber spatula to break it up into bits, and seared it hard to produce crispy bits that clung to the noodles. Next, we stirred in minced garlic and grated ginger, plus a big scoop of the Sichuan pickle called ya cai, for added unique tang. If you can't find Sichuan chili flakes, substitute gochugaru (Korean red pepper flakes). Sichuan peppercorns provide a tingly, numbing sensation that's important to this dish. We prefer the chewy texture of fresh, eggless Chinese wheat noodles here. If they aren't available, substitute fresh lo mein or ramen noodles or 4 ounces of dried lo mein noodles. Ya cai, Sichuan preserved mustard greens, gives these noodles a savory and pungent boost; you can buy it online or at an Asian market. If ya cai is unavailable, increase the soy sauce in step 2 to 1 teaspoon.

SAUCE

- 2 tablespoons vegetable oil
- 1½ teaspoons Sichuan chili flakes
- 1 teaspoon Sichuan peppercorns, ground fine
- ⅛ teaspoon ground cinnamon
- 1 tablespoon soy sauce
- 1 teaspoon Chinese black vinegar
- 1 teaspoon sweet wheat paste or hoisin sauce
- ¾ teaspoon Chinese sesame paste or tahini

NOODLES

- 4 ounces ground pork
- 1 teaspoon Shaoxing wine or dry sherry
- ½ teaspoon soy sauce
- 1 small head baby bok choy (about 3 ounces)
- 1½ teaspoons vegetable oil, divided
- 2 garlic cloves, minced
- 1 teaspoon grated fresh ginger
- 8 ounces fresh Chinese wheat noodles
- 3 tablespoons ya cai
- 1 scallion, sliced thin on bias

1. FOR THE SAUCE Heat oil, chili flakes, peppercorns, and cinnamon in 14-inch flat-bottomed wok or 10-inch non-stick skillet over low heat for 10 minutes. Using rubber spatula, transfer oil mixture to bowl (do not wash wok). Whisk soy sauce, vinegar, wheat paste, and sesame paste into oil mixture. Divide evenly among 2 shallow bowls.

2. FOR THE NOODLES Bring 2 quarts water to boil in large pot. While water comes to boil, combine pork, Shaoxing wine, and soy sauce in medium bowl and toss with your hands until well combined. Set aside. Trim base from bok choy (larger leaves will fall off); halve lengthwise through core. Rinse well.

3. Heat 1 teaspoon oil in now-empty wok over medium-high heat until shimmering. Add reserved pork mixture and use rubber spatula to smear into thin layer across surface of wok. Break up meat into ¼-inch chunks with side of spatula and cook, stirring frequently, until pork is firm and well browned, about 4 minutes. Push pork mixture to far side of wok and add garlic, ginger, and remaining ½ teaspoon oil to cleared space. Cook, stirring constantly, until garlic mixture begins to brown, about 30 seconds. Stir to combine pork mixture with garlic mixture. Remove wok from heat.

Dan Dan Mian

4. Add bok choy to boiling water and cook until leaves are vibrant green and stems are crisp-tender, about 1 minute. Using slotted spoon or spider skimmer, transfer bok choy to plate; set aside. Add noodles to boiling water and cook, stirring often, until almost tender (center should still be firm with slightly opaque dot). Drain noodles. Rinse under hot running water, tossing with tongs, for 1 minute. Drain well.

5. Divide noodles evenly among prepared bowls. Return wok to medium heat. Add ya cai and cook, stirring frequently, until warmed through, about 1 minute. Spoon equal amounts of pork topping over noodles. Divide bok choy evenly among bowls, shaking to remove excess moisture as you portion. Top with scallions and serve, leaving each diner to stir components together before eating.

Lemongrass Beef and Rice Noodle Bowl

Serves 2

Total time 45 minutes

WHY THIS RECIPE WORKS Inspired by Vietnamese bun bo xao, this dish consists of dressed rice noodles topped with beef, crunchy vegetables, herbs, and peanuts. To start, we soaked the noodles in boiling water off the heat and then drained and rinsed them twice. Then we assembled a pungent dressing (for serving) of lime juice, fish sauce, lemongrass, sugar, and chili-garlic sauce. We tossed the flank steak with a marinade made with the same ingredients, seared it over high heat, then sliced it thinly. To serve, two bowls of noodles were topped with the steak, carrot, cucumber, and sprouts and drizzled with the reserved sauce. To prepare lemongrass, trim stalk to bottom 6 inches, trim root end, and remove any dried outer layers; mince.

　6　ounces rice vermicelli

1½　teaspoons vegetable oil, divided

　2　tablespoons lime juice, plus lime wedges for serving

　2　tablespoons fish sauce, divided

　1　tablespoon minced lemongrass, divided

1½　teaspoons sugar, divided

　1　teaspoon chili-garlic sauce, divided

　8　ounces flank steak, trimmed

　1　carrot, peeled and cut into 2-inch-long matchsticks

　¼　English cucumber, cut into 2-inch-long matchsticks

　1　ounce (½ cup) bean sprouts

　2　tablespoons Thai basil and/or mint leaves

　1　tablespoon dry-roasted peanuts, chopped

Lemongrass Beef and Rice Noodle Bowl

1. Bring 2 quarts water to boil in large saucepan. Off heat, add noodles and let sit, stirring occasionally, until tender, about 5 minutes. Drain noodles, rinse well, and drain again. Toss noodles with ½ teaspoon oil; set aside. Whisk lime juice, 5 teaspoons fish sauce, 1½ teaspoons lemongrass, 1 teaspoon sugar, and ½ teaspoon chili-garlic sauce together in small bowl until sugar is dissolved; set sauce aside.

2. Whisk remaining 1 teaspoon fish sauce, remaining 1½ teaspoons lemongrass, remaining ½ teaspoon sugar, and remaining ½ teaspoon chili-garlic sauce together in bowl. Add steak and toss to coat. Heat remaining 1 teaspoon oil in 10- or 12-inch skillet over medium- high heat until just smoking. Add steak and cook until well browned and meat registers 120 to 125 degrees (for medium-rare) or 130 to 135 degrees (for medium), 3 to 6 minutes per side. Transfer steak to cutting board, tent loosely with aluminum foil, and let rest for 5 minutes.

3. Slice steak thin against grain. Divide noodles between serving bowls, then top each portion with steak, carrot, cucumber, and sprouts. Whisk any accumulated juices from steak into reserved sauce and drizzle evenly over each portion. Sprinkle with basil and peanuts. Serve with lime wedges.

Ramen with Pork and Cabbage

Serves 2

Total time 1 hour

WHY THIS RECIPE WORKS Instant ramen might come with microwave instructions, but the quick preparation doesn't do these Japanese noodles justice. For our recipe, we kept the instant noodles but ditched the salty seasoning packet in favor of building our own sauce. We started by stir-frying marinated thinly sliced country-style pork ribs in a 12-inch nonstick skillet, which was big enough to hold the pork, vegetables, and noodles. Next, we added scallions, cooking until softened before adding garlic, ginger, and red pepper flakes. Chicken broth, oyster sauce, and sesame oil created a sauce with savory, sweet flavor in which we simmered the ramen until it was tender and the sauce was thickened. Green cabbage, stirred in at the end, added freshness. It doesn't matter which flavor of ramen noodles you buy since you won't be using the seasoning packets sold with the noodles. To make the pork easier to slice, freeze it for 15 minutes. The sauce in this dish will seem a bit brothy when finished, but the liquid will be absorbed quickly by the noodles when serving. You will need a 12-inch nonstick skillet with a tight-fitting lid for this recipe.

1½ teaspoons water

⅛ teaspoon baking soda

8 ounces boneless country-style pork ribs, trimmed and sliced thin crosswise

4 teaspoons soy sauce, divided

¼ teaspoon cornstarch

1 tablespoon vegetable oil, divided

6 scallions, white and green parts separated, sliced thin on bias

3 garlic cloves, minced

1 teaspoon grated fresh ginger

Pinch red pepper flakes

1¾ cups chicken broth

1 tablespoon oyster sauce

1 teaspoon toasted sesame oil

2 (3-ounce) packages ramen noodles, seasoning packets discarded

1½ cups shredded green cabbage

1. Combine water and baking soda in medium bowl. Add pork and toss to coat; let sit for 5 minutes. Add 1 teaspoon soy sauce and cornstarch and toss until well combined.

2. Heat 1½ teaspoons vegetable oil in 12-inch nonstick skillet over medium-high heat until just smoking. Add pork in single layer, breaking up any clumps, and cook, without stirring, until browned on bottom, about 1 minute. Stir and continue to cook until pork is no longer pink, about 1 minute; transfer to clean bowl.

3. Heat remaining 1½ teaspoons vegetable oil in now-empty skillet over medium-high heat until shimmering. Add scallion whites and cook until softened, about 2 minutes. Stir in garlic, ginger, and pepper flakes and cook until fragrant, about 30 seconds. Stir in broth, oyster sauce, sesame oil, and remaining 1 tablespoon soy sauce and bring to boil. Arrange noodles in skillet in even layer; you may need to break noodles to fit. Cover; reduce heat to medium; and simmer until noodles have softened on bottoms (tops will still be dry), about 3 minutes.

4. Uncover pot and, using tongs, flip noodles and stir to separate. Stir in cabbage and scallion greens and cook until noodles are tender and cabbage is wilted, about 2 minutes. Stir in pork along with any accumulated juices and cook until heated through, about 30 seconds. Serve.

CHAPTER 10
Grilling

■ **FAST** (Start to finish in 30 minutes or less)
■ **VEGETARIAN**

Opposite: Grilled Shrimp and Vegetable Kebabs

Grilling Basics

SETTING UP A FIRE

The fire setup—how much charcoal or how many burners you're using and where the heat is located in relation to the food—allows you to control the heat level and the rate of cooking. Using the wrong setup can cause food to burn before it's cooked through or cook through without developing any flavorful browning or char.

BEST PRACTICE Use the fire setup that's appropriate for the type of food you're grilling. We use four main fire setups, and we follow these guidelines when choosing which to use.

FIRE TYPE

SINGLE-LEVEL FIRE A single-level fire delivers a uniform level of heat across the entire cooking surface and is often used for small, quick-cooking pieces of food, such as sausages, some fish, and some vegetables.

HALF-GRILL FIRE Like a two-level fire, this fire has two cooking zones. One side is intensely hot, and the other side is comparatively cool. It's great for cooking fatty foods, because the cooler zone provides a place to set food while flare-ups die down. For foods that require long cooking times, you can brown the food on the hotter side, then set it on the cooler side to finish with indirect heat. It's also good for cooking chicken breasts gently over the cooler side, then giving them a quick sear on the hotter side.

CONCENTRATED FIRE Corralling the coals in a disposable pan concentrates the heat to create an intense fire ideal for quick-cooking foods that we want to give a substantial char.

TWO-LEVEL FIRE Like a half-grill fire, this setup creates two cooking zones: a hotter area for searing and a slightly cooler area to cook food more gently. It is often used for thick chops and bone-in chicken pieces.

FOUR BASIC FIRE SETUPS

SINGLE-LEVEL FIRE

Charcoal Setup	Distribute the lit coals in an even layer across the bottom of the grill.
Gas Setup	After preheating the grill, turn all the burners to the heat setting as directed in the recipe.

HALF-GRILL FIRE

Charcoal Setup	Distribute the lit coals over half of the grill, piling them in an even layer. Leave the other half of the grill free of coals.
Gas Setup	After preheating the grill, adjust primary burner (or, if using 3-burner grill, primary burner and second burner) as needed.

CONCENTRATED FIRE

| Charcoal Setup | Poke holes in bottom of large disposable aluminum pan, place pan in center of grill, and pour lit coals into pan. |
| Gas Setup | After preheating the grill, turn all the burners to the heat setting as directed in the recipe. |

TWO-LEVEL FIRE

| Charcoal Setup | Evenly distribute two-thirds of the lit coals over half of the grill, then distribute the remainder of the coals in an even layer over the other half of the grill. |
| Gas Setup | After preheating the grill, leave the primary burner on high and turn the other(s) to medium. The primary burner is the one that must be left on. |

DON'T COOK ON A GUNKED-UP GRILL

Food debris, grease, and smoke that build up on various parts of the grill can cause sticking and impart off-flavors to food; full grease traps can ignite; and built-up grease on the interior basin and underside of the grill lid can carbonize and turn into a patchy layer that flakes off and lands on your food.

HOW TO CLEAN YOUR GRILL

COOKING GRATE After preheating the grill, scrape the cooking grate clean with a grill brush.

INTERIOR BASIN AND LID Lightly scrub the cool grill and lid with steel wool and water.

ASH CATCHER (CHARCOAL ONLY) Empty the cooled ash regularly.

GREASE TRAPS (GAS ONLY) Remove the cool shallow pan from under your grill and scrub it with hot soapy water. To make cleanup easier, line the pan with aluminum foil before use.

OILING THE COOKING GRATE

Most cooking grates are made of steel or cast iron and must be oiled before grilling to keep food from sticking.

BEST PRACTICE Using tongs, dip a wad of paper towels in vegetable oil and thoroughly wipe the preheated, scrubbed cooking grate before adding food.

Grilled Chicken Fajitas

Serves 2

Total time 50 minutes, plus 15 minutes marinating

WHY THIS RECIPE WORKS We wanted fajitas with a combination of smoky grilled vegetables and strips of juicy chicken wrapped up in warm flour tortillas. Marinating the chicken gave it a bright, tangy flavor. We built a two-level fire by pouring two-thirds of the coals over one half of the grill and the remaining one-third of the coals over the other half. Creating a hotter side and a cooler side allowed us to grill the chicken and the peppers and onions simultaneously. When both the chicken and vegetables were spottily browned, we finished them with a burst of fresh flavor by tossing them with some reserved marinade. Do not marinate the chicken for longer than 15 minutes or the lime juice will make the meat mushy. To make this dish spicier, reserve and add the chile seeds as desired. You will need one 12-inch metal skewer for this recipe. See page 259 for information on how to set up a two-level fire. Serve with your favorite fajita toppings.

Grilled Chicken Fajitas

5 tablespoons vegetable oil, divided

¼ cup lime juice (2 limes)

2 tablespoons chopped fresh cilantro

3 garlic cloves, minced

1 tablespoon Worcestershire sauce

1½ teaspoons packed brown sugar

1 jalapeño chile, stemmed, seeded, and minced

1 teaspoon table salt for the marinade

½ teaspoon plus pinch pepper, divided

2 (6- to 8-ounce) boneless, skinless chicken breasts, trimmed and pounded to even thickness

1 small red onion, sliced into ½-inch rings (do not separate rings)

1 red, yellow, or orange bell pepper, stemmed, seeded, and quartered

⅛ teaspoon table salt

6 (6-inch) flour tortillas

1. Whisk ¼ cup oil, lime juice, cilantro, garlic, Worcestershire, sugar, jalapeño, ½ teaspoon salt, and ½ teaspoon pepper together in bowl. Transfer ¼ cup marinade to separate bowl; set aside for serving.

2. Add ½ teaspoon salt to remaining marinade, combine with chicken in 1-gallon zipper-lock bag, seal bag tightly, and toss to coat. Let chicken marinate in refrigerator for 15 minutes. Thread onion rings, from side to side, onto 12-inch metal skewer. Brush onion and bell pepper with remaining 1 tablespoon oil and sprinkle with ⅛ teaspoon salt and remaining pinch pepper.

3A. FOR A CHARCOAL GRILL Open bottom vent completely. Light large chimney starter filled with charcoal briquettes (6 quarts). When top coals are partially covered with ash, pour two-thirds evenly over half of grill, then pour remaining coals over other half of grill. Set cooking grate in place, cover, and open lid vent completely. Heat grill until hot, about 5 minutes.

3B. FOR A GAS GRILL Turn all burners to high; cover; and heat grill until hot, about 15 minutes. Leave primary burner on high and turn other burner(s) to medium. (Adjust burners as needed to maintain hot fire and medium fire on separate sides of grill.)

4. Clean and oil cooking grate. Remove chicken from marinade and place on hotter side of grill. Place onion rings and bell pepper on cooler side of grill. Cook (covered if using gas), turning chicken and vegetables as needed, until chicken is browned and registers 160 degrees and vegetables are spottily charred, 8 to 12 minutes. Transfer chicken and vegetables to cutting board, tent loosely with aluminum foil, and let rest while grilling tortillas.

5. Place tortillas on hotter side of grill in single layer and cook until warmed and lightly browned on both sides, about 15 seconds per side. Stack grilled tortillas in foil packet to keep warm and soft until serving.

6. Separate onion rings and slice bell pepper into ¼-inch strips. Toss vegetables with half of reserved marinade in bowl. Slice chicken into ¼-inch strips and toss with remaining marinade in separate bowl. Arrange chicken and vegetables on serving platter and serve with warm tortillas.

VARIATION
Grilled Beef Fajitas

Substitute 12 ounces flank steak for chicken. Grill steak over hotter side of grill, turning as needed, until well browned and registers 120 to 125 degrees (for medium-rare), about 8 minutes. Slice steak thin against grain before tossing with marinade.

GRILLING TORTILLAS

Grill tortillas in single layer until soft and lightly charred, about 15 seconds per side. Stack grilled tortillas in foil packet to keep them warm and soft until serving time.

Grilled Herbed Chicken and Vegetable Kebabs

Serves 2

Total time 45 minutes, plus 30 minutes marinating

WHY THIS RECIPE WORKS Chicken kebabs are an obvious choice when cooking for two—they cook quickly and are a snap to assemble. We wanted moist, well-seasoned chicken alongside a mix of lightly charred vegetables. We preferred boneless chicken thighs to breasts, as they stayed juicy on the grill. To give the chicken a head start on flavor, we marinated it with fresh herbs and garlic. Reserving some marinade to drizzle over the chicken at the end added another layer of flavor. For the vegetables, a zucchini, a red pepper, and a small onion gave us a great mix of flavors and textures without any leftovers. You will need four 12-inch metal skewers for this recipe. If the chicken pieces are smaller than 1½ inches, thread two small pieces together. See page 258 for information on how to set up a single-level fire.

¼ cup extra-virgin olive oil
2 tablespoons minced fresh parsley, chives, basil, tarragon, or oregano
3 garlic cloves, minced
¾ teaspoon table salt for the marinade
½ teaspoon pepper
2 teaspoons lemon juice
1 pound boneless, skinless chicken thighs, trimmed and cut into 1½-inch pieces
1 red bell pepper, stemmed, seeded, and cut into 1½-inch pieces
1 small red onion, quartered through root end, each quarter cut into 1-inch pieces
1 zucchini, sliced ½ inch thick

1. Whisk oil, parsley, garlic, salt, and pepper together in large bowl. Transfer 1½ tablespoons marinade to separate bowl and stir in lemon juice; set aside for serving. Transfer 2 tablespoons marinade to 1-gallon zipper-lock bag, add chicken, seal bag tightly, and toss to coat. Let chicken marinate in refrigerator for at least 30 minutes or up to 1 hour.

2. Add bell pepper, onion, and zucchini to remaining marinade and toss to coat. Thread chicken and vegetables evenly onto four 12-inch metal skewers, starting and ending with chicken.

3A. FOR A CHARCOAL GRILL Open bottom vent completely. Light large chimney starter filled with charcoal briquettes (6 quarts). When top coals are partially covered with ash, pour evenly over grill. Set cooking grate in place, cover, and open lid vent completely. Heat grill until hot, about 5 minutes.

3B. FOR A GAS GRILL Turn all burners to high; cover; and heat grill until hot, about 15 minutes.

4. Clean and oil cooking grate. Place kebabs on grill and cook (covered if using gas) until chicken is well browned on all sides and vegetables are tender, 8 to 12 minutes, turning as needed. Transfer kebabs to serving platter, tent loosely with aluminum foil, and let rest for 5 to 10 minutes. Drizzle with reserved marinade and serve.

VARIATIONS
Grilled Curried Chicken and Vegetable Kebabs

Substitute 2 tablespoons minced fresh cilantro or mint for parsley and 2 teaspoons lime juice for lemon juice. In step 1, whisk 1 teaspoon curry powder into oil mixture before reserving some for serving.

Grilled Southwestern Chicken and Vegetable Kebabs

Substitute 2 tablespoons minced fresh cilantro for parsley and 2 teaspoons lime juice for lemon juice. In step 1, whisk 1 tablespoon minced chipotle chile and 1 teaspoon chili powder into oil mixture before reserving some for serving.

PREPARING ONION FOR KEBABS

1. Peel onion, trim off stem and root ends, then quarter onion.

2. Pull onion apart into sections that are 3 layers thick.

3. Cut each 3-layered section into 1-inch pieces.

4. Skewer onion through center of each piece.

Grilled Bone-In Chicken Breasts with Cherry Tomatoes

Serves 2

Total time 1 hour 5 minutes

WHY THIS RECIPE WORKS For the perfect easy summer meal, we wanted juicy, tender chicken breasts and bright cherry tomatoes together on the grill. Grilling bone-in chicken breasts over blazing hot coals caused flare-ups from the rendered fat and dried out the delicate meat. Instead, we spread the coals on one half of the grill to make a hotter side for crisping the skin and a cooler side where the chicken could cook gently. Tenting it with foil helped it to cook more evenly. Then, while the chicken rested, we tossed the tomatoes in oil and grilled them until they were nicely blistered but still fresh-tasting. You will need two or three 12-inch metal skewers for this recipe depending on the size of your tomatoes. See page 258 for information on how to set up a half-grill fire.

12 ounces cherry tomatoes
¼ cup extra-virgin olive oil, divided
2 tablespoons chopped fresh basil, cilantro, or tarragon
1 tablespoon red wine vinegar
1 garlic clove, minced
½ teaspoon table salt, divided
¼ teaspoon pepper, divided
2 (10- to 12-ounce) bone-in split chicken breasts, trimmed

1. Toss tomatoes with 1 tablespoon oil and thread, through stem ends, onto two or three 12-inch metal skewers. Mix remaining 3 tablespoons oil, basil, vinegar, garlic, ¼ teaspoon salt, and ⅛ teaspoon pepper together in small bowl; set aside for serving. Pat chicken breasts dry with paper towels and sprinkle with remaining ¼ teaspoon salt and remaining ⅛ teaspoon pepper.

2A. FOR A CHARCOAL GRILL Open bottom vent completely. Light large chimney starter three-quarters filled with charcoal briquettes (4½ quarts). When top coals are partially covered with ash, pour evenly over half of grill. Set cooking grate in place, cover, and open lid vent completely. Heat grill until hot, about 5 minutes.

2B. FOR A GAS GRILL Turn all burners to high; cover; and heat grill until hot, about 15 minutes. Turn primary burner to medium-high and turn off other burner(s). (Adjust primary burner as needed to maintain grill temperature around 350 degrees.)

3. Clean and oil cooking grate. Place chicken, skin side down, on cooler side of grill with thicker ends of breasts facing hotter side of grill. Tent chicken loosely with aluminum foil; cover grill; and cook until chicken is browned and registers 150 degrees, 25 to 35 minutes.

4. Discard foil and slide chicken to hotter side of grill. Cook (covered if using gas), turning as needed, until chicken is well browned; skin is crisp; and chicken registers 160 degrees, 5 to 10 minutes. Transfer chicken to serving platter and let rest while grilling tomatoes.

5. Place tomato skewers on hotter side of grill and cook, turning skewers as needed, until skins begin to blister and wrinkle, 3 to 6 minutes. Remove skewers from grill and carefully slide tomatoes off skewers and onto platter with chicken. Drizzle vinaigrette over chicken and tomatoes. Serve.

Barbecued Dry-Rubbed Chicken

Serves 2

Total time 1 hour 10 minutes, plus 30 minutes salting

WHY THIS RECIPE WORKS Simply brushing grilled chicken with barbecue sauce only flavors the surface of the meat, and worse, it turns the skin flabby. We wanted classic barbecued chicken that was flavored through and though. Our solution was to swap the barbecue sauce for a dry spice rub. Spread over and under the skin before cooking, it flavored the chicken down to the bone, and it didn't prevent the skin from crisping on the grill. To keep the chicken juicy, we let it rest while the salt in the rub penetrated the meat. We also added a generous amount of sugar to the rub; as it melted in the heat, it gave our chicken the glazed sweetness of a sauce. A second coating of the rub partway through cooking thickened the glaze even more. To keep the sugar from burning, we cooked the chicken over indirect heat. Apply the second coating of spices with a light hand or it won't melt into a glaze. See page 258 for information on how to set up a half-grill fire.

- 1 tablespoon packed dark brown sugar
- 1 teaspoon paprika
- ¾ teaspoon chili powder
- ¾ teaspoon pepper
- ½ teaspoon dry mustard
- ½ teaspoon onion powder
- ¼ teaspoon table salt
  Pinch cayenne pepper
- 2 (10- to 12-ounce) bone-in split chicken breasts, trimmed

1. Combine sugar, paprika, chili powder, pepper, mustard, onion powder, salt, and cayenne in bowl. Transfer 1½ tablespoons spice mixture to shallow dish; set aside. Pat chicken dry with paper towels. Use your fingers to gently loosen center portion of skin covering each breast, then rub remaining spice mixture over and underneath skin. Transfer chicken to large plate, cover with plastic wrap, and refrigerate for at least 30 minutes or up to 1 hour.

2A. FOR A CHARCOAL GRILL Open bottom vent completely. Light large chimney starter three-quarters filled with charcoal briquettes (4½ quarts). When top coals are partially covered with ash, pour evenly over half of grill. Set cooking grate in place, cover, and open lid vent completely. Heat grill until hot, about 5 minutes.

2B. FOR A GAS GRILL Turn all burners to high; cover; and heat grill until hot, about 15 minutes. Turn primary burner to medium-high and turn off other burner(s). (Adjust primary burner as needed to maintain grill temperature around 350 degrees.)

3. Clean and oil cooking grate. Place chicken, skin side down, on cooler side of grill with thicker ends of breasts facing hotter side of grill. Tent chicken loosely with aluminum foil; cover grill; and cook until chicken is browned and registers 140 degrees, 20 to 25 minutes.

Barbecued
Dry-Rubbed
Chicken

4. Discard foil. Using tongs, lightly dredge skin side of breasts in reserved spice rub. Return chicken, skin side up, to cooler side of grill with thicker ends of breasts facing hotter side of grill. Cover grill and cook until rub has melted into glaze and chicken registers 160 degrees, about 15 minutes. Transfer chicken to serving platter and let rest for 5 to 10 minutes. Serve.

Spiced Grilled
Chicken with Raita

Spiced Grilled Chicken with Raita

Serves 2

Total time 1 hour 5 minutes, plus 1 hour marinating

WHY THIS RECIPE WORKS Inspired by Indian tandoori chicken, yogurt-marinated chicken cooked in a tandoor oven, this dish packs in surprising flavor from a short ingredient list. As with traditional tandoori recipes, we marinated the chicken in yogurt. For the spice rub, curry powder alone tasted harsh and one-dimensional. Garam masala added complexity, but the raw taste remained. Adding the spices to the yogurt marinade solved the problem—the yogurt kept the chicken moist and tender; plus, it helped to bloom, or deepen, the flavor of the spices once they hit the grill. To prevent the yogurt marinade from burning, we built a half-grill fire and started the chicken on the cooler side of the grill, then finished it on the hotter side so that it would get an authentic char. A raita, made with yogurt flavored with garlic and cilantro, provided a cool, creamy counterpoint to the grilled meat. Do not substitute nonfat yogurt. See page 258 for information on how to set up a half-grill fire.

⅔ cup plain whole-milk yogurt, divided
1½ teaspoons curry powder
1½ teaspoons garam masala
½ teaspoon table salt for the marinade
   Pinch pepper
2 (10- to 12-ounce) bone-in split chicken breasts, trimmed
1 tablespoon minced fresh cilantro
1 small garlic clove, minced

1. Combine ⅓ cup yogurt, curry powder, garam masala, salt, and pepper in 1-gallon zipper-lock bag. Add chicken to bag, seal bag tightly, and toss to coat. Let chicken marinate in refrigerator for at least 1 hour or up to 6 hours. To make the raita, combine cilantro, garlic, and remaining ⅓ cup yogurt in bowl and season with salt and pepper to taste; cover and refrigerate.

2A. FOR A CHARCOAL GRILL Open bottom vent completely. Light large chimney starter three-quarters filled with charcoal briquettes (4½ quarts). When top coals are partially covered with ash, pour evenly over half of grill. Set cooking grate in place, cover, and open lid vent completely. Heat grill until hot, about 5 minutes.

2B. FOR A GAS GRILL Turn all burners to high; cover; and heat grill until hot, about 15 minutes. Turn primary burner to medium-high and turn off other burner(s). (Adjust primary burner as needed to maintain grill temperature around 350 degrees.)

3. Clean and oil cooking grate. Remove chicken from marinade and place, skin side down, on cooler side of grill with thicker ends of breasts facing hotter side of grill. Tent chicken loosely with aluminum foil, cover grill, and cook until chicken is browned and registers 150 degrees, 25 to 35 minutes.

4. Discard foil and slide chicken to hotter side of grill. Cook (covered if using gas), turning as needed, until chicken is lightly charred; skin is crisp; and chicken registers 160 degrees, 5 to 10 minutes. Transfer chicken to serving platter and let rest for 5 to 10 minutes. Serve with raita.

Grilled Jerk Chicken Breasts

Serves 2
Total time 1 hour 10 minutes, plus 2 hours marinating
WHY THIS RECIPE WORKS For this version of jerk chicken, thyme and allspice mimicked the unique smoke of Jamaican pimento wood. We mixed the spices with habanero, scallions, garlic, and molasses to make a potent paste, rubbed the paste under and over the skin, and let the chicken rest to absorb the flavors. A half-grill fire let us cook the chicken

gently, then char it over the hotter side. This dish is very spicy; to make it less spicy, remove the habanero seeds and ribs. Be careful when handling the habanero, as it can cause your skin to burn; use latex gloves when handling the chile mixture in step 1. If you cannot find a habanero, substitute two jalapeños. See page 258 for information on how to set up a half-grill fire.

4 scallions, chopped
2 tablespoons vegetable oil
1 tablespoon light or mild molasses
1 habanero chile, stemmed
2 garlic cloves, peeled
1½ teaspoons dried thyme
1 teaspoon ground allspice
1 teaspoon table salt for the marinade
2 (10- to 12-ounce) bone-in split chicken breasts, trimmed
   Lime wedges

1. Process scallions, oil, molasses, habanero, garlic, thyme, allspice, and salt together in food processor (or blender) until almost smooth, about 15 seconds. Use your fingers to gently loosen center portion of skin covering each breast. Wearing latex gloves, rub 1 tablespoon marinade underneath skin of each breast. Combine chicken and remaining marinade in 1-gallon zipper-lock bag, seal bag tightly, and toss to coat. Let chicken marinate in refrigerator for at least 2 hours or up to 24 hours.

2A. FOR A CHARCOAL GRILL Open bottom vent completely. Light large chimney starter three-quarters filled with charcoal briquettes (4½ quarts). When top coals are partially covered with ash, pour evenly over half of grill. Set cooking grate in place, cover, and open lid vent completely. Heat grill until hot, about 5 minutes.

2B. FOR A GAS GRILL Turn all burners to high; cover; and heat grill until hot, about 15 minutes. Turn primary burner to medium-high and turn off other burner(s). (Adjust primary burner as needed to maintain grill temperature around 350 degrees.)

3. Clean and oil cooking grate. Remove chicken from marinade and place, skin-side down, on cooler side of grill with thicker ends of breasts facing hotter side of grill. Tent chicken loosely with aluminum foil; cover grill; and cook until chicken is browned and registers 150 degrees, 25 to 35 minutes.

4. Discard foil and slide chicken to hotter side of grill. Cook (covered if using gas), turning as needed, until chicken is lightly charred; skin is crisp; and chicken registers 160 degrees, 5 to 10 minutes. Transfer chicken to serving platter and let rest for 5 to 10 minutes. Serve with lime wedges.

Best Grilled Chicken Thighs with Gochujang

Serves 2

Total time 1 hour 20 minutes

WHY THIS RECIPE WORKS We found that the best way to grill chicken thighs was also the easiest. Cooking the chicken over indirect heat until it registered 185 to 190 degrees, which took about an hour, allowed collagen in the meat to break down into gelatin, which lubricated the meat so that it tasted moist and silky. And grilling the thighs skin sides down enabled fat under the skin's surface to thoroughly render, turning it paper-thin, and collagen in the skin to break down and soften—both of which allowed the skin to get nicely crisp once we seared it over direct heat for the last few minutes of cooking. We coated the thighs with a bold-flavored paste, applying most of it to the flesh side so as not to introduce too much extra moisture to the skin, which would interfere with crisping. Briefly searing the flesh side before serving took the raw edge off the paste on that side. See page 258 for information on how to set up a half-grill fire.

2 tablespoons gochujang
1½ teaspoons soy sauce
1 garlic clove, minced
1 teaspoon sugar
½ teaspoon kosher salt
4 (5- to 7-ounce) bone-in chicken thighs, trimmed

1. Combine gochujang, soy sauce, garlic, and sugar in bowl.

2. Place chicken, skin side up, on large plate. Sprinkle skin side with salt and spread evenly with one-third of gochujang paste. Flip chicken and spread remaining two-thirds of gochujang paste evenly over flesh side. Refrigerate while preparing grill. (Chicken can be refrigerated for up to 2 hours.)

3A. FOR A CHARCOAL GRILL Open bottom vent halfway. Light large chimney starter mounded with charcoal briquettes (7 quarts). When top coals are partially covered with ash, pour evenly over half of grill. Set cooking grate in place, cover, and open lid vent halfway. Heat grill until hot, about 5 minutes.

3B. FOR A GAS GRILL Turn all burners to high; cover; and heat grill until hot, about 15 minutes. Leave primary burner on high and turn off other burner(s). (Adjust primary burner [or, if using 3-burner grill, primary burner and second burner] as needed to maintain grill temperature around 350 degrees.)

4. Clean and oil cooking grate. Place chicken, skin side down, on cooler side of grill. Cover and cook for 20 minutes. Rearrange chicken, keeping skin side down, so that pieces that were closest to edge are now closer to heat source and vice versa. Cover and continue to cook until chicken registers 185 to 190 degrees, 15 to 20 minutes.

5. Move all chicken, skin side down, to hotter side of grill and cook until skin is nicely charred, about 5 minutes. Flip chicken and cook until flesh side is lightly browned, 1 to 2 minutes. Transfer to platter, tent with aluminum foil, and let rest for 10 minutes. Serve.

Grilled Turkey Burgers

Serves 2

Total time 45 minutes

WHY THIS RECIPE WORKS A lean, fully cooked turkey burger simply seasoned with salt and pepper is a dry, tasteless stand-in for an all-beef burger. Add the dry heat of the grill to the equation, and things only get worse. We wanted a turkey burger that grilled up juicy and full of flavor—one that would rival a beef burger. We started with easy ground turkey and found that mixing in moist, rich ricotta cheese greatly improved the texture and flavor of the meat. A little Worcestershire sauce and Dijon mustard seasoned the burgers nicely. The burgers cooked up quickly on the hot grill and stayed tender and juicy thanks to the ricotta and seasonings. Be sure to use ground turkey, not ground turkey breast (also labeled 99 percent fat free), in this recipe. We prefer the richer flavor and softer texture of whole-milk ricotta here, but part-skim or fat-free will also work. See page 259 for information on how to set up a two-level fire. Serve with your favorite burger toppings.

12 ounces ground turkey
2 ounces (¼ cup) whole-milk ricotta cheese
1 teaspoon Worcestershire sauce
1 teaspoon Dijon mustard
¼ teaspoon table salt
¼ teaspoon pepper
2 hamburger buns

1. Break turkey into small pieces in bowl. Add ricotta, Worcestershire, mustard, salt, and pepper and gently knead until well incorporated. Divide meat mixture into 2 lightly packed balls, gently flatten each ball into 1-inch-thick patty, and press shallow divot in center of each patty. Transfer to plate, cover with plastic wrap, and refrigerate until grill is ready.

2A. FOR A CHARCOAL GRILL Open bottom vent completely. Light large chimney starter filled with charcoal briquettes (6 quarts). When top coals are partially covered with ash, pour two-thirds evenly over half of grill, then pour remaining coals over other half of grill. Set cooking grate in place, cover, and open lid vent completely. Heat grill until hot, about 5 minutes.

2B. FOR A GAS GRILL Turn all burners to high; cover; and heat grill until hot, about 15 minutes. Leave primary burner on high and turn other burner(s) to medium. (Adjust burners as needed to maintain hot fire and medium fire on separate sides of grill.)

3. Clean and oil cooking grate. Place burgers on hotter side of grill and cook (covered if using gas) until well browned on both sides, 5 to 7 minutes, flipping burgers halfway through cooking.

4. Slide burgers to cooler side of grill. Cover grill and cook, turning as needed, until burgers register 160 degrees, 5 to 7 minutes. Transfer burgers to serving platter, tent loosely with aluminum foil, and let rest for 5 minutes. While burgers rest, cook buns until warm and lightly charred, about 30 seconds. Serve on buns.

VARIATION

Grilled Southwestern Turkey Burgers

Omit Worcestershire sauce. Add 1 minced garlic clove, 1 teaspoon minced chipotle chile in adobo sauce, and ½ teaspoon cumin to meat mixture.

Grilled Turkey Burgers

Grilled Steak Burgers

Serves 2

Total time 1 hour

WHY THIS RECIPE WORKS We wanted a moist and juicy burger with a texture that was tender and cohesive. Just as important, we wanted a flavorful, deeply caramelized crust and a nice flat surface capable of holding lots of condiments. For robustly flavored meat, we opted for ultrabeefy ground sirloin. Because sirloin is about 90 percent lean, we kneaded in some melted butter to ensure that our patties stayed tender. We formed the meat into thick patties and indented the center of each so they wouldn't puff up on the grill. For a rich, flavorful steak sauce, we simmered more butter with tomato paste, beef broth, raisins, mustard, balsamic vinegar, and Worcestershire sauce. See page 258 for information on how to set up a single-level fire. We prefer these burgers cooked to medium-rare, but if you prefer them more or less done, see our guidelines on page 161. Serve with your favorite burger toppings.

Grilled Steak Burgers

4 tablespoons unsalted butter
1 garlic clove, minced
½ teaspoon table salt
½ teaspoon pepper
1 tablespoon tomato paste
⅓ cup beef broth
3 tablespoons raisins
1 tablespoon Dijon mustard
1 tablespoon balsamic vinegar
1½ teaspoons Worcestershire sauce
12 ounces 90 percent lean ground sirloin
2 hamburger buns

1. Melt butter in 8-inch skillet over medium-low heat. Add garlic, salt, and pepper and cook until fragrant, about 1 minute. Pour all but 1 tablespoon butter mixture into bowl and let cool, about 5 minutes.

2. Meanwhile, add tomato paste to skillet with remaining butter mixture and cook over medium heat until paste begins to darken, 1 to 2 minutes. Stir in broth, raisins, mustard, vinegar, and Worcestershire and simmer until raisins plump, about 5 minutes. Transfer sauce to blender and process until smooth, about 30 seconds; transfer to bowl.

3. Combine 2 tablespoons cooled butter mixture with ground sirloin and gently knead until well incorporated. Divide meat mixture into 2 lightly packed balls, gently flatten each ball into ¾-inch-thick patty, and press shallow divot in center of each patty; transfer to plate. Measure out 1 tablespoon sauce and brush onto both sides of patties; cover burgers and refrigerate until grill is ready. Combine remaining 1 tablespoon butter mixture with 2 tablespoons sauce and brush onto cut sides of buns.

4A. FOR A CHARCOAL GRILL Open bottom vent completely. Light large chimney starter filled with charcoal briquettes (6 quarts). When top coals are partially covered with ash, pour evenly over grill. Set cooking grate in place, cover, and open lid vent completely. Heat grill until hot, about 5 minutes.

4B. FOR A GAS GRILL Turn all burners to high; cover; and heat grill until hot, about 15 minutes.

5. Clean and oil cooking grate. Place burgers on grill and cook (covered if using gas) until they register 120 to 125 degrees (for medium-rare), 6 to 8 minutes, flipping burgers halfway through cooking. Transfer burgers to plate, tent loosely with aluminum foil, and let rest for 5 to 10 minutes.

6. While burgers rest, cook buns until warm and lightly charred, about 30 seconds. Serve burgers on buns with remaining sauce.

Grilled Beef and Vegetable Kebabs with Lemon-Rosemary Marinade

Grilled Beef and Vegetable Kebabs with Lemon-Rosemary Marinade

Serves 2

Total time 1 hour, plus 1 hour marinating

WHY THIS RECIPE WORKS We wanted a failproof approach for kebabs with chunks of marinated beef with caramelized char on the outside and a juicy interior paired with nicely browned vegetables. We chose well-marbled steak tips for their beefy flavor; and for the marinade, we included salt for moisture, oil for flavor, and sugar for browning. For even more depth, we used tomato paste, lemon zest, rosemary, and beef broth. Steak tips, also known as flap meat, are sold as whole steak, cubes, and strips; look for either whole steak tips or strips that are easy to cut into small pieces. You will need three 12-inch metal skewers for this recipe. See page 259 for information on how to set up a concentrated fire.

MARINADE

- 1 small onion, chopped coarse
- 3 tablespoons beef broth
- 3 tablespoons vegetable oil
- 1½ tablespoons tomato paste
- 3 garlic cloves, chopped
- 2 teaspoons minced fresh rosemary
- 1½ teaspoons grated lemon zest
- 1 teaspoon table salt
- ¾ teaspoon sugar
- ½ teaspoon pepper

BEEF AND VEGETABLES

- 12 ounces sirloin steak tips, trimmed and cut into 2-inch pieces
- 1 zucchini or summer squash, halved lengthwise and sliced 1 inch thick
- 1 red or green bell pepper, stemmed, seeded, and cut into 1½-inch pieces
- 1 small red onion, quartered through root end, each quarter cut into 1-inch pieces

1. FOR THE MARINADE Process all ingredients together in blender until smooth, about 45 seconds. Transfer ½ cup marinade to medium bowl; set aside.

2. FOR THE BEEF AND VEGETABLES Pat steak tips dry with paper towels and prick on all sides with fork. Combine remaining marinade and beef in 1-gallon zipper-lock bag, seal bag tightly, and toss to coat. Let meat marinate in refrigerator for at least 1 hour or up to 2 hours. Meanwhile, toss zucchini, bell pepper, and onion with reserved marinade, cover, and let sit at room temperature for 30 minutes.

3. Remove beef from marinade and pat dry with paper towels. Thread beef tightly onto one 12-inch metal skewer. Thread vegetables onto two 12-inch metal skewers in alternating pattern of zucchini, pepper, and onion.

4A. FOR A CHARCOAL GRILL Using kitchen shears, poke twelve ½-inch holes in bottom of disposable pan. Open bottom vent completely and place disposable pan in center of grill. Light large chimney starter two-thirds filled with charcoal briquettes (4 quarts). When top coals are partially covered with ash, pour into even layer in disposable pan. Set cooking grate in place with bars parallel to long side of disposable pan, cover, and open lid vent completely. Heat grill until hot, about 5 minutes.

4B. FOR A GAS GRILL Turn all burners to high; cover; and heat grill until hot, about 15 minutes. Leave all burners on high.

5. Clean and oil cooking grate. Place meat skewer over hotter side of grill (directly over coals) and vegetable skewers on cooler part of grill (outside of edge of aluminum pan if using charcoal). Cook (covered if using gas), turning skewers every 3 to 4 minutes, until beef is well browned and vegetables are tender and lightly charred, 17 to 21 minutes. Transfer skewers to serving platter, tent loosely with aluminum foil, and let rest for 5 to 10 minutes. Serve.

VARIATIONS
Grilled Beef and Vegetable Kebabs with North African Marinade

Omit lemon zest and rosemary from marinade and add 10 cilantro sprigs, 1 teaspoon paprika, ¾ teaspoon ground cumin, and ¼ teaspoon cayenne pepper.

Grilled Beef and Vegetable Kebabs with Red Curry Marinade

Omit lemon zest and rosemary from marinade and add ¼ cup fresh basil leaves, 1½ tablespoons red curry paste, 1½ teaspoons grated lime zest, and 1 teaspoon grated ginger.

SKEWERING THINNER PIECES OF BEEF

To ensure that thinner pieces cook at same rate as larger chunks, slice tapered beef into 2-inch by 4-inch pieces and roll or fold to create thicker pieces for skewer.

Grilled Steakhouse Steak Tips

Serves 2

Total time 40 minutes, plus 2 hours marinating

WHY THIS RECIPE WORKS Grilled steak tips are a steakhouse favorite for a reason: This tender cut of beef takes well to potent marinades and easily picks up flavorful char. Plus, steak tips are a perfect cut for serving two. We wanted steak tips with deep flavor and tender texture. For the meat, we chose sirloin steak tips, also known as flap meat, an affordable cut that stayed tender and moist during a brief stint on the grill. To further tenderize and season the meat, we used a soy sauce–based marinade flavored with garlic, paprika, cayenne, and tomato paste. Letting the steak tips rest for five to

**Grilled Steakhouse
Steak Tips**

1. Whisk soy sauce, oil, sugar, garlic, tomato paste, paprika, pepper, and cayenne together in bowl until sugar dissolves. Pat steak tips dry with paper towels and prick on all sides with fork. Combine marinade and steak in 1-gallon zipper-lock bag, seal bag tightly, and toss to coat. Let meat marinate in refrigerator for at least 2 hours or up to 24 hours.

2A. FOR A CHARCOAL GRILL Open bottom vent completely. Light large chimney starter filled with charcoal briquettes (6 quarts). When top coals are partially covered with ash, pour evenly over grill. Set cooking grate in place, cover, and open lid vent completely. Heat grill until hot, about 5 minutes.

2B. FOR A GAS GRILL Turn all burners to high; cover; and heat grill until hot, about 15 minutes.

3. Clean and oil cooking grate. Remove meat from marinade and place on grill. Cook (covered if using gas), turning as needed, until beef is charred on both sides and registers 130 to 135 degrees (for medium), 8 to 10 minutes. Transfer to serving platter, tent loosely with aluminum foil, and let rest for 5 to 10 minutes. Serve.

Grilled Smoky Spice-Rubbed Steaks

Serves 2
Total time 40 minutes

WHY THIS RECIPE WORKS The big, beefy flavor of strip steaks holds up well to spice rubs. To that end, we set out to develop a recipe for grilled strip steaks imbued with a smoky, spicy Southwestern-flavored rub. We rubbed the steaks evenly with an assertive mixture of chili powder, paprika, brown sugar, and garlic and threw them on a blazing hot grill to sear. Placing a packet of soaked wood chips directly on the coals gave the steaks a subtle smokiness. Resting the steaks before serving was key—if sliced into right off the grill, the meat would lose its flavorful juices and be dry. Although we prefer hickory wood chips, any variety of chip except mesquite will work. See page 258 for information on how to set up a single-level fire. We prefer these steaks cooked to medium-rare, but if you prefer them more or less done, see our guidelines on page 161.

10 minutes after grilling helped to ensure juicy meat. Steak tips are sold as whole steak, cubes, and strips; look for either whole steak tips or strips that are easy to cut into small pieces for this recipe. We also prefer these steak tips cooked to medium, but if you prefer them more or less done, see our guidelines on page 161. See page 258 for information on how to set up a single-level fire.

- 3 tablespoons soy sauce
- 3 tablespoons vegetable oil
- 1½ tablespoons packed dark brown sugar
- 3 garlic cloves, minced
- 1½ teaspoons tomato paste
- 1½ teaspoons paprika
- ¼ teaspoon pepper
- ⅛ teaspoon cayenne pepper
- 12 ounces sirloin steak tips, trimmed and cut into 2½-inch pieces

¼ cup wood chips, soaked in water for 15 minutes and drained
1 tablespoon paprika
1½ teaspoons packed light brown sugar
1½ teaspoons chili powder
½ teaspoon garlic powder
¼ teaspoon table salt
¼ teaspoon pepper
⅛ teaspoon cayenne pepper
2 (8-ounce) boneless strip steaks, ¾ inch thick, trimmed
1 tablespoon vegetable oil

1. Using piece of heavy-duty aluminum foil, wrap soaked chips in foil packet and cut several vent holes in top. Combine paprika, sugar, chili powder, garlic powder, salt, pepper, and cayenne in bowl. Pat steaks dry with paper towels, brush both sides with oil, and rub spice mixture evenly over both sides.

2A. FOR A CHARCOAL GRILL Open bottom vent halfway. Light large chimney starter filled with charcoal briquettes (6 quarts). When top coals are partially covered with ash, pour evenly over grill. Place wood chip packet on coals. Set cooking grate in place, cover, and open lid vent halfway. Heat grill until hot and wood chips are smoking, about 5 minutes.

2B. FOR A GAS GRILL Remove cooking grate and place wood chip packet directly on primary burner. Set grate in place; turn all burners to high; cover; and heat grill until hot and wood chips are smoking, about 15 minutes.

3. Clean and oil cooking grate. Place steaks on grill and cook (covered if using gas), turning as needed, until well browned and meat registers 120 to 125 degrees (for medium-rare), 6 to 8 minutes. Transfer steaks to cutting board, tent loosely with foil, and let rest for 5 to 10 minutes. Serve.

MAKING A FOIL PACKET FOR WOOD CHIPS

After soaking wood chips in water for 15 minutes, spread drained chips in center of 15 by 12-inch piece of heavy-duty aluminum foil. Fold to seal edges, then cut slits to allow smoke to escape.

Grilled Flank Steak with Chimichurri Sauce

Serves 2

Total time 50 minutes

WHY THIS RECIPE WORKS Traditionally, Argentine steaks are thick-cut and slow-smoked to give them a nice char and smoky flavor, but we wanted to speed things up. We chose quick-cooking flank steak for its beefy flavor and moist meat. Then, to give our steaks that authentic smoky flavor, we rubbed them with smoked paprika, sugar, salt, and pepper. Carefully patting them dry ensured that they took on lots of char over the hot fire. But when we added the spice rub directly to the dry steaks, it was dusty and raw-tasting. An easy fix was to brush the steaks with oil before adding the spice rub, allowing the flavors of the rub to bloom and deepen as the steaks cooked. Finally, we whipped up the traditional chimichurri sauce, made with parsley, cilantro, oregano, garlic, red wine vinegar, salt, and pepper and emulsified with extra-virgin olive oil. See page 258 for information on how to set up a single-level fire. We prefer this steak cooked to medium-rare, but if you prefer it more or less done, see our guidelines on page 161.

1 teaspoon hot water
¼ teaspoon dried oregano
3 tablespoons extra-virgin olive oil, divided
3 tablespoons minced fresh parsley
2 tablespoons minced fresh cilantro
1 tablespoon red wine vinegar
1 small garlic clove, minced
½ teaspoon table salt, divided
  Pinch plus ⅛ teaspoon pepper, divided
  Pinch plus ⅛ teaspoon sugar, divided
1 (1-pound) flank steak, trimmed
1 tablespoon smoked paprika

1. Combine hot water and oregano in small bowl and let sit for 5 minutes. Whisk in 2 tablespoons oil, parsley, cilantro, vinegar, garlic, ¼ teaspoon salt, pinch pepper, and pinch sugar; set aside for serving. Pat steak dry with paper towels, then brush with remaining 1 tablespoon oil. Combine paprika, remaining ¼ teaspoon salt, remaining ⅛ teaspoon pepper, and remaining ⅛ teaspoon sugar in bowl, then rub evenly over steak.

2A. FOR A CHARCOAL GRILL Open bottom vent completely. Light large chimney starter filled with charcoal briquettes (6 quarts). When top coals are partially covered with ash, pour evenly over grill. Set cooking grate in place, cover, and open lid vent completely. Heat grill until hot, about 5 minutes.

2B. FOR A GAS GRILL Turn all burners to high; cover; and heat grill until hot, about 15 minutes. Leave all burners on high.

3. Clean and oil cooking grate. Place steak on grill. Cook (covered if using gas), turning as needed, until steak is lightly charred on both sides and registers 120 to 125 degrees (for medium-rare), 6 to 8 minutes. Transfer to cutting board, tent loosely with aluminum foil, and let rest for 5 to 10 minutes. Slice steak thin against grain. Serve with sauce.

Grilled Marinated Skirt Steak

Serves 2

Total time 40 minutes

WHY THIS RECIPE WORKS Intensely beefy skirt steak is a popular cut because its shaggy grain makes it ideal for soaking up a flavorful marinade. But while a marinade might add flavor, it usually causes the meat to steam on the grill. To achieve a charred crust, we seasoned our steak with salt, pepper, and sugar before grilling and didn't marinate it until after it came off the grate. And since the marinade never touched raw meat, we also could serve it as a sauce on the side. Keep the marinade at room temperature or it will cool down the steak. See page 258 for information on how to set up a half-grill fire. We prefer this steak cooked to medium-rare, but if you prefer it more or less done, see our guidelines on page 161.

¼ cup soy sauce
2 tablespoons Worcestershire sauce
4 teaspoons sugar, divided
1 scallion, sliced thin
2 garlic cloves, minced
1½ teaspoons Dijon mustard
1 teaspoon balsamic vinegar
1 teaspoon pepper, divided
2 tablespoons extra-virgin olive oil
1 (12-ounce) skirt steak, cut crosswise into 4-inch pieces and trimmed
¼ teaspoon table salt

1. Combine soy sauce, Worcestershire, 1 tablespoon sugar, scallion, garlic, mustard, vinegar, and ¾ teaspoon pepper in bowl. Slowly whisk in oil until incorporated and sugar has dissolved. Pat steak dry with paper towels and sprinkle with ¼ teaspoon salt, remaining ¼ teaspoon pepper, and remaining 1 teaspoon sugar.

2A. FOR A CHARCOAL GRILL Open bottom vent completely. Light large chimney starter mounded with charcoal briquettes (7 quarts). When top coals are partially covered with ash, pour evenly over half of grill. Set cooking grate in place, cover, and open lid vent completely. Heat grill until hot, about 5 minutes.

2B. FOR A GAS GRILL Turn all burners to high; cover; and heat grill until hot, about 15 minutes.

3. Clean and oil cooking grate. Place steak on grill (directly over coals if using charcoal). Cook (covered if using gas) until well browned and meat registers 120 to 125 degrees (for medium-rare), 2 to 4 minutes per side.

4. Transfer steak to 8-inch square baking pan and poke all over with fork. Pour marinade over steak, tent with aluminum foil, and let rest for 5 to 10 minutes. Transfer steak to cutting board and slice thin against grain. Pour marinade into serving vessel and serve with steak.

Bistecca alla Fiorentina

Serves 2

Total time 50 minutes

WHY THIS RECIPE WORKS A famous dish in Tuscan cuisine, bistecca alla fiorentina is a simple recipe that consists of a beautifully grilled steak lightly dressed with extra-virgin olive oil and lemon juice. The grassy oil complements the beef while the acidic lemon juice sharpens the flavors. To bring out the full, fresh flavor of the olive oil and lemon juice, we drizzled them over the steak after cooking rather than before, as many recipes recommend. Be sure to buy steaks that are at least 1 inch thick. See page 258 for information on how to set up a half-grill fire. For even deeper flavor, grill lemon halves on hot grill until caramelized about 6 minutes. We prefer this steak cooked to medium-rare, but if you prefer it more or less done, see our guidelines on page 161.

1 (1¾-pound) porterhouse or T-bone steak, 1 to 1½ inches thick, trimmed
½ teaspoon table salt
¼ teaspoon pepper
1 garlic clove, cut in half
2 tablespoons extra-virgin olive oil
Lemon wedges

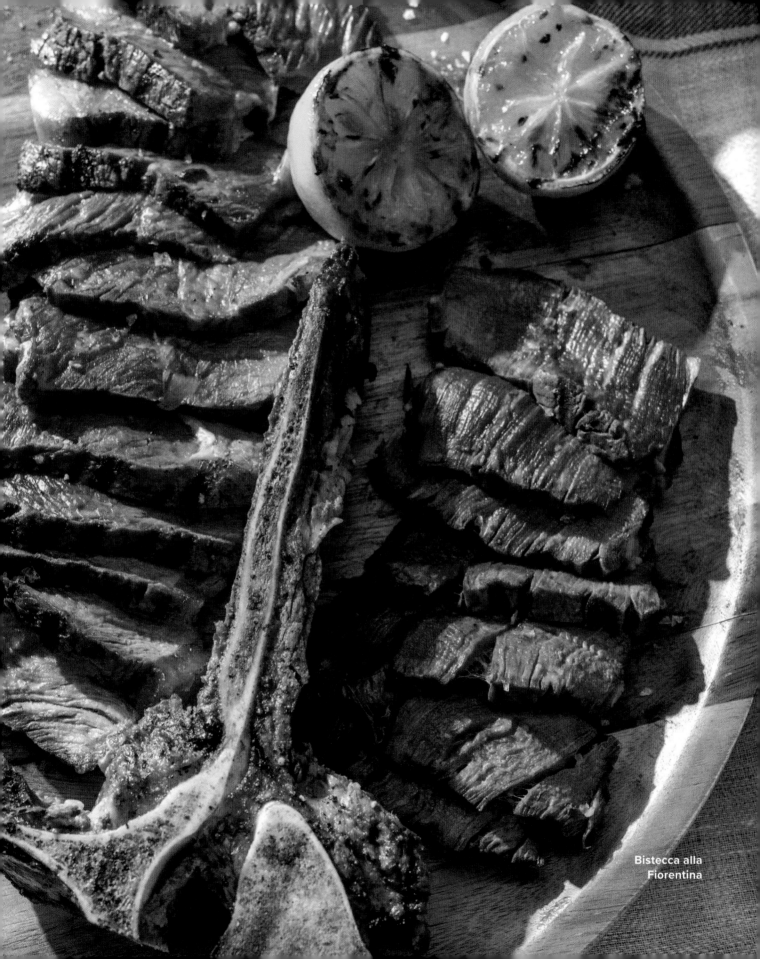

Bistecca alla Fiorentina

1. Pat steak dry with paper towels, sprinkle with salt and pepper, and rub cut sides of garlic clove over bone and meat.

2A. FOR A CHARCOAL GRILL Open bottom vent completely. Light large chimney starter three-quarters filled with charcoal briquettes (4½ quarts). When top coals are partially covered with ash, pour evenly over half of grill. Set cooking grate in place, cover, and open lid vent completely. Heat grill until hot, about 5 minutes.

2B. FOR A GAS GRILL Turn all burners to high; cover; and heat grill until hot, about 15 minutes. Leave primary burner on high and turn other burner(s) to low.

3. Clean and oil cooking grate. Place steak on hotter part of grill with tenderloin sides (smaller side of T-bone) facing cooler part of grill. Cook (covered if using gas) until dark crust forms, 6 to 8 minutes. Flip steak and turn so that tenderloin side is facing cooler side of grill. Continue to cook (covered if using gas) until dark brown crust forms on second side, 6 to 8 minutes.

4. Slide steak to cooler side of grill with bone side facing hotter side of grill. Cover grill and continue to cook until meat registers 120 to 125 degrees (for medium-rare), 2 to 4 minutes longer, flipping halfway through cooking.

5. Transfer steak to cutting board, tent loosely with aluminum foil, and let rest for 5 to 10 minutes. Cut strip and tenderloin pieces off bone, then cut each piece crosswise into ¼-inch-thick slices. Transfer to serving platter and drizzle with oil. Serve with lemon wedges.

CARVING A BONE-IN STEAK

1. After meat has rested, cut along bone to remove large top loin, or strip, section.

2. Cut smaller tenderloin section off bone. Cut each large piece crosswise into ¼-inch-thick slices for serving.

Grilled Glazed Pork Chops

Serves 2

Total time 50 minutes

WHY THIS RECIPE WORKS Quick-cooking pork chops are great for two, but because they're lean, they can easily overcook and turn dry. For chops with deeply browned crusts and tender, juicy meat all the way to the bone, we started with well-marbled bone-in, thick-cut rib chops. As with chicken breasts, we found that a two-level fire allowed us to sear the chops and then finish cooking them gently over the cooler side of the grill. To flavor the chops, we made a sweet and tangy maple and mustard glaze. We brushed the seared chops with the glaze and tented them with foil on the cooler side of the grill. See page 259 for information on how to set up a two-level fire.

2 tablespoons maple syrup
2 tablespoons Dijon mustard
2 tablespoons whole-grain mustard
2 tablespoons extra-virgin olive oil
  Pinch cayenne pepper
  Pinch plus ½ teaspoon table salt, divided
  Pinch plus ¼ teaspoon pepper, divided
2 (12- to 14-ounce) bone-in pork rib or center-cut chops, about 1½ inches thick, trimmed

1. Whisk maple syrup, Dijon mustard, whole-grain mustard, oil, cayenne, pinch salt, and pinch pepper together in bowl. Transfer ¼ cup glaze to separate bowl; set aside for serving.

2. Cut 2 slits about 2 inches apart through outer layer of fat and silverskin on each chop. Pat chops dry with paper towels and sprinkle with remaining ½ teaspoon salt and remaining ¼ teaspoon pepper.

3A. FOR A CHARCOAL GRILL Open bottom vent completely. Light large chimney starter filled with charcoal briquettes (6 quarts). When top coals are partially covered with ash, pour two-thirds evenly over half of grill, then pour remaining coals over other half of grill. Set cooking grate in place, cover, and open lid vent completely. Heat grill until hot, about 5 minutes.

3B. FOR A GAS GRILL Turn all burners to high; cover; and heat grill until hot, about 15 minutes. Leave primary burner on high and turn other burner(s) to medium. (Adjust burners as needed to maintain hot fire and medium fire on separate sides of grill.)

4. Clean and oil cooking grate. Place chops on hotter side of grill. Cook (covered if using gas), turning as needed, until well browned on both sides, 6 to 10 minutes. Slide chops to cooler side of grill and brush with glaze. Tent loosely with aluminum foil; cover grill; and cook until chops register 145 degrees, 7 to 9 minutes, flipping and brushing them with glaze halfway through cooking.

5. Transfer chops to serving platter, tent loosely with foil, and let rest for 5 to 10 minutes. Serve with reserved glaze.

Grill-Smoked Pork Chops

Serves 2

Total time 1 hour 10 minutes

WHY THIS RECIPE WORKS For great grill-smoked bone-in pork chops with rosy, ultramoist meat and smoke flavor throughout, we built a half-grill fire and started the chops on the cooler side of the grill. Then we brushed on a few coats of sauce and seared the glazed chops over the hotter side to give them a beautiful crust. Bone-in chops worked best; the bones lent flavor and suppleness to the meat, and we used this cut to our advantage by cooking each chop upright on its bone instead of laying it flat. To keep the chops from toppling over, we speared them together with skewers. You will need two 12-inch metal skewers for this recipe. If desired, a disposable aluminum roasting pan can be placed under the grate on a charcoal grill to catch the pork drippings. See page 258 for information on how to set up a half-grill fire.

¼ cup ketchup

2 tablespoons light or mild molasses

1 tablespoon grated onion

1 tablespoon Worcestershire sauce

1 tablespoon Dijon mustard

1 tablespoon cider vinegar

1½ teaspoons packed brown sugar

1 cup wood chips, soaked in water for 15 minutes and drained

2 (12- to 14-ounce) bone-in pork rib or center-cut chops, about 1½ inches thick, trimmed

½ teaspoon table salt

¼ teaspoon pepper

1. Simmer ketchup, molasses, onion, Worcestershire, mustard, vinegar, and sugar in small saucepan over medium heat, stirring often, until sauce is thickened and measures ½ cup, 3 to 5 minutes. Season with salt and pepper to taste. Transfer ¼ cup glaze to bowl; set aside for serving. Using piece of heavy-duty aluminum foil, wrap soaked chips in foil packet and cut several vent holes in top (see page 271).

2. Cut 2 slits, about 2 inches apart, through outer layer of fat and silverskin on each chop. Pat chops dry with paper towels and sprinkle with salt and pepper. Stand chops on their rib bones, side by side and facing in same direction. Pass two 12-inch metal skewers through loin muscle of each chop, close to bone, about 1 inch from each end. Once chops have been threaded onto skewers, pull them apart to create 2-inch space between them.

3A. FOR A CHARCOAL GRILL Open bottom vent halfway. Light large chimney starter filled with charcoal briquettes (6 quarts). When top coals are partially covered with ash, pour evenly over half of grill. Place wood chip packet on coals. Set cooking grate in place, cover, and open lid vent halfway. Heat grill until hot and wood chips are smoking, about 5 minutes.

3B. FOR A GAS GRILL Remove cooking grate and place wood chip packet directly on primary burner. Set grate in place; turn all burners to high; cover; and heat grill until hot and wood chips are smoking, about 15 minutes. Leave primary burner on high and turn off other burner(s). (Adjust burner as needed to maintain grill temperature around 350 degrees.)

4. Clean and oil cooking grate. Stand chops, bone side down, on cooler side of grill. Cover (positioning lid vent over chops if using charcoal) and cook until chops register 120 degrees, 20 to 25 minutes.

5. Carefully remove chops from skewers and brush one side with half of glaze. Grill, glazed side down, over hotter side of grill (covered if using gas) until browned, 3 to 6 minutes. Brush second side of chops with remaining glaze; flip; and cook until second side is browned and chops register 145 degrees, 3 to 6 minutes. Transfer chops to serving platter, tent loosely with foil, and let rest for 5 to 10 minutes. Serve with reserved glaze.

GRILL-SMOKING PORK CHOPS

1. To stand pork chops on grill, pass two skewers through loin muscle of each chop. Then pull chops apart to create space to allow smoke to circulate.

2. Stand skewered chops, bone side down, on cooking grate on cooler side of grill.

Grilled Coriander-Rubbed Pork Tenderloin with Herbs

Serves 2

Total time 50 minutes

WHY THIS RECIPE WORKS Thanks to its compact size and shape, pork tenderloin is a good candidate for both the grill and dinner for two. But its leanness can make it a challenge to cook: Less fat translates to little flavor and meat that easily dries out. We needed a technique that would yield pork with a well-browned crust and a perfectly cooked interior. A half-grill fire was an easy solution. We browned the pork over the hotter side of the grill, then moved it to the cooler side to cook through gently. Tenting the pork with foil helped it to cook through more quickly. To flavor the lean pork, we rubbed it with bright, citrusy coriander, brown sugar, and salt before grilling, then drizzled it with a fresh herb oil before serving. See page 258 for information on how to set up a half-grill fire.

- 3 tablespoons extra-virgin olive oil, divided
- 1 tablespoon minced fresh parsley
- ½ teaspoon minced fresh rosemary
- 1 small garlic clove, minced
- ⅛ teaspoon plus ½ teaspoon table salt, divided
- ⅛ teaspoon plus ¼ teaspoon pepper, divided
- ¾ teaspoon brown sugar
- ½ teaspoon ground coriander
- 1 (12-ounce) pork tenderloin, trimmed

1. Whisk 2 tablespoons oil, parsley, rosemary, garlic, ⅛ teaspoon salt, and ⅛ teaspoon pepper together in bowl; set aside for serving. In separate bowl, combine sugar, coriander, remaining ½ teaspoon salt, and remaining ¼ teaspoon pepper. Pat tenderloin dry with paper towels; rub with remaining 1 tablespoon oil; and coat with sugar mixture, pressing to help it adhere.

2A. FOR A CHARCOAL GRILL Open bottom vent completely. Light large chimney starter filled with charcoal briquettes (6 quarts). When top coals are partially covered with ash, pour evenly over half of grill. Set cooking grate in place, cover, and open lid vent completely. Heat grill until hot, about 5 minutes.

2B. FOR A GAS GRILL Turn all burners to high; cover; and heat grill until hot, about 15 minutes. Leave primary burner on high and turn off other burner(s).

3. Clean and oil cooking grate. Place pork on hotter side of grill. Cook (covered if using gas), turning as needed, until well browned on all sides, 10 to 12 minutes. Slide pork to cooler side of grill, tent loosely with aluminum foil, and cook until pork registers 145 degrees, 5 to 8 minutes.

4. Transfer pork to cutting board, tent loosely with foil, and let rest for 5 to 10 minutes. Slice pork into ¼-inch-thick slices and drizzle with herb-oil mixture. Serve.

CHECKING THE FUEL LEVEL IN A GAS TANK

1. Bring about 1 cup of water to boil. Pour water over side of tank.

2. Where water has warmed metal, the tank is empty; where metal remains cool to touch, there is propane inside.

Bun Cha

Serves 2

Total time 1 hour 10 minutes

WHY THIS RECIPE WORKS Vietnamese bun cha is a vibrant mix of grilled pork, crisp salad, and delicate rice vermicelli, united by a potent sauce. We started by boiling dried rice vermicelli, after which we rinsed the noodles well and spread them on a platter to dry. Then we mixed up the zesty sauce known as nuoc cham using lime juice, sugar, and fish sauce. For juicy pork patties, we mixed baking soda into supermarket ground pork, which helped the meat retain moisture and brown during the grilling time. We also seasoned the pork with shallot, fish sauce, sugar, and pepper. Briefly soaking the grilled patties in the sauce further flavored the patties and imbued the sauce with grill flavor. We prefer the more delicate springiness of vermicelli made from 100 percent rice flour to those that include a secondary starch such as cornstarch. If you can find only the latter, just cook them longer—up to 12 minutes. For a less spicy sauce, use only one-quarter of the Thai chile. For the cilantro, use the leaves and the thin, delicate stems, not the thicker ones close to the root. See page 258 for information on how to set up a half-grill fire.

NOODLES AND SALAD

 4 ounces rice vermicelli
 ½ head Boston lettuce (4 ounces), torn into
     bite-size pieces
 ½ English cucumber, peeled, quartered lengthwise,
     seeded, and sliced thin on bias
 ½ cup fresh cilantro leaves and stems
 ½ cup fresh mint leaves, torn if large

SAUCE

 ½ small Thai chile, stemmed and minced
 1½ tablespoons sugar, divided
 1 small garlic clove, minced
 ⅓ cup hot tap water
 2½ tablespoons fish sauce
 2 tablespoons lime juice

PORK PATTIES

 1 small shallot, minced
 1½ teaspoons fish sauce
 ¾ teaspoon sugar
 ¼ teaspoon baking soda
 ¼ teaspoon pepper
 8 ounces ground pork

1. FOR THE NOODLES AND SALAD Bring 2 quarts water to boil in large pot. Stir in noodles and cook until tender but not mushy, 4 to 12 minutes. Drain noodles and rinse under cold running water until cool. Drain noodles very well, spread on large plate, and let stand at room temperature to dry. Arrange lettuce, cucumber, cilantro, and mint separately on platter and refrigerate until needed.

2. FOR THE SAUCE Using mortar and pestle (or on cutting board using flat side of chef's knife), mash Thai chile, 1½ teaspoons sugar, and garlic to fine paste. Transfer to medium bowl and add hot water and remaining 1 tablespoon sugar. Stir until sugar is dissolved. Stir in fish sauce and lime juice; set aside.

3. FOR THE PORK PATTIES Combine shallot, fish sauce, sugar, baking soda, and pepper in medium bowl. Add pork and mix until well combined. Shape pork mixture into 6 patties, each about 2½ inches wide and ½ inch thick.

4A. FOR A CHARCOAL GRILL Open bottom vent completely. Light large chimney starter filled with charcoal briquettes (6 quarts). When top coals are partially covered with ash, pour evenly over half of grill. Set cooking grate in place, cover, and open lid vent completely. Heat grill until hot, about 5 minutes.

**Grilled Coriander-Rubbed
Pork Tenderloin with Herbs**

Bun Cha

Grilled Lamb Chops with Shaved Zucchini Salad

4B. FOR A GAS GRILL Turn all burners to high; cover; and heat grill until hot, about 15 minutes. Leave all burners on high.

5. Clean and oil cooking grate. Cook patties (directly over coals if using charcoal; covered if using gas) until well charred, 3 to 4 minutes per side. Transfer grilled patties to bowl with sauce and toss gently to coat. Let stand for 5 minutes.

6. Transfer patties to serving plate, reserving sauce. Serve noodles, salad, sauce, and pork patties separately.

Grilled Lamb Chops with Shaved Zucchini Salad

Serves 2

Total time 35 minutes

WHY THIS RECIPE WORKS Lamb doesn't need to be reserved for weekends or special occasions. Our quick-cooking lamb loin chops can be on the table in just over 30 minutes for an easy and delicious weeknight meal. Lamb loin chops are especially tender and tend to dry out if cooked past medium-rare, so we used a medium-hot fire and cooked the chops for only a few minutes per side. A quick, fresh zucchini salad, with the bright flavor and acidity of lemon juice tamed by cool mint, was the perfect complement to the mild gaminess of the lamb. We sliced zucchini into ribbons so that it didn't need to be cooked; the thin slices were tender, with a pleasing bite. We finished the salad with a drizzle of extra-virgin olive oil and thin shavings of salty Parmesan that mimicked the zucchini ribbons in shape and texture. Look for small zucchini, which are younger and have thinner skins than large zucchini. See page 258 for information on how to set up a single-level fire.

2½ tablespoons extra-virgin olive oil, divided
 2 teaspoons minced fresh rosemary
 1 garlic clove, minced
 ⅛ teaspoon plus ¼ teaspoon table salt, divided
   Pinch plus ⅛ teaspoon pepper, divided
 4 (4-ounce) lamb loin or rib chops, ¾ to 1 inch thick, trimmed
 1 zucchini
1½ teaspoons lemon juice
 1 ounce Parmesan cheese, shaved
 1 tablespoon minced fresh mint or basil

1. Combine 1 tablespoon oil, rosemary, garlic, ⅛ teaspoon salt, and pinch pepper in bowl; set aside. Pat chops dry with paper towels, rub chops with ½ tablespoon oil, and season with remaining ¼ teaspoon salt and remaining ⅛ teaspoon pepper.

ESSENTIAL EQUIPMENT FOR THE GRILL

Outdoor cooking requires some specialized equipment, starting with the grill. If you are using a charcoal grill, it's also helpful to keep a water-filled spray bottle handy to squelch any flare-ups from fat dripping on the coals (if using a gas grill, check the drip pan and empty excess fat regularly).

CHARCOAL GRILL The test kitchen's charcoal grill standard is the 22-inch kettle grill. Some grills also have features that make them easier to use. A generous cooking surface is always best; a deep lid can cover large foods such as a whole turkey; a built-in thermometer is a handy tool; and a side table is the ultimate convenience.

CHARCOAL We prefer regular charcoal briquettes to hardwood charcoal (aka lump charcoal), which burns too quickly. We avoid using instant-lighting briquettes because they have a slightly off-odor as they burn, and we prefer to use a less-processed product.

CHIMNEY STARTER For igniting charcoal briquettes, nothing is safer or more effective than a chimney starter (aka flue starter). We prefer large chimney starters—ones that can hold at least 6 quarts of briquettes. See page 264 for instructions on lighting a grill with a chimney starter.

GAS GRILL When choosing a grill, even heat distribution and good fat drainage are two important factors. We also like our gas grills to have a generous cooking surface area—at least 350 square inches—and three independently operating burners.

GRILL BRUSH Nothing works better than a good grill brush for getting burnt-on gunk off a cooking grate. Most feature stiff metal bristles, but sticky goo can quickly get stuck in the bristles. We prefer grill brushes with replaceable scouring pads as the scrubbers. Make sure that the brush has a long, preferably wooden, handle.

TONGS Tongs are the most useful tool for turning anything from slender asparagus spears to racks of ribs. But tongs made especially for grilling are cumbersome to use, particularly for smaller items. We prefer 16-inch kitchen tongs.

BARBECUE MITT A good grilling mitt should have enough heat resistance to keep hands from burning and enough pliability to keep you from inadvertently dropping grates or smashing food.

BASTING BRUSH Look for a basting brush with an angled head and long handle made from a heat-resistant material. We prefer silicone brush bristles, which won't melt or singe.

2A. FOR A CHARCOAL GRILL Open bottom vent completely. Light large chimney starter filled with charcoal briquettes (6 quarts). When top coals are partially covered with ash, pour evenly over grill. Set cooking grate in place, cover, and open lid vent completely. Heat grill until hot, about 5 minutes.

2B. FOR A GAS GRILL Turn all burners to high; cover; and heat grill until hot, about 15 minutes.

3. Clean and oil cooking grate. Place chops on grill and cook, brushing with rosemary-garlic oil and flipping as needed, until both sides are well browned and chops register 120 to 125 degrees (for medium-rare), 4 to 8 minutes. Transfer chops to serving platter; tent loosely with aluminum foil and let rest while making salad.

4. Use vegetable peeler or mandoline to slice zucchini lengthwise into very thin ribbons. Gently toss zucchini with salt and pepper to taste and arrange attractively on serving platter. Drizzle with remaining 1 tablespoon oil and lemon juice, then sprinkle with Parmesan and mint. Serve with lamb chops, passing rosemary-garlic oil separately.

MAKING ZUCCHINI RIBBONS

Using vegetable peeler or mandoline, slice zucchini lengthwise into very thin ribbons.

Grilled Fish Tacos

Grilled Blackened Red Snapper

Grilled Fish Tacos

Serves 2

Total time 50 minutes

WHY THIS RECIPE WORKS Southwestern fish tacos combine grilled pieces of fish and crisp shredded cabbage with a tangy white sauce, all wrapped up in warm, soft corn tortillas. Tasters liked the meaty flavor and firm texture of mahi-mahi. To flavor the fish, we rubbed it with a mix of chili powder, salt, and pepper. Over the blazing heat of the grill, the fish developed a nicely crisped crust before its quick-cooking interior was overdone. We liked the crisp crunch of raw cabbage, but its flavor was a bit bland. Tossing it with cilantro, lime juice, and salt and pepper gave it just enough bright flavor. Halibut, swordfish, or red snapper can be substituted for the mahi-mahi. See page 258 for information on how to set up a single-level fire. Be sure to oil the cooking grate well in step 4.

¼ small head green cabbage, cored and shredded (2 cups)

3 tablespoons chopped fresh cilantro, divided

2 tablespoons vegetable oil, divided

1½ tablespoons lime juice, divided

⅛ teaspoon plus ¼ teaspoon table salt, divided

Pinch plus ⅛ teaspoon pepper, divided

⅓ cup mayonnaise

1–2 teaspoons minced canned chipotle chiles in adobo sauce

1 small garlic clove, minced

2 (6- to 8-ounce) skinless mahi-mahi fillets, 1 inch thick

1 teaspoon chili powder

6 (6-inch) corn tortillas

Sliced avocado

Lime wedges

1. Toss cabbage, 2 tablespoons cilantro, 1 tablespoon oil, 1 tablespoon lime juice, ⅛ teaspoon salt, and pinch pepper together in bowl; set aside for serving. In separate bowl, combine mayonnaise, chipotle, garlic, remaining 1 tablespoon cilantro, and remaining 1½ teaspoons lime juice and season with salt and pepper to taste; set aside for serving.

2. Pat mahi-mahi dry with paper towels and brush with remaining 1 tablespoon oil. Combine chili powder, remaining ¼ teaspoon salt, and remaining ⅛ teaspoon pepper, then rub evenly over fillets.

3A. FOR A CHARCOAL GRILL Open bottom vent completely. Light large chimney starter filled with charcoal briquettes (6 quarts). When top coals are partially covered with ash, pour evenly over grill. Set cooking grate in place, cover, and open lid vent completely. Heat grill until hot, about 5 minutes.

3B. FOR A GAS GRILL Turn all burners to high; cover; and heat grill until hot, about 15 minutes. Leave all burners on high.

4. Clean cooking grate, then repeatedly brush grate with well-oiled paper towels until grate is black and glossy, 5 to 10 times. Place fillets on grill and cook (covered if using gas) until fish flakes apart when gently prodded with paring knife and registers 130 degrees, 10 to 14 minutes, gently flipping fillets with 2 spatulas halfway through cooking. Transfer fillets to cutting board and tent loosely with aluminum foil.

5. Place tortillas on grill in single layer and cook until warmed and lightly browned on both sides, about 15 seconds per side. Stack grilled tortillas in foil packet to keep warm and soft. To serve, cut each fillet into 3 equal pieces. Smear warm tortillas with mayonnaise mixture, top with cabbage and fish, and serve with lime wedges and avocado.

PREVENTING FISH FROM STICKING

Scrape grate clean with brush, then wipe it 5 to 10 times with paper towels dipped in vegetable oil until grate is black and glossy, dipping paper towels in oil between applications.

Grilled Blackened Red Snapper

Serves 2

Total time 50 minutes

WHY THIS RECIPE WORKS Blackened fish is usually prepared in a cast-iron skillet, but it can lead to a relentlessly smoky kitchen. We thought we'd solve this issue by moving our fish to the grill, but this introduced a host of new challenges—curled fillets that stuck to the grill and spices that tasted raw and harsh. To prevent curling fillets, we simply scored the skin. We solved the sticking problem by thoroughly oiling the grate. Finally, to give the fish a flavorful blackened—but not burnt—coating, we bloomed our spice mixture in melted butter, allowed it to cool, then brushed it on the fish. Once on the grill, the spice crust acquired depth and richness while the fish cooked through. Striped bass, halibut, or grouper can be substituted for the snapper. See page 258 for information on how to set up a half-grill fire. Be sure to oil the grate well in step 4; fish is delicate and tends to stick to the grill. Serve with Creamy Chipotle Chili Sauce (page 310), if desired.

1 tablespoon paprika

1 teaspoon onion powder

1 teaspoon garlic powder

½ teaspoon ground coriander

⅛ teaspoon cayenne pepper

½ teaspoon table salt

¼ teaspoon pepper

2 tablespoons unsalted butter

2 (6- to 8-ounce) skin-on red snapper fillets, ¾ inch thick
   Lime wedges

1. Combine paprika, onion powder, garlic powder, coriander, cayenne, salt, and pepper in bowl. Melt butter in 8-inch skillet over medium heat. Stir in spice mixture and cook, stirring constantly, until fragrant and spices turn dark rust color, about 2 minutes. Transfer mixture to shallow dish and let cool to room temperature, then use fork to break up any large clumps.

2. Using sharp knife, make 3 or 4 shallow slashes about 1 inch apart along skin side of each fillet, being careful not to cut into flesh. Pat fillets dry with paper towels. Rub spice mixture evenly over both sides of fillets. Lay fish on wire rack set over baking sheet and refrigerate until grill is ready.

3A. FOR A CHARCOAL GRILL Open bottom vent completely. Light large chimney starter three-quarters filled with charcoal briquettes (4½ quarts). When top coals are partially covered with ash, pour evenly over half of grill. Set cooking grate in place, cover, and open lid vent completely. Heat grill until hot, about 5 minutes.

3B. FOR A GAS GRILL Turn all burners to high; cover; and heat grill until hot, about 15 minutes.

4. Clean cooking grate, then repeatedly brush grate with well-oiled paper towels until grate is black and glossy, 5 to 10 times. Place snapper on hotter side of grill, skin side down and perpendicular to bars of cooking grate. Cook until exterior is dark brown and fish is opaque and flakes apart when gently prodded with paring knife, 10 to 14 minutes, gently flipping fillets with 2 spatulas halfway through cooking. Serve with lime wedges.

Grilled Swordfish and Artichoke Skewers with Olive Caponata

Serves 2

Total time 40 minutes

WHY THIS RECIPE WORKS For these skewers, we paired swordfish with artichoke hearts, chunks of lemon, and an olive caponata infused with basil and garlic. Once grilled, the artichoke hearts softened slightly yet retained some texture, and the lemon flavor went from tart and acidic to intensely sweet and rich. A simple olive caponata, brushed over our skewers once they came off the grill, complemented the bright lemon flavor. We tossed the swordfish with a bit of ground coriander, which added complexity and provided a base of flavor. You can substitute other sturdy, firm-fleshed fish such as mahi-mahi or halibut. You will need two 12-inch metal skewers for this recipe. See page 258 for information on how to set up a single-level fire. To thaw the artichokes quickly, microwave them in a covered bowl for about 3 minutes and pat dry before using. Be sure to oil the cooking grate well in step 3 to keep the fish from sticking.

- ¼ cup pitted kalamata olives, chopped
- 3 tablespoons extra-virgin olive oil, divided
- 1 tablespoon chopped fresh basil
- ½ garlic clove, minced
- ½ teaspoon table salt, divided
  Pinch plus ⅛ teaspoon pepper, divided
- 1 (12-ounce) skinless swordfish steak, cut into ¾-inch pieces
- 2 teaspoons ground coriander
- 4 ounces frozen artichoke hearts, thawed and patted dry
- ½ lemon, quartered

1. Combine olives, 2 tablespoons oil, basil, garlic, ¼ teaspoon salt, and pinch pepper in bowl; set aside for serving. Pat swordfish dry with paper towels and sprinkle with coriander, remaining ¼ teaspoon salt, and remaining ⅛ teaspoon pepper. Thread fish, artichokes, and lemon evenly onto two 12-inch metal skewers in alternating pattern. Brush skewers with remaining 1 tablespoon oil.

2A. FOR A CHARCOAL GRILL Open bottom vent completely. Light large chimney starter three-quarters filled with charcoal briquettes (4½ quarts). When top coals are partially covered with ash, pour evenly over grill. Set cooking grate in place, cover, and open lid vent completely. Heat grill until hot, about 5 minutes.

2B. FOR A GAS GRILL Turn all burners to high; cover; and heat grill until hot, about 15 minutes. Turn all burners to medium-high.

3. Clean cooking grate, then repeatedly brush grate with well-oiled paper towels until grate is black and glossy, 5 to 10 times. Place skewers on grill and cook (covered if using gas), turning as needed, until fish is lightly charred and registers 130 degrees, 10 to 12 minutes. Transfer skewers to serving platter and brush with olive caponata. Serve.

Grilled Salmon Steaks

Serves 2

Total time 45 minutes

WHY THIS RECIPE WORKS Salmon steaks are perfect for the grill: They're sturdier than a fillet, but they still cook relatively quickly. We started our testing by developing a method for evenly cooked steaks. Because salmon steaks have thinner belly flaps that can easily overcook, we wrapped and tied our steaks into neat medallions that would cook evenly. A half-grill fire allowed us to sear the steaks over the hot side of the grill and then finish cooking them gently on the cooler side. To flavor our rich salmon, we made a lemon and shallot butter sauce in a disposable aluminum pie plate set alongside the steaks. Once the steaks were nicely seared, we transferred them to the pie plate to finish cooking through right in the sauce, flavoring the fish all the way through. See page 258 for information on how to set up a half-grill fire. Before serving, lift out the small circular bone from the center of each steak. Be sure to oil the grate well in step 3; fish is delicate and tends to stick to the grill. If using wild salmon, decrease cook time slightly and cook steaks to 120 degrees (for medium-rare).

- 2 (10-ounce) salmon steaks, 1 to 1½ inches thick
- 1 tablespoon extra-virgin olive oil
- ½ teaspoon plus ⅛ teaspoon table salt, divided
- ¼ teaspoon pepper
- 1 small shallot, minced
- 2 tablespoons unsalted butter, cut into 2 pieces
- 1½ teaspoons capers, rinsed
- ½ teaspoon grated lemon zest plus 3 tablespoons juice
- 1 (9-inch) disposable aluminum pie plate
- 1 tablespoon minced fresh parsley

1. Pat salmon dry with paper towels. Working with 1 steak at a time, carefully trim 1½ inches of skin from 1 tail. Tightly wrap other tail around skinned portion and tie steaks with kitchen twine. Brush steaks with oil and sprinkle with ½ teaspoon salt and pepper. Combine shallot, butter, capers, lemon zest and juice, and remaining ⅛ teaspoon salt in disposable pie plate.

2A. FOR A CHARCOAL GRILL Open bottom vent completely. Light large chimney starter filled with charcoal briquettes (6 quarts). When top coals are partially covered with ash, pour evenly over half of grill. Set cooking grate in place, cover, and open lid vent completely. Heat grill until hot, about 5 minutes.

2B. FOR A GAS GRILL Turn all burners to high; cover; and heat grill until hot, about 15 minutes. Leave primary burner on high and turn off other burner(s).

3. Clean cooking grate, then repeatedly brush grate with well-oiled paper towels until grate is black and glossy, 5 to 10 times. Place steaks on hotter side of grill and cook (covered if using gas) until browned, 2 to 3 minutes per side. Meanwhile, place pie plate on cooler side of grill and heat until butter has melted, about 2 minutes.

4. Transfer steaks to pie plate and gently turn to coat with melted butter. Cover grill and cook until center of fish is still translucent when checked with tip of paring knife and registers 125 degrees (for medium-rare), 6 to 14 minutes, flipping steaks and rotating pie plate halfway through grilling.

5. Transfer salmon to serving platter, leaving sauce in pan, and remove twine. Whisk parsley into sauce and drizzle over steaks. Serve.

PREPARING SALMON STEAKS

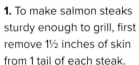

1. To make salmon steaks sturdy enough to grill, first remove 1½ inches of skin from 1 tail of each steak.

2. Next, tuck skinned portion into center of steak, wrap other tail around it, and tie with kitchen twine.

NOTES FROM THE TEST KITCHEN

HOW HOT IS YOUR FIRE?

If you don't have a grill thermometer on hand, you can use this simple method to check the intensity of a fire. Once the grill is preheated, take the temperature of the fire by holding your hand 5 inches above the cooking grate and counting how long you can comfortably leave it in place.

INTENSITY OF FIRE	TIME YOU CAN HOLD YOUR HAND 5 INCHES ABOVE GRATE
Hot fire	2 seconds
Medium-hot fire	3 to 4 seconds
Medium fire	5 to 6 seconds
Medium-low fire	7 seconds

Grilled Shrimp and Vegetable Kebabs

Grilled Shrimp and Vegetable Kebabs

Serves 2

Total time 1 hour, plus 15 minutes brining

WHY THIS RECIPE WORKS Combining shrimp and vegetable kebabs is notoriously difficult because the shrimp inevitably overcooks in the time it takes most vegetables to pass from raw to crisp-tender. We nestled mushrooms into the curve of the shrimp on the skewer to insulate the shrimp and extend their cooking time, and we cut the vegetables to mimic the profile of the shrimp so that the entire skewer made contact with the grill. Finally, we precooked some vegetables in the microwave before we skewered them to give them a head start. We dressed the cooked kebabs with a lemon-herb vinaigrette, which finished the dish in style. Small mushrooms measuring about 1¼ to 1½ inches in diameter work best here. You will need four 12-inch metal skewers for this recipe. Be sure to oil the grate well in step 3. See page 258 for information on how to set up a single-level fire.

SHRIMP

- 1 tablespoon table salt, for brining
- 1 tablespoon sugar, for brining
- 12 ounces jumbo shrimp (16 to 20 per pound), peeled and deveined
- 1½ large red or yellow bell peppers, stemmed, seeded, and cut into ¾-inch-wide by 3-inch-long strips
- ¼ teaspoon table salt, divided
- 12 cremini mushrooms, trimmed
- 6 scallions, cut into 3-inch lengths
- 1 tablespoon vegetable oil

VINAIGRETTE

- 2 tablespoons lemon juice
- 2 tablespoons extra-virgin olive oil
- 1 teaspoon minced fresh thyme
- ½ teaspoon minced garlic
- ¼ teaspoon table salt
- ⅛ teaspoon Dijon mustard
  Pinch pepper

1. FOR THE SHRIMP Dissolve 1 tablespoon salt and sugar in 2 cups cold water in large container. Submerge shrimp in brine, cover, and refrigerate for 15 minutes. Remove shrimp from brine and pat dry with paper towels.

2. Line large microwave-safe plate with double layer of paper towels. Spread bell peppers skin side down in even layer on plate and sprinkle with ⅛ teaspoon salt. Microwave for 2 minutes. Transfer bell peppers, still on towels, to cutting board and let cool.

3. Line second plate with double layer of paper towels. Spread mushrooms in even layer on plate and sprinkle with remaining ⅛ teaspoon salt. Microwave for 3 minutes. Transfer mushrooms, still on towels, to cutting board and let cool.

4. Lay 1 shrimp on cutting board and run 12-inch metal skewer through center. Thread mushroom onto skewer through sides of cap, pushing so it nestles tightly into curve of shrimp. Follow mushroom with 2 pieces scallion and 2 pieces bell pepper, skewering so vegetables and shrimp form even layer. Repeat shrimp and vegetable sequence 2 more times. When skewer is full, gently press ingredients so they fit snugly together in center of skewer. Thread remaining shrimp and vegetables on 3 more skewers for total of 4 kebabs. Brush each side of kebabs with oil and season with pepper.

5A. FOR A CHARCOAL GRILL Open bottom vent completely. Light large chimney starter mounded with charcoal briquettes (7 quarts). When top coals are partially covered with ash, pour evenly over grill. Set cooking grate in place, cover, and open lid vent completely. Heat grill until hot, about 5 minutes.

5B. FOR A GAS GRILL Turn all burners to high; cover; and heat grill until hot, about 15 minutes. Leave all burners on high.

6. FOR THE VINAIGRETTE While grill heats, whisk all ingredients together in bowl.

7. Clean cooking grate, then repeatedly brush grate with well-oiled paper towels until grate is black and glossy, 5 to 10 times. Place kebabs on grill and cook (covered if using gas) until charred, about 2½ minutes. Flip kebabs and cook until second side is charred and shrimp are cooked through, 2 to 3 minutes, moving kebabs as needed to ensure even cooking. Transfer kebabs to serving platter. Rewhisk vinaigrette and drizzle over kebabs. Serve.

Grilled Scallops with Fennel and Orange Salad

Serves 2

Total time 40 minutes

WHY THIS RECIPE WORKS Grilled scallops need little embellishment—their sweet, briny richness becomes even more intense on a hot grill, and their exterior develops a flavorful, nicely charred crust. With just oil, salt, and pepper plus a sprinkling of crushed pink peppercorns for color and fruity flavor, our scallops were ready for the grill. To turn our tender scallops into a satisfying supper, we created a simple salad to go with them. A trio of fresh fennel, orange pieces, and minced basil kept the dish bright and fresh-tasting. You will need four 12-inch metal skewers for this recipe. We recommend buying "dry" scallops, which don't have chemical additives and taste better than "wet." See page 258 for information on how to set up a single-level fire. Be sure to oil the grate well in step 3; scallops are delicate and tend to stick to the grill.

- 1 orange
- 1 fennel bulb, stalks discarded, bulb halved, cored, and sliced thin
- 1 tablespoon minced fresh basil
- 2 tablespoons extra-virgin olive oil, divided
- 8 large sea scallops, tendons removed
- 2 teaspoons pink peppercorns, crushed
- ¼ teaspoon table salt
- ⅛ teaspoon pepper

Grilled Scallops with Fennel and Orange Salad

To double-skewer scallops, thread 4 scallops onto one 12-inch metal skewer, then place second skewer through scallops parallel to and about ¼ inch from first skewer.

1. Cut away peel and pith from orange. Quarter orange, then slice crosswise into ¼-inch-thick pieces. Toss orange, fennel, basil, and 1 tablespoon oil in bowl and season with salt and pepper to taste; set aside for serving.

2. Pat scallops dry with paper towels and thread onto doubled 12-inch metal skewers, 4 scallops per doubled skewer. Brush scallops with remaining 1 tablespoon oil and sprinkle with peppercorns, salt, and pepper.

3A. FOR A CHARCOAL GRILL Open bottom vent completely. Light large chimney starter mounded with charcoal briquettes (7 quarts). When top coals are partially covered with ash, pour evenly over grill. Set cooking grate in place, cover, and open lid vent completely. Heat grill until hot, about 5 minutes.

3B. FOR A GAS GRILL Turn all burners to high; cover; and heat grill until hot, about 15 minutes.

4. Clean cooking grate, then repeatedly brush grate with well-oiled paper towels until grate is black and glossy, 5 to 10 times. Place scallop skewers on grill and cook (covered if using gas), turning as needed, until lightly charred and centers of scallops are opaque, about 6 minutes. Serve with salad.

Grilled Vegetable and Bread Salad

Serves 2   **VEGETARIAN**

Total time 45 minutes

WHY THIS RECIPE WORKS Grilled vegetables are the perfect basis for a summer supper, when all kinds of produce are at the height of ripeness. We wanted to pair nicely charred vegetables with chunks of rustic bread, fresh herbs, and a bright vinaigrette. We chose zucchini, red bell pepper, and sweet red onion for the vegetables. After 10 minutes on the grill, the vegetables were perfectly browned and tender and full of smoky flavor. We brushed slices of rustic Italian bread with oil and quickly toasted them over the grill. Then we simply tossed everything with a vinaigrette of basil, lemon, garlic, and mustard. A rustic round loaf, or a baguette sliced on the extreme bias, works best for this recipe. Be sure to use high-quality bread. You will need one 12-inch metal skewer for this recipe. See page 258 for information on how to set up a single-level fire.

¼ cup extra-virgin olive oil, divided
1 tablespoon chopped fresh basil
½ teaspoon grated lemon zest plus 2 teaspoons juice
1 small garlic clove, minced
½ teaspoon Dijon mustard
⅛ teaspoon plus ¼ teaspoon table salt, divided
¼ teaspoon pepper, divided
1 small red onion, sliced into ¾-inch-thick rounds
1 red bell pepper, stemmed, seeded, and quartered
1 zucchini, halved lengthwise
3 ounces Italian or French bread, cut into 1-inch-thick slices
2 ounces goat cheese, crumbled (½ cup)

1. Whisk 2 tablespoons oil, basil, lemon zest and juice, garlic, mustard, ⅛ teaspoon salt, and ⅛ teaspoon pepper together in large bowl; set vinaigrette aside.

2. Thread onion rounds from side to side onto 12-inch metal skewer. Brush onion, bell pepper, zucchini, and bread with remaining 2 tablespoons oil and sprinkle with remaining ¼ teaspoon salt and remaining ⅛ teaspoon pepper.

3A. FOR A CHARCOAL GRILL Open bottom vent completely. Light large chimney starter half filled with charcoal briquettes (3 quarts). When top coals are partially covered with ash, pour evenly over grill. Set cooking grate in place, cover, and open lid vent completely. Heat grill until hot, about 5 minutes.

3B. FOR A GAS GRILL Turn all burners to high; cover; and heat grill until hot, about 15 minutes. Turn all burners to medium.

4. Clean and oil cooking grate. Place vegetables on 1 side of grill and cook (covered if using gas) until spottily charred on both sides, 10 to 15 minutes, flipping them halfway through cooking. Transfer vegetables to cutting board and carefully remove onion from skewer.

5. While vegetables cook, place bread slices on grill, opposite vegetables, and cook (covered if using gas) until golden brown on both sides, about 4 minutes, flipping them halfway through cooking. Transfer bread to cutting board with vegetables.

6. Cut vegetables and bread into 1-inch pieces. Add vegetables and bread to bowl with vinaigrette and toss to coat. Divide salad evenly between 2 plates and sprinkle evenly with goat cheese. Serve.

Grilled Portobello Burgers with Garlicky Eggplant

Serves 2   **VEGETARIAN**
Total time 50 minutes

WHY THIS RECIPE WORKS For a hearty vegetarian entrée off the grill, we turned to portobello mushroom burgers. But in our initial tests, the mushrooms oozed moisture, turning the buns soggy; and even worse, they tasted bland. Luckily, the solutions to these problems were simple. To rid the mushroom caps of their excess moisture, we scored them before grilling. For bold flavor, we brushed them with a garlic and thyme oil halfway through cooking. Then we topped the burgers with grilled onion, creamy goat cheese, baby arugula, and juicy tomato. For an easy side dish, we drizzled thick rounds of eggplant with more of the garlicky oil and grilled them alongside the burgers. If your mushrooms are larger or smaller, you may need to adjust the cooking time accordingly. You will need one 12-inch metal skewer for this recipe. See page 258 for information on how to set up a single-level fire.

 6 tablespoons extra-virgin olive oil
 3 garlic cloves, minced
 1 teaspoon minced fresh thyme or ¼ teaspoon dried
 ½ teaspoon plus pinch table salt
 ¼ teaspoon plus ⅛ teaspoon plus pinch pepper, divided
12 ounces eggplant, sliced into ¼-inch-thick rounds
 1 small red onion, sliced into ¾-inch-thick rounds
 2 large portobello mushroom caps (4 to 5 inches in diameter)
 2 ounces goat cheese, crumbled (½ cup)
 2 hamburger buns
 ½ cup baby arugula
 1 tomato, cored and sliced thin

1. Cook oil, garlic, thyme, ¼ teaspoon salt, and ¼ teaspoon pepper in 8-inch skillet over medium heat until fragrant, about 1 minute; transfer to bowl. Brush both sides of eggplant rounds with 2 tablespoons garlic oil and sprinkle with ¼ teaspoon salt and ⅛ teaspoon pepper. Thread onion rounds from side to side onto 12-inch metal skewer, brush with 1 tablespoon garlic oil, and sprinkle with remaining pinch salt and remaining pinch pepper. Using paring knife, lightly score top of each mushroom cap in diagonal crosshatch pattern.

2A. FOR A CHARCOAL GRILL Open bottom grill vent completely. Light large chimney starter three-quarters filled with charcoal briquettes (4½ quarts). When top coals are partially covered with ash, pour evenly over grill. Set cooking grate in place, cover, and open lid vent completely. Heat grill until hot, about 5 minutes.

2B. FOR A GAS GRILL Turn all burners to high; cover; and heat grill until hot, about 15 minutes. Turn all burners to medium-high.

3. Clean and oil cooking grate. Place mushrooms, gill side down; onion skewer; and eggplant rounds on grill. Cook mushrooms (covered if using gas) until lightly charred and beginning to soften, 4 to 6 minutes. Flip mushrooms, brush with 1 tablespoon garlic oil, and cook until tender and browned on second side, 4 to 6 minutes. Sprinkle goat cheese over mushrooms and cook until cheese softens, about 2 minutes.

4. Meanwhile, cook onion and eggplant, turning as needed, until spottily charred on both sides, about 10 minutes. Transfer mushrooms, onion, and eggplant to large plate and tent loosely with aluminum foil. Grill buns until warm and lightly charred, about 30 seconds; transfer to separate plate.

5. Toss arugula with 1 teaspoon garlic oil in bowl and season with salt and pepper to taste. Carefully remove onion from skewer and separate rings. Assemble mushroom caps, onion rings, arugula, and tomato on buns. Drizzle remaining garlic oil over eggplant rounds. Serve with burgers.

Grilled Eggplant with Ginger-Sesame Vinaigrette

Serves 2 `FAST` `VEGETARIAN`

Total time 25 minutes

WHY THIS RECIPE WORKS Eggplant is a natural fit for the grill: it turns soft and silken over the intense heat of the fire and picks up complex charred flavors that complement its earthy taste. To achieve grilled eggplant that wasn't leathery or spongy, the size of the slice proved crucial; grilled over high heat, ¼ inch was just the right thickness to produce a charred exterior and tender flesh. Instead of marinating the eggplant slices before grilling, we saved time and effort by simply oiling and salting them before popping them on the grill, and then we drizzled the rounds with a flavorful ginger and sesame vinaigrette off the heat. See page 258 for information on how to set up a single-level fire.

GINGER-SESAME VINAIGRETTE

- 1 tablespoon unseasoned rice vinegar
- 1 teaspoon minced shallot
- 2 tablespoons extra-virgin olive oil
- 1 tablespoon toasted sesame oil
- 1 teaspoon sugar
- ½ teaspoon mayonnaise
- ½ teaspoon chili-garlic sauce
- ½ teaspoon grated fresh ginger
- ⅛ teaspoon table salt
- ⅛ teaspoon pepper

EGGPLANT

- 1 pound eggplant, sliced into ¼-inch-thick rounds
- 3 tablespoons extra-virgin olive oil
- ¼ teaspoon table salt
- ⅛ teaspoon pepper
- 2 tablespoons chopped roasted peanuts
- 1 scallion, sliced thin

1. FOR THE VINAIGRETTE Combine vinegar and shallot in small jar; let sit for 5 minutes. Add olive oil, sesame oil, sugar, mayonnaise, chili-garlic sauce, ginger, salt, and pepper to jar, secure lid, and shake vigorously until emulsified, about 30 seconds. (Vinaigrette can be refrigerated for up to 3 days.)

2. FOR THE EGGPLANT Brush eggplant all over with oil and sprinkle with salt and pepper.

3A. FOR A CHARCOAL GRILL Open bottom vent completely. Light large chimney starter filled with charcoal briquettes (6 quarts). When top coals are partially covered

Grilled Eggplant with Ginger-Sesame Vinaigrette

with ash, pour evenly over grill. Set cooking grate in place, cover, and open lid vent completely. Heat grill until hot, about 5 minutes.

3B. FOR A GAS GRILL Turn all burners to high; cover; and heat grill until hot, about 15 minutes. Turn all burners to medium-high.

4. Clean and oil cooking grate. Arrange eggplant on grill and cook (covered if using gas) until tender and grill marks appear, about 4 minutes per side. Transfer to serving platter, drizzle with vinaigrette, and sprinkle with peanuts and scallion. Serve.

VARIATION
Grilled Eggplant with Lemon-Herb Yogurt Sauce

Substitute ⅓ cup plain yogurt, ½ teaspoon grated lemon zest plus 2 teaspoons juice, 2 teaspoons extra-virgin olive oil, 1 small minced garlic clove, 1 tablespoon minced fresh cilantro, 1 tablespoon minced fresh mint, and ⅛ teaspoon table salt for ginger-sesame vinaigrette. Substitute pomegranate seeds for peanuts and ¼ cup fresh cilantro leaves for scallion.

Grilled Tofu with
Charred Broccoli
and Peanut Sauce

Grilled Tofu with Charred Broccoli and Peanut Sauce

Serves 2 `FAST` `VEGETARIAN`

Total time 30 minutes

WHY THIS RECIPE WORKS For a vibrant vegetarian dinner from the grill, we paired firm slabs of tofu with broccoli wedges, both of which do well after exposure to the high heat and char of the grill. Thai red curry paste added complex flavor; a single spoonful contains an assortment of aromatic ingredients including chiles, lemongrass, galangal, and makrut lime leaves. We brushed it over the tofu as a makeshift marinade, and stirred it into a quick peanut sauce that we used as a last-minute drizzle to unite the tofu and broccoli. See page 258 for information on how to set up a single-level fire.

- 14 ounces firm or extra-firm tofu
- 2 tablespoons hot water, plus extra as needed
- 2 tablespoons creamy peanut butter
- 1 tablespoon Thai red curry paste, divided
- ¼ teaspoon grated lime zest plus ½ teaspoon juice, plus lime wedges for serving
- 12 ounces broccoli crowns, cut into 4 wedges if 3 to 4 inches in diameter, or 6 wedges if 4 to 5 inches in diameter
- 2 tablespoons vegetable oil, divided
- ½ teaspoon table salt, divided
- ⅛ teaspoon pepper, divided
- 2 tablespoons chopped fresh cilantro
- 1 tablespoon chopped dry-roasted peanuts

1. Slice tofu lengthwise into 4 even slabs. Arrange tofu in even layer on paper towel–lined plate; set aside.

2. Whisk hot water, peanut butter, 1 teaspoon curry paste, and lime zest and juice in bowl until smooth. Add extra hot water, 1 teaspoon at a time, as needed until sauce is thick but pourable. Season with salt and pepper to taste; set aside.

3. Toss broccoli with 1 tablespoon oil, ¼ teaspoon salt, and pinch pepper in bowl; set aside. Whisk remaining 2 teaspoons curry paste, 1 tablespoon oil, ¼ teaspoon salt, and pinch pepper together in bowl. Pat tofu dry with paper towels and brush tofu all over with curry mixture.

4A. FOR A CHARCOAL GRILL Open bottom vent completely. Light large chimney starter filled with charcoal briquettes (6 quarts). When top coals are partially covered with ash, pour evenly over grill. Set cooking grate in place, cover, and open lid vent completely. Heat grill until hot, about 5 minutes.

4B. FOR A GAS GRILL Turn all burners to high; cover; and heat grill until hot, about 15 minutes. Leave all burners on high.

5. Clean and oil cooking grate. Grill broccoli and tofu until broccoli is charred in spots and tofu is well browned, 6 to 10 minutes, turning broccoli as needed and gently flipping tofu halfway through grilling. Transfer tofu and broccoli to serving platter. Drizzle with peanut sauce and sprinkle with cilantro and peanuts. Serve with lime wedges and crispy shallots, if desired.

Crispy Shallots

Makes ½ cup `FAST` `VEGETARIAN`

Total Time 20 minutes

- 3 shallots, sliced thin
- ½ cup vegetable oil for frying

1. Combine shallots and oil in medium bowl. Microwave for 5 minutes. Stir and continue to microwave for 2 minutes. Repeat stirring and microwaving in 2-minute increments until beginning to brown, 4 to 6 minutes.

2. Repeat stirring and microwaving in 30-second increments until deep golden brown, 30 seconds to 2 minutes. Using slotted spoon, transfer shallots to paper towel–lined plate; season with salt to taste. Let drain and crisp for about 5 minutes.

Grilled Pizza with Charred Romaine and Red Onion Salad

Serves 2 `VEGETARIAN`

Total time 1 hour, plus 15 minutes salting

WHY THIS RECIPE WORKS Pizza is a natural fit for the grill: The superhot fire mimics a professional pizza oven, giving the crust great char and crispness. We made a batch of our basic pizza dough, shaped it into two individual crusts, and grilled them over a medium-hot fire. We left one-quarter of the grill bottom free of coals, which gave us a cooler zone to move the crusts to if they started to burn. After cooking the dough on one side, we flipped the crusts and topped them with mozzarella, Parmesan, and tomato sauce. A quick charred romaine salad rounded out our meal. You can substitute store-bought pizza dough for the dough in this recipe. Let the dough sit out at room temperature while preparing the remaining ingredients; otherwise, it will be difficult to stretch. You will need one 12-inch metal skewer for this recipe. Do not remove the core from the lettuce; it will help keep the leaves together on the grill.

PIZZA
- 12 ounces plum tomatoes, cored, seeded, and cut into ½-inch pieces
- ¼ teaspoon table salt
- 2 tablespoons chopped fresh basil
- 2 tablespoons extra-virgin olive oil
- 1 small garlic clove, minced
- ⅛ teaspoon red pepper flakes
- 3 ounces mozzarella cheese, shredded (¾ cup)
- ¼ cup grated Parmesan cheese
- 1 recipe Basic Pizza Dough (page 101), room temperature

SALAD
- 3 tablespoons extra-virgin olive oil, divided
- 2 teaspoons balsamic vinegar
- 1 teaspoon honey
- ½ teaspoon Dijon mustard
- 1 small garlic clove, minced
- 1 red onion, sliced into ¾-inch-thick rounds
- ⅛ teaspoon table salt
  Pinch pepper
- 1 large romaine lettuce heart, halved lengthwise through core
- 1 ounce Parmesan cheese, shaved

1. FOR THE PIZZA Toss tomatoes with salt, spread on paper towel–lined plate, and let drain for 15 minutes. Combine drained tomatoes, basil, 1 tablespoon oil, garlic, and pepper flakes in bowl and season with salt and pepper to taste. In separate bowl, combine mozzarella and Parmesan.

2. Place dough on lightly floured counter and divide into 2 equal pieces. Working with 1 piece at a time, press and roll dough into 9-inch rounds. (If dough shrinks when rolled out, cover with plastic wrap and let rest for 5 minutes.) Lay dough rounds on separate pieces of parchment paper dusted with flour; they can be stacked on top of one another. Cover with plastic wrap.

3. FOR THE SALAD Whisk 2 tablespoons oil, vinegar, honey, mustard, and garlic together in small bowl. Season with salt and pepper to taste; set dressing aside. Thread onion rounds from side to side onto 12-inch metal skewer. Brush skewered onion and romaine with remaining 1 tablespoon oil and sprinkle with salt and pepper.

Grilled Pizza with Charred Romaine and Red Onion Salad

4A. FOR A CHARCOAL GRILL Open bottom vent completely. Light large chimney starter filled with charcoal briquettes (6 quarts). When top coals are partially covered with ash, pour in even layer over three-quarters of grill, leaving one quadrant free of coals. Set cooking grate in place, cover, and open lid vent completely. Heat grill until hot, about 5 minutes.

4B. FOR A GAS GRILL Turn all burners to high; cover; and heat grill until hot, about 15 minutes. Leave primary burner on high and turn off other burner(s). (Adjust primary burner as needed to maintain hot fire on one side.)

5. Clean and oil cooking grate. Place skewered onion on hotter part of grill and cook (covered if using gas) until spottily charred on both sides, 8 to 10 minutes, flipping onion halfway through cooking. Meanwhile, cook romaine on hotter part of grill next to onion until spottily charred on all sides, about 2 minutes, turning as needed. Transfer onion and romaine to serving platter. Carefully remove onion from skewer, separate rings, and tent vegetables loosely with aluminum foil to keep warm.

6. Lightly flour rimless (or inverted) baking sheet. Invert 1 dough round onto prepared sheet, peel off parchment, and reshape as needed. Working quickly, carefully slide round onto hotter part of grill. Repeat with second dough round. Cook (covered if using gas) until top of dough is covered with bubbles and bottom is spotty brown, about 1 minute, poking large bubbles with tongs as needed. (Check bottom of crust continually and slide to cooler part of grill if browning too quickly.)

7. Using tongs, return crusts to inverted sheet, browned sides up. Brush with remaining 1 tablespoon oil, sprinkle with cheese mixture, then top with tomato mixture. Return pizzas to hotter part of grill, cover, and cook until bottoms are well browned and cheese is melted, 2 to 4 minutes, checking bottoms frequently to prevent burning. Transfer pizzas to cutting board.

8. Drizzle onion and romaine with reserved dressing and sprinkle with Parmesan. Slice pizzas and serve with salad.

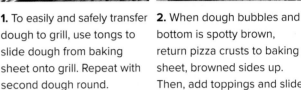

1. To easily and safely transfer dough to grill, use tongs to slide dough from baking sheet onto grill. Repeat with second dough round.

2. When dough bubbles and bottom is spotty brown, return pizza crusts to baking sheet, browned sides up. Then, add toppings and slide rounds back onto grill.

NOTES FROM THE TEST KITCHEN

GRILLING VEGETABLES AT A GLANCE

To easily grill a vegetable to serve alongside dinner, use this chart as a guide. Brush or toss the vegetables with oil before grilling. Grill vegetables over a medium-hot fire (see page 258).

VEGETABLE	PREPARATION	GRILLING DIRECTIONS
Asparagus	Snap off tough ends.	Grill, turning once, until tender and streaked with light grill marks, 5 to 7 minutes.
Bell Pepper	Core, seed, and cut into large wedges.	Grill, turning every 2 minutes, until streaked with dark grill marks, 8 to 10 minutes.
Corn	Remove all but last layer of husk.	Grill, turning every 2 minutes, until husk chars and peels away at tip, 8 to 10 minutes.
Endive	Cut in half lengthwise through stem end.	Grill, flat side down, until streaked with dark grill marks, 5 to 7 minutes.
Eggplant	Remove ends. Cut into ¼-inch-thick rounds or strips.	Grill, turning once, until flesh is darkly colored, 8 to 10 minutes.
Fennel	Slice bulb through base into ¼-inch-thick pieces.	Grill, turning once, until streaked with dark grill marks and quite soft, 7 to 9 minutes.
White or Cremini Mushrooms	Trim thin slice from stems then thread onto skewers.	Grill, turning several times, until golden brown, 6 to 7 minutes.
Onions	Peel and cut into ½-inch-thick slices.	Grill, turning occasionally, until lightly charred, 10 to 12 minutes.
Cherry Tomatoes	Remove stems then thread onto skewers.	Grill, turning several times, until streaked with dark grill marks, 3 to 6 minutes.
Plum Tomatoes	Cut in half lengthwise and seed.	Grill, turning once, until streaked with dark grill marks, about 6 minutes.
Zucchini or Summer Squash	Remove ends. Slice lengthwise into ½-inch-thick strips.	Grill, turning once, until streaked with dark grill marks, 8 to 10 minutes.

CHAPTER 11

Slow Cooker & Air Fryer Favorites

▪ **FAST** (Start to finish in 30 minutes or less)
▪ **VEGETARIAN**

Opposite: Air-Fryer Shoestring Fries

Slow-Cooker Beef and Noodle Soup

Serves 2

Cooking time 9 to 10 hours on low or 6 to 7 hours on high

WHY THIS RECIPE WORKS This soup makes a hearty beefy meal for two, the kind of recipe that can withstand up to 10 hours in the slow cooker so you can come home at the end of a long day and dinner will be waiting for you. For this old-fashioned soup, we chose blade steak, which contributed beefy flavor. We found that cremini mushrooms gave our soup a rich, earthy dimension. A traditional mirepoix, for which we jump-started the onion in the microwave with a little oil and tomato paste, formed the base of the soup, while store-bought beef broth, enhanced with soy sauce, imparted deep flavor.

- 1 small onion, chopped fine
- 4 teaspoons vegetable oil, divided
- 1 garlic clove, minced
- 1 teaspoon tomato paste
- ¾ teaspoon minced fresh thyme or ¼ teaspoon dried
- 3 cups beef broth
- 6 ounces cremini mushrooms, trimmed and sliced ½ inch thick
- 1 carrot, peeled and chopped
- 1 celery rib, chopped
- 2 teaspoons soy sauce
- 1 bay leaf
- 1 (8-ounce) beef blade steak, ¾ to 1 inch thick, trimmed
- ⅛ teaspoon table salt plus salt for cooking egg noodles
  Pinch pepper
- 1 ounce (⅔ cup) wide egg noodles
- 1 tablespoon chopped fresh parsley

1. Lightly spray inside of slow cooker with vegetable oil spray. Microwave onion, 1 tablespoon oil, garlic, tomato paste, and thyme in bowl, stirring occasionally, until onion is softened, about 5 minutes; transfer to slow cooker. Stir in broth, mushrooms, carrot, celery, soy sauce, and bay leaf. Sprinkle steak with salt and pepper and nestle into slow cooker. Cover and cook until beef is tender, 9 to 10 hours on low or 6 to 7 hours on high.

2. Bring 2 quarts water to boil in large saucepan. Add noodles and 1½ teaspoons salt and cook, stirring often, until al dente. Drain noodles, rinse with cold water, then toss with remaining 1 teaspoon oil in bowl.

3. Transfer steak to cutting board, let cool slightly, then shred into bite-size pieces using 2 forks; discard fat and gristle.

4. Discard bay leaf. Stir noodles and beef into soup and let sit until heated through, about 5 minutes. Stir in parsley and season with salt and pepper to taste. Serve.

Slow-Cooker Creamy Butternut Squash and Apple Soup

Serves 2   VEGETARIAN

Cooking time 6 to 7 hours on low or 4 to 5 hours on high

WHY THIS RECIPE WORKS We wanted to make things easy and prepare this classic soup in the slow cooker. We started by microwaving chopped onion in a bowl with butter and salt. After transferring that mixture to the slow cooker, we added freshly peeled butternut squash, which we cut into 1-inch pieces; broth; and a Golden Delicious apple. After the soup had cooked for 6 to 7 hours on low (or 4 to 5 hours on high), we pureed it to a silky-smooth texture. A dollop of sour cream works really well on this soup, but you can also sprinkle it with crumbled blue cheese or goat cheese, or crispy bacon. You can use an immersion blender to puree the soup directly in the slow cooker instead of using a blender. Serve with Garlic Croutons (page 15), if desired.

- ½ onion, chopped fine
- 2 tablespoons unsalted butter
- ¼ teaspoon table salt
- 1 pound butternut squash, peeled, seeded, and cut into 1-inch pieces (3 cups)
- 1 Golden Delicious apple, peeled, cored, and chopped
- 2 cups vegetable or chicken broth

1. Lightly spray inside of slow cooker with vegetable oil spray. Microwave onion, butter, and ¼ teaspoon salt in bowl, stirring occasionally, until onion is softened, about 5 minutes; transfer to slow cooker. Stir in squash, apple, and broth. Cover and cook until squash is tender, 6 to 7 hours on low or 4 to 5 hours on high.

2. Process soup in blender until smooth, 1 to 2 minutes. Season with salt and pepper to taste.

Slow-Cooker Chicken Stew with Chickpeas and Apricots

Serves 2

Cooking time 3 to 4 hours on low

WHY THIS RECIPE WORKS For a Moroccan-style slow-cooked chicken stew for two that delivered big flavor, we started with chicken thighs and added chickpeas and dried apricots, which softened during the long cooking time and permeated the stew with their flavor. To keep our prep work to a minimum, we chose boneless, skinless chicken thighs, which could be simply seasoned and added to the stew; once they were tender, we shredded them into bite-size pieces. Chicken broth and white wine infused the chicken with flavor, while tomato paste added savory depth. Since there is no opportunity for stews to thicken naturally in the moist environment of the slow cooker, a bit of tapioca ensured that the sauce thickened nicely. Serve over couscous or white rice.

- 2 tablespoons tomato paste
- 1 tablespoon vegetable oil
- 1 tablespoon paprika
- 1 teaspoon garam masala
- 1½ cups chicken broth, plus extra as needed
- 1 (14-ounce) can chickpeas, rinsed
- ¼ cup dry white wine
- 1 tablespoon instant tapioca
- 1 pound boneless, skinless chicken thighs, trimmed
- ¼ teaspoon table salt
- ⅛ teaspoon pepper
- 3 tablespoons chopped dried apricots

1. Lightly spray inside of slow cooker with vegetable oil spray. Microwave tomato paste, oil, paprika, and garam masala in bowl, stirring occasionally, until fragrant, about 1 minute; transfer to prepared slow cooker. Stir in broth, chickpeas, wine, and tapioca. Sprinkle chicken with salt and pepper and nestle into slow cooker. Cover and cook until chicken is tender, 3 to 4 hours on low.

2. Using large spoon, skim excess fat from surface of stew. Break chicken into 1-inch pieces with tongs. Stir in apricots and let sit until heated through, about 5 minutes. Adjust stew consistency with extra broth as needed. Season with salt and pepper to taste, and serve.

Slow-Cooker Creamy Butternut Squash and Apple Soup

Slow-Cooker Chicken Stew with Chickpeas and Apricots

Slow-Cooker Hearty Beef Stew

Serves 2

Cooking time 6 to 7 hours on low or 4 to 5 hours on high

WHY THIS RECIPE WORKS For such a humble dish, beef stew requires a lot of work. We wanted a small-batch stew with maximum flavor for minimum effort. To start, we swapped the traditional chuck roast for convenient steak tips, which were easy to cut into pieces and came out tender and flavorful. We skipped browning the meat and instead bolstered the beefy, savory notes of our broth with tomato paste and soy sauce. For the vegetables, we stuck with the traditional lineup of potatoes, carrots, and peas. Steak tips, also known as flap meat, are sold as whole steak, cubes, and strips; look for either whole steak tips or strips that are easy to cut into small pieces for this recipe. Use small red potatoes measuring 1 to 2 inches in diameter; if your potatoes are larger, cut them into 1-inch pieces to ensure that they cook through.

- 1 tablespoon vegetable oil
- 1 tablespoon tomato paste
- 2 garlic cloves, minced
- 1 teaspoon minced fresh thyme or ¼ teaspoon dried
- 2 cups beef broth, plus extra as needed
- 8 ounces small red potatoes, unpeeled
- 2 carrots, peeled and sliced ½ inch thick
- 1 tablespoon instant tapioca
- 1 tablespoon soy sauce
- ½ teaspoon table salt
- ¾ teaspoon pepper, divided
- 1 pound sirloin steak tips, trimmed and cut into 1½-inch pieces
- ⅔ cup frozen peas

1. Lightly spray inside of slow cooker with vegetable oil spray. Microwave oil, tomato paste, garlic, and thyme in bowl, stirring occasionally, until fragrant, about 1 minute; transfer to prepared slow cooker. Stir in broth, potatoes, carrots, tapioca, soy sauce, ½ teaspoon salt, and ½ teaspoon pepper. Sprinkle beef with remaining ¼ teaspoon pepper and stir into slow cooker. Cover and cook until beef is tender, 6 to 7 hours on low or 4 to 5 hours on high.

2. Using large spoon, skim excess fat from surface of stew. Stir in peas and let sit until heated through, about 5 minutes. Adjust stew consistency with extra broth as needed. Season with salt and pepper to taste, and serve.

Slow-Cooker Weeknight Beef Chili

Slow-Cooker Weeknight Beef Chili

Serves 2

Cooking time 5 to 6 hours on low or 3 to 4 hours on high

WHY THIS RECIPE WORKS We wanted to scale down our big batch chili, but it still had to offer all the rich, long-simmered flavor we were craving. The trio of tomato sauce, diced tomatoes, and tomato paste ensured that our chili tasted complex and was the right consistency. For big flavor, we incorporated generous amounts of chili powder, garlic, and cumin; minced chipotle added smoky undertones and heat. We also reached for soy sauce to boost the meaty, savory notes. Ground beef turned gritty after hours of slow cooking; we microwaved it briefly so that it became firm enough to break into coarse crumbles that didn't turn grainy in the slow cooker. Serve with your favorite chili garnishes.

- 1 pound 85 percent lean ground beef
- 2 tablespoons chili powder
- 2 tablespoons tomato paste

3 garlic cloves, minced

1½ teaspoons ground cumin

1 (15-ounce) can kidney beans, rinsed

1 (15-ounce) can tomato sauce

1 (14.5-ounce) can diced tomatoes

1½ tablespoons soy sauce

1½ teaspoons packed brown sugar

1 teaspoon minced canned chipotle chile in adobo sauce

½ teaspoon table salt

½ teaspoon pepper

1. Lightly spray inside of slow cooker with vegetable oil spray. Microwave ground beef, chili powder, tomato paste, garlic, and cumin in bowl, stirring occasionally, until beef is no longer pink, about 5 minutes. Transfer mixture to prepared slow cooker, breaking up any large pieces of meat with wooden spoon. Stir in beans, tomato sauce, tomatoes and their juice, soy sauce, sugar, chipotle, salt, and pepper. Cover and cook until beef is tender, 5 to 6 hours on low or 3 to 4 hours on high.

2. Using large spoon, skim excess fat from surface of chili. Break up any remaining large pieces of beef with spoon. Season with salt and pepper to taste, and serve.

VARIATION

Slow-Cooker Weeknight Turkey Chili

Be sure to use ground turkey, not ground turkey breast (also labeled 99 percent fat free), in this recipe. Do not cook this chili on high as it will cause the turkey to dry out.

Substitute 1 pound ground turkey for ground beef and 1 (15-ounce) can pinto beans for kidney beans. Cook chili until turkey is tender, 3 to 4 hours on low.

NOTES FROM THE TEST KITCHEN

CHOOSING A SMALLER SLOW COOKER
The **Cuisinart 4-Quart Cook Central 3-in-1 Multicooker** was our favorite small slow cooker. A slow cooker that can also brown, sauté, and steam, it produced perfect chicken, steaks, and ribs. Its programmable timer can be set to cook for up to 24 hours then automatically switches to "keep warm." We liked its lightweight, easy-clean, sturdy metal insert with extra-large handles and its oval shape, clear lid, and intuitive controls. The browning function is a nice plus for searing food or reducing sauces.

Slow Cooker Black Bean Chili

Slow-Cooker Black Bean Chili

Serves 2 [VEGETARIAN]

Cooking time 8 to 9 hours on high

WHY THIS RECIPE WORKS Vegetarian chilis are tricky since there are no ham products, like meaty, smoky ham hocks, to build flavor over the long cooking time. To achieve the full flavors we expected from a traditional black bean chili, we started by blooming a generous amount of aromatics and spices first in a skillet and then deglazed the skillet with broth to capture all the browned bits; this extra step ensured that our chili had deep flavor. Though a bit odd for a chili, a surprise ingredient, mustard seeds, added an appealing pungency and the level of complexity we were looking for. To bulk up the chili, we added white mushrooms and canned tomatoes. We added the tomatoes at the end, because their acidity prevented the beans from cooking through fully when added at the beginning. To make this dish spicier, reserve and add the chile seeds as desired. Serve with your favorite chili garnishes.

Slow-Cooker Meatballs and Marinara

Slow-Cooker Braised Short Ribs with Hoisin Sauce

1 tablespoon vegetable oil
½ onion, chopped fine
½ red bell pepper, minced
½ jalapeño chile, seeded and minced
2 garlic cloves, minced
1 tablespoon chili powder
1 teaspoon mustard seeds
1 teaspoon minced canned chipotle chile
  in adobo sauce
1 teaspoon ground cumin
1 teaspoon dried oregano
2 cups vegetable or chicken broth, divided,
  plus extra as needed
¾ cup dried black beans, picked over and rinsed
3 ounces white mushrooms, trimmed and halved if
  small or quartered if large
1 bay leaf
1 (14.5-ounce) can whole peeled tomatoes,
  drained and chopped
1 tablespoon chopped fresh cilantro

1. Lightly spray inside of slow cooker with vegetable oil spray. Heat oil in 12-inch skillet over medium heat until shimmering. Add onion and bell pepper and cook until vegetables are softened and lightly browned, 5 to 7 minutes. Stir in jalapeño, garlic, chili powder, mustard seeds, chipotle, cumin, and oregano and cook until fragrant, about 1 minute. Stir in 1 cup broth, scraping up any browned bits; transfer to slow cooker.

2. Stir remaining 1 cup broth, beans, mushrooms, and bay leaf into slow cooker. Cover and cook until beans are tender, 8 to 9 hours on high.

3. Discard bay leaf. Transfer ½ cup cooked beans to bowl and mash with potato masher until mostly smooth. Stir mashed beans and tomatoes into chili and let sit until heated through, about 5 minutes. Adjust consistency with extra hot broth as needed. Stir in cilantro and season with salt and pepper to taste. Serve.

Slow-Cooker Meatballs and Marinara

Makes 6 meatballs and 2½ cups sauce; enough for
8 ounces pasta
Cooking time 3 to 4 hours on low
WHY THIS RECIPE WORKS Our slow-cooker version of meatballs and marinara involves some prep work, but once everything is in the slow cooker, you've bought yourself hours of freedom, with the promise of a great dinner waiting in the

wings. To build a sauce with long-simmered flavor, we started by microwaving onion, tomato paste, garlic, and oregano. Clean-flavored crushed tomatoes were all we needed to add to this base. For the meatballs, a combination of ground beef, some of the sautéed aromatics, Parmesan, and parsley was a solid start, but they were still a bit dry. So we added a panade—a paste of bread and water—which provided the moisture they needed. Microwaving the meatballs before adding them to the slow cooker helped render just enough fat to ensure that our sauce wasn't greasy.

- ½ onion, chopped fine
- 1 tablespoon tomato paste
- 1 tablespoon extra-virgin olive oil
- 2 garlic cloves, minced
- 2 teaspoons minced fresh oregano or ½ teaspoon dried
- ½ slice hearty white sandwich bread, torn into 1-inch pieces
- 2 tablespoons water
- ½ teaspoon table salt, divided
- ¼ teaspoon pepper
- ¼ cup grated Parmesan cheese
- 1 tablespoon minced fresh parsley
- 1 large egg yolk
- 8 ounces 85 percent lean ground beef
- 1 (28-ounce) can crushed tomatoes
- 1 tablespoon chopped fresh basil
- ½ teaspoon sugar, plus extra for seasoning

1. Lightly spray inside of slow cooker with vegetable oil spray. Microwave onion, tomato paste, oil, garlic, and oregano in bowl, stirring occasionally, until onion is softened, about 5 minutes; transfer half of onion mixture to slow cooker.

2. Add bread, water, ¼ teaspoon salt, and ¼ teaspoon pepper to remaining onion mixture in bowl and mash into paste using fork. Stir in Parmesan, parsley, and egg yolk until combined. Add ground beef and knead with hands until well combined. Pinch off and roll mixture into 2-inch meatballs (about 6 meatballs) and arrange on large plate. Microwave meatballs until firm and no longer pink, about 5 minutes; discard rendered fat.

3. Add tomatoes and remaining ¼ teaspoon salt to slow cooker. Gently nestle meatballs into slow cooker; cover; and cook until meatballs are tender, 3 to 4 hours on low. Stir in basil and sugar. Season with salt, pepper, and extra sugar to taste. Serve.

Slow-Cooker Braised Short Ribs with Hoisin Sauce

Serves 2

Cooking Time 8 to 9 hours on low or 5 to 6 hours on high

WHY THIS RECIPE WORKS For a boldly flavored, seriously satisfying dinner for two, we slow-cooked short ribs until meltingly tender in a sweet, spicy, and savory sauce. The well-marbled ribs cooked down significantly, so to compensate we started with over a pound of ribs. Hoisin sauce and chili-garlic sauce provided an intensely flavored sauce with a nice sweetness and subtle heat, and chicken broth added meatiness. To ensure a nicely thickened sauce by the end of the cooking time, we stirred in 2 teaspoons of tapioca. Thinly sliced scallion whites gave the sauce an aromatic presence. Once the ribs were tender, we defatted the sauce, then stirred the ribs back in and sprinkled the finished dish with scallion greens for freshness and a burst of color. Look for boneless short ribs that are well marbled and measure about 2 inches wide and 1 inch thick. Serve over egg noodles or rice.

- ½ cup chicken broth
- ⅓ cup hoisin sauce
- 3 scallions, white parts minced, green parts sliced thin
- 1 tablespoon chili-garlic sauce
- 2 teaspoons instant tapioca
- 2 (10-ounce) boneless beef short ribs, trimmed
- ¼ teaspoon table salt
- ⅛ teaspoon pepper

1. Lightly spray inside of slow cooker with vegetable oil spray. Combine broth, hoisin, scallion whites, chili-garlic sauce, and tapioca in prepared slow cooker. Sprinkle beef with salt and pepper and nestle into slow cooker. Cover and cook until beef is tender, 8 to 9 hours on low or 5 to 6 hours on high.

2. Transfer short ribs to serving platter, tent loosely with aluminum foil, and let rest for 5 minutes. Using large spoon, skim excess fat from surface of sauce. Pour sauce over short ribs and sprinkle with scallion greens. Serve.

Slow-Cooker Sweet-and-Sour Sticky Ribs

2 tablespoons ketchup
2 tablespoons soy sauce
2 tablespoons unseasoned rice vinegar
1 tablespoon minced fresh cilantro

1. Mix garlic powder, ginger, salt, and pepper together in bowl and rub evenly over ribs.

2. Lightly spray inside of slow cooker with vegetable oil spray. Arrange ribs along bottom and sides of prepared slow cooker, meaty side facing down. Cover and cook until ribs are tender, 5 to 6 hours on low.

3. Adjust oven rack 10 inches from broiler element and heat broiler. Set wire rack in aluminum foil–lined rimmed baking sheet and spray with oil spray. Whisk preserves, ketchup, soy sauce, and vinegar together. Transfer ribs meaty side up to prepared rack. Brush ribs with sauce, then broil until browned and sticky, 10 to 15 minutes, flipping and brushing with additional sauce every few minutes. Sprinkle with cilantro. Serve with remaining sauce.

ARRANGING RIBS IN A SLOW COOKER

Arrange rack with meaty side down across bottom of slow cooker. Ends of rack will come up against sides of slow cooker.

Slow-Cooker Sweet-and-Sour Sticky Ribs

Serves 2

Cooking time 5 to 6 hours on low

WHY THIS RECIPE WORKS Chinese-style sweet-and-sour ribs are a party favorite, but we wanted to scale this irresistible dish down for two. Leaving the membrane attached to the underside of our baby back ribs helped the rack hold together as it cooked and, as a bonus, shortened our prep time. We rubbed the ribs with a mixture of garlic powder and ground ginger, which infused them with flavor. Once the ribs were tender, we brushed them with a tangy sauce and broiled them to develop a caramelized, lightly charred exterior. Avoid racks of baby back ribs that are larger than 2 pounds; they will be difficult to maneuver into the slow cooker.

1½ teaspoons garlic powder
1 teaspoon ground ginger
1 teaspoon table salt
1 teaspoon pepper
1 (1½- to 2-pound) rack baby back ribs, trimmed
⅓ cup apricot preserves

Slow-Cooker Pulled Pork Tacos with Radish-Apple Slaw

Serves 2

Cooking time 6 to 7 hours on low or 4 to 5 hours on high

WHY THIS RECIPE WORKS Pulled pork tacos tend to be a dish that serves a crowd and uses a large pork butt roast. But this scaled-down recipe makes it practical for just two. Here, we used convenient boneless country-style ribs, which became meltingly tender in the slow cooker. To give our pulled pork an equally rich sauce, we deployed just the right pantry staples—chili powder, cumin, chipotle chiles, canned tomato sauce, and raisins—to produce a quick mole with complex flavor. Blending the sauce gave it the perfect consistency. For a topping with plenty of crunch, we created a slaw featuring tart apples, peppery radishes, and red onion. Avocado added creamy richness, while a dressing spiked with lime brightened things up, and cilantro lent a bright, grassy note. For more information on warming tortillas, see page 124. You can use an immersion blender to puree the sauce directly in the slow cooker instead of using a blender.

PORK

- 2 teaspoons extra-virgin olive oil
- 2 teaspoons chili powder
- 2 teaspoons ground cumin
- 1 teaspoon minced canned chipotle chile in adobo sauce
- 1 garlic clove, lightly crushed and peeled
- 1 pound boneless country-style pork ribs, trimmed and cut into 2-inch pieces
- 1 (8-ounce) can tomato sauce
- ⅓ cup raisins
- ¼ teaspoon table salt
- ¼ teaspoon pepper

RADISH-APPLE SLAW

- 2 tablespoons extra-virgin olive oil
- 1 tablespoon lime juice
- 1½ teaspoons cider vinegar
- ½ teaspoon table salt
- 6 ounces radishes, trimmed and cut into ¼-inch wedges
- ½ Granny Smith apple, cored and cut into 2-inch-long matchsticks
- ¼ cup thinly sliced red onion
- 1 avocado, halved, pitted, and cut into ½-inch pieces
- 2 ounces cotija cheese, crumbled (½ cup)
- ½ cup fresh cilantro leaves
- 4–6 (6-inch) corn tortillas, warmed

1. FOR THE PORK Lightly spray inside of slow cooker with vegetable oil spray. Microwave oil, chili powder, cumin, chipotle, and garlic in small bowl until fragrant, about 1 minute. Combine pork, oil mixture, tomato sauce, raisins, salt, and pepper in slow cooker. Cover and cook until tender, 6 to 7 hours on low or 4 to 5 hours on high.

2. Transfer pork to cutting board, let cool slightly, then shred into bite-size pieces using 2 forks; discard excess fat.

3. Using wide, shallow spoon, skim excess fat from surface of sauce. Process sauce in blender until smooth, about 1 minute. (Adjust sauce consistency with hot water as needed.) Combine ¾ cup sauce and pork in now-empty slow cooker and season with salt and pepper to taste.

4. FOR THE RADISH-APPLE SLAW Whisk oil, lime juice, vinegar, and salt together in large bowl. Add radishes, apple, and onion and toss to coat. Gently fold in avocado, cotija, and cilantro. Season with salt and pepper to taste. Serve pork with tortillas, remaining sauce, and slaw.

NOTES FROM THE TEST KITCHEN

TIPS FOR ENSURING SLOW-COOKER SUCCESS

Here are some tips for turning out satisfying, full-flavored slow-cooker dishes.

SPRAY YOUR SLOW COOKER When cooking a smaller amount of food in the slow cooker, more evaporation can occur, leading some dishes to stick to the sides of the slow-cooker insert and burn. To avoid this, be sure to spray the sides of the slow-cooker insert with vegetable oil spray before adding any food.

DON'T SKIMP ON THE AROMATICS You'll see hefty amounts of onions, garlic, herbs, and other flavorful ingredients in our recipes. This is because the moist heat environment and long cooking times that come with the slow cooker tend to dull flavors. Also, many recipes need a flavor boost at the end of the cooking time, which is why we often finish with fresh herbs, lemon juice, or other flavorful ingredients.

USE FLAVOR ENHANCERS To replicate the meaty flavor usually achieved by browning meat and vegetables, we turn to umami-rich ingredients like tomato paste and soy sauce, which offer savory depth and rich flavor to many of our recipes.

ADD DELICATE VEGETABLES AT THE RIGHT TIME Delicate vegetables, like frozen peas, baby spinach, and chopped tomatoes turn mushy when added at the beginning, so we usually stir them in at the end, ensuring that they are perfectly tender.

SKIM AWAY EXCESS FAT To remove excess fat, simply turn off the slow cooker and let the food sit for a few minutes so the fat can rise to the top. Use a large spoon to skim the excess fat off the surface.

Air-Fryer Roasted Bone-In Chicken Breasts

Serves 2 `FAST`

Total time 30 minutes

WHY THIS RECIPE WORKS Roasting a pair of bone-in chicken breasts in the air fryer is a snap, and there are no leftovers to deal with. Bone-in chicken cooks beautifully in the air fryer, and the circulated hot air does nearly all the work. We rubbed the breasts with just a teaspoon of oil to ensure crispy skin and flipped and rotated them halfway through cooking. Starting them skin side down helped the fat in the skin to render, then we flipped them so the skin could brown. A moderate 350 degrees minimized moisture loss and resulted in perfectly juicy meat. For a sauce to drizzle over our roasted breasts, we created two bright, fresh options, either of which can be prepared while the chicken cooks (one enlists the microwave but neither requires a pan or even a blender, keeping the prep minimal and cutting down on dishes to wash). For an elegant presentation, cut the chicken breasts off the bone before serving.

- 2 (12-ounce) bone-in split chicken breasts, trimmed
- 1 teaspoon extra-virgin olive oil
- ½ teaspoon table salt
- ¼ teaspoon pepper

Pat chicken dry with paper towels, rub with oil, and sprinkle with salt and pepper. Arrange breasts skin side down in air-fryer basket, spaced evenly apart, alternating ends. Place basket into air fryer and set temperature to 350 degrees. Cook until chicken registers 160 degrees, 20 to 25 minutes, flipping and rotating breasts halfway through cooking. Transfer chicken to serving platter, tent loosely with aluminum foil, and let rest for 5 minutes. Serve.

Lemon-Basil Salsa Verde

Makes about 1 cup `FAST`

Total time 10 minutes

Whisk ¼ cup minced fresh parsley, ¼ cup chopped fresh basil, 3 tablespoons extra-virgin olive oil, 1 tablespoon rinsed and minced capers, 1 tablespoon water, 2 minced garlic cloves, 1 rinsed and minced anchovy fillet, ½ teaspoon grated lemon zest and 2 teaspoons juice, and ⅛ teaspoon table salt together in bowl.

Peach-Ginger Chutney

Makes 2 cups `FAST` `VEGETARIAN`

Total time 15 minutes

Microwave 1 teaspoon extra-virgin olive oil, 1 small minced shallot, 1 minced garlic clove, 1 teaspoon grated fresh ginger, ⅛ teaspoon table salt, and pinch red pepper flakes in medium bowl until shallot has softened, about 1 minute. Stir in 1½ cups frozen peaches, thawed and cut into ½-inch pieces; 2 tablespoons packed light brown sugar; and 1½ tablespoons cider vinegar. Microwave until peaches have softened and liquid is thick and syrupy, 6 to 8 minutes, stirring occasionally. Stir in 1 tablespoon chopped crystallized ginger.

Air-Fried Chicken

Serves 2

Total time 50 minutes

WHY THIS RECIPE WORKS Our air-fried chicken comes out golden and crispy on the outside and moist and juicy on the inside, and needed only a light spray of vegetable oil to become crisp. The secret was removing the fatty skin and finding a coating that would become crunchy without needing to be fried in a pan of hot oil. In a side-by-side taste test, crushed cornflakes won out over bread crumbs and Melba toast, offering the best color and crispness, but the results tasted a bit like breakfast cereal. We spiced up the cornflakes with poultry seasoning, paprika, and cayenne pepper. Dipping the floured chicken pieces in buttermilk added tang and ensured that the crumbs stuck to the chicken.

- Vegetable oil spray
- 2 (12-ounce) bone-in split chicken breasts, trimmed
- ¾ teaspoon table salt, divided
- ¼ teaspoon pepper
- ⅓ cup buttermilk
- ½ teaspoon dry mustard
- ½ teaspoon garlic powder
- ¼ cup all-purpose flour
- 2 cups (2 ounces) cornflakes, finely crushed
- 1½ teaspoons poultry seasoning
- ½ teaspoon paprika
- ⅛ teaspoon cayenne pepper

1. Lightly spray bottom of air-fryer basket with vegetable oil spray. Remove skin from chicken and trim any excess fat. Halve each breast crosswise, pat dry with paper towels, and sprinkle with ½ teaspoon salt and pepper. Whisk buttermilk, mustard, garlic powder, ½ teaspoon salt, and ¼ teaspoon pepper together in medium bowl. Spread flour in shallow dish. Combine cornflakes, poultry seasoning, paprika, remaining ¼ teaspoon salt, and cayenne in second shallow dish.

2. Working with 1 piece of chicken at a time, dredge in flour; dip in buttermilk mixture, letting excess drip off; then coat with cornflake mixture, pressing gently to adhere; transfer to large plate. Lightly spray chicken with oil spray.

3. Arrange chicken pieces in prepared basket, spaced evenly apart. Place basket into air fryer and set temperature to 400 degrees. Cook until chicken is crisp and registers 160 degrees, 16 to 24 minutes, flipping and rotating pieces halfway through cooking. Serve.

Air-Fryer Lemon-Pepper Chicken Wings

Serves 2   FAST

Total time 30 minutes

WHY THIS RECIPE WORKS Once you make chicken wings in your air fryer, you may never go back to conventional frying or oven roasting again. With their delicate skin and paper-thin layer of fat, chicken wings are a perfect candidate for air frying. In the intense, evenly circulating heat, the fat renders as the skin crisps, then conveniently accumulates at the bottom of the air fryer without smoking up your kitchen. We didn't want to toss our wings in gloppy, sugar- or fat-heavy sauces, so once cooked, we tossed them with a simple combination of lemon zest and herbs. If you buy chicken wings that are already split, with the tips removed, you will need only 1 pound.

1¼	pounds chicken wings, halved at joints, wingtips discarded
⅛	teaspoon table salt
¼	teaspoon pepper
1	tablespoon grated lemon zest, plus lemon wedges for serving
1	tablespoon minced fresh parsley, dill, and/or tarragon

Air-Fryer Lemon-Pepper Chicken Wings

1. Pat wings dry with paper towels and sprinkle with salt and pepper. Arrange wings in even layer in air-fryer basket. Place basket into air fryer and set temperature to 400 degrees. Cook until wings are golden brown and crisp, 18 to 24 minutes, flipping wings halfway through cooking.

2. Combine lemon zest and parsley in large bowl. Add wings and toss until evenly coated. Serve with lemon wedges.

VARIATIONS
Air-Fryer Parmesan-Garlic Chicken Wings
Add 1 tablespoon grated Parmesan cheese and 1 minced garlic clove to lemon zest–parsley mixture.

Air-Fryer Cilantro-Lime Chicken Wings
To make this dish spicier, reserve and add the chile seeds as desired.

Substitute lime zest and wedges for lemon and cilantro for parsley. Add 1 tablespoon minced jalapeño chile to lime zest–cilantro mixture.

TIPS FOR AIR FRYER SUCCESS

BETTER BROWNING While cooking in the air fryer is low fat, it isn't no fat. We spray or brush meat and fish with vegetable oil (spraying makes it easy to focus the oil on top of the protein). Fat isn't the only way to boost browning. Glazes using honey, preserves, and hoisin sauce all add flavor, and they also help food brown.

SKEWER IT Threading pieces of chicken or vegetables onto wooden skewers provides an easy way to space food out in the basket and maximize air exposure. It also helps generate some flavorful charring.

A WORD ABOUT PREHEATING We found preheating unnecessary. To allow for differences across models, the cooking times in our recipes are meant to be counted as soon as you press "start."

FORGET ABOUT ATTACHMENTS Some air fryers come with rotisserie baskets or frying baskets with auto-stir attachments. These accessories are fussy to use and don't make better food.

CHOOSING A SMALLER AIR FRYER

We love the **Philips Premium Airfryer with Fat Removal Technology.** This 3-quart airfryer is perfect for the for-two household and will work with all the recipes in this chapter. This machine has a slim, compact footprint, and we liked that its nonstick cooking basket was simple to clean and had a removable bottom for deeper cleaning. Its digital controls and dial-operated menu made setting the time and temperature easy and intuitive. It automatically stopped cooking as soon as the set time was up, and its drawer allowed us to remove its cooking basket without exposing our hands to the heating element.

Air-Fryer Spiced Chicken Kebabs with Vegetable and Bulgur Salad

Serves 2

Total time 1 hour

WHY THIS RECIPE WORKS For this recipe, we used skewers to raise the vegetables and chicken in the air fryer, allowing heat to circulate around them to generate better browning and charring. Partway through cooking, we stacked the chicken kebabs on the vegetable kebabs, placed crosswise for maximum air circulation, which brought the chicken closer to the heat source. A garlicky yogurt mixture spiced with baharat, an East Mediterranean spice blend, acted as a marinade for the chicken and sauce for the finished dish. Using bigger pieces of chicken and packing them tightly onto skewers kept the meat juicy. Skewering the vegetables separately allowed us to tailor cooking times so that the chicken and vegetables were ready at the same time. Look for medium-grind bulgur (labeled "#2"). Avoid coarsely ground bulgur; it will not cook through in time. You can use store-bought baharat or make your own (see page 205). For an accurate measurement of boiling water, bring a kettle of water to a boil and then measure out the desired amount. Serve with warmed pitas or naans, if desired.

- ½ cup medium-grind bulgur, rinsed
- ⅓ cup boiling water
- 1 teaspoon baharat, divided
- ½ teaspoon table salt, divided
- ⅔ cup plain Greek yogurt
- 2 teaspoons grated lemon zest plus ¼ cup juice, divided (2 lemons)
- 2 tablespoons extra-virgin olive oil, divided
- 1 small garlic clove, minced to paste
- 12 ounces boneless, skinless chicken breasts, trimmed and cut into 1½-inch pieces
- ½ cup coarsely chopped fresh mint, divided
- ½ cup coarsely chopped fresh parsley, divided
- 1 small red bell pepper, stemmed, seeded, and cut into 1½-inch pieces
- 1 small red onion, halved and cut through root end into 6 equal wedges
  Vegetable oil spray
- 5 (6-inch) wooden skewers
- 2 tablespoons toasted chopped pistachios, almonds, or walnuts

1. Combine bulgur, boiling water, ¾ teaspoon baharat, and ¼ teaspoon salt in large bowl. Cover tightly with plastic wrap and let sit while preparing kebabs.

2. Combine yogurt, lemon zest, 2 tablespoons lemon juice, 1 tablespoon oil, garlic, remaining ¼ teaspoon baharat, and remaining ¼ teaspoon salt in bowl. Transfer ¼ cup yogurt mixture to medium bowl, add chicken, and toss to coat; let marinate for at least 15 minutes or up to 1 hour. Stir ¼ cup mint and ¼ cup parsley into remaining yogurt mixture and season with salt and pepper to taste; set aside for serving.

3. Thread bell pepper and onion evenly onto 3 skewers; lightly spray with oil spray. Arrange kebabs in air-fryer basket, parallel to each other and spaced evenly apart. Place basket into air fryer, set temperature to 375 degrees, and cook for 5 minutes.

4. Meanwhile, thread chicken evenly onto remaining 2 skewers. Arrange chicken kebabs on top of vegetable kebabs, perpendicular to bottom layer. Return basket to air fryer and cook until chicken is lightly browned and registers 160 degrees, 15 to 20 minutes, flipping and rotating chicken kebabs halfway through cooking. Transfer chicken kebabs to plate, tent with aluminum foil, and let rest while finishing salad.

5. Transfer vegetable kebabs to cutting board. When cool enough to handle, slide vegetables off skewers and chop coarse. Add vegetables, pistachios, remaining 2 tablespoons lemon juice, remaining 1 tablespoon oil, remaining ¼ cup mint, and remaining ¼ cup parsley to bulgur and toss to combine. Season with salt and pepper to taste. Serve chicken kebabs and salad with yogurt sauce.

Air-Fryer Turkey-Zucchini Meatballs with Orzo, Spiced Tomato Sauce, and Feta

Air-Fryer Turkey-Zucchini Meatballs with Orzo, Spiced Tomato Sauce, and Feta

Serves 2

Total time 1 hour

WHY THIS RECIPE WORKS Cooking pasta or grains in the air fryer can be tricky since the environment encourages rapid evaporation, which can lead to uneven cooking. Enter orzo—a rice-shaped pasta with a rare talent for maintaining its shape and texture when cooked, especially when pretoasted. So we pretoasted the orzo in olive oil and garlic, using a 6-inch cake pan. Then we parcooked the pasta in a warmly spiced tomato sauce. Meanwhile, we shaped our turkey meatballs using shredded zucchini, which replaced the traditional panade and gave the meatballs moisture and tenderness. We nestled the meatballs into the parcooked orzo and sauce, then air-fried the meatballs until they had simmered on the bottom and were lightly roasted on the top. Finally, we added crumbled feta and air-fried everything together for the last few minutes.

Be sure to use ground turkey, not ground turkey breast (also labeled 99 percent fat-free), in this recipe. You will need a 6-inch round nonstick or silicone cake pan for this recipe; before starting this recipe, confirm your air fryer allows enough space for the pan.

- ½ cup traditional or whole-wheat orzo
- 1 tablespoon extra-virgin olive oil, plus extra for drizzling
- 2 garlic cloves, minced, divided
- 1 (8-ounce) can tomato sauce
- ¾ cup water
- ¼ teaspoon pepper, divided
- ⅛ teaspoon ground cinnamon
  Pinch ground cloves
- 8 ounces ground turkey
- 4 ounces zucchini, grated (¾ cup)
- 1 tablespoon minced fresh oregano, plus extra for serving
- ⅛ teaspoon table salt
- 1 ounce crumbled feta cheese (¼ cup)

Air-Fryer Roasted
Bone-In Pork Chop
with Chermoula

1. Combine orzo, oil, and half of garlic in 6-inch round nonstick cake pan, then spread into even layer. Place pan into air-fryer basket and place basket into air fryer. Set temperature to 400 degrees and cook until orzo is lightly browned and fragrant, 3 to 5 minutes, stirring halfway through cooking.

2. Stir tomato sauce, water, ⅛ teaspoon pepper, cinnamon, and cloves into orzo mixture until evenly combined. Return basket to air fryer and cook until orzo is al dente, 18 to 22 minutes.

3. Using your hands, lightly knead turkey, zucchini, oregano, salt, remaining garlic, and remaining ⅛ teaspoon pepper in medium bowl until mixture forms cohesive mass. With lightly moistened hands, pinch off and roll mixture into 8 meatballs. (Meatballs can be refrigerated for up to 24 hours.)

4. Stir orzo mixture gently to recombine. Nestle meatballs into orzo and cook until meatballs are lightly browned, 8 to 10 minutes. Sprinkle feta over meatballs and cook until meatballs register 160 degrees and feta is spotty brown, 2 to 4 minutes.

5. Transfer pan to wire rack and let meatballs and orzo rest for 5 minutes. Drizzle with extra oil and sprinkle with extra oregano before serving.

Air-Fryer Roasted Bone-In Pork Chop

Serves 2

Total time 40 minutes

WHY THIS RECIPE WORKS Aiming to roast bone-in pork chops for two in our air fryer, we first tried using two 8-ounce chops, but rotating and flipping them proved too awkward; they didn't quite fit. Since bone-in chops are often found thick-cut, we switched to a single 1-pound chop, which was easier to fit in the basket. With such a thick chop, however, we needed a way to cook the meat through without the exterior drying out. Roasting at a moderate 350 degrees resulted in an evenly cooked, juicy chop, and—to our pleasant surprise—also gave the chop more color because of the longer roasting time. Cutting two slits in the sides of the chop prevented it from curling during cooking. To contrast with the rich, roasted meat, we created two bold sauces, a peach-mustard sauce (made with frozen peaches) and an herbaceous, smoky chermoula. If making the chermoula, prepare it before roasting the chop to allow its flavors to meld.

1 (1-pound) bone-in pork rib or center-cut chop, 1½ to 1¾ inches thick, trimmed
1 teaspoon vegetable oil
¼ teaspoon table salt
⅛ teaspoon pepper

1. Pat chop dry with paper towels. Using sharp knife, cut 2 slits, about 2 inches apart, through fat on edge of chop. Rub with oil and sprinkle with salt and pepper.

2. Place chop in air-fryer basket, then place basket into air fryer. Set temperature to 350 degrees and cook until pork registers 140 degrees, 20 to 25 minutes, flipping and rotating chop halfway through cooking.

3. Transfer chop to cutting board, tent with aluminum foil, and let rest for 5 minutes. Carve pork from bone and slice ½ inch thick. Serve alone or with one of the sauces below.

Peach-Mustard Sauce

Makes 1½ cups **FAST** **VEGETARIAN**
Total time 15 minutes

Microwave 5 ounces frozen sliced peaches, cut into 1-inch pieces, 2 tablespoons water, 1 tablespoon sugar, and 2 teaspoons white wine vinegar in medium bowl, stirring occasionally, until peaches have softened and mixture is slightly thickened, about 8 minutes. Let cool slightly, then stir in ¾ teaspoon whole-grain mustard and ½ teaspoon minced fresh thyme or rosemary.

Chermoula

Makes ¾ cup **FAST** **VEGETARIAN**
Total time 10 minutes

Whisk ⅓ cup extra-virgin olive oil, ⅓ cup minced fresh cilantro, 1 tablespoon lemon juice, 2 minced garlic cloves, ½ teaspoon ground cumin, ½ teaspoon paprika, and ⅛ teaspoon cayenne in bowl until combined. Season with salt and pepper to taste.

Air-Fryer Fennel-Rubbed Pork Tenderloin with Zucchini Ribbon Salad

Serves 2

Total time 50 minutes

WHY THIS RECIPE WORKS Mild, buttery pork tenderloin is a favorite choice for a weeknight meal, but its long shape wasn't an obvious fit for the air fryer. The solution? We cut it in half and found we could accommodate two tenderloins in the basket that way. We wanted to give the pork a crust, so we brushed on a mixture of garlic, honey, lemon zest, and fennel seeds. Coarsely ground whole fennel seeds gave the meat a beautiful flavor and aroma. For an easy side dish, we shaved ribbons of zucchini, showcasing the squash's crunchier side. We tossed it with toasted pine nuts, basil, and shaved Parmesan, dressing the salad just before serving to avoid wilting. Use a spice grinder to coarsely grind the fennel seeds (about six 1-second pulses); you can also pound the seeds with a skillet or meat mallet. Use a vegetable peeler or a mandoline to shave the zucchini.

2 tablespoons extra-virgin olive oil, divided
2 garlic cloves, minced
1½ teaspoons honey
½ teaspoon grated lemon zest plus 1 tablespoon juice
¼ teaspoon plus ⅛ teaspoon table salt, divided
¼ teaspoon pepper, divided
1 (1-pound) pork tenderloin, trimmed and halved crosswise
1 tablespoon fennel seeds, coarsely ground
2 small zucchini (6 ounces each), shaved lengthwise into ribbons
1 ounce Parmesan cheese, shaved
1 tablespoon shredded fresh basil
1 tablespoon pine nuts, toasted (optional)

1. Microwave 1½ teaspoons oil, garlic, honey, lemon zest, ¼ teaspoon salt, and ⅛ teaspoon pepper in large bowl until fragrant, about 30 seconds, stirring once halfway through. Pat pork dry with paper towels, add to oil mixture, and toss to coat.

2. Sprinkle pork pieces with fennel seeds, pressing to adhere, then arrange in air fryer basket. (Tuck thinner tail end of tenderloin under itself as needed to create uniform pieces.) Place basket into air fryer and set temperature to 350 degrees. Cook until pork is lightly browned and registers 140 degrees, 16 to 21 minutes, flipping and rotating tenderloin pieces halfway through cooking. Transfer pork to cutting board, tent with aluminum foil, and let rest while preparing salad.

3. Gently toss zucchini with remaining 1½ tablespoons oil, lemon juice, remaining ⅛ teaspoon salt, and remaining ⅛ teaspoon pepper in clean bowl. Arrange attractively on serving platter and sprinkle with Parmesan, basil, and pine nuts, if using. Slice pork ½ inch thick and serve with salad.

Air-Fryer Orange-Mustard Glazed Salmon

Serves 2 FAST

Total time 30 minutes

WHY THIS RECIPE WORKS A sweet, tangy glaze offers appealing contrast to rich, meaty salmon, but most recipes stumble by calling for broiling the fish, which can result in unevenly cooked salmon and a burnt glaze. So we were happy to find that the air fryer produced failproof results; the direct heat from above caramelized the glaze's sugars, while the circulated air cooked the fish from all sides. We liked the idea of an orange glaze, which we made with juice and zest, orange marmalade, and mustard. We brushed the mixture on the fillets before cooking and after 10 minutes were met with crispy glazed fish boasting beautiful browned edges and a velvety pink interior. This technique lends itself to a variety of flavors, so we also developed a glaze made with hoisin and rice vinegar and a sweet-smoky honey-chipotle glaze. If using wild salmon, decrease cook time slightly and cook fillet to 120 degrees (for medium-rare). For more information on making a foil sling, see page 309.

1 tablespoon orange marmalade
¼ teaspoon grated orange zest plus 1 tablespoon juice
2 teaspoons whole-grain mustard
2 (8-ounce) skin-on salmon fillets, 1½ inches thick
¼ teaspoon table salt
⅛ teaspoon pepper

1. Make foil sling for air-fryer basket by folding 1 long sheet of aluminum foil so it is 4 inches wide. Lay sheet of foil widthwise across basket, pressing foil into and up sides of basket. Fold excess foil as needed so that edges of foil are flush with top of basket. Lightly spray foil and basket with vegetable oil spray.

2. Combine marmalade, orange zest and juice, and mustard in bowl. Pat salmon dry with paper towels and sprinkle with salt and pepper. Brush tops and sides of fillets evenly with glaze. Arrange fillets skin side down on sling in prepared basket, spaced evenly apart. Place basket into air fryer and set temperature to 400 degrees. Cook salmon until center is still translucent

when checked with tip of paring knife and registers 125 degrees (for medium-rare), 10 to 14 minutes, using sling to rotate fillets halfway through cooking.

3. Using sling, carefully remove salmon from air fryer. Slide fish spatula along underside of fillets and transfer to individual serving plates, leaving skin behind. Serve.

VARIATIONS
Air-Fryer Hoisin Glazed Salmon
Omit orange zest. Substitute 2 tablespoons hoisin sauce for marmalade, 1 tablespoon unseasoned rice vinegar for orange juice, and ⅛ teaspoon ground ginger for mustard.

Air-Fryer Honey-Chipotle Glazed Salmon
Omit orange zest and juice. Substitute 2 tablespoons honey for marmalade and 2 teaspoons minced canned chipotle chile in adobo sauce for mustard.

Air-Fried
Crunchy Cod
Fillets

MAKING AN ALUMINUM FOIL SLING

1. Fold one long sheet of foil so that it is 4 inches wide. Lay the sheet of foil width-wise across the basket or rack. Press the foil up and into the sides and fold any excess foil so that the edges of the foil are flush with the lip of the basket.

2. After cooking, use the sling to carefully remove the fish from the air-fryer basket.

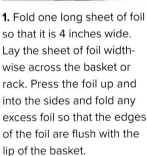

Air-Fried Crunchy Cod Fillets

Serves 2

Total time 45 minutes

WHY THIS RECIPE WORKS Fish is so moist that any attempt to give it a crisp crust (short of deep frying) is likely to end up soggy. So we avoided breading the fish all over and simply pressed pretoasted panko crumbs onto the top, which gave us crunch in every bite. A coating of mayonnaise, egg yolk, and lemon zest boosted flavor and helped the crumbs

adhere. But the flaky cod was too delicate to lift from the air-fryer basket without breaking. A foil sling enabled us to rotate and later remove the fillets in one piece. You can substitute halibut or haddock for the cod. For more information on making a foil sling, see left. Serve with Creamy Chipotle Chile Sauce (page 310), if desired.

- ⅓ cup panko bread crumbs
- 1 teaspoon vegetable oil
- 1 small shallot, minced
- 1 small garlic clove, minced
- ½ teaspoon minced fresh thyme or ⅛ teaspoon dried
- ½ teaspoon table salt
- ⅜ teaspoon pepper, divided
- 1 tablespoon minced fresh parsley
- 1 tablespoon mayonnaise
- 1 large egg yolk
- ¼ teaspoon grated lemon zest, plus lemon wedges for serving
- 2 (8-ounce) skinless cod fillets, 1¼ inches thick

1. Make foil sling for air-fryer basket by folding 1 long sheet of aluminum foil so it is 4 inches wide. Lay sheet of foil width-wise across basket, pressing foil into and up sides of basket. Fold excess foil as needed so that edges of foil are flush with top of basket. Lightly spray foil and basket with vegetable oil spray.

2. Toss panko with oil in bowl until evenly coated. Stir in shallot, garlic, thyme, ¼ teaspoon salt, and ⅛ teaspoon pepper. Microwave, stirring frequently, until panko is light golden brown, about 2 minutes. Transfer to shallow dish and let cool slightly; stir in parsley. Whisk mayonnaise, egg yolk, lemon zest, and ⅛ teaspoon pepper together in bowl.

3. Pat cod dry with paper towels and sprinkle with remaining ¼ teaspoon salt and remaining ⅛ teaspoon pepper. Arrange fillets skinned side down on plate and brush tops evenly with mayonnaise mixture. (Tuck thinner tail ends of fillets under themselves as needed to create uniform pieces.) Working with 1 fillet at a time, dredge coated side in panko mixture, pressing gently to adhere. Arrange fillets crumb side up on sling in prepared basket, spaced evenly apart. Place basket into air fryer and set temperature to 300 degrees. Cook until cod registers 140 degrees, 12 to 16 minutes, using sling to rotate fillets half-way through cooking. Using sling, carefully remove cod from air fryer. Serve with lemon wedges.

Air-Fryer Harissa-Rubbed Haddock with Brussels Sprouts and Leek

Creamy Chipotle Chile Sauce

Makes about ⅔ cup `FAST` `VEGETARIAN`
Total time 15 minutes

Whisk ¼ cup mayonnaise, ¼ cup sour cream, 2 teaspoons minced canned chipotle chile in adobo sauce, 2 teaspoons minced fresh cilantro, 1 teaspoon lime juice, and 1 small minced garlic clove together in bowl.

Air-Fryer Harissa-Rubbed Haddock with Brussels Sprouts and Leek

Serves 2
Total time 35 minutes

WHY THIS RECIPE WORKS For this beautifully satisfying dinner, we air-fried a hearty pile of vegetables—earthy brussels sprouts and a tender leek—with halibut. We used harissa to create a zesty crust on the mild-flavored fish. We gave the vegetables a head start so that they could begin to soften, and then they finished cooking underneath the fish at a hotter temperature, which rendered them crispy with char around the edges. We decided to cut the leek into large pieces, 1-inch thick, which helped it cook alongside the hardier sprouts without getting overly charred. Look for small brussels sprouts no bigger than a golf ball. If you can find only large sprouts, quarter them. Black sea bass, cod, hake, and pollack are good substitutes for the haddock. Tail-end fillets can be folded to achieve the proper thickness. You can use store-bought harissa or our Harissa (page 311) in this recipe.

12 ounces brussels sprouts, trimmed and halved
 1 large leek, white and light green parts only, halved lengthwise, sliced 1 inch thick, and washed thoroughly
 3 tablespoons extra-virgin olive oil, divided
 ½ teaspoon table salt, divided
 4 teaspoons harissa
 2 (6- to 8-ounce) skinless haddock fillets, 1 to 1½ inches thick
 1 teaspoon grated lemon zest, plus lemon wedges for serving

1. Toss brussels sprouts and leek with 2 tablespoons oil and ¼ teaspoon salt in bowl. Arrange vegetables in even layer in air-fryer basket. Place basket into air fryer; set temperature to 350 degrees; and cook for 10 minutes, stirring vegetables halfway through cooking.

2. Combine harissa paste, remaining 1 tablespoon oil, and remaining ¼ teaspoon salt in small bowl. Pat haddock dry with paper towels and rub with harissa mixture. Stir vegetables, then place fillets, skinned side down, on top, spaced evenly apart. (Tuck thinner tail ends of fillets under themselves as needed to create uniform pieces.) Return basket to air fryer; increase temperature to 400 degrees; and cook until haddock is lightly browned, flakes apart when prodded gently with paring knife, and registers 135 degrees, 8 to 14 minutes.

3. Transfer haddock to serving platter. Stir lemon zest into vegetables and season with salt and pepper to taste. Transfer vegetables to platter with haddock and serve with lemon wedges.

Harissa

Makes about ½ cup FAST VEGETARIAN
Total time 25 minutes

A spicy, aromatic paste, harissa is used as both an ingredient and a condiment throughout North Africa. If you can't find Aleppo pepper, you can substitute ¾ teaspoon paprika and ¾ teaspoon finely chopped red pepper flakes.

  6 tablespoons extra-virgin olive oil
  6 garlic cloves, minced
  2 tablespoons paprika
  1 tablespoon ground coriander
  1 tablespoon ground dried Aleppo pepper
  1 teaspoon ground cumin
  ¾ teaspoon caraway seeds
  ½ teaspoon table salt

Combine all ingredients in bowl and microwave until bubbling and very fragrant, about 1 minute, stirring halfway through microwaving. Let cool completely.

Air-Fried Brussels Sprouts

Air-Fried Brussels Sprouts

Serves 2 FAST VEGETARIAN
Total time 25 minutes

WHY THIS RECIPE WORKS Fried brussels sprouts have become a menu staple—and for good reason. The tiny cabbages become caramelized and crispy while maintaining enough structure to work as a dipping vessel. Our first attempts to make them in an air fryer were promising but not perfect. Since we usually achieve crispiness (when not frying) by using a very hot oven, we tossed the brussels sprouts in a little oil and roasted them in the air fryer at 400 degrees. They crisped up quickly but tasted raw inside. The solution turned out to be more obvious: Lowering the heat to 350 degrees gave the sprouts time to soften on the inside while the outside crisped. The results mimicked the deep-fried sprouts so well that we were inspired to create a version with another beloved fried vegetable: crispy shallots. The brussels sprouts are delicious with just a squeeze of lemon, but irresistible with Lemon-Chive Dipping Sauce (page 312). If you are buying loose brussels sprouts, select those that are about 1½ inches long. Quarter brussels sprouts longer than 2½ inches.

½ pound brussels sprouts, trimmed and halved
1½ teaspoons extra-virgin olive oil
⅛ teaspoon table salt
   Pinch pepper
   Lemon wedges

Toss brussels sprouts with oil, salt, and pepper in bowl; transfer to air-fryer basket. Place basket into air fryer and set temperature to 350 degrees. Cook brussels sprouts until tender, well browned, and crispy, 20 to 25 minutes, tossing halfway through cooking. Season with salt and pepper to taste. Serve with lemon wedges.

VARIATION
Air-Fried Brussels Sprouts with Crispy Shallots
Add 1 thinly sliced shallot to bowl with brussels sprouts along with oil, salt, and pepper.

Lemon-Chive Dipping Sauce
Makes about 3 tablespoons   FAST
Total time 10 minutes

Whisk 2 tablespoons mayonnaise, 1½ teaspoons minced fresh chives, ¼ teaspoon grated lemon zest plus 1 teaspoon juice, ¼ teaspoon Worcestershire sauce, ¼ teaspoon Dijon mustard, and ⅛ teaspoon garlic powder together in bowl.

Air-Fryer Shoestring Fries
Serves 2   VEGETARIAN
Total time 45 minutes

WHY THIS RECIPE WORKS In the realm of fries, the flavor of shoestring fries is hard to beat. Their thinner shape allows for more of our favorite part—the crunch. Instead of cutting them by hand, we used a spiralizer to quickly cut potatoes into thin, even strings. Then we cut them into manageable 4-inch lengths. We removed excess starch by rinsing and then drying them with paper towels. We coated the fries with just 2 tablespoons of oil, which made them perfectly golden, although they maintained a dry, crisp exterior. To mix up the flavor, try one of our seasoning variations. Serve with Lemon-Chive Dipping Sauce, if desired. You will need a spiralizer with a ¼-inch (6mm) noodle attachment for this recipe.

1 pound russet potatoes, unpeeled
2 tablespoons vegetable oil
¼ teaspoon table salt
⅛ teaspoon pepper

1. Use chef's knife to trim off ends of potatoes. Using spiralizer fitted with ¼-inch (6mm) noodle attachment, cut potatoes into ribbons, cutting ribbons into 4-inch lengths with kitchen shears as you spiralize. Submerge potatoes in large bowl of water and rinse to remove excess starch. Drain potatoes and repeat process as needed until water remains clear. Drain potatoes, transfer to paper towel–lined rimmed baking sheet, and thoroughly pat dry.

2. Toss potatoes with oil, salt, and pepper. Arrange potatoes in even layer in air-fryer basket. Place basket into air fryer and set temperature to 350 degrees. Cook for 15 to 20 minutes, using tongs to toss gently and separate potatoes every 5 minutes to prevent sticking. Season with salt and pepper to taste, and serve.

VARIATIONS
Air-Fryer Shoestring Fries with Rosemary and Lemon Zest
Sprinkle 1 teaspoon minced fresh rosemary over potatoes and toss to combine before final 5 minutes of cooking. Before serving, toss fries with 1 teaspoon grated lemon zest.

Air-Fryer Shoestring Fries with Coriander and Dill
Sprinkle 1 teaspoon ground coriander and ½ teaspoon pepper over potatoes and toss to combine before final 5 minutes of cooking. Before serving, toss fries with 1 teaspoon minced fresh dill.

Air-Fryer Crispy Baked Potato Fans
Serves 2   VEGETARIAN
Total time 45 minutes

WHY THIS RECIPE WORKS Essentially baked potatoes but par-sliced into thin, even segments that create a fanlike shape, our air-fried potato fans became extra-crispy on the outside while their interiors remained fluffy and moist. We turned to olive oil to help crisp the segments and added flavor with aromatic smoked paprika and garlic powder. We found that using the right kind of potato was key. The russet, or Idaho, potato was the best choice because of its starchy flesh and creamy texture. We found it was critical to rinse the potatoes of surface

**Air-Fryer Crispy
Baked Potato Fans**

¼ inch from bottom of potato. Repeat with second potato. Rinse potatoes gently under running water, let drain, and transfer to plate. Microwave until slightly tender when squeezed gently, 6 to 12 minutes, flipping potatoes halfway through cooking.

2. Combine oil, paprika, garlic powder, salt, and pepper in bowl. Brush potatoes with portion of oil mixture, then drizzle remaining oil in between slices. Arrange potatoes cut side up in air-fryer basket, spaced evenly apart. Place basket into air fryer and set temperature to 400 degrees. Cook until potato skins are crisp and golden brown and potato interiors register 205 degrees, 25 to 30 minutes. Sprinkle potatoes with scallions and serve with lemon wedges.

Air-Fryer Make-Ahead Breakfast Burritos

Makes 6 burritos **VEGETARIAN**

Total time 45 minutes (30 minutes from frozen)

WHY THIS RECIPE WORKS If you love a good breakfast burrito, this recipe is for you. Though the filling is made in a skillet, shaped burritos can be warmed in the air fryer from refrigerated or frozen. Unlike the microwave, the air fryer heats evenly, so there are no soggy or cold bits. While store-bought breakfast burritos often rely on greasy meat for bulk and flavor, we filled our burrito with refried black beans and added frozen chopped kale to our fluffy scrambled eggs. To build a flavorful base for the beans, we sautéed aromatic scallions, cumin, and chili powder. We added our beans, mashing them while they cooked, which created a cohesive mixture. To freeze the burritos, wrap each one in foil. The number of burritos you can cook at one time will depend on the size of your air fryer. Serve with salsa, Greek yogurt, lime wedges, and hot sauce.

starch after they were sliced, as it prevented them from sticking together, and we trimmed off the ends of each potato, which gave the slices room to fan out. To prevent overcooking or burning our spuds in the heat of the air fryer, we precooked them briefly in the microwave. To ensure that the potatoes fan out evenly, look for uniformly shaped potatoes. Chopsticks or thick skewers provide a failproof guide for slicing the potato petals without cutting all the way through the potato in step 1.

 2 russet potatoes, unpeeled
 2 tablespoons extra-virgin olive oil
 ¼ teaspoon smoked paprika
 ¼ teaspoon garlic powder
 ¼ teaspoon table salt
 ⅛ teaspoon pepper
 2 tablespoons minced scallions, fresh chives,
     fresh dill, and/or fresh parsley
     Lemon wedges

1. Cut ¼ inch from bottoms and ends of potatoes. Place 1 chopstick or thick skewer lengthwise on each side of 1 potato, then slice potato crosswise at ¼-inch intervals, stopping

 8 large eggs
 ¼ cup milk
 ⅛ teaspoon table salt
 2 tablespoons extra-virgin olive oil, divided
 8 ounces frozen chopped kale or spinach,
     thawed and squeezed dry
 6 scallions, sliced thin
 1½ teaspoons ground cumin
 ½ teaspoon chili powder
 1 (15-ounce) can black beans
 ¼ cup chopped fresh cilantro
 2 tablespoons lime juice
 6 (10-inch) white or 100 percent whole-wheat tortillas

1. Whisk eggs, milk, and salt in large bowl until well combined. Heat 1 tablespoon oil in 12-inch nonstick skillet over medium heat until shimmering. Add egg mixture and, using rubber spatula, constantly and firmly scrape along bottom and sides of skillet until eggs are just set, 2 to 4 minutes. Off heat, fold in kale. Transfer egg mixture to plate and wipe skillet clean with paper towels.

2. Heat remaining 1 tablespoon oil in now-empty skillet over medium heat until shimmering. Add scallions, cumin, and chili powder and cook until fragrant, about 1 minute. Stir in beans and their canning liquid and cook, mashing beans with back of spoon, until mixture is heated through and thickened, 3 to 5 minutes. Off heat, stir in cilantro and lime juice. Season with salt and pepper to taste.

3. Wrap tortillas in damp dish towel and microwave until warm and pliable, about 1 minute. Lay tortillas on counter and spread bean mixture evenly across each tortilla, close to bottom edge. Top with egg-kale mixture. Working with 1 tortilla at a time, fold sides, then bottom of tortilla over filling, then continue to roll tightly into wrap.

4. Arrange up to 4 burritos, seam side down, in air-fryer basket, spaced evenly apart. Place basket into air fryer; set temperature to 400 degrees; and cook until crisp, 5 to 8 minutes.

5. Individually wrap remaining burritos in greased aluminum foil. Transfer to zipper-lock bags and freeze for up to 2 months. To bake from frozen, place foil-wrapped burritos into air-fryer basket. Place basket into air fryer; set temperature to 325 degrees; and cook until heated through, about 30 minutes, flipping burritos halfway through cooking. Let rest, wrapped in foil, for 5 minutes before serving. (Alternatively, frozen wrapped burritos can be thawed in refrigerator overnight and baked for about 15 minutes.)

Air-Fryer Kale, Roasted Red Pepper, and Goat Cheese Frittata

Air-Fryer Kale, Roasted Red Pepper, and Goat Cheese Frittata

Serves 2 `FAST` `VEGETARIAN`

Total time 25 minutes

WHY THIS RECIPE WORKS This frittata highlights the incredible convenience and even cooking offered by the air fryer. In about fifteen minutes of cooking time, it transformed a simple egg-and-cheese custard packed with kale, roasted red peppers, and scallions into a delightful meal for two—fluffy and tender on the inside, golden and delicately sealed on the outside. The compact size and even heat of a nonstick cake pan made the occasional stirring of the egg mixture during cooking unnecessary. Using frozen vegetables (which are blanched before freezing) meant we didn't have to precook them. Any worries we had that frozen vegetables might taste soggy were put to rest by the air fryer's rapidly circulating hot air, which gently roasted the vegetables at the surface and edges of the frittata. You will need a 6-inch round nonstick or silicone cake pan for this recipe; before starting this recipe, confirm your air fryer allows enough space for the pan.

- 4 large eggs
- 1 tablespoon milk
- ⅛ teaspoon table salt
- 4 ounces frozen chopped kale or spinach, thawed and squeezed dry
- ¼ cup jarred roasted red peppers, rinsed, patted dry, and chopped
- 1 ounce goat cheese, crumbled (¼ cup)
- 2 scallions, sliced thin

1. Generously spray 6-inch round nonstick cake pan with vegetable oil spray. Whisk eggs, milk, and salt in medium bowl until well combined, then stir in kale, peppers, goat cheese, and scallions.

2. Transfer egg mixture to prepared pan and place pan in air-fryer basket. Place basket into air fryer; set temperature to 350 degrees; and cook until frittata is deep golden brown and registers 180 to 190 degrees, 15 to 25 minutes.

3. Transfer pan to wire rack and let rest for 5 minutes. Using rubber spatula, loosen frittata from pan and transfer to cutting board. Cut into wedges and serve.

VARIATIONS
Air-Fryer Ham, Pea, and Swiss Cheese Frittata
Substitute 2 ounces chopped deli ham and ½ cup thawed frozen peas for kale and red peppers, and Swiss cheese for goat cheese.

Air-Fryer Broccoli, Sun-Dried Tomato, and Cheddar Frittata
Substitute 4 ounces frozen chopped broccoli florets, thawed and patted dry, and 2 tablespoons chopped oil-packed sun-dried tomatoes, rinsed and patted dry, for kale and red peppers, and cheddar cheese for goat cheese.

Air-Fryer Make-Ahead Fruit, Nut, and Oat Scones
Makes 10 scones   VEGETARIAN

Total time 45 minutes (20 minutes from frozen)

WHY THIS RECIPE WORKS Who wouldn't want a breakfast scone that can be made ahead of time? Our scones can be easily baked in the air fryer, even directly from frozen. We toasted both oats and nuts in the air fryer to enhance their flavor. We developed this recipe with raisins and walnuts, but any dried fruit and nuts will work. The number of scones you can cook at one time will depend on the size of your air fryer. For the variations, extra glaze can be stored in an airtight container for up to a week.

- ½ cup whole milk
- 1 large egg
- 1½ cups (7½ ounces) all-purpose flour
- ¼ cup (1¾ ounces) plus 1 tablespoon sugar, divided
- 2 teaspoons baking powder
- ½ teaspoon table salt
- 8 tablespoons unsalted butter, chilled, cut into ½-inch pieces
- 1¼ cups (3¾ ounces) old-fashioned rolled oats, toasted
- ½ cup raisins
- ¼ cup walnuts, toasted and chopped

1. Whisk milk and egg together in bowl; measure out and reserve 1 tablespoon milk mixture. Pulse flour, ¼ cup sugar, baking powder, and salt in food processor until combined, about 4 pulses. Scatter butter over top and pulse until mixture resembles coarse cornmeal, 12 to 14 pulses. Transfer mixture to large bowl and stir in oats, raisins, and walnuts. Stir in remaining milk mixture until large clumps form. Continue to mix dough by hand in bowl until dough forms cohesive mass.

2. Turn dough and any floury bits onto lightly floured counter; pat gently into 7-inch circle. Cut dough into 10 wedges. Brush tops with reserved 1 tablespoon milk mixture and sprinkle with remaining 1 tablespoon sugar.

3. Lightly spray base of air-fryer basket with canola oil spray. Space desired number of scones at least ½ inch apart in prepared basket; evenly space remaining scones on parchment paper–lined rimmed baking sheet. Place basket into air fryer and set temperature to 350 degrees. Bake until scones are golden brown, 10 to 15 minutes. Transfer scones to wire rack and let cool for at least 5 minutes before serving.

4. Freeze remaining sheet of scones until firm, about 1 hour. Transfer scones to 1-gallon zipper-lock bag and freeze for up to 1 month. To bake from frozen, place scones into air-fryer basket. Place basket into air fryer, set temperature to 250 degrees, and bake for 10 minutes. Increase temperature to 350 degrees and continue to bake until golden brown, about 10 minutes.

VARIATIONS
Air-Fryer Currant, Almond, and Oat Scones with Earl Grey Glaze
Substitute currants for raisins and almonds for walnuts. Microwave 1 tablespoon milk and ½ teaspoon crumbled Earl Grey tea leaves in medium bowl until steaming, about 30 seconds. Let cool completely, about 10 minutes. Whisk in ½ cup confectioners' sugar until smooth and let sit until thick but pourable, about 10 minutes. Omit sugar for sprinkling. Let scones cool to room temperature, about 20 minutes, then drizzle with glaze. Let glaze set for 10 minutes before serving.

Air-Fryer Apricot, Pistachio, and Oat Scones with Garam Masala Glaze
Substitute chopped dried apricots for raisins and pistachios for walnuts. Microwave 1 tablespoon milk and ½ teaspoon garam masala in medium bowl until steaming, about 30 seconds. Let cool completely, about 10 minutes. Whisk in ½ cup confectioners' sugar until smooth and let sit until thick but pourable, about 10 minutes. Omit sugar for sprinkling. Let scones cool to room temperature, about 20 minutes, then drizzle with glaze. Let glaze set for 10 minutes before serving.

CHAPTER 12

Vegetable Side Dishes

▦ **FAST** (Start to finish in 30 minutes or less)
▦ **VEGETARIAN**

Opposite: Beets with Hazelnuts and Chives

Roasted Artichoke Hearts with Lemon and Basil

Pan-Roasted Asparagus

Roasted Artichoke Hearts with Lemon and Basil

Serves 2 `FAST` `VEGETARIAN`

Total time 30 minutes

WHY THIS RECIPE WORKS For this quick side dish, we wanted to bring out the delicate, vegetal flavor of tender artichoke hearts without extensive hands-on time. Frozen artichoke hearts eliminated the tedious prep work that fresh artichokes required, but the frozen hearts contained a considerable amount of water, which prevented browning and diluted the flavor of our dish. To encourage deep caramelization, we preheated the baking sheet in a 450-degree oven. The excess water quickly evaporated on the sizzling-hot pan, giving us golden-brown, deeply flavored artichokes. Lining the baking sheet with foil made cleanup a snap. While the hearts roasted, we tossed together a simple dressing with just lemon juice, olive oil, basil, and roasted garlic to highlight the artichokes' flavor without overpowering them. To thaw the artichokes quickly, microwave them in a covered bowl for about 3 minutes and pat dry before using.

- 9 ounces frozen artichoke hearts, thawed and patted dry
- 1 garlic clove, peeled
- 5 teaspoons extra-virgin olive oil, divided
- ¼ teaspoon table salt
  Pinch pepper
- 2 teaspoons lemon juice
- 2 teaspoons chopped fresh basil

1. Adjust oven rack to middle position, place aluminum foil–lined rimmed baking sheet on rack, and heat oven to 450 degrees. Toss artichokes with garlic, 1 tablespoon oil, salt, and pepper and carefully arrange in single layer on hot sheet. Roast artichokes until browned around edges, 15 to 20 minutes.

2. Mince roasted garlic. Whisk remaining 2 teaspoons oil, lemon juice, basil, and minced garlic together in large bowl. Add roasted artichokes and toss to coat. Season with salt and pepper to taste, and serve.

VARIATION

Roasted Artichoke Hearts with Fennel, Mustard, and Tarragon

Roast 1 small fennel bulb, cored and thinly sliced, along with artichokes and garlic. Substitute 2 teaspoons minced fresh tarragon for basil and add 1 teaspoon whole-grain mustard to dressing in step 2.

Pan-Roasted Asparagus

Serves 2 FAST VEGETARIAN

Total time 20 minutes

WHY THIS RECIPE WORKS Asparagus can be a perfect no-fuss, quick-cooking side dish for two, but getting it right can be a challenge. To avoid overcooking, we started with thicker spears. To help the asparagus release moisture, encouraging caramelization and better flavor, we parcooked the spears, covered, with butter and oil. The water evaporating from the butter helped to steam the asparagus, cooking it through evenly. Then we removed the lid and turned up the heat to brown the spears. We found that we preferred the flavor of asparagus that had been browned on only one side, keeping the other side green and crisp-tender. This also allowed us to skip the tedious step of rotating individual spears. This recipe works best with asparagus that is at least ½ inch thick near the base. Do not use pencil-thin asparagus; it will overcook. You will need a 12-inch skillet with a tight-fitting lid for this recipe.

 1 tablespoon unsalted butter
 2 teaspoons extra-virgin olive oil
 1 pound thick asparagus, trimmed
 1 teaspoon lemon juice

 1. Heat butter and oil in 12-inch skillet over medium heat until butter is melted. Add half of asparagus to skillet with tips pointed in 1 direction and add remaining asparagus with tips pointed in opposite direction. Using tongs, distribute spears in even layer; cover; and cook until asparagus is bright green and still crisp, about 7 minutes.

 2. Uncover; increase heat to medium-high; and cook until asparagus is tender and well browned on one side, 3 to 4 minutes, using tongs to transfer spears from center of skillet to edge of skillet to ensure even browning. Season with salt and pepper to taste, drizzle with lemon juice, and serve.

VARIATION

Pan-Roasted Asparagus with Toasted Garlic and Parmesan

Cook 2 thinly sliced garlic cloves and oil in 12-inch skillet over medium heat until garlic is crisp and golden, about 4 minutes. Transfer garlic to paper towel–lined plate and set aside, leaving oil in skillet. Add butter to garlic oil left in skillet and proceed with recipe. Sprinkle toasted garlic and 2 tablespoons grated Parmesan cheese over asparagus before serving.

TRIMMING ASPARAGUS

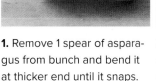

1. Remove 1 spear of asparagus from bunch and bend it at thicker end until it snaps.

2. With broken asparagus spear as guide, trim tough ends from remaining asparagus bunch using chef's knife.

Garlicky Green Beans

Serves 2 FAST VEGETARIAN

Total time 20 minutes

WHY THIS RECIPE WORKS Garlicky green beans are a classic side dish, but they run the risk of quickly becoming overcomplicated—or overcooked. We wanted to streamline the process to make this dish fresh, flavorful, and fast for two. We love the rich, mellow flavor of roasted garlic, but in the oven it takes the better part of an hour. We discovered that microwaving the garlic with oil and sugar gave us creamy, caramelized garlic (plus a flavorful cooking oil) in only 1 minute. To ensure crisp-tender beans, we added some water directly to a covered skillet so that they could steam gently for a few minutes, then we uncovered the pan so they could brown in our flavorful garlic oil. Microwave temperatures can vary, so be sure to check the garlic after 30 seconds to see if it has softened. You will need a 12-inch nonstick skillet with a tight-fitting lid for this recipe.

 6 garlic cloves, peeled and halved lengthwise
 1 tablespoon extra-virgin olive oil
   Pinch sugar
 8 ounces green beans, trimmed
 2 tablespoons water
 1½ teaspoons red or white wine vinegar

 1. Microwave garlic, oil, and sugar in small bowl until garlic is softened and fragrant, 30 to 60 seconds.

 2. Heat 2 teaspoons garlic oil in 12-inch nonstick skillet over medium heat until shimmering. Add green beans and water; cover; and cook until green beans are bright green, about 3 minutes. Add remaining garlic oil without stirring and cook, covered, until green beans are almost tender, about 2 minutes.

3. Uncover and continue to cook, stirring occasionally, until green beans are spotty brown and garlic is golden, 3 to 4 minutes. Off heat, stir in vinegar, season with salt and pepper to taste, and serve.

VARIATION
Lemony Green Beans with Toasted Almonds
Omit garlic, sugar, and step 1. Substitute ⅛ teaspoon grated lemon zest plus 1½ teaspoons juice for vinegar. Sprinkle green beans with 2 tablespoons toasted sliced almonds before serving.

TRIMMING GREEN BEANS QUICKLY

Line up several green beans in row on cutting board. Trim about ½ inch from each end, then cut beans as directed in recipe.

Beets with Hazelnuts and Chives
Serves 2   VEGETARIAN

Total time 40 minutes

WHY THIS RECIPE WORKS When it comes to storage vegetables, beets are hard to beat: The jewel-toned root vegetables, which pack a punch of earthy sweetness, will last for weeks in your fridge, perfect for the weeks you didn't make it to the grocery store. Rather than wrapping and roasting—typical beet protocol—we halved whole unpeeled beets and simmered them gently in a small amount of liquid in a covered saucepan. This method gave us tender beets with concentrated flavor in less than half an hour, just enough time to whisk together a quick vinaigrette for the still-warm beets to drink up and to chop some nuts and fresh herbs. The skins slip right off when the beets are tender and slightly cooled. Use beets that are 2 to 3 inches in diameter for this recipe. You will need a medium saucepan with a tight-fitting lid for this recipe.

3 beets (10 ounces), trimmed and halved
¼ teaspoon table salt, divided
1 tablespoon balsamic vinegar
1 tablespoon extra-virgin olive oil
  Pinch pepper
1 tablespoon chopped skinned toasted hazelnuts, pistachios, or walnuts
1 tablespoon chopped fresh chives, mint, or parsley

1. Place beets, cut side down, in single layer in medium saucepan. Add 1 cup water and ⅛ teaspoon salt, then bring to simmer over medium-high heat. Reduce heat to low; cover; and simmer until beets are tender and tip of paring knife inserted into beets meets no resistance, 18 to 26 minutes.

2. Drain beets, then transfer to cutting board. When beets are cool enough to handle, rub off skins with paper towel or dish towel, then cut into ½-inch wedges.

3. Whisk vinegar, oil, remaining ⅛ teaspoon salt, and pepper together in medium bowl. Add beets and toss to coat, then season with salt and pepper to taste and sprinkle with nuts and herbs. Serve.

Skillet Broccoli with Olive Oil and Garlic
Serves 2   FAST   VEGETARIAN

Total time 20 minutes

WHY THIS RECIPE WORKS Broccoli florets are quick-cooking, easy to prep, and sold in smaller quantities—perfect when cooking for two. The trick is getting the cores to cook through before the delicate outer buds overcook and begin to fall apart. Our solution was to use a two-step stir-fry method. An initial sear in hot oil browned the florets, adding color and flavor. Then we added water to the skillet to quickly steam the tough cores. To flavor the crisp-tender broccoli, we added garlic and thyme at the end of cooking, quickly blooming them in the hot skillet to deepen their flavor before stirring everything together. You will need a 10-inch skillet with a tight-fitting lid for this recipe.

2 tablespoons extra-virgin olive oil, divided
1 garlic clove, minced
¼ teaspoon minced fresh thyme
8 ounces broccoli florets, cut into 1-inch pieces
¼ teaspoon table salt
2 tablespoons water

Skillet Broccoli with Olive Oil and Garlic

1. Combine 1 tablespoon oil, garlic, and thyme in bowl. Heat remaining 1 tablespoon oil in 10-inch skillet over medium-high heat until just smoking. Add broccoli and salt and cook, without stirring, until beginning to brown, about 2 minutes.

2. Add water; cover; and cook until broccoli is bright green but still crisp, about 2 minutes. Uncover and continue to cook until water has evaporated and broccoli is crisp-tender, about 2 minutes.

3. Push broccoli to sides of skillet. Add garlic mixture and cook, mashing mixture into skillet, until fragrant, about 30 seconds. Stir garlic mixture into broccoli. Season with salt and pepper to taste, and serve.

VARIATION

Skillet Broccoli with Sesame Oil and Ginger

Omit thyme. Substitute 2 teaspoons toasted sesame oil for 2 teaspoons of olive oil in garlic mixture in step 1; add 2 teaspoons grated fresh ginger to garlic mixture.

Broiled Broccoli Rabe

Serves 2 FAST VEGETARIAN
Total time 20 minutes

WHY THIS RECIPE WORKS There's no reason to be bitter about broccoli rabe when you cook the notoriously sharp-tasting vegetable with our superfast method. Most of broccoli rabe's bitterness comes from an enzymatic reaction triggered when the florets are cut or chewed, so we kept the leafy parts of the vegetable whole—they charred beautifully in the oven, adding crunch and savory depth. Because the heat from broiling deactivated the enzyme, much of the bitterness was tamed. Tossing the pieces with garlicky oil gave an extra layer of spiciness that contrasted nicely with the assertive broccoli rabe,

    8 ounces broccoli rabe, trimmed
    1 tablespoon extra-virgin olive oil
    1 garlic clove, minced
    ¼ teaspoon table salt
       Pinch red pepper flakes
       Lemon wedges

1. Adjust oven rack 4 inches from broiler element and heat broiler. Cut tops (leaves and florets) of broccoli rabe from stalks, keeping tops whole, then cut stalks into 1-inch pieces. Transfer to aluminum foil–lined rimmed baking sheet.

2. Combine oil, garlic, salt, and pepper flakes in bowl, then pour over broccoli rabe and toss to coat. Broil until exposed leaves are well browned, 2 to 2½ minutes. Using tongs, toss to expose unbrowned leaves. Return sheet to oven and continue to broil until most leaves are lightly charred and stalks are crisp-tender, 2 to 2½ minutes. Season with salt and pepper to taste. Serve with lemon wedges.

Roasted Brussels Sprouts

Serves 2 VEGETARIAN
Total time 40 minutes

WHY THIS RECIPE WORKS For a streamlined recipe for roasted brussels sprouts, we halved the sprouts to speed cooking and to create a flat surface for browning. Since we were making just enough sprouts for two, we found that a regular baking sheet was too big; the oil burned where the sheet was empty. So we roasted the sprouts in a 12-inch ovensafe skillet with a tight-fitting cover, eliminating the need for foil. We tossed the sprouts with a little water to create a steamy environment to cook the sprouts through plus a tablespoon of oil to ensure that they didn't stick. Uncovering the pan partway through allowed the exteriors to caramelize, giving us tender sprouts with nicely browned exteriors. Look for brussels sprouts that are about 1½ inches long; quarter sprouts longer than 2½ inches. Be careful not to cut off too much of the stem end when trimming the sprouts, or the leaves will fall away from the core. You will need a 12-inch ovensafe skillet with a tight-fitting lid for this recipe.

8 ounces brussels sprouts, trimmed and halved
4 teaspoons water
1 tablespoon extra-virgin olive oil
⅛ teaspoon table salt
  Pinch pepper

1. Adjust oven rack to upper-middle position and heat oven to 500 degrees. Toss brussels sprouts with water, oil, salt, and pepper and arrange cut side down in 12-inch ovensafe skillet.

2. Cover and roast sprouts for 10 minutes. Uncover and continue to roast until sprouts are well browned and tender, 10 to 12 minutes. Season with salt and pepper to taste, and serve.

VARIATIONS
Roasted Brussels Sprouts with Garlic, Red Pepper Flakes, and Parmesan

While brussels sprouts roast, heat 2 teaspoons extra-virgin olive oil in 8-inch skillet over medium-low heat until shimmering. Add 1 small minced garlic clove and pinch red pepper flakes and cook until garlic is golden and fragrant, about 1 minute. Remove from heat. Toss roasted sprouts with garlic oil, then season with salt and pepper to taste. Sprinkle with 1 tablespoon grated Parmesan cheese before serving.

Roasted Brussels Sprouts with Bacon and Pecans

While brussels sprouts roast, halve 1 slice bacon crosswise and cook in 8-inch skillet over medium heat until crispy, 5 to 7 minutes. Using slotted spoon, transfer bacon to paper towel–lined plate and reserve bacon fat. Finely chop bacon. After transferring sprouts to platter, toss with 1½ teaspoons extra-virgin olive oil, reserved bacon fat, chopped bacon, and 2 tablespoons finely chopped toasted pecans. Season with salt and pepper to taste, and serve.

Skillet-Roasted Cabbage with Mustard and Thyme
Serves 2 VEGETARIAN
Total time 35 minutes

WHY THIS RECIPE WORKS Vegetables that store well, like cabbage, are great for when life gets in the way of our best grocery shopping intentions. But if you think cabbage is good only for shredding into coleslaw or sauerkraut, think again. When we cut it into thick wedges and seared it in a skillet, the cabbage was transformed into a sweet, silky vegetable whose caramelized layers created the perfect nooks and crannies for soaking up a quick, flavorful sauce of butter, fresh thyme, and mustard. When halving the cabbage, turn it core side up to help ensure that you slice evenly through it; each wedge needs a piece of intact core so the wedges don't fall apart. You will need a 12-inch nonstick skillet with a tight-fitting lid for this recipe.

6 tablespoons water, divided
3 tablespoons unsalted butter, divided
½ head (1 pound) green, napa, or savoy cabbage, cut into 4 (2-inch) wedges
¼ teaspoon table salt
½ teaspoon minced fresh thyme or ¼ teaspoon dried
⅛ teaspoon pepper
1½ teaspoons Dijon mustard

1. Combine ¼ cup water and 1 tablespoon butter in 12-inch nonstick skillet. Arrange cabbage wedges in single layer in skillet, cut side down. Sprinkle wedges with salt and cook over medium heat, uncovered, until water has evaporated and wedges are well browned, 15 to 18 minutes.

2. Flip wedges to second cut side; add remaining 2 tablespoons water to skillet; and cook, covered, until wedges are tender and second side is well browned, 2 to 4 minutes longer.

3. Transfer wedges to plate. Reduce heat under skillet to medium-low, then add remaining 2 tablespoons butter and cook until butter is melted and bubbling, 30 seconds to 1 minute. Stir in thyme and pepper and cook until fragrant, about 30 seconds. Off heat, stir in mustard. Return cabbage wedges to skillet and gently turn to coat in butter mixture; season with salt and pepper to taste. Serve.

Roasted Carrots

1. Adjust oven rack to middle position and heat oven to 425 degrees. Line rimmed baking sheet with aluminum foil. Toss carrots with melted butter, salt, and pepper and arrange in single layer on prepared sheet. Cover sheet tightly with foil and roast carrots until almost tender, about 15 minutes.

2. Carefully remove top piece of foil and continue to roast carrots, uncovered, until well browned and tender, 20 to 25 minutes, stirring twice during roasting. Season with salt and pepper to taste, and serve.

VARIATION
Roasted Carrots and Shallots with Lemon and Thyme

Reduce number of carrots to 3. Toss 3 shallots, peeled and halved lengthwise, and ½ teaspoon minced fresh thyme with carrots, butter, and seasonings. Toss roasted vegetables with ¾ teaspoon lemon juice before serving.

PREPARING CARROTS FOR ROASTING

Cutting carrots to a uniform size is key to evenly cooked results when roasting.

A. For large carrots (over 1 inch in diameter), cut carrot in half crosswise, then quarter each section lengthwise to create total of 8 pieces.

B. For medium carrots (½ to 1 inch in diameter), cut carrot in half crosswise, then halve wider section lengthwise to create total of 3 pieces.

C. For small carrots (less than ½ inch in diameter), cut carrot in half crosswise, then leave both sections whole.

Roasted Carrots
Serves 2   VEGETARIAN

Total time 45 minutes

WHY THIS RECIPE WORKS Roasting carrots draws out their natural sugars and intensifies their flavor. We precooked the carrots before roasting, which kept their moisture in and minimized withering. We avoided dirtying a second pan by precooking the buttered, seasoned carrots right on the baking sheet, covered with foil, which kept them from drying out. The butter helped create a steamy cooking environment. When the carrots were almost tender, we removed the foil to caramelize them.

 4   carrots, peeled, halved crosswise, and cut lengthwise into ½-inch-wide batons
 1   tablespoon unsalted butter, melted
 ¼   teaspoon table salt
 ⅛   teaspoon pepper

Roasted Cauliflower

Roasted Celery Root with Yogurt
and Sesame Seeds

Roasted Cauliflower

Serves 2 **VEGETARIAN**

Total time 45 minutes

WHY THIS RECIPE WORKS We wanted to add flavor to cauliflower without drowning it in a blanket of cheese sauce, so we developed a recipe for roasted cauliflower with golden, nutty, well-browned edges and a sweet, tender interior. Since browning took place only where the cauliflower was in contact with the hot baking sheet, we sliced half a head of cauliflower into four wedges, creating more flat surface area than you'd get with florets. To keep the cauliflower from drying out, we started it covered in a hot oven, which allowed it to steam until barely soft. Then we removed the foil to caramelize and brown the wedges. Flipping each slice halfway through roasting ensured even cooking and color. Thanks to its natural sweetness and flavor, our roasted cauliflower needed little enhancement— just a drizzle of olive oil and a sprinkle of salt and pepper.

½ head cauliflower (1 pound)
2 tablespoons extra-virgin olive oil, divided
¼ teaspoon table salt, divided
⅛ teaspoon pepper, divided

1. Adjust oven rack to lowest position and heat oven to 475 degrees. Line rimmed baking sheet with aluminum foil.

2. Trim outer leaves off cauliflower and cut stem flush with bottom. Cut cauliflower into 4 equal wedges. Arrange wedges cut side down on prepared sheet, drizzle with 1 tablespoon oil, and sprinkle with ⅛ teaspoon salt and pinch pepper. Gently rub seasonings and oil into cauliflower, then flip cauliflower and season other cut side with remaining 1 tablespoon oil, remaining ⅛ teaspoon salt, and remaining pinch pepper.

3. Cover sheet tightly with foil and roast cauliflower for 10 minutes. Carefully remove top piece of foil and continue to roast, uncovered, until bottoms of cauliflower pieces are golden, about 4 minutes. Remove sheet from oven, and, using spatula, carefully flip cauliflower. Return sheet to oven and continue to roast cauliflower until golden all over, about 4 minutes. Season with salt and pepper to taste. Serve.

VARIATIONS

Roasted Cauliflower with Lemon and Capers

Add 1 teaspoon minced fresh thyme to oil before rubbing on cauliflower. In medium bowl, whisk 1 tablespoon rinsed and chopped capers, additional 1 teaspoon extra-virgin olive oil, 1 teaspoon lemon juice, and ¼ teaspoon grated lemon zest together. Gently toss roasted cauliflower in oil mixture before serving.

Roasted Cauliflower with Chorizo and Smoked Paprika

Add 1 teaspoon smoked paprika to oil before rubbing on cauliflower. Spread 1 small red onion, halved and sliced ½ inch thick, and 3 ounces chorizo, halved lengthwise and sliced ½ inch thick, on baking sheet with cauliflower before roasting. In medium bowl, whisk 1 tablespoon minced fresh parsley, additional 1 teaspoon extra-virgin olive oil, and 1 teaspoon sherry vinegar together. Gently toss roasted cauliflower in oil mixture before serving.

CUTTING CAULIFLOWER INTO WEDGES

1. Trim off outer leaves of cauliflower and cut stem flush with bottom of head. Place head upside down and cut in half through central stalk. Set aside one half for another use.

2. Lay remaining cauliflower half on its cut side and cut it into 4 wedges, keeping florets attached to pieces of central stalk.

Cauliflower Gratin

Serves 2   VEGETARIAN

Total time 40 minutes

WHY THIS RECIPE WORKS We wanted an effortless version of this casserole that would serve two, not 10. We cooked the cauliflower in the microwave, which gave us a head start (no need to drag out a pot to steam it on the stovetop) and meant that our gratin needed just a short stint in the oven. For a speedy cheese sauce, we microwaved garlic-and-herb Boursin cheese with a small amount of heavy cream; after just a minute, it had thickened to the right consistency. Toasted panko bread crumbs ensured that our easy cauliflower gratin offered the same golden, crisp topping as traditional versions. You will need an 8½ by 5½-inch baking dish for this recipe.

½ cup panko bread crumbs
1½ teaspoons extra-virgin olive oil
10 ounces cauliflower florets, cut into 1-inch pieces
1 tablespoon water
½ (5.2-ounce) package Boursin Garlic and Fine Herbs cheese
¼ cup heavy cream
¼ teaspoon table salt
⅛ teaspoon pepper
1 tablespoon finely minced fresh chives

1. Adjust oven rack to middle position and heat oven to 450 degrees. Combine panko and oil in 8-inch nonstick skillet. Toast panko over medium-high heat, stirring often, until golden, about 3 minutes.

2. Meanwhile, microwave cauliflower and water together in covered bowl until tender, about 3 minutes; drain cauliflower.

3. Wipe bowl dry with paper towels. Microwave Boursin, cream, salt, and pepper in cleaned bowl until cheese is melted, about 1 minute. Whisk Boursin mixture until smooth, then add drained cauliflower and toss to coat.

4. Transfer cauliflower mixture to 8½ by 5½-inch baking dish and sprinkle with toasted panko. Bake until hot and lightly bubbling around edges, about 7 minutes. Transfer gratin to wire rack and let cool for 5 to 10 minutes. Sprinkle with chives before serving.

Roasted Celery Root with Yogurt and Sesame Seeds

Serves 2   VEGETARIAN

Total time 55 minutes

WHY THIS RECIPE WORKS We wanted to bring celery root, an often overlooked vegetable, to the table and highlight its herbal flavor and pleasant, creamy texture. To unlock its unique flavor, roasting was best. We cooked the slices on the bottom oven rack, which helped caramelize the exteriors. Yogurt, reinforced with both lemon juice and zest, complemented the savory celery root. To finish, we sprinkled an aromatic combination of toasted sesame seeds, coriander, and dried thyme over the top before adding cilantro leaves.

1 celery root (1 pound), peeled, halved, and sliced ½ inch thick
1 tablespoon extra-virgin olive oil
⅛ teaspoon plus 2 pinches table salt, divided
   Pinch pepper
1½ tablespoons plain yogurt
⅛ teaspoon grated lemon zest plus ¼ teaspoon juice
¼ teaspoon sesame seeds, toasted
¼ teaspoon coriander seeds, toasted and crushed
   Pinch dried thyme
1½ tablespoons fresh cilantro leaves

1. Adjust oven rack to lowest position and heat oven to 425 degrees. Toss celery root with oil, ⅛ teaspoon salt, and pinch pepper and arrange in rimmed baking sheet in single layer. Roast celery root until sides touching sheet toward back of oven are well browned, 15 to 20 minutes. Rotate sheet and continue to roast until sides touching sheet toward back of oven are well browned, 6 to 10 minutes.

2. Use metal spatula to flip each piece and continue to roast until celery root is very tender and sides touching sheet are browned, 8 to 12 minutes.

3. Transfer celery root to serving platter. Whisk yogurt, lemon zest and juice, and pinch salt together in bowl. In separate bowl, combine sesame seeds, coriander seeds, thyme, and remaining pinch salt. Drizzle celery root with yogurt sauce and sprinkle with seed mixture and cilantro. Serve.

PEELING CELERY ROOT

1. Using chef's knife, cut ½ inch from both root end and opposite end of celery root.

2. Turn celery root so 1 cut side rests on board. To peel, cut from top to bottom, rotating celery root while removing wide strips of skin.

Elote
Serves 2 `VEGETARIAN`
Total time 45 minutes

WHY THIS RECIPE WORKS In Mexico, street vendors add kick to grilled corn by slathering it with a creamy mixture of crema, spices, cilantro, and lime juice, along with a sprinkle of queso fresco. To bring this delightfully messy street food into our kitchen, we broiled corn on the cob in the oven instead of heading out to the grill. But first, we brushed the cobs with oil to keep them from drying out so that the high heat of the oven's broiler could mimic the grill and create good charring. Flipping the corn halfway through allowed us to char all sides. For the flavorful topping, mayonnaise made a good substitute for traditional Mexican crema, especially when dressed up with cilantro, garlic, lime, and chili powder. To keep the crumbly queso fresco from sliding right off the corn and ending up only on the plate, we mixed it in with the mayonnaise just before slathering all over the charred corn, letting it melt into the kernels for a creamy, crunchy side. Feta cheese can be substituted for the queso fresco.

2 ears corn, husks and silk removed, stalks left intact
1 teaspoon extra-virgin olive oil
3 tablespoons mayonnaise
1 tablespoon crumbled queso fresco
1 tablespoon minced fresh cilantro
1 teaspoon lime juice, plus lime wedges for serving
1 small garlic clove, minced
¼ teaspoon chili powder
   Pinch table salt

1. Adjust oven rack to middle position and heat broiler. Brush corn all over with oil and transfer to aluminum foil–lined rimmed baking sheet. Broil corn until well browned on 1 side, 15 to 20 minutes. Flip corn and broil until browned on opposite side, 15 to 20 minutes.

2. Meanwhile, whisk mayonnaise, queso fresco, cilantro, lime juice, garlic, chili powder, and salt in bowl until incorporated. Remove corn from oven and brush evenly on all sides with mayonnaise mixture. Season with salt and pepper to taste. Serve corn with lime wedges and any extra mayonnaise mixture.

Simple Ratatouille

Serves 2   `FAST`

Total time 25 minutes

WHY THIS RECIPE WORKS   This version of the classic Provençal dish celebrates late summer's bounty of vegetables. We streamlined it by omitting some of the traditional watery vegetables (bell peppers and zucchini) that required time to eradicate their excess moisture. Instead, we focused on three essential components: eggplant, garlic, and tomatoes. Browning cubes of eggplant and then adding halved cherry or grape tomatoes gave us flavorful caramelization and softened the vegetables without making them mushy. A touch of anchovy paste with the garlic and a few spoonfuls of briny capers at the end added complexity and depth of flavor. We prefer to use globe eggplant because it is easy to find, but using a whole Italian or Japanese eggplant would also work (and help you avoid extra raw eggplant). Serve alone as a side dish, toss with pasta, or slather on toast and top with a poached or fried egg.

- 2 tablespoons plus 2 teaspoons extra-virgin olive oil, divided
- ½ eggplant (8 ounces), cut into ¾-inch pieces
- ⅛ teaspoon table salt
   Pinch pepper
- 2 garlic cloves, minced
- ⅛ teaspoon anchovy paste
- 6 ounces cherry or grape tomatoes, halved (1 cup)
- ½ cup chicken or vegetable broth
- 2 teaspoons capers, rinsed and minced
- 1 tablespoon chopped fresh basil, mint, or parsley

1. Heat 2 tablespoons oil in 12-inch nonstick skillet over medium-high heat until shimmering. Add eggplant, salt, and pepper and cook until eggplant is browned and tender, 6 to 8 minutes.

2. Reduce heat to medium-low, then stir in remaining 2 teaspoons oil, garlic, and anchovy paste and cook until fragrant, about 30 seconds. Stir in tomatoes and broth and simmer until liquid has evaporated and tomatoes have broken down slightly, 5 to 7 minutes. Stir in capers, season with salt and pepper to taste, and sprinkle with basil. Serve.

Simple Ratatouille

Braised Hearty Greens

Serves 2   VEGETARIAN

Total time 35 minutes

WHY THIS RECIPE WORKS The traditional Southern method for making braised greens—simmering the greens with a ham hock for hours—results in a rich and tasty dish, but the greens lose their deep color, firm texture, and earthy flavor. We wanted an easy one-pot recipe for fresh and flavorful braised greens. Since we needed just enough for two, we were able to cook all the greens at once instead of in batches. We wilted kale in a small amount of broth and then, when it was tender, we removed the lid to allow the liquid to evaporate. Shallot, brown sugar, cider vinegar, and cayenne pepper rounded out the flavors. Don't dry the greens completely after washing; a little extra water clinging to the leaves will help them wilt when cooking. You can substitute mustard, turnip, or collard greens for the kale; if using collard greens, allow 2 to 3 extra minutes of cooking time in step 1. You will need a medium saucepan with a tight-fitting lid for this recipe.

- 2 tablespoons unsalted butter, divided
- 1 shallot, sliced thin
- 1 pound kale, stemmed and cut into 1-inch pieces
- ½ cup vegetable or chicken broth
- 1½ teaspoons packed brown sugar
- ¼ teaspoon table salt
- ⅛ teaspoon cayenne pepper
- 1½ teaspoons cider vinegar

1. Melt 1 tablespoon butter in medium saucepan over medium heat. Add shallot and cook until softened, about 2 minutes. Add kale, broth, sugar, salt, and cayenne. Cover; reduce heat to medium-low; and cook, stirring occasionally, until kale is completely tender, about 10 minutes.

2. Uncover; increase heat to medium-high; and cook, stirring occasionally, until liquid is nearly evaporated, 10 to 12 minutes. Off heat, stir in remaining 1 tablespoon butter and vinegar. Season with salt and pepper to taste and serve.

VARIATIONS

Braised Hearty Greens with Pancetta and Pine Nuts

Cook 2 ounces chopped thinly sliced pancetta in medium saucepan over medium heat until browned and crisp, 6 to 8 minutes. Using slotted spoon, transfer pancetta to paper towel–lined plate; substitute fat left in saucepan for butter in step 1. Substitute 1½ teaspoons red wine vinegar for cider vinegar and top braised greens with 1 tablespoon toasted pine nuts and crisp pancetta before serving.

Braised Hearty Greens with White Beans

Substitute 1 small onion, halved and thinly sliced, for shallot in step 1; cook until softened and lightly browned, 5 to 7 minutes. Add 1 minced garlic clove and cook until fragrant, about 30 seconds. Add 1 cup rinsed canned small white beans to kale after removing lid in step 2.

Sautéed Mushrooms

Serves 2   VEGETARIAN

Total time 35 minutes

WHY THIS RECIPE WORKS Browned and ultrasavory, sautéed mushrooms make a great side dish, but the mushrooms can quickly turn from silky to rubbery. The first step was choosing the mushrooms. We paired cremini with a smaller amount of rich, earthy shiitakes. To keep the high water content of the cremini from inhibiting browning, we cooked them in a covered skillet until they released their liquid, then we uncovered the skillet to let the liquid evaporate and the mushrooms brown. A generous amount of butter kept the mushrooms from burning, and deglazing the pan with white wine increased flavor and provided welcome acidity. Choose shiitakes with caps between 2 and 2½ inches in diameter. You will need a 10-inch skillet with a tight-fitting lid for this recipe.

- 2 tablespoons unsalted butter, divided
- 1 small shallot, sliced thin
- 8 ounces cremini or white mushrooms, trimmed and halved if small or quartered if large
- 4 ounces shiitake mushrooms, stemmed and sliced ½ inch thick
- ¼ teaspoon table salt
- ¾ teaspoon minced fresh thyme or ⅛ teaspoon dried
- 1 small garlic clove, minced
- 2½ tablespoons dry white wine

1. Melt 1 tablespoon butter in 10-inch skillet over medium heat. Add shallot and cook until softened, about 2 minutes. Add cremini mushrooms, shiitake mushrooms, and salt; cover; and cook, stirring occasionally, until mushrooms have released their moisture, 8 to 10 minutes.

Sautéed Mushrooms

2. Remove lid; add remaining 1 tablespoon butter; and cook, stirring occasionally, until mushrooms are deep golden brown and tender, 10 to 12 minutes. Stir in thyme and garlic and cook until fragrant, about 30 seconds. Stir in wine and cook, scraping up any browned bits, until liquid is nearly evaporated, about 30 seconds. Season with salt and pepper to taste, and serve.

Sautéed Snow Peas with Lemon and Parsley

Serves 2   `FAST`   `VEGETARIAN`

Total time 20 minutes

WHY THIS RECIPE WORKS To amplify the delicate flavor of sweet, grassy peas, we browned them to caramelize their flavor. We tried a traditional stir-fry technique, but the constant stirring gave us greasy, overcooked pods without any browning. Adding a sprinkle of sugar and cooking the peas without stirring for a short time helped to achieve a flavorful sear, then we continued to cook them until they were just crisp-tender. To boost flavor, we sautéed minced shallot flavored with lemon zest and then stirred everything together. Lemon juice and parsley kept this dish fresh and bright.

    2   teaspoons vegetable oil, divided
    1   small shallot, minced
    ¾   teaspoon grated lemon zest plus ½ teaspoon juice
    ¼   teaspoon table salt
    ⅛   teaspoon pepper
    ⅛   teaspoon sugar
    6   ounces snow peas, strings removed
    1   tablespoon minced fresh parsley, chives, or tarragon

1. Combine 1 teaspoon oil, shallot, and lemon zest in small bowl. Combine salt, pepper, and sugar in separate small bowl.

2. Heat remaining 1 teaspoon oil in 10-inch nonstick skillet over high heat until just smoking. Add snow peas, sprinkle with salt mixture, and cook, without stirring, for 30 seconds. Stir, then continue to cook, without stirring, until snow peas are beginning to brown, about 30 seconds. Continue to cook, stirring constantly, until peas are crisp-tender, 1 to 2 minutes.

3. Push peas to sides of skillet. Add shallot mixture and cook, mashing mixture into skillet, until fragrant, about 30 seconds. Stir shallot mixture into peas, transfer to bowl, and stir in lemon juice and parsley. Season with salt and pepper to taste, and serve.

VARIATIONS
Sautéed Snow Peas with Ginger and Scallion
Substitute 2 minced scallion whites, 1½ teaspoons grated fresh ginger, and 1 minced small garlic clove for shallot and lemon zest. Substitute pinch red pepper flakes for pepper in step 1. Substitute ½ teaspoon unseasoned rice vinegar for lemon juice and 2 thinly sliced scallion greens for parsley.

Sautéed Snow Peas with Cumin and Cilantro
Substitute 1 minced small garlic clove and ¼ teaspoon toasted cumin seeds for shallot. Substitute ½ teaspoon lime zest for lemon zest, ½ teaspoon lime juice for lemon juice, and 1 tablespoon minced fresh cilantro for parsley.

Potato Gratin
Serves 2   VEGETARIAN
Total time 45 minutes

WHY THIS RECIPE WORKS This potato gratin features tender sliced potatoes napped with a velvety cream sauce. Heavy cream thickened with flour gave us a rich-tasting sauce that could withstand the baking time without breaking. We enriched the sauce with garlic, shallot, thyme, and a pinch each of nutmeg and cayenne. We skipped tediously layering the potato slices; we simply poured them into the dish and gently pressed into an even layer. A sprinkle of grated Gruyère imparted a nutty flavor. Parmesan can be used in place of the Gruyère. Use a mandoline, a V-slicer, or a food processor fitted with a ⅛-inch-thick slicing blade to slice the potatoes. You will need a shallow 8½ by 5½-inch baking dish with sides that are no more than 2 inches high for this recipe.

    1   large russet potato (12 ounces), peeled and
        sliced ⅛ inch thick
    1   tablespoon unsalted butter
    1   small shallot, minced
    ½   teaspoon table salt
    1   garlic clove, minced
    1   teaspoon minced fresh thyme or ¼ teaspoon dried
    ¼   teaspoon pepper
        Pinch ground nutmeg
        Pinch cayenne pepper
    2   teaspoons all-purpose flour
    ¾   cup heavy cream
    ¼   cup finely grated Gruyère cheese

1. Adjust oven rack to upper-middle position and heat oven to 400 degrees. Grease 8½ by 5½-inch baking dish. Place potato slices in medium bowl.

2. Melt butter in small saucepan over medium heat. Add shallot and salt and cook until softened, about 2 minutes. Stir in garlic, thyme, pepper, nutmeg, and cayenne and cook until fragrant, about 30 seconds. Stir in flour and cook until incorporated, about 10 seconds. Whisk in cream, scraping up any browned bits and smoothing out any lumps; bring to simmer; and cook until beginning to thicken, about 30 seconds.

3. Pour sauce over potato slices and toss to coat thoroughly. Transfer potato mixture to prepared dish and gently press potato slices into even layer, removing any air pockets. Cover dish tightly with aluminum foil and bake until potatoes are almost tender, 35 to 40 minutes.

4. Carefully remove foil and sprinkle with Gruyère. Continue to bake, uncovered, until cheese is lightly browned and potatoes are tender, about 10 minutes. Transfer gratin to wire rack and let cool for 5 to 10 minutes before serving.

Best Baked Potatoes

Serves 2 `VEGETARIAN`

Total time 1 hour 30 minutes

WHY THIS RECIPE WORKS Baked potatoes are one of those dishes most home cooks think they don't need a recipe for, but following our precise roasting technique guarantees a perfect potato—with a fluffy interior, crispy skin, and even seasoning—every time. For starters, our testing pointed us to an ideal doneness temperature: 205 degrees. Baking russet potatoes in a hot oven propped up on a wire rack prevented a leathery ring from forming beneath the peel, and taking the potato's temperature with an instant-read thermometer ensured that we hit the 205-degree sweet spot every time. Coating the potatoes in salty water before baking was all the effort required to season the skin; brushing on vegetable oil once the potatoes were cooked through and then baking the potatoes for an additional 10 minutes promised the crispest exterior possible. Potatoes this good deserve an accompaniment, so we came up with some simple but sophisticated toppings to serve with them. Open up the potatoes immediately after removal from the oven in step 3 so steam can escape. Top the potatoes as desired, or with one of our flavorful toppings.

    Table salt for soaking potatoes
2   (7- to 9-ounce) russet potatoes, unpeeled,
    each lightly pricked with fork in 6 places
2   teaspoons vegetable oil

1. Adjust oven rack to middle position and heat oven to 450 degrees. Dissolve 2 tablespoons salt in ½ cup water in medium bowl. Place potatoes in bowl and toss so exteriors of potatoes are evenly moistened. Transfer potatoes to wire rack set in rimmed baking sheet and bake until center of largest potato registers 205 degrees, 45 minutes to 1 hour.

2. Remove potatoes from oven and brush tops and sides with oil. Return potatoes to oven and bake for 10 minutes.

3. Remove potatoes from oven and, using paring knife, make 2 slits, forming X, in each potato. Using clean dish towel, hold ends and squeeze slightly to push flesh up and out. Season with salt and pepper to taste. Serve immediately.

Best Baked Potatoes

VARIATIONS

Best Baked Potatoes with Herbed Goat Cheese

Mash 2 ounces softened goat cheese with fork. Stir in 1 tablespoon extra-virgin olive oil, 1 tablespoon minced fresh parsley, 1½ teaspoons minced shallot, and ¼ teaspoon lemon zest. Season with salt and pepper to taste, and dollop on potatoes before serving.

Best Baked Potatoes with Creamy Egg Topping

Stir 2 chopped hard-cooked eggs, 2 tablespoons sour cream, 2 teaspoons minced cornichons, 1½ teaspoons minced fresh parsley, 1½ teaspoons Dijon mustard, 1½ teaspoons rinsed and minced capers, and 1½ teaspoons minced shallot together in bowl. Season with salt and pepper to taste, and dollop on potatoes before serving.

Easier French Fries

Serves 2 `FAST` `VEGETARIAN`

Total time 30 minutes

WHY THIS RECIPE WORKS Even with their short ingredient list, making fries at home can seem daunting. And filling a pot with oil to make fries for only two felt wasteful. We wanted a recipe that would require fewer steps and less oil. We discovered that starting our fries in cold oil, then heating it, was an easy solution to both problems: The gradual increase in temperature gave the fries a chance to cook through and soften before the exteriors crisped, and this method required only 3 cups of oil versus the 2 to 3 quarts called for in most recipes. Compared to traditional russets, the higher water content of Yukon Gold potatoes made for crisp fries with creamy interiors, and thanks to their thin skins, we didn't even have to peel them. You will need a saucepan with a 4-quart capacity for this recipe; if your pan is larger you may need more oil to cover the potatoes. If desired, serve with Belgian-Style Dipping Sauce or Garlic Mayonnaise.

> 1½ pounds Yukon gold potatoes, unpeeled, sides squared, and cut lengthwise into ¼-inch-thick batons
> 3 cups peanut oil or vegetable oil, for frying

1. Set wire rack in rimmed baking sheet lined with triple layer of paper towels. Combine potatoes and oil in large saucepan. Cook over high heat until oil has reached rolling boil, about 5 minutes. Continue to cook, without stirring, until potatoes are limp but exteriors are beginning to firm, 12 to 14 minutes.

2. Using tongs, stir potatoes, gently scraping up any that stick, and continue to cook, stirring occasionally, until fries are golden and crisp, 5 to 10 minutes. Using slotted spoon, transfer fries to prepared rack. Season with salt to taste, and serve immediately.

Belgian-Style Dipping Sauce

Makes about ¼ cup `FAST` `VEGETARIAN`

Total time 20 minutes

For a spicier sauce, use the larger quantity of hot sauce.

> 3 tablespoons mayonnaise
> 1 tablespoon ketchup
> ¼–½ teaspoon hot sauce
> ¼ teaspoon minced garlic
> ⅛ teaspoon table salt

Whisk all ingredients together in bowl. Refrigerate until flavors meld, about 15 minutes.

Garlic Mayonnaise

Makes about ¼ cup `FAST` `VEGETARIAN`

Total time 20 minutes

> ¼ cup mayonnaise
> 1 teaspoon lemon juice
> ½ teaspoon Dijon mustard
> ½ small garlic clove, minced

Whisk all ingredients together in bowl and season with salt and pepper to taste. Refrigerate until flavors meld, about 15 minutes.

CUTTING POTATOES FOR FRENCH FRIES

1. Square off potato by cutting ¼-inch-thick slice from each of its 4 long sides. Then cut potato lengthwise into ¼-inch-thick planks.

2. Stack 3 or 4 planks and cut into ¼-inch-thick batons. Repeat with remaining planks.

Mashed Potatoes

Serves 2 FAST VEGETARIAN

Total time 30 minutes

WHY THIS RECIPE WORKS We wanted creamy yet fluffy mashed potatoes with plenty of buttery richness, and we didn't want to spend a lot of time or effort pulling this simple side together. We sped things up by swapping the usual russet potatoes for Yukon Golds. Because Yukon Golds have less starch and are less absorbent than russets, they don't become soggy when simmered without their skins. This meant we were able to peel and slice the potatoes before cooking, cutting our simmering time in half. We returned the drained potatoes to the hot pan to mash them, which helped the remaining water evaporate before the potatoes became gluey. We mashed the potatoes by hand, which prevented overbeating and kept them from turning pasty. And melting the butter before folding it in along with the half-and-half allowed it to coat the starch molecules quickly and easily, so the potatoes turned out creamy and light. You can substitute whole milk for the half-and-half here, but the potatoes will taste a bit leaner. Make sure to cook the potatoes thoroughly; they are done if they break apart when a knife is inserted and gently wiggled.

1 pound Yukon Gold potatoes, peeled and
   sliced ½ inch thick
   Table salt for cooking potatoes
⅓ cup half-and-half, room temperature
3 tablespoons unsalted butter, melted and cooled

1. Place potatoes and 1 tablespoon salt in medium saucepan and add water to cover by 1 inch. Bring to boil over medium-high heat, then reduce to simmer and cook, stirring once or twice, until potatoes are tender, 12 to 15 minutes.

2. Drain potatoes and return to saucepan set on still-hot burner. Using potato masher, mash potatoes until a few small lumps remain. Gently mix half-and-half and melted butter together in small bowl until combined. Add half-and-half mixture to potatoes and, using rubber spatula, fold gently to incorporate. Season with salt and pepper to taste, and serve immediately.

VARIATION

Buttermilk Mashed Potatoes

Substitute ⅓ cup buttermilk for half-and-half.

Easier French Fries

Mashed Potatoes

**Rustic Smashed
Red Potatoes**

12 ounces small red potatoes, unpeeled
¼ teaspoon table salt plus salt for cooking potatoes
1 bay leaf
3 tablespoons cream cheese, softened
1 tablespoon unsalted butter, melted
¼ teaspoon pepper
1 tablespoon minced fresh chives (optional)

1. Place potatoes, 1 teaspoon salt, and bay leaf in medium saucepan and add water to cover by 1 inch. Bring to boil over medium-high heat, then reduce to simmer and cook, stirring once or twice, until potatoes are tender, 10 to 15 minutes. Reserve ½ cup cooking water, then drain potatoes. Return potatoes to saucepan, discard bay leaf, and let steam escape for 2 minutes.

2. Meanwhile, whisk softened cream cheese and melted butter together in small bowl until smooth and fully incorporated. Stir in 2 tablespoons reserved cooking water; ¼ teaspoon salt; pepper; and chives, if using.

3. Using rubber spatula or back of wooden spoon, smash potatoes just enough to break skins. Fold in cream cheese mixture until most of liquid has been absorbed and chunks of potatoes remain. Add remaining reserved cooking water as needed, 1 tablespoon at a time, until potatoes are slightly looser than desired (potatoes will thicken slightly with sitting). Season with salt and pepper to taste, and serve immediately.

Rustic Smashed Red Potatoes

Serves 2   VEGETARIAN

Total time 35 minutes

WHY THIS RECIPE WORKS For our version of rustic smashed potatoes, we wanted chunks of potato textured with skins and bound by a rich, creamy puree. Moist, low-starch red potatoes had pleasantly tender, thin skins that gave us the perfect chunky texture. Cooking the potatoes whole helped them retain their naturally creamy character and kept the dish from getting waterlogged. A spatula or wooden spoon worked best to smash the potatoes without making them overly smooth. A combination of tangy cream cheese and melted butter complemented the rich, earthy potatoes without dulling their flavor, and adding some of the starchy cooking water thinned the mash just enough to keep it from turning gluey as it cooled. Use small red potatoes measuring 1 to 2 inches in diameter. Try to purchase potatoes of equal size; if that's not possible, test the larger potatoes for doneness. White potatoes can be used instead of red, but their skins will lack the rosy color.

Roasted Red Potatoes

Serves 2   VEGETARIAN

Total time 55 minutes

WHY THIS RECIPE WORKS To arrive at our ideal roasted potatoes—ones with deep golden, crisp crusts and creamy, soft interiors—we took advantage of the naturally high moisture content of red potatoes. We covered them for part of the cooking time which allowed the trapped moisture to steam the potatoes, and gave them creamy flesh and allowed us to skip the extra step of parboiling, a welcome timesaver. We finished the potatoes uncovered which crisped the outsides to a perfect golden brown. We knew from past recipes that contact with the baking sheet was important to browning, so we flipped the potatoes partway through the browning process to achieve multi-sided crispness. We made these simple potatoes even easier by lining the baking sheet with foil, making for quick cleanup.

1 pound red potatoes, unpeeled, cut into
    ¾-inch wedges
1½ tablespoons extra-virgin olive oil
¼ teaspoon table salt
⅛ teaspoon pepper

1. Adjust oven rack to middle position and heat oven to 425 degrees. Line rimmed baking sheet with aluminum foil. Toss potatoes with oil, salt, and pepper and arrange cut side down in single layer on prepared sheet. Cover sheet tightly with foil and roast potatoes for 20 minutes.

2. Carefully remove top piece of foil and continue to roast, uncovered, until bottoms of potatoes are golden and crusty, 8 to 10 minutes. Remove sheet from oven, and, using spatula, flip potatoes. Return sheet to oven and continue to roast potatoes until crusty and golden on second side, about 5 minutes. Season with salt and pepper to taste. Serve.

VARIATION
Roasted Red Potatoes with Garlic and Rosemary
Sprinkle potatoes with 1 tablespoon minced fresh rosemary during final 5 minutes of roasting in step 2. Toss roasted potatoes with 1 minced garlic clove before serving.

Sautéed Radishes with Crispy Bacon

Sautéed Radishes with Crispy Bacon
Serves 2 FAST
Total time 30 minutes

WHY THIS RECIPE WORKS Radishes generally serve one of two purposes: tossed raw on top of a salad for crunch, or pickled and added to a taco for piquant bite. This sells this vegetable short, however; the real magic happens when you cook and caramelize radishes. To give cooked radishes another flavor element beyond sweet-spicy, we started with one of our favorite foods, bacon. This provided our crispy garnish, and the rendered fat gave us a smoky base for cooking. A finishing touch of red wine vinegar woke everything up, and with the addition of a little bit of fresh herbs, we were satisfied with our not-so-ordinary take on the peppery radish. Oh, and try not to snack on the crispy bacon before you're ready to serve. Maybe cook two pieces, just in case. Serve with lemon wedges, a smear of hummus, and pita bread for a casual dinner.

1 slice bacon, chopped fine
8 ounces radishes, trimmed and halved if small or quartered if large
¼ teaspoon table salt
   Pinch pepper
1 garlic clove, minced
1 teaspoon red wine vinegar
1 teaspoon minced fresh chives, parsley, or scallions
   Lemon wedges

Cook bacon in 8- or 10-inch nonstick skillet over medium heat until crispy, 5 to 7 minutes. Using slotted spoon, transfer bacon to paper towel–lined plate. Pour off all but 1 teaspoon fat from skillet. (If necessary, add oil to equal 1 teaspoon.) Add radishes, salt, and pepper; reduce heat to medium-low; and cook, stirring occasionally, until radishes are lightly browned and crisp-tender, 12 to 16 minutes. Stir in garlic and vinegar and cook until fragrant, about 30 seconds. Off heat, stir in chives, season with salt and pepper to taste, and sprinkle with bacon. Serve.

Spinach with Garlic Chips and Red Pepper Flakes

Serves 2 `FAST` `VEGETARIAN`

Total time 15 minutes

WHY THIS RECIPE WORKS To create a quick and healthy spinach side dish, we wilted the spinach in a saucepan and added garlic and red pepper flakes to complement the earthy, mineral flavor of the greens. First, we sliced the garlic thin and fried it in hot oil until golden and crisp. The garlic chips added a nice, flavorful crunch, and we wilted the spinach in the rich garlic oil, which added another layer of flavor. One pound of flat-leaf spinach (about 1½ bunches) can be substituted for the curly-leaf spinach, but do not use baby spinach; it is too delicate. Do not heat the oil before adding the garlic in step 1; heating them together over gentle heat prevents the garlic from burning. Don't dry the spinach completely after washing; a little extra water clinging to the leaves will help them wilt when cooking. You will need a large saucepan with a tight-fitting lid for this recipe.

- 1   tablespoon extra-virgin olive oil
- 2   garlic cloves, sliced thin
      Pinch red pepper flakes
- 10 ounces curly-leaf spinach, stemmed and chopped coarse

1. Cook oil and garlic in large saucepan over medium heat, stirring occasionally, until garlic is golden and very crisp, about 5 minutes. Using slotted spoon, transfer garlic chips to paper towel–lined plate.

2. Add pepper flakes to garlic oil and cook over medium heat until fragrant, about 30 seconds. Add spinach in handfuls, stirring and tossing each handful to wilt slightly before adding next. Cover saucepan; increase heat to medium-high; and cook, stirring occasionally, until spinach is tender and wilted but still bright green, 1 to 3 minutes. Off heat, season with salt and pepper to taste and toss with garlic chips. Serve.

Easy Creamed Spinach

Serves 2 `FAST` `VEGETARIAN`

Total time 15 minutes

WHY THIS RECIPE WORKS We wanted super-easy, one-pot creamed spinach that still offered the rich flavor and creamy texture of an authentic steakhouse version. After wilting our spinach in a covered pot, we set it in a colander to drain the excess liquid while we used the same pot to make the sauce. We bypassed the usual work-intensive béchamel and started with creamy Boursin cheese flavored with garlic and herbs. Just 2 tablespoons of cream ensured that our sauce was the right thickness to coat our spinach nicely. One pound of flat-leaf spinach (about 1½ bunches) can be substituted for the curly-leaf spinach, but do not use baby spinach because it is too delicate. Don't dry the spinach completely after washing; a little extra water clinging to the leaves will help them wilt when cooking.

- 1½ teaspoons extra-virgin olive oil
- 10 ounces curly-leaf spinach, stemmed and chopped coarse
- ½   (5.2-ounce) package Boursin Garlic and Fine Herbs cheese
- 2   tablespoons heavy cream

1. Heat oil in large saucepan over high heat until shimmering. Add spinach in handfuls, stirring and tossing each handful to wilt slightly before adding next. Continue to cook spinach, stirring constantly, until uniformly wilted, about 1 minute. Transfer spinach to colander and squeeze between tongs to release excess liquid.

2. Wipe saucepan dry with paper towels. Whisk Boursin and cream together in now-empty saucepan; bring to simmer over medium-high heat; and cook until thickened, about 2 minutes. Off heat, stir in spinach until evenly coated. Season with salt and pepper to taste, and serve.

Maple-Glazed Acorn Squash

Serves 2 `VEGETARIAN`

Total time 45 minutes

WHY THIS RECIPE WORKS Maple syrup is a natural counterpart for earthy and sweet acorn squash, but many recipes leave the glaze in pools in the squash halves—or stuck on the baking sheet. To taste the syrup in every bite, we needed the syrup to stick but not burn. We cut our acorn squash into wedges, which increased its surface area and gave the glaze more to stick to (and smaller pieces of squash also resulted in a shorter roasting time). Tossing the wedges with vegetable oil and a small amount of sugar before baking ensured that they browned quickly. At first, our simple glaze of maple syrup and melted butter—with salt and a little cayenne for kick—ran right off the squash, but slightly reducing the glaze in the microwave helped it coat the squash nicely. Avoid using pancake syrup here; pure maple syrup is important to the flavor of this dish.

1 acorn squash (1½ pounds), halved lengthwise, seeded, and cut into 8 wedges
1 tablespoon vegetable oil
1 teaspoon sugar
¼ teaspoon table salt
¼ teaspoon pepper
2 tablespoons maple syrup
2 tablespoons unsalted butter
Pinch cayenne pepper

1. Adjust oven rack to middle position and heat oven to 475 degrees. Line rimmed baking sheet with aluminum foil. Toss squash with oil, sugar, salt, and pepper and arrange cut side down in single layer on prepared sheet. Roast until bottoms of squash wedges are deep golden brown, about 15 minutes.

2. Meanwhile, microwave maple syrup, butter, cayenne, and pinch salt in bowl, stirring occasionally, until butter is melted and mixture is slightly thickened, about 90 seconds; cover to keep warm.

3. Remove sheet from oven, and, using spatula, carefully flip squash. Brush with half of glaze and continue to roast until squash is tender and deep golden, 5 to 8 minutes. Carefully flip squash, brush with remaining glaze, and serve.

PREPARING ACORN SQUASH FOR ROASTING

1. Set squash on dish towel and cut slice off the bottom so it will sit level. Position chef's knife on top of squash and strike with mallet to drive it into squash and all the way through.

2. Remove seeds and place squash halves cut side down on cutting board and cut in half, lengthwise.

3. Using your hand to steady squash quarters, carefully cut each into 2 wedges.

Butternut Squash Puree

Butternut Squash Puree
Serves 2   VEGETARIAN
Total time 50 minutes

WHY THIS RECIPE WORKS With a silky-smooth texture and lightly sweet flavor, pureed butternut squash is a surefire winner. And although it requires a relatively long cooking time, it's almost entirely hands-off. Our first instinct was to braise the squash, but we found that the squash's subtle flavor was washed away and its texture was watery. It turned out that the squash exuded so much liquid as it cooked that we didn't need to include braising liquid at all. So we simply cooked the squash pieces over low heat, which created a perfect steamy environment and coaxed the flavor out of the squash while breaking down its tough starches. A little cream and butter were all we needed to enrich the squash without overpowering its delicate flavor. Pureeing the squash in the food processor yielded a sumptuous, creamy texture. You can substitute delicata squash for the butternut squash.

Roasted Sweet Potato Wedges

1 pound butternut squash, peeled, seeded, and cut into 1-inch pieces
2 tablespoons unsalted butter, cut into 2 pieces
2 tablespoons heavy cream, divided
½ teaspoon sugar
¼ teaspoon table salt
⅛ teaspoon pepper
Pinch cayenne pepper

1. Combine squash, butter, 1 tablespoon cream, sugar, salt, pepper, and cayenne in medium saucepan. Cover and cook squash over low heat until fall-apart tender, 40 to 50 minutes.

2. Transfer squash mixture to food processor, add remaining 1 tablespoon cream, and process until smooth, about 20 seconds, scraping down sides of bowl as needed. Transfer squash puree to bowl, season with salt and pepper to taste, and serve.

VARIATIONS
Butternut Squash Puree with Orange
Add 1½ teaspoons packed brown sugar and 1½ teaspoons orange marmalade to food processor with cream in step 2.

Butternut Squash Puree with Honey and Chipotle Chile
Add 1½ teaspoons honey and ½ teaspoon minced chipotle chile in adobo sauce to food processor with cream in step 2.

Tomato Gratin

Mashed Sweet Potatoes
Serves 2 VEGETARIAN
Total time 50 minutes

WHY THIS RECIPE WORKS Deeply flavored, earthy, and subtly sweet, mashed sweet potatoes hardly need a layer of marshmallows to make them into a tempting side. For a silky and full-flavored mash, we found that the secret was to thinly slice the potatoes and cook them covered on the stovetop over low heat with just a little butter and cream. This method allowed the potatoes to cook evenly in their own moisture, retaining all of their flavor. A teaspoon of sugar was all the enhancement the potatoes needed. Once the potatoes were fall-apart tender, they could be mashed to a silky-smooth texture right in the pot—no draining, no straining, no fuss. Adding another spoonful of cream when we mashed the potatoes enriched them even more. You will need a medium saucepan with a tight-fitting lid for this recipe.

1 pound sweet potatoes, peeled, quartered lengthwise and sliced ¼ inch thick
2 tablespoons unsalted butter, cut into 2 pieces
2 tablespoons heavy cream, divided
1 teaspoon sugar
¼ teaspoon table salt
⅛ teaspoon pepper

1. Combine potatoes, butter, 1 tablespoon cream, sugar, salt, and pepper in medium saucepan. Cover and cook potatoes over low heat until fall-apart tender, 40 to 50 minutes.

2. Add remaining 1 tablespoon cream and mash sweet potatoes with potato masher until a few small lumps remain. Season with salt and pepper to taste, and serve.

Roasted Sweet Potato Wedges

Serves 2   VEGETARIAN

Total time 35 minutes

WHY THIS RECIPE WORKS We love roasting wedges: They require minimal prep, and their generous size gives them eat-with-your-hands appeal. But while potato wedges feel like a steakhouse side, roasted sweet potato wedges have a more distinctive—yet still complementary—flavor that made them an unexpected match for a wide variety of dishes. With nothing more than olive oil, salt, and pepper and a quick visit to a hot 450-degree oven (you don't even need to flip them!), the wedges became caramelized and sweet on the outside and soft and creamy on the inside. Be sure to scrub and dry the whole potatoes thoroughly before cutting it into wedges. For even more flavor, toss wedges with your favorite spice blend (barbecue, Latin, curry powder, Cajun, or Old Bay), or give them smoky heat (try smoked paprika or chipotle chile powder) before roasting.

2 sweet potatoes (12 ounces each), unpeeled, cut lengthwise into 1½-inch-wide wedges
2 tablespoons vegetable oil
½ teaspoon table salt
¼ teaspoon pepper

1. Adjust oven rack to middle position and heat oven to 450 degrees. Line rimmed baking sheet with aluminum foil and spray with vegetable oil spray. Toss all ingredients together in bowl.

2. Arrange potato wedges, cut sides down, in single layer on prepared sheet. Roast until sides in contact with sheet are dark golden brown and wedges are tender, 20 to 25 minutes. Season with salt and pepper to taste. Serve.

Tomato Gratin

Serves 2   VEGETARIAN

Total time 1 hour 5 minutes, plus 30 minutes salting

WHY THIS RECIPE WORKS It's hard to go wrong with a creamy, cheesy, vegetable side, yet most tomato gratins end up waterlogged and flavorless. We solved the problem of a watery gratin by salting the tomatoes for 30 minutes before whirling them in a salad spinner to remove excess moisture. Sautéed onion, flavored with garlic and fresh thyme, amped up the savory notes of the dish, and panko plus grated Parmesan cheese delivered a crispy, cheesy topping. Since the panko browned before the tomatoes were cooked, we gave the tomatoes a head start in the oven before sprinkling on the topping. You will need an 8½ by 5½-inch baking dish for this recipe.

12 ounces plum tomatoes, cored and sliced ¼ inch thick
½ teaspoon plus ⅛ teaspoon table salt, divided
⅛ teaspoon sugar
¼ cup panko bread crumbs
¼ cup grated Parmesan cheese
4 teaspoons extra-virgin olive oil, divided
2 pinches pepper, divided
1 small onion, halved and sliced thin
1 small garlic clove, minced
½ teaspoon minced fresh thyme or ⅛ teaspoon dried

1. Adjust oven racks to lower-middle and upper-middle positions and heat oven to 450 degrees. Toss tomatoes, ½ teaspoon salt, and sugar together in bowl and let sit for 30 minutes. Combine panko, Parmesan, 2 teaspoons oil, remaining ⅛ teaspoon salt, and pinch pepper in second bowl.

2. Heat remaining 2 teaspoons oil in 8-inch skillet over medium-high heat until shimmering. Add onion and cook, stirring occasionally, until softened, about 5 minutes. Stir in garlic and thyme and cook until fragrant, about 30 seconds. Season with salt and pepper to taste. Spread onion mixture in bottom of 8½ by 5½-inch baking dish.

3. Transfer tomatoes to salad spinner and spin to remove excess moisture. Arrange tomatoes in even layer over onion mixture and sprinkle with remaining pinch pepper. Transfer baking dish to lower rack and bake until tomatoes are tender and starting to bubble, about 15 minutes. Sprinkle evenly with panko mixture; transfer to upper rack; and bake until topping is golden brown, about 10 minutes. Transfer gratin to wire rack and let cool for 5 to 10 minutes before serving.

CHAPTER 13

Rice, Grains & Beans

■ **FAST** (Start to finish in 30 minutes or less)
■ **VEGETARIAN**

Opposite: Dal with Tofu and Spinach

Simple White Rice

1. Heat oil in small saucepan over medium heat until shimmering. Stir in rice and cook until edges of grains begin to turn translucent, about 2 minutes. Stir in water and salt and bring to boil. Reduce heat to low; cover; and simmer until all liquid is absorbed, 18 to 22 minutes.

2. Remove saucepan from heat. Remove lid, place folded clean dish towel over saucepan, then replace lid. Let rice sit for 10 minutes, then gently fluff with fork. Serve.

Classic Rice Pilaf

Serves 2 **VEGETARIAN**

Total time 40 minutes

WHY THIS RECIPE WORKS Rice pilaf should be fragrant, fluffy, and tender. For the best pilaf, we started with traditional basmati rice. We tried a standard 1:2 ratio of rice to water, but we got the best results with a little less water. Bringing the water to a boil before measuring it, so that we didn't lose any to evaporation, was also key. We rinsed the rice before cooking, which gave us beautifully separated grains, and sautéing the raw rice in butter before steaming gave our pilaf great flavor. Minced shallot added a subtle aromatic flavor. Long-grain white rice can be substituted here. For an accurate measurement of boiling water, bring a kettle of water to a boil and then measure out the desired amount.

- 1 tablespoon unsalted butter or extra-virgin olive oil
- 1 small shallot, minced
- ¾ cup basmati rice, rinsed
- 1¼ cups boiling water
- ¼ teaspoon table salt
- ⅛ teaspoon pepper

1. Melt butter in small saucepan over medium heat. Add shallot and cook until softened, about 2 minutes. Stir in rice and cook until edges of grains begin to turn translucent, about 2 minutes. Stir in boiling water, salt, and pepper, and bring rice to boil. Reduce heat to low; cover; and simmer until all liquid is absorbed, 12 to 15 minutes.

2. Remove saucepan from heat. Remove lid, place folded clean dish towel over saucepan, then replace lid. Let rice sit for 10 minutes, then gently fluff with fork. Serve.

Simple White Rice

Serves 2 **VEGETARIAN**

Total time 50 minutes

WHY THIS RECIPE WORKS White rice seems like an easy enough dish to make, but it can be deceptively temperamental, quickly dissolving into unpleasant, gummy grains. For really great long-grain rice with distinct, separate grains that didn't clump together, we rinsed the rice of excess starch first. Then, to add a rich dimension, we sautéed the grains in oil before covering them with boiling water. We simmered the rice until all of the liquid was absorbed, then we placed a dish towel between the lid and pot to absorb excess moisture and ensure dry, fluffy grains.

- 1 teaspoon vegetable oil
- ¾ cup long-grain white, basmati, or jasmine rice, rinsed
- 1¼ cups water
- ¼ teaspoon table salt

Classic Rice Pilaf with Pine Nuts, Basil, and Lemon

Add ¼ cup shredded fresh basil, 2 tablespoons toasted pine nuts, and ¼ teaspoon grated lemon zest to saucepan when fluffing rice in step 2.

Classic Rice Pilaf with Saffron and Toasted Almonds

Add pinch saffron to saucepan with shallot. Add 2 tablespoons toasted sliced almonds to saucepan when fluffing rice in step 2.

NOTES FROM THE TEST KITCHEN

GETTING TO KNOW RICE

All rice (except wild rice) starts out as brown rice. A grain of rice is made up of endosperm, germ, bran, and a hull or husk. Brown rice is simply husked and cleaned. White rice has the germ and bran removed. This makes the rice cook up faster and softer, and it's more shelf-stable, but this process also removes much of the fiber, protein, and other nutrients, as well as flavor.

LONG-GRAIN WHITE RICE This broad category includes generic long-grain rice as well as aromatic varieties such as basmati (see below), Texmati, and jasmine. The grains are slender and elongated and measure four to five times longer than they are wide. The rice cooks up light and fluffy with firm, distinct grains, making it good for pilafs and salads. Avoid converted rice, which is parboiled during processing. In our opinion, this tan-colored rice cooks up too separate, and the flavor is a bit off.

MEDIUM-GRAIN WHITE RICE Shorter and squatter than long-grain, medium-grain rice is tender with grains that clump together. This category includes a wide variety of specialty rices used to make risotto (Arborio) and paella (Valencia), as well as many Japanese and Chinese brands. The grains are fat, measuring two to three times longer than they are wide. This rice cooks up a bit sticky (the starch is what makes risotto so creamy), and when simmered, the grains clump together.

SHORT-GRAIN WHITE RICE These are opaque, almost round grains, that are softer and stickier than long- or medium-grain rice thanks to low amylose and high amylopectin. It's often sold as sushi rice. (Although many medium-grain rices have that label as well.) The category includes numerous Japanese and Korean brands. The grains of short-grain rice are almost round, and the texture is quite sticky and soft when cooked.

BROWN RICE As with white rice, brown rice comes in a variety of grain sizes: short, medium, and long. Long-grain brown rice, the best choice for pilafs, cooks up fluffy, with separate grains. Medium-grain brown rice is a bit more sticky, perfect for risotto, paella, and similar dishes. Short-grain brown rice is the most sticky, ideal for sushi and other Asian dishes where getting the grains to clump together is desired.

BASMATI RICE Prized for its nutty flavor and sweet aroma, basmati rice is eaten in pilafs and biryanis and with curries. Indian basmati is aged for a minimum of one year, though often much longer, before being packaged. Aging dehydrates the rice, which translates into grains that, once cooked, expand greatly. We don't recommend American-grown basmati.

WILD RICE Wild rice is technically not in the same family as other rices; it's actually an aquatic grass. Wild rice is North America's only native grain. It grows naturally in lakes and also is cultivated in manmade paddies in Minnesota, California, and Canada. We prefer brands that parboil the grains during processing.

RED RICE Red rice is a special variety of rice with a red husk rather than the more common brown. It is usually unhulled or partially hulled and has a high nutritional value and a nutty flavor.

BLACK RICE Like brown rice, black rice is sold unhulled. But only black rice contains anthocyanins, the same antioxidant compounds in blueberries and blackberries. These compounds are what turn the rice a deep purple as it cooks.

Foolproof Baked White Rice

Serves 2   `VEGETARIAN`

Total time 45 minutes

WHY THIS RECIPE WORKS A hands-off recipe for perfect rice is a cook's ace in the hole, so we wanted to use the enclosed heat of the oven for a fuss-free way to evenly cook rice while freeing up our stovetop. When we tried to use our usual stovetop ratio of liquid to rice for this easy baked rice, we found that the grains were a bit too crunchy. Adding a little extra liquid was necessary for the high heat of the oven and greatly improved the texture—producing distinct, clump-free, fluffy grains. At the end of baking we simply fluffed the rice with a fork, sealed the dish with aluminum foil, and let it sit on the counter to finish cooking for 10 minutes. Do not substitute basmati rice for the long-grain white rice. For an accurate measurement of boiling water, bring a kettle of water to a boil and then measure out the desired amount.

1¾   cups boiling water
1   cup long-grain white or jasmine rice, rinsed
1   teaspoon extra-virgin olive oil
¼   teaspoon table salt

1. Adjust oven rack to middle position and heat oven to 450 degrees. Combine all ingredients in 8-inch square baking dish or pan. Cover dish tightly with aluminum foil and bake until liquid is absorbed and rice is tender, 20 to 30 minutes, rotating dish halfway through baking.

2. Remove dish from oven; uncover; and fluff rice with fork, scraping up any rice that has stuck to bottom. Re-cover dish with foil and let rice sit for 10 minutes. Season with salt and pepper to taste. Serve.

VARIATION
Foolproof Baked Brown Rice

Substitute long-grain or medium-grain brown rice for white rice and increase cooking time to 45 to 55 minutes.

Parmesan Risotto

Serves 2   `VEGETARIAN`

Total time 55 minutes

WHY THIS RECIPE WORKS Classic Parmesan risotto is incredibly satisfying, rich in both flavor and texture. But try to adapt this finicky recipe for two and you'll most likely be disappointed by sticky, gummy, and bland rice. For foolproof risotto for two, we had to find just the right proportion of liquid to rice. We settled on ¾ cup of Arborio rice as the right

Parmesan Risotto

amount for two, and after lots of tests and tinkering, we found that 2½ cups water, 2 cups broth, and ½ cup white wine (for acidity and complexity) gave us tender, creamy risotto with a little bite. Although the liquid is traditionally added incrementally with constant stirring, we found we could simplify things by adding half of the liquid and cooking the rice hands-off until the liquid was absorbed. Then we added the rest of the broth in stages, stirring constantly, until the rice was perfectly cooked. The texture of the risotto will stiffen substantially as it sits; loosen with additional hot broth or water as needed before serving. Garnish with parsley and shaved Parmesan, if desired.

2½   cups water
2   cups vegetable or chicken broth
2   tablespoons unsalted butter, divided
1   small onion, chopped fine
¼   teaspoon table salt
1   garlic clove, minced
¾   cup Arborio rice
½   cup dry white wine
1   ounce Parmesan cheese, grated (½ cup)

1. Bring water and broth to simmer in small saucepan over medium heat. Remove from heat, cover, and keep warm.

2. Melt 1 tablespoon butter in medium saucepan over medium-high heat. Add onion and salt and cook until softened, about 5 minutes. Stir in garlic and cook until fragrant, about 30 seconds. Add rice and cook, stirring constantly, until grains are translucent around edges, about 1 minute. Add wine and cook, stirring frequently, until fully absorbed, 3 to 5 minutes.

3. Stir in 2 cups reserved warm broth. Reduce heat to medium-low; cover; and simmer until almost all liquid is absorbed, about 12 minutes.

4. Stir in ½ cup reserved warm broth and cook, stirring constantly, until absorbed, about 3 minutes. Repeat with additional broth 2 or 3 more times until rice is al dente (you may have broth left over). Off heat, stir in remaining 1 tablespoon butter and Parmesan. Season with salt and pepper to taste, and serve.

VARIATION
Pesto Risotto

You can make your own pesto (page 235) or use your favorite store-bought brand from the refrigerated section of the supermarket—they have a fresher flavor than jarred pesto sold in the grocery aisles.

Substitute ¼ cup basil pesto for remaining 1 tablespoon butter and Parmesan in step 4.

No-Fuss Parmesan Polenta

Serves 2 FAST VEGETARIAN

Total time 30 minutes

WHY THIS RECIPE WORKS Polenta is a make-it-a-meal mainstay—it's a hearty, creamy base that pairs nicely with just about any topping. It is also wonderful as a creamy side dish for just about any roast. But traditional recipes require that you are chained to the stove, stirring the polenta constantly until it reaches the right consistency; otherwise it will burn. Not so with this version that we developed to give the cook a break. Our trick? We added a pinch of baking soda—it allowed us to cut cooking time in half and eliminated the need for constant stirring, giving us the best quick polenta recipe. While you might not expect it, polenta reheats well—cover and warm in the microwave, adjusting consistency with hot water as needed. It is important to cook the polenta over very low heat, so use a flame tamer if your stovetop runs hot.

2½ cups water
¼ teaspoon table salt
  Pinch baking soda
½ cup coarse-ground cornmeal
1 ounce Parmesan cheese, grated (½ cup)
1 tablespoon unsalted butter

1. Bring water to boil in small saucepan over medium-high heat. Stir in salt and baking soda. Slowly add cornmeal in steady stream, stirring constantly. Bring mixture to boil, stirring constantly, about 30 seconds. Reduce heat to lowest possible setting and cover.

2. After 5 minutes, whisk cornmeal to smooth out any lumps, making sure to scrape down sides and bottom of saucepan. Cover and continue to cook, without stirring, until cornmeal is tender but slightly al dente, 8 to 10 minutes longer. (Polenta should be loose and barely hold its shape; it will continue to thicken as it cools.)

3. Off heat, stir in Parmesan and butter and season with salt and pepper to taste. Cover and let sit for 5 minutes.

NOTES FROM THE TEST KITCHEN

SORTING OUT POLENTA

In the supermarket, cornmeal can be labeled anything from yellow grits to corn semolina. Forget the names. When shopping for the right product to make polenta, there are three things to consider: "instant" or "quick-cooking" versus the traditional style, degerminated or full-grain meal, and grind size.

Instant and quick-cooking cornmeals are parcooked and comparatively bland—leave them on the shelf. Though we loved the full corn flavor of whole-grain cornmeal, it remains slightly gritty no matter how long you cook it. We prefer degerminated cornmeal, in which the hard hull and germ are removed from each kernel (check the back label or ingredient list to see if your cornmeal is degerminated; if it's not explicitly labeled as such, you can assume it's whole grain).

As for grind, we found coarser grains brought the most desirable and pillowy texture to our No-Fuss Parmesan Polenta. However, grind coarseness can vary dramatically from brand to brand since there are no standards to ensure consistency—one manufacturer's "coarse" may be another's "fine." To identify coarse polenta as really coarse, the grains should be about the size of couscous.

Cheesy Baked Grits

Serves 2   VEGETARIAN

Total time 1 hour plus 10 minutes cooling

WHY THIS RECIPE WORKS A staple of the Southern table, grits are a simple but satisfying side dish. We wanted a rich and cheesy version, baked until it was brown on the top and creamy in the middle. We began building flavor by sautéing some chopped onion in butter. Then we brought water—enriched with cream and spiked with a dash of hot sauce—to a boil and whisked in the grits. We found that convenient quick grits had a creamy yet substantial texture that tasters preferred over old-fashioned grits. Once they were thickened, we stirred in plenty of tangy extra-sharp cheddar cheese along with a beaten egg, which gave the finished dish an airy texture, and moved the grits to the oven to develop a nicely browned crust. A sprinkle of scallions was the finishing touch. Do not substitute instant grits or old-fashioned grits for the quick-cooking grits in this recipe, as they require different amounts of liquid for cooking. You will need an 8-inch ovensafe nonstick skillet for this recipe.

    1 tablespoon unsalted butter
    ¼ cup finely chopped onion
    ¾ cup water
    ¼ cup heavy cream
    ½ teaspoon table salt
    ¼ teaspoon hot sauce
    ¼ cup quick-cooking grits
    1 large egg, lightly beaten
    ⅛ teaspoon pepper
    3 ounces extra-sharp cheddar cheese,
      shredded (¾ cup), divided
    1 scallion, sliced thin

1. Adjust oven rack to middle position and heat oven to 375 degrees. Melt butter in 8-inch ovensafe nonstick skillet over medium heat. Add onion and cook until softened and lightly browned, 5 to 7 minutes. Stir in water, cream, salt, and hot sauce and bring to boil. Slowly whisk in grits. Reduce heat to low and cook, stirring often, until grits are thick and creamy, 5 to 7 minutes.

2. Off heat, stir in egg, pepper, and ½ cup cheddar until combined. Smooth grits into even layer and sprinkle with remaining ¼ cup cheddar. Transfer skillet to oven and bake until cheese is melted and golden, 15 to 20 minutes.

3. Using potholders (skillet handle will be hot), remove skillet from oven and transfer to wire rack. Let cool for 10 minutes, sprinkle with scallion, and serve.

Toasted Orzo with Chives and Lemon

Serves 2   VEGETARIAN

Total time 50 minutes

WHY THIS RECIPE WORKS Most versions of orzo pilaf are bland at best, little more than a stodgy starch used to bulk up a meal. We wanted a flavorful orzo pilaf that would hold its own when paired with any main dish. We toasted the orzo until golden brown before cooking it, which was the key to an outstanding pilaf. After sautéing an onion in butter, we added a combination of white wine and broth and simmered the orzo over moderate heat. A handful of minced chives added fresh flavor and a shot of color. Lemon zest and juice brightened the dish, nicely balancing the hearty, nutty orzo. In step 1, watch the orzo closely toward the end of the toasting time—it can quickly go from browned to burnt.

    ⅔ cup orzo
    1 tablespoon unsalted butter
    1 small onion, chopped fine
    1 garlic clove, minced
    2 cups vegetable or chicken broth
    ½ cup water
    2 tablespoons dry white wine
    1 tablespoon minced fresh chives
    ½ teaspoon grated lemon zest plus 1 teaspoon juice

1. Toast orzo in 10-inch skillet over medium heat, stirring frequently, until golden brown, 6 to 8 minutes; transfer to bowl.

2. Melt butter in now-empty skillet over medium-high heat. Add onion and cook until softened, about 5 minutes. Stir in garlic and cook until fragrant, about 30 seconds. Stir in toasted orzo, broth, water, and wine and bring to simmer. Reduce heat to medium-low and cook, stirring every 5 minutes, until liquid has been absorbed and orzo is tender, about 15 minutes.

3. Stir in chives and lemon zest and juice and cook until heated through, about 1 minute. Season with salt and pepper to taste, and serve.

VARIATION

Toasted Orzo with Tomatoes and Basil

Omit lemon juice. Substitute 2 tablespoons chopped fresh basil for chives. Add ½ cup chopped tomatoes and ¼ cup grated Parmesan cheese with basil and lemon zest in step 3.

Herbed Couscous

1. Toast couscous in small saucepan over medium-high heat, stirring often, until some grains begin to brown, about 3 minutes. Transfer couscous to medium bowl.

2. Heat 1½ teaspoons oil in now-empty saucepan over medium heat until shimmering. Add shallot and cook until softened, about 2 minutes. Stir in garlic and cayenne and cook until fragrant, about 30 seconds. Stir in broth and bring to boil.

3. Pour boiling broth mixture over couscous in bowl; cover bowl tightly with plastic wrap; and let sit until couscous is tender, about 12 minutes. Uncover and fluff couscous with fork. Stir in parsley and remaining 1½ teaspoons oil. Season with salt and pepper to taste. Serve.

VARIATIONS

Couscous with Tomato, Scallion, and Lemon
Substitute 2 thinly sliced scallions for parsley. Add 1 cored and chopped tomato, 1 teaspoon lemon juice, and ¼ teaspoon grated lemon zest to couscous with oil in step 3.

Couscous with Saffron, Raisins, and Almonds
Substitute pinch crumbled saffron threads and pinch ground cinnamon for garlic. Add ¼ cup raisins and 2 tablespoons toasted sliced almonds to couscous with oil in step 3.

Herbed Couscous

Serves 2 VEGETARIAN

Total Time: 35 minutes

WHY THIS RECIPE WORKS Couscous is one of our go-tos when we want a fast, easy side or light dinner. For a basic version that we could easily translate into additional flavor variations, we started by considering the spice. A single pinch of cayenne pepper bloomed in oil gave the couscous a friendly warmth, and aromatic shallot and garlic added depth. We also quickly toasted the couscous to coax out more of its natural nuttiness before adding a splash of flavorful hot vegetable broth. We simply let the couscous and broth sit until the grains became tender and hydrated before giving the mixture a quick fluff with a fork and a final enriching addition of oil.

⅓ cup couscous
1 tablespoon extra-virgin olive oil, divided
1 shallot, minced
1 garlic clove, minced
  Pinch cayenne pepper
½ cup vegetable or chicken broth
¼ cup minced fresh parsley

Quinoa Pilaf

Serves 2 VEGETARIAN

Total time 55 minutes

WHY THIS RECIPE WORKS With its hearty flavor, chewy texture, and complete protein properties, quinoa has increasingly become a popular side dish. We set out to put this "super-grain" to work in a quick and easy quinoa pilaf. We rinsed the quinoa (to remove its bitter saponin coating), and we toasted it in extra-virgin olive oil to deepen its flavor. This step also ensured that the pilaf had distinct individual grains, rather than cooking up in dense clumps. For rich, savory flavor, we simmered the toasted quinoa in chicken broth along with a little thyme. Once the grains were tender, we removed the pot from the heat and let it sit for 10 minutes before fluffing the grains with a fork. Placing a kitchen towel under the lid absorbed the steam and kept the grains from getting soggy. We like the convenience of prewashed quinoa; rinsing removes the quinoa's bitter protective coating. If you buy unwashed quinoa, rinse it and then spread it out on a clean dish towel to dry for 15 minutes.

Quinoa Salad with Red Bell Pepper and Cilantro

Tabbouleh

- 1 tablespoon extra-virgin olive oil
- 1 small onion, chopped fine
- ¼ teaspoon table salt
- ¾ cup prewashed white quinoa
- 1¼ cups vegetable or chicken broth
- 1 teaspoon minced fresh thyme or ¼ teaspoon dried

1. Heat oil in medium saucepan over medium-high heat until shimmering. Add onion and salt and cook until onion is softened, about 5 minutes.

2. Add quinoa and cook, stirring often, until quinoa is lightly toasted and aromatic, about 5 minutes. Stir in broth and thyme and bring to simmer. Reduce heat to low; cover; and simmer until quinoa is translucent and tender, 16 to 18 minutes.

3. Remove saucepan from heat. Remove lid, place folded clean kitchen towel over saucepan, then replace lid. Let quinoa sit for 10 minutes, then gently fluff with fork. Season with salt and pepper to taste, and serve.

VARIATION

Quinoa Pilaf with Goat Cheese and Chives

Substitute 2 minced garlic cloves for onion; cook until fragrant, about 30 seconds, before adding quinoa. Add 1 tablespoon minced chives to saucepan when fluffing quinoa in step 3. Sprinkle with ¼ cup crumbled goat cheese before serving.

Quinoa Salad with Red Bell Pepper and Cilantro

Serves 2   **VEGETARIAN**

Total time 40 minutes plus 20 minutes cooling

WHY THIS RECIPE WORKS To take advantage of the versatility of quinoa, we wanted to make a protein-packed quinoa salad. We started by using our pilaf method to cook the grains until just tender. Then we spread the cooked quinoa over a baking sheet to cool it to room temperature quickly. Crisp, sweet bell pepper; jalapeño; red onion; and fresh cilantro provided a sweet and spicy contrast to the hearty, chewy quinoa. We tossed the vegetables and grains with a bright dressing flavored with lime juice, mustard, garlic, and cumin. After 12 minutes of cooking, there will still be a little bit of water in the pan, but this will evaporate as the quinoa cools. To make this dish spicier, reserve and add the chile seeds as desired. We like the convenience of prewashed quinoa; rinsing removes the quinoa's bitter protective coating (called saponin). If you buy unwashed quinoa, rinse it and then spread it out on a clean dish towel to dry for 15 minutes.

⅔ cup prewashed white quinoa
1 cup water
⅛ teaspoon table salt
2 tablespoons finely chopped red bell pepper
¼ jalapeño chile, stemmed, seeded, and minced
3 tablespoons finely chopped red onion
1 tablespoon minced fresh cilantro
2 tablespoons extra-virgin olive oil
2 teaspoons lime juice
1 teaspoon Dijon mustard
1 small garlic clove, minced
¼ teaspoon ground cumin

1. Toast quinoa in small saucepan over medium heat, stirring often, until lightly toasted and aromatic, about 5 minutes. Stir in water and salt and bring to simmer. Reduce heat to low; cover; and simmer until quinoa has absorbed most of water and is just tender, 12 to 14 minutes. Spread quinoa on rimmed baking sheet lined with clean dish towel and let cool for about 20 minutes.

2. When quinoa is cool, transfer to serving bowl. Stir in bell pepper, jalapeño, onion, and cilantro. In separate bowl, whisk oil, lime juice, mustard, garlic, and cumin together until well combined. Pour over quinoa and toss to coat. Season with salt and pepper to taste, and serve.

Tabbouleh

Serves 2 VEGETARIAN
Total time 45 minutes plus 1 hour resting
WHY THIS RECIPE WORKS Tabbouleh is a traditional Middle Eastern salad made of bulgur, parsley, tomato, and onion steeped in a penetrating mint and lemon dressing. For tabbouleh for two, we started by salting the tomatoes to rid them of excess moisture that otherwise would make our salad soggy. We soaked the bulgur in lemon juice and some of the drained tomato liquid, rather than water, which allowed it to soak up lots of flavor. A whole chopped onion overwhelmed the salad, but a single scallion added just the right amount of oniony flavor. Bright parsley, mint, and a bit of cayenne pepper rounded out the dish. We added the herbs and vegetables while the bulgur was still soaking so that the components had time to mingle, resulting in a cohesive, balanced dish. Serve the salad with the crisp inner leaves of romaine lettuce and wedges of pita bread. This salad tastes best the day it's made. Look for medium-grind bulgur (labeled "#2"), which is roughly the size of mustard seeds. Avoid coarsely ground bulgur; it will not cook through in time.

1 tomato, cored and cut into ½-inch pieces
¼ teaspoon table salt, divided
¼ cup medium-grind bulgur, rinsed and dried well
2 tablespoons lemon juice, divided
¾ cup chopped fresh parsley
¼ cup chopped fresh mint
1 scallion, sliced thin
3 tablespoons extra-virgin olive oil
Pinch cayenne pepper

1. Toss tomato with ⅛ teaspoon salt and let drain in fine-mesh strainer set over bowl, tossing occasionally, about 30 minutes.

2. In separate bowl, combine bulgur, 1 tablespoon lemon juice, and 1 tablespoon juice from drained tomatoes. Let stand until grains begin to soften, 30 to 40 minutes.

3. Layer drained tomato, parsley, mint, and scallion on top of bulgur. Whisk remaining 1 tablespoon lemon juice, oil, cayenne, and remaining ⅛ teaspoon salt together, then drizzle over top and toss gently to combine. Cover and let sit at room temperature until flavors meld and bulgur is tender, about 1 hour. Before serving, toss to recombine and season with salt and pepper to taste.

NOTES FROM THE TEST KITCHEN

GETTING TO KNOW BULGUR
Adding recipes using bulgur to your repertoire is a great way to add fiber, protein, iron, and magnesium to your diet. But cooking with bulgur requires an understanding of what it is and how to buy it. A product of the wheat berry, bulgur has been steamed, dried, ground, and then sorted by size (fine-grain, medium-grain, and coarse-grain). The result of this process is a fast-cooking, highly nutritious grain that can be used many ways. We like medium-grind bulgur for tabbouleh and salads because it requires little more than a soak to become tender and flavorful. Soaking it in flavorful liquids, such as lemon or lime juice, also imbues it with bright flavor. Coarse-grind bulgur, which requires simmering, is best for cooked applications like pilaf. Note that medium-grind bulgur can work in cooked applications if you make adjustments to cooking times. Do not substitute cracked wheat for bulgur. Be sure to rinse bulgur, regardless of grain size, to remove excess starches that can turn the grain gluey.

Simple Farro

Serves 2   `FAST`   `VEGETARIAN`

Total time 30 minutes

WHY THIS RECIPE WORKS Farro, an ancient form of wheat that predates our modern bread wheat, comes in a few different forms, but our favorite is minimally processed whole farro, in which the grain's germ and bran have been retained. Whole farro has a nutty flavor and delicately chewy texture, and it cooks in only 15 to 20 minutes, which makes it one of the fastest cooking whole grains. We found that the simplest cooking method was best: Boil in salted water until tender; drain well; and add to salads, soups, and side dishes, or store in the refrigerator for up to five days. Pearled farro can be used, but cooking times vary, so start checking for doneness after 10 minutes. Do not use quick-cooking farro in this recipe. Warm farro can be tossed with butter or olive oil and salt and pepper for a simple yet hearty side dish. It can also be added to soups or, when cooled, added to salads.

   1 cup whole farro, rinsed
   ½ teaspoon table salt

Bring 2 quarts water to boil in large saucepan. Add farro and salt. Return to boil; reduce heat; and simmer until grains are tender with slight chew, 15 to 20 minutes. Drain well.

Kimchi Bokkeumbap

Serves 2

Total time 45 minutes

WHY THIS RECIPE WORKS Iconic, quick-cooking Korean comfort food, kimchi bokkeumbap, is typically made with leftover cooked short-grain rice and well-fermented kimchi, but from there, seasonings and additions to bulk it up vary widely from cook to cook. We started by stir-frying some aromatics (chopped onion and sliced scallions) with chopped ham—a popular addition that we liked for its smoky flavor and pleasantly springy texture. Then we added lots of chopped cabbage kimchi along with some of its savory, punchy juice and a little water and seasoned it with soy sauce, toasted sesame oil, and gochujang to add savoriness, rich nuttiness, and a little more heat. We simmered the cabbage leaves so that they softened a bit; stirred in the rice and cooked the mixture until the liquid had been absorbed; and topped the rice with small strips of gim (seaweed paper), sesame seeds, and scallion greens. This recipe works best with day-old rice; alternatively, cook your rice 2 hours ahead, spread it on a rimmed baking sheet, and let it cool completely before chilling it for 30 minutes.

Plain pretoasted seaweed snacks can be substituted for the gim; omit the toasting in step 1. If your kimchi doesn't yield 2 tablespoons of juice, make up the difference with water. If using soft, well-aged kimchi, omit the water and reduce the cooking time at the end of step 2 to 2 minutes. If desired, top each portion of rice with a Fried Egg (page 360).

   ½ (8-inch square) sheet gim
   1 tablespoon vegetable oil, divided
   1 (¼-inch-thick) slice deli ham, cut into ¼-inch pieces
       (about 2 ounces)
   1 small onion, chopped
   3 scallions, white and green parts separated
       and sliced thin on bias
   ⅔ cup cabbage kimchi, drained with 2 tablespoons juice
       reserved, cut into ¼-inch strips
   2 tablespoons water
   2 teaspoons soy sauce
   2 teaspoons gochujang paste
   ¼ teaspoon pepper
   1½ cups cooked Short-Grain White Rice (page 351)
   2 teaspoons toasted sesame oil
   2 teaspoons sesame seeds, toasted

   1. Grip gim with tongs and hold about 2 inches above low flame on gas burner. Toast gim, turning every 3 to 5 seconds, until gim is aromatic and shrinks slightly, about 20 seconds. (If you do not have a gas stove, toast gim on rimmed baking sheet in 275-degree oven until gim is aromatic and shrinks slightly, 20 to 25 minutes, flipping gim halfway through toasting.) Using kitchen shears, cut gim into four 2-inch-wide strips. Stack strips and cut crosswise into thin strips.

   2. Heat 1½ teaspoons vegetable oil in 14-inch flat-bottomed wok or 12-inch nonstick skillet over medium-high heat until shimmering. Add ham, onion, and scallion whites and cook, stirring frequently, until onion is softened and ham is beginning to brown at edges, 5 to 7 minutes. Stir in kimchi and reserved juice, water, soy sauce, gochujang, and pepper. Cook, stirring occasionally, until kimchi turns soft and translucent, 3 to 5 minutes.

   3. Add rice; reduce heat to medium-low; and cook, stirring and folding constantly until mixture is evenly coated, about 3 minutes. Stir in sesame oil and remaining 1½ teaspoons vegetable oil. Increase heat to medium-high and cook, stirring occasionally, until mixture begins to stick to wok, about 3 minutes. Transfer to serving bowl. Sprinkle with sesame seeds, scallion greens, and gim and serve.

Short-Grain White Rice

Makes about 2 cups **VEGETARIAN**
Total time 35 minutes

For rice that is soft and sticky to soak up savory sauces, turn to steamed short-grain rice. Short-grain rice varieties (except for glutinous rice) such as sushi rice work well here.

    1 cup water
    1 cup short-grain white rice, rinsed
    ⅛ teaspoon table salt

Bring water, rice, and salt to boil in large saucepan over medium-high heat. Reduce heat to low; cover; and simmer until water is absorbed, about 10 minutes. Off heat, let rice sit until fully tender, about 15 minutes.

Braised Chickpeas with Garlic and Parsley

Serves 2 **FAST** **VEGETARIAN**
Total time 20 minutes

WHY THIS RECIPE WORKS For many people, chickpeas are synonymous with hummus, but with their buttery, nutty flavor, these beans also make a great side dish. Convenient canned chickpeas needed only a few minutes of cooking to warm through, keeping our dish quick and simple. To develop a rich foundation of flavor, we first toasted garlic and red pepper flakes in oil, then added a minced shallot and cooked it until all was lightly browned and aromatic. We added the chickpeas and some chicken broth to this mixture and simmered it covered until the flavors blended, then turned up the heat and reduced the liquid to a light, flavorful glaze. A little parsley and lemon juice brightened and balanced the flavors. You will need a 10-inch skillet with a tight-fitting lid for this recipe.

    2 tablespoons extra-virgin olive oil
    2 garlic cloves, sliced thin
      Pinch red pepper flakes
    1 large shallot, minced
    1 (15-ounce) can chickpeas, rinsed
    ½ cup vegetable or chicken broth
    1 tablespoon minced fresh parsley
    1 teaspoon lemon juice

Braised Chickpeas with Garlic and Parsley

1. Cook oil, garlic, and pepper flakes in 10-inch skillet over medium heat, gently shaking pan to prevent garlic from sticking, until garlic turns pale gold, about 1 minute. Stir in shallot and cook until softened and lightly browned, about 3 minutes. Stir in chickpeas and broth; cover; and cook until chickpeas have warmed through and flavors meld, about 2 minutes.

2. Uncover; increase heat to high; and simmer until liquid has reduced slightly, about 3 minutes. Off heat, stir in parsley and lemon juice. Season with salt and pepper to taste, and serve.

VARIATIONS
Braised Chickpeas with Red Bell Pepper and Basil

You will need a 10-inch skillet with a tight-fitting lid for this recipe.

Add ½ red bell pepper, cut into ½-inch pieces, to skillet with shallot; cook until softened, about 5 minutes, before adding chickpeas. Substitute 1 tablespoon chopped fresh basil for parsley.

Braised Chickpeas with Smoked Paprika and Cilantro

You will need a 10-inch skillet with a tight-fitting lid for this recipe.

Omit red pepper flakes. Add ¼ teaspoon smoked paprika to skillet once shallot has softened. Substitute 1 tablespoon minced fresh cilantro for parsley and ½ teaspoon sherry vinegar for lemon juice.

SLICING GARLIC THIN

Place flattest side of peeled garlic clove down on cutting board. Holding garlic securely, slice garlic thin using paring knife. Use tip of knife to pull out green stem, if present.

Braised White Beans with Rosemary and Parmesan

Serves 2 VEGETARIAN

Total time 35 minutes

WHY THIS RECIPE WORKS This Tuscan-inspired white bean braise should boast a rustic, rich texture and be lightly seasoned with garlic and rosemary. In traditional versions of this dish, dried beans are gently cooked for hours over low heat, allowing the beans to break down and bind together. To make it more practical as a side dish for two, we wanted to re-create this dish with convenient, time-saving canned beans. Mashing some of the beans before adding them to the pot gave the finished dish the creamy, saucy texture of long-simmered beans in just 10 minutes. Simmering the beans in chicken broth allowed them to absorb rich, savory flavor.

 1 (15-ounce) can white or cannellini beans, rinsed, divided
 1 tablespoon extra-virgin olive oil
 1 small onion, chopped fine
 1 garlic clove, minced
 1 teaspoon minced fresh rosemary or ¼ teaspoon dried
 ¾ cup vegetable or chicken broth
 1 ounce Parmesan cheese, grated (½ cup)

1. Mash ⅔ cup beans in bowl with potato masher until smooth. Heat oil in small saucepan over medium-high heat until shimmering. Add onion and cook until softened and

lightly browned, 5 to 7 minutes. Stir in garlic and rosemary and cook until fragrant, about 30 seconds.

2. Stir in broth, mashed beans, and remaining whole beans. Bring to simmer and cook until slightly thickened, about 10 minutes. Off heat, sprinkle with Parmesan and season with salt and pepper to taste. Serve.

RINSING CANNED BEANS

Before using canned beans, rinse beans thoroughly in fine-mesh strainer.

Cuban Black Beans

Serves 2 FAST VEGETARIAN

Total time 20 minutes

WHY THIS RECIPE WORKS Recipes using canned beans are quick and easy, but in some instances also provide the added bonus of using their body-building bean liquid, also known as aquafaba. But we wanted to do a little more than simply open a can, so we drew inspiration from Cuba, where spiced black beans are a staple of the cuisine. We found that a quick sofrito of shallots, garlic, and bell pepper, combined with cumin and oregano, added plenty of earthy, fragrant flavor to our simple canned black beans. Mashing part of the beans gave them a creamy texture, but leaving a portion whole kept the dish from becoming soup. Serve with chopped cilantro, sliced scallions, and shredded cheese, if desired. To turn this into a meal, serve with rice or other grains, or with plantain chips, sliced avocado, a dollop of sour cream, and hot sauce.

 1 tablespoon vegetable oil
 1 large shallot, minced
 ½ green bell pepper, chopped fine
 2 garlic cloves, minced
 ¼ teaspoon dried oregano
 ¼ teaspoon ground cumin
 ⅛ teaspoon pepper
 1 (15-ounce) can black beans, drained with liquid reserved, divided

1. Heat oil in medium saucepan over medium heat until shimmering. Add shallot and bell pepper and cook until softened and beginning to brown, 4 to 6 minutes. Stir in garlic, oregano, cumin, and pepper and cook until fragrant, about 30 seconds.

2. Off heat, add ½ cup beans and all reserved bean liquid and mash with potato masher until mostly smooth. Stir in remaining beans. Cook over medium heat until warmed through, 2 to 3 minutes. Season with salt and pepper to taste. Serve.

Black Bean Salad with Corn and Avocado

Serves 2 `FAST` `VEGETARIAN`

Total time 25 minutes

WHY THIS RECIPE WORKS For a great black bean salad, restraint, rather than a kitchen-sink approach, is important. We didn't want to lose the beans among an endless array of Tex-Mex ingredients. We found that a judicious mixture of black beans, corn, avocado, tomato, and cilantro gave us just the right combination of flavors and textures. Toasting the corn before we added it gave the salad deep, well-rounded flavor. And to give our simple dressing plenty of kick, we used a generous amount of bright lime juice, some spicy minced chipotle chile, and a little honey for balancing sweetness. Fresh corn is important for the flavor of this salad—don't substitute frozen or canned corn.

  2 tablespoons extra-virgin olive oil, divided
  1 tablespoon lime juice
  ½ teaspoon minced canned chipotle chile in adobo sauce
  ¼ teaspoon honey
  ¼ teaspoon table salt
  ¼ teaspoon pepper
  1 ear corn, kernels cut from cob
  ¾ cup canned black beans, rinsed
  1 small tomato, cored, seeded, and chopped fine
  2 tablespoons minced fresh cilantro
  ½ avocado, cut into ½-inch pieces

Whisk 1 tablespoon oil, lime juice, chipotle, honey, salt, and pepper together in medium bowl. Heat remaining 1 tablespoon oil in 10-inch skillet over medium-high heat until shimmering. Add corn and cook, stirring occasionally, until golden brown, 6 to 8 minutes. Transfer corn to bowl with dressing. Stir in beans, tomato, and cilantro. Gently fold in avocado. Season with salt and pepper to taste. Serve.

Cuban Black Beans

Black Bean Salad with Corn and Avocado

Spiced Lentil and Rice Pilaf

Lentil Salad with Olives, Mint, and Feta

Serves 2 `VEGETARIAN`

Total time 1 hour plus 1 hour brining

WHY THIS RECIPE WORKS We wanted a bright-tasting lentil salad with lentils that retained their shape and boasted a firm-tender bite. We brined the lentils in warm salted water to soften the lentils' skins, which led to fewer blowouts. Then we baked the lentils to heat them gently and uniformly. Once we had perfectly cooked lentils, all we had to do was pair the earthy legumes with a tart vinaigrette and a few boldly flavored additions. We chose kalamata olives, fresh mint, and creamy feta cheese for a Mediterranean flair. Although we prefer lentilles du Puy (also called French green lentils) for this recipe, it will work with any type of lentil except red or yellow. Note that cooking times may vary depending on the type of lentils you use. Brining helps keep the lentils intact, but this step can be skipped if you're in a hurry. The salad can be served warm or at room temperature.

½ cup lentils, picked over and rinsed
½ teaspoon table salt, for brining
1 cup vegetable or chicken broth
2 garlic cloves, lightly crushed and peeled
1 bay leaf
¼ teaspoon table salt
2½ tablespoons extra-virgin olive oil
1½ tablespoons white wine vinegar
¼ cup coarsely chopped pitted kalamata olives
¼ cup chopped fresh mint
1 shallot, minced
2 tablespoons crumbled feta cheese

1. Place lentils and ½ teaspoon salt in bowl. Cover with 2 cups warm water and soak for 1 hour. Drain well. (Drained lentils can be refrigerated for up to 2 days before cooking.)

2. Adjust oven rack to middle position and heat oven to 325 degrees. Place drained lentils, 1 cup warm water, broth, garlic, bay leaf, and ¼ teaspoon salt in medium saucepan. Cover and bake until lentils are tender but remain intact, 40 minutes to 1 hour. Meanwhile, whisk oil and vinegar together in large bowl.

3. Drain lentils well, discarding garlic and bay leaf. Add drained lentils, olives, mint, and shallot to dressing and toss to combine. Season with salt and pepper to taste. Sprinkle with feta and serve.

Lentil Salad with Goat Cheese

Omit olives. Substitute red wine vinegar for white wine vinegar and add 1 teaspoon Dijon mustard to dressing in step 2. Substitute 2 tablespoons chopped fresh parsley for mint and 1 ounce crumbled goat cheese for feta.

Spiced Lentil and Rice Pilaf

Serves 2   `VEGETARIAN`

Total time 1½ hours

WHY THIS RECIPE WORKS The hearty combination of lentils and rice appears in dishes across the globe. The humble ingredients come together to create a dish that's satisfying and complex, and this versatile base can take on a variety of substitution and add-in options. Lentils and rice cook at different rates, so we knew that making a one-pot recipe would require staggering the cooking. We started by precooking brown lentils, which needed longer to cook through than the rice. For the pot, a saucepan was big enough for a recipe to serve two. After setting the lentils aside, we added shallot to the pot to soften along with a fragrant mix of garlic, turmeric, coriander, and cayenne to bloom. Adding the rice and cooked lentils to this aromatic base gave them a flavorful backbone as they cooked. A sprinkle of toasted pistachios provided much-needed textural contrast, cilantro leaves added freshness, and cooling yogurt provided the perfect finishing touch. Allow the rice to cook for the full 12 minutes before lifting the lid to check it. Sprinkle with pomegranate seeds, if desired.

½ cup brown lentils, picked over and rinsed

⅛ teaspoon table salt, plus salt for cooking lentils

1 tablespoon extra-virgin olive oil

1 shallot, minced

1 garlic clove, minced

¾ teaspoon ground turmeric

½ teaspoon ground coriander

Pinch cayenne pepper

¾ cup long-grain white rice, rinsed

1¼ cups vegetable broth

2 tablespoons chopped toasted pistachios

2 tablespoons fresh cilantro leaves

¼ cup plain Greek yogurt

1. Bring lentils, 2 cups water, and ½ teaspoon salt to boil in small saucepan over high heat. Reduce heat to low and cook until lentils are tender, 12 to 15 minutes. Drain and set aside. Wipe saucepan clean with paper towels.

2. Heat oil in now-empty saucepan over medium heat until shimmering. Add shallot and ⅛ teaspoon salt and cook until softened, about 3 minutes. Stir in garlic, turmeric, coriander, and cayenne and cook until fragrant, about 30 seconds. Add rice and cook, stirring frequently, until edges begin to turn translucent, about 2 minutes. Stir in broth and lentils and bring to boil. Reduce heat to low; cover; and cook until rice is tender and water is absorbed, 12 to 15 minutes.

3. Let sit off heat for 10 minutes. Fluff rice and lentils with fork. Transfer to serving platter and sprinkle with pistachios and cilantro. Serve with yogurt.

NOTES FROM THE TEST KITCHEN

GETTING TO KNOW LENTILS

Lentils come from many parts of the world, in dozens of sizes and colors, with considerable differences in flavor and texture. Because they are thin-skinned, they require no soaking, which makes them a highly versatile legume. Here are the most commonly available types of lentils.

BROWN AND GREEN LENTILS These larger lentils are what you'll find in every supermarket. They are a uniform drab brown or green. They have a mild, light, earthy flavor and a creamy texture. Because they hold their shape well when cooked, they are good all-purpose lentils, great in soups and salads or simmered and then tossed with olive oil and herbs.

LENTILLES DU PUY These dark green French lentils from the city of Le Puy are smaller than the more common brown and green varieties. They are a dark olive green, almost black. They have a rich, earthy, complex flavor and a firm but tender texture. This is the kind to use if you are looking for lentils that will keep their shape and look beautiful on the plate when cooked, so they're perfect for salads and dishes where the lentils take center stage.

RED AND YELLOW LENTILS These Indian lentils are small and orange-red or golden yellow. They come split and skinless, so they completely disintegrate into a uniform consistency when cooked. If you are looking for lentils that will quickly break down into a thick puree, as in our recipe for Dal with Tofu and Spinach, this is the kind to use.

Dal with Tofu and Spinach

Serves 2 VEGETARIAN

Total time 40 minutes

WHY THIS RECIPE WORKS Dal is an Indian dish of red lentils simmered to a porridgelike consistency and seasoned with spices, tomatoes, and onions. Traditional recipes call for a mix of spices, and while that's delicious, we wanted to streamline this meal for the for-two cook. We found that we got complex flavor with just garam masala and ginger. It took some trial and error to get the consistency of the dal just right—too much water and it wound up thin and soupy; too little and it was thick and pasty. Two cups of broth to ½ cup of lentils turned out to be just right. Tofu and spinach rounded out the meal, and tomatoes, lime juice, and fresh herbs brightened everything up. Do not substitute brown or green lentils for the red lentils. Dollop with yogurt and sprinkle with scallions or pickled jalapenos if desired. Serve with naan or pita bread.

- 2 tablespoons vegetable oil, divided
- 1 small onion, chopped fine
- 2 garlic cloves, minced
- 1¼ teaspoons garam masala
- 1 teaspoon grated fresh ginger or ⅛ teaspoon ground ginger
  Pinch cayenne pepper
- 2 cups vegetable or chicken broth
- ½ cup red lentils, picked over and rinsed
- 3 ounces cherry or grape tomatoes, quartered (½ cup)
- 2 tablespoons minced fresh cilantro or parsley
- 1 teaspoon lime juice
- 7 ounces firm tofu, cut into ¾-inch pieces
- 1 cup baby spinach

1. Heat 1 tablespoon oil in medium saucepan over medium heat until shimmering. Add onion and cook until softened, about 5 minutes. Stir in garlic, garam masala, ginger, and cayenne and cook until fragrant, about 30 seconds. Stir in broth and lentils; bring to simmer; and cook over low heat until lentils are tender and resemble thick, coarse puree, 12 to 15 minutes. Season with salt and pepper to taste.

2. Meanwhile, combine tomatoes, cilantro, lime juice, and remaining 1 tablespoon oil in bowl. Season with salt and pepper to taste; set aside until ready to serve.

3. Stir tofu and spinach into lentils and cook until spinach is wilted and tofu is warmed through, 2 to 3 minutes. Top dal with tomato mixture.

Red Lentil Kibbeh

Serves 2 VEGETARIAN

Total time 1 hour

WHY THIS RECIPE WORKS Kibbeh is a popular Middle Eastern dish made from bulgur, onions, varying spices, and, traditionally, ground meat. During Lent, however, kibbeh is often prepared with lentils in lieu of meat. Our version uses red lentils for their vibrant hue, and we enhanced both their color and flavor with two red pastes: Tomato paste brought sweetness and umami, and harissa added smoky complexity. Once the lentils were cooked, we whisked the mixture until the lentils partially broke down. The cohesive mash that formed was perfect for spooning into lettuce leaves and drizzling with yogurt for a dinner you can eat with your hands. You can use store-bought harissa or make your own (see page 311). Do not substitute brown or green lentils for the red lentils. Look for medium-grind bulgur (labeled "#2"), which is roughly the size of mustard seeds.

- 4 teaspoons extra-virgin olive oil, divided
- 1 small onion, chopped fine
- 1 small red bell pepper, stemmed, seeded, and chopped fine
- ¾ teaspoon table salt
- 1 tablespoon harissa
- 1 tablespoon tomato paste
- ½ cup medium-grind bulgur
- 2 cups water
- ⅓ cup dried red lentils, picked over and rinsed
- ¼ cup chopped fresh parsley
- 1 tablespoon lemon juice, plus lemon wedges for serving
  Bibb or Boston lettuce leaves
  Plain yogurt

1. Heat 2 teaspoons oil in large saucepan over medium heat until shimmering. Add onion, bell pepper, and salt and cook until vegetables are softened, about 5 minutes. Stir in harissa and tomato paste and cook until fragrant, about 1 minute.

2. Stir in bulgur and water and bring to boil. Reduce heat to low; cover; and simmer until bulgur is just tender, about 8 minutes. Stir in lentils; cover; and cook, stirring occasionally, until lentils and bulgur are fully tender, 8 to 10 minutes.

3. Off heat, lay clean folded dish towel underneath lid and let sit for 10 minutes. Sprinkle parsley, lemon juice, and remaining 2 teaspoons oil over lentil mixture and stir vigorously until mixture is cohesive. Season with salt and pepper to taste. Serve kibbeh with lettuce leaves, passing yogurt and lemon wedges separately.

Red Lentil Kibbeh

CHAPTER 14

Eggs &
Breakfast

Eggs, Omelets, and More

Pancakes, Waffles, and More

■ **FAST** (Start to finish in 30 minutes or less)

■ **VEGETARIAN**

Opposite: Congee with Jammy Eggs, Peanuts, and Scallions

Perfect Fried Eggs

Serves 2 `FAST` `VEGETARIAN`

Total time 20 minutes

WHY THIS RECIPE WORKS In our search for the perfect fried egg, we realized that cracking the eggs one by one into the pan would caused them to cook unevenly, so we cracked them into bowls and tipped them into the pan all at once. We heated the oil for a full 5 minutes, which ensured that the whites set quickly. After we covered the eggs and cooked them for 1 minute, we let them sit off the heat for an additional 15 to 45 seconds, which gave us tender whites and warm, runny yolks. When checking the eggs for doneness, lift the lid just a crack to prevent loss of steam. To cook two eggs, use an 8- or 9-inch nonstick skillet and halve the amounts of oil and butter. You will need a 12-inch skillet with a tight-fitting lid for this recipe.

- 2 teaspoons vegetable oil
- 4 large eggs
- ⅛ teaspoon table salt
  Pinch pepper
- 2 teaspoons unsalted butter, cut into 4 pieces and chilled

Perfect Fried Eggs

1. Heat oil in 12-inch nonstick skillet over low heat for 5 minutes. Meanwhile, crack eggs into 2 small bowls (2 eggs in each), and sprinkle with salt and pepper.

2. Increase heat to medium-high and heat until oil is shimmering. Add butter and quickly swirl to coat skillet. Working quickly, pour 1 bowl of eggs in 1 side of skillet and second bowl of eggs in other side. Cover and cook for 1 minute. Remove skillet from burner and let stand, covered, for 15 to 45 seconds for runny yolks (white around edge of yolk will be barely opaque), 45 to 60 seconds for soft but set yolks, and about 2 minutes for medium-set yolks. Slide eggs onto warm plates and serve immediately.

Easy-Peel Hard-Cooked Eggs

Serves 2 `VEGETARIAN`

Total time 35 minutes

WHY THIS RECIPE WORKS Boiled eggs that start in cold water are hard to peel because the proteins in the egg white set slowly, which gives them time to fuse to the surrounding membrane. When you try to remove the shell, parts of the white cling to the membrane, and the surface of the egg becomes pockmarked. The solution? We placed cold eggs into hot steam, which denatured the outermost egg white proteins; this caused them to form a solid gel that shrunk and pulled away from the membrane. The shells now slipped off easily. You can double this recipe as long as you use a pot large enough to hold the eggs in a single layer. Be sure to use eggs that have no cracks and are cold from the refrigerator. The eggs can be stored in their shells stored in their shells for up to five days and peeled when needed. You will need a medium saucepan with a tight-fitting lid for this recipe.

- 4 large eggs

1. Bring 1 inch water to rolling boil in medium saucepan over high heat. Place eggs in steamer basket and transfer basket to saucepan. Cover, reduce heat to medium-low, and steam eggs for 13 minutes.

2. Combine 2 cups ice cubes and 2 cups cold water in bowl. Using tongs or slotted spoon, transfer eggs to ice bath and let sit for 15 minutes. Peel before using.

VARIATION

Easy-Peel Jammy Eggs

Cook over medium-high heat in step 1, and decrease cooking time to 8 minutes. In step 2, submerge eggs in ice bath just until cool enough to handle, about 30 seconds.

BUYING EGGS

When eggs are the focal point of a dish, their quality and size make a big difference. We use large eggs in all our recipes. But even beyond size, there are numerous—and often confusing—options when buying eggs at the supermarket. Here's what we've learned.

FARM FRESH AND ORGANIC In our taste tests, farm-fresh eggs were standouts. The large yolks were bright orange and sat very high above the comparatively small whites, and the flavor of these eggs was exceptionally rich and complex. Organic eggs followed in second place, eggs from hens raised on a vegetarian diet in came in third, and standard supermarket eggs finished last. Tasters easily detected differences in egg-based dishes such as an omelet or a frittata but not in cakes or cookies.

EGGS AND OMEGA-3S Many companies market eggs with a high level of omega-3 fatty acids, the healthful unsaturated fats also found in some fish. In our taste test, we found that eggs with more omega-3s had a richer egg flavor and a deeper yolk color. Why? Commercially raised chickens usually peck on corn and soy, while chickens on an omega-3-enriched diet also eat greens, flaxseeds, and algae, which add flavor, complexity, and color to their eggs. Look for products that guarantee at least 200 milligrams of omega-3s per egg.

HOW OLD ARE MY EGGS? Egg cartons are marked with a sell-by date and a pack date. The pack date is the day the eggs were packed, which is generally within a week of when they were laid but may be as much as 30 days later. The sell-by date is within 30 days of the pack date, which is the legal limit set by the U.S. Department of Agriculture. A carton of eggs may be up to two months old by the sell-by date. But eggs are still fit for consumption for an additional three to five weeks past the sell-by date.

ANATOMY OF AN EGG

VITELLINE This membrane contains and protects the yolk. It weakens as the egg ages.

YOLK The yolk contains most of the egg's vitamins and minerals as well as all the fat and some of the protein.

AIR CELL This void results from contraction as the interior cools after the egg is laid. It increases in size as the egg ages.

CHALAZAE These whitish cords extend from each pole end and center the yolk. As an egg ages, the chalazae weaken and the yolk can become off-center.

SHELL The shell and inner membrane keep the contents in place and keep out bacteria. The shell is permeable, and over time the contents of an egg can evaporate. Never use an egg with a cracked or split shell.

WHITE The white, also called the albumin, is made of protein and water and is divided into thick and thin layers, with the thickest layer closest to the yolk. A slight cloudiness indicates extreme freshness. As eggs age, the white becomes thinner and clearer.

EGG SIZES Eggs vary in size, and that variance can make a difference in recipes, especially those that call for several eggs. We call for large eggs in all our recipes, but you can substitute one size for another. See the Emergency Substitution Chart on page 30 for details.

Soft-Cooked Eggs

Serves 2 FAST VEGETARIAN

Total time 15 minutes

WHY THIS RECIPE WORKS Most methods for making soft-cooked eggs are hit or miss. We wanted a recipe that would produce any number of perfect eggs with set whites and fluid yolks. To eliminate temperature variables, we used fridge-cold eggs and boiling water. This also created the steepest temperature gradient, ensuring that the yolk at the center stayed fluid while the white cooked through. To keep the temperature of the water from dropping when we added the cold eggs, we decided to steam the eggs rather than boil them. This minimized the contact between the hot water and the cold surface of the eggs, maintaining the temperature of the water whether we cooked one egg or six. You can cook one to six large, extra-large, or jumbo eggs without altering the cooking time. Be sure to use eggs that have no cracks and are cold from the refrigerator. Because precise timing is vital to the success of this recipe, we strongly recommend using a digital timer. We recommend serving these eggs in egg cups with buttered toast for dipping.

4 large eggs

1. Bring ½ inch water to boil in medium saucepan over medium-high heat. Using tongs, gently place eggs in boiling water (eggs will not be submerged). Cover saucepan and cook eggs for 6½ minutes.

2. Remove cover, transfer saucepan to sink, and place under cold running water for 30 seconds. Remove eggs from saucepan and serve immediately, seasoning with salt and pepper to taste.

VARIATIONS

Soft-Cooked Eggs with Sautéed Mushrooms

Heat 2 tablespoons extra-virgin olive oil in 12-inch skillet over medium-high heat until shimmering. Add 12 ounces sliced white mushrooms and pinch table salt and cook, stirring occasionally, until liquid has evaporated and mushrooms are lightly browned, 5 to 6 minutes. Stir in 2 teaspoons chopped fresh herbs (chives, tarragon, parsley, or combination). Season with salt and pepper to taste and divide between 2 plates. Top each serving with 2 peeled soft-cooked eggs, split cross-wise to release yolks, and season eggs with salt and pepper to taste.

Soft-Cooked Eggs

Soft-Cooked Eggs with Steamed Asparagus

Look for asparagus that is at least ½ inch thick near the base.

Steam 12 ounces asparagus, trimmed, over medium heat until crisp-tender, 4 to 5 minutes. Divide asparagus between 2 plates, then top each serving with 1 tablespoon extra-virgin olive oil and 1 tablespoon grated Parmesan cheese. Top each serving with 2 peeled soft-cooked eggs, split crosswise to release yolks, and season eggs with salt and pepper to taste.

Soft-Cooked Eggs with Salad

Combine 3 tablespoons extra-virgin olive oil, 1 tablespoon balsamic vinegar, 1 teaspoon Dijon mustard, and 1 teaspoon minced shallot in jar; seal lid; and shake vigorously until emulsified, 20 to 30 seconds. Toss 5 ounces assertively flavored salad greens (arugula, radicchio, watercress, or frisée) with dressing. Season with salt and pepper to taste and divide between 2 plates. Top each serving with 2 peeled soft-cooked eggs, split crosswise to release yolks, and season eggs with salt and pepper to taste.

Ultimate Scrambled Eggs

Serves 2 `FAST` `VEGETARIAN`

Total time 15 minutes

WHY THIS RECIPE WORKS For scrambled eggs that were fluffy and moist, not dried-out and tough, we put some science to work. The first step was to add salt to the uncooked eggs; salt dissolved some of the egg proteins, creating more tender curds. To avoid overbeating the eggs, we beat them until just combined using the gentle action of a fork rather than a whisk. For the dairy, we found that half-and-half produced clean-tasting curds that were both fluffy and stable. To replicate the richer flavor of farm-fresh eggs, we added extra yolks. Finally, we started the eggs on medium-high heat, which created puffy curds, then finished them over low heat to ensure that they wouldn't overcook. It's important to follow visual cues, as pan thickness will affect cooking times. If using an electric stove, heat one burner on low heat and a second burner on medium-high heat; move the skillet between the burners for temperature adjustment. If you don't have half-and-half, you can substitute 4 teaspoons of whole milk and 2 teaspoons of heavy cream.

- 4 large eggs plus 1 large yolk
- 2 tablespoons half-and-half
- ⅛ teaspoon table salt
- ⅛ teaspoon pepper
- ½ tablespoon unsalted butter, chilled

1. Beat eggs and yolk, half-and-half, salt, and pepper with fork until eggs are thoroughly combined and color is pure yellow; do not overbeat.

2. Heat butter in 10-inch nonstick skillet over medium-high heat until foaming just subsides (butter should not brown), swirling to coat skillet. Add egg mixture and, using heat-resistant rubber spatula, constantly and firmly scrape along bottom and sides of skillet until eggs begin to clump and spatula just leaves trail on bottom of skillet, 45 to 75 seconds.

3. Reduce heat to low and continue to cook, gently but constantly folding eggs, until clumped and just slightly wet, 30 to 60 seconds. Transfer eggs to warm plates and season with salt to taste. Serve immediately.

MAKING SCRAMBLED EGGS

Once spatula just leaves a trail through eggs, that's your cue to turn heat to low and continue to cook until large, shiny, wet curds form.

Tofu Scramble with Shallot and Herbs

Serves 2 `FAST` `VEGETARIAN`

Total time 15 minutes

WHY THIS RECIPE WORKS Tofu scrambles are increasingly common on restaurant breakfast menus as an alternative to scrambled eggs, but they often turn out dry and dull. We wanted to come up with a version of this dish that would appeal to carnivores and vegans alike. Soft tofu was essential for a creamy texture; we crumbled it into smaller and larger pieces to resemble different size egg curds. A small amount of curry powder added depth of flavor and a touch of color to the tofu without overwhelming the other flavors. A minced shallot added just the right amount of aromatic flavor, and fresh herbs gave a pop of brightness. Do not substitute firm tofu for the soft tofu in this recipe. Be sure to press the tofu dry thoroughly before cooking.

- 14   ounces soft tofu
- 2   teaspoons vegetable oil
- 1   shallot, minced
- ¼   teaspoon curry powder
- ¾   teaspoon table salt
- ⅛   teaspoon pepper
- 2   tablespoons minced fresh basil, parsley, tarragon, or marjoram

Gently pat tofu dry with paper towels, then crumble into ¼- to ½-inch pieces. Heat oil in 10-inch nonstick skillet over medium heat until shimmering. Add shallot and cook until softened, about 2 minutes. Stir in tofu, curry powder, salt, and pepper and cook until tofu is hot, about 2 minutes. Off heat, stir in basil and serve.

VARIATIONS

Tofu Scramble with Spinach and Feta

Before adding tofu to skillet, cook 4 ounces baby spinach until wilted, about 1 minute. Add ½ cup crumbled feta cheese with tofu.

Tofu Scramble with Tomato, Scallions, and Parmesan

Add 1 tomato, seeded and chopped fine, and 1 minced garlic clove with shallot and cook until tomato is no longer wet, 3 to 5 minutes. Add ¼ cup grated Parmesan cheese and 2 tablespoons minced scallions with tofu.

Tofu Scramble with Shiitakes, Bell Pepper, and Goat Cheese

Add 4 ounces shiitake mushrooms, stemmed and sliced thin, 1 finely chopped small red bell pepper, and pinch red pepper flakes with shallot; cover and cook until mushrooms have released their liquid, about 5 minutes. Uncover and continue to cook until mushrooms are dry, about 2 minutes. Stir in tofu and seasonings along with ¼ cup crumbled goat cheese and continue to cook as directed.

Classic Filled Omelet

Serves 2   VEGETARIAN

Total time 35 minutes

WHY THIS RECIPE WORKS Omelets seem simple, but cooking the eggs properly in a hot pan can be a delicate matter. Add in cheese, which must melt before the omelet turns brown and rubbery, and you've got a truly temperamental dish on your hands. We wanted a failproof cooking method for a

creamy, supple omelet with perfectly melted cheese that didn't leak all over the pan. We found that a good-quality nonstick skillet and an easy-melting cheese were essential. A heatproof rubber spatula kept the eggs from tearing as we shaped the omelet with the sides of the pan. To ensure that the cheese melted before the eggs overcooked, we shredded it fine for quick melting and removed the pan from the heat after adding the cheese. The residual heat was enough to melt the cheese without overcooking the eggs. This technique gave us the omelet we had been looking for: moist and creamy with plenty of perfectly melted cheese. You can substitute cheddar, Monterey Jack, or any semisoft, grateable cheese for the Gruyère.

- 6   large eggs
- ¼   teaspoon table salt, divided
- ⅛   teaspoon pepper, divided
- 1   tablespoon unsalted butter, divided, plus 1 tablespoon melted butter for brushing omelets, divided
- 6   tablespoons finely shredded Gruyère cheese, divided
- 1   recipe filling (recipes follow), divided

1. Add 3 eggs to small bowl, sprinkle with ⅛ teaspoon salt and pinch pepper, and beat with fork until thoroughly combined. Repeat with remaining 3 eggs, remaining ⅛ teaspoon salt and remaining pinch pepper in separate bowl.

2. Melt 1½ teaspoons butter in 10-inch nonstick skillet over medium-high heat. Add 1 bowl of egg mixture and cook until edges begin to set, 2 to 3 seconds. Using heat-resistant rubber spatula, stir eggs in circular motion until slightly thickened, about 10 seconds. Use spatula to pull cooked edges of eggs in toward center, then tilt skillet to 1 side so that uncooked eggs run to edge of skillet. Repeat until omelet is just set but still moist on surface, 20 to 25 seconds. Sprinkle 3 tablespoons Gruyère and half of filling across center of omelet.

3. Off heat, use spatula to fold lower third (portion nearest you) of omelet over filling; press gently with spatula to secure seams, maintaining fold.

4. Run spatula between outer edge of omelet and skillet to loosen. Pull skillet sharply toward you few times to slide unfolded edge of omelet up far side of skillet. Jerk skillet again so that unfolded edge folds over itself, or use spatula to fold edge over. Invert omelet onto warm plate. Tidy edges with spatula, brush with melted butter, and serve immediately.

5. Wipe out skillet and repeat with remaining 1½ teaspoons butter, remaining egg mixture, remaining 3 tablespoons Gruyère, remaining filling, and remaining melted butter.

Omelet Fillings

MUSHROOM AND THYME

`FAST` `VEGETARIAN`

Total time 15 minutes

- 1 tablespoon unsalted butter
- 1 small shallot, minced
- 2 ounces white mushrooms, trimmed and sliced ¼ inch thick
- 1 teaspoon minced fresh thyme

Melt butter in 10-inch skillet over medium heat. Add shallot and cook until softened, about 2 minutes. Add mushrooms and cook until lightly browned, about 3 minutes. Off heat, stir in thyme and season with salt and pepper to taste. Transfer to small bowl, cover, and set aside until needed.

BACON, ONION, AND SCALLION

`FAST`

Total time 15 minutes

Smoked Gouda cheese is a good match for this filling.

- 2 slices bacon, cut into ½-inch pieces
- ½ small onion, chopped fine
- 1 scallion, sliced thin

Cook bacon in 10-inch skillet over medium heat until crispy, 5 to 7 minutes. Using slotted spoon, transfer bacon to paper towel–lined plate. Pour off all but 1 tablespoon fat from skillet; add onion; and cook over medium heat until softened and golden brown, about 3 minutes. Off heat, stir in scallion. Combine crispy bacon and onion mixture in small bowl, cover, and set aside until needed.

BELL PEPPER, MUSHROOM, AND ONION

`FAST` `VEGETARIAN`

Total time 15 minutes

Monterey Jack or pepper Jack cheese will taste good with this filling.

- 1 tablespoon unsalted butter
- ½ small onion, chopped fine
- 1 ounce white mushrooms, trimmed and sliced ¼ inch thick
- ¼ red bell pepper, cut into ½-inch pieces
- 1 teaspoon minced fresh parsley

Melt butter in 10-inch skillet over medium heat. Add onion and cook until softened, about 2 minutes. Add mushrooms and cook until softened and beginning to brown, about 2 minutes. Add bell pepper and cook until softened, about 2 minutes. Off heat, stir in parsley and season with salt and pepper to taste. Transfer mixture to small bowl, cover, and set aside until needed.

MAKING A FILLED OMELET

1. Pull cooked eggs from edges of skillet toward center, tilting skillet so any uncooked eggs run to skillet's edges.

2. Sprinkle cheese and filling across center of omelet. Off heat, fold lower third of omelet over filling, then press seam to secure.

3. Pull skillet sharply toward you so that unfolded edge of omelet slides up far side of skillet.

4. Fold far edge of omelet toward center and press to secure seam. Invert omelet onto plate.

Poached Egg Sandwiches with Goat Cheese, Tomato, and Spinach

Serves 2　**VEGETARIAN**

Total time 1 hour

WHY THIS RECIPE WORKS Poached eggs are often written off for being too finicky, but we were determined to make them failproof. We poached the eggs in a shallow skillet, which was easier to maneuver than a deep saucepan. Cracking the eggs into teacups made it easy to pour the eggs into the skillet all at once. As soon as we added the eggs, we took the skillet off the heat to allow the eggs to cook gently in the residual heat without the simmering water making the whites ragged. A splash of vinegar lowered the pH of the water, helping the eggs to cook more gently at a lower temperature. Once we had our perfectly poached eggs, we served them on crisp toasted English muffins spread with lemony goat cheese and topped with fresh tomato and lightly sautéed spinach. Do not omit the vinegar in the egg poaching water—in addition to adding flavor, it helps to ensure that the egg whites stay intact during cooking.

- 2 ounces goat cheese, crumbled and softened (½ cup)
- 4 teaspoons extra-virgin olive oil, divided
- 1 teaspoon lemon juice
- 2 English muffins, split, toasted, and still warm
- 1 small tomato, cored and sliced thin
- 1 shallot, minced
- ¼ teaspoon table salt, plus salt for poaching eggs
- 1 small garlic clove, minced
- 4 ounces (4 cups) baby spinach
- 2 tablespoons distilled white vinegar
- 4 large eggs

1. Adjust oven rack to middle position and heat oven to 300 degrees. Combine goat cheese, 1 teaspoon oil, and lemon juice in bowl until smooth and season with salt and pepper to taste. Spread mixture evenly over warm English muffin halves, top with tomato slices, and arrange on rimmed baking sheet. Keep warm in oven.

2. Heat remaining 1 tablespoon oil in 12-inch nonstick skillet over medium heat until shimmering. Add shallot and salt and cook until softened, about 2 minutes. Stir in garlic and cook until fragrant, about 30 seconds. Stir in spinach, 1 handful at a time, until wilted. Continue to cook, stirring frequently, until spinach is uniformly wilted and glossy, about 30 seconds. Using tongs, squeeze out any excess moisture from spinach, then divide evenly among English muffins and return to oven to keep warm.

Poached Egg Sandwiches with Goat Cheese, Tomato, and Spinach

3. Wipe skillet clean, then fill it nearly to rim with water. Add vinegar and 1 teaspoon salt and bring to boil. Meanwhile, crack eggs into 2 teacups (2 eggs in each).

4. Reduce water to gentle simmer. Lower rims of teacups into water and gently tip eggs into skillet simultaneously. Remove skillet from heat, cover, and poach eggs for 4 minutes (add 30 seconds for firm yolks).

5. Using slotted spoon, gently lift eggs from water and let drain before laying them on top of each English muffin. Season with salt and pepper to taste, and serve immediately.

POURING EGGS INTO SKILLET

To add eggs to water at same time for poaching, crack 2 eggs each into 2 teacups. Simultaneously lower lips of cups into simmering water and tip eggs into water.

Broccoli and Feta Frittata

Serves 2   VEGETARIAN

Total time 45 minutes

WHY THIS RECIPE WORKS We started with a well-seasoned filling made with bold ingredients and combined it with six eggs to make a substantial dinner. To ensure that the frittata was cohesive, we chopped the filling ingredients small so that they were held in place by the eggs. To help the eggs stay tender even when cooked to a relatively high temperature, we added milk and salt. The liquid diluted the proteins, making it harder for them to coagulate and turn the eggs rubbery, and salt weakened the interactions between proteins, which produced a softer curd. Finally, for eggs that were cooked fully and evenly, we started the frittata on the stovetop, stirring until a spatula left a trail in the curds, and then transferred the skillet to the oven to gently finish. You will need an 8-inch ovensafe nonstick skillet for this recipe.

6 large eggs

2 tablespoons whole milk

¼ teaspoon plus ⅛ teaspoon table salt, divided

1½ teaspoons extra-virgin olive oil

6 ounces broccoli florets, cut into ½-inch pieces (2 cups)

Pinch red pepper flakes

1½ tablespoons water

¼ teaspoon grated lemon zest plus ¼ teaspoon juice

2 ounces feta cheese, crumbled into ½-inch pieces (½ cup)

1. Adjust oven rack to middle position and heat oven to 350 degrees. Whisk eggs, milk, and ¼ teaspoon salt in bowl until well combined.

2. Heat oil in 8-inch ovensafe nonstick skillet over medium-high heat until shimmering. Add broccoli, pepper flakes, and remaining ⅛ teaspoon salt and cook, stirring frequently, until broccoli is crisp-tender and spotty brown, 4 to 6 minutes. Add water and lemon zest and juice and cook, stirring constantly, until broccoli is just tender and no water remains in skillet, about 30 seconds.

3. Add feta and egg mixture and cook, using heat-resistant rubber spatula to stir and scrape bottom of skillet until large curds form and spatula leaves trail through eggs but eggs are still very wet, about 30 seconds. Smooth curds into even layer and cook, without stirring, for 30 seconds. Transfer skillet to oven and bake until frittata is slightly puffy and surface bounces back when lightly pressed, 6 to 9 minutes. Using rubber spatula, loosen frittata from skillet and transfer to cutting board. Let sit for 5 minutes before slicing and serving.

Shakshuka

Serves 2   VEGETARIAN

Total time 1 hour

WHY THIS RECIPE WORKS This classic Tunisian dish is a satisfying one-pot meal consisting of eggs cooked in a long-simmered, spiced tomato and pepper sauce. For the sauce, we blended whole peeled tomatoes and jarred roasted red peppers for a mix of sweetness, smokiness, and acidity. Pita bread prevented the silky-smooth sauce from weeping. A combination of garlic, tomato paste, and ground spices created the distinct flavor profile. We poured the sauce into a skillet and simmered it until thickened; after removing the pan from the heat we used the back of a spoon to make indentations in the sauce, cracked the eggs into the wells, and covered the whites with sauce, which ensured even cooking. We covered the skillet after bringing everything back to a simmer, which created a steamy environment that cooked the eggs from both above and below. Chopped cilantro, crumbled feta, and sliced kalamata olives on top provided brightness, texture, and flavor. You will need a 10-inch skillet with a tight-fitting lid for this recipe.

2 (8-inch) pita breads, divided

1 (14-ounce) can whole peeled tomatoes, drained

1½ cups jarred roasted red peppers, divided

2 tablespoons extra-virgin olive oil

2 garlic cloves, sliced thin

1½ teaspoons tomato paste

1 teaspoon ground coriander

1 teaspoon smoked paprika

½ teaspoon ground cumin

¼ teaspoon table salt

⅛ teaspoon pepper

⅛ teaspoon cayenne pepper

4 large eggs

¼ cup coarsely chopped fresh cilantro leaves and stems

2 tablespoons crumbled feta cheese

2 tablespoons pitted kalamata olives, sliced

1. Cut enough pita bread into ½-inch pieces to make ¼ cup (about one-eighth of 1 pita bread). Cut remaining pita breads into wedges for serving. Process pita pieces, tomatoes, and half of red peppers in blender until smooth, 1 to 2 minutes, scraping down sides of blender jar as needed. Cut remaining red peppers into ¼-inch pieces and set aside.

2. Heat oil in 10-inch skillet over medium heat until shimmering. Add garlic and cook, stirring occasionally, until golden, about 1 minute. Add tomato paste, coriander, paprika, cumin, salt, pepper, and cayenne and cook, stirring constantly, until rust-colored and fragrant, about 1 minute. Stir in tomato–red pepper puree and reserved red peppers (mixture may sputter) and bring to simmer. Reduce heat to maintain simmer; cook, stirring occasionally, until slightly thickened (spatula will leave trail that slowly fills in behind it, but sauce will still slosh when skillet is shaken), 6 to 8 minutes.

3. Remove skillet from heat. Using back of spoon, make 4 shallow dime-size indentations in sauce. Crack 1 egg into small bowl and pour into 1 indentation (it will hold yolk in place but not fully contain egg). Repeat with remaining 3 eggs. Spoon sauce over edges of egg whites so that whites are partially covered and yolks are exposed.

4. Bring to simmer over medium heat (there should be small bubbles across entire surface). Reduce heat to maintain simmer. Cover and cook until yolks film over, 3 to 4 minutes. Continue to cook, covered, until whites are softly but uniformly set (if skillet is shaken lightly, each egg should jiggle as a single unit), 1 to 2 minutes. Off heat, sprinkle with cilantro, feta, and olives. Serve immediately, passing pita wedges separately.

NOTES FROM THE TEST KITCHEN

STORING EGGS
We've tasted two- and three-month-old eggs and found them perfectly palatable. However, at four months, the white was very loose and the yolk had off-flavors, though it was still edible. Older eggs lack the structure-lending properties of fresh eggs.

IN THE REFRIGERATOR If your refrigerator has an egg tray in the door, don't use it—eggs should be stored on a shelf, where the temperature is below 40 degrees (the average refrigerator door temperature in our kitchen is closer to 45 degrees). Eggs are best stored in their cardboard carton, which protects them from absorbing flavors from other foods and helps maintain humidity, which slows down the evaporation of the eggs' moisture.

IN THE FREEZER Extra whites can be frozen, but their rising properties will be compromised. Frozen whites are best in recipes at call for small amounts (like an egg wash) or don't depend on whipping (an omelet). Yolks can't be frozen as is, but adding sugar syrup (microwave 2 parts sugar to 1 part water, stirring to dissolve sugar) to the yolks allows them to be frozen. Stir a scant ¼ teaspoon sugar syrup per yolk into the yolks before freezing.

Skillet Strata with Cheddar
Serves 2 VEGETARIAN
Total time 55 minutes

WHY THIS RECIPE WORKS To downsize our strata to serve two, we switched from a casserole dish to an 8-inch skillet. Whole milk provided richness without overwhelming the dish. Toasting bite-size squares of bread in the skillet ensured that they maintained some structure when doused in custard. We liked cheddar cheese for its sharp flavor, and sautéed onion and thyme lent aromatic notes. Baking the strata in the same skillet in which we sautéed the onions and toasted the bread made for easier cleanup. Do not trim the crusts from the bread or the strata will be too dense and eggy. Make sure to remove the strata from the oven when it is still slightly loose; it will continue to set as it cools. You will need an 8-inch ovensafe nonstick skillet for this recipe.

3 large eggs
¾ cup whole milk
1 teaspoon minced fresh thyme or ¼ teaspoon dried
¼ teaspoon table salt
¼ teaspoon pepper
2 ounces cheddar cheese, shredded (½ cup)
2 tablespoons unsalted butter
1 small onion, chopped fine
2 slices hearty white sandwich bread, cut into 1-inch pieces

1. Adjust oven rack to middle position and heat oven to 425 degrees. Whisk eggs, milk, thyme, salt, and pepper together in bowl. Stir in cheese and set aside.

2. Melt butter in 8-inch ovensafe nonstick skillet over medium heat. Add onion and cook until softened and lightly browned, 5 to 7 minutes. Add bread and cook, using heat-resistant rubber spatula to fold bread and onion together, until bread is lightly toasted, about 3 minutes.

3. Off heat, fold in egg mixture until slightly thickened and well combined with bread. Gently press down on bread to help it soak up egg mixture. Bake until edges and center of strata are puffed and edges have pulled away slightly from sides of skillet, 12 to 15 minutes.

4. Using potholders (skillet handle will be hot), remove skillet from oven. Let sit for 5 minutes before serving.

VARIATION
Skillet Strata with Sausage and Gruyère
Substitute ½ cup shredded Gruyère cheese for cheddar cheese. Reduce amount of butter to 1 tablespoon and add 4 ounces crumbled raw breakfast sausage to skillet with onion in step 2.

Skillet Strata
with Cheddar

Classic Cheese Quiche

Serves 2 VEGETARIAN

Total time 1¼ hours, plus 20 minutes freezing and 30 minutes cooling

WHY THIS RECIPE WORKS To tailor a classic quiche to serve two, we first needed to ditch our full-size pie plate. A 6-inch pie plate produced a perfect-size quiche for two people. For a crisp, flaky crust, we parbaked the dough to keep the filling from turning the crust soggy. For the filling, two eggs and ⅔ cup of half-and-half gave us a creamy texture and lightly eggy flavor. Cheddar cheese and minced herbs rounded out the flavor. Taking the quiche out of the oven when the center looked slightly underdone allowed carryover cooking to produce a perfectly cooked quiche. You will need a 6-inch pie plate for this recipe. We prefer the buttery flavor and flaky texture of homemade pie dough; however, you can substitute 1 (9-inch) store-bought pie dough round if desired. It is important to add the custard to the crust while it is still warm; if the crust has cooled, rewarm it in the oven for 5 minutes before adding the custard.

> 1 recipe Classic Single-Crust Pie Dough (page 400)
> ⅔ cup half-and-half
> 2 large eggs, lightly beaten
> 2 teaspoons minced fresh chives or parsley
> ⅛ teaspoon table salt
> ⅛ teaspoon pepper
> 2 ounces cheddar cheese, shredded (½ cup)

1. Roll dough into 10-inch circle, about ⅛ inch thick, on lightly floured counter. Loosely roll dough around rolling pin and gently unroll it onto 6-inch pie plate, letting excess dough hang over edge. Ease dough into plate by gently lifting edge of dough with your hand while pressing into plate bottom with your other hand, letting excess dough overhang plate.

2. Trim overhang to ½ inch beyond lip of pie plate. Tuck overhang under itself; folded edge should be flush with edge of pie plate. Crimp dough evenly around edge of pie using your fingers. Wrap dough-lined pie plate loosely in plastic wrap and place in freezer until dough is fully chilled and firm, about 20 minutes.

3. Adjust oven rack to lower-middle position and heat oven to 375 degrees. Line chilled pie shell with parchment paper or double layer of aluminum foil, covering edges to prevent burning, and fill with pie weights. Bake until pie dough looks dry and is light in color, 25 to 30 minutes. Transfer pie plate to wire rack and remove weights and parchment. (Crust must still be warm when custard filling is added.)

4. Reduce oven temperature to 350 degrees. Line rimmed baking sheet with aluminum foil. Whisk half-and-half, eggs, chives, salt, and pepper together in 4-cup liquid measuring cup. Stir in cheddar until well combined.

5. Place warm baked pie crust on prepared sheet and return shell to oven. Carefully pour egg mixture into crust until it reaches about ½ inch from top edge of crust (you may have extra egg mixture). Bake quiche until top is lightly browned; very center still jiggles and looks slightly underdone; and knife inserted about 1 inch from edge comes out clean, 30 to 40 minutes. Let quiche cool on wire rack for 30 minutes to 1 hour. Serve slightly warm or at room temperature.

VARIATIONS
Quiche Lorraine

While crust bakes in step 3, cook 2 slices bacon, cut into ¼-inch pieces, in 8-inch skillet over medium-low heat until crispy, about 10 minutes. Using slotted spoon, transfer bacon to paper towel–lined plate. Pour off all but 1 tablespoon fat from skillet; add ¼ cup finely chopped onion; and cook over medium heat until softened and lightly browned, 5 to 7 minutes; set aside. Substitute 2 ounces Gruyère cheese for cheddar cheese and whisk bacon and onion into egg mixture in step 4.

Ham and Swiss Quiche

Substitute 2 ounces Swiss cheese for cheddar cheese. Whisk 2 ounces thinly sliced deli ham, cut into ¼-inch pieces, into egg mixture in step 4.

Buttermilk Pancakes

Serves 2 VEGETARIAN

Total time 35 minutes, plus 10 minutes resting

WHY THIS RECIPE WORKS We wanted truly tangy buttermilk pancakes with a slightly crisp, golden crust surrounding a fluffy, tender center. We loved the tangy flavor that the buttermilk imparted, but too much made our batter runny; we found that supplementing the buttermilk with sour cream gave us the tang we were after without diluting the batter. For pancakes that were lightly sweet, we decided that 1 tablespoon of sugar was the perfect amount. A combination of baking powder and baking soda provided the best rise. Gently folding the wet and dry ingredients together was essential for a tender texture; overmixed batter made for tough pancakes. Letting the batter sit while the skillet heated allowed the batter to thicken slightly, resulting in perfect light, fluffy pancakes.

Buttermilk Pancakes

1 cup (5 ounces) all-purpose flour
1 tablespoon sugar
½ teaspoon baking powder
¼ teaspoon baking soda
¼ teaspoon table salt
1 cup buttermilk
2 tablespoons sour cream
2 tablespoons unsalted butter, melted and cooled
1 large egg
1 teaspoon vegetable oil, plus extra as needed

1. Adjust oven rack to middle position and heat oven to 200 degrees. Set wire rack in rimmed baking sheet, spray with vegetable oil spray, and place in oven.

2. Whisk flour, sugar, baking powder, baking soda, and salt together in medium bowl. Whisk buttermilk, sour cream, melted butter, and egg together in separate bowl until smooth. Make well in center of dry ingredients, add buttermilk mixture to well, and stir gently with rubber spatula until just combined. (Batter will be lumpy with a few spots of dry flour; do not overmix.) Let batter rest for 10 minutes before cooking.

NOTES FROM THE TEST KITCHEN

KEY TIPS TO BETTER PANCAKES
Here are our tips for getting perfectly fluffy, golden-brown pancakes every time.

MAKE A WELL WHEN MIXING Make a well in the center of the dry ingredients, pour the liquid ingredients into the well, and stir gently together until just incorporated. We like this method when making liquidy batters, because it helps incorporate the wet ingredients into the dry without overmixing.

LEAVE SOME LUMPS When stirring the batter, be careful not to overmix it—the batter should actually have a few lumps. Overmixed batter makes for dense pancakes.

GET THE SKILLET HOT BUT NOT SCORCHING
Heat the oil in a 12-inch nonstick skillet over medium heat for 3 to 5 minutes. If the skillet is not hot enough before cooking the pancakes, the pancakes will be pale and dense. Knowing when the skillet is hot enough can take some practice; if you're not sure if the skillet is ready, try cooking just one small pancake to check.

WIPE OUT EXCESS OIL Before adding the batter, use a wad of paper towels to carefully wipe out the excess oil, leaving a thin film of oil in the pan. If you use too much oil, the delicate cakes will taste greasy and dense.

USE A ¼-CUP MEASURE Add the batter to the skillet in ¼-cup increments (two or three pancakes will fit at a time). Using a measuring cup ensures that the pancakes are the same size and that they cook at the same rate. Don't crowd the pan or the pancakes will run together and be difficult to flip.

FLIP WHEN YOU SEE BUBBLES Cook the pancakes on the first side until large bubbles begin to appear, about 2 minutes. The bubbles indicate that the pancakes are ready to be flipped. If the pancakes are not browned when flipped, the skillet needs to be hotter; if the pancakes are overly browned, turn down the heat.

3. Heat oil in 12-inch nonstick skillet over medium heat until shimmering. Using wad of paper towels, carefully wipe out oil, leaving thin film of oil on bottom and sides of skillet. Using ¼-cup dry measure, portion batter into skillet in 3 places. Cook until edges are set, first side is golden brown, and bubbles on surface are just beginning to break, 2 to 3 minutes.

4. Using thin, wide spatula, flip pancakes and continue to cook until second side is golden brown, 1 to 2 minutes. Transfer pancakes to prepared wire rack (don't overlap them) in warm oven. Repeat with remaining batter, using more oil as needed. Serve.

GETTING PERFECTLY COOKED PANCAKES

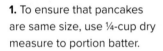

1. To ensure that pancakes are same size, use ¼-cup dry measure to portion batter.

2. Cook pancakes until large bubbles begin to appear, about 2 minutes. Flip pancakes and cook until golden brown on second side, about 1½ minutes.

Buttermilk Waffles

Serves 2   VEGETARIAN

Total time 35 minutes

WHY THIS RECIPE WORKS Most "waffle" recipes are merely repurposed pancake recipes that rely on butter and maple syrup to mask the mediocre results. Our waffles had to have a crisp, golden-brown crust with a moist, fluffy interior. We started by adapting buttermilk pancake batter, but this produced a gummy, wet interior and not much crust. We needed a drier batter with much more leavening oomph. We found the key to lightening our waffles in recipes for tempura batter, which often call for seltzer, because the tiny bubbles inflate the batter the same way as a chemical leavener. We tried replacing the buttermilk in our recipe with a mixture of seltzer and powdered buttermilk, plus baking soda for browning. The resulting waffles were light and crisp. Buttermilk powder is available in the baking aisle. Do not substitute sparkling water such as Perrier for the seltzer water.

1 cup (5 ounces) all-purpose flour
¼ cup (1¼ ounces) buttermilk powder
1½ teaspoons sugar
¼ teaspoon table salt
¼ teaspoon baking soda
¼ cup sour cream
1 large egg
2 tablespoons vegetable oil
⅛ teaspoon vanilla extract
⅔ cup seltzer water

1. Adjust oven rack to middle position and heat oven to 200 degrees. Set wire rack in rimmed baking sheet, spray with vegetable oil spray, and place in oven.

2. Whisk flour, buttermilk powder, sugar, salt, and baking soda together in large bowl. Whisk sour cream, egg, oil, and vanilla together in medium bowl, then gently stir in seltzer. Make well in center of dry ingredients, add seltzer mixture to well, and stir gently with rubber spatula until just combined. (Batter will be lumpy with a few spots of dry flour; do not overmix.)

3. Heat waffle iron and bake waffles according to manufacturer's instructions (use about ⅓ cup batter for 7-inch round iron). Transfer waffles to prepared wire rack in warm oven; repeat with remaining batter. Serve.

Almond Granola with Dried Fruit

Makes about 5 cups   VEGETARIAN

Total time 1 hour, plus 1 hour cooling

WHY THIS RECIPE WORKS Store-bought granola suffers from many shortcomings. It's often loose and gravelly and infuriatingly expensive. We wanted to make our own granola at home with big, satisfying clusters and a crisp texture. The secret was to firmly pack the granola mixture into a 13 by 9-inch pan before baking. Once it was baked, we had granola "bark" that we could break into crunchy clumps of any size. A combination of just a few tablespoons each of maple syrup and brown sugar gave us granola with a subtle, not cloying, sweetness. Chopping the almonds by hand proved best for superior texture and crunch. If you prefer not to hand-chop, substitute an equal quantity of slivered or sliced almonds. (A food processor does a poor job of chopping whole nuts evenly.) Do not use quick oats. You can substitute 1 cup of your favorite dried fruit(s) for the raisins.

2½	tablespoons maple syrup
2½	tablespoons packed light brown sugar
2	teaspoons vanilla extract
¼	teaspoon table salt
¼	cup vegetable oil
2½	cups (7½ ounces) old-fashioned rolled oats
1	cup whole almonds, chopped coarse
1	cup raisins, chopped

1. Adjust oven rack to upper-middle position and heat oven to 325 degrees. Make parchment paper sling for 13 by 9-inch baking pan by folding 2 long sheets of parchment; first sheet should be 13 inches wide and second sheet should be 9 inches wide. Lay sheets of parchment in pan perpendicular to each other, with extra parchment hanging over edges of pan. Push parchment into corners and up sides of pan, smoothing parchment flush to pan.

2. Whisk maple syrup, sugar, vanilla, and salt together in large bowl, then whisk in oil. Fold in oats and almonds until thoroughly coated.

3. Transfer oat mixture to prepared pan and spread across bottom into thin, even layer. Using stiff metal spatula, compress oat mixture until very compact. Bake until lightly browned, 30 to 35 minutes, rotating pan halfway through baking.

4. Remove granola from oven and let cool on wire rack to room temperature, about 1 hour. Using parchment overhang, lift granola out of pan. Break cooled granola into pieces of desired size and transfer to large clean bowl. Add raisins and toss gently to combine. (Granola can be stored in airtight container for up to 2 weeks.)

Buttermilk Waffles

VARIATIONS
Pecan-Orange Granola with Dried Cranberries
Add 1 tablespoon grated orange zest and 1¼ teaspoons ground cinnamon to maple syrup mixture in step 2. Substitute 1 cup pecans for almonds and 1 cup dried cranberries for raisins.

Tropical Granola with Dried Mango
Reduce amount of vanilla extract to 1 teaspoon and add ¾ teaspoon ground ginger and ¼ teaspoon ground nutmeg to maple syrup mixture in step 2. Substitute 1 cup macadamia nuts for almonds and ¾ cup unsweetened shredded coconut for ½ cup of oats. Substitute 1 cup chopped dried mango or pineapple for raisins.

Hazelnut Granola with Dried Pear
Substitute 1 cup toasted and skinned hazelnuts for almonds and 1 cup chopped dried pears for raisins.

Almond Granola with Dried Fruit

Steel-Cut Oatmeal

Serves 2 VEGETARIAN

Total time 30 minutes, plus 12 hours resting

WHY THIS RECIPE WORKS Most oatmeal fanatics agree that steel-cut oats offer the best flavor and texture, but many balk at the 40-minute cooking time. We were determined to find a way to make really good oatmeal that would take just 10 minutes before serving. Our solution was to jump-start the oats' cooking by stirring them into boiling water the night before, so they gently hydrated and softened overnight. In the morning, we simply added more water and simmered the oats for just 4 to 6 minutes. Then we briefly rested the oatmeal off the heat so that it could thicken to the perfect consistency: creamy with a subtle chew and nutty flavor. The oatmeal will thicken as it cools. If you prefer a looser consistency, thin the oatmeal with boiling water. Serve with toppings such as brown sugar, toasted nuts, maple syrup, or dried fruit.

- 2 cups water, divided
- ½ cup steel-cut oats
  Pinch table salt

1. Bring 1½ cups water to boil in small saucepan over high heat. Off heat, stir in oats and salt, cover, and let sit overnight.

2. Stir remaining ½ cup water into oats and bring to boil over medium-high heat. Reduce heat to medium and cook, stirring occasionally, until oats are softened but still retain some chew and mixture thickens and resembles warm pudding, 4 to 6 minutes. Remove saucepan from heat and let sit for 5 minutes. Stir and then serve, passing desired toppings separately.

VARIATION
Apple-Cinnamon Steel-Cut Oatmeal
Increase salt to ¼ teaspoon. Substitute ¼ cup apple cider and ¼ cup whole milk for water in step 2. Stir ¼ cup peeled and grated Golden Delicious, Fuji, or Gala apple; 1 tablespoon packed dark brown sugar; and ¼ teaspoon ground cinnamon into oatmeal with cider and milk. Sprinkle each serving with 1 tablespoon coarsely chopped toasted walnuts.

Congee with Jammy Egg, Peanuts, and Scallions

Serves 2 VEGETARIAN

Total time 1 hour

WHY THIS RECIPE WORKS Savory, warming rice porridge is a welcome breakfast throughout China and neighboring countries. Topping options are numerous: We went with salty, tangy, and savory additions such as scallions, rice vinegar, and soy sauce, which enhanced the richness of the jammy eggs and unsalted peanuts. Congee consistencies vary across versions; this thicker congee is hearty and super filling. Jasmine rice can be substituted for conventional long-grain white rice; do not use basmati. You will need a large saucepan with a tight-fitting lid for this recipe.

- 4 cups water
- ¾ cup long-grain white rice, rinsed
- ½ cup vegetable or chicken broth
- ¼ teaspoon table salt
- 2 Easy-Peel Jammy Eggs (page 360), halved
- 2 tablespoons dry-roasted unsalted peanuts, chopped coarse
- 2 scallions, sliced thin
- 2 teaspoons unseasoned rice vinegar
- 1 teaspoon soy sauce
- 1 teaspoon chili oil (optional)

1. Combine water, rice, broth, and salt in large saucepan and bring to boil over high heat. Reduce heat to maintain vigorous simmer. Cover pot, tucking wooden spoon horizontally between pot and lid to hold lid ajar. Cook, stirring occasionally, until mixture is thickened, glossy, and reduced to about 3 cups, 35 to 40 minutes.

2. Top each 1½-cup portion with 1 jammy egg; 1 tablespoon peanuts; half the scallions; 1 teaspoon vinegar; ½ teaspoon soy sauce; and ½ teaspoon chili oil, if using.

Mangú Breakfast Bowl with Tempeh

Serves 2 VEGETARIAN

Total time 45 minutes

WHY THIS RECIPE WORKS Mangú, a rich Dominican breakfast of mashed plantains, is often served with a trio of accompaniments known as "tres golpes," or "three hits" of flavor—salami, cheese, and eggs. In this vegetarian version, the subtly sweet, silky plantain mash is pure magic when paired with spiced tempeh, our pleasantly chewy-crispy stand-in for the sausage in traditional recipes. Topped with the tempeh, onion, creamy avocado, and citrusy fresh cilantro, it's a plant-based Dominican feast. Look for unripe plantains that are green to yellow green and feel firm and full in their skins. You can speed up the breakfast prep by cooking and mashing the plantains the night before.

Mangú Breakfast Bowl with Tempeh

1. Place the plantains on a cutting board. Use a chef's knife to cut off the ends of each plantain.

2. With the plantain on its side, slice along the vein lengthwise (the long way) to split the peel open, making sure not to cut into the fruit.

3. Use a spoon or your hands to peel back the skin from the plantains and slice as directed.

1 pound unripe plantains, peeled and sliced ½ inch thick

¼ teaspoon table salt, divided, plus salt for cooking plantains

2 tablespoons extra-virgin olive oil, divided

1 small red onion, halved through root end and sliced ½ inch thick

¼ cup plus ¼ teaspoon red wine vinegar, divided

4 ounces tempeh, cut into ½-inch pieces

2 teaspoons soy sauce

1 teaspoon garlic powder

½ teaspoon dried oregano

½ teaspoon ground cumin

½ avocado, sliced thin

2 tablespoons chopped fresh cilantro

1. Place plantains and ½ teaspoon salt in large saucepan, add cold water to cover by 2 inches, and bring to boil over high heat. Reduce heat to medium-high and cook until plantains are tender and easily pierced with tip of knife, 15 to 20 minutes. Reserve 1 cup cooking water. Drain plantains and return to now-empty saucepan.

2. Add 2 teaspoons oil, ½ cup of reserved cooking water, and ⅛ teaspoon salt to plantains and mash with potato masher until mostly smooth. Season with salt and pepper to taste. Cover to keep warm. (Plantain mixture will thicken as it cools. Completely cooled mixture can be refrigerated for up to 2 days; reheat in saucepan over medium heat, adjusting consistency with water as desired.)

3. Meanwhile, heat 1 teaspoon oil in 10- or 12-inch non-stick skillet over medium heat until shimmering. Add onion and remaining ⅛ teaspoon salt and cook until softened, 3 to 5 minutes. Stir in ¼ cup vinegar and cook until evaporated, about 1 minute. Transfer onion mixture to small bowl; set aside. Wipe skillet clean with paper towels.

4. Toss tempeh with soy sauce, garlic powder, oregano, cumin, 1 teaspoon oil, and remaining ¼ teaspoon vinegar in medium bowl. Heat remaining 2 teaspoons oil in now-empty skillet over medium heat until shimmering. Add tempeh and cook until browned on all sides, 3 to 5 minutes. Stir plantain mixture to recombine and adjust consistency with remaining ½ cup reserved cooking water as needed. Top each portion of plantains with tempeh, onion mixture, avocado, and cilantro. Serve.

CHAPTER 15

Quick Breads

Biscuits and Scones

Muffins and Coffee Cake

Quick Loaves

■ VEGETARIAN

Opposite: Corn Muffins

Simple Drop Biscuits

Makes 4 biscuits VEGETARIAN

Total time 40 minutes

WHY THIS RECIPE WORKS We wanted a drop biscuit recipe we could make anytime—and this would be no ordinary drop biscuit. It should possess the same rich flavor and tender crumb of a rolled and cut biscuit, but with less work. We replaced the usual milk with buttermilk, which gave the biscuits a rich, buttery tang. The buttermilk also encouraged a crisp crust and a fluffy interior. Stirring melted butter into the buttermilk created clumps that seemed problematic at first, but when we tried making a batch with the lumpy buttermilk, the result was a surprisingly better biscuit. The water in the lumps of butter turned to steam in the oven, creating additional height. A combination of baking powder and baking soda gave us even more rise for the lightest, fluffiest biscuits. If you have one, a spring-loaded ice cream scoop makes portioning these biscuits particularly easy. You will need about 1 teaspoon of melted butter for brushing the tops of the biscuits.

- ⅔ cup (3⅓ ounces) all-purpose flour
- ¾ teaspoon baking powder
- ¼ teaspoon baking soda
- ⅛ teaspoon sugar
- ⅛ teaspoon table salt
- ⅓ cup buttermilk, chilled
- 2 tablespoons unsalted butter, melted and hot, plus extra for brushing

1. Adjust oven rack to middle position and heat oven to 450 degrees. Line baking sheet with parchment paper.

2. Whisk flour, baking powder, baking soda, sugar, and salt together in medium bowl. In separate bowl, stir chilled buttermilk and melted butter together until butter forms small clumps. Stir buttermilk mixture into flour mixture with rubber spatula until just incorporated and dough pulls away from sides of bowl.

3. Using greased ¼-cup dry measure or #16 ice cream scoop, scoop out and drop 4 mounds of dough onto prepared sheet, spacing them about 1½ inches apart. Bake until biscuit tops are golden brown and crisp, 12 to 15 minutes, rotating sheet halfway through baking.

4. Brush baked biscuits with extra melted butter, transfer to wire rack, and let cool for 5 minutes. Serve warm.

VARIATIONS

Fresh Herb Simple Drop Biscuits

Whisk 2 teaspoons minced fresh mild herbs (such as tarragon, cilantro, chives, parsley, or dill) or 1 teaspoon minced fresh hearty herbs (such as thyme, sage, or rosemary) into the flour mixture.

Black Pepper and Bacon Simple Drop Biscuits

Whisk 2 slices fried, crumbled bacon and ¼ teaspoon coarsely ground black pepper into flour mixture.

Rosemary and Parmesan Simple Drop Biscuits

Whisk ¼ cup grated Parmesan and pinch minced fresh rosemary into flour mixture.

MAKING DROP BISCUITS

When melted butter is stirred into cold buttermilk, the butter clumps. Although it looks like a mistake, it's not; the clumps of butter turn to steam in the oven, ensuring that the biscuits have a light and fluffy interior.

NOTES FROM THE TEST KITCHEN

JUDGING DONENESS IN QUICK BREADS

Fully baked items should feel springy and resilient when the center is gently pressed. If your finger leaves an impression—or if the center jiggles—the item is not done. This works best with biscuits, scones, and loaf-style quick breads. The other option is to insert a skewer or toothpick into the center of the item; it should emerge fairly clean, with perhaps just a few crumbs attached. If you see moist batter, the item needs to bake longer.

STORING QUICK BREADS AND MUFFINS

Most biscuits, scones, and muffins can be stored in a zipper-lock bag at room temperature for up to three days. If the they include perishable flavorings like bacon, it is best to refrigerate them, but in general the refrigerator causes baked goods to dry out and so is not our first choice for storage. When ready to serve, warm them in a 300-degree oven for 10 minutes.

Simple Currant Cream Scones

Simple Currant Cream Scones

Makes 4 scones VEGETARIAN

Total time 45 minutes, plus 10 minutes cooling

WHY THIS RECIPE WORKS Traditional British scones are essentially fluffy biscuits. They should be sweet, but not too sweet, so that they can be enjoyed with jam and perhaps clotted cream. For a light, tender texture, we tried cake flour, but it made gummy scones. All-purpose flour, on the other hand, gave us light, feathery scones. Heavy cream gave our scones a rich, not-too-dry character. A food processor made quick work of incorporating the butter into the flour; we stirred in the cream by hand and then lightly kneaded the dough before cutting it into wedges. We also found that it was important to get the scones into the oven immediately after cutting them out for the best rise. Resist the urge to eat the scones hot out of the oven; letting them cool for at least 10 minutes allows them to firm up and improves their texture.

- 1 cup (5 ounces) all-purpose flour
- 2 tablespoons sugar
- 1½ teaspoons baking powder
- ¼ teaspoon table salt
- 3 tablespoons unsalted butter, cut into ¼-inch pieces and chilled
- ¼ cup dried currants
- ½ cup heavy cream

1. Adjust oven rack to middle position and heat oven to 375 degrees. Line baking sheet with parchment paper.

2. Process flour, sugar, baking powder, and salt in food processor until combined, about 5 seconds. Scatter butter over top and pulse until mixture resembles coarse cornmeal with some slightly larger butter lumps, about 6 pulses. Transfer mixture to large bowl and stir in currants. Stir in cream with rubber spatula until dough begins to form, about 30 seconds.

3. Turn dough and any floury bits onto lightly floured counter and knead until rough, slightly sticky ball forms, 5 to 10 seconds. Shape dough into 5-inch round, about ¾ inch thick. Cut dough into 4 wedges.

4. Place wedges on prepared sheet. Bake until scone tops are light golden brown, 18 to 22 minutes, rotating sheet halfway through baking. Transfer scones to wire rack and let cool for at least 10 minutes before serving.

VARIATIONS

Simple Maple-Pecan Cream Scones

Omit sugar. Substitute ¼ cup pecans, toasted and chopped, for currants. Whisk 1½ tablespoons maple syrup into heavy cream before adding to flour mixture. While scones bake, whisk 3 tablespoons confectioners' sugar and 1 tablespoon maple syrup together in bowl to make glaze. Let baked scones cool to room temperature, about 20 minutes, then drizzle with glaze. Let glaze set for 5 to 10 minutes before serving.

Simple Ginger Cream Scones

Substitute ¼ cup chopped crystallized ginger for currants.

MAKING SIMPLE CREAM SCONES

1. Pat dough into 5-inch round, about ¾ inch thick.

2. Using metal bench scraper or knife, cut dough into 4 evenly sized wedges.

TROUBLESHOOTING MUFFINS

Here are a few tricks that will help you become a muffin master.

PROBLEM Overflowing muffin tins
SOLUTION Portion the batter carefully

Our failproof way for filling muffin tins is to portion ⅓ cup of the batter into each cup, and then circle back and evenly add the remaining batter using a spoon. A spring-loaded #12 ice cream scoop (which holds ⅓ cup batter) makes it easy to portion batter into the cups without making a mess. Whether you are using an ice cream scoop or a measuring cup, spray it first with vegetable oil spray so that all the batter slides off easily.

PROBLEM Tough, squat muffins
SOLUTION Don't overmix the batter

Overmixing encourages gluten development, which inhibits rise and makes tougher muffins. To avoid this, blend the wet and dry ingredients separately and mix the two gently until just combined.

PROBLEM Stuck muffins
SOLUTION Give the tin a good greasing

A good nonstick muffin tin will make a huge difference in your success rate with muffins. Next, it's important to grease the tin thoroughly; we like to use baking spray with flour. We get this pan prep out of the way first, before we start making the batter. To prevent the spray from getting all over the counter or floor, we suggest spraying the muffin tin over the sink, a garbage can, or even an open dishwasher door.

PROBLEM Overdone or underdone muffins
SOLUTION Poke them with a toothpick

The best way to test a muffin for doneness is to poke it with a toothpick. A toothpick inserted into the center of the muffin should come out with only a few crumbs attached.

PROBLEM Broken muffins
SOLUTION Cool them in the tins

Be sure to let the muffins cool in the tins for at least 10 minutes to help them set up so that they are easier to remove without breaking.

Corn Muffins

Makes 4 muffins VEGETARIAN
Total time 35 minutes, plus 20 minutes cooling

WHY THIS RECIPE WORKS A corn muffin should taste like corn, but not overpoweringly so, and should be moist, with a tender crumb and a crunchy top. We wanted a recipe that struck just the right balance in both texture and flavor. The cornmeal itself proved to be an important factor; degerminated cornmeal just didn't have enough corn flavor. A fine-ground, whole-grain meal provided better flavor and texture. Butter, milk, and sour cream provided moisture and richness plus acidity for its tenderizing effect. We tried mixing the ingredients with both the quick-bread and creaming methods; creaming resulted in overly airy, cakey muffins, so we stuck with the easier quick-bread method. We got our crunchy browned top from a 400-degree oven. Any muffin tin with standard-size cups will work here, and the batter can be placed in any of the cups. We prefer stone-ground cornmeal because it has a full flavor.

⅔ cup (3⅓ ounces) all-purpose flour
⅓ cup (1⅔ ounces) stone-ground cornmeal
½ teaspoon baking powder
½ teaspoon baking soda
¼ teaspoon table salt
⅓ cup sour cream
¼ cup (1¾ ounces) sugar
1 large egg, room temperature
3 tablespoons unsalted butter, melted and cooled
2 tablespoons whole milk

1. Adjust oven rack to middle position and heat oven to 400 degrees. Spray 4 cups of muffin tin with baking spray with flour.

2. Whisk flour, cornmeal, baking powder, baking soda, and salt together in large bowl. In separate bowl, whisk sour cream, sugar, egg, melted butter, and milk together until smooth. Gently fold sour cream mixture into flour mixture with rubber spatula until just combined. (Batter will be lumpy with a few spots of dry flour; do not overmix.)

3. Using dry measuring cup or ice cream scoop, divide batter evenly among prepared muffin cups. Bake until muffins are golden brown and toothpick inserted in center of muffin comes out clean, 12 to 17 minutes, rotating muffin tin halfway through baking.

4. Let muffins cool in muffin tin on wire rack for 10 minutes. Remove muffins from muffin tin and let cool for at least 10 minutes before serving.

Apricot-Orange Corn Muffins

Add ¼ teaspoon finely grated orange zest and ⅓ cup dried apricots, chopped fine, to sour cream mixture in step 2.

Cheddar Cheese and Scallion Corn Muffins

Reduce sugar to 2 tablespoons. Add 2 thinly sliced scallions and ½ cup shredded cheddar cheese to sour cream mixture in step 2. Sprinkle muffins with 2 tablespoons shredded cheddar cheese before baking.

Blueberry Muffins

Makes 4 muffins `VEGETARIAN`

Total time 45 minutes, plus 20 minutes cooling

WHY THIS RECIPE WORKS Blueberry muffins, for all of their simple, warm appeal, have a host of problems, as they often emerge from the oven too sweet, too dense, or just plain bland, with little blueberry flavor. We wanted delicate muffins with a balanced, fresh blueberry flavor. To achieve a delicate texture, we decided to forgo creaming the butter and sugar and instead folded melted butter into the batter. Plain yogurt added moisture and a nice tang, and a little lemon zest complemented the sweet blueberries nicely. Sprinkling the muffins with lemon-sugar topping was the perfect finishing touch. Any muffin tin with standard-size cups will work here, and the batter can be placed in any of the cups. Frozen blueberries can be substituted for the fresh blueberries; rinse and dry the frozen blueberries (do not thaw) before folding into the batter.

TOPPING

  1   tablespoon sugar
 ¼   teaspoon finely grated lemon zest

MUFFINS

 ¾   cup (3¾ ounces) all-purpose flour
 ¼   cup (1¾ ounces) sugar
  1   teaspoon baking powder
 ⅛   teaspoon baking soda
 ⅛   teaspoon table salt
 ¼   cup whole-milk or low-fat plain yogurt
  1   large egg, room temperature
 ¼   teaspoon finely grated lemon zest
  3   tablespoons unsalted butter, melted and cooled
2½   ounces (½ cup) fresh blueberries

Blueberry Muffins

1. FOR THE TOPPING Adjust oven rack to middle position and heat oven to 325 degrees. Spray 4 cups of muffin tin with baking spray with flour. Combine sugar and lemon zest in bowl; set aside.

2. FOR THE MUFFINS Whisk flour, sugar, baking powder, baking soda, and salt together in large bowl. In separate bowl, whisk yogurt, egg, and lemon zest together until smooth. Gently fold yogurt mixture into flour mixture with rubber spatula until just combined, then fold in melted butter and blueberries.

3. Using dry measure or ice cream scoop, divide batter evenly among prepared muffin cups. Sprinkle sugar topping over muffins. Bake until muffins are golden brown and toothpick inserted in center of muffin comes out clean, 20 to 24 minutes, rotating muffin tin halfway through baking.

4. Let muffins cool in muffin tin on wire rack for 10 minutes. Remove muffins from muffin tin and let cool for at least 10 minutes before serving.

Morning Glory Muffins

Makes 4 muffins VEGETARIAN

Total time 1 hour, plus 20 minutes cooling

WHY THIS RECIPE WORKS Morning glory muffins are chock-full of nuts, fruit, carrots, and spices. But all these tasty add-ins can make for heavy, sodden muffins, so we aimed to lighten them up. Our first move was to strain the fruit and press out the extra juice to prevent our muffins from being soggy. To keep the bright, fruity flavor intact, we saved the fruit juice, reduced it on the stovetop, and added the concentrated syrup back to the batter. To keep the nuts and coconut from becoming mealy or soggy in the finished muffins, we toasted and processed them. At last, our muffins were truly glorious. Any muffin tin with standard-size cups will work here, and the batter can be placed in any of the cups. We prefer golden raisins in these muffins but ordinary raisins will work too.

⅓ cup canned crushed pineapple
1 small Granny Smith apple, peeled and shredded
¼ cup (¾ ounce) sweetened shredded coconut, toasted
¼ cup walnuts, toasted
¾ cup (3¾ ounces) all-purpose flour
¼ cup (1¾ ounces) sugar
½ teaspoon baking soda
¼ teaspoon baking powder
¼ teaspoon ground cinnamon
¼ teaspoon table salt
3 tablespoons unsalted butter, melted and cooled
1 large egg, room temperature
¼ teaspoon vanilla extract
⅓ cup shredded carrot (1 carrot)
⅓ cup golden raisins

1. Adjust oven rack to middle position and heat oven to 350 degrees. Spray 4 cups of muffin tin with baking spray with flour. Place pineapple and shredded apple in fine-mesh strainer set over liquid measuring cup. Press fruit dry, reserving juice; juice should measure about ⅓ cup. Bring juice to boil in 8-inch skillet over medium-high heat and cook until reduced to 2 tablespoons, 3 to 5 minutes; let cool slightly.

2. Process coconut and walnuts in food processor until finely ground, about 15 seconds. Add flour, sugar, baking soda, baking powder, cinnamon, and salt and process until combined, about 5 seconds; transfer to medium bowl.

3. In separate bowl, whisk cooled juice, melted butter, egg, and vanilla together until smooth. Gently fold juice mixture into flour mixture with rubber spatula until just combined, then fold in drained pineapple-apple mixture, carrot, and raisins.

4. Using dry measuring cup or ice cream scoop, divide batter evenly among prepared muffin cups. Bake until muffins are golden brown and toothpick inserted in center of muffin comes out clean, 24 to 28 minutes, rotating muffin tin halfway through baking.

5. Let muffins cool in muffin tin on wire rack for 10 minutes. Remove muffins from muffin tin and let cool for at least 10 minutes before serving.

NOTES FROM THE TEST KITCHEN

MUFFIN TIN MYTH BUSTER

Did your mother ever tell you that if you're baking a small batch of muffins using a 12-cup tin, you should fill the empty cups with water? The theory is that the water acts as a "heat sink" to ensure that muffins next to empty cups heat evenly (avoiding stunted growth or spotty browning). But when we tested this theory by baking a small batch of muffins and leaving the extra cups empty, all the muffins had the same height, texture, and color, and none of the tins warped. The reason? In a full 12-cup muffin tin, all but the two center muffins are directly exposed to the oven's heat on at least one side to no ill effect. So when making a small batch of muffins, you can place the batter in any of the cups and your muffins will bake just fine.

Cinnamon Streusel Coffee Cake

Makes one 6-inch cake VEGETARIAN

Total time 1 hour, plus 20 minutes cooling

WHY THIS RECIPE WORKS For a well-balanced coffee cake sized for two that delivered both tender cake and a crunchy, cinnamon-y streusel topping, we started by building a simple cake with just the right amount of moisture and structure. We cut back on the butter so our cake wouldn't be greasy, but we needed to find another ingredient to bump up the moistness and richness. Buttermilk worked perfectly and it imparted a nice subtle tang. All-purpose flour ensured that our cake was sturdy enough to support a generous amount of pecan-and-cinnamon streusel topping. You will need a 6-inch round cake pan for this recipe. You can substitute 3 tablespoons of plain whole-milk or low-fat yogurt mixed with 1 tablespoon of milk for the buttermilk if necessary.

Cinnamon Streusel Coffee Cake

1. **FOR THE STREUSEL TOPPING** Adjust oven rack to middle position and heat oven to 350 degrees. Grease 6-inch round cake pan, line with parchment paper, grease parchment, and flour pan. Mix flour, granulated sugar, brown sugar, butter, and cinnamon together with your fingers in medium bowl until mixture resembles wet sand. Stir in pecans; set aside.

2. **FOR THE CAKE** Whisk flour, baking powder, baking soda, cinnamon, and salt together in separate medium bowl. Whisk buttermilk, granulated sugar, brown sugar, egg, and melted butter together in small bowl until smooth. Gently fold egg mixture into flour mixture with rubber spatula until combined.

3. Scrape batter into prepared pan and smooth top. Sprinkle streusel evenly over top of cake. Bake until cake is golden brown and toothpick inserted in center comes out with a few moist crumbs attached, about 30 minutes, rotating pan halfway through baking.

4. Let cake cool in pan on wire rack for 10 minutes. Remove cake from pan, discarding parchment, and let cool for at least 10 minutes before serving.

Banana Bread

Makes one 5½ by 3-inch loaf `VEGETARIAN`

Total time 55 minutes, plus 1 hour 5 minutes cooling

WHY THIS RECIPE WORKS Our ideal banana bread is a moist, tender loaf that really tastes like bananas. We set out to scale down banana bread to fit in a mini loaf pan but keep all the flavor intact. One ultraripe banana infused the bread with flavor. A combination of butter and a little yogurt kept our loaf rich and moist. We liked the addition of toasted walnuts for crunch and a little vanilla to enhance the overall flavor. Creaming the butter and sugar resulted in overmixed batter and a dense loaf, so we gently folded everything together to ensure that our loaf stayed tender. You will need a 5½ by 3-inch loaf pan or a pan of similar size for this recipe. The key to this recipe is using a very ripe, darkly speckled banana.

STREUSEL TOPPING

- 1½ tablespoons all-purpose flour
- 1½ tablespoons granulated sugar
- 1½ tablespoons packed light brown sugar
- 1 tablespoon unsalted butter, softened
- ¾ teaspoon ground cinnamon
- ⅓ cup pecans or walnuts, chopped

CAKE

- ¾ cup (3¾ ounces) all-purpose flour
- ¼ teaspoon baking powder
- ¼ teaspoon baking soda
- ¼ teaspoon ground cinnamon
  Pinch table salt
- ¼ cup buttermilk
- ¼ cup (1¾ ounces) granulated sugar
- ¼ cup packed (1¾ ounces) light brown sugar
- 1 large egg, room temperature
- 2 tablespoons unsalted butter, melted and cooled

- ½ cup (2½ ounces) all-purpose flour
- ¼ cup walnuts, toasted and chopped coarse
- ¼ cup sugar
- ½ teaspoon baking soda
- ⅛ teaspoon table salt
- 1 small ripe banana, peeled and mashed well (¼ cup)
- 1 large egg, room temperature
- 1 tablespoon unsalted butter, melted and cooled
- 1 tablespoon plain yogurt
- ½ teaspoon vanilla extract

Banana Bread

1. Adjust oven rack to middle position and heat oven to 350 degrees. Grease 5½ by 3-inch loaf pan.

2. Whisk flour, walnuts, sugar, baking soda, and salt together in medium bowl. In separate bowl, whisk mashed banana, egg, melted butter, yogurt, and vanilla together until smooth. Gently fold banana mixture into flour mixture with rubber spatula until just combined. (Batter will be lumpy with a few spots of dry flour; do not overmix.)

3. Scrape batter into prepared pan and smooth top. Bake until loaf is golden brown and toothpick inserted in center comes out clean, 30 to 40 minutes, rotating pan halfway through baking.

4. Let loaf cool in pan on wire rack for 5 minutes. Remove loaf from pan and let cool for at least 1 hour before serving.

VARIATION
Banana-Chocolate Bread
Add ¾ ounce grated bittersweet chocolate to flour mixture in step 2.

NOTES FROM THE TEST KITCHEN

STORING BANANAS

MAKING BANANAS LAST Most people store bananas on the countertop, but we wondered if chilling the fruit could slow ripening. To find out, we left 12 pounds of bananas at room temperature for three days until they were perfectly ripe (with a firm but yielding texture). We then moved half of the bananas into the refrigerator, leaving the remainder at room temperature.

After four days, the room-temperature fruit became markedly soft and mushy, while the refrigerated fruit remained firm, despite blackened skins. We continued to taste the refrigerated bananas after the room-temperature samples had been discarded and were delighted to discover that they lasted an additional five days (almost two weeks after purchase). The explanation is simple: As a banana ripens, it emits a gas called ethylene and develops acids that aid in ripening. Cool temperatures slow down this process, thereby decelerating ripening. Note that refrigeration also causes the cell walls of the peel to break down, releasing enzymes that cause the formation of black-brown pigments.

RIPENING BANANAS The abundance of natural sugars in overripe bananas is the secret to big flavor and serious moisture in baked goods. Yellow bananas don't have as much sweet flavor and will remain starchy even after baking. Strategies for speeding ripening in bananas abound, but we've found most of them ineffective. One theory, for example, holds that freezing or roasting underripe bananas in their skins will quickly render them sweet and soft enough for baking. While these methods do turn the bananas black—giving them the appearance of their super-sweet, overripe brethren—they actually do little to encourage the necessary conversion of starch to sugar. The best way to ripen bananas is to enclose them in a paper bag for a few days. The bag will trap the ethylene gas produced by fruit that hastens ripening, while still allowing some moisture to escape. Since fully ripe fruit emits the most ethylene, placing a ripe banana or other ripe fruit in the bag will speed the process along by a day or two.

Zucchini Bread

½ zucchini (4 ounces)
½ cup (2½ ounces) all-purpose flour
½ teaspoon baking powder
½ teaspoon baking soda
¼ teaspoon ground cinnamon
¼ teaspoon ground allspice
⅛ teaspoon table salt
½ cup (3½ ounces) sugar
1 large egg, room temperature
1 tablespoon unsalted butter, melted and cooled
1 tablespoon plain yogurt
1 teaspoon lemon juice
¼ cup pecans or walnuts, toasted and chopped coarse

1. Adjust oven rack to middle position and heat oven to 350 degrees. Grease 5½ by 3-inch loaf pan.

2. Shred zucchini on large holes of box grater. Squeeze shredded zucchini in clean dish towel or several layers of paper towels until very dry.

3. Whisk flour, baking powder, baking soda, cinnamon, allspice, and salt together in medium bowl. In separate bowl, whisk sugar, egg, melted butter, yogurt, and lemon juice together until smooth. Gently fold shredded zucchini, yogurt mixture, and pecans into flour mixture with rubber spatula until just combined. (Do not overmix.)

4. Scrape batter into prepared pan and smooth top. Bake until loaf is golden brown and toothpick inserted into center comes out clean, 35 to 45 minutes, rotating pan halfway through baking.

5. Let loaf cool in pan on wire rack for 5 minutes. Remove loaf from pan and let cool for at least 1 hour before serving.

Zucchini Bread

Makes one 5½ by 3-inch loaf   VEGETARIAN

Total time 1 hour, plus 1 hour 5 minutes cooling

WHY THIS RECIPE WORKS It can be difficult to muster enthusiasm for your typical bland, soggy loaf of zucchini bread. We wanted a zucchini bread worth eating: subtly spiced, with great summery zucchini flavor, and with a moist—but not wet—crumb. To start, we had to confront the downfall of most zucchini breads—the excess moisture from the zucchini. Shredding the zucchini and then squeezing it dry in a dish towel not only rid the zucchini of excess moisture but also intensified the zucchini flavor for a better-tasting bread. Many zucchini bread recipes use oil, but we preferred the rich flavor of butter. Cinnamon and allspice along with lemon juice perked the flavor up further, as did the tang of yogurt. Finally, for nutty flavor in every bite, we stirred toasted chopped nuts into the batter. You will need a 5½ by 3-inch loaf pan or a pan of similar size for this recipe. Be sure to squeeze the zucchini thoroughly of moisture before adding it to the batter, or the bread will turn out soggy.

REMOVING MOISTURE FROM ZUCCHINI

1. To prevent soggy zucchini bread, it's important to remove excess moisture. Shred zucchini on large holes of box grater.

2. Squeeze shredded zucchini in clean dish towel or several layers of paper towels until dry.

Cheddar Cheese Bread

Skillet Olive Bread

Cheddar Cheese Bread

Makes one 5½ by 3-inch loaf   VEGETARIAN
Total time 55 minutes, plus 1 hour 5 minutes cooling

WHY THIS RECIPE WORKS We were after the ultimate cheese bread, one that was cheesy inside and out. To find the best recipe, we tested lots of cheese and techniques. First, for the batter, we found that extra-sharp cheddar cheese worked best, and cutting it into small chunks rather than shredding it gave the bread luscious, chewy pockets of cheese. For a cheesy crust on top and bottom, we sprinkled Parmesan in the bottom of our loaf pan before filling it with batter and then topped the batter with more Parmesan. You will need a 5½ by 3-inch loaf pan or a pan of similar size for this recipe. Use the large holes of a box grater to shred the Parmesan; do not substitute finely grated or pregrated Parmesan. A mild, soft Asiago cheese, crumbled into ¼-inch pieces, is a nice substitute for the cheddar. The texture of the bread improves as it cools.

1 ounce Parmesan cheese, shredded (⅓ cup)
¾ cup plus 2 tablespoons (4⅜ ounces) all-purpose flour
1 teaspoon baking powder
¼ teaspoon table salt
  Pinch cayenne pepper
  Pinch pepper
2 ounces extra-sharp cheddar cheese, cut into ¼-inch cubes (½ cup)
¼ cup whole milk
3 tablespoons sour cream
1 large egg, room temperature
1 tablespoon unsalted butter, melted and cooled

1. Adjust oven rack to middle position and heat oven to 350 degrees. Grease 5½ by 3-inch loaf pan, then sprinkle 2 tablespoons Parmesan evenly over bottom of pan.

2. Whisk flour, baking powder, salt, cayenne, and pepper together in medium bowl. Fold in cheddar, breaking up any clumps, until cheese is coated with flour mixture. In separate bowl, whisk milk, sour cream, egg, and melted butter together until smooth. Gently fold milk mixture into flour mixture with rubber spatula until just combined. (Batter will be heavy and thick; do not overmix.)

3. Scrape batter into prepared pan, smooth top, and sprinkle with remaining Parmesan. Bake until loaf is golden brown and toothpick inserted into center comes out with a few crumbs attached, 30 to 40 minutes, rotating pan halfway through baking.

4. Let loaf cool in pan on wire rack for 5 minutes. Remove loaf from pan and let cool for at least 1 hour before serving.

Skillet Olive Bread

Serves 2 VEGETARIAN

Total time 50 minutes

WHY THIS RECIPE WORKS Most savory breads serve a crowd and require long rest periods and kneading. Not ours. We stirred together an effortless quick bread and baked it in a small cast-iron skillet, which gave us just enough for two. We started with all-purpose flour and added whole milk and sour cream for a moist texture. A whole egg lent richness and structure. Shredded Parmesan, minced garlic, chopped kalamata olives, and fresh basil ensured that our bread was robustly flavored. Use the large holes of a box grater to shred the Parmesan; do not substitute finely grated or pregrated Parmesan. We prefer to use an 8-inch cast-iron skillet because it makes the best crust, but you can also use an 8-inch oven-safe skillet; increase the baking time by 10 to 15 minutes.

  1 cup (5 ounces) all-purpose flour
  1 tablespoon chopped fresh basil
  1 teaspoon baking powder
  ¼ teaspoon table salt
  1½ ounces Parmesan cheese, shredded (½ cup)
  ½ cup whole milk
  3 tablespoons sour cream
  1 large egg, room temperature
  2 tablespoons extra-virgin olive oil
  1 garlic clove, minced
  ¼ cup pitted kalamata olives, chopped

1. Adjust oven rack to lower-middle position and heat oven to 450 degrees.

2. Whisk flour, basil, baking powder, and salt together in medium bowl. Stir in ⅓ cup Parmesan, breaking up any clumps, until cheese is coated with flour. In separate bowl, whisk milk, sour cream, and egg together until smooth.

3. Heat oil in 8-inch cast-iron skillet over medium-high heat until shimmering. Add garlic and cook until fragrant, about 30 seconds. Pour all but 2 teaspoons garlic oil into milk mixture and whisk to incorporate. Gently fold milk mixture into flour mixture with rubber spatula until just combined, then fold in olives. (Batter will be heavy and thick; do not overmix.)

4. Working quickly, scrape batter into hot skillet, smooth top, and sprinkle with remaining Parmesan. Bake until loaf is golden brown and toothpick inserted into center comes out clean, 15 to 20 minutes, rotating skillet halfway through baking.

5. Let bread cool slightly in skillet on wire rack for 5 minutes. Remove loaf from skillet and serve warm or at room temperature.

NOTES FROM THE TEST KITCHEN

BAKING SODA VERSUS BAKING POWDER

Baking Soda

Baking soda is a leavener that provides lift to muffins, biscuits, cakes, and other baked goods. When baking soda, which is alkaline, encounters an acidic ingredient (such as sour cream, buttermilk, or brown sugar), carbon and oxygen combine to form carbon dioxide. The tiny bubbles of carbon dioxide then lift up the dough. Baking soda also promotes browning.

Baking Powder

Baking powder also creates carbon dioxide to provide lift to a wide range of baked goods. The active ingredients in baking powder are baking soda and an acidic element, such as cream of tartar. It also contains cornstarch to absorb moisture and keep the powder dry. Cooks use baking powder rather than baking soda when there is no natural acidity in the batter.

There are two kinds of baking powder. A single-acting baking powder has only one acid combined with the baking soda: a quick-acting acid that begins to work when liquid is added to the batter. A double-acting baking powder (like most supermarket brands) has two acids added to the baking soda: The second acid (often sodium aluminum sulfate) begins to work only when the dish is put in the oven, after the temperature has climbed above 120 degrees.

We recommend using double-acting baking powder in all recipes—baked goods rise higher since most of the rise with baking powder occurs at oven temperatures. Double-acting baking powder also provides sufficient lift in the oven to allow you to bake frozen dough. Also, we have found that single-acting baking powder doesn't provide sufficient leavening for doughs with little liquid, such as scones or muffins.

STORING CHEMICAL LEAVENERS Keep baking powder and baking soda in a cool, dark, dry place in the pantry. Despite most manufacturer claims of one year, our tests have proven baking powder loses its potency after six months.

CHAPTER 16

Fruit Desserts, Pies & Tarts

■ **FAST** (Start to finish in 30 minutes or less)
■ **VEGETARIAN**

Opposite: Individual Blueberry Crumbles

White Wine–Poached Pears with Lemon and Herbs

Serves 2 VEGETARIAN

Total time 45 minutes, plus 2 hours chilling

WHY THIS RECIPE WORKS Poached pears are a classic French dessert that is surprisingly simple to make at home. We wanted a recipe for meltingly tender pears that we could serve chilled, and we planned to reuse the poaching liquid as an aromatic sauce to keep the preparation contained to just one pot. Bartlett and Bosc won tasters over with their honeyed sweetness and clean appearance. Cutting the pears in half ensured that they cooked evenly. We poached the fruit in white wine, which offered a nuanced flavor, especially when enhanced with lemon, mint, and thyme. We turned the pears several times as they cooked, then removed them from the pot and reduced the cooking liquid. Letting the pears cool in the syrup prevented them from drying out; it also allowed them to absorb some of the syrup, so that they were plump and spiced. Select pears that yield slightly when pressed. Use a medium-bodied dry white wine such as Sauvignon Blanc. The fruit can be served as is or with crème fraîche. You will need a medium saucepan with a tight-fitting lid for this recipe.

½ vanilla bean
2 cups dry white wine
⅓ cup (2⅓ ounces) sugar
5 (2-inch) strips lemon zest
4 sprigs fresh mint
3 sprigs fresh thyme
   Pinch table salt
2 ripe but firm Bosc or Bartlett pears (8 ounces each), peeled, halved, and cored

1. Cut vanilla bean in half lengthwise. Using tip of paring knife, scrape out seeds. Bring wine, sugar, lemon zest, mint sprigs, thyme sprigs, salt, and vanilla seeds and pod to boil in medium saucepan over high heat and cook, stirring occasionally, until sugar has dissolved, about 5 minutes.

2. Add pears and return to boil. Reduce heat to medium-low; cover; and simmer until pears are tender and toothpick slips easily in and out of pears, 10 to 20 minutes, gently turning pears over every 5 minutes.

3. Using slotted spoon, transfer pears to plate; discard solids. Bring syrup to simmer over medium heat and cook, stirring occasionally, until slightly thickened and measures ½ cup, about 15 minutes. Return pears and any accumulated juices to syrup and let cool to room temperature. Cover and refrigerate until well chilled, at least 2 hours or up to 3 days. Serve.

White Wine–Poached Pears with Lemon and Herbs

Crepes with Honey and Toasted Almonds

Serves 2 FAST VEGETARIAN

Total time 30 minutes

WHY THIS RECIPE WORKS Crepes have a reputation for being difficult, but we were determined to make a failproof version that required just a 12-inch nonstick skillet (rather than a specialized pan). Heating the pan properly was essential. If too hot, the batter set up before it evenly coated the surface. If too cool, the crepes were pale (read: bland) and too flimsy to flip without tearing. Using just enough of our crepe batter to coat the bottom of the pan was also important, as was the tilt-and-shake method that we employed to distribute it. To avoid singed fingertips, we loosened the crepe with a rubber spatula before grasping its edge and nimbly turning it to the flip side to cook until spotty brown. We heated the stack of finished crepes in the microwave briefly, which guaranteed that they were all warm when served. A drizzle of honey and sprinkling of almonds made a sweet filling. Crepes will give off steam as they cook, but if at any point the skillet begins to smoke, remove it from the heat immediately and turn down the heat. Stacking the crepes on a wire rack allows excess steam to escape, so they won't stick together. To allow for practice, the recipe yields 5 crepes; only 4 are needed for the filling.

½ teaspoon vegetable oil
½ cup (2½ ounces) all-purpose flour
½ teaspoon sugar
⅛ teaspoon plus ¼ teaspoon table salt, divided
¾ cup whole milk
1 large egg
1 tablespoon unsalted butter, melted and cooled
4 teaspoons honey, divided
2 teaspoons finely chopped toasted sliced almonds, divided

1. Heat oil in 12-inch nonstick skillet over low heat for at least 10 minutes.

2. Whisk flour, sugar, and ⅛ teaspoon salt together in medium bowl. Whisk milk and egg together in second bowl. Add half of milk mixture to dry ingredients and whisk until smooth. Add melted butter and whisk until incorporated. Whisk in remaining milk mixture until smooth.

3. Wipe out skillet with paper towels, leaving thin film of oil on bottom and sides of pan. Increase heat to medium and let skillet heat for 1 minute. After 1 minute, test heat of skillet by placing 1 teaspoon batter in center of pan and cooking for 20 seconds. If mini crepe is golden brown on bottom, skillet is properly heated; if it is too light or too dark, adjust heat accordingly and retest.

4. Pour ¼ cup batter into far side of skillet and tilt and shake gently until batter evenly covers bottom of pan. Cook crepe without moving it until top surface is dry and edges are starting to brown, about 25 seconds. Using heat-resistant rubber spatula, loosen crepe from side of skillet. Gently slide spatula underneath edge of crepe, grasp edge with your fingertips, and flip crepe. Cook until second side is lightly spotted, about 20 seconds. Transfer cooked crepe, spotted side up, to wire rack. Return skillet to heat and heat for 10 seconds before repeating with remaining batter. As crepes are done, stack on wire rack.

5. Transfer stack of crepes to large plate and invert second plate over crepes. Microwave until crepes are warm, 30 to 45 seconds (45 to 60 seconds if crepes have cooled completely). Remove top plate and wipe dry with paper towel. Drizzle half of top crepe with 1 teaspoon honey and sprinkle with ¼ teaspoon almonds and pinch salt. Fold uncoated bottom half over covered half, then fold in half again. Transfer filled crepe to second plate. Repeat with remaining crepes. Serve immediately.

1. Pour ¼ cup batter into far side of skillet.

2. Tilt and shake skillet gently until batter evenly covers bottom of skillet.

3. Gently slide spatula underneath edge of crêpe, grasp edge with your fingertips, and flip crêpe.

Berry Gratins

Serves 2 VEGETARIAN

Total time 40 minutes, plus 10 minutes chilling

WHY THIS RECIPE WORKS When the occasion demands something a bit more dressed up than berries with a dollop of whipped cream, our thoughts turn to berry gratin. While toppings for this baked dessert vary, our favorite is the light and creamy Italian custard, zabaglione. To ensure our zabaglione had the perfect, creamy consistency every time, we cooked the egg yolk, sugar, and wine in a glass bowl set over a pan of barely simmering water until it was nicely thickened, then folded in a little whipped cream. Broiling—rather than baking—the gratin ensured that the crust browned before the berries overcooked. Do not substitute frozen berries in this recipe. Make sure to cook the egg mixture in a glass bowl; glass conducts heat more evenly and gently than metal. To prevent scorching, pay close attention to the gratins when broiling. You will need two shallow 6-ounce gratin dishes for this recipe, but a 3-cup broiler-safe baking dish (measuring approximately 7¼ by 5¼ inches) will also work.

BERRY MIXTURE

7½ ounces (1½ cups) blackberries, blueberries, raspberries, and/or strawberries (strawberries hulled and halved lengthwise if small, quartered if large)

1 teaspoon granulated sugar

Pinch table salt

ZABAGLIONE

1 large egg yolk

1 tablespoon granulated sugar, divided

1 tablespoon dry white wine

2 teaspoons packed light brown sugar

2 tablespoons heavy cream, chilled

1. FOR THE BERRY MIXTURE Line rimmed baking sheet with aluminum foil. Gently toss berries, sugar, and salt together in bowl. Divide berry mixture evenly between 2 shallow 6-ounce gratin dishes and set on prepared sheet; set aside.

2. FOR THE ZABAGLIONE Whisk egg yolk, 2 teaspoons granulated sugar, and wine together in medium glass bowl until sugar is dissolved, about 1 minute. Set bowl over small saucepan of barely simmering water (water should not touch bottom of bowl) and cook, whisking constantly, until mixture is frothy.

3. Continue to cook, whisking constantly, until mixture is slightly thickened, creamy, and glossy, 5 to 10 minutes (mixture will form loose mounds when dripped from whisk). Remove bowl from saucepan and whisk constantly for 30 seconds to cool slightly. Transfer bowl to refrigerator and chill until egg mixture is completely cool, about 10 minutes.

4. Meanwhile, adjust oven rack 6 inches from broiler element and heat broiler. Combine brown sugar and remaining 1 teaspoon granulated sugar in bowl.

5. In separate bowl, whisk cream until soft peaks form. Using rubber spatula, gently fold whipped cream into cooled egg mixture until incorporated and no streaks remain. Spoon zabaglione over berries and sprinkle sugar mixture evenly on top; let sit at room temperature until sugar dissolves, about 10 minutes.

6. Broil gratins until sugar is bubbly and caramelized, 1 to 4 minutes. Serve immediately.

Berry Gratins

MAKING ZABAGLIONE

When making zabaglione, it's important to pay attention to the visual cues to know when it's ready and prevent overcooking.

Once zabaglione is slightly thickened, creamy, and glossy, that's your cue to remove it from heat and begin whisking constantly to cool slightly.

NOTES FROM THE TEST KITCHEN

WASHING AND STORING BERRIES

Washing berries before you use them is always a safe practice, because they are prone to mold. Swish them in a solution of 3 parts water and 1 part vinegar, rinse, then dry thoroughly in a colander or paper towel–lined salad spinner.

It's particularly important to store berries carefully, because they are apt to rot quickly. We recommend storing them loosely covered in a paper towel–lined container.

Strawberry Shortcakes

1. **FOR THE STRAWBERRIES** Using potato masher, mash one-third of strawberries with sugar in bowl to coarse pulp. Stir in remaining strawberries; cover; and let sit while making shortcakes, at least 30 minutes or up to 2 hours.

2. **FOR THE SHORTCAKES** Adjust oven rack to middle position and heat oven to 475 degrees. Line rimmed baking sheet with parchment paper. Whisk flour, 1 ½ teaspoons sugar, baking powder, baking soda, and salt together in large bowl. Whisk milk, melted butter, and lemon juice together in second bowl. Stir milk mixture into flour mixture until just incorporated. (Dough will be quite sticky.)

3. Using greased ¼-cup dry measuring cup, gently scoop dough into 2 even mounds on prepared sheet, about 1 ½ inches apart. Sprinkle evenly with remaining ¾ teaspoon sugar. Bake until tops are golden, 12 to 14 minutes, rotating sheet halfway through baking. Transfer biscuits to wire rack and let cool completely, about 30 minutes. (Cooled biscuits can be stored in airtight container for up to 1 day.)

4. Split each biscuit in half and place bottoms on individual plates. Using slotted spoon, portion strawberries over biscuit bottoms. Top with whipped cream and biscuit tops and serve.

VARIATION
Peach Shortcakes

Peel, pit, and cut 2 ripe peaches into ¼-inch-thick wedges; substitute peaches for strawberries. Toss one-third of peaches with sugar and microwave, stirring occasionally, until bubbling, 1 to 2 minutes. Using potato masher, mash hot peaches to coarse pulp before stirring in remaining peaches.

Strawberry Shortcakes

Serves 2   VEGETARIAN

Total time 40 minutes, plus 30 minutes cooling

WHY THIS RECIPE WORKS Strawberry shortcakes are a whimsical summertime treat, but they can take a while to make. To simplify them for two, we used rustic drop biscuits instead of cake as the base. Butter, milk, and lemon juice give the biscuits richness and buttermilk-style tang.

STRAWBERRIES
- 8 ounces strawberries, hulled and quartered, divided
- 1½ tablespoons sugar

SHORTCAKES
- ½ cup (2½ ounces) all-purpose flour
- 2¼ teaspoons sugar, divided
- ½ teaspoon baking powder
- ⅛ teaspoon baking soda
- ⅛ teaspoon table salt
- 3 tablespoons milk, chilled
- 2 tablespoons butter, melted and cooled
- ¾ teaspoon lemon juice

Whipped Cream

Makes about ¾ cup   FAST   VEGETARIAN
Total time 5 minutes

The whipped cream can be refrigerated in a fine-mesh strainer set over a small bowl, wrapped tightly with plastic wrap, for up to 8 hours.

- ⅓ cup heavy cream, chilled
- 1 teaspoon sugar
- ¼ teaspoon vanilla extract

Using hand-held mixer set at medium-low speed, beat cream, sugar, and vanilla in medium bowl until foamy, about 1 minute. Increase speed to high and beat until soft peaks form, 1 to 3 minutes.

WORKING WITH PHYLLO DOUGH

Phyllo dough, tissue-thin layers of pastry dough, can be used in a variety of recipes, both sweet and savory. Phyllo is available in two sheet sizes: full-size sheets that measure 18 by 14 inches (about 20 large sheets per box) and half-size sheets that are 14 by 9 inches (about 40 small sheets per box). The smaller sheets are more convenient for scaled-down desserts, but if you happen to buy the large sheets, simply cut them half. Here are some tips that make working with this delicate dough easier.

THAW THE PHYLLO DOUGH COMPLETELY BEFORE USING Frozen phyllo dough must be thawed before using, and we've found that thawing it quickly in the microwave doesn't work—it makes the delicate sheets of dough stick together. We've had the best luck thawing the dough in the refrigerator overnight. (Our second choice is to thaw phyllo on the counter for 4 to 5 hours.) When the dough is completely thawed, it will be very flexible and will unfold easily without tearing.

THROW OUT BADLY TORN SHEETS OF DOUGH Usually there are one or two badly torn sheets of phyllo per box that just can't be salvaged—throw them out. There are always a few extra sheets of phyllo in the package, so you won't come up short. But don't worry about small rips; just make sure to adjust the orientation of the sheets as you stack them so that cracks in different sheets don't line up. And if phyllo sheets emerge from the box fused at their edges, don't try to separate the sheets. Instead, trim and discard the fused portion.

KEEP THE PHYLLO COVERED WHILE WORKING Because each sheet is paper-thin, it dries out very quickly when exposed to air. As soon as the phyllo is removed from its plastic sleeve, unfold the dough and carefully smooth it with your hands to flatten. Cover with plastic wrap, then a damp dish towel.

DON'T REFREEZE LEFTOVER DOUGH Leftover sheets can be rerolled, wrapped in plastic wrap, and stored in the refrigerator for up to five days. Don't try refreezing phyllo dough because it will become brittle and impossible to work with.

Apple Strudel

Apple Strudel

Serves 2 VEGETARIAN

Total time 1 hour 15 minutes, plus 20 minutes cooling

WHY THIS RECIPE WORKS Most modern phyllo-based versions of strudel have tough layers of phyllo on the underside, while the sheets on top shatter before you even cut a slice. Meanwhile, fillings collapse and leak everywhere, despite the bread crumbs supposedly added to soak up liquid. We warmed our apples through in the microwave in order to activate an enzyme that allows them to bake until tender without collapsing, and we stirred in ultradry panko bread crumbs to soak up a comparable amount of liquid. To avoid a compressed, tough underside, we used fewer sheets of phyllo and changed the typical wrapping technique, so the seam was on the top instead of on the bottom. To minimize the flyaways on top, we dusted a small amount of confectioners' sugar between the phyllo layers so that they fused in the oven, and we sliced our strudel while it was warm. Gala apples can be substituted for Golden Delicious apples. Phyllo dough is also available in larger 18 by 14-inch sheets; if using, cut them in half to make 14 by 9-inch sheets. Thaw phyllo in the refrigerator overnight or on the counter for 4 to 5 hours; don't thaw it in the microwave.

2 Golden Delicious apples (7 ounces each), peeled, cored, and cut into ½-inch pieces

1½ tablespoons granulated sugar

¼ teaspoon grated lemon zest plus ¾ teaspoon juice

⅛ teaspoon ground cinnamon

⅛ teaspoon ground ginger

2 pinches table salt, divided

1½ tablespoons golden raisins

2¼ teaspoons panko bread crumbs

3½ tablespoons unsalted butter, melted

1½ teaspoons confectioners' sugar, plus extra for serving

7 (14 by 9-inch) phyllo sheets, thawed

1. Toss apples, granulated sugar, lemon zest and juice, cinnamon, ginger, and pinch salt together in large bowl. Cover and microwave until apples are warm to touch, 60 to 75 seconds, stirring once halfway through microwaving. Let apples stand, covered, for 5 minutes. Transfer apples to colander set in second large bowl and let drain, reserving liquid. Return apples to bowl; stir in raisins and panko.

2. Adjust oven rack to upper-middle position and heat oven to 375 degrees. Spray rimmed baking sheet with vegetable oil spray. Stir pinch salt into melted butter.

3. Place 16½ by 12-inch sheet of parchment paper on counter with long side parallel to edge of counter. Place 1 phyllo sheet on parchment with long side parallel to edge of counter. Place confectioners' sugar in fine-mesh strainer (rest strainer in bowl to prevent making a mess). Lightly brush sheet with melted butter and dust sparingly with confectioners' sugar. Repeat with 6 more phyllo sheets, melted butter, and confectioners' sugar, stacking sheets one on top of other as you go.

4. Arrange apple mixture in 2½ by 10-inch rectangle 2 inches from bottom of phyllo and about 2 inches from each side. Using parchment, fold sides of phyllo over filling, then fold bottom edge of phyllo over filling. Brush folded portions of phyllo with reserved apple liquid. Fold top edge over filling, making sure top and bottom edges overlap by about 1 inch. (If they do not overlap, unfold, rearrange filling into slightly narrower strip, and refold.) Press firmly to seal. Using thin metal spatula, transfer strudel to prepared sheet. Lightly brush top and sides of strudel with remaining apple liquid.

5. Bake until golden brown, 25 to 30 minutes, rotating sheet halfway through baking. Using thin metal spatula, immediately transfer strudel to cutting board. Let cool for 3 minutes. Slice strudel into quarters and let cool for at least 20 minutes. Serve warm or at room temperature, dusting with extra confectioners' sugar before serving.

MAKING QUICK APPLE STRUDEL

1. On parchment paper, layer phyllo sheets atop one another, brushing each sheet with melted butter and dusting lightly with confectioners' sugar. Repeat 6 times stacking sheets atop one another.

2. Arrange filling in 2½ by 10-inch rectangle 2 inches from bottom of phyllo.

3. Using parchment, fold sides and then bottom over filling; brush folded portions with reserved apple liquid and continue to roll dough around filling to form strudel. Press firmly to seal.

4. Transfer strudel to prepared sheet using thin metal spatula. Brush top and sides of strudel with remaining apple liquid.

Skillet Cherry Cobbler

Serves 2 VEGETARIAN

Total time 55 minutes, plus 15 minutes cooling

WHY THIS RECIPE WORKS We wanted a streamlined, scaled-down recipe for cherry cobbler we could make any time of year. Jarred sour cherries are plump, tart, and available year-round. They're also already pitted and packed in a flavorful juice we could incorporate into our recipe. Switching from a baking dish to a skillet allowed us to simmer the sauce on the stovetop before adding the other elements and moving the skillet to the oven. Buttermilk contributed a light, tender texture to the biscuits, and dropping small spoonfuls of dough—rather than the standard large mounds—over the cherries allowed the biscuits to cook through in just 20 minutes. The amount of sugar you use in the filling will depend on the sweetness of your cherries. We prefer the crunchy texture of turbinado sugar sprinkled over the biscuits before baking, but granulated sugar can be substituted. You will need a 10-inch ovensafe skillet for this recipe. Serve with vanilla ice cream or Whipped Cream (page 393).

TOPPING

- ½ cup (2½ ounces) all-purpose flour
- 3 tablespoons granulated sugar
- ½ teaspoon baking powder
- ⅛ teaspoon baking soda
- ⅛ teaspoon table salt
- ¼ cup buttermilk, chilled
- 2 tablespoons unsalted butter, melted and cooled

FILLING

- ¼–⅓ cup (1¾ to 2⅓ ounces) granulated sugar
- 1 tablespoon cornstarch
- Pinch table salt
- 1⅓ cups jarred sour cherries in light syrup, drained with ¼ cup syrup reserved
- ¼ cup dry red wine
- ¼ teaspoon vanilla extract
- 1 small cinnamon stick
- 1 teaspoon turbinado sugar

1. FOR THE TOPPING Adjust oven rack to middle position and heat oven to 400 degrees. Whisk flour, sugar, baking powder, baking soda, and salt together in medium bowl. In separate bowl, stir chilled buttermilk and melted butter together until butter forms small clumps. Stir buttermilk mixture into flour mixture with rubber spatula until just incorporated. Cover and set aside.

2. FOR THE FILLING Whisk granulated sugar, cornstarch, and salt together in 10-inch ovensafe skillet. Whisk in reserved cherry syrup, wine, and vanilla, then add cinnamon stick. Bring mixture to simmer over medium-high heat and cook, whisking frequently, until slightly thickened, 1 to 3 minutes. Off heat, remove cinnamon stick and stir in cherries.

3. Using large spoon, scoop and drop 1-inch pieces of dough, spaced about ½ inch apart, over cherry filling, then sprinkle with turbinado sugar. Bake until biscuits are golden brown and filling is thick and glossy, 20 to 25 minutes. Let cobbler cool in skillet on wire rack for at least 15 minutes before serving.

Skillet Apple Crisp

Skillet Apple Crisp

Serves 2 `VEGETARIAN`

Total time 55 minutes, plus 15 minutes cooling

WHY THIS RECIPE WORKS Most recipes for apple crisp result in unevenly cooked apples and a topping that's anything but crisp. To drive off excess moisture and allow the fruit to caramelize, we sautéed the apples in a little butter. Apple cider provided intense fruity flavor. Chewy rolled oats and crunchy pecans made a substantial crisp topping that was the perfect contrast to the tender apples underneath. We like Golden Delicious apples for this recipe, but any sweet, crisp apple such as Honeycrisp or Braeburn can be substituted; do not use Granny Smith apples. You will need a 10-inch ovensafe skillet for this recipe. Serve with vanilla ice cream or Whipped Cream (page 393).

TOPPING

¼ cup (1¼ ounces) all-purpose flour
¼ cup pecans, chopped fine
¼ cup (¾ ounce) old-fashioned rolled oats
3 tablespoons packed light brown sugar
1 tablespoon granulated sugar
¼ teaspoon ground cinnamon
¼ teaspoon table salt
3 tablespoons unsalted butter, melted

FILLING

1½ pounds Golden Delicious apples, peeled, cored, halved, and cut into ½-inch-thick wedges
2 tablespoons granulated sugar
¼ teaspoon ground cinnamon (optional)
½ cup apple cider
1 teaspoon lemon juice
1 tablespoon unsalted butter

1. FOR THE TOPPING Adjust oven rack to middle position and heat oven to 450 degrees. Combine flour, pecans, oats, brown sugar, granulated sugar, cinnamon, and salt in medium bowl. Stir in melted butter until mixture is thoroughly moistened and crumbly; set aside.

2. FOR THE FILLING In separate bowl, toss apples; sugar; and cinnamon; if using, together; set aside. Bring cider to simmer in 10-inch ovensafe skillet over medium heat and cook until reduced to ⅓ cup, 2 to 3 minutes. Transfer reduced cider to small bowl and stir in lemon juice.

3. Melt butter in now-empty skillet over medium heat. Add apple mixture and cook, stirring frequently, until apples begin to soften and become translucent, 12 to 14 minutes. (Do not fully cook apples.) Off heat, gently stir in cider mixture until apples are coated.

4. Sprinkle topping evenly over fruit, breaking up any large chunks. Place skillet on baking sheet and bake until fruit is tender and topping is deep golden brown, 15 to 20 minutes. Let crisp cool on wire rack for 15 minutes before serving.

VARIATION

Skillet Apple Crisp with Raspberries and Almonds

Substitute ¼ cup slivered almonds for pecans. Add ⅛ teaspoon almond extract to reduced cider with lemon juice in step 2. Stir ¼ cup raspberries into apple mixture along with reduced cider in step 3.

CORING APPLES

A. CORING WITH A CORER Cut small slice from top and bottom of apple. Hold apple steady and push corer through. Peel and cut apple according to recipe.

B. CORING WITHOUT A CORER Cut sides of apple squarely away from core. Cut each piece of apple according to recipe.

Individual Pear Crisps

Serves 2   VEGETARIAN

Total time 50 minutes, plus 15 minutes cooling

WHY THIS RECIPE WORKS Simply substituting pears for apples in this classic American dessert is a recipe for disaster; pears exude so much moisture that a traditional crisp topping will sink into the filling. To solve this problem, we found that selecting ripe yet firm pears of the right variety (Bartlett or Bosc worked best) was key. To compensate for all the liquid they released, we added a slurry of cornstarch and lemon juice. We also developed an extra-sturdy topping; melting the butter helped bind the flour to the other ingredients, and a generous amount of nuts guaranteed a thick, crunchy crust. For this crisp, the pears should be ripe but firm, which means the flesh at the base of the stem should give slightly when gently pressed with a finger. You will need two 12-ounce ramekins for this recipe, but an 8½ by 5½-inch baking dish will also work. Serve with vanilla ice cream or Whipped Cream (page 393).

2 tablespoons granulated sugar, divided
1 teaspoon lemon juice
¼ teaspoon cornstarch
2 pinches table salt, divided
2 ripe but firm Bartlett or Bosc pears, peeled, halved, cored, and cut into 1½-inch pieces
⅓ cup whole almonds or pecans, chopped fine
¼ cup (1¼ ounces) all-purpose flour
2 tablespoons packed light brown sugar
⅛ teaspoon ground cinnamon
Pinch ground nutmeg
3 tablespoons unsalted butter, melted and cooled

1. Adjust oven rack to lower-middle position and heat oven to 425 degrees. Line rimmed baking sheet with aluminum foil. Combine 1 tablespoon granulated sugar, lemon juice, cornstarch, and pinch salt in medium bowl. Gently toss pears with sugar mixture and divide evenly between two 12-ounce ramekins.

2. Mix almonds, flour, brown sugar, cinnamon, nutmeg, remaining pinch salt, and remaining 1 tablespoon granulated sugar together in medium bowl. Drizzle melted butter over top and stir until mixture resembles crumbly wet sand. Pinch mixture between your fingers into small pea-size pieces (with some smaller loose bits). Sprinkle topping evenly over pears, breaking up any large chunks.

3. Place crisps on prepared sheet and bake until filling is bubbling around edges and topping is deep golden brown, 20 to 25 minutes, rotating sheet halfway through baking. Let crisps cool on wire rack for 15 minutes before serving.

VARIATION
Individual Peach Crisps
Microwave 1 pound frozen peaches in bowl at 50 percent power, stirring occasionally, until thawed and slightly warm, 5 to 7 minutes; drain peaches well. Substitute thawed and drained peaches for pears.

Garam Masala–Spiced Mango Crisp
Serves 2 VEGETARIAN

Total time 1 hour, plus 15 minutes cooling

WHY THIS RECIPE WORKS Our secret weapon for a stellar crisp that we can enjoy any time of year? Frozen fruit. It's convenient and consistently high-quality; here, we opted to use frozen mangos and garam masala for a warmly spiced, nectary-sweet, any-season dessert. We microwaved and drained the fruit to thaw it and eliminate excess liquid. We then added sugar, garam masala, and a bit of cornstarch for thickening. To make the topping, we mixed chilled butter with flour and oats until slightly clumpy crumbs formed. Baking the crisp in a hot oven ensured that the topping became golden brown and crunchy and the mango filling bubbly and thickened; a loaf pan kept things easy and casual; served up in bowls, there's room for a big scoop of ice cream. The test kitchen's preferred loaf pan measures 8½ by 4½ inches; if you use a 9 by 5-inch loaf pan, start checking for doneness 5 minutes early. Serve with vanilla ice cream, if desired.

3 cups frozen mango chunks
¼ cup packed brown sugar, divided
1½ teaspoons cornstarch
¼ teaspoon plus ⅛ teaspoon garam masala, divided
  Pinch table salt
¼ cup (1¼ ounces) all-purpose flour
2 tablespoons old-fashioned rolled oats
2 tablespoons butter, cut into 4 pieces and chilled

1. Adjust oven rack to lower-middle position and heat oven to 425 degrees. Microwave mangos in bowl until steaming and juices start to bubble, about 3 minutes, stirring occasionally. Drain off any liquid, then toss mangos with 2 tablespoons sugar, cornstarch, ¼ teaspoon garam masala, and salt. Spread mango filling in 8½-by 4½-inch loaf pan.

2. Whisk flour, oats, remaining 2 tablespoons sugar, and remaining ⅛ teaspoon garam masala together in medium bowl. Add butter and, using your fingers, blend into dry ingredients until dime-size clumps form. Pinch together any powdery parts, then sprinkle topping evenly over filling.

3. Bake until filling is bubbling around edges and topping is golden brown, about 30 minutes, rotating pan halfway through baking. Let cool on wire rack for 15 minutes before serving.

Individual Blueberry Crumbles
Serves 2 VEGETARIAN

Total time 1 hour, plus 15 minutes cooling

WHY THIS RECIPE WORKS We wanted an easy blueberry crumble with fresh flavor and a substantial crumble topping. To avoid a soupy filling, we preferred to add a thickener rather than cook the berries; a little cornstarch thickened the blueberry filling nicely. A combination of butter, flour, brown sugar, oats, and a sprinkle of cinnamon delivered the best streusel topping. Leaving the streusel in dime-size pieces kept it from sinking into the filling. Avoid instant or quick oats here. In step 2, do not press the topping into the berry mixture or it may sink and become soggy. Do not substitute frozen berries in this recipe. You will need two 12-ounce ramekins for this recipe, but an 8½ by 5½-inch baking dish will also work. Serve with vanilla ice cream or Whipped Cream (page 393).

Garam Masala–Spiced
Mango Crisp

¼–⅓ cup (1¾ to 2⅓ ounces) granulated sugar

1½ teaspoons cornstarch

2 pinches table salt, divided

10 ounces (2 cups) blueberries

½ cup (2½ ounces) all-purpose flour

⅓ cup (1 ounce) old-fashioned rolled oats

¼ cup packed (1¾ ounces) light brown sugar

¼ teaspoon ground cinnamon

4 tablespoons unsalted butter, cut into
4 pieces and chilled

1. Adjust oven rack to lower-middle position and heat oven to 375 degrees. Line rimmed baking sheet with aluminum foil. Combine ¼ cup granulated sugar, cornstarch, and pinch salt in medium bowl. Gently toss blueberries with sugar mixture. (If blueberries taste tart, add up to 4 teaspoons more sugar.) Divide blueberries evenly between two 12-ounce ramekins.

2. Mix flour, oats, brown sugar, cinnamon, and remaining pinch salt together in medium bowl. Add butter and, using your fingers, blend butter into dry ingredients until dime-size clumps form. Pinch together any powdery parts, then sprinkle topping evenly over blueberries.

3. Place crumbles on prepared sheet and bake until filling is bubbling around edges and topping is deep golden brown, about 30 minutes, rotating sheet halfway through baking. Let crumbles cool on wire rack for 15 minutes before serving.

Classic Double-Crust Pie Dough

Makes enough for one 6-inch pie VEGETARIAN

Total time 25 minutes, plus 1 hour chilling

WHY THIS RECIPE WORKS Vegetable shortening makes pie dough easy to handle and yields a crust that is remarkably flaky. But nothing beats the rich flavor of a crust made with butter. We set out to create a basic pie dough that combined the right fats and the right proportion of fat to flour to give us a supremely tender and flaky crust that was also rich and buttery. We experimented with a variety of combinations and ultimately settled on 5 tablespoons of butter to 3 tablespoons of shortening for the best flavor and texture. We found that 1¼ cups of flour was just the right amount, producing a dough that was easy to work and a baked crust that was extremely tender and flavorful. While this pie dough can be made by hand, the food processor is faster and easier and does the best job of cutting the fat into the flour. If you don't have a food processor, see "Hand-Mixing Pie Dough" on page 401.

1¼ cups (6¼ ounces) all-purpose flour

1 tablespoon sugar

½ teaspoon table salt

3 tablespoons vegetable shortening, cut into
½-inch pieces and chilled

5 tablespoons unsalted butter, cut into
¼-inch pieces and chilled

4–6 tablespoons ice water

1. Process flour, sugar, and salt in food processor until combined, about 5 seconds. Scatter shortening over top and process until mixture resembles coarse cornmeal, about 10 seconds. Scatter butter over top and pulse until mixture resembles coarse crumbs, about 10 pulses.

2. Transfer mixture to bowl. Sprinkle 4 tablespoons ice water over mixture. Using rubber spatula, stir and press dough until it sticks together. If dough does not come together, stir in remaining water, 1 tablespoon at a time, until it does.

3. Divide dough in half and form each half into 3-inch disk. Wrap disks tightly in plastic wrap and refrigerate for 1 hour. Let chilled dough sit on counter to soften slightly, about 10 minutes, before rolling. (Wrapped dough can be refrigerated for up to 2 days or frozen for up to 2 months. If frozen, let dough thaw completely on counter before rolling.)

VARIATION
Classic Single-Crust Pie Dough

Makes enough for one 6-inch pie

Total time 25 minutes, plus 1 hour chilling

If you don't have a food processor, see "Hand-Mixing Pie Dough" on page 401.

1 cup (5 ounces) all-purpose flour

1 teaspoon sugar

½ teaspoon table salt

2 tablespoons vegetable shortening, cut into
½-inch pieces and chilled

4 tablespoons unsalted butter, cut into
¼-inch pieces and chilled

3–5 tablespoons ice water

1. Process flour, sugar, and salt in food processor until combined, about 5 seconds. Scatter shortening over top and process until mixture resembles coarse cornmeal, about 10 seconds. Scatter butter over top and pulse until mixture resembles coarse crumbs, about 10 pulses.

TIPS FOR BETTER PIE CRUSTS

Pie dough seems easy enough to prepare. Mix flour, salt, and sugar together, cut in some fat, add water just until the dough sticks together, roll it out, and bake. Yet it can all go wrong so easily, resulting in a crust that's dense and tough instead of tender and flaky. To ensure a perfect pie crust every time, we use these tricks.

KEEP EVERYTHING COLD Keeping the fat cold when mixing it into the flour is the key to a tender, flaky dough. Always chill the butter and shortening before making the dough and make sure that your water is ice cold. On particularly warm days, we even recommend chilling the flour and mixing bowl. And once the dough comes together, wrap it in plastic wrap and refrigerate it for at least one hour before attempting to roll it out. Cool dough is easier to manage and less apt to break or tear. Before rolling it out, let the dough soften slightly on counter for about 10 minutes. If it softens too much when rolling or shaping, slide it onto a baking sheet and place it in the refrigerator or freezer to firm up.

ROLL IT OUT RIGHT Keeping the dough as evenly round as possible when rolling makes fitting it into a pie plate easy. The dough should be in the shape of a flat disk before you start to roll it, and the counter should be lightly floured. Every few times you roll the dough, rotate it a quarter turn and lightly flour the counter to prevent it from sticking. Keep checking the dough as you roll it: If it starts becoming lopsided, use your hands or a bench scraper to reshape the dough.

CHILL THE CRUST The biggest risk when baking a pie crust is that the dough can shrink in the oven and your pie may overflow. A cold pie shell will hold its shape better in the oven, in part because the chilling gives the gluten in the dough time to relax.

BAKE ON A FOIL-LINED BAKING SHEET Juicy, fruit-filled pies can be prone to bubbling over, and the sugary juice will burn and smoke if it hits the bottom of the oven. To avoid this, place the pie on a rimmed baking sheet that has been lined with foil and bake on the lowest oven rack. The sheet catches any splatters and the foil makes cleanup easy and reduces the risk of spills smoking and burning. The sheet also conducts heat well and thus promotes better browning, preventing a soggy bottom crust. Placing the sheet on the lowest rack ensures that it gets nice and hot.

PROTECT THE CRUST Sometimes the crimped crust around the edge of the pie can get quite brown before the pie has finished baking. If this happens, simply wrap a piece of foil loosely around the rim of the pie.

---

2. Transfer mixture to bowl. Sprinkle 3 tablespoons ice water over mixture. Using rubber spatula, stir and press dough until it sticks together. If dough does not come together, stir in remaining water, 1 tablespoon at a time, until it does.

3. Form dough into 3-inch disk, wrap tightly in plastic wrap, and refrigerate for 1 hour. Let chilled dough sit on counter to soften slightly, about 10 minutes, before rolling. (Wrapped dough can be refrigerated for up to 2 days or frozen for up to 2 months. If frozen, let dough thaw completely on counter before rolling.)

HAND-MIXING PIE DOUGH

1. Freeze butter until firm. Whisk flour, sugar, and salt together in large bowl. Sprinkle chilled vegetable shortening over flour mixture and press into flour using fork.

2. Grate frozen butter on into flour mixture. Using two butter or dinner knives, cut mixture together until it resembles coarse crumbs. Add water, stirring with rubber spatula.

Raspberry-Nectarine Pie

1 recipe Classic Double-Crust Pie Dough (page 401)
2 nectarines, halved, pitted, and sliced ⅓ inch thick
5 ounces (1 cup) raspberries
¼–⅓ cup (1¾ to 2⅓ ounces) plus 1 teaspoon sugar, divided
2 teaspoons cornstarch
¼ teaspoon grated lemon zest plus ¾ teaspoon juice
Pinch table salt
1 large egg white, lightly beaten

Raspberry-Nectarine Pie

Makes one 6-inch pie VEGETARIAN

Total time 1 hour 20 minutes, plus 30 minutes chilling and 1½ hours cooling

WHY THIS RECIPE WORKS For a fresh take on summer fruit pie, we turned to a vibrant combination of nectarines and raspberries. Granulated sugar sweetened our pie without competing with the fruit's flavor, and a little lemon juice added brightness. To account for the varying ripeness and juiciness of the nectarines, we found that macerating the fruit and sugar for 20 minutes and then draining off most of the liquid prevented a soupy filling. A little cornstarch helped thicken the filling nicely. Starting with a hot oven and lowering the temperature partway through baking ensured that both the top and bottom crusts were baked to golden-brown perfection. We prefer the buttery flavor and flaky texture of homemade pie dough here; however, you can substitute two 9-inch store-bought pie dough rounds, if desired. You will need a 6-inch pie plate for this recipe.

1. Adjust oven rack to lowest position and heat oven to 425 degrees. Roll 1 disk of dough into 9-inch circle on lightly floured counter. Loosely roll dough around rolling pin and gently unroll it onto 6-inch pie plate, letting excess dough hang over edge. Ease dough into plate by gently lifting edge of dough with your hand while pressing into plate bottom with your other hand. Leave any dough that overhangs plate in place. Wrap dough-lined pie plate loosely in plastic wrap and refrigerate until dough is firm, about 30 minutes. Roll other disk of dough into 9-inch circle on lightly floured counter, then transfer to parchment paper–lined baking sheet; cover with plastic and refrigerate for 30 minutes.

2. Meanwhile, gently toss nectarines, raspberries, and ¼ cup sugar together in bowl and let sit, tossing occasionally, until fruit releases its juice, about 20 minutes.

3. Drain fruit in colander set in large bowl. Measure out and reserve 1 tablespoon juice; discard remaining juice. Add drained fruit, reserved juice, cornstarch, lemon zest and juice, and salt to now-empty bowl and toss gently to combine. (If fruit tastes tart, add up to 4 teaspoons more sugar.)

4. Transfer fruit mixture to dough-lined pie plate, mounding it slightly in middle. Loosely roll remaining dough round around rolling pin and gently unroll it onto filling. Trim overhang to ½ inch beyond lip of pie plate. Pinch edges of top and bottom crusts firmly together. Tuck overhang under itself; folded edge should be flush with edge of pie plate. Crimp dough evenly around edge of pie plate using your fingers. Cut three 1-inch vents in center of top crust. Brush surface with beaten egg white and sprinkle with remaining 1 teaspoon sugar.

5. Place pie on foil-lined rimmed baking sheet and bake until crust is light golden brown, 20 to 25 minutes. Reduce oven temperature to 375 degrees, rotate sheet, and continue to bake until juices are bubbling and crust is deep golden brown, 20 to 25 minutes. Let pie cool on wire rack until filling has set, about 1½ hours; serve slightly warm or at room temperature.

1. Unroll untrimmed top piece of dough over filled pie, taking care not to stretch it and create thin spots.

2. Trim overhanging edges of both crusts to about ½ inch beyond lip of pie plate.

3. Pinch edges of top and bottom crusts firmly together to prevent leaking, then tuck overhang under itself to make it flush with edge of pie plate.

4. Use index finger of one hand and thumb and index finger of other hand to create fluted ridges perpendicular to edge of pie plate. Use small knife to make 1-inch vents in center of top crust, depending on recipe.

Sweet Cherry Pie

Makes one 6-inch pie   VEGETARIAN

Total time 1 hour 25 minutes, plus 2 hours 20 minutes chilling, freezing, and cooling

WHY THIS RECIPE WORKS While sweet cherries are typically best eaten out of hand, sour cherries are more suited to baking, where their bright fruit flavor shines. But fresh sour cherries can be hard to find, so we set out to develop a cherry pie that would taste great using easily available sweet cherries. Adding a plum in with the cherries provided a subtle tartness that tamed the cherries' sweetness. We processed the plum with a small portion of the cherries to create a puree that we mixed in with the unprocessed cherries for a moist, juicy

filling. We prefer the buttery flavor and flaky texture of home-made pie dough here; however, you can substitute two 9-inch store-bought pie dough rounds, if desired. You can substitute 12 ounces frozen sweet cherries for the fresh cherries; to preserve their juice, thaw them only partway before using. You will need a 6-inch pie plate for this recipe. Grind the tapioca to a fine powder in a spice grinder for 30 seconds or in a mortar and pestle.

1 recipe Classic Double-Crust Pie Dough (page 400)
14 ounces fresh sweet cherries, pitted and halved
1 red plum, quartered and pitted
¼ cup (1¾ ounces) sugar
2 teaspoons instant tapioca, ground
1½ teaspoons lemon juice
   Pinch table salt
   Pinch ground cinnamon (optional)
1 tablespoon unsalted butter, cut into ¼-inch pieces
1 large egg white, lightly beaten

1. Adjust oven rack to lowest position and heat oven to 425 degrees. Roll 1 disk of dough into 9-inch circle on lightly floured counter. Loosely roll dough around rolling pin and gently unroll it onto 6-inch pie plate, letting excess dough hang over edge. Ease dough into plate by gently lifting edge of dough with your hand while pressing into plate bottom with your other hand. Leave any dough that overhangs plate in place. Wrap dough-lined pie plate loosely in plastic wrap and refrigerate until dough is firm, about 30 minutes. Roll other disk of dough into 9-inch circle on lightly floured counter, then transfer to parchment paper–lined baking sheet; cover with plastic and refrigerate for 30 minutes.

2. Meanwhile, process ½ cup cherries and plum together in food processor until smooth, about 1 minute, scraping down sides of bowl as necessary. Strain puree through fine-mesh strainer into large bowl, pressing on solids to extract liquid; discard solids. Stir remaining halved cherries; sugar; ground tapioca; lemon juice; salt; and cinnamon, if using, into puree and let sit for 15 minutes.

3. Transfer cherry mixture with its juices to dough-lined pie plate, mounding it slightly in middle (pie plate will be very full). Scatter butter pieces over top. Loosely roll remaining dough round around rolling pin and gently unroll it onto filling. Trim overhang to ½ inch beyond lip of pie plate. Pinch edges of top and bottom crusts firmly together. Tuck overhang under itself; folded edge should be flush with edge of pie plate. Crimp dough evenly around edge of pie plate using your fingers. Cut five 1-inch vents in center of top crust. Brush surface with beaten egg white and freeze for 20 minutes.

4. Place pie on foil-lined rimmed baking sheet and bake until crust is light golden brown, 20 to 25 minutes. Reduce oven temperature to 350 degrees; rotate sheet; and continue to bake until juices are bubbling and crust is deep golden brown, 25 to 35 minutes. Let pie cool on wire rack until filling has set, about 1½ hours; serve slightly warm or at room temperature.

Icebox Strawberry Pie

Makes one 6-inch pie

Total time 1 hour, plus 5 hours 20 minutes freezing, cooling, and chilling

WHY THIS RECIPE WORKS For a no-bake strawberry pie bursting with berry flavor and boasting a firm, sliceable texture, we discovered a few key steps. Simmering a portion of the berries concentrated their juice, which reinforced the strawberry flavor of our filling and made it less watery. Leaving some berries uncooked added a freshness that was missing when we cooked all the berries. But since the fresh berries released some water as the pie chilled, we added a small amount of unflavored gelatin to help our filling firm up to just the right consistency. We prefer the buttery flavor and flaky texture of homemade pie dough here; however, you can substitute one 9-inch store-bought pie dough round, if desired. You will need a 6-inch pie plate for this recipe. In step 4, be sure to cook the strawberry mixture until it measures ½ cup in a liquid measuring cup.

1 recipe Classic Single-Crust Pie Dough (page 400)

FILLING

8 ounces (1¾ cups) frozen strawberries
1½ teaspoons lemon juice
1 teaspoon water
¾ teaspoon unflavored gelatin
⅓ cup (2⅓ ounces) sugar
Pinch table salt
5 ounces fresh strawberries, hulled and sliced thin (¾ cup)

TOPPING

½ cup heavy cream, chilled
1 ounce cream cheese, softened
1 tablespoon sugar
¼ teaspoon vanilla extract

1. Roll dough into 10-inch circle, about ⅜ inch thick, on lightly floured counter. Loosely roll dough around rolling pin and gently unroll it onto 6-inch pie plate, letting excess dough hang over edge. Ease dough into plate by gently lifting edge of dough with your hand while pressing into plate bottom with your other hand. Leave any dough that overhangs plate in place.

2. Trim overhang to ½ inch beyond lip of pie plate. Tuck overhang under itself; folded edge should be flush with edge of pie plate. Crimp dough evenly around edge of pie plate using your fingers. Wrap dough-lined pie plate loosely in plastic wrap and place in freezer until dough is fully chilled and firm, about 20 minutes, before using.

FITTING THE DOUGH AND FINISHING A SINGLE-CRUST PIE

1. Loosely roll dough around rolling pin, then gently unroll it onto pie plate, letting excess hang over plate.

2. Lift dough around edges and gently press it into corners of pie plate.

3. To finish, trim overhanging edge of crust to about ½ inch beyond lip of pie plate, then tuck overhang under itself to make it flush with edge of pie plate.

4. Use index finger of one hand and thumb and index finger of other hand to create fluted ridges perpendicular to edge of pie plate.

3. Adjust oven rack to lower-middle position and heat oven to 375 degrees. Line chilled pie shell with parchment paper or double layer of aluminum foil, covering edges to prevent burning, and fill with pie weights. Bake until pie dough looks dry and is light in color, 25 to 30 minutes. Remove weights and parchment and continue to bake crust until deep golden brown, 10 to 12 minutes. Transfer pie plate to wire rack and let crust cool completely, about 1 hour.

4. FOR THE FILLING Meanwhile, cook frozen strawberries in small saucepan over low heat until berries begin to release their juice, about 3 minutes. Increase heat to medium-low and continue to cook, stirring frequently, until mixture measures ½ cup and is thick and jamlike, 10 to 15 minutes.

5. Combine lemon juice and water in small bowl, sprinkle gelatin over liquid, and let sit until gelatin softens, about 5 minutes. Stir gelatin mixture, sugar, and salt into cooked berry mixture, return to simmer, and cook for about 1 minute. Transfer to medium bowl and let cool to room temperature, about 30 minutes.

6. Fold fresh strawberries into cooled berry mixture. Spread filling evenly over bottom of baked and cooled pie crust and refrigerate until set, at least 4 hours or up to 24 hours.

7. FOR THE TOPPING Using hand-held mixer set at medium-low speed, beat cream, cream cheese, sugar, and vanilla in medium bowl until combined, about 1 minute. Increase speed to high and beat until stiff peaks form, 1 to 3 minutes. Spread topping evenly over pie and serve.

Icebox
Strawberry Pie

Banana Cream Pie

Makes one 6-inch pie VEGETARIAN

Total time 1¼ hours, plus 6 hours 20 minutes freezing, cooling, and chilling

WHY THIS RECIPE WORKS Banana cream pie is utterly irresistible—unless the pastry cream ends up soupy, stiff, and bland. Using cornstarch instead of flour gave us a nicely thickened pastry cream that held up to slicing. Rather than relying on artificial banana extract or liqueur (an impractical purchase when we needed only a splash), we got roasted banana flavor by infusing the pastry cream with sautéed bananas. Be sure to buy all-yellow to lightly spotted bananas for this recipe. We prefer the buttery flavor and flaky texture of homemade pie dough here; however, you can substitute one 9-inch store-bought pie dough round, if desired. You will need a 6-inch pie plate for this recipe. Peel and slice the bananas just before using. When straining the half-and-half mixture in step 5, do not press on the bananas or the custard will turn gray as it sits.

Banana Cream Pie

1 recipe Classic Single-Crust Pie Dough (page 400)
2 ripe bananas, divided
2 tablespoons unsalted butter, divided
1¼ cups half-and-half
5 tablespoons (2¼ ounces) granulated sugar
3 large egg yolks
⅛ teaspoon table salt
1 tablespoon cornstarch
¾ teaspoon vanilla extract, divided
1 tablespoon orange juice
¼ cup heavy cream, chilled
2 teaspoons confectioners' sugar

1. Roll dough into 10-inch circle, about ⅜ inch thick, on lightly floured counter. Loosely roll dough around rolling pin and gently unroll it onto 6-inch pie plate, letting excess dough hang over edge. Ease dough into plate by gently lifting edge of dough with your hand while pressing into plate bottom with your other hand. Leave any dough that overhangs plate in place.

2. Trim overhang to ½ inch beyond lip of pie plate. Tuck overhang under itself; folded edge should be flush with edge of pie plate. Crimp dough evenly around edge of pie plate using your fingers. Wrap dough-lined pie plate loosely in plastic wrap and place in freezer until dough is fully chilled and firm, about 20 minutes, before using.

3. Adjust oven rack to lower-middle position and heat oven to 375 degrees. Line chilled pie shell with parchment paper or double layer of aluminum foil, covering edges to prevent burning, and fill with pie weights. Bake until pie dough looks dry and is light in color, 25 to 30 minutes. Remove weights and parchment and continue to bake crust until deep golden brown, 10 to 12 minutes. Transfer pie plate to wire rack and let crust cool completely, about 1 hour.

4. Meanwhile, peel and slice 1 banana ½ inch thick. Melt 1 tablespoon butter in small saucepan over medium-high heat. Add banana slices and cook until they begin to soften, about 2 minutes. Add half-and-half, bring to boil, and cook for 30 seconds. Remove pot from heat, cover, and let sit for 40 minutes.

5. Whisk granulated sugar, egg yolks, and salt together in medium bowl until smooth. Whisk in cornstarch. Strain cooled half-and-half mixture through fine-mesh strainer into yolk mixture—do not press on banana—and whisk until incorporated; discard cooked banana.

6. Transfer mixture to clean saucepan. Cook over medium heat, whisking constantly, until thickened to consistency of warm pudding (180 degrees), 4 to 6 minutes. Off heat, whisk in remaining 1 tablespoon butter and ½ teaspoon vanilla. Transfer pastry cream to bowl, press greased parchment directly against surface, and let cool for about 1 hour.

7. Peel and slice remaining banana ¼ inch thick and toss with orange juice. Whisk pastry cream briefly, then spread half over bottom of baked and cooled pie crust. Arrange sliced bananas on pastry cream. Top with remaining pastry cream.

8. Using hand-held mixer set at medium-low speed, beat cream, confectioners' sugar, and remaining ¼ teaspoon vanilla in medium bowl until foamy, about 1 minute. Increase speed to high and beat until soft peaks form, 1 to 3 minutes. Spread whipped cream attractively over center of pie. Refrigerate until set, at least 5 hours or up to 24 hours. Serve.

Key Lime Pie

Makes one 6-inch pie   VEGETARIAN

Total time 45 minutes, plus 4 hours cooling and chilling

WHY THIS RECIPE WORKS For a Key lime pie with bold lime flavor, we used a combination of lime juice and zest in the filling. Sweetened condensed milk provided a creamy richness, and two egg yolks thickened our filling to just the right consistency. A buttery graham cracker crust contributed caramel notes that complemented the sweet-tart filling. We developed our recipe using regular supermarket Persian limes. Feel free to use Key limes if desired; note that you'll need about 10 Key limes to yield ¼ cup juice. You will need a 6-inch pie plate for this recipe. It is important to add the filling to the crust while it is still warm.

FILLING
2 large egg yolks
2 teaspoons grated lime zest plus ¼ cup juice (2 limes) plus extra zest for serving
⅔ cup sweetened condensed milk

CRUST
4 whole graham crackers, broken into 1-inch pieces
2 tablespoons unsalted butter, melted and cooled
4 teaspoons granulated sugar

TOPPING
¼ cup heavy cream, chilled
2 teaspoons confectioners' sugar
⅛ teaspoon vanilla extract

1. FOR THE FILLING Whisk egg yolks and 2 teaspoons lime zest together in medium bowl until mixture has light green tint, about 1 minute. Whisk in condensed milk until smooth, then whisk in lime juice. Cover mixture and set aside at room temperature until thickened, about 30 minutes.

Key Lime Pie

To make graham cracker crust, press crumb mixture firmly and evenly across bottom and up sides of pie plate, using bottom of measuring cup.

Easy Apple Galette

Serves 2 VEGETARIAN

Total time 1 hour 5 minutes, plus 15 minutes cooling

WHY THIS RECIPE WORKS For an ultraeasy apple galette for two, we bypassed the labor-intensive, time-consuming homemade pastry and reached for store-bought frozen puff pastry instead. Forming an attractive crust was as easy as folding over the edges of the pastry. We found that a Granny Smith apple worked best; the slices stayed moist in the oven and maintained their shape throughout cooking. Sprinkling a little sugar on the apples prevented them from drying out and also helped them brown nicely. A simple glaze made from apricot preserves and a small amount of water was the perfect finishing touch, contributing an attractive sheen and fruity tartness to our scaled-down apple galette. Be sure to let the puff pastry thaw completely before using; otherwise, it can crack and break apart. To thaw frozen puff pastry, let it sit either in the refrigerator for 24 hours or on the counter for 30 minutes to 1 hour.

½ (9½ by 9-inch) sheet puff pastry, thawed
1 large Granny Smith apple (8 ounces), peeled, cored, halved, and sliced ⅛ inch thick
½ tablespoon unsalted butter, cut into ¼-inch pieces
2 teaspoons sugar
1 tablespoon apricot preserves
1 teaspoon water

1. Adjust oven rack to middle position and heat oven to 400 degrees. Line rimmed baking sheet with parchment paper. Transfer puff pastry to prepared sheet and fold edges over by ¼ inch; crimp to create ¼-inch-thick border.

2. Starting in 1 corner of tart, shingle apple slices into crust in tidy diagonal rows, overlapping them by about half, until surface is completely covered. Dot apple with preserves and sprinkle evenly with sugar. Bake until bottom of tart is deep golden brown and apple has caramelized, 40 to 45 minutes, rotating sheet halfway through baking.

2. FOR THE CRUST Meanwhile, adjust oven rack to middle position and heat oven to 325 degrees. Process graham cracker pieces in food processor to fine, even crumbs, about 30 seconds. Sprinkle melted butter and sugar over crumbs and pulse to incorporate, about 5 pulses.

3. Sprinkle mixture into 6-inch pie plate. Using bottom of measuring cup, press crumbs into even layer on bottom and sides of pie plate. Bake until crust is fragrant and beginning to brown, 13 to 18 minutes. Transfer pie plate to wire rack; do not turn oven off. (Crust must still be warm when filling is added.)

4. Pour thickened filling into warm pie crust. Bake pie until center is firm but jiggles slightly, 15 to 20 minutes. Let pie cool slightly on wire rack, about 1 hour; cover loosely with plastic wrap and refrigerate until filling is chilled and set, about 3 hours.

5. FOR THE TOPPING Using hand-held mixer set at medium-low speed, beat cream, sugar, and vanilla in medium bowl until foamy, about 1 minute. Increase speed to high and beat until soft peaks form, 1 to 3 minutes. Spread whipped cream attractively over top of chilled pie, sprinkle with extra lime zest, and serve.

3. Combine apricot preserves and water in bowl and microwave until mixture begins to bubble, about 30 seconds. Brush glaze over apple and let tart cool slightly on sheet for 15 minutes. Serve warm or at room temperature.

MAKING EASY APPLE GALETTE

1. Fold edges of dough over by ¼ inch and crimp to create ¼-inch-thick border.

2. Starting in 1 corner, shingle sliced apples to form even rows across dough, overlapping each slice by about half.

Free-Form Summer Fruit Tartlets

Serves 2   VEGETARIAN

Total time 1½ hours, plus 1 hour 25 minutes chilling and cooling

WHY THIS RECIPE WORKS For an easy yet elegant take on summer fruit pie, we wanted a recipe for individual free-form fruit tarts. We started with an all-butter crust for the best flavor and tender texture. We turned to the French fraisage method to make the pastry, which calls for smearing the dough with the heel of your hand to spread the butter into long, thin streaks, creating lots of flaky layers when the dough is baked. Then we simply rolled out the chilled dough and pleated it loosely around the fruit filling. Taste the fruit before adding sugar to it; use the lesser amount if the fruit is very sweet, more if it is tart. However much sugar you use, do not add it to the fruit until you are ready to fill and form the tart. Serve with vanilla ice cream or Whipped Cream (page 400).

DOUGH

- ¾ cup (3¾ ounces) all-purpose flour
- ¼ teaspoon table salt
- 5 tablespoons unsalted butter, cut into ½-inch pieces and chilled
- 2–3 tablespoons ice water

Free-Form Summer Fruit Tartlets

FILLING

- 8 ounces peaches, nectarines, apricots, or plums, halved, pitted, and cut into ½-inch wedges
- 2½ ounces (½ cup) blackberries, blueberries, or raspberries
- 3–5 tablespoons sugar, divided

1. FOR THE DOUGH Process flour and salt in food processor until combined, about 5 seconds. Scatter butter over top and pulse until mixture resembles coarse crumbs and butter pieces are about size of small peas, 6 to 8 pulses. Continue to pulse, adding 1 tablespoon ice water at a time, until dough begins to form small curds and holds together when pinched with fingers (dough will be crumbly), about 10 pulses.

2. Turn dough crumbs onto lightly floured counter and gather into rectangular-shaped pile about 8 inches long and 3 inches wide, with short side facing you. Starting at farthest end, use heel of your hand to smear small amount of dough against counter. Continue to smear dough until all crumbs have been worked. Gather smeared crumbs together into another rectangular-shaped pile and repeat process. Divide dough in half and form each half into 3-inch disk. Wrap disks tightly in plastic wrap and refrigerate for 1 hour. Let chilled dough sit on counter to soften slightly, about 10 minutes, before rolling. (Wrapped dough can be refrigerated for up to 2 days or frozen for up to 2 months. If frozen, let dough thaw completely on counter before rolling.)

3. Roll each disk of dough into 7-inch circle between 2 small sheets of floured parchment. (If dough sticks to parchment, gently loosen and lift sticky area with bench scraper and dust parchment with additional flour.) Slide dough circles, still between parchment sheets, onto rimmed baking sheet and refrigerate until firm, 15 to 30 minutes. (If refrigerated longer and dough is hard and brittle, let sit at room temperature until pliant.)

4. FOR THE FILLING Adjust oven rack to lower-middle position and heat oven to 400 degrees. Gently toss peaches and blackberries and 2 tablespoons sugar together in bowl. (If fruit tastes tart, add up to 2 tablespoons more sugar.) Remove top sheet of parchment from each dough circle. Mound half of fruit in center of 1 circle, leaving 1½-inch border around edge of fruit. Being careful to leave ½-inch border of dough around edge of fruit, fold outermost 1 inch of dough over fruit, pleating it every 1 to 2 inches as needed; gently pinch pleated dough to secure, but do not press dough into fruit. Repeat with remaining fruit and dough circle.

5. Working quickly, brush top and sides of dough with water and sprinkle tartlets evenly with remaining 1 tablespoon sugar. Bake until crust is deep golden brown and fruit is bubbling, 40 to 45 minutes, rotating sheet halfway through baking.

6. Transfer tartlets with sheet to wire rack and let cool for 10 minutes, then use parchment to gently transfer tartlets to wire rack. Use metal spatula to loosen tartlets from parchment and remove parchment. Let tartlets cool on rack until juices have thickened, about 20 minutes; serve slightly warm or at room temperature.

MAKING FREE-FORM SUMMER FRUIT TARTLETS

1. Roll chilled disks of dough into 7-inch circle between sheets of floured parchment paper. Slide dough circles with parchment onto rimmed baking sheet and refrigerate until firm.

2. Mound half of fruit in center of each circle, leaving 1½-inch border around edge of fruit.

3. Being careful to leave ½-inch border of dough around edge of fruit, fold outermost 1 inch of dough over fruit, pleating it every 1 to 2 inches as needed.

4. Quickly brush top and sides of dough with water and sprinkle with sugar.

Pear Tarte Tatin

Serves 2 `VEGETARIAN`

Total time 1 hour 5 minutes, plus 30 minutes cooling

WHY THIS RECIPE WORKS This classic French dessert is the original skillet dessert—fruit is caramelized, topped with a crust, then served upside down. To streamline it, we used convenient store-bought puff pastry. To give it a modern spin, we used pears in place of the traditional apples. Quartering them before cooking them in the caramel gave the fruit time to absorb the buttery flavor without turning to mush. Then we simply topped the pears with the puff pastry and baked it until golden brown. The pears should be ripe but firm. Be sure to let the puff pastry thaw completely before using; otherwise, it can crack and break apart. To thaw frozen puff pastry, let it sit either in the refrigerator for 24 hours or on the counter for 30 minutes to 1 hour. Use caution around the caramel—it is extremely hot. You will need an ovensafe 8-inch nonstick skillet for this recipe. Serve with vanilla ice cream or Whipped Cream (page 393).

1 (9½ by 9-inch) sheet puff pastry, thawed
2 tablespoons unsalted butter
½ cup (3½ ounces) sugar
3 small ripe but firm Bosc or Bartlett pears (6 ounces each), peeled, halved, cored, and each half halved lengthwise

1. Adjust oven rack to upper-middle position and heat oven to 425 degrees. Roll puff pastry into 10-inch square on lightly floured counter. Using sharp knife, cut pastry into 10-inch circle, then cut four 1-inch vents in center of dough. Slide pastry onto lightly floured large plate, cover, and refrigerate until needed.

2. Melt butter in 8-inch ovensafe nonstick skillet over medium-high heat. Stir in sugar and cook until sugar has dissolved completely and mixture is light golden, about 2 minutes.

3. Off heat, place 1 pear quarter cut side down around edge of skillet, with peeled side touching skillet wall. Continue to shingle 9 more pear quarters around edge of skillet, with narrow ends slightly raised. Place remaining pear quarters cut side down in skillet middle. Cook pears over medium heat until they are light golden brown and caramel is darkly colored, 9 to 11 minutes, turning pears over so peeled sides are facing down halfway through cooking.

4. Off heat, slide chilled dough circle over pears in skillet. Being careful not to burn your fingers, fold back edge of dough so that it fits snugly into skillet. Bake tart until crust is golden brown and crisp, 20 to 25 minutes, rotating skillet halfway through baking.

5. Using potholder (skillet handle will be hot), remove skillet from oven. Let tart cool in skillet for 30 minutes. Run thin knife around edge; place inverted serving platter (or cutting board) over top; and gently flip tart onto platter, using mitts or dish towels if skillet is still hot. Scrape out any pears that stick to skillet and put them back into place on tart. Serve.

MAKING PEAR TARTE TATIN

1. Arrange pear quarters cut side down around edge of skillet, with narrow ends slightly raised. Then place remaining pear quarters cut side down in middle of skillet.

2. After cooking pears in skillet until light golden brown and caramel is darkly colored, slide chilled dough circle over pears.

3. Carefully fold back edge of dough so that it fits snugly into skillet.

4. Once baked tart has cooled, run thin knife around edge of skillet. Place serving platter over skillet, hold tightly, and invert skillet and platter. Set platter on counter and lift skillet off, leaving tart behind.

All-Butter Tart Shells

Makes two 4-inch tart shells   VEGETARIAN
Total time 50 minutes, plus 30 minutes freezing
WHY THIS RECIPE WORKS While pie crust is tender and flaky, classic tart crust should be rich, crisp, and crumbly—almost like shortbread. We love the flavor of an all-butter crust, but the dough can be difficult to work with. To make it easier, we skipped rolling out the dough and instead turned to a pat-in-the-pan-style crust. We started by cutting the butter into the flour (the food processor was an easy way to speed up this task). Once the dough came together, we simply tore it into pieces and pressed it into the pan until we had a cohesive crust. The dough baked as evenly as traditional rolled tart dough, and since the butter was evenly distributed throughout the dough, the crust was exceptionally rich and crisp. You will need two 4-inch fluted tart pans with removable bottoms for this recipe.

½ cup plus 2 tablespoons (3⅛ ounces) all-purpose flour
1½ teaspoons sugar
¼ teaspoon table salt
4 tablespoons unsalted butter, cut into ½-inch pieces and chilled
2–3 tablespoons ice water

1. Grease two 4-inch tart pans with removable bottoms. Process flour, sugar, and salt in food processor until combined, about 5 seconds. Scatter butter over top and pulse until mixture resembles coarse cornmeal, about 15 pulses. Add 2 tablespoons ice water and continue to pulse until large clumps of dough form and no powdery bits remain, about 5 pulses. If dough doesn't clump, add remaining water, 1 teaspoon at a time, and pulse until it does.

2. Divide dough into 2 equal pieces. Tear each piece of dough into walnut-size clumps and spread evenly in bottom of prepared pans. Working outward from center of each pan, press dough into even layer, then press it up sides and into fluted edges of pan. Use your thumb to level off top edges and remove excess dough; use excess dough to patch any holes. Lay plastic wrap over dough in each pan and smooth out any bumps or shallow areas using your fingertips. Place dough-lined tart pans on large plate and freeze until fully chilled and firm, at least 30 minutes or up to 1 day.

3. Adjust oven rack to middle position and heat oven to 375 degrees. Set dough-lined tart pans on rimmed baking sheet. Press parchment paper or double layer of aluminum foil into frozen tart shells, covering edges to prevent burning, and fill with pie weights.

4. Bake tart shells until top edges of dough just start to color and surface of dough under parchment no longer looks wet, about 30 minutes. Carefully remove weights and parchment and continue to bake tart shells until golden brown, 5 to 10 minutes. Transfer tart shells with sheet to wire rack. Use shells while still warm or let cool completely (see individual recipe instructions.)

MAKING A TART SHELL

1. Tear 1 piece of dough into clumps and distribute evenly in bottom of prepared tart pan.

2. Working from center, press dough into even layer and up sides into fluted edges of pan.

3. Use your thumb to level off top edge. Use excess dough to patch any holes.

4. Lay plastic wrap over dough and smooth out any bumps using your fingertips.

Lemon Tarts

Nutella Tarts

Lemon Tarts

Serves 2 VEGETARIAN

Total time 40 minutes, plus 1½ hours cooling

WHY THIS RECIPE WORKS We wanted a proper lemon tart, filled with a creamy lemon curd that possessed a perfectly balanced sweet-tart flavor. For serious lemon flavor, we used ¼ cup of juice and a whopping tablespoon of zest. Then we added just enough sugar—⅓ cup—to balance the bracing acidity of the lemons. To ensure our lemon curd was creamy and dense, with a vibrant yellow color, we used one whole egg along with three egg yolks. A little butter added richness. For a smooth, light texture, we strained the curd and then stirred in heavy cream just before baking. Once the lemon curd ingredients are combined, cook the curd immediately; otherwise, it will have a grainy consistency. It is important to add the filling to the tart shell while it is still warm; if the shell has cooled, rewarm it in the oven for 5 minutes before adding the filling. Dust with confectioners' sugar or serve with Whipped Cream (page 393).

- 1 large egg plus 3 large yolks
- ⅓ cup (2⅓ ounces) sugar
- 1 tablespoon grated lemon zest plus ¼ cup juice (2 lemons)
  Pinch table salt
- 2 tablespoons unsalted butter, cut into 2 pieces
- 1 tablespoon heavy cream, chilled
- 1 recipe All-Butter Tart Shells (page 411), still warm

1. Adjust oven rack to middle position and heat oven to 375 degrees. Whisk egg and yolks together in small saucepan. Whisk in sugar until combined, then whisk in lemon zest and juice and salt. Add butter and cook over medium-low heat, stirring constantly, until mixture thickens slightly and registers 170 degrees, 5 to 7 minutes. Immediately pour mixture through fine-mesh strainer into bowl and stir in cream.

2. Divide warm lemon filling evenly between warm prebaked tart shells and smooth tops. Place tarts on rimmed baking sheet and bake until filling is opaque and centers jiggle slightly when gently shaken, about 10 minutes, rotating sheet halfway through baking.

3. Transfer tarts with sheet to wire rack and let cool to room temperature, about 1½ hours. To serve, remove outer metal ring of tart pans, slide thin metal spatula between tarts and tart pan bottoms, and carefully slide tarts onto individual plates.

Nutella Tarts

Serves 2   `VEGETARIAN`

Total time 15 minutes, plus 1¾ hours chilling

WHY THIS RECIPE WORKS For amazingly simple yet showstopping individual tarts, we started with our flaky and flavorful All-Butter Tart Shells. For the base of the filling, we relied on Nutella, a creamy and incredibly crave-worthy hazelnut-chocolate spread. To the Nutella we added heavy cream, butter, and a little bittersweet chocolate for silky richness. A sprinkling of chopped hazelnuts in the bottom of each tart shell added a welcome crunch and textural contrast to the smooth, creamy filling. And because this easy filling required no baking, all we had to do was pour it into the tart shells and let it set. Garnished with whole toasted hazelnuts, these tarts are sure to impress. Serve with Whipped Cream (page 393).

⅓ cup hazelnuts, toasted and skinned, divided
1 recipe All-Butter Tart Shells (page 411), cooled
½ cup Nutella
3 tablespoons heavy cream
1 ounce bittersweet chocolate, chopped
1 tablespoon unsalted butter

1. Reserve 16 whole hazelnuts for garnish, then chop remaining hazelnuts coarse. Sprinkle half of chopped hazelnuts in bottom of each cooled prebaked tart shell.

2. Microwave Nutella, cream, chocolate, and butter together in covered bowl at 30 percent power, stirring often, until mixture is smooth and glossy, about 1 minute (do not overheat). Divide warm Nutella filling evenly between tart shells and smooth tops.

3. Refrigerate tarts until filling is just set, about 15 minutes. Arrange reserved whole hazelnuts evenly around edge of tarts and continue to refrigerate until filling is firm, about 1½ hours. To serve, remove outer metal ring of tart pans, slide thin metal spatula between tarts and tart pan bottoms, and carefully slide tarts onto individual plates.

Pecan Tarts

Serves 2   `VEGETARIAN`

Total time 40 minutes, plus 1½ hours cooling

WHY THIS RECIPE WORKS We wanted a recipe for individual pecan tarts with a rich, smooth, cohesive filling that was subtly sweet. We used our easy pat-in-the-pan All-Butter Tart Shells as the base for the filling. Dark brown sugar added rich caramel notes that nicely complemented the pecans, and swapping some of the sugar for a little corn syrup ensured that the filling was smooth, not gritty. A pinch of salt balanced the sweetness, preventing the tarts from being cloying. A little vanilla extract rounded out all the flavors, and just one egg yolk was all we needed to ensure that the filling set up properly. Because the pecans were the star the show, we chopped them coarse before adding them to the filling to ensure that we had nuts in every bite. Serve with vanilla ice cream or Whipped Cream (page 393).

¼ cup packed (1¾ ounces) dark brown sugar
3 tablespoons light corn syrup
2 tablespoons unsalted butter
   Pinch table salt
1 large egg yolk
½ teaspoon vanilla extract
½ cup pecans, toasted and chopped coarse
1 recipe All-Butter Tart Shells (page 411), cooled

1. Adjust oven rack to middle position and heat oven to 325 degrees. Heat sugar and corn syrup together in small saucepan over medium heat, stirring occasionally, until sugar dissolves, about 2 minutes. Off heat, whisk in butter and salt until butter is melted. Whisk in egg yolk and vanilla until combined. Stir in pecans.

2. Divide warm pecan mixture evenly between cooled prebaked tart shells and smooth tops. Place tarts on rimmed baking sheet and bake until centers jiggle slightly when gently shaken, 10 to 15 minutes, rotating sheet halfway through baking.

3. Transfer tarts with sheet to wire rack and let cool to room temperature, about 1½ hours. To serve, remove outer metal ring of tart pans, slide thin metal spatula between tarts and tart pan bottoms, and carefully slide tarts onto individual plates.

CHAPTER 17

Cookies, Cakes & Custards

▦ **FAST** (Start to finish in 30 minutes or less)
▦ **VEGETARIAN**

Opposite: Rustic Peach Cakes

Chewy Chocolate Chip Cookies

Makes 12 cookies VEGETARIAN
Total time 50 minutes

WHY THIS RECIPE WORKS Most cookie recipes leave the baker with a yield that's far larger than what can be eaten by two before they go stale. We wanted to develop a recipe for the perfect chewy chocolate chip cookie that would yield a mini batch of 12 cookies. To keep our recipe quick and convenient, we also wanted to eliminate the need to lug out an electric mixer. Rather than creaming the butter and sugar, we melted the butter so that we could simply stir everything together in one bowl. Gently folding the dry ingredients into the wet ingredients ensured that our cookies were tender and chewy, not tough. A combination of granulated and brown sugars plus a dash of vanilla extract gave the cookies a subtle caramelized flavor. To avoid overbaking, pull the cookies out of the oven when they are still slightly underbaked in the center; they will finish cooking on the baking sheet.

    1 cup (5 ounces) all-purpose flour
    ½ teaspoon baking soda
    ¼ teaspoon table salt
    ½ cup packed (3½ ounces) light brown sugar
    ¼ cup (1¾ ounces) granulated sugar
    5 tablespoons unsalted butter, melted and cooled
    1 large egg
    1½ teaspoons vanilla extract
    1 cup (6 ounces) semisweet chocolate chips

1. Adjust oven rack to middle position and heat oven to 350 degrees. Line baking sheet with parchment paper. Whisk flour, baking soda, and salt together in bowl.

2. Whisk brown sugar and granulated sugar together in medium bowl. Whisk in melted butter until combined. Whisk in egg and vanilla until smooth. Gently stir in flour mixture with rubber spatula until soft dough forms. Fold in chocolate chips.

3. Working with 2 tablespoons dough at a time, roll into balls and space them 2 inches apart on prepared sheet.

4. Bake cookies until edges are set but centers are still soft and puffy, about 14 minutes, rotating sheet halfway through baking. Let cookies cool slightly on sheet. Serve warm or at room temperature. (Cookies can be stored at room temperature for up to 3 days.)

Edible Cookie Dough

Serves 2 FAST VEGETARIAN
Total time 25 minutes

WHY THIS RECIPE WORKS Whether you're nurturing a bout of childhood nostalgia or you simply don't want to turn on your oven, look to this recipe, which is easily (and safely) made using pantry ingredients. The key to making edible dough is more than just nixing the egg and leaveners, though. Flour is also unsafe to eat raw, so microwave it to zap any potential bacteria. Brown sugar delivers the caramelized flavor that you'd normally get from baking. Mini chocolate chips distribute themselves evenly throughout the dough, but feel free to use any chips you have on hand, or chop up a bar. Or substitute Reese's Pieces, peanut butter chips, chopped nuts, crushed Oreos, or sprinkles. Best of all, you can easily double or triple this recipe, freeze the extra dough balls, and save them for a rainy day.

    ¼ cup (1¼ ounces) all-purpose flour
    2 tablespoons unsalted butter, softened
    2 tablespoons packed brown sugar
    2 tablespoons mini chocolate chips
    2 teaspoons milk
    ¼ teaspoon vanilla extract
    ⅛ teaspoon table salt

1. Microwave flour in small bowl for 45 seconds; set aside to cool, about 3 minutes.

2. Using rubber spatula, mash butter and sugar together in separate bowl until well combined and lightened in color. Stir in cooled flour, chocolate chips, milk, vanilla, and salt until combined. Refrigerate until firm, about 15 minutes. Roll into 6 balls and serve.

NOTES FROM THE TEST KITCHEN

FREEZING COOKIE DOUGH
Keeping frozen cookie dough on hand means that you can bake as many, or as few, cookies as you like. To freeze the dough, form it into balls, arrange the balls on a baking sheet, and place the sheet in the freezer. Once the individual balls of dough are frozen, place them in a zipper-lock freezer bag and store them in the freezer. To bake, line a baking sheet with parchment paper and place on top of a second baking sheet. Arrange the frozen cookies (do not thaw) on the prepared sheet and bake as directed, increasing the baking time by 5 to 10 minutes.

Oatmeal-Raisin Cookies

Makes 12 cookies VEGETARIAN

Total time 50 minutes

WHY THIS RECIPE WORKS It took 30 batches of oatmeal cookies before we figured out how to make our ideal oatmeal cookie—with lots of oat flavor, crisp around the edges, and chewy in the middle. To pack the cookies with oat flavor, we used a high ratio of oats to flour. Old-fashioned rolled oats provided the best flavor; instant and quick oats lacked oat flavor and made the cookies dry and mealy. Swapping some of the granulated sugar for brown sugar complemented the nutty oats and gave us moister, chewier cookies. Since the oats weighed down the batter, we needed to add extra liquid to get the cookies to spread correctly and to ensure that they weren't dry or crumbly. Milk added more body and flavor than plain water; just a couple of tablespoons did the trick. Do not substitute quick or instant oats in this recipe.

1¼ cups (3¾ ounces) old-fashioned rolled oats

½ cup plus 2 tablespoons (3⅛ ounces) all-purpose flour

¼ teaspoon baking powder

¼ teaspoon table salt

⅛ teaspoon ground cinnamon

½ cup packed (3½ ounces) brown sugar

¼ cup (1¾ ounces) granulated sugar

6 tablespoons unsalted butter, melted and cooled

1 large egg yolk

2 tablespoons whole milk

¾ teaspoon vanilla extract

⅓ cup raisins

1. Adjust oven rack to middle position and heat oven to 350 degrees. Line baking sheet with parchment paper. Whisk oats, flour, baking powder, salt, and cinnamon together in bowl.

2. Whisk brown sugar and granulated sugar together in medium bowl. Whisk in melted butter until combined. Whisk in egg yolk, milk, and vanilla until smooth. Gently stir in oat mixture with rubber spatula until soft dough forms. Fold in raisins.

3. Working with heaping 1½ tablespoons dough at a time, roll into balls and space them 2 inches apart on prepared sheet. Using bottom of greased drinking glass, flatten dough balls until 2½ inches in diameter.

4. Bake cookies until edges are set and beginning to brown, about 15 minutes, rotating sheet halfway through baking. Let cookies cool slightly on sheet. Serve warm or at room temperature. (Cookies can be stored at room temperature for up to 3 days.)

Edible Cookie Dough

Oatmeal-Raisin Cookies

Molasses Spice Cookies

¼ teaspoon ground cloves
⅛ teaspoon finely ground pepper
⅛ teaspoon table salt
2 tablespoons plus ¼ cup (1¾ ounces) granulated sugar, divided
3 tablespoons packed dark brown sugar
6 tablespoons unsalted butter, melted and cooled
¼ cup molasses
1 large egg yolk
½ teaspoon vanilla extract

1. Adjust oven rack to middle position and heat oven to 350 degrees. Line baking sheet with parchment paper. Whisk flour, cinnamon, ginger, baking soda, cloves, pepper, and salt together in bowl. Place 2 tablespoons granulated sugar in shallow dish.

2. Whisk brown sugar and remaining ¼ cup granulated sugar together in medium bowl. Whisk in melted butter until combined. Whisk in molasses, egg yolk, and vanilla until smooth. Gently stir in flour mixture with rubber spatula until soft dough forms.

3. Working with heaping 1½ tablespoons dough at a time, roll into balls. Roll dough balls in granulated sugar to coat, then space balls 2 inches apart on prepared sheet. Using bottom of greased drinking glass, flatten dough balls until 2 inches in diameter. Sprinkle tops of cookies evenly with 2 teaspoons of granulated sugar remaining in shallow dish from rolling. Discard remaining sugar.

4. Bake cookies until edges are set and beginning to brown, 10 to 12 minutes, rotating sheet halfway through baking. Let cookies cool slightly on sheet. Serve warm or at room temperature. (Cookies can be stored at room temperature for up to 3 days.)

Molasses Spice Cookies

Makes 12 cookies VEGETARIAN
Total time 50 minutes

WHY THIS RECIPE WORKS Our ultimate molasses spice cookie is soft, chewy, and gently spiced with deep, dark molasses flavor. Using just the right amount of molasses and brown sugar and flavoring the cookies with a combination of vanilla, ginger, cinnamon, cloves, and black pepper gave these spiced cookies the warm flavor and subtle bite that we were after. Baking soda was essential to create the traditional cracks and crinkles so characteristic of these charming cookies, and rolling the dough in granulated sugar before baking gave the soft cookies sparkling sweet crunch. We pulled the cookies from the oven when the edges were just set; residual heat finished the baking and kept the cookies chewy and moist. Light or mild molasses gives the cookies a milder flavor; for a stronger flavor, use robust or full molasses.

1 cup plus 2 tablespoons (5⅔ ounces) all-purpose flour
¾ teaspoon ground cinnamon
¾ teaspoon ground ginger
½ teaspoon baking soda

SHAPING MOLASSES SPICE COOKIES

1. Take 1½ tablespoons dough and roll it between your palms into ball. Roll ball of dough in sugar, then place it on prepared sheet.

2. Use greased drinking glass with flat bottom or measuring cup to flatten balls of dough until 2 inches in diameter. Sprinkle tops with sugar.

ALL ABOUT SUGAR

Sugar not only adds sweetness to baked goods, it affects texture too. The amount or type of sugar can make a cookie crisp or chewy. Here are the most common types of sugar we use in baking.

WHITE GRANULATED SUGAR Made either from sugar cane or sugar beets, this is the type of sugar used most often in our recipes. It has a clean flavor, and its evenly ground, loose texture ensures that it incorporates well with butter when creaming and dissolves easily into batters.

CONFECTIONERS' SUGAR Also called powdered sugar, this is the most finely ground sugar. It is most commonly used for dusting cakes and cookies and for making quick glazes and icings. To prevent clumping, confectioners' sugar contains a small amount of cornstarch. You can also approximate confectioners' sugar with this method: For 1 cup of confectioners' sugar, process 1 cup of granulated sugar with 1 tablespoon of cornstarch in a blender (not a food processor) until fine, 30 to 40 seconds.

TURBINADO AND DEMERARA SUGAR These "raw" sugars have large crystals that do not readily dissolve—a reason to avoid them in dough. Instead, we like to sprinkle them on muffin tops to create crunch or use them to form the caramel crust on Crème Brûlée (page 444).

BROWN SUGAR Brown sugar is simply granulated white sugar that has been combined with molasses. (When necessary, our ingredient list will indicate "light" or "dark" brown sugar. If either can be used, we simply list "brown sugar.") Store brown sugar in an airtight container to prevent it from drying out. To approximate 1 cup of light brown sugar, pulse 1 cup of granulated sugar with 1 tablespoon of mild molasses in a food processor until blended. Use 2 tablespoons of molasses for dark brown sugar.

MEASURING SUGAR

Weighing sugar is always the most accurate, but if you're measuring sugar by volume, it's important to use the best method. White sugar should be measured with the dip-and-sweep method: Dip the measuring cup into the sugar and sweep away the excess with a straight-edged object like the back of a butter knife. Brown sugar, on the other hand, is so moist and clumpy that it must be packed into the measuring cup to get an accurate measurement. Fill the dry measure with brown sugar and use the next smallest cup to pack it down. For instance, if you need ⅓ cup of packed brown sugar, use the bottom of the ¼-cup measure to pack it down. When properly packed, 1 cup of brown sugar should weigh the same as 1 cup of granulated sugar: 7 ounces.

REVIVING HARDENED BROWN SUGAR

If your brown sugar dries out, place the sugar in a zipper-lock bag, add a slice of bread, and set it aside overnight until the sugar is soft again. Or, quicker yet, put the brown sugar in a microwave-safe bowl with the bread and tightly cover with plastic wrap. Microwave until the sugar is moist, 15 to 30 seconds.

Cornmeal Olive Oil Cookies

Makes 12 cookies   VEGETARIAN

Total time 50 minutes

WHY THIS RECIPE WORKS For these lightly sweetened Italian-style cookies, we combined subtly sweet cornmeal and aromatic rosemary with peppery extra-virgin olive oil. To hold the savory flavors of these cookies in check, we used two different types of sugar. One-quarter cup of granulated sugar in the dough contributed a mild sweetness and cakey texture, while rolling the warm cookies in confectioners' sugar lent a second layer of sweetness. Fresh rosemary provided deep floral and herbal notes. These sophisticated cookies pair equally well with a hot cup of tea or coffee, or a glass of wine.

- ¾ cup (3¾ ounces) all-purpose flour
- ¼ cup (1¼ ounces) cornmeal
- ½ teaspoon baking powder
- ⅛ teaspoon table salt
- ⅓ cup extra-virgin olive oil
- ¼ cup (1¾ ounces) granulated sugar
- 1 large egg
- ½ teaspoon minced fresh rosemary
- ⅓ cup (1⅓ ounces) confectioners' sugar, plus extra as needed

1. Adjust oven rack to middle position and heat oven to 375 degrees. Line baking sheet with parchment paper. Whisk flour, cornmeal, baking powder, and salt together in bowl.

2. Whisk oil and granulated sugar together in medium bowl until combined. Whisk in egg and rosemary until smooth. Gently stir in flour mixture with rubber spatula until soft dough forms.

3. Working with 1 tablespoon dough at a time, roll into balls and space them 2 inches apart on prepared sheet.

4. Bake cookies until edges are lightly golden and centers puff and split open, about 13 minutes, rotating sheet halfway through baking. Let cookies cool slightly on sheet. Place confectioners' sugar in bowl, then gently roll warm cookies in sugar to coat. Dust with extra confectioners' sugar as desired before serving. Serve warm or at room temperature. (Cookies can be stored at room temperature for up to 3 days.)

Peanut Butter–Chocolate Quesadillas

Serves 2 ‎ **FAST** ‎ **VEGETARIAN**
Total time 20 minutes

WHY THIS RECIPE WORKS A flour tortilla serves as a cross between a crepe and a pancake in this warm, satisfying dessert (or anytime snack) that comes together in just a few minutes and offers far greater rewards—but no greater effort—than making a PB&J. There's no queso in this quesadilla; instead, you'll spread peanut butter (creamy or crunchy) over half of a tortilla, top the nut butter with a handful of chocolate chips, and fold the tortilla in half. Toast the quesadilla in a little butter until it's crispy and browned, the peanut butter is warmed through, and the chocolate chips are melty. As you might imagine, this template lends itself beautifully to improvisation with other fillings and toppings. Add some thinly sliced bananas, apples, or strawberries along with the chocolate chips. Sprinkle with confectioners' sugar, if you like.

2 (10-inch) flour tortillas
¼ cup creamy or chunky peanut butter
2 tablespoons chocolate chips
2 tablespoons unsalted butter, divided

1. Lay tortillas on cutting board. Spread 2 tablespoons peanut butter over half of each tortilla, leaving ½-inch border around edge. Sprinkle 1 tablespoon chocolate chips over peanut butter on each tortilla, then fold other half of tortilla over top.

Peanut Butter–Chocolate Quesadillas

2. Melt 1 tablespoon butter in 10- or 12-inch nonstick skillet over medium-low heat. Place 1 filled tortilla in skillet and cook until crispy and well browned, about 2 minutes. Flip tortilla and cook until second side is crispy and well browned, 1 to 2 minutes. Transfer quesadilla to cutting board and let cool slightly. Repeat with remaining 1 tablespoon butter and remaining filled tortilla. Cut into wedges and serve.

Fudgy Brownies

Makes 8 brownies   VEGETARIAN

Total time 55 minutes, plus 30 minutes cooling

WHY THIS RECIPE WORKS Everyone loves brownies, but a full pan of brownies for two is way too much for even the most ardent brownie lovers. To scale back our batch of fudgy brownies, we ditched the large baking dish in favor of a loaf pan, which made just eight brownies—perfect for two people to enjoy over a few days. Two types of chocolate—semisweet chocolate and cocoa powder—gave us plenty of fudgy flavor. To make our batter easy to mix by hand, we melted the semi-sweet chocolate quickly in the microwave. A whole egg plus an extra yolk made our brownies rich, moist, and chewy. The deep sides of the loaf pan made it hard to cut the brownies neatly, so we lined the pan with a foil sling that allowed us to lift the brownies out in one piece before cutting. Be careful not to overbake these brownies or they will have a very dry, cakey texture. The test kitchen's preferred loaf pan measures 8½ by 4½ inches; if you use a 9 by 5-inch loaf pan, start checking for doneness 5 minutes earlier than advised in the recipe.

3½ ounces semisweet chocolate, chopped
4 tablespoons unsalted butter, cut into 4 pieces
1 tablespoon unsweetened cocoa powder
½ cup plus 2 tablespoons (4⅓ ounces) sugar
1 large egg plus 1 large yolk
1 teaspoon vanilla extract
¼ teaspoon table salt
½ cup (2½ ounces) all-purpose flour

1. Adjust oven rack to middle position and heat oven to 350 degrees. Make foil sling for 8½ by 4½-inch loaf pan by folding 2 long sheets of aluminum foil; first sheet should be 8½ inches wide and second sheet should be 4½ inches wide. Lay sheets of foil in pan perpendicular to each other, with extra foil hanging over edges of pan. Push foil into corners and up sides of pan, smoothing foil flush to pan. Grease foil.

2. Microwave chocolate, butter, and cocoa in bowl at 50 percent power, stirring occasionally, until melted and smooth, 1 to 3 minutes; let cool slightly. Whisk sugar, egg and yolk, vanilla, and salt together in medium bowl until combined. Whisk in melted chocolate mixture until combined. Stir in flour with rubber spatula until just combined.

3. Transfer batter to prepared pan; spread batter into corners of pan and smooth surface. Bake until toothpick inserted in center comes out with a few moist crumbs attached, 24 to 28 minutes, rotating pan halfway through baking. Let brownies cool completely in pan on wire rack. Remove brownies from pan using foil, loosening sides with paring knife, if needed. Cut brownies into 2-inch squares and serve. (Brownies can be stored at room temperature for up to 3 days.)

Blondies

Makes 8 bars   VEGETARIAN

Total time 50 minutes, plus 30 minutes cooling

WHY THIS RECIPE WORKS Although blondies are baked in a pan like brownies, the flavorings are similar to those in chocolate chip cookies—vanilla, butter, and brown sugar, often laced with nuts and chocolate chips. But blondies can be bland, floury, and dry. We set out to fix the blondie so it would be chewy but not dense, sweet but not cloying, and loaded with nuts and chocolate. For deep caramelized flavor, we eliminated the granulated sugar and used only brown sugar to make our bars. A combination of semisweet and white chocolate chips highlighted the vanilla and caramel flavors, and chopped pecans added crunch and nutty richness. Walnuts can be substituted for the pecans. The test kitchen's preferred loaf pan measures 8½ by 4½ inches; if you use a 9 by 5-inch loaf pan, start checking for doneness 5 minutes earlier than advised in the recipe.

½ cup (2½ ounces) all-purpose flour
½ teaspoon baking powder
¼ teaspoon table salt
½ cup packed (3½ ounces) light brown sugar
3 tablespoons unsalted butter, melted and cooled
1 large egg
1½ teaspoons vanilla extract
⅓ cup pecans, toasted and chopped
2 tablespoons semisweet chocolate chips
2 tablespoons white chocolate chips

1. Adjust oven rack to middle position and heat oven to 350 degrees. Make foil sling for 8½ by 4½-inch loaf pan by folding 2 long sheets of aluminum foil; first sheet should be 8½ inches wide and second sheet should be 4½ inches wide. Lay sheets of foil in pan perpendicular to each other, with extra foil hanging over edges of pan. Push foil into corners and up sides of pan, smoothing foil flush to pan. Grease foil.

2. Whisk flour, baking powder, and salt together in bowl. In large bowl, whisk sugar and melted butter until combined. Whisk in egg and vanilla until smooth. Stir in flour mixture with rubber spatula until just combined. Fold in pecans and semisweet and white chocolate chips.

3. Transfer batter to prepared pan; spread batter into corners of pan and smooth surface. Bake until toothpick inserted in center comes out clean, 20 to 25 minutes, rotating pan halfway through baking. Let bars cool completely in pan on wire rack. Remove bars from pan using foil, loosening sides with paring knife, if needed. Cut into 2-inch squares and serve. (Bars can be stored at room temperature for up to 3 days.)

Chocolate and Peanut Butter Oatmeal Bars

Makes 8 bars `VEGETARIAN`

Total time 20 minutes, plus 30 minutes freezing

WHY THIS RECIPE WORKS Chocolate and peanut butter are an irresistible combination. Add nutty, buttery oats to make easy no-cook treats and you've got a surefire winner. But old-fashioned, instant, and quick-cooking oats each tasted dry and dusty in the bars. Granola, which is already fully cooked, proved to be the solution; it tasted great right out of the package. For the chocolate, we mixed crumbled chocolate wafers in with the oats and peanut butter, then topped the bars with a layer of melted semisweet chocolate. Look for a simply flavored oat-and-nut-based granola; avoid granola with dried fruit. If the granola has large clumps, place it in a zipper-lock bag and gently break it into small pieces with a mallet or rolling pin. Do not substitute crunchy peanut butter here. You can substitute ⅓ cup semisweet chocolate chips for the semisweet chocolate.

3 ounces chocolate wafer cookies, crumbled
½ cup (2 ounces) granola, crushed into small pieces
¼ cup (1 ounce) confectioners' sugar
2 tablespoons unsalted butter
½ cup smooth peanut butter, divided
2 ounces semisweet chocolate, chopped

1. Make foil sling for 8½ by 4½-inch loaf pan by folding 2 long sheets of aluminum foil; first sheet should be 8½ inches wide and second sheet should be 4½ inches wide. Lay sheets of foil in pan perpendicular to each other, with extra foil hanging over edges of pan. Push foil into corners and up sides of pan, smoothing foil flush to pan. Grease foil.

2. Process crumbled chocolate wafers in food processor to fine, even crumbs, about 30 seconds. Combine wafer crumbs, granola, and sugar in medium bowl. Microwave butter in second medium bowl until melted, about 30 seconds, then whisk in 6 tablespoons peanut butter until combined. Stir peanut butter mixture into wafer-granola mixture until combined. Scrape mixture into prepared pan and press firmly into even layer with greased spatula. Freeze, uncovered, until firm, about 20 minutes.

3. Microwave chocolate in bowl at 50 percent power, stirring occasionally, until melted and smooth, about 2 minutes. Spread melted chocolate evenly over top of frozen mixture. Microwave remaining 2 tablespoons peanut butter in clean bowl until warm, about 1 minute, then drizzle attractively over top. Freeze, uncovered, until chocolate has hardened, about 10 minutes.

4. Remove bars from pan using foil, loosening sides with paring knife, if needed. Cut into 2-inch squares and serve. (Bars can be stored at room temperature for up to 2 days.)

MAKING A FOIL SLING

1. Place 2 sheets of aluminum foil perpendicular to each other in loaf pan, pushing foil into corners. Smooth foil flush to pan.

2. Use foil handles to lift baked brownies or bars from pan.

Summer Berry Snack Cakes

Serves 2   VEGETARIAN

Total time 50 minutes, plus 1 hour 10 minutes cooling

WHY THIS RECIPE WORKS Unlike fancy layer cakes, snack cakes come together in just minutes with little effort, making them a perfect no-fuss dessert for two. We wanted to make two simple single-serving vanilla-scented cakes dotted with juicy bites of fresh berries. Getting the right ratio of tart berries to sweet cake was key; too many berries made the cakes wet and dense, but ½ cup of berries gave us just the right balance. To give the cakes a light, airy texture, we creamed the softened butter and sugar together before adding egg, vanilla, flour, and milk. Dusting the cooled cakes with powdered sugar gave them a delicate finish. You will need a tray-style mini Bundt pan or two single 1-cup Bundt pans for this recipe—the center tube is necessary for even baking.

½ cup (2½ ounces) all-purpose flour
½ teaspoon baking powder
⅛ teaspoon table salt
3 tablespoons unsalted butter, softened
¼ cup (1¾ ounces) granulated sugar
1 large egg, room temperature
¼ teaspoon vanilla extract
2 tablespoons whole milk, room temperature
2½ ounces (½ cup) blueberries and/or raspberries
   Confectioners' sugar

1. Adjust oven rack to middle position and heat oven to 350 degrees. Spray two 1-cup Bundt pans with baking spray with flour. Whisk flour, baking powder, and salt together in bowl.

2. Using hand-held mixer set at low speed, beat butter and granulated sugar in medium bowl until sugar is moistened, about 1 minute. Increase speed to medium-high and beat mixture until pale and fluffy, about 3 minutes, scraping down sides of bowl as needed. Add egg and vanilla and beat until combined, about 30 seconds. Reduce speed to low and add flour mixture in 3 additions, alternating with milk in 2 additions (batter will be quite thick). Gently fold in blueberries with rubber spatula.

3. Divide batter evenly between prepared pans, smooth tops, and gently tap each pan on counter to release air bubbles. Wipe any drops of batter off sides of pans. Place pans on rimmed baking sheet and bake cakes until toothpick inserted in center comes out clean, 20 to 30 minutes, rotating sheet halfway through baking.

4. Let cakes cool in pans on wire rack for 10 minutes. Remove cakes from pans and let cool completely on rack, about 1 hour. Dust with confectioners' sugar and serve.

Angel Food Cakes

Angel Food Cakes

Serves 2   VEGETARIAN

Total time 1 hour, plus 1 hour cooling

WHY THIS RECIPE WORKS Because it requires a delicate balance of ingredients, angel food cake is particularly tricky to scale for two. Two small, 2-cup tube pans made elegant single-serving cakes. For voluminous whipped egg whites, cream of tartar offered extra insurance against deflation. Cake flour was essential for a delicate crumb. Inverting the pans while the cakes rested ensured that the cakes didn't sink as they cooled. You will need two 2-cup tube pans and either two 5- or 6-inch kitchen funnels or two chopsticks and two empty beer bottles for this recipe. If your tube pans do not have removable bottoms, line the bottoms with parchment paper. Serve with fresh berries and Whipped Cream (page 393).

6 tablespoons (1½ ounces) cake flour
½ cup (3½ ounces) sugar, divided
   Pinch table salt
3 large egg whites, room temperature
½ teaspoon cream of tartar
¼ teaspoon vanilla extract

1. Adjust oven rack to lower-middle position and heat oven to 325 degrees. Whisk flour, ¼ cup sugar, and salt together in bowl.

2. Using hand-held mixer set at medium-low speed, beat egg whites and cream of tartar in large bowl until foamy, about 1 minute. Increase speed to medium-high and beat whites to soft, billowy mounds, about 1 minute. Gradually add remaining ¼ cup sugar and beat until glossy, soft peaks form, 1 to 3 minutes. Whisk in vanilla by hand.

3. Sift flour mixture over egg whites in 2 additions, folding gently with rubber spatula after each addition until combined.

4. Divide batter evenly between two 2-cup tube pans and smooth tops. Wipe any drops of batter off sides of pans. Place pans on rimmed baking sheet and bake cakes until toothpick inserted in center comes out clean and any cracks in cakes appear dry, 30 to 35 minutes.

5. Invert each cake pan over upside-down kitchen funnel or over empty beer bottle with chopstick set inside. Let cakes cool completely in pans, about 1 hour. Run thin knife around edges of cakes to loosen, then gently tap pans upside down on counter to release cakes. Turn cakes right side up onto plates and serve.

VARIATIONS
Chocolate-Almond Angel Food Cakes

Substitute ¼ teaspoon almond extract for vanilla extract and add ½ ounce finely grated bittersweet chocolate to egg whites with flour mixture in step 3.

Café au Lait Angel Food Cakes

Add ½ teaspoon instant espresso powder to flour mixture in step 1. Substitute ½ teaspoon coffee liqueur, such as Kahlúa, for vanilla extract in step 2.

TWO WAYS TO COOL ANGEL FOOD CAKES

A. Set two 5- or 6-inch kitchen funnels upside down on counter. Invert 1 cake over each funnel.

B. Place chopstick in empty bottle; repeat setup. Invert each cake over 1 chopstick, balancing it on mouth of bottle.

Lemon–Poppy Seed Pound Cake

Lemon–Poppy Seed Pound Cake

Makes one 5½ by 3-inch loaf   **VEGETARIAN**
Total time 1 hour, plus 1 hour 10 minutes cooling

WHY THIS RECIPE WORKS Lemon–poppy seed pound cake is a classic, but most versions lack true lemon flavor. We wanted an easy recipe for a truly lemony pound cake that would serve just two. Adjusting the size was an easy fix: We ditched our regular loaf pan in favor of a small, 5½ by 3-inch loaf pan. Next, we set out to make the cake failproof. Cake flour and baking powder produced a tender crumb. Mixing the poppy seeds with a small amount of flour helped to distribute them evenly in the cake. For bold lemon flavor throughout, we used both lemon zest and fresh lemon juice. To finish it off, we brushed the cake with a simple lemon glaze, poking small holes in the cake to help the glaze sink in. Substituting all-purpose flour for cake flour will result in a denser cake. You will need a 5½ by 3-inch loaf pan or a 2½-cup pan of a similar shape for this recipe.

CAKE

½ cup (2 ounces) cake flour

¼ teaspoon baking powder

⅛ teaspoon table salt

4 teaspoons poppy seeds

⅓ cup (2⅓ ounces) sugar

4 tablespoons unsalted butter, melted and cooled

1 large egg, room temperature

1½ teaspoons grated lemon zest plus ½ teaspoon juice

¼ teaspoon vanilla extract

LEMON GLAZE

2 tablespoons sugar

1 tablespoon lemon juice

1. FOR THE CAKE Adjust oven rack to middle position and heat oven to 325 degrees. Grease and flour 5½ by 3-inch loaf pan.

2. Whisk flour, baking powder, and salt together in bowl. In small bowl, combine 1 tablespoon flour mixture and poppy seeds.

3. In medium bowl, whisk sugar, melted butter, egg, lemon zest and juice, and vanilla together until smooth. Whisk in remaining flour mixture in 2 additions until a few streaks of flour remain. Gently whisk in poppy seed mixture until most of lumps are gone (do not overmix). Give batter final stir with rubber spatula.

4. Scrape batter into prepared pan and smooth top. Wipe any drops of batter off sides of pan and gently tap pan on counter to release air bubbles. Bake cake until toothpick inserted in center comes out with a few moist crumbs attached, 30 to 40 minutes, rotating pan halfway through baking. Let cake cool in pan on wire rack for 10 minutes, then turn onto rack. Poke cake's top and sides with toothpick.

5. FOR THE LEMON GLAZE Combine sugar and lemon juice in bowl and microwave until sugar dissolves and mixture thickens slightly, about 1 minute, stirring halfway through microwaving. Brush top and sides of cake with warm glaze and let cool completely on rack, about 1 hour, before serving.

NOTES FROM THE TEST KITCHEN

THE IMPORTANCE OF TEMPERATURE IN BAKING

EGGS AND MILK Temperature plays an important role in the behavior of ingredients in baking. Cakes often use room-temperature eggs and milk. Room-temperature eggs and milk are more easily incorporated than cold, and the additional mixing necessary to incorporate cold ingredients may adversely affect the batter and, ultimately, the texture of the baked good. Because recipes for two call for only small amounts of liquid ingredients like milk and butter-milk, you can simply set them on the counter while you prep the rest of the recipe. Eggs, however, take about an hour to come to room temperature on their own. To warm them quickly, put whole eggs in a small bowl of warm water (about 110 degrees) for about 5 minutes.

BUTTER The temperature of butter in particular makes a difference in many recipes and can dramatically affect the texture of finished baked goods. For example, pie dough made with warm or room-temperature butter rather than chilled butter will be nearly impossible to roll out, and the resulting crust will be hard and tough rather than tender and flaky. On the other hand, many cakes and cookies require softened butter for creaming; softened butter blends easily with the sugar, and this action incorporates air into the dough or batter, creating tender baked goods.

Generally, recipes will call for butter chilled, softened, or melted and cooled. Chilled butter (about 35 degrees) should be cold and unyielding when pressed with a finger. To chill butter quickly, cut it into small pieces and freeze until very firm, 10 to 15 minutes. Softened butter (65 to 67 degrees) will bend easily without breaking and will give slightly when pressed. To soften butter quickly, you can place cold butter in a plastic bag and use a rolling pin to pound it to the desired consistency, or you can cut the butter into small pieces and let it sit until softened. For melted and cooled butter (85 to 90 degrees), melt the butter on the stovetop or in the microwave then let it cool for about 5 minutes.

RESCUING OVERSOFTENED BUTTER The fat in butter is partially crystalline and highly sensitive to temperature changes. When butter is properly softened to 65 or 70 degrees, the tiny crystals surround and stabilize the air bubbles that are generated during creaming. When heated to the melting point, however, these crystals are destroyed. They can be reestablished but only if the butter is rapidly chilled. To quickly cool partially melted butter, mix the butter with a few ice cubes. Once the butter has cooled to a softened stage—right below 70 degrees—remove the ice.

Glazed Lemon Bundt Cakes

Serves 2 `VEGETARIAN`

Total time 1 hour 20 minutes, plus
1 hour 10 minutes cooling

WHY THIS RECIPE WORKS For a simple Bundt cake with potent lemon flavor, we had to keep the acidity of the lemon juice from ruining its texture. To maximize the lemon flavor, we turned to lemon zest; 2 teaspoons gave the cake a perfumed lemon flavor. Increasing the butter and replacing the milk with buttermilk gave us a rich, tender cake with a light crumb. Creaming the butter and sugar was essential to creating a light and even crumb. For the glaze, a simple mixture of lemon zest and juice and confectioners' sugar gave our cakes an extra burst of citrus flavor. Mini Bundt pans produced perfect single-serving cakes. You will need a tray-style mini Bundt pan or two single 1-cup Bundt pans for this recipe—the center tube is necessary to facilitate even baking.

CAKES

- ½ cup (2½ ounces) all-purpose flour
- ¼ teaspoon table salt
- ¼ teaspoon baking powder
- ⅛ teaspoon baking soda
- 2 tablespoons buttermilk, room temperature
- 2 teaspoons grated lemon zest plus 1 teaspoon juice
- ½ teaspoon vanilla extract
- 3 tablespoons unsalted butter, softened
- ⅓ cup (2⅓ ounces) granulated sugar
- 1 large egg, room temperature

LEMON GLAZE

- ⅓ cup (1⅓ ounces) confectioners' sugar, plus extra as needed
- ¼ teaspoon grated lemon zest plus 2¾ teaspoons juice
  Pinch table salt

1. FOR THE CAKES Adjust oven rack to lower-middle position and heat oven to 350 degrees. Spray two 1-cup Bundt pans with baking spray with flour.

2. Whisk flour, salt, baking powder, and baking soda together in bowl. In small bowl, whisk buttermilk, lemon zest and juice, and vanilla together.

3. Using hand-held mixer set at low speed, beat butter and sugar in medium bowl until sugar is moistened, about 1 minute. Increase speed to medium-high and beat mixture until pale and fluffy, about 3 minutes, scraping down sides of bowl as needed. Add egg and beat until combined, about 30 seconds. Reduce speed to low and add flour mixture in 3 additions, alternating with buttermilk mixture in 2 additions. Increase speed to medium-high and beat until mixture is completely smooth, about 30 seconds. Give batter final stir by hand.

4. Divide batter evenly between prepared pans, smooth tops, and gently tap each pan on counter to release air bubbles. Wipe any drops of batter off sides of pans. Place pans on rimmed baking sheet and bake cakes until light golden brown and toothpick inserted in center comes out clean, 20 to 22 minutes, rotating sheet halfway through baking.

5. Let cakes cool in pans on wire rack set over baking sheet for 10 minutes. Remove cakes from pans and let cool completely on rack, about 1 hour.

6. FOR THE LEMON GLAZE Whisk sugar, lemon zest and juice, and salt together in bowl until smooth, adding extra sugar as needed to achieve thick but still pourable consistency. Pour glaze over tops of cooled cakes, letting glaze drip down sides. Let glaze set before serving, about 25 minutes.

Rich Chocolate Bundt Cakes

Serves 2 `VEGETARIAN`

Total time 1 hour 5 minutes, plus
1 hour 10 minutes cooling

WHY THIS RECIPE WORKS Too often, chocolate Bundt cakes look better than they taste: All those pretty fluted edges usually boast only muted chocolate flavor. To infuse our Bundt cake with serious chocolate flavor, we used both bittersweet chocolate and cocoa powder. Borrowing a technique from devil's food cake, we poured boiling water over the chocolate to bloom its flavor and help the cocoa particles distribute more evenly through the batter. Vanilla and espresso powder complemented the floral nuances of the chocolate, adding more depth of flavor. For deeper caramelized flavor and extra moisture, we swapped out white sugar for brown. As a final touch, we greased the cups or pans using cocoa powder instead of flour to avoid an unattractive white film. You will need a tray-style mini Bundt pan or two single 1-cup Bundt pans for this recipe—the center tube is necessary to facilitate even baking. For an accurate measurement of boiling water, bring a full kettle of water to a boil and then measure out the desired amount.

- 3 tablespoons unsweetened cocoa powder, divided
- 2 tablespoons unsalted butter, softened, plus 1 tablespoon melted, for pans
- 1½ ounces bittersweet chocolate, chopped fine
- ¼ teaspoon instant espresso powder or instant coffee powder
- 2 tablespoons boiling water

Rich Chocolate Bundt Cakes

and beat mixture until pale and fluffy, about 3 minutes, scraping down sides of bowl as needed. Add egg and beat until combined, about 30 seconds (batter may look slightly curdled). Reduce speed to low and add flour mixture in 2 additions, alternating with chocolate mixture. Give batter final stir by hand.

4. Divide batter evenly between prepared pans, smooth tops, and gently tap each pan on counter to release air bubbles. Wipe any drops of batter off sides of pans. Place pans on rimmed baking sheet and bake cakes until toothpick inserted in center comes out with a few moist crumbs attached, 20 to 22 minutes, rotating sheet halfway through baking.

5. Let cakes cool in pans on wire rack for 10 minutes. Remove cakes from pans and let cool completely on rack, about 1 hour. Dust with confectioners' sugar and serve.

PREPARING A BUNDT PAN

Make paste with 1 tablespoon flour or cocoa powder (for chocolate cakes) and 1 tablespoon melted butter. Apply paste to Bundt pans with pastry brush, reaching all nooks and crannies.

- 3 tablespoons sour cream, room temperature
- ½ teaspoon vanilla extract
- ⅓ cup (1⅔ ounces) all-purpose flour
- ¼ teaspoon baking soda
- ¼ teaspoon table salt
- ⅓ cup packed (2⅓ ounces) light brown sugar
- 1 large egg, room temperature
  Confectioners' sugar

1. Adjust oven rack to middle position and heat oven to 350 degrees. Mix 1 tablespoon cocoa and melted butter into paste. Using pastry brush, thoroughly coat interior of two 1-cup Bundt pans with paste.

2. Combine chocolate, espresso powder, and remaining 2 tablespoons cocoa in small bowl. Pour boiling water over mixture; cover; and let sit until chocolate is melted, 3 to 5 minutes. Whisk mixture gently until smooth. Let cool to room temperature, then whisk in sour cream and vanilla. In separate bowl, whisk flour, baking soda, and salt together.

3. Using hand-held mixer set at low speed, beat brown sugar and softened butter in medium bowl until sugar is moistened, about 1 minute. Increase speed to medium-high

Bold and Spicy Gingerbread Cakes

Serves 2 `VEGETARIAN`

Total time 1 hour 20 minutes, plus 1 hour 10 minutes cooling

WHY THIS RECIPE WORKS Most gingerbread cakes miss the mark, with a cloying sweetness and ginger that is either too harsh or too muted. We wanted a moist cake with bold, spicy ginger flavor and balanced sweetness. Creaming the butter and sugar made the cakes too fluffy, but simply melting the butter and mixing everything together gave us a rich, dense texture. We liked robust molasses for a fuller flavor. A combination of ground dried ginger and grated fresh ginger was key to creating the bite we were after. Cinnamon, allspice, and a pinch of pepper complemented the ginger nicely, and blooming the spices in the melted butter rounded out their flavors. If desired, you can substitute 1 teaspoon water for the bourbon in the glaze. You will need a tray-style mini Bundt pan or two single 1-cup Bundt pans for this recipe—the center tube is necessary to facilitate even baking.

CAKES

⅓ cup (1⅔ ounces) all-purpose flour
¼ teaspoon baking powder
⅛ teaspoon baking soda
⅛ teaspoon table salt
2 tablespoons unsalted butter
¼ teaspoon ground ginger
¼ teaspoon ground cinnamon
⅛ teaspoon ground allspice
  Pinch finely ground pepper
1 large egg, room temperature
3 tablespoons granulated sugar
½ teaspoon grated fresh ginger
2 tablespoons robust or full molasses
1 tablespoon water

BOURBON GLAZE

½ cup (2 ounces) confectioners' sugar,
  plus extra as needed
1½ teaspoons water
1 teaspoon bourbon

1. FOR THE CAKES Adjust oven rack to middle position and heat oven to 375 degrees. Spray two 1-cup Bundt pans with baking spray with flour.

2. Whisk flour, baking powder, baking soda, and salt together in bowl. Melt butter in small saucepan over medium heat. Add ground ginger, cinnamon, allspice, and pepper and cook until fragrant, about 30 seconds. Off heat, let cool slightly.

3. Whisk egg, sugar, and fresh ginger together in medium bowl until light and frothy. Whisk in cooled butter mixture, molasses, and water until smooth and thoroughly combined. Gently whisk in flour mixture until just combined. Give batter final stir with rubber spatula.

4. Divide batter evenly between prepared pans, smooth tops, and gently tap each pan on counter to release air bubbles. Wipe any drops of batter off sides of pans. Place pans on rimmed baking sheet and bake cakes until toothpick inserted in center comes out with a few moist crumbs attached, 20 to 25 minutes, rotating sheet halfway through baking.

5. Let cakes cool in pans on wire rack set over baking sheet for 10 minutes. Remove cakes from pans and let cool completely on rack, about 1 hour.

6. FOR THE BOURBON GLAZE Whisk sugar, water, and bourbon together in bowl until smooth, adding extra sugar as needed to achieve thick but still pourable consistency. Pour glaze over tops of cooled cakes, letting glaze drip down sides. Let glaze set before serving, about 25 minutes.

Almond Cakes
Serves 2 `VEGETARIAN`
Total time 1 hour, plus 40 minutes cooling
WHY THIS RECIPE WORKS Almond cake is a versatile dessert, as good eaten plain as it is adorned with a simple sauce, whipped cream, or fresh berries. It should be lightly sweet, with a texture like coarse pound cake. We found that a cup of ground almonds and ¼ cup of cake flour created the rustic texture we were after without making the cake too heavy and dense. To prevent the almonds from turning into nut butter when ground, we processed them with 2 tablespoons of sugar. Another 5 tablespoons of sugar in the cake provided just enough sweetness—any more and the cake formed a sickly sweet, candylike crust. Adding 2 tablespoons of milk gave our batter just the right consistency without dulling any of the almond flavor. You will need two 4½-inch springform pans for this recipe. Be careful not to overtoast the almonds or the cakes will have a dry, crumbly texture. Serve with Whipped Cream (page 393) and fresh berries.

1 cup slivered almonds, toasted
7 tablespoons (3 ounces) granulated sugar, divided
  Pinch table salt
¼ cup (1 ounce) cake flour
¼ teaspoon baking powder
2 tablespoons unsalted butter, softened
1 large egg, room temperature
2 tablespoons whole milk, room temperature
  Confectioners' sugar

1. Adjust oven rack to middle position and heat oven to 325 degrees. Grease two 4½-inch springform pans.

2. Process almonds, 2 tablespoons granulated sugar, and salt in food processor until very finely ground, about 15 seconds. Add flour and baking powder and pulse to incorporate, about 5 pulses.

3. Using hand-held mixer set at low speed, beat butter and remaining 5 tablespoons granulated sugar in medium bowl until sugar is moistened, about 1 minute. Increase speed to medium-high and beat mixture until pale and fluffy, about 3 minutes, scraping down sides of bowl as needed. Add egg and beat until combined, about 30 seconds. Reduce speed to low and slowly add ground almond mixture until combined, 15 to 30 seconds. Add milk and beat until combined, 15 to 30 seconds. Give batter final stir by hand.

4. Divide batter evenly between prepared pans, smooth tops, and gently tap each pan on counter to release air bubbles. Wipe any drops of batter off sides of pans. Place pans on rimmed baking sheet and bake cakes until tops are golden brown and toothpick inserted in center comes out with a few moist crumbs attached, 25 to 30 minutes, rotating sheet halfway through baking.

5. Let cakes cool in pans on wire rack for 10 minutes. Run thin knife around edges of cakes, remove sides of pans, and let cool slightly, about 30 minutes. Slide thin metal spatula between cakes and pan bottoms to loosen, then slide cakes onto individual serving plates. Dust with confectioners' sugar and serve warm.

Almond Cake

Rustic Peach Cakes

Serves 2 　VEGETARIAN

Total time 1 hour 20 minutes, plus 1½ hours cooling

WHY THIS RECIPE WORKS We wanted a recipe for a rustic yellow cake studded with chunks of juicy fresh peaches. To develop a cake sturdy enough to support the peaches, we altered our recipe for yellow cake. Substituting all-purpose flour for the cake flour gave the cake a sturdier crumb, as did replacing the milk with sour cream. Swapping some of the white sugar for light brown sugar added a subtle caramel flavor. To get rid of some of the peaches' excess moisture, we tossed them with cinnamon and sugar and let them sit while we prepared the batter. Scattering dried peaches over the batter added an extra layer of peach flavor without adding more moisture. Look for barely ripe peaches that give slightly to the touch; overly ripe peaches will make this cake soggy. You will need two 4½-inch springform pans for this recipe. Serve with vanilla ice cream or Whipped Cream (page 393).

　¼　cup (1¾ ounces) granulated sugar, divided
　⅛　teaspoon ground cinnamon
　1　peach, peeled, halved, pitted, and cut into 8 wedges
　½　cup (2½ ounces) all-purpose flour
　½　teaspoon baking powder
　⅛　teaspoon table salt
　4　tablespoons unsalted butter, softened
　2　tablespoons packed light brown sugar
　1　large egg, room temperature
　1　tablespoon sour cream, room temperature
　½　teaspoon vanilla extract
　3　tablespoons finely chopped dried peaches or apricots

1. Adjust oven rack to middle position and heat oven to 350 degrees. Grease two 4½-inch springform pans.

Rustic Peach Cakes

2. Combine 2 tablespoons granulated sugar and cinnamon in medium bowl. Measure out and reserve 1 tablespoon cinnamon sugar. Add peach wedges to bowl with remaining cinnamon sugar and toss to coat.

3. In separate bowl, whisk flour, baking powder, and salt together. Using hand-held mixer set at low speed, beat butter, brown sugar, and remaining 2 tablespoons granulated sugar in second medium bowl until sugar is moistened, about 1 minute. Increase speed to medium-high and beat mixture until pale and fluffy, about 3 minutes, scraping down sides of bowl as needed. Add egg, sour cream, and vanilla and beat until combined, about 30 seconds. Reduce speed to low and slowly add flour mixture. Give batter final stir by hand.

4. Divide batter evenly between prepared pans, smooth tops, and gently tap each pan on counter to release air bubbles. Wipe any drops of batter off sides of pans. Scatter dried peaches evenly over batter, then arrange 4 sugared peach wedges in pinwheel pattern over top in each pan. Sprinkle reserved cinnamon-sugar mixture evenly over peaches.

5. Place pans on rimmed baking sheet and bake cakes until tops are golden brown and toothpick inserted in center comes out with a few moist crumbs attached, 30 to 35 minutes, rotating sheet halfway through baking.

6. Let cakes cool completely in pans on wire rack, about 1½ hours. Run thin knife around edges of cakes and remove sides of pans. Slide thin metal spatula between cakes and pan bottoms to loosen, then slide cakes onto individual serving plates. Serve.

NOTES FROM THE TEST KITCHEN

FLOUR AND BAKING

Flour is essential for providing structure to most baked goods. The amount and type of flour that you use can be the difference between a tough, leaden cake and a light, tender one.

ALL-PURPOSE FLOUR VERSUS CAKE FLOUR

The main difference between types of flour is their protein content. All-purpose is by far the most versatile flour available. With a protein content between 10 percent and 11.7 percent, it provides enough structure to make good sandwich bread, yet it's light enough to use for cakes of a medium-to-coarse crumb. Cake flour has a lower protein content—about 6 to 8 percent—and thus yields cakes and pastries with less gluten, which translates to a finer, more delicate crumb. We use cake flour for light or fine-grained cakes, such as pound cake and angel food cake. It is possible to approximate 1 cup of cake flour by using 2 tablespoons of cornstarch plus ⅞ cup of all-purpose flour. Cake flour is usually bleached, but when buying all-purpose flour, we prefer unbleached. Bleached flours in our tests did not perform as well as the unbleached flours and were sometimes criticized for tasting flat or carrying off-flavors.

MEASURING FLOUR
The way you measure flour can make a big difference in your recipe. Too little flour can turn out baked goods that are flat, wet, or lacking in structure. Too much flour can result in tough, dry baked goods. For the ultimate in accuracy, nothing beats weighing flour, but our research has shown that the dip-and-sweep method is also reliable. You might be surprised to learn that if you are spooning your flour into a measuring cup and then leveling it off, you could end up with 20 percent less flour than with the dip-and-sweep method. For the dip-and-sweep method, simply dip the measuring cup into the container of flour and sweep away the excess with a straight-edged object like the back of a butter knife.

STORING FLOUR
Refined flours, including all-purpose, bread, and cake flour, can be stored in airtight containers in your pantry for up to one year. A wide-mouthed plastic container allows you to scoop out what you need without making a floury mess of your countertop. Make sure the container can hold the entire contents of a 5-pound bag. A tight-fitting lid is also essential.

Whole-wheat flour and others made from whole grains contain more fat than refined flours and can turn rancid quickly at room temperature. For this reason, we recommend storing these flours in the freezer. In various tests, we found that using flour straight from the freezer inhibited rise and yielded denser baked goods. Therefore, it's best to bring chilled flour to room temperature before baking.

Fluffy Yellow Layer Cake

Makes one 6-inch cake VEGETARIAN

Total time 55 minutes, plus 1 hour 10 minutes cooling

WHY THIS RECIPE WORKS We wanted a scaled-down yellow layer cake with the same ethereal texture and supreme fluffiness as the cakes that come from a box—without the mysterious chemical additives. We found that the secret was to use a chiffon cake method (whipping egg whites separately and folding them into the batter at the end) to lighten the cake and a combination of fats (butter plus vegetable oil) to keep the butter flavor intact while improving the moistness of the cake. For extra tenderness, we increased the sugar and substituted buttermilk for milk. Be sure to bring all of the ingredients to room temperature before beginning this recipe. You will need two 6-inch round cake pans for this recipe. We recommend using a small offset spatula to easily and neatly frost the cake. You can use Chocolate Frosting (page 433) or Vanilla Frosting (page 433) in this recipe.

- 1 large egg white plus 2 large yolks, room temperature
- ½ cup (3½ ounces) sugar, divided
- ¾ cup (3 ounces) cake flour
- ½ teaspoon baking powder
- ⅛ teaspoon baking soda
- ¼ teaspoon table salt
- ⅓ cup buttermilk, room temperature
- 3 tablespoons unsalted butter, melted and cooled
- 1 tablespoon vegetable oil
- ¾ teaspoon vanilla extract
- 2 cups frosting

1. Adjust oven rack to middle position and heat oven to 350 degrees. Grease two 6-inch round cake pans, line with parchment paper, grease parchment, and flour pans.

2. Using hand-held mixer set at medium-low speed, beat egg white in medium bowl until foamy, about 1 minute. Increase speed to medium-high and beat white to soft, billowy mounds, about 1 minute. Gradually add 2 tablespoons sugar and beat until glossy, stiff peaks form, 1 to 2 minutes, scraping down sides of bowl as needed; set aside.

3. Whisk flour, baking powder, baking soda, salt, and remaining 6 tablespoons sugar together in second medium bowl. In small bowl, whisk buttermilk, melted butter, oil, vanilla, and egg yolks together. Using hand-held mixer set at low speed, gradually pour butter mixture into flour mixture and mix until almost combined (a few streaks of dry flour will remain), 15 to 30 seconds. Scrape down bowl, then beat on medium-low speed until smooth and fully combined, 10 to 15 seconds.

4. Using rubber spatula, stir one-third of whites into batter, then add remaining whites and gently fold into batter until no white streaks remain. Divide batter evenly between prepared pans, smooth tops, and gently tap each pan on counter to release air bubbles. Wipe any drops of batter off sides of pans. Bake cakes until toothpick inserted in center comes out with a few moist crumbs attached, 16 to 18 minutes, rotating pans halfway through baking.

5. Let cakes cool in pans on wire rack for 10 minutes. Run knife around edge of cakes to loosen. Remove cakes from pans, discarding parchment, and let cool completely on rack, about 1 hour. (Cooled cakes can be wrapped tightly in plastic wrap and stored at room temperature for up to 1 day. Wrapped tightly in plastic, then aluminum foil, cakes can be frozen for up to 1 month. Defrost cakes at room temperature before unwrapping and frosting.)

6. Line edges of cake platter with 4 strips of parchment paper to keep platter clean. Place 1 cake layer on platter. Spread ½ cup frosting evenly over top, right to edge of cake. Top with second cake layer, press lightly to adhere, then spread ½ cup frosting evenly over top. Spread remaining 1 cup frosting evenly over sides of cake. To smooth frosting, run edge of offset spatula around cake sides and over top, or create billows by pressing back of spoon into frosting and twirling spoon as you lift away. Carefully remove parchment strips before serving. (Assembled cake can be refrigerated for up to 1 day. Bring to room temperature before serving.)

Chocolate Layer Cake

Makes one 6-inch cake VEGETARIAN

Total time 1 hour 10 minutes, plus 1 hour 10 minutes cooling

WHY THIS RECIPE WORKS A beautifully frosted chocolate layer cake is the perfect dessert for any special occasion, but in a small household, most of it will go stale and dry out before it can be enjoyed. To make a petite layer cake suited for two, we needed to scale back our recipe to fill two 6-inch cake pans. For rich chocolate flavor, we used both cocoa powder and unsweetened chocolate. A small amount of instant espresso powder further enhanced the chocolate flavor. We added boiling water to the chocolate mixture to dissolve the espresso powder and intensify the chocolate flavor. Sour cream ensured that the cake stayed moist, and brown sugar provided subtle caramelized notes. You will need two 6-inch round cake pans for this recipe. For an accurate measurement of boiling water, bring a full kettle of water to a boil and then measure out the desired amount. We recommend using a small offset spatula to easily and neatly frost the cake. You can use Vanilla Frosting (page 433) or Chocolate Frosting (page 433) in this recipe.

- 1½ ounces unsweetened chocolate, chopped
- 3 tablespoons unsweetened cocoa powder
- ¼ teaspoon instant espresso powder or instant coffee powder
- ½ cup boiling water
- ¼ cup sour cream, room temperature
- ¼ teaspoon vanilla extract
- ½ cup (2½ ounces) all-purpose flour
- ½ teaspoon baking soda
- ⅛ teaspoon baking powder
- ¼ teaspoon table salt
- 4 tablespoons unsalted butter, softened
- ½ cup packed (3½ ounces) light brown sugar
- 1 large egg, room temperature
- 2 cups frosting

Chocolate Layer Cake

1. Adjust oven rack to middle position and heat oven to 350 degrees. Grease two 6-inch round cake pans, line with parchment paper, grease parchment, and flour pans.

2. Combine chocolate, cocoa, and espresso powder in small bowl. Pour boiling water over mixture, cover, and let sit until chocolate is melted, 3 to 5 minutes. Whisk mixture gently until smooth. Let cool to room temperature, then whisk in sour cream and vanilla. In separate bowl, whisk flour, baking soda, baking powder, and salt together.

3. Using hand-held mixer set at low speed, beat butter and sugar in medium bowl until sugar is moistened, about 1 minute. Increase speed to medium-high and beat mixture until pale and fluffy, about 3 minutes, scraping down sides of bowl as needed. Add egg and beat until combined, about 30 seconds. Reduce speed to low and add flour mixture in 2 additions, alternating with chocolate mixture. Give batter final stir by hand.

4. Divide batter evenly between prepared pans, smooth tops, and gently tap each pan on counter to release air bubbles. Wipe any drops of batter off sides of pans. Bake cakes until toothpick inserted in center comes out with a few moist crumbs attached, 20 to 25 minutes, rotating pans halfway through baking.

5. Let cakes cool in pans on wire rack for 10 minutes. Run knife around edge of cakes to loosen. Remove cakes from pans, discarding parchment, and let cool completely on rack, about 1 hour. (Cooled cakes can be wrapped tightly in plastic wrap and stored at room temperature for up to 1 day. Wrapped tightly in plastic, then aluminum foil, cakes can be frozen for up to 1 month. Defrost cakes at room temperature before unwrapping and frosting.)

6. Line edges of cake platter with 4 strips of parchment paper to keep platter clean. Place 1 cake layer on platter. Spread ½ cup frosting evenly over top, right to edge of cake. Top with second cake layer, press lightly to adhere, then spread ½ cup frosting evenly over top. Spread remaining 1 cup frosting evenly over sides of cake. To smooth frosting, run edge of offset spatula around cake sides and over top, or create billows by pressing back of spoon into frosting and twirling spoon as you lift away. Carefully remove parchment strips before serving. (Assembled cake can be refrigerated for up to 1 day. Bring to room temperature before serving.)

Chocolate Frosting

Makes about 2 cups FAST VEGETARIAN
Total time 20 minutes

To make this frosting for cupcakes, cut all ingredients in half.

- 6 ounces milk, bittersweet, or semisweet chocolate, chopped
- 14 tablespoons unsalted butter, softened
- ⅔ cup (2⅔ ounces) confectioners' sugar
- ½ cup (1½ ounces) unsweetened cocoa powder
  Pinch table salt
- ½ cup light corn syrup
- 1 teaspoon vanilla extract

Microwave chocolate in bowl at 50 percent power, stirring occasionally, until melted and smooth, 2 to 4 minutes. Let cool slightly. Process butter, sugar, cocoa, and salt in food processor until smooth, about 10 seconds, scraping down sides of bowl as needed. Add corn syrup and vanilla and process until just combined, 5 to 10 seconds. Add melted chocolate and pulse until smooth and creamy, about 5 pulses. (Frosting can be kept at room temperature for up to 3 hours before using or refrigerated for up to 3 days. If refrigerated, let sit at room temperature for 1 hour before using.)

TWO WAYS TO CHOP CHOCOLATE

A. WITH A KNIFE Hold knife at 45-degree angle to corner chocolate block and bear down evenly. After cutting about 1 inch from corner, repeat with other corners. Chop as directed in recipe.

B. WITH A LARGE FORK Alternatively, use sharp 2-tined meat fork to break chocolate into smaller pieces. Chop as directed in recipe.

Vanilla Frosting

Makes about 2 cups FAST VEGETARIAN
Total time 15 minutes

To make this frosting for cupcakes, cut all ingredients in half. Be sure to use unsalted butter here. For fun, consider adding some color to the frosting by stirring in a few drops of food coloring.

- 2 tablespoons heavy cream
- 1½ teaspoons vanilla extract
- ⅛ teaspoon table salt
- 16 tablespoons unsalted butter, softened
- 2 cups (8 ounces) confectioners' sugar

Stir cream, vanilla, and salt together in bowl until salt dissolves. Using hand-held mixer set at medium-high speed, beat butter in medium bowl until smooth, 30 to 60 seconds, scraping down sides of bowl as needed. Reduce speed to medium-low, gradually add sugar, and beat until smooth, about 2 minutes. Add cream mixture and beat until combined, about 30 seconds. Increase speed to medium-high and beat until frosting is pale and fluffy, about 5 minutes.

VARIATIONS
Coffee Frosting
Add 4 teaspoons instant espresso powder or instant coffee powder to cream mixture.

Coconut Frosting
Add 2 teaspoons coconut extract to cream mixture.

CHECKING A CAKE FOR DONENESS

To check cake for doneness, insert toothpick into center; it should come out with just a few moist crumbs attached. If you see raw batter, continue to bake cake, checking every few minutes.

Carrot Cake with Cream Cheese Frosting

Carrot Cake with Cream Cheese Frosting

Serves 2   `VEGETARIAN`

Total time 1 hour 10 minutes, plus
1 hour 10 minutes cooling

WHY THIS RECIPE WORKS We wanted a carrot cake that was moist and rich—not soggy or greasy—with a tender crumb and balanced spice flavor. Getting the ingredient proportions just right was tricky. Too much oil made the cake heavy and greasy; too little made it lean and lacking in richness. Too much spice overpowered the sweet carrot flavor, but too little left the cake bland. And the shredded carrots could quickly turn the whole thing soggy. We tried precooking the carrots to rid them of some of their moisture, but precooked carrots turned to mush in the cake. Instead, we scaled back the carrots until we had just the right amount of moisture; one small carrot was enough to give the cake its distinct flavor. For a rich, decadent cream cheese frosting, we added vanilla extract and a pinch of salt to give the frosting a rich flavor that wasn't cloying.

CAKE
- ⅔ cup (3⅓ ounces) all-purpose flour
- ½ teaspoon ground cinnamon
- ¼ teaspoon baking powder
- ⅛ teaspoon baking soda
- ⅛ teaspoon table salt
- ⅛ teaspoon ground nutmeg
- Pinch ground cloves
- ⅓ cup (2⅓ ounces) granulated sugar
- ¼ cup vegetable oil
- 1 large egg, room temperature
- 2 tablespoons packed light brown sugar
- 1 small carrot, peeled and shredded

FROSTING
- 4 ounces cream cheese, softened
- 2 tablespoons unsalted butter, softened
- ½ teaspoon vanilla extract
- Pinch table salt
- ½ cup (2 ounces) confectioners' sugar

1. FOR THE CAKE Adjust oven rack to middle position and heat oven to 350 degrees. Grease 7¼ by 5¼-inch baking dish, line with parchment paper, grease parchment, and flour dish.

2. Whisk flour, cinnamon, baking powder, baking soda, salt, nutmeg, and cloves together in bowl. In medium bowl, whisk granulated sugar, oil, egg, and brown sugar together until smooth and thoroughly combined. Gently whisk in flour mixture until just combined. Stir in carrot.

3. Scrape batter into prepared dish, smooth top, and gently tap dish on counter to release air bubbles. Wipe any drops of batter off side of dish. Bake cake until toothpick inserted in center comes out with a few moist crumbs attached, 30 to 40 minutes, rotating dish halfway through baking.

4. Let cake cool in dish on wire rack for 10 minutes. Run knife around edge of cake to loosen. Remove cake from dish, discarding parchment, and let cool completely on rack, about 1 hour.

5. FOR THE FROSTING Using hand-held mixer set at medium-high speed, beat cream cheese, butter, vanilla, and salt in medium bowl until smooth, 1 to 2 minutes, scraping down sides of bowl as needed. Reduce speed to medium-low, gradually add sugar, and beat until smooth, 2 to 3 minutes. Increase speed to medium-high and beat until frosting is pale and fluffy, 2 to 3 minutes. Spread frosting evenly over cake and serve. (Cake can be refrigerated for up to 1 day. Bring to room temperature before serving.)

Vanilla Cupcakes

Makes 4 cupcakes VEGETARIAN

Total time 45 minutes, plus 1 hour 10 minutes cooling

WHY THIS RECIPE WORKS Cupcakes are a natural choice when you want a small-scale dessert, but most recipes produce at least a dozen. We wanted a recipe for just four fluffy, tender, snowy-white cupcakes. Using cake flour and doubling up on leaveners ensured that our cupcakes had golden, rounded tops and a tender crumb. Buttermilk gave the cupcakes a tangy richness. To avoid having to pull out our electric mixer, we melted the butter and simply stirred everything together by hand. Make sure not to overmix the batter or the cupcakes will turn out tough. Any muffin tin with standard-size cups will work here, and the batter can be placed in any of the cups. We recommend using a small offset spatula to easily and neatly frost the cupcakes. You can use Vanilla Frosting (page 433) or Chocolate Frosting (page 433) in this recipe.

¾ cup (3 ounces) cake flour
¼ teaspoon baking powder
⅛ teaspoon baking soda
⅛ teaspoon table salt
¼ cup (1¾ ounces) sugar
1 large egg, room temperature
3 tablespoons unsalted butter, melted and cooled
¼ cup buttermilk, room temperature
½ teaspoon vanilla extract
1 cup frosting

1. Adjust oven rack to middle position and heat oven to 325 degrees. Line 4 cups of muffin tin with paper or foil liners.

2. Whisk flour, baking powder, baking soda, and salt together in bowl. In medium bowl, whisk sugar, egg, and melted butter together until smooth. Whisk in buttermilk and vanilla until thoroughly combined. Sift flour mixture over egg mixture in 2 additions, whisking gently after each addition until a few streaks of flour remain. Continue to whisk batter until most of lumps are gone (do not overmix).

3. Using dry measuring cup or ice cream scoop, divide batter evenly among prepared muffin cups. Bake cupcakes until golden brown and toothpick inserted in center comes out clean, 18 to 22 minutes, rotating muffin tin halfway through baking.

4. Let cupcakes cool in muffin tin on wire rack for 10 minutes. Remove cupcakes from muffin tin and let cool completely on rack, about 1 hour. Spread 3 to 4 tablespoons frosting over each cooled cupcake and serve.

Vanilla Cupcakes

Chocolate Cupcakes

Makes 4 cupcakes VEGETARIAN

Total time 55 minutes, plus 1 hour 10 minutes cooling

WHY THIS RECIPE WORKS Developing a recipe for decadent chocolate cupcakes wasn't as easy as adding chocolate to our white cupcakes. We found that cake flour didn't provide enough structure to support the added chocolate, giving us crumbly cupcakes that fell apart in our hands. All-purpose flour proved to be a better option. The flavor of the buttermilk was out of place here, but a few tablespoons of whole milk gave us a tender crumb without affecting the flavor. A combination of bittersweet chocolate and cocoa powder gave us decadent chocolate flavor. A little salt and vanilla extract rounded out the flavors. Any muffin tin with standard-size cups will work here, and the batter can be placed in any of the cups. We recommend using a small offset spatula to easily and neatly frost the cupcakes. You can use Vanilla Frosting (page 433) or Chocolate Frosting (page 433) in this recipe.

- ¼ cup (1¼ ounces) all-purpose flour
- ¼ teaspoon baking powder
- ⅛ teaspoon baking soda
- ⅛ teaspoon table salt
- 4 tablespoons unsalted butter, cut into 3 pieces
- 1½ ounces bittersweet chocolate, chopped
- 3 tablespoons unsweetened cocoa powder
- ¼ cup (1¾ ounces) sugar
- 1 large egg, room temperature
- 3 tablespoons whole milk, room temperature
- ½ teaspoon vanilla extract
- 1 cup frosting

1. Adjust oven rack to middle position and heat oven to 325 degrees. Line 4 cups of muffin tin with paper or foil liners. Whisk flour, baking powder, baking soda, and salt together in bowl.

2. In separate bowl, microwave butter, chocolate, and cocoa at 50 percent power, stirring occasionally, until melted and smooth, about 1 minute; let cool slightly. Whisk sugar and egg together in medium bowl until smooth. Whisk in milk and vanilla until combined. Whisk in cooled chocolate mixture until well combined. Sift flour mixture over chocolate mixture in 2 additions, whisking gently after each addition until a few streaks of flour remain (batter will be thick). Continue to whisk batter until most of lumps are gone (do not overmix).

3. Using dry measuring cup or ice cream scoop, divide batter evenly among prepared muffin cups. Bake cupcakes until toothpick inserted into center comes out clean, 18 to 22 minutes, rotating muffin tin halfway through baking.

4. Let cupcakes cool in pan on wire rack for 10 minutes. Remove cupcakes from muffin tin and let cool completely on rack, about 1 hour. Spread 3 to 4 tablespoons frosting over each cooled cupcake and serve.

Lemon Pudding Cake

Serves 2 VEGETARIAN

Total time 1 hour 40 minutes, plus 30 minutes cooling

WHY THIS RECIPE WORKS Somewhere between a cake and a custard, lemon pudding cake should separate into two layers as it bakes, with light, airy cake topping a creamy, lemony pudding. The cakey top layer depends on whipped egg whites to rise to the top while baking, so stabilizing the egg whites with some sugar was important. A high proportion of liquid—½ cup of milk—was necessary to get the pudding layer to sink. To make sure that our pudding was thick and rich, not soupy, we added a bit of cornstarch. To get the burst of bright lemon flavor we wanted, we added both lemon zest and juice. You will need a 3-cup baking dish (measuring approximately 7¼ by 5¼ inches) or dish of a similar size for this recipe. It's important to use a metal pan for the water bath—a glass baking dish may crack when you add the boiling water.

- 2 large eggs, separated, room temperature
- ½ cup (3½ ounces) sugar, divided
- 4 teaspoons all-purpose flour
- ½ teaspoon cornstarch
- 2 tablespoons unsalted butter, softened
- 2 teaspoons grated lemon zest plus ¼ cup juice (2 lemons)
- ½ cup whole milk, room temperature

1. Adjust oven rack to lowest position and heat oven to 325 degrees. Place dish towel in bottom of 13 by 9-inch baking pan. Grease 7¼ by 5¼-inch baking dish and set on towel. Bring kettle of water to boil.

2. Using hand-held mixer set at medium-low speed, beat egg whites in large bowl until foamy, about 1 minute. Increase speed to medium-high and beat whites to soft, billowy mounds, about 1 minute. Gradually add 6 tablespoons sugar and beat until glossy, stiff peaks form, 2 to 6 minutes; set aside.

3. Whisk flour and cornstarch together in small bowl. Using hand-held mixer set at medium-high speed, beat butter, lemon zest, and remaining 2 tablespoons sugar in medium bowl until pale and fluffy, about 3 minutes, scraping down sides of bowl as needed. Add egg yolks and beat until combined, about 30 seconds. Reduce speed to low and slowly add flour mixture until combined, about 30 seconds. Add milk and lemon juice and beat until just combined.

4. Using rubber spatula, stir one-third of whites into batter, then add remaining whites and gently fold into batter until no white streaks remain. Scrape batter into prepared dish and smooth top. Set pan on oven rack. Taking care not to splash water into dish, pour enough boiling water into pan to reach halfway up sides of dish. Bake cake until surface is golden brown and edges are set (center should jiggle slightly when gently shaken), about 1 hour.

5. Carefully transfer baking dish to wire rack and let cake cool until warm, about 30 minutes. Serve warm or at room temperature.

MAKING A WATER BATH

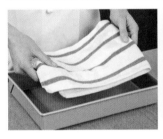

1. To prevent baking dish (or ramekins) from sliding, line bottom of metal baking pan with dish towel. Then place baking dish on top.

2. Add batter to baking dish set inside baking pan; transfer pan to oven. Then carefully pour boiling water into pan, halfway up sides of baking dish.

Molten Chocolate Microwave Mug Cakes

Serves 2 FAST VEGETARIAN

Total time 20 minutes

WHY THIS RECIPE WORKS Molten chocolate cake is a restaurant classic that has long held a spot on many a dessert menu. These little cakes are refined, but since the craving for decadent, fudgy cake and warm chocolate filling can strike at

Molten Chocolate Microwave Mug Cake

any moment, we needed a way to satisfy it regularly—and fast. Enter: the microwave. We'd heard a lot about mug cakes, and the promise of homemade molten chocolate cake in about 10 minutes from start to finish was alluring. But while the recipes we tried did indeed deliver on the time front, the hype was unwarranted: These cakes were rubbery, heavy, chalky, and bland. Even worse, they often exploded over the brim. To keep our cakes from overflowing, we had to supplement bittersweet chocolate with cocoa powder; because cocoa powder has less fat, it produces less steam, thus decreasing the chance of an overflow. (The cocoa powder also provided a flavor boost, of course.) For a light, tender crumb, we found we needed to microwave the cakes gently at 50 percent power. Stirring the batter halfway through ensured even cooking. Finally, we created the requisite gooey, molten center by simply dropping a couple of pieces of bittersweet chocolate into each cake. We developed this recipe in a full-size 1200-watt microwave. If the wattage of your microwave is less than 1200 watts, you will need to increase the cooking times throughout. Use a mug that holds at least 12 ounces, or the batter will overflow.

- 4 tablespoons unsalted butter
- 1 ounce bittersweet chocolate, chopped, plus 1 ounce broken into 4 equal pieces
- ¼ cup (1¾ ounces) sugar
- 2 large eggs
- 2 tablespoons unsweetened cocoa powder
- 1 teaspoon vanilla extract
- ¼ teaspoon table salt
- ¼ cup (1¼ ounces) all-purpose flour
- ½ teaspoon baking powder

1. Microwave butter and chopped chocolate in large bowl at 50 percent power, stirring often, until melted, about 1 minute. Whisk sugar, eggs, cocoa, vanilla, and salt into chocolate mixture until smooth. In separate bowl, combine flour and baking powder. Whisk flour mixture into chocolate mixture until combined. Divide batter evenly between 2 (12-ounce) coffee mugs.

2. Place mugs on opposite sides of microwave turntable. Microwave at 50 percent power for 45 seconds. Stir batter and microwave at 50 percent power for 45 seconds (batter will rise to just below rim of mug).

3. Press 2 chocolate pieces into center of each cake until chocolate is flush with top of cake. Microwave at 50 percent power for 30 seconds to 1 minute (chocolate pieces should be melted and cake should be slightly wet around edges of mug and somewhat drier toward center). Let cakes sit for 2 minutes before serving.

VARIATION

S'mores Molten Microwave Mug Cakes

Reduce salt to ⅛ teaspoon. Substitute 2 marshmallows for broken chocolate pieces in step 3. After submerging marshmallows, sprinkle each mug with 2 tablespoons crushed graham crackers. Garnish with broken pieces of graham cracker.

Lemon–Poppy Seed Mug Cakes

Serves 2 FAST VEGETARIAN

Total time 15 minutes

WHY THIS RECIPE WORKS Mug cakes aren't just an excuse to eat gooey, decadent chocolate—the technique can apply to even the lightest and fluffiest of cakes. We created a simple cake batter full of lemon zest and juice, with an egg contributing a lovely yellow hue and a few spoonfuls of poppy seeds adding pleasing texture and contrasting color. After less than

2 minutes in the microwave, we had a soft, pillowy, lemon cake. We developed this recipe in a full-size 1200-watt microwave. If the wattage of your microwave is less than 1200 watts, you will need to increase the cooking times throughout. Use a mug that holds at least 12 ounces, or the batter will overflow. Serve topped with Whipped Cream (page 393), fresh berries, or a berry compote.

- 6 tablespoons (1¾ ounces) all-purpose flour
- ¼ cup (1¾ ounces) sugar
- 4 teaspoons poppy seeds (optional)
- 1 tablespoon grated lemon zest plus 4 teaspoons juice
- ½ teaspoon baking powder
- ¼ teaspoon table salt
- 4 tablespoons unsalted butter, melted
- 2 large eggs
- 1 teaspoon vanilla extract

1. Whisk flour; sugar; poppy seeds, if using; lemon zest; baking powder; and salt together in bowl; set aside. Stir melted butter, egg, vanilla, and lemon juice in separate bowl and whisk in flour mixture until combined. Divide batter evenly between 2 (12-ounce) coffee mugs.

2. Place mugs on opposite sides of microwave turntable. Microwave at 50 percent power until cake has doubled in size and is firm, but top is just wet to the touch, 1 minute 30 seconds to 2 minutes (cake may rise above edge of mug but will not overflow). Let cake rest for 2 minutes before serving.

Warm Chocolate Fudge Cakes

Serves 2 VEGETARIAN

Total time 50 minutes

WHY THIS RECIPE WORKS To bring this restaurant favorite home for two, we started by building a rich, brownie-like cake batter with an intense chocolate flavor. Moderate amounts of vegetable oil and chocolate ensured that our cakes were plenty moist and boasted a good jolt of chocolaty flavor. An egg contributed to our cakes' moistness and richness, and a small amount of flour gave them more structure and lift. Finally, for a gooey center, we pressed a square of chocolate into each ramekin before baking, giving us individual cakes with a big burst of chocolate and a rich, fudgy center. You will need two 6-ounce ramekins for this recipe. Serve these cakes warm in their ramekins dusted with confectioners' sugar or top with vanilla ice cream, if desired.

Lemon–Poppy Seed Mug Cakes

Warm Chocolate Fudge Cakes

6 tablespoons (1¾ ounces) all-purpose flour
¼ teaspoon baking powder
⅛ teaspoon baking soda
⅛ teaspoon table salt
2½ ounces bittersweet chocolate (2 ounces chopped, ½ ounce broken into two ¼-ounce pieces)
¼ cup whole milk, room temperature
3 tablespoons packed light brown sugar
2 tablespoons vegetable oil
1 large egg, lightly beaten
¼ teaspoon vanilla extract

1. Adjust oven rack to middle position and heat oven to 350 degrees. Grease and flour two 6-ounce ramekins. Whisk flour, baking powder, baking soda, and salt together in bowl.

2. Microwave chopped chocolate and milk in medium bowl at 50 percent power, stirring occasionally, until chocolate is melted and mixture is smooth, 1 to 3 minutes. Stir in sugar until dissolved; let cool slightly. Whisk in oil, egg, and vanilla until combined. Gently whisk in flour mixture until just combined. Give batter final stir with rubber spatula.

3. Divide batter evenly between prepared ramekins and gently tap each ramekin on counter to release air bubbles. Wipe any drops of batter off sides of ramekins. Gently press chocolate pieces evenly into center of each ramekin to submerge in batter. Place ramekins on rimmed baking sheet and bake cakes until tops are just firm to touch and center is gooey when pierced with toothpick, 10 to 15 minutes, rotating sheet halfway through baking. Let cool for 2 to 3 minutes before serving.

Tiramisu

Serves 2 VEGETARIAN

Total time 40 minutes, plus 6 hours chilling

WHY THIS RECIPE WORKS Tiramisu features delicate ladyfingers soaked in a spiked coffee mixture and layered with a sweet, creamy filling. To scale it down, we used a cup of mascarpone lightened with some cream and just a tablespoon of dark rum. Soaking the ladyfingers in a mixture of water, instant espresso powder and rum achieved the ideal saturated texture. A sprinkling of cocoa and grated chocolate made for an elegant finish. Be sure to use hard, not soft, ladyfingers. Brandy or whiskey can be substituted for the rum. You will need a 3-cup baking dish (measuring approximately 7¼ by 5¼ inches) or dish of a similar size for this recipe. Do not allow the mascarpone to warm to room temperature before using it or it may curdle.

⅔ cup water, room temperature

2 tablespoons instant espresso powder

2 tablespoons dark rum, divided

2 large egg yolks

¼ cup (1¾ ounces) sugar

Pinch table salt

8 ounces (1 cup) mascarpone

¼ cup heavy cream, chilled

10–15 dried ladyfingers (savoiardi)

1 tablespoon unsweetened cocoa powder

1 tablespoon grated bittersweet or semisweet chocolate (optional)

Tiramisu

1. Stir water, espresso powder, and 1 tablespoon rum together in shallow dish until espresso dissolves; set aside.

2. Using hand-held mixer set at low speed, beat egg yolks in large bowl until just combined, about 30 seconds. Increase speed to medium-high, add sugar and salt, and beat until pale yellow, 1 to 2 minutes, scraping down sides of bowl as needed. Add remaining 1 tablespoon rum and beat until combined, 15 to 30 seconds. Reduce speed to low, add mascarpone, and beat until no lumps remain, 15 to 30 seconds.

3. Using hand-held mixer set at medium-low speed, beat cream in small bowl until frothy, about 1 minute. Increase speed to high and beat until stiff peaks form, 1 to 3 minutes. Using rubber spatula, stir one-third of whipped cream into mascarpone mixture, then add remaining whipped cream and gently fold into mascarpone mixture until no white streaks remain.

4. Working with one at a time, drop half of ladyfingers into espresso mixture, roll to coat, remove, and transfer to 7¼ by 5¼-inch baking dish. (Do not submerge ladyfingers in espresso mixture; entire process should take no longer than 2 to 3 seconds for each cookie.) Arrange soaked cookies in single layer in dish, breaking or trimming ladyfingers as necessary to fit.

5. Spread half of mascarpone mixture over ladyfingers with spatula, spreading mixture to sides and into corners of dish, then smooth surface. Place 1½ teaspoons cocoa in fine-mesh strainer and dust cocoa over mascarpone mixture.

6. Repeat dipping and arrangement with remaining ladyfingers; spread remaining mascarpone mixture over ladyfingers and dust with remaining 1½ teaspoons cocoa. Wipe edges of dish clean with paper towel. Cover with plastic wrap and refrigerate for at least 6 hours or up to 24 hours. Sprinkle with grated chocolate, if using, and serve chilled. (Tiramisu can be refrigerated for up to 1 day.)

VARIATION

Tiramisu with Cooked Eggs

This recipe involves cooking the yolks in a double boiler, which requires a little more effort and makes for a slightly thicker mascarpone filling, but the results are just as good as with our traditional method. You will need an additional 2 tablespoons heavy cream.

In step 2, add 2 tablespoons cream to egg yolks after sugar and salt; do not whisk in rum. Set bowl with egg yolks over medium saucepan of barely simmering water (water should not touch bottom of bowl); cook, constantly scraping along bottom and sides of bowl with heat-resistant rubber spatula, until mixture coats back of spoon and registers 160 degrees, 3 to 5 minutes. Remove bowl from saucepan and stir vigorously to cool slightly, then set aside and let cool to room temperature, about 15 minutes. Whisk in remaining 1 tablespoon rum until combined. Using hand-held mixer set at low speed, beat egg yolk mixture and mascarpone together in large bowl until no lumps remain, 15 to 30 seconds. Proceed with recipe from step 3, using full amount of heavy cream specified (¼ cup).

New York Cheesecakes
Serves 2 `VEGETARIAN`

Total time 1 hour 20 minutes, plus 3½ hours cooling, chilling, and resting

WHY THIS RECIPE WORKS A full-size cheesecake, as luscious as it is, will mostly go to waste in a two-person household. For failproof individual cheesecakes for two, we started with a simple graham-cracker crust and prebaked it to ensure that it wouldn't turn soggy once we added the filling. We thinned the cream cheese with just a little tangy sour cream. One whole egg plus an extra yolk gave the cakes a lush texture that was dense but not heavy. A pinch of salt, a small dose of vanilla, and a squeeze of lemon juice perfected the flavors. Finally, we baked the cheesecakes using the classic New York method—first at 500 degrees to get a nicely browned top, then at 200 degrees to cook through gently. You will need two 4½-inch springform pans for this recipe. Serve as is or with fresh berries.

New York Cheesecakes

CRUST
- 3 whole graham crackers, broken into 1-inch pieces
- 3 tablespoons unsalted butter, melted and cooled, divided
- 1 tablespoon sugar

FILLING
- 10 ounces cream cheese, softened
- ⅓ cup (2⅓ ounces) sugar, divided
- Pinch table salt
- 4 teaspoons sour cream
- ½ teaspoon lemon juice
- ½ teaspoon vanilla extract
- 1 large egg plus 1 large yolk

1. FOR THE CRUST Adjust oven rack to middle position and heat oven to 325 degrees. Process graham cracker pieces in food processor to fine, even crumbs, about 30 seconds. Sprinkle 2 tablespoons melted butter and sugar over crumbs and pulse to incorporate, about 5 pulses. Divide mixture evenly between two 4½-inch springform pans. Using bottom of spoon, press crumbs firmly into even layer on bottom of pans, keeping sides as clean as possible. Bake crusts until fragrant and beginning to brown, about 10 minutes. Let crusts cool in pans on wire rack while making filling.

2. FOR THE FILLING Increase oven temperature to 500 degrees. Using hand-held mixer set at medium-low speed, beat cream cheese in large bowl until smooth, 1 to 2 minutes. Scrape down sides of bowl. Add ¼ cup sugar and salt and beat until combined, 30 to 60 seconds. Scrape down bowl, add remaining sugar, and beat until combined, 30 to 60 seconds.

Scrape down bowl, add sour cream, lemon juice, and vanilla and beat until combined, 15 to 30 seconds. Scrape down bowl, add egg and egg yolk and beat until combined, 30 to 60 seconds.

3. Being careful not to disturb baked crusts, brush inside of pans with remaining 1 tablespoon melted butter and place pans on rimmed baking sheet. Pour filling evenly into cooled crusts, smooth tops, and bake cheesecakes for 5 minutes. Without opening oven door, reduce temperature to 200 degrees and continue to bake until cakes register 150 degrees, 10 to 15 minutes, rotating sheet halfway through baking.

4. Let cheesecakes cool in pans on wire rack for 5 minutes, then run thin knife around edge of each cake. Let cakes continue to cool to room temperature, about 1 hour. Wrap pans tightly in plastic wrap and refrigerate until cold, at least 2 hours or up to 4 days.

5. To unmold cheesecakes, wrap hot dish towel around pans and let sit for 1 minute. Remove sides of pans. Slide thin metal spatula between crusts and pan bottoms to loosen, then slide cakes onto individual serving plates. Let cakes sit at room temperature for 30 minutes before serving. (Cheesecakes can be made up to 3 days in advance; however, crust will begin to lose its crispness after only 1 day.)

SOFTENING CREAM CHEESE QUICKLY

To speed up the softening of cold cream cheese, simply submerge the foil-wrapped package in a bowl of warm water for about 10 minutes.

MAKING A GRAHAM-CRACKER CRUST

To get an even, firmly packed graham-cracker crust for our New York-style cheese-cake, use a spoon to press the crumb mixture firmly and evenly across the bottom of the pan.

Chocolate Pots de Crème

Chocolate Pots de Crème

Serves 2 VEGETARIAN

Total time 30 minutes, plus 5 hours 20 minutes cooling, chilling, and resting

WHY THIS RECIPE WORKS Classic pots de crème recipes can be finicky and laborious but deliver a dessert with a satiny texture and intense chocolate flavor. We wanted a user-friendly recipe for two. Since we were making only two custards, we decided that making them on the stovetop would be simpler than using the oven. First, we cooked a simple custard in a small saucepan, then we poured the warm custard over the chocolate. Once the chocolate was melted, we divided the decadent mixture between two ramekins and refrigerated the custards until chilled. Tasters liked bittersweet chocolate for its moderate sweetness, and a little instant espresso powder deepened the chocolate flavor. We prefer pots de crème made with 60 percent cacao bittersweet chocolate (our favorite brands are Ghirardelli and Callebaut). A teaspoon of strong brewed coffee may be substituted for the instant espresso and water. You will need two 5-ounce ramekins for this recipe.

POTS DE CRÈME

2½ ounces bittersweet chocolate, chopped fine
2 large egg yolks
4 teaspoons granulated sugar
Pinch table salt

¾ cup heavy cream
1 teaspoon water
⅛ teaspoon instant espresso powder
1 teaspoon vanilla extract

WHIPPED CREAM AND GARNISH

¼ cup heavy cream, chilled
2 teaspoons confectioners' sugar
⅛ teaspoon vanilla extract
Cocoa powder (optional)
Chocolate shavings (optional)

1. FOR THE POTS DE CRÈME Place chocolate in medium bowl; set fine-mesh strainer over bowl and set aside.

2. Whisk egg yolks, sugar, and salt together in second medium bowl until combined, then whisk in cream. Transfer mixture to small saucepan and cook over medium-low heat, stirring constantly and scraping bottom of pot with heat-resistant rubber spatula, until it is thickened and silky and registers 175 to 180 degrees, 3 to 6 minutes. (Do not let custard overcook or simmer.)

3. Immediately pour custard through fine-mesh strainer over chocolate. Let mixture stand to melt chocolate, about 5 minutes; whisk gently until smooth. Combine water and espresso powder and stir to dissolve, then whisk dissolved espresso and vanilla into chocolate mixture. Pour mixture evenly into two 5-ounce ramekins. Gently tap ramekins on counter to release air bubbles.

4. Let pots de crème cool to room temperature, about 1 hour. Cover ramekins tightly with plastic wrap and refrigerate until chilled, at least 4 hours or up to 3 days. Before serving, let pots de crème stand at room temperature for 20 to 30 minutes.

5. FOR THE WHIPPED CREAM AND GARNISH Using hand-held mixer set at medium-low speed, beat cream, sugar, and vanilla in small bowl until foamy, about 1 minute. Increase speed to high and beat until soft peaks form, 1 to 3 minutes. Dollop pots de crème with whipped cream and garnish with cocoa powder and/or chocolate shavings, if desired. Serve.

MAKING CHOCOLATE SHAVINGS

Use vegetable peeler and peel shavings off block of chocolate at least 1 inch thick. Softened chocolate will be easier to shave; microwave on lowest power setting for 1 minute.

Crème Brûlée

Serves 2   VEGETARIAN

Total time 1½ hours, plus 4½ hours cooling and chilling

WHY THIS RECIPE WORKS Crème brûlée is all about the contrast between the crisp, caramelized sugar crust and the silky custard underneath. The secret to getting a custard with a soft, supple texture was to use only egg yolks rather than whole eggs. To make tempering the egg yolks easier, we heated just half of the cream until the sugar was fully dissolved, then added the remaining cold cream to bring the temperature down so that we could add the egg yolks. Crunchy turbinado sugar made for an incredibly crackly crust. To substitute vanilla extract for the vanilla bean, skip the steeping time in step 2 and stir ½ teaspoon vanilla extract into the yolk mixture in step 3. Granulated sugar can be substituted for the

turbinado sugar. You will need two 6-ounce ramekins for this recipe (two 4- to 5-ounce shallow fluted ramekins can also be used; you will have some custard left over). It's important to use a metal pan for the water bath—a glass baking pan may crack when you add the boiling water. Note that the custard will firm up as it cools.

    1 (3-inch) piece vanilla bean
    1 cup heavy cream, chilled, divided
    3 tablespoons granulated sugar
       Pinch table salt
    3 large egg yolks, room temperature
  2–3 teaspoons turbinado sugar

1. Adjust oven rack to middle position and heat oven to 300 degrees. Place dish towel in bottom of 8-inch square baking pan and place two 6-ounce ramekins on towel (they should not touch). Bring kettle of water to boil.

2. Cut vanilla bean in half lengthwise. Using tip of paring knife, scrape out seeds. Combine vanilla bean pod and seeds, ½ cup cream, granulated sugar, and salt in small saucepan. Bring mixture to simmer over medium heat, stirring occasionally to dissolve sugar. Off heat, let steep for 15 minutes.

3. After cream has steeped, stir in remaining ½ cup cream. Place egg yolks in medium bowl and slowly whisk in ½ cup of cream mixture until smooth. Whisk in remaining cream mixture until thoroughly combined. Strain custard through fine-mesh strainer into 2-cup liquid measuring cup; discard solids in strainer. Pour custard evenly into ramekins.

4. Set pan on oven rack. Taking care not to splash water into ramekins, pour enough boiling water into pan to reach halfway up sides of ramekins. Bake until centers of custards are just barely set and register 170 to 175 degrees, 30 to 35 minutes (25 to 30 minutes for shallow fluted dishes), checking temperature 5 minutes before recommended minimum time.

5. Carefully transfer ramekins to wire rack and let custards cool to room temperature, about 2 hours. Cover ramekins tightly with plastic wrap and refrigerate until cold, at least 2 hours or up to 3 days.

6. Uncover ramekins; if condensation has collected on custards, blot moisture with paper towel. Sprinkle each with about 1 teaspoon turbinado sugar (1½ teaspoons for shallow fluted dishes); tilt and tap each ramekin to distribute sugar evenly, dumping out excess sugar. Ignite torch and, holding flame about 2 inches from surface of custard, sweep over custard until sugar melts and turns golden brown, proceeding until entire surface is deeply golden. Refrigerate ramekins, uncovered, to rechill, 30 to 40 minutes. Serve.

Espresso Crème Brûlée

Add ½ teaspoon instant espresso powder or instant coffee powder to egg yolks in step 3.

REMOVING SEEDS FROM A VANILLA BEAN

1. Use small knife to cut piece of vanilla bean in half lengthwise.

2. Scrape vanilla seeds out of bean using tip of knife.

CARAMELIZING CRÈME BRÛLÉE

1. Sprinkle sugar over surface of custard, then tilt and tap ramekin to distribute sugar into thin, even layer. Pour out any excess sugar and wipe inside rim clean.

2. To caramelize sugar, sweep flame of torch from perimeter of custard toward middle, keeping flame about 2 inches above ramekin, until sugar is bubbling and deep golden brown.

Easy Lemon Soufflé

Serves 2   `VEGETARIAN`

Total time 40 minutes

WHY THIS RECIPE WORKS Lemon soufflé, with its ethereal, airy texture and bright, tart lemon flavor, requires a precise balance of ingredients. To size this recipe for two and make it failproof, we ditched the soufflé dish in favor of a small skillet. Using an equal number of egg whites and yolks made our soufflé lofty but still rich and creamy. Sugar and cream of tartar

Easy Lemon Soufflé

helped stabilize the whipped egg whites, ensuring that our soufflé stayed tall. We started cooking our batter on the stovetop, then allowed it to rise in the oven until beautifully puffed and golden. An 8-inch traditional (not nonstick) skillet is essential to getting the right texture and height here. Don't open the oven door during the first 5 minutes of baking, but do check the soufflé for doneness regularly during the final few minutes in the oven. The center of the soufflé should be creamy and slightly liquid when properly cooked. You will need an 8-inch ovensafe traditional skillet for this recipe.

- 3 large eggs, separated
- ⅛ teaspoon cream of tartar
- 6 tablespoons (2⅔ ounces) granulated sugar, divided
- ⅛ teaspoon table salt
- 1 tablespoon all-purpose flour
- ¾ teaspoon grated lemon zest plus 3 tablespoons juice
- 2 teaspoons unsalted butter
  Confectioners' sugar

1. Adjust oven rack to middle position and heat oven to 375 degrees. Using hand-held mixer set at medium-low speed, beat egg whites and cream of tartar in large bowl until foamy, about 1 minute. Increase speed to medium-high and beat whites to soft, billowy mounds, about 1 minute. Gradually add 2 tablespoons granulated sugar and salt and beat until glossy, stiff peaks form, 1 to 3 minutes.

2. Using hand-held mixer set at medium-high speed, beat egg yolks and remaining ¼ cup granulated sugar in second large bowl until pale and thick, about 2 minutes, scraping down sides of bowl as needed. Add flour and lemon zest and juice and beat until combined, about 30 seconds.

3. Fold one-quarter of whipped egg whites into yolk mixture until almost no white streaks remain. Gently fold in remaining egg whites until just combined.

4. Melt butter in 8-inch ovensafe skillet over medium-low heat. Swirl skillet to coat it evenly with melted butter, then gently scrape soufflé batter into skillet and cook until edges begin to set, about 1 minute.

5. Transfer skillet to oven and bake soufflé until puffed; center jiggles slightly when shaken; and surface is golden, 6 to 8 minutes. Using potholder (skillet handle will be hot), remove skillet from oven. Dust soufflé with confectioners' sugar and serve immediately.

SEPARATING EGGS

To separate eggs, use either the broken shell halves or your hand.

A. To use broken shell halves, gently transfer egg yolk from one shell half to other, so white will drip into bowl and leave intact yolk behind.

B. To use your hand (make sure it's very clean), cup your hand over small bowl, transfer egg into your palm, and slowly allow white to slide through fingers, leaving yolk intact.

Bourbon Bread Pudding

Serves 2 | VEGETARIAN

Total time 2 hours, plus 35 minutes sitting and cooling time

WHY THIS RECIPE WORKS The best bourbon bread pudding features a rich, scoopable custard that envelops the bread with a perfect balance of sweetness, spice, and bourbon flavor. We wanted to do justice to each element, while scaling the recipe for two individual servings. To avoid a soggy structure, we used a sturdy baguette, torn into 1-inch pieces, that would hold up to our eggy custard. Brown sugar gave the custard a rounded, caramelized flavor, while a couple tablespoons of bourbon was enough for punch without making the pudding too boozy. Swapping out whole eggs for yolks and covering the ramekins with foil kept the pudding from curdling. We removed the foil for the last 10 minutes of baking to form a crisp, golden crust. This recipe uses two 12-ounce ramekins; you can also assemble the bread pudding in a single 3-cup oven-safe casserole or soufflé dish and increase the covered baking time to 40 minutes.

- 6 ounces baguette, torn into 1-inch pieces (4 cups)
- ¼ cup raisins
- 2 tablespoons bourbon
- ¾ cup heavy cream
- ⅓ cup packed (2⅓ ounces) light brown sugar
- ¼ cup whole milk
- 2 large egg yolks
- 1 teaspoon vanilla extract
- ½ teaspoon ground cinnamon, divided
- ⅛ teaspoon table salt
  Pinch ground nutmeg
- 2 tablespoons unsalted butter, cut into ¼-inch pieces
- 1 tablespoon granulated sugar

1. Adjust oven rack to middle position and heat oven to 375 degrees. Spread bread in single layer on small rimmed baking sheet and bake until golden brown and crisp, 10 to 20 minutes, tossing halfway through baking. Let bread cool completely.

2. Meanwhile, microwave raisins and bourbon in covered bowl until bubbling, 30 to 60 seconds. Let sit until softened, about 15 minutes.

3. Whisk cream, brown sugar, milk, egg yolks, vanilla, ¼ teaspoon cinnamon, salt, and nutmeg together in large bowl. Add bread and raisin mixture and toss until evenly coated. Let mixture sit, tossing occasionally, until bread begins to absorb custard and is softened, about 20 minutes.

4. Grease two 12-ounce ramekins. Divide bread mixture evenly between prepared ramekins and sprinkle with butter, granulated sugar, and remaining ¼ teaspoon cinnamon. Cover each ramekin with aluminum foil, place on small rimmed baking sheet, and bake for 30 minutes.

5. Remove foil from bread puddings and continue to bake until tops are crisp and golden brown, 10 to 15 minutes. Let bread puddings cool for 15 minutes before serving.

Rice Pudding

Serves 2 VEGETARIAN

Total time 1¼ hours

WHY THIS RECIPE WORKS Rice pudding is one of those simple, unassuming desserts that, when done just right, can be truly sublime. Tasting of little more than milk and good vanilla, the pudding has a short ingredient list, but the ratio of ingredients is key. We liked the results we got from 4 cups of milk to ¼ cup of medium-grain white rice, which gave us completely cooked, tender grains of rice and pudding with a creamy, thick—but not stodgy—consistency. Although this recipe requires a relatively long cooking time, it's low-maintenance time, requiring just a bit of stirring to prevent scorching.

- 4 cups milk, plus extra as needed
- 3 tablespoons sugar
- ¼ teaspoon table salt
- ⅛ teaspoon ground cinnamon
- ¼ cup medium-grain white rice
- ½ teaspoon vanilla extract

Combine milk, sugar, salt, and cinnamon in large saucepan and bring to boil over medium-high heat. Stir in rice and reduce heat to low. Cook, adjusting heat to maintain gentle simmer and stirring regularly to prevent scorching, until rice is soft and pudding has thickened to consistency of yogurt, 50 minutes to 1 hour. Stir in vanilla and adjust consistency with extra milk as needed. Serve warm or chilled.

VARIATIONS

Coconut-Cardamom Rice Pudding

Substitute coconut milk for milk and ground cardamom for cinnamon. Sprinkle with ¼ cup toasted coconut before serving.

Lemon–Bay Leaf Rice Pudding

Add 1 bay leaf to saucepan with milk; discard after rice pudding is fully cooked. Add 1 teaspoon grated lemon zest with vanilla.

Nutritional Information for Our Recipes

To calculate the nutritional values of our recipes per serving, we used The Food Processor SQL by ESHA research. When using this program, we entered all the ingredients, using weights wherever possible. We also used our preferred brands in these analyses. Any ingredient listed as "optional" was excluded from the analyses. If there is a range in the serving size, we used the highest number of servings to calculate nutritional values. We did not include additional salt or pepper for food that's seasoned to taste.

	CALORIES	TOTAL FAT (G)	SAT FAT (G)	CHOL (MG)	SODIUM (MG)	CARBS (G)	FIBER (G)	TOTAL SUGAR (G)	ADDED SUGAR (G)	PROTEIN (G)
Introduction										
Quick Pickled Vegetables	5	0	0	0	10	1	0	1	0	0
Vegetable Scrap Broth	15	0	0	0	470	4	1	2	0	0
Strawberry Refrigerator Jam	30	0	0	0	0	8	0	7	6	0
Pan-Roasted Asparagus	50	2.5	0	0	290	7	3	3	0	4
Creamy Asparagus Soup	120	7	4.5	20	310	10	3	4	0	6
Stir-Fried Asparagus with Shiitake Mushrooms	110	5	0	0	140	14	5	8	2	7
Garlic Croutons	70	0.5	0	0	380	14	0	1	0	2
Summer Berry Gratin	170	8	4.5	115	85	22	2	15	11	2
Individual Chocolate Bread Puddings	530	27	16	135	360	62	3	26	20	13
Very Berry Smoothie	200	2	1	10	280	40	4	27	6	8
Ranch Dressing	42	4	2	10	69	1	0	1	0	1
Muffin Tin Doughnuts	470	16	9	85	190	77	1	43	42	6
Roasted Butternut Squash Salad	310	15	2	0	320	45	7	21	0	4
Butternut Squash Breakfast Hash	180	5	2	10	190	32	6	7	0	6
Creamy New York Deli Coleslaw	250	20	3	10	560	15	6	8	1	3
Roasted Cabbage Wedges	210	14	1	0	350	18	6	11	1	3
Quick Kimchi	60	0	0	0	370	11	3	6	3	3
Crispy Spiced Chickpeas	140	9	0.5	0	250	13	4	0	0	4
Kidney Bean Salad	140	7	1	0	520	15	4	3	0	5
Refried Beans	210	14	2	0	320	16	4	2	0	5
Garlicky Sautéed White Beans with Tomatoes	220	14	2	0	550	18	5	3	0	7
Quick Tomato Salsa	1	0	0	0	160	4	1	1	0	1
Spicy Chipotle Barbecue Sauce	110	4	2.5	10	370	19	1	16	13	1
Easy Tomato Chutney	70	0	0	0	260	16	1	13	8	1
Chavela	100	0	0	0	580	12	2	4	0	2
Cauliflower Rice	90	3	0.5	0	430	13	5	5	0	5
Whipped Cauliflower	150	11	10	0	360	11	5	4	0	4
Skillet-Roasted Cauliflower with Capers and Pine Nuts	240	21	2.5	0	460	13	5	5	0	6

	CALORIES	TOTAL FAT (G)	SAT FAT (G)	CHOL (MG)	SODIUM (MG)	CARBS (G)	FIBER (G)	TOTAL SUGAR (G)	ADDED SUGAR (G)	PROTEIN (G)
Introduction (cont.)										
Cream of Celery Soup	230	14	9	40	580	23	3	6	1	4
Celery Salad with Red Onion and Orange	190	14	2	0	65	15	3	10	3	1
Dehydrated Citrus Zest	0	0	0	0	0	0	0	0	0	0
Coconut Rice Pudding	420	8	5	20	230	79	0	42	34	9
No-Churn Coconut Ice Milk	510	33	21	100	300	48	0	52	45	3
Piña Coladas	240	2	1.5	0	5	42	2	35	19	1
Smashed Sichuan Cucumbers	25	1.5	0	0	430	2	1	1	1	1
Quick Pickle Chips	40	0	0	0	420	9	0	6	0	1
Easy Ratatouille	277	22	3	3	801	18	5	9	8	0
Easy Eggplant Dip	180	16	3.5	5	300	8	3	4	0	2
Quick Pickled Fennel	110	0	0	0	930	25	5	17	0	2
Fennel Confit	150	14	2	0	180	5	2	2	0	1
Fennel Salad with Oranges and Olives	140	8	1	0	180	15	3	9	0	2
Spicy Whipped Feta	140	13	5	25	260	2	0	1	0	4
Watermelon and Feta Salad with Mint	120	6	4	25	320	15	1	14	0	5
Creamy Feta Dressing	410	40	13	65	770	5	0	4	1	9
Easy Dried Herbs	0	0	0	0	0	0	0	0	0	0
Lemon and Herb Compound Butter	80	9	6	25	230	0	0	0	0	0
Simplest Ground Turkey Tacos	340	15	6	60	790	22	5	2	0	34
Mango-Turkey Sloppy Joes	390	10	2	20	840	57	4	30	4	22
Baguette with Radishes, Butter, and Herbs	160	13	7	30	140	9	1	1	0	2
Braised Radishes	80	6	2	10	280	5	2	3	0	3
Quick Pickled Radishes	5	0	0	0	25	1	0	0	0	0
Herbed Ricotta Spread	170	15	6	30	50	3	0	0	0	7
Lemon-Herb Ricotta Fritters	140	10	4.5	55	320	5	0	0	0	8
Sweet Ricotta Cheese Dip	210	12	8	45	80	14	0	11	11	10
Rotisserie Chicken Stock	5	0	0	5	5	0	0	0	0	0
Quick Shrimp Shell Stock	10	0.5	0	5	10	0	0	0	0	1
Miso Soup with Tofu	150	8	1	0	1060	9	1	4	0	14
Sriracha-Lime Tofu Bowl	280	14	1	0	540	23	5	14	7	14
Soups and Chowders										
Hearty Chicken Noodle Soup	350	10	2	130	1170	18	2	6	0	47
Beef and Barley Soup	520	17	4	80	2320	58	11	11	0	35
Escarole, Sausage, and Orzo Soup	370	19	5	75	1590	23	1	4	0	26
Potato-Leek Soup with Crispy Ham and Jammy Eggs	410	11	2.5	205	880	58	5	8	0	21
New England Clam Chowder	720	24	12	190	3390	49	3	4	0	74

	CALORIES	TOTAL FAT (G)	SAT FAT (G)	CHOL (MG)	SODIUM (MG)	CARBS (G)	FIBER (G)	TOTAL SUGAR (G)	ADDED SUGAR (G)	PROTEIN (G)
Soups and Chowders (cont.)										
Hot-and-Sour Soup	250	2.5	0	105	1700	38	2	9	2	18
Miso-Ginger Udon Noodle Soup	460	12	0.5	0	850	69	3	6	0	21
Soupe au Pistou	290	15	4	5	840	28	8	7	0	11
Farmhouse Vegetable and Barley Soup	370	12	7	30	1240	56	9	5	0	7
Butternut Squash Soup with Blue Cheese and Pepitas	370	22	8	30	940	39	7	9	0	11
Creamy Curried Cauliflower Soup	250	19	8	35	790	17	6	7	0	7
Creamless Creamy Tomato Soup	290	15	2	0	930	31	1	18	4	5
Gazpacho	120	5	0.5	0	380	16	3	10	0	4
Corn Chowder with Chorizo and Poblanos	420	23	4.5	25	930	46	7	14	0	20
Pasta e Fagioli	380	6	2.5	10	1570	64	9	10	0	17
5-Ingredient Black Bean Soup	210	2.5	1.5	5	1080	43	1	3	0	13
Tuscan White Bean Soup	230	5	2	10	1770	32	10	6	0	15
Moong Dal Soup with Coconut Milk and Spinach	490	19	11	0	750	58	11	5	0	26
Lentil Soup	430	13	4	20	960	53	12	12	0	20
Moroccan-Style Chickpea Soup	230	8	3.5	15	1180	34	7	13	0	7
Stews, Curries, and Chilis										
Weeknight Beef Stew	607	34	11	134	1316	28	4	6	0	42
Classic Beef Stew	640	31	10	135	1250	34	5	8	0	49
Catalan Beef Stew	1100	82	30	250	1180	18	3	8	1	64
Brazilian Pork and Black Bean Stew	670	35	9	175	2070	32	7	5	0	54
Chicken Tagine	490	15	2	105	1000	56	12	19	0	33
Ras el Hanout (per 1 tablespoon)	30	1	0	0	0	5	3	0	0	1
Shrimp and Sausage Gumbo	450	23	7	215	1420	22	2	6	0	39
Fish Stew with Chorizo and Fennel	580	30	9	125	1840	20	6	9	0	47
Ciambotta	410	26	6	5	880	39	6	10	0	7
Quinoa and Vegetable Stew	310	10	1	0	610	50	6	11	0	7
Thai Red Curry with Chicken	430	17	12	105	1250	38	2	11	4	30
Vindaloo-Style Pork	480	25	4.5	125	2040	21	5	8	0	40
Thai Red Curry with Beef and Eggplant	340	19	2.5	50	1010	17	3	14	4	23
Classic Beef Chili	630	35	11	115	1940	41	13	14	0	42
Texas Chili	1120	74	29	250	2040	46	14	10	0	70
Five-Alarm Chili	700	40	11	115	780	42	5	8	1	42
Turkey Chili	370	8	3	45	1810	41	10	12	0	40
White Chicken Chili	430	13	2	125	1370	31	6	5	0	46
Tempeh Chili	530	12	2	0	1740	77	10	19	0	32

	CALORIES	TOTAL FAT (G)	SAT FAT (G)	CHOL (MG)	SODIUM (MG)	CARBS (G)	FIBER (G)	TOTAL SUGAR (G)	ADDED SUGAR (G)	PROTEIN (G)
Side Salads and Dinner Salads										
Foolproof Vinaigrette	93	10	1	0	38	0	0	0	0	0
Greek Chopped Salad	250	14	2.5	10	880	22	5	6	0	8
Wilted Spinach Salad with Radishes, Feta, and Pistachios	230	20	4	10	150	9	3	4	2	5
Roasted Beet Salad with Goat Cheese and Pistachios	310	21	4.5	5	540	25	7	16	0	8
Cucumber Salad with Olives, Oregano, and Almonds	90	5	0.5	0	610	8	2	5	2	2
Garlicky Broccoli and Chickpea Salad	410	28	3.5	0	930	33	11	8	0	13
Cherry Tomato Salad with Basil and Fresh Mozzarella	150	12	4.5	20	310	7	1	4	1	6
Panzanella	896	48	9	10	1211	94	7	15	0	24
Fennel, Apple, and Chicken Chopped Salad	320	13	3.5	70	750	28	7	17	0	25
Charred Chicken Caesar Salad	930	47	8	180	1220	56	0	6	0	67
Fattoush with Butternut Squash and Apple	420	18	4	15	960	58	9	16	0	13
Baked Pita Chips	170	0.5	0	0	390	33	0	1	0	5
Steak, Mushroom, and Blue Cheese Salad	510	38	9	75	500	8	2	4	0	33
Steak and Rice Noodle Salad	510	25	4	70	1260	41	2	9	6	33
Chef's Salad with Capicola and Provolone	500	38	13	60	1420	14	3	7	0	27
Poached Shrimp Salad with Avocado and Grapefruit	280	14	2	160	1200	21	8	9	2	21
Seared Scallop Salad with Snap Peas and Radishes	358	21	3	41	857	17	4	5	0	24
Freekeh Salad with Sweet Potato and Walnuts	560	28	3.5	0	770	66	14	3	0	14
Tortellini Salad with Bell Pepper, Pine Nuts, and Basil	560	32	6	55	1040	56	2	7	0	14
Classic Tuna Salad	260	11	1.5	60	840	3	1	1	0	34
Classic Chicken Salad	400	25	4	135	450	3	1	1	0	39
Classic Potato Salad	430	23	4	105	480	48	4	6	0	9
Sweet and Tangy Coleslaw	170	7	1	0	640	25	5	20	13	2
Roasted Grape and Cauliflower Salad with Chermoula	420	31	4.5	0	960	33	8	19	0	7
Charred Cabbage Salad with Torn Tofu and Plantain Chips	390	23	3	0	890	35	6	12	2	14
Burgers, Pizzas, Sandwiches, and More										
Juicy Pub-Style Burgers	740	41	13	155	870	23	2	7	2	57
Turkey Burgers	470	23	5	125	750	26	0	4	0	37
Make-Ahead Lentil and Mushroom Burgers	370	16	2.5	0	500	49	7	7	0	12
Salmon Tacos with Cabbage Slaw and Lime Crema	420	16	3.5	50	830	46	3	7	0	25

	CALORIES	TOTAL FAT (G)	SAT FAT (G)	CHOL (MG)	SODIUM (MG)	CARBS (G)	FIBER (G)	TOTAL SUGAR (G)	ADDED SUGAR (G)	PROTEIN (G)
Burgers, Pizzas, Sandwiches, and More (cont.)										
Steamed Bao with Hoisin Chicken and Cucumber	150	3.5	0	20	200	22	0	7	3	10
Grilled Cheese Sandwiches with Caramelized Onion and Apple	420	22	11	0	1120	52	2	9	0	7
Portobello Panini	570	37	13	70	1100	36	2	7	0	22
Tofu Katsu Sandwiches	700	25	2	0	1130	90	1	114	1	23
Lamb Pita Sandwiches with Tzatziki	700	43	20	130	1110	41	1	4	0	41
Basic Pizza Dough	260	3.5	0.5	0	590	44	2	0	0	9
Easy Skillet Cheese Pizza	650	39	13	45	1400	50	5	4	0	24
Ultimate Thin-Crust Pizza	730	22	10	55	1760	92	5	4	2	35
Spinach Calzone	600	31	13	150	1430	51	6	2	0	31
Salami, Capicola, and Provolone Stromboli	560	26	11	75	1990	46	4	1	0	33
Chicken										
Chicken Saltimbocca	570	27	7	195	1060	13	0	1	0	59
Sautéed Chicken Breasts with White Wine and Herb Pan Sauce	480	24	5	140	700	15	0	3	0	40
Quick Salsa Verde (per 1 tablespoon)	60	7	0.5	0	65	0	0	0	0	0
Chicken Marsala	590	28	12	170	450	25	1	7	0	42
Chicken Piccata	460	24	5	140	500	13	1	1	0	41
Crispy Chicken Breasts	620	28	3.5	215	470	41	0	1	0	47
Chicken Parmesan	860	30	8	245	1340	81	7	10	1	62
Chicken Tikka Masala	530	29	4.5	135	1400	21	1	14	2	44
Braised Chicken with Green Olives and Figs	280	13	2	95	470	19	3	12	0	22
Three-Cup Chicken	390	20	2.5	135	1900	12	1	6	2	38
Chicken Teriyaki	440	31	8	165	830	6	0	3	3	30
Chicken Mole	570	24	4.5	200	940	22	4	11	0	65
Murgh Makhani	681	45	25	330	1174	19	3	12	3	51
Roasted Chicken Breasts with Lemon and Thyme	540	32	15	210	720	0	0	0	0	59
Pan-Roasted Chicken Breasts with Garlic and Sherry Sauce	590	35	11	190	900	3	0	0	57	59
Skillet-Roasted Chicken Breasts with Harissa-Mint Carrots	572	31	7	160	1246	18	5	9	0	54
Weeknight Roast Chicken	1320	97	31	425	2450	4	1	2	0	98
Chicken Fajitas	570	22	2	125	480	51	2	10	1	44
Gai Pad Krapow	240	10	1.5	85	570	9	1	5	3	28
Gōngbǎo Jīdīng	450	27	3.5	135	1180	11	2	5	3	42
Chicken Pot Pie	1026	60	29	168	1488	85	6	7	0	38
Lemon-Herb Couscous with Chicken and Dried Cherries	540	13	2	60	770	75	4	7	0	32
Chicken and Orzo with Spinach and Feta	580	19	6	150	1030	48	1	4	0	52

	CALORIES	TOTAL FAT (G)	SAT FAT (G)	CHOL (MG)	SODIUM (MG)	CARBS (G)	FIBER (G)	TOTAL SUGAR (G)	ADDED SUGAR (G)	PROTEIN (G)
Chicken (cont.)										
Chicken and Chorizo Paella	710	37	9	135	1500	48	4	4	0	46
Chicken and Rice	760	43	11	235	1430	42	1	2	0	45
Pomegranate Chicken with Farro and Cucumber Salad	540	20	2.5	40	750	71	8	15	0	23
Braised Chicken Thighs with Potatoes, Fennel, and Tarragon	860	53	13	280	1300	39	7	11	0	52
Chicken Scarpariello	693	46	13	221	1086	17	3	6	0	52
Crispy Chicken with Cabbage Slaw and Tonkatsu Sauce	650	19	2	110	730	86	2	5	0	30
Parmesan and Basil-Stuffed Chicken with Roasted Carrots	570	28	11	200	1080	19	4	11	3	58
Goat Cheese and Olive–Stuffed Chicken with Roasted Carrots	520	23	12	205	950	20	4	11	3	57
Chicken Sausage Hash	500	28	6	280	1460	34	2	5	0	30
Beef, Pork, and Lamb										
Pan-Seared Rib Eye Steaks with Sweet-Tart Red Wine Sauce	760	60	24	150	520	7	1	5	2	41
One-Pan Coffee-Rubbed Steak with Sweet Potatoes and Apples	530	19	3.5	45	800	68	12	30	2	25
Perfect Filets Mignons with Horseradish Sauce	610	40	14	190	610	7	1	3	0	52
Steak Tips with Red Wine Pan Sauce	500	31	11	135	730	6	0	3	1	40
Seared Steak with Crispy Potatoes and Herb Sauce	830	54	10	120	890	30	4	3	0	56
Sirloin Steak with Boursin Mashed Potatoes	690	39	17	150	660	34	2	4	0	47
Seared Flank Steak with Oat Berries, Zucchini, and Peppers	570	18	4	60	790	67	10	16	0	32
Pot-Roasted Steaks with Root Vegetables	500	25	6	115	660	29	5	7	1	38
Modern Beef Pot Pie with Mushrooms and Sherry	740	43	14	150	1000	289	2	5	0	56
Prime Rib for Two	760	48	17	220	860	4	1	2	0	67
Glazed Meatloaf with Root Vegetables	680	38	13	220	1510	37	5	14	0	44
Bò Lúc Lắc	250	14	3.5	60	710	9	1	4	2	22
Stir-Fried Beef and Gai Lan	412	27	8	120	632	4	0	1	0	36
Stir-Fried Cumin Beef	346	24	5	77	402	7	1	3	2	25
Steak Fajitas	750	36	11	115	1340	58	3	7	0	47
Keema	350	19	5	75	600	19	4	5	0	26
Sautéed Pork Cutlets with Mustard-Cider Sauce	450	32	11	125	530	8	1	6	1	29
Sautéed Boneless Pork Chops with Sage-Butter Sauce	530	38	15	130	580	5	1	2	0	37
Crispy Sesame Pork Chops with Wilted Napa Cabbage Salad	910	60	10	195	380	41	5	4	0	51

	CALORIES	TOTAL FAT (G)	SAT FAT (G)	CHOL (MG)	SODIUM (MG)	CARBS (G)	FIBER (G)	TOTAL SUGAR (G)	ADDED SUGAR (G)	PROTEIN (G)
Beef, Pork, and Lamb (cont.)										
Pan-Seared Thick-Cut, Bone-In Pork Chop	160	6	2	65	70	0	0	0	0	26
Pork Schnitzel	660	35	7	385	1010	33	2	4	0	49
Sautéed Pork Chops with Pears and Blue Cheese	440	27	12	115	750	16	3	11	1	33
Pan-Seared Pork Chops with Dirty Rice	870	46	13	165	1920	45	2	4	0	64
Roasted Pork Chops and Zucchini with Basil Vinaigrette	700	38	9	190	950	9	2	6	0	77
Smothered Pork Chops	360	21	7	100	530	7	1	2	0	32
Maple-Glazed Pork Tenderloin	470	10	1.5	110	980	48	0	40	40	36
Spice-Rubbed Pork Tenderloin with Mango Relish	290	9	1.5	105	510	17	3	12	0	35
Herb-Rubbed Pork Tenderloin with Fennel and Artichokes	340	12	2.5	110	830	17	6	8	0	40
Smoky Indoor Ribs	1510	98	30	320	3010	91	1	57	45	62
Garlicky Pork with Eggplant	460	25	2.5	105	700	21	4	2	7	37
Stir-Fried Pork with Shiitakes	490	26	3	105	1280	23	3	11	0	42
Pork Fajitas	540	11	4	105	1870	56	2	6	0	44
Pork Tacos with Mango Salsa	820	48	17	135	630	61	3	23	0	37
Braised Lamb Chops with Tomatoes, Olives, and Rosemary	790	57	25	170	1010	15	4	7	0	46
Mustard-Rosemary Lamb Chops with Roasted Parsnips	640	30	7	125	750	50	11	19	8	42
Roast Rack of Lamb with Whiskey Sauce	770	59	27	170	630	4	1	2	0	36
Lamb Meatballs with Lemony Rice and Artichokes	490	17	6	40	850	66	2	3	0	19
Fish and Seafood										
Fish Meunière	420	33	12	110	115	11	0	0	0	19
Steamed Sole and Vegetable Bundles with Tarragon	220	9	4.5	90	960	11	4	5	0	25
Braised Cod Peperonata	260	6	1	75	840	12	2	7	0	32
Oven-Steamed Fish with Scallions and Ginger	260	10	1	75	1120	7	1	3	2	32
Baked Sole Fillets with Herbs and Bread Crumbs	250	14	8	95	790	13	4	1	0	43
Nut-Crusted Cod Fillets	370	18	2.5	165	410	15	2	3	0	37
Lemon-Herb Cod with Crispy Garlic Potatoes	500	21	6	90	390	42	3	1	0	35
Lemon-Poached Halibut with Roasted Fingerling Potatoes	490	15	2	40	810	66	9	5	0	23
Baked Snapper with Roasted Ratatouille	540	31	4.5	65	1030	25	8	13	0	40
Pan-Roasted Thick-Cut Fish Fillets	180	6	0.5	75	380	1	0	1	1	30
Cod and Couscous Packets with Chermoula	530	17	3	70	960	54	5	1	0	38

	CALORIES	TOTAL FAT (G)	SAT FAT (G)	CHOL (MG)	SODIUM (MG)	CARBS (G)	FIBER (G)	TOTAL SUGAR (G)	ADDED SUGAR (G)	PROTEIN (G)
Fish and Seafood (cont.)										
Halibut and Creamy Coconut Rice Packets	517	16	11	98	1015	50	2	0	0	43
Spiced Swordfish with Avocado-Grapefruit Salsa	420	26	5	110	490	11	4	6	0	35
Sesame-Crusted Tuna with Wasabi Dressing	490	30	2.5	70	630	3	2	0	0	45
Pesce all'Acqua Pazza	221	8	1	92	846	5	1	2	0	29
Pan-Seared Salmon with Braised Lentils and Swiss Chard	700	43	13	125	860	33	9	4	0	48
Chili-Glazed Salmon with Bok Choy	582	41	7	109	1063	9	3	4	0	43
Roast Salmon with Broccoli Rabe and Pistachio Gremolata	510	36	7	95	720	6	4	1	0	40
Pomegranate-Glazed Salmon with Black-Eyed Peas and Walnuts	850	49	9	95	1210	57	8	25	2	47
Salmon and Black Rice Salad with Snap Peas and Radishes	520	21	3.5	45	860	60	7	7	3	26
Crispy Salmon Cakes with Sweet and Tangy Tartar Sauce	880	72	11	95	1140	24	1	4	0	32
Shrimp Saganaki	520	25	9	250	1870	28	2	17	0	32
Pan-Seared Shrimp with Spicy Orange Glaze	150	6	0.5	160	1050	6	0	4	2	18
Stir-Fried Shrimp with Lemon-Ginger Sauce	210	6	1	160	1470	15	4	5	0	22
Shrimp and Grits with Andouille Cream Sauce	742	53	30	377	1451	28	2	3	0	37
Pan-Seared Scallops	230	13	4.5	55	960	6	0	0	0	21
Turmeric Scallops with Mango Noodle Salad	430	12	1.5	25	750	64	5	30	5	20
Clams with Pearl Couscous, Kielbasa, and Fennel	900	19	8	170	2560	100	5	10	0	74
Steamed Mussels in White Wine with Parsley	310	13	6	85	660	12	0	1	0	28
Maryland Crab Cakes	290	17	7	160	610	10	0	0	0	22
Fried Calamari	562	33	3	267	530	42	1	2	0	24
Quick Marinara Sauce	100	7	1	0	230	9	2	5	0	2
Spicy Mayonnaise	402	45	7	23	520	0	0	0	0	0
Couscous with Smoked Trout, Apricots, and Pickled Peppers	510	12	2.5	45	750	72	7	16	0	26
Cataplana	819	38	12	274	3792	30	7	10	0	81
Vegetarian Mains										
Roasted Acorn Squash with Bulgur and Chickpeas	680	38	6	0	1020	77	15	13	0	15
Stuffed Eggplant with Lentils, Pomegranate, and Ricotta	560	31	4.5	0	950	58	16	17	2	16
Baharat	15	1	0	0	0	3	2	0	0	1

	CALORIES	TOTAL FAT (G)	SAT FAT (G)	CHOL (MG)	SODIUM (MG)	CARBS (G)	FIBER (G)	TOTAL SUGAR (G)	ADDED SUGAR (G)	PROTEIN (G)
Vegetarian Mains (cont.)										
Skillet Eggplant Parmesan	950	61	16	240	1750	63	6	16	0	38
Stuffed Tomatoes with Goat Cheese and Zucchini	600	40	9	20	1060	45	10	16	0	20
Vegetable and Bean Tostadas	580	18	6	30	570	83	5	12	0	21
Zucchini, Tomato, and Ricotta Tarts	570	41	19	75	350	41	1	6	3	10
Fennel, Olive, and Goat Cheese Tarts	331	26	11	26	417	8	2	2	0	12
Savory Spinach Strudel	400	16	8	40	650	49	2	17	0	15
Risotto Primavera	466	21	8	28	1163	53	4	4	0	18
Skillet Brown Rice and Beans with Corn and Tomatoes	430	13	1.5	0	980	70	9	13	0	11
Farro Risotto with Arugula, Cherry Tomatoes, and Lemon	450	17	5	20	720	66	8	12	0	14
Savory Dutch Baby with Shaved Mushroom and Celery Salad	470	30	7	200	600	33	1	3	0	17
Quinoa Cakes	290	23	6	105	760	14	1	1	0	9
Chickpea Cakes with Cucumber-Yogurt Sauce	300	15	3.5	95	760	27	4	8	0	15
Black Bean Burgers	560	19	3	95	1130	81	1	7	0	20
Mushroom, Brussels Sprout, and White Bean Gratin	480	22	3	0	980	53	12	7	0	13
Roasted Cauliflower Steaks with Chimichurri	470	43	6	0	690	19	7	6	0	7
Chimichurri	140	14	2	0	10	2	1	0	0	1
Curry Roasted Cabbage Wedges with Tomatoes and Chickpeas	460	26	3.5	0	940	48	17	11	1	14
Crispy Tempeh with Sambal	860	32	0	0	1140	98	0	5	5	24
Panang Curry with Eggplant, Broccolini, and Tofu	720	27	10	0	1160	99	6	12	0	26
Braised Tofu with Butternut Squash and Eggplant	300	15	3	0	570	32	6	10	0	12
Pasta and Noodle Dishes										
Spaghetti with Garlic and Olive Oil	500	23	3	0	590	65	3	2	0	11
Cacio e Pepe	870	38	22	116	1191	88	4	4	0	41
Pasta with Tomato and Almond Pesto	610	30	5	10	1130	67	5	4	0	19
Linguine with Quick Tomato Sauce	480	13	2	0	900	73	9	11	0	12
Hands-Off Spaghetti and Meatballs	780	32	10	80	1410	86	0	11	0	37
Pasta alla Norma	670	28	6	20	1500	87	13	14	0	18
Rigatoni with Quick Mushroom Ragu	500	13	1.5	0	1000	77	5	9	0	16
Classic Pork Ragu	830	27	5	126	1770	88	12	16	0	49
Pasta with Roasted Cauliflower, Garlic, and Walnuts	670	33	6	10	1150	75	6	4	0	21
Pasta with Roasted Cherry Tomatoes, Garlic, and Basil	490	15	2.5	0	740	77	6	12	2	14

	CALORIES	TOTAL FAT (G)	SAT FAT (G)	CHOL (MG)	SODIUM (MG)	CARBS (G)	FIBER (G)	TOTAL SUGAR (G)	ADDED SUGAR (G)	PROTEIN (G)
Pasta and Noodle Dishes (cont.)										
Spaghetti and Turkey-Pesto Meatballs	800	24	6	50	1600	104	11	21	1	49
Basil Pesto	110	11	1.5	0	80	2	1	0	0	1
Pasta with Chicken, Broccoli, and Sun-Dried Tomatoes	830	30	14	140	1080	87	10	7	0	47
Orecchiette with Broccoli Rabe and Italian Sausage	700	30	8	45	1370	70	6	2	0	40
Spaghetti al Tonno	550	17	2.5	30	1510	68	4	5	0	30
Spaghetti with Lemon, Basil, and Shrimp	690	33	9	170	1000	65	3	2	0	32
Garlicky Spaghetti with Clams	510	17	3.5	40	860	58	9	2	0	32
Cheese Ravioli with Roasted Red Pepper and Pistachio Pesto	540	35	10	130	1700	34	2	5	0	22
Classic Lasagna	970	60	28	270	2040	50	5	13	0	56
Baked Macaroni and Cheese	960	46	25	140	1440	90	0	23	0	44
Baked Ziti with Creamy Leeks, Kale, and Sun-Dried Tomatoes	660	17	2	0	850	108	9	11	0	17
Baked Manicotti	1027	54	29	235	1443	71	6	9	0	64
Ultracreamy Spaghetti with Zucchini	598	24	11	40	845	72	5	8	0	25
Skillet Pasta with Fresh Tomato Sauce	230	4.5	0.5	0	300	39	3	6	0	7
Skillet Penne with Chicken, Mushrooms, and Gorgonzola	740	29	9	110	1090	68	3	4	0	41
Skillet Weeknight Bolognese with Linguine	760	28	12	90	800	87	9	16	1	34
Skillet Mussels Marinara with Spaghetti	140	3	0.5	15	310	19	1	3	0	9
Skillet Tortellini with Crispy Prosciutto and Spring Vegetables	850	52	10	75	1430	76	4	10	0	24
Meaty Skillet Lasagna	830	39	17	135	1880	68	7	17	0	49
Fideos with Chickpeas and Goat Cheese	530	17	3.5	5	910	73	11	10	0	18
Chilled Soba Noodles with Cucumber, Snow Peas, and Radishes	329	9	1	0	934	52	2	3	6	0
Japchae	400	23	2	0	1000	44	5	13	3	6
Dan Dan Mian	790	36	7	136	678	89	6	4	1	28
Lemongrass Beef and Rice Noodle Bowl	550	13	3	60	840	82	4	7	3	27
Ramen with Pork and Cabbage	570	17	3	85	1940	67	3	6	0	36
Grilling										
Grilled Chicken Fajitas	740	42	3.5	125	910	48	2	9	3	43
Grilled Herbed Chicken and Vegetable Kebabs	580	38	7	215	1100	12	3	6	0	47
Grilled Bone-In Chicken Breasts with Cherry Tomatoes	550	34	5	160	980	7	2	4	0	51
Barbecued Dry-Rubbed Chicken	310	6	1.5	160	420	9	1	7	7	50
Spiced Grilled Chicken with Raita	510	27	9	180	350	4	1	3	0	59

	CALORIES	TOTAL FAT (G)	SAT FAT (G)	CHOL (MG)	SODIUM (MG)	CARBS (G)	FIBER (G)	TOTAL SUGAR (G)	ADDED SUGAR (G)	PROTEIN (G)
Grilling (cont.)										
Grilled Jerk Chicken Breasts	440	20	2.5	160	260	12	1	8	8	51
Best Grilled Chicken Thighs with Gochujang	590	41	12	235	770	9	0	4	2	43
Grilled Turkey Burgers	360	7	5	80	800	24	0	4	0	50
Grilled Steak Burgers	700	41	21	170	1290	38	0	17	0	40
Grilled Beef and Vegetable Kebabs with Lemon-Rosemary Marinade	470	26	3.5	85	1320	17	4	10	2	40
Grilled Steakhouse Steak Tips	480	31	4	80	1630	16	1	12	10	33
Grilled Smoky Spice-Rubbed Steaks	410	19	5	120	510	7	2	4	3	53
Grilled Flank Steak with Chimichurri Sauce	350	15	6	155	430	3	2	1	0	50
Grilled Marinated Skirt Steak	540	38	10	125	2400	10	1	8	5	39
Bistecca alla Fiorentina	600	41	11	190	730	1	0	0	0	53
Grilled Glazed Pork Chops	500	25	5	115	860	13	0	12	12	45
Grill-Smoked Pork Chops	400	10	3.5	115	1070	30	0	28	18	45
Grilled Coriander-Rubbed Pork Tenderloin with Herbs	390	25	4	110	820	3	0	2	2	36
Bun Cha	630	25	9	80	1630	73	2	17	15	28
Grilled Lamb Chops with Shaved Zucchini Salad	410	29	7	90	780	4	1	2	0	33
Grilled Fish Tacos	670	36	4.5	140	940	51	4	10	0	38
Grilled Blackened Red Snapper	290	14	7	95	700	4	2	0	0	36
Grilled Swordfish and Artichoke Skewers with Olive Caponata	480	34	6	110	820	7	5	0	0	35
Grilled Salmon Steaks	670	45	10	155	610	4	1	1	0	58
Grilled Shrimp and Vegetable Kebabs	403	23	3	214	1096	25	3	9	0	27
Grilled Scallops with Fennel and Orange Salad	320	15	2	40	1020	23	6	11	0	23
Grilled Vegetable and Bread Salad	490	36	8	15	570	32	3	7	0	11
Grilled Portobello Burgers with Garlicky Eggplant	730	53	12	20	810	48	9	17	0	10
Grilled Eggplant with Ginger-Sesame Vinaigrette	310	25	3.5	0	440	22	6	14	2	3
Grilled Tofu with Charred Broccoli and Peanut Sauce	460	33	5	0	980	18	4	5	0	25
Crispy Shallots	50	5	0	0	0	2	0	1	0	0
Grilled Pizza with Charred Romaine and Red Onion Salad	910	57	16	50	1740	69	7	17	3	34
Slow Cooker and Air Fryer Favorites										
Slow-Cooker Beef and Noodle Soup	407	21	5	65	1585	28	4	7	0	28
Slow-Cooker Creamy Butternut Squash and Apple Soup	260	11	7	30	1100	38	6	16	0	6
Slow-Cooker Chicken Stew with Chickpeas and Apricots	590	18	3.5	215	1220	45	8	17	0	55
Slow-Cooker Hearty Beef Stew	520	13	3.5	115	1260	38	6	7	0	59

	CALORIES	TOTAL FAT (G)	SAT FAT (G)	CHOL (MG)	SODIUM (MG)	CARBS (G)	FIBER (G)	TOTAL SUGAR (G)	ADDED SUGAR (G)	PROTEIN (G)
Slow-Cooker and Air-Fryer Favorites (cont.)										
Slow-Cooker Weeknight Beef Chili	720	36	13	155	2090	45	14	14	3	55
Slow-Cooker Black Bean Chili	410	8	1	0	960	62	4	16	0	22
Slow-Cooker Meatballs and Marinara	560	31	10	180	1560	34	1	16	1	36
Slow-Cooker Braised Short Ribs with Hoisin Sauce	810	56	23	210	1190	26	1	14	0	51
Slow-Cooker Sweet-and-Sour Sticky Ribs	1061	65	23	274	1402	43	1	27	8	78
Slow-Cooker Pulled Pork Tacos with Radish-Apple Slaw	1050	65	17	150	1910	76	13	34	0	47
Air-Fryer Roasted Bone-In Chicken Breasts	49	28	8	175	460	0	0	0	0	57
Lemon-Basil Salsa Verde	200	21	3	0	320	2	1	0	0	1
Peach-Ginger Chutney	140	2.5	0	0	150	30	2	27	13	1
Air-Fried Chicken	670	28	8	175	1330	39	2	5	0	62
Air-Fryer Lemon-Pepper Chicken Wings	310	21	6	170	370	1	0	0	0	28
Air-Fryer Spiced Chicken Kebabs with Vegetable and Bulgur Salad	590	24	4.5	130	700	42	8	8	0	52
Air-Fryer Turkey-Zucchini Meatballs with Orzo, Spiced Tomato Sauce, and Feta	410	13	5	60	880	40	2	7	0	37
Air-Fryer Roasted Bone-In Pork Chop	210	9	2.5	75	370	0	0	0	0	30
Peach-Mustard Sauce	50	0	0	0	40	13	1	12	6	1
Chermoula	340	37	5	0	0	2	1	0	0	0
Air-Fryer Fennel-Rubbed Pork Tenderloin with Zucchini Ribbon Salad	500	27	14	230	900	13	3	8	4	56
Air-Fryer Orange-Mustard Glazed Salmon	520	32	7	125	550	8	0	7	0	46
Air-Fried Crunchy Cod Fillets	340	12	2	190	490	12	1	1	0	43
Creamy Chipotle Chile Sauce	230	25	5	25	190	2	0	1	0	1
Air-Fryer Harissa-Rubbed Haddock with Brussels Sprouts and Leek	330	22	3	30	830	21	7	6	0	15
Harissa (per 1 teaspoon)	110	11	1.5	0	150	2	1	0	0	1
Air-Fried Brussels Sprouts	80	4	0.5	0	170	9	4	2	0	3
Lemon-Chive Dipping Sauce (per 2 tablespoons)	90	10	1.5	5	115	1	0	0	0	0
Air-Fryer Shoestring Fries	310	14	2	0	300	41	3	1	0	5
Air-Fryer Crispy Baked Potato Fans	300	14	2	0	300	40	3	2	0	5
Air-Fryer Make-Ahead Breakfast Burritos	420	16	4	250	940	45	4	2	0	21
Air-Fryer Kale, Roasted Red Pepper, and Goat Cheese Frittata	230	14	6	385	460	5	2	2	0	18
Air-Fryer Make-Ahead Fruit, Nut, and Oat Scones	320	12	6	45	230	30	1	24	6	5

	CALORIES	TOTAL FAT (G)	SAT FAT (G)	CHOL (MG)	SODIUM (MG)	CARBS (G)	FIBER (G)	TOTAL SUGAR (G)	ADDED SUGAR (G)	PROTEIN (G)
Vegetable Side Dishes										
Roasted Artichoke Hearts with Lemon and Basil	180	13	2	0	390	13	9	1	0	3
Pan-Roasted Asparagus	140	10	4	15	0	9	4	4	0	6
Garlicky Green Beans	110	7	1	0	10	11	3	4	0	3
Beets with Hazelnuts and Chives	300	19	1.5	0	770	30	8	22	0	5
Skillet Broccoli with Olive Oil and Garlic	170	14	2	0	330	8	3	2	0	3
Broiled Broccoli Rabe	180	15	1	0	660	7	6	1	0	7
Roasted Brussels Sprouts	110	7	1	0	170	10	4	2	0	4
Skillet-Roasted Cabbage with Mustard and Thyme	220	17	11	45	440	14	5	8	0	3
Roasted Carrots	110	6	3.5	15	390	14	4	7	0	1
Roasted Cauliflower	180	15	2.5	0	360	11	5	4	0	4
Cauliflower Gratin	390	31	19	80	600	24	3	4	0	8
Roasted Celery Root with Yogurt and Sesame Seeds	160	8	1.5	0	490	19	4	4	0	3
Elote	260	21	3	10	250	19	2	5	0	5
Simple Ratatouille	220	19	1.5	0	380	11	4	6	0	2
Braised Hearty Greens	240	13	7	30	520	26	9	10	3	10
Sautéed Mushrooms	170	11	7	30	310	10	2	5	0	4
Sautéed Snow Peas with Lemon and Parsley	80	5	0.5	0	300	8	2	4	0	3
Potato Gratin	570	43	27	130	710	38	3	4	0	11
Best Baked Potatoes	180	2.5	0	0	10	36	3	1	0	4
Easier French Fries	530	28	2	0	20	60	0	0	0	8
Belgian-Style Dipping Sauce (per 1 tablespoon)	70	8	1	5	190	1	0	1	0	0
Garlic Mayonnaise (per 1 tablespoon)	90	10	1.5	5	105	0	0	0	0	0
Mashed Potatoes	390	21	13	60	330	42	0	2	0	7
Rustic Smashed Red Potatoes	250	13	8	35	680	28	3	3	0	5
Roasted Red Potatoes	250	11	1.5	0	330	35	4	3	0	4
Sautéed Radishes with Crispy Bacon	80	6	2	10	430	5	2	3	0	3
Spinach with Garlic Chips and Red Pepper Flakes	100	7	1	0	115	6	3	1	0	4
Easy Creamed Spinach	270	25	15	60	340	7	3	0	0	6
Maple-Glazed Acorn Squash	330	18	8	30	300	43	4	20	14	2
Butternut Squash Puree	220	13	8	35	310	27	5	6	0	3
Mashed Sweet Potatoes	350	17	10	45	420	48	7	12	2	4
Roasted Sweet Potato Wedges	390	14	2	0	760	60	11	18	0	5
Tomato Gratin	230	14	3.5	10	1000	18	3	6	0	9
Rice, Grains, and Beans										
Simple White Rice	250	2.5	0	0	300	52	0	0	0	5
Classic Rice Pilaf	330	6	3.5	15	300	60	0	1	0	6
Foolproof Baked White Rice	320	2.5	0	0	300	70	0	0	0	6

	CALORIES	TOTAL FAT (G)	SAT FAT (G)	CHOL (MG)	SODIUM (MG)	CARBS (G)	FIBER (G)	TOTAL SUGAR (G)	ADDED SUGAR (G)	PROTEIN (G)
Rice, Grains, and Beans (cont.)										
Parmesan Risotto	480	17	9	40	1130	58	2	3	0	15
No-Fuss Parmesan Polenta	200	10	6	25	590	20	2	0	0	8
Cheesy Baked Grits	450	34	20	185	900	18	1	2	0	15
Toasted Orzo with Chives and Lemon	300	6	3.5	15	520	47	3	6	0	12
Herbed Couscous	190	7	1	0	200	27	2	2	0	4
Quinoa Pilaf	320	11	1.5	0	650	44	5	3	0	10
Quinoa Salad with Red Bell Pepper and Cilantro	360	18	2.5	0	230	41	5	3	0	9
Tabbouleh	280	22	3	0	310	21	5	3	0	4
Simple Farro	280	0	0	0	200	60	6	0	0	12
Kimchi Bokkeumbap	450	16	1.5	15	1160	62	4	4	0	17
Short Grain White Rice	320	2	0	0	150	70	2	0	0	10
Braised Chickpeas with Garlic and Parsley	270	17	2.5	0	540	24	7	2	0	8
Braised White Beans with Rosemary and Parmesan	260	11	3	10	670	25	7	4	0	17
Cuban Black Beans	200	8	0.5	0	530	31	1	3	0	9
Black Bean Salad with Corn and Avocado	340	23	3	0	600	29	9	5	1	8
Lentil Salad with Olives, Mint, and Feta	360	22	4	10	590	32	8	3	0	12
Spiced Lentil and Rice Pilaf	590	19	4.5	5	370	87	9	3	0	20
Dal with Tofu and Spinach	330	14	4	15	580	36	9	6	0	15
Red Lentil Kibbeh	500	23	3.5	0	1030	59	11	7	0	17
Eggs and Breakfast										
Perfect Fried Eggs	219	18	6	382	255	1	0	0	0	13
Easy-Peel Hard-Cooked Eggs	70	5	1.5	185	70	0	0	0	0	6
Soft-Cooked Eggs	72	5	2	186	71	0	0	0	0	6
Ultimate Scrambled Eggs	210	16	7	475	300	2	0	1	0	14
Tofu Scramble with Shallot and Herbs	200	12	0	0	870	5	1	1	0	16
Classic Omelet with Mushroom and Thyme Filling	460	37	19	625	510	4	0	2	0	26
Classic Omelet with Bacon, Onion, and Scallion Filling	460	36	18	620	670	3	0	1	0	28
Classic Omelet with Bell Pepper, Mushroom, and Onion Filling	460	37	19	625	510	4	1	2	0	25
Poached Egg Sandwiches with Goat Cheese, Tomato, and Spinach	430	21	8	385	660	33	2	2	0	24
Broccoli and Feta Frittata	237	16	7	390	463	5	0	2	0	17
Shakshuka	550	28	6	380	1610	50	2	11	0	23
Skillet Strata with Cheddar	245	16	9	174	322	13	1	4	0	12
Classic Cheese Quiche	840	56	30	305	1030	59	0	6	2	23
Buttermilk Pancakes	500	19	10	140	720	65	0	13	6	15
Buttermilk Waffles	550	22	6	125	630	65	0	13	3	18
Almond Granola with Dried Fruit	290	14	1	0	65	37	4	19	6	6

	CALORIES	TOTAL FAT (G)	SAT FAT (G)	CHOL (MG)	SODIUM (MG)	CARBS (G)	FIBER (G)	TOTAL SUGAR (G)	ADDED SUGAR (G)	PROTEIN (G)
Eggs and Breakfast (cont.)										
Ten-Minute Steel-Cut Oatmeal	170	3	0	0	200	29	5	0	0	7
Congee with Jammy Egg, Peanuts, and Scallions	380	9	2.5	185	670	58	1	1	0	15
Mangú Breakfast Bowl with Tempeh	240	6	1.5	5	390	37	3	18	0	12
Quick Breads										
Simple Drop Biscuits	150	6	3.5	15	250	19	1	1	0	3
Simple Currant Cream Scones	350	19	12	55	650	39	1	13	6	5
Corn Muffins	290	12	7	75	300	38	2	13	12	5
Blueberry Muffins	270	10	6	70	250	38	0	18	16	5
Morning Glory Muffins	450	24	15	70	290	55	3	29	12	7
Cinnamon Streusel Coffee Cake	800	32	13	140	360	117	2	71	68	12
Banana Bread	460	18	5	110	490	68	2	34	25	10
Zucchini Bread	510	18	5	110	600	80	2	52	50	9
Cheddar Cheese Bread	530	26	15	160	1000	47	0	2	0	24
Skillet Olive Bread	590	29	10	130	1040	57	0	4	0	22
Fruit Desserts, Pies, and Tarts										
White Wine–Poached Pears with Lemon and Herbs	450	0	0	0	85	69	6	54	34	1
Crêpes with Honey and Toasted Almonds	330	13	6	115	510	54	0	17	13	10
Berry Gratins	170	8	4.5	110	85	22	2	19	13	3
Strawberry Shortcakes	330	12	7	30	340	50	2	21	14	5
Whipped Cream (per ¼ cup)	100	10	6	30	5	2	0	2	1	1
Apple Strudel	620	21	12	55	500	103	4	36	9	10
Skillet Cherry Cobbler	610	11	7	30	450	113	1	50	48	6
Skillet Apple Crisp	730	34	15	60	300	111	11	77	39	5
Individual Pear Crisps	550	29	11	45	150	72	9	44	26	8
Garam Masala–Spiced Mango Crisp	470	11	4.5	0	200	93	1	69	27	4
Individual Blueberry Crumbles	660	24	14	60	80	108	5	63	49	6
Classic Double-Crust Pie Dough (per ¼ pie)	370	23	11	40	290	35	0	3	3	5
Classic Single-Crust Pie Dough (per ¼ pie)	280	17	9	30	290	27	0	1	1	4
Raspberry-Nectarine Pie (per ¼ pie)	480	23	11	40	340	62	4	24	17	7
Sweet Cherry Pie (per ¼ pie)	340	14	7	25	200	49	2	28	14	4
Icebox Strawberry Pie (per ¼ pie)	390	22	13	55	210	46	2	26	20	4
Banana Cream Pie (per ¼ pie)	510	31	17	210	270	52	2	29	18	7
Key Lime Pie (per ¼ pie)	340	16	9	130	80	41	0	38	5	6
Easy Apple Galette	350	17	9	10	210	54	1	23	4	5
Free-Form Summer Fruit Tartlets	570	28	18	75	290	72	3	30	19	7
Pear Tarte Tatin	890	41	22	30	410	143	10	75	50	10
All-Butter Tart Shells	360	22	14	60	290	35	0	3	3	5
Lemon Tarts	740	45	26	470	410	72	0	37	36	12

	CALORIES	TOTAL FAT (G)	SAT FAT (G)	CHOL (MG)	SODIUM (MG)	CARBS (G)	FIBER (G)	TOTAL SUGAR (G)	ADDED SUGAR (G)	PROTEIN (G)
Fruit Desserts, Pies, and Tarts (cont.)										
Nutella Tarts	1090	77	35	100	330	89	3	45	3	13
Pecan Tarts	870	55	23	180	400	89	3	54	53	8
Cookies, Cakes, and Custards										
Chewy Chocolate Chip Cookies	200	9	6	30	110	29	1	21	21	2
Edible Cookie Dough	270	15	9	30	150	34	0	21	13	2
Oatmeal-Raisin Cookies	190	7	4	45	70	27	1	16	12	3
Molasses Spice Cookies	160	6	3.5	30	80	25	0	15	15	2
Cornmeal Olive Oil Cookies	130	7	1	15	50	16	0	7	7	2
Peanut Butter–Chocolate Quesadillas	580	38	13	35	460	48	2	10	7	14
Fudgy Brownies	220	10	6	60	85	30	0	23	15	3
Blondies	190	10	4.5	35	115	23	1	16	14	2
Chocolate and Peanut Butter Oatmeal Bars	240	14	5	10	170	25	1	15	5	5
Summer Berry Snack Cakes	430	19	12	140	300	57	1	29	25	8
Angel Food Cakes	300	0	0	0	160	67	0	50	50	7
Lemon–Poppy Seed Pound Cake (per ¼ cake)	280	13	8	75	120	35	1	23	23	3
Glazed Lemon Bundt Cakes	520	19	11	140	550	80	0	53	52	7
Rich Chocolate Bundt Cakes	530	30	18	60	480	67	1	33	32	5
Bold and Spicy Gingerbread Cakes	470	13	8	125	320	80	0	62	62	6
Almond Cakes	720	44	10	125	170	66	6	45	42	19
Rustic Peach Cakes	590	26	16	160	310	81	2	51	38	8
Fluffy Yellow Layer Cake (per ¼ cake)	1090	68	39	225	350	124	0	75	55	9
Chocolate Layer Cake (per ¼ cake)	1840	113	71	370	870	201	3	161	160	12
Chocolate Frosting (per ½ cup)	770	53	33	110	70	81	0	49	31	4
Vanilla Frosting (per ½ cup)	650	47	30	130	75	57	0	56	56	0
Carrot Cake with Cream Cheese Frosting	1060	61	21	180	880	117	1	78	74	12
Vanilla Cupcakes	550	33	21	135	210	58	0	41	40	4
Chocolate Cupcakes	580	40	24	140	200	57	0	46	40	4
Lemon Pudding Cake	430	18	10	220	100	59	0	53	50	9
Molten Chocolate Microwave Mug Cakes	570	36	20	245	470	59	0	38	25	10
Lemon–Poppy Seed Mug Cakes	490	29	16	245	470	46	1	26	25	10
Warm Chocolate Fudge Cakes	500	28	8	95	330	62	0	37	20	8
Tiramisu	1070	74	39	405	250	85	0	54	25	16
New York Cheesecakes	950	72	46	425	710	56	0	47	39	16
Chocolate Pots de Crème	700	62	38	320	115	34	2	15	11	8
Crème Brûlée	580	50	30	410	120	27	0	26	23	7
Easy Lemon Soufflé	310	11	4.5	290	250	43	0	39	38	10
Bourbon Bread Pudding	490	26	15	160	250	55	3	31	21	8
Rice Pudding	460	16	9	50	500	62	0	43	19	17

Conversions and Equivalents

Some say cooking is a science and an art. We would say that geography has a hand in it, too. Flours and sugars manufactured in the United Kingdom and elsewhere will feel and taste different from those manufactured in the United States. So we cannot promise that the loaf of bread you bake in Canada or England will taste the same as a loaf baked in the States, but we can offer guidelines for converting weights and measures. We also recommend that you rely on your instincts when making our recipes. Refer to the visual cues provided. If the dough hasn't "come together in a ball" as described, you may need to add more flour—even if the recipe doesn't tell you to. You be the judge.

The recipes in this book were developed using standard U.S. measures following U.S. government guidelines. The charts below offer equivalents for U.S. and metric measures. All conversions are approximate and have been rounded up or down to the nearest whole number.

example

1 teaspoon	=	4.9292 milliliters, rounded up to 5 milliliters
1 ounce	=	28.3495 grams, rounded down to 28 grams

volume conversions

U.S.	Metric
1 teaspoon	5 milliliters
2 teaspoons	10 milliliters
1 tablespoon	15 milliliters
2 tablespoons	30 milliliters
¼ cup	59 milliliters
⅓ cup	79 milliliters
½ cup	118 milliliters
¾ cup	177 milliliters
1 cup	237 milliliters
1¼ cups	296 milliliters
1½ cups	355 milliliters
2 cups (1 pint)	473 milliliters
2½ cups	591 milliliters
3 cups	710 milliliters
4 cups (1 quart)	0.946 liter
1.06 quarts	1 liter
4 quarts (1 gallon)	3.8 liters

weight conversions

Ounces	Grams
½	14
¾	21
1	28
1½	43
2	57
2½	71
3	85
3½	99
4	113
4½	128
5	142
6	170
7	198
8	227
9	255
10	283
12	340
16 (1 pound)	454

conversions for common baking ingredients

Baking is an exacting science. Because measuring by weight is far more accurate than measuring by volume, and thus more likely to produce reliable results, in our recipes we provide ounce measures in addition to cup measures for many ingredients. Refer to the chart below to convert these measures into grams.

Ingredient	Ounces	Grams
Flour		
1 cup all-purpose flour*	5	142
1 cup cake flour	4	113
1 cup whole-wheat flour	5½	156
Sugar		
1 cup granulated (white) sugar	7	198
1 cup packed brown sugar (light or dark)	7	198
1 cup confectioners' sugar	4	113
Cocoa Powder		
1 cup cocoa powder	3	85
Butter†		
4 tablespoons (½ stick or ¼ cup)	2	57
8 tablespoons (1 stick or ½ cup)	4	113
16 tablespoons (2 sticks or 1 cup)	8	227

* U.S. all-purpose flour, the most frequently used flour in this book, does not contain leaveners, as some European flours do. These leavened flours are called self-rising or self-raising. If you are using self-rising flour, take this into consideration before adding leaveners to a recipe.

† In the United States, butter is sold both salted and unsalted. We generally recommend unsalted butter. If you are using salted butter, take this into consideration before adding salt to a recipe.

oven temperatures

Fahrenheit	Celsius	Gas Mark
225	105	¼
250	120	½
275	135	1
300	150	2
325	165	3
350	180	4
375	190	5
400	200	6
425	220	7
450	230	8
475	245	9

converting temperatures from an instant-read thermometer

We include doneness temperatures in many of the recipes in this book. We recommend an instant-read thermometer for the job. Refer to the table above to convert Fahrenheit degrees to Celsius. Or, for temperatures not represented in the chart, use this simple formula:

Subtract 32 degrees from the Fahrenheit reading, then divide the result by 1.8 to find the Celsius reading.

example

"Cook burger patties until meat registers 130 to 135 degrees."

To convert:
130°F − 32 = 98°
98° ÷ 1.8 = 54.44°C, rounded down to 54°C

Index

Note: Page references in *italics* indicate photographs.

G

Gai Lan
    and Beef, Stir-Fried, *148,* 148–49
    prepping, for stir-frying, 149
Gai Pad Krapow, 124, *125*
Galette, Easy Apple, 407–8
Garlic
    Chips and Red Pepper Flakes, Spinach
        with, 336
    Croutons, 15
    freezing, 8
    Harissa, 311
    Mayonnaise, 332
    mincing to a paste, 226
    Picada, 56
    preparing for roasting, 233
    slicing thin, 352
    storing, 13
    Toasted, and Parmesan, Pan-Roasted
        Asparagus with, 319
Gas grill, 279
Gazpacho, 46
Gazpacho with Shrimp, 46
Ginger
    Bold and Spicy Gingerbread Cakes,
        427–28
    Cream Scones, Simple, 379
    and Five-Spice, Roasted Chicken Breasts
        with, 121
    freezing, 8
    -Hoisin Glaze, Pan-Seared Shrimp
        with, 191
    -Miso Udon Noodle Soup, 42
    Molasses Spice Cookies, 418, *418*
    -Peach Chutney, 302
    and Scallion, Sautéed Snow Peas
        with, 330
    and Scallions, Oven-Steamed Fish with,
        174–75, *175*
    Sesame, and Scallions, Cucumber Salad
        with, 74
    and Sesame Oil, Skillet Broccoli with, 321
    -Sesame Vinaigrette, Grilled Eggplant
        with, 287, *287*
    and Smoked Paprika, Maple-Glazed Pork
        Tenderloin with, 160
    -Soy Sauce, Sesame-Crusted Tuna
        with, 183
    storing, 13
    -Tomato Sauce, Pan-Seared Scallops
        with, 194
Gingerbread Cakes, Bold and Spicy,
    427–28
Glass bowls, 29

Goat Cheese
    Cherries, and Almonds, Wilted Spinach
        Salad with, 74
    and Chickpeas, Fideos with, 250, *250*
    and Chives, Quinoa Pilaf with, 348
    Fennel, and Olive Tarts, *210,* 211
    Grilled Vegetable and Bread Salad,
        285–86
    Herbed, Best Baked Potatoes with, 331
    Kale, and Roasted Red Pepper Frittata,
        Air-Fryer, *314,* 314–15
    Lentil Salad with, 355
    Olives, and Spicy Garlic Oil, Easy Skillet
        Pizza with, 103
    and Olive–Stuffed Chicken with Roasted
        Carrots, 135
    and Pistachios, Roasted Beet Salad with,
        74–75, *75*
    Shiitakes, and Bell Pepper, Tofu Scramble
        with, 364
    Tomato, and Spinach, Poached Egg
        Sandwiches with, 366, *366*
    and Zucchini, Stuffed Tomatoes with,
        202, 208
Gochujang
    Best Grilled Chicken Thighs with, 266
    bottom-of-the-jar, ideas for, 7
Gōngbāo Jīdīng, 126
Graham cracker(s)
    crust, preparing, 407, 443
    Key Lime Pie, 406–7, *407*
    New York Cheesecakes, 442, *442*
    S'mores Molten Microwave Mug
        Cakes, 438
Grains, 215
    see also specific types
Granola
    Almond, with Dried Fruit, 372–73, *373*
    Chocolate and Peanut Butter Oatmeal
        Bars, 422
    Hazelnut, with Dried Pear, 373
    Pecan-Orange, with Dried
        Cranberries, 373
    Tropical, with Dried Mango, 373
Grape and Cauliflower, Roasted, Salad
    with Chermoula, 90
Grapefruit
    and Avocado, Poached Shrimp Salad
        with, *70,* 84–85
    -Avocado Salsa, Spiced Swordfish with,
        182, *182*
    segmenting, 85
Gratins
    Berry, 391–92
    Cauliflower, 325

Gratins (*cont.*)
    Mushroom, Brussels Sprout, and White
        Bean, *219,* 219–20
    Potato, 330–31
    Summer Berry, 15
    Tomato, *338,* 339
Green Beans
    Garlicky, 319–20
    Lemony, with Toasted Almonds, 320
    Soupe au Pistou, *34,* 43
    trimming quickly, 320
Greens
    package-free, buying, 5
    Soft-Cooked Eggs with Salad, 363
    storing, 13
    see also specific greens
Gremolata, Pistachio, and Broccoli Rabe,
    Roast Salmon with, 186
Grill brush, 279
Grilling
    checking fuel level in gas tank, 276
    cleaning the grill, 259
    essential equipment, 279
    fire setups, 258–59
    fire types, 258
    how to light a grill, 264
    list of recipes, 257
    making a foil packet for wood chips, 271
    oiling the cooking grate, 259
    preventing fish from sticking, 281
    setting up a fire, 258
    testing intensity of fire, 283
Grits
    Cheesy Baked, 346
    and Shrimp with Andouille Cream Sauce,
        192, 193
Gumbo, Shrimp and Sausage, 58

H

Haddock
    Harissa-Rubbed, Air-Fryer, with Brussels
        Sprouts and Leek, *310,* 310–11
    Pesce all'Acqua Pazza, *182,* 183–84
Half-and-half, substitutes for, 30
Halibut
    and Creamy Coconut Rice Packets, 181
    Lemon-Poached, with Roasted Fingerling
        Potatoes, 178, *178*
Ham
    and Cheddar Stromboli, 107
    Crispy, and Jammy Eggs, Potato-Leek
        Soup with, *38,* 39
    Kimchi Bokkeumbap, 350

W

Y

Z